THE GOOD COUNTRY

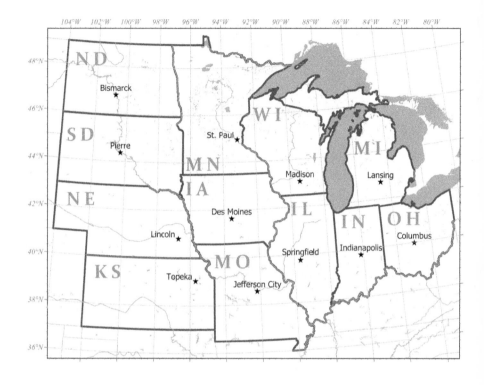

THE GOOD COUNTRY
A History of the American Midwest,
1800–1900

JON K. LAUCK

UNIVERSITY OF OKLAHOMA PRESS : NORMAN

Publication of this book is made possible through the generosity of Edith Kinney Gaylord.

Library of Congress Cataloging-in-Publication Data

Names: Lauck, Jon, 1971– author.
Title: The good country : a history of the American Midwest, 1800–1900 / Jon K. Lauck.
Other titles: History of the American Midwest, 1800–1900
Description: Norman : University of Oklahoma Press, [2022] | Includes bibliographical references and index. | Summary: "A history of the US Midwest in the nineteenth century, describing and analyzing a rich civic culture that prized education, literature, libraries, and the arts; developed a stable social order grounded in Victorian norms, republican virtue, and Christian teachings; was marred by overt racism but made significant progress toward racial equality; and generally put democratic ideals into practice further than any nation to date"—Provided by publisher.
Identifiers: LCCN 2021057702 | ISBN 978-0-8061-9063-1 (hardcover) | ISBN 978-0-8061-9064-8 (paperback)
Subjects: LCSH: Middle West—Civilization—19th century. | Middle West—Politics and government—19th century. | Political culture—Middle West—History—19th century. | Middle West—Intellectual life—19th century.
Classification: LCC F351 .L325 2022 | DDC 977—dc23/eng/20220114
LC record available at https://lccn.loc.gov/2021057702

The paper in this book meets the guidelines for permanence and durability of the Committee on Production Guidelines for Book Longevity of the Council on Library Resources, Inc. ∞

To Amy
le grá mór

This country is in a state of bewilderment that cries out for good history. How are we to account for liberating thoughts and movements, things that have gone well? What has been the thinking behind our great institutions? I have found little help in answering these questions. . . . It seems to me that for the survival of our experiment to be even imaginable the country must know itself better.

Marilynne Robinson

CONTENTS

Acknowledgments

I want to extend special thanks to all my friends and colleagues involved in the movement to revive midwestern history. This effort started in earnest in a bar in Wisconsin in the fall of 2013 with the formation of a working group that would blossom into the Midwestern History Association the next year, which also saw the beginning of the annual MHA conferences focused on midwestern history. These conferences would not have been possible without the generous support of my friend Gleaves Whitney, then director of the Hauenstein Center in Grand Rapids, Michigan, which became home to the conference. Without the financial support of the Hauenstein Center (named for Ralph Hauenstein, a midwesterner, World War II veteran, and editor of the *Grand Rapids Herald*, who attended our early conferences before passing at age 103) and the organizational prowess of Gleaves, these midwestern history conferences would not have been possible. The fateful year of our first conference, 2014, also saw the launch of *Middle West Review*, the only scholarly journal dedicated to the study of the Midwest as a region and a place where critical discussions about the nature of the Midwest continue to take place. An organized scholarly association, an annual conference where ideas can be exchanged, and a scholarly journal to carry on the discussion and debate are all crucial ingredients to building an academic field of study. I hope this book can serve as another signpost indicating how far we have come on our journey.

For their patience as this book came together I thank my family, midwesterners all, who routinely live up to the region's historical precedents of democratic virtue. In particular, I thank Amy for her love, support, good cheer, and tolerance for our ever-burgeoning bookshelves and ever-diminishing storeroom, where only a few more file boxes will fit. I thank our children, Brendtly, Abigail, and Henry, who keep it all lively. And I thank my mom and dad, both products of the deep civic culture of the rural Midwest.

ACKNOWLEDGMENTS

Finally, I want to remember some gentlemen we have lost along the way. Since the effort to bring more attention to the Midwest took shape nearly a decade ago, fine scholars such as Terry Barnhart, Al Bogue, Drew Cayton, Ellis Hawley, and John E. Miller have left us, and it is fitting to recall that we could not have made it as far as we did without them. They were fine sons of the Good Country and worthy of remembrance.

Sioux Falls, South Dakota
August 2021

INTRODUCTION

THE EXCEPTIONALISM OF
THE OLD SQUARE WORLD

During the fall of 2017, while driving to some destination in the American Midwest, I listened to Terry Gross's National Public Radio show *Fresh Air*. Since Hugh Hefner had recently died, she ran a snippet of an old interview of him taped in 1999. The clip began with Hefner commenting that his Playboy empire was launched as a "direct result of my response to my own Puritan upbringing. My parents are—or were—typically Midwestern Methodist Puritans."[1] At the same time that the *Fresh Air* interview played, the *Omaha World-Herald* ran a story about Hefner's parents growing up in south-central Nebraska in Phelps County and attending Nebraska Wesleyan University, as good Methodists would do. Glenn Hefner graduated from Nebraska Wesleyan in 1918 and Grace graduated in 1920. They left nearly a million dollars when they died to help poor students attend the college. They also donated to various causes back in Holdrege, the county seat of Phelps County, including nearly $200,000 to an assisted living center.[2]

After hearing Hugh Hefner's comments to Terry Gross about his "Midwestern Methodist Puritan" parents, I expected a grim tale of parental oppression to follow. But Hefner then reported that his mother was kindly and loving and highly supportive of his success and that she was proud of him. She was an early investor in her son's famous magazine. This is not to say that she endorsed the results of his particular line of work, however. "That isn't our lifestyle," she said. "We're on the conservative side. You can't live your children's lives." Hefner's parents came across as good people—they worked hard, supported their children, gave generously to charity—yet Hefner criticized them and the world that produced them. This irony

1

caused me to think more about the invocation of frequent shibboleths about the repressed and repressive and backward Midwest, or what Hefner deemed the world of "Midwestern Methodist Puritans." I set out to understand the old midwestern world in which Hefner's parents matured and from where, in 1918 and 1920 in Lincoln, Nebraska, they graduated from college. I set out to describe and give an accounting of the old square world of the American Midwest that continues to hold a place in the American imagination.

Consider another case, also from Hefner's era. In late November 1962, Professor Allan Bogue, a historian at the University of Iowa who was on a trip out west, wrote a colorful letter to "Kit" Lasch back in Iowa City. Bogue considered himself a midwesterner and always included a strong emphasis on the Midwest in his course on western history; he was about to publish his book of midwestern economic history titled *From Prairie to Corn Belt* (1963), a title and treatment that would now be an unlikely product of academia. Bogue had hired Christopher "Kit" Lasch, a Nebraska native, to teach at Iowa the previous spring.[3] Bogue ended his letter by asking Lasch in a postscript if he had seen a "rather disappointing" article about Iowa by the emerging writer Philip Roth that had recently been published in *Esquire*. Lasch duly reported that the article had caused a "minor sensation" and "great indignation" in Iowa and agreed that "Philip's article wasn't very good."[4] Roth, who was then teaching at the Iowa Writer's Workshop (he had been "frog-marched to the Midwest" by an unhappy spouse), had found Iowa anti-whiskey, anti-"girlie magazine," anti-communist, anti-intellectual, cold, Republican, and "white"; a place with bland food and an orientation toward the Chamber of Commerce and the PTA and where people used the phrase "real good" too much; and a state generally inhibited by an enveloping "smallness." Iowans were too nice, chatty, and "folksy." In Iowa, "grown men" and respectable "merchants" wore "BEAT MINNESOTA" buttons to Iowa Hawkeye football games and "demure housewives" baked cakes and made fudge.[5] Roth complained about parking tickets and hated the newspaper scene. The *Des Moines Register* was too Republican (it reported on President Kennedy "staying up late at parties") and ran "photos of hogs, of corn, of cheerleaders," and the local *Iowa City Press-Citizen* was printed in multiple colors ("a kind of flash I don't happen to go for"). Roth said he was on a "list" because he received the Sunday *New York Times* (a "short list," he emphasized) and was flustered and even infuriated by delays in the delivery of the *Times*. He confessed that he "lived mostly at the periphery of Iowa life" and that, when he moved there, he expected Iowa to be "Kansas," since he had "only a simple vision of America without cities, trees or hills, which I called Kansas."[6] Roth wrote to his friend William Styron to "warn you to keep clear of Iowa if you KNOW whats gd. for you."[7]

A chronicle of the disregard of the Midwest consistent with Hefner and Roth could go on for volumes, and indeed it has in the form of the "revolt from the village" genre of literature and school of commentary, but that is well-trod soil. Instead, it is past time to analyze the object of the critics' attacks critically. It is time to focus on whether Hefner and Roth and a long train of other intellectuals and writers were right about the American Midwest. Specifically, it is time to look at the Midwest during the long nineteenth century—or from roughly the era after the American Revolution until the era before World War I—and to judge the veracity of the critics' claims about the traditional Midwest. There is no book on the Midwest during this formative era. In fact, in keeping with the past derision of the region, the Midwest has been greatly neglected by historians, a condition that a small group of academics and other writers, mostly located in the Midwest, has been attempting to remedy in recent years by way of new study groups, journals, and other publications. I count this book in that number.

Given the prevailing atmosphere of disdain and indifference, readers may be surprised at what a new look at midwestern history reveals. Once the cobwebs are cleared off old journals, long-forgotten records consulted, and the veil of stereotypes pierced, a remarkable world is discovered. In contrast to prevailing clichés and the modern platitudes about backwardness, sterility, racial injustice, and oppression, an in-depth look at the history of the American Midwest reveals a land of democratic vigor, cultural strength, racial and gender progress, and civic energy—a Good Country, a place lost to the mists of time by chronic neglect but one well worth recovering, for the sake of both the accuracy of our history and our own well-being. The Midwest of the long nineteenth century, to state it boldly, constituted the most advanced democratic society that the world had seen to date, but its achievements are rarely highlighted in history texts and indeed seldom mentioned.

In this old and forgotten Midwest, where theories of democracy advanced so far in practice, there were also, dare I say, elements of idealism. These stemmed from the democratic nature of the Northwest Ordinance but also from the emergence of New Americans, people born and raised in the young republic who had escaped the bonds and constraints of Europe and colonial life with its indentures, slavery, and persisting aristocracy. They scoffed at those who tried to reestablish Old World privileges out on the open frontier of Ohio and Indiana. They recognized the absence of privation, the natural bounty of the region, and the access to fruitful land, a precious rarity in feudal Europe, so the degree to which they embraced boosting and promoting their new region and its expansion and fecundity makes sense. To invoke midwestern idealism is not to imply naiveté. Pragmatism and common sense reigned. But there was a communally agreed to ideal, a model for behavior, a goal to be striven for, a moral code, a way of inspiring the young, a motivation for civic duty, a virtuous patriotism, a recognition of civic obligations, and, perhaps most telling, a willingness to bleed and die for one's home, especially as against sinful rebels who put the young republic at risk. Above all, there was little of modernity's corrosive cynicism, the kind that yields indifference and decay. It is hard to pin it down and dissect and quantify it, but this idealism runs through the record of the Midwest and it is a key part of its history, despite its elusiveness to the written word. It is why, during the rocky decades of the later twentieth century, when hard times came, there was so much nostalgia for the old Midwest. This is not to say false feelings or empty sentiment, but a nostalgia grounded in a lived and real experience.

As profound and successful as midwestern development was, it failed on some fronts. This book is titled *The Good Country*, not *The Perfect Country*. Chapter 4 and parts of chapters 2 and 5 are specifically designed to examine the failures of the Midwest with regard to women, Native Americans, racial and ethnic minorities, and other matters while also recognizing the context, complexity, and ambiguity of this history along with evidence of substantive advances to remedy these failures. This exercise represents the great challenge of modern historiography, one met by or even acknowledged by too few historians. The history profession in the United States, many would concede, has become too one-sided, too critical, and too focused on American faults and not sufficiently attentive to what would have been considered great achievements in their proper historical setting.

It is past time for a great correction in the field of American history. A rebalancing of what we think we know is needed to place people and events properly, to understand better what worked and what failed, and to provide hope from the past to those who seek democratic progress in the present. American history was not one long train of abuses and suffering, as it would sometimes seem based on the prevailing sentiments in and outputs from American history departments. Nor was it an uninterrupted ascendance toward perfection, as some critics of academia might presume. It was a mixture of advances and defeats, but more of the former than many recent historians admit. By looking with fresh eyes at the history of the American Midwest, the most historically neglected region in the United States, we can begin to see elements of American history that have nearly vanished from the main currents of historical work in recent decades and begin the great correction that may rebalance our view of the past and rectify the recent distortion of the American story.[8]

Beyond the historical record and the interpretative agendas and disputes of scholars—and more important to all our daily lives—is the need to reflect on the political culture in which we are now immersed. For several decades at least, a common way to frame cultural and political conflict in the United States is to pit the traditions and practices of Old America against the new and rising and youthful forces of change, to contrast the square against the hip. This has become our most foundational political dynamic and what we continue to fuss about in most of our political and cultural debates. If the assumptions surrounding the Old World are wrong, however, it rescrambles a prevalent framing device for modern American politics. A different framing based on a more accurate history might reduce social tensions and democratic logjams by causing the upstart forces of change to instead draw on the successes of the past instead of dismissing them or, worse, denying their existence. After a long and tortured intellectual journey after he had left the University of Iowa, Christopher Lasch came to these realizations and began to worry about the cost of forgetting our once-prevalent civic and communal traditions. He came to see that "his parents' early-twentieth-century Midwestern world" was rooted and decent and democratic and worth remembering.[9]

It would help the rebalancing of American history and memory and the rejiggering of our public discourse and accompanying political impasse if it was realized that much of our present dilemma is based on a misunderstanding of the American Midwest. In 1921, about the time this study ends, a young man from a midwestern country town set us off on the wrong course. Carl Van Doren, born and raised on a farm near Hope, Illinois, wrote an essay about the "revolt from the village" by young midwesterners, much like Hefner a few decades later, who wanted more adventure and excitement and so sought wider vistas.[10] Van Doren's analysis was deeply flawed, but it caught on and generated a whole school of thought grounded in attacking the supposed sins and villainies of the Midwest, and this school persists to the present. The great irony, however, is that Van Doren did not intend to unleash the forces of prejudice and condescension against the Midwest. In fact, his original thoughts for his essay demonstrate that he considered his home quite kind and lovely. His complaint was that it was "dull," so he ran off to New York to become a writer, as many young writers tend to do. But dullness is not villainy. It can simply be the reassuring rhythm and rituals of civic affairs in an old democracy.

As this book was being written, mostly in the hurly burly of 2020, a year frequently compared to 1968 and all its convulsions and acrimony, dull sounded rather good—and still does. A stronger grounding in the dull but decent and routine world of old-time midwestern civic culture might be just what we need, a modern version of what the Ohioan Warren Harding called normalcy. That means we should not accept Van Doren's designation of empty dullness. The history of the Midwest reveals much genuine progress when properly viewed in the context of world history. Enjoying the fruits of a long and hard-won struggle for democratic progress should not be casually dismissed as dull. It should be seen as a sweet victory against centuries of tyranny and abuse, and the costs of that victory should never be dismissed or forgotten, lest we lose our bearings in the stream of time. The most critical step one can take when beginning a good-faith reconsideration of the Midwest is to think deeply about the world the young Midwest entered.

The importance of this crucial step came home to me on December 7, 2019, when I stopped in at an upstart used bookstore in Watertown, South Dakota, owned by a retired high school debate coach. In the far back of the store, in the foreign affairs section, I ran across a copy of *Impressions of Russia* by Georg Brandes. Later research revealed that Brandes was a historian and literary critic from Denmark (he introduced the West to Kierkegaard and Ibsen) who visited Russia during the 1880s and published his Russo-observations in 1889.[11] Brandes reminds us that it is essential to place the Midwest in a global perspective and a *longue durée*. We need to capture the Midwest's "significance," to use Frederick Jackson Turner's favorite designation, and not be distracted by the interesting but trivial, a common temptation for many historians these days. In his sprawling masterpiece on the global nineteenth century, the German historian Jurgen Osterhammel emphasizes that it is imperative "to have a feel for proportions" when surveying the historical landscape, a sense of the big moments and critical accomplishments of a place and time.[12] This includes the development of sustainable democratic institutions in the American Midwest in the nineteenth century, which, when viewed widely, was highly unique and praiseworthy. Brandes and others can help us to see these general truths by liberating the historical gaze from the narrow framework of American history and the agendas of contemporary politics and culture.

Grand judgments require a wide perspective because "generalizations can only be validated by comparison."[13] It is a "common-sense proposition that nothing should be studied in a vacuum."[14] "Without comparisons to make," said de Tocqueville during his work on France and the United States, "the mind doesn't know how to proceed."[15] From a global point of view, the advanced degree of democratic development in the Midwest was exceptionally rare and thus significant and therefore deserving of a preponderance of our attention and, yes, our praise.[16] This is not to say that the democratic failures in the Midwest should not be recorded and analyzed, but only to say that these failings must be placed in a broader global perspective, one that considers the full weight and power of existing monarchical systems and other tyrannies. Before turning to the development of the nineteenth-century Midwest, we must consider the conditions that prevailed in the rest of the world at the same time. Only then can we see how precious the midwestern democratic heritage has been and why its history is so urgent now.

Brandes's descriptions of Russia are stark and grim. In Russia, there was "a constant exertion on the part of the rulers to make real knowledge impossible and to destroy all individual and independent will." The condition of the peasants was "of profound ignorance and of an Asiatic spirit of submission." Peasants and other members of the lower classes, upon encountering someone of greater status, would immediately grovel, fall on their knees, and touch their foreheads to the dirt. Workers slept in crammed barracks akin to dog kennels with no chairs, tables, carpets, or pillows and ate uncooked porridge. The children of peasants and workers received no education, yet the female children of the nobility could attend the Imperial Girls' School (in a country of twenty-eight million people there were only twenty thousand pupils). If the tsar visited the school, the custom was for him to drop his handkerchief and watch the "girls all scramble for it, and it is torn in pieces, so that each one can get a fragment." The tsar then takes the most favored girl to his table and gives her the leftovers on his plate: "It is the custom and usage for her to swallow it with delight shown in all her features."[17]

Deference to the tsar was fierce, and the absolutist tradition in Russia ran deep.[18] In the 1880s, when Brandes visited and Tsar Alexander III came to power, he witnessed some familiar Russian authoritarianism.[19] Alexander consolidated power even more, bolstered the Orthodox church, and emboldened anti-democratic officials.[20] So persisted the "pillars of Old Russia—autocracy, orthodoxy, and the institution of serfdom."[21] The vast majority of Russians were peasants, serfs either controlled by large landowners or in direct bondage to the tsar. Landowners could sell their serfs at auction, discipline them via flogging and other torture, or send them to prison or Siberian labor camps.[22] The "grey peasant mass," said one historian, was "delivered body and soul to the mercies of the master," who managed a form of "slavery in its harshest aspects, symbolized best by the rod" and known as the "worst form of serfdom in Europe."[23] Fear of the secret police was also pervasive.[24] The most hideous side of Alexander's reign was the treatment of Russian Jews. In the early 1880s, an anti-Semitic pogrom led to the death and displacement of thousands of Russian Jews and the destruction of Jewish property.[25] Less calamitous, but equally disruptive, was the tsar's treatment of German farmers who had settled in southwestern Russia. To avoid conscription into the Russian army, they fled to the Midwest and Canada.[26]

Halfway around the globe from Russia, in tropical Brazil, the 1880s brought momentous change after centuries of struggle for the average Brazilian.[27] After its creation as a Portuguese colony in 1500, Brazil was dominated by massive patriarchal sugar plantations on which labored thousands of African slaves.[28] Brazil was ruled by Portuguese colonial viceroys and administrators for centuries. Absolutism prevailed, church and state were fused together, and there was no separation between branches of government. Even after independence came in 1822, the country was ruled by the Portuguese king's son, the emperor Pedro, and the planter aristocracy, the *mazombos,* who controlled Brazilian life. The historian Leslie Bethell explains that after independence there was "never any intention of establishing in Brazil anything that, even at the time, looked remotely like liberal representative democracy based, however theoretically, on the sovereignty of the people."[29] A new legislative assembly, which was chosen by only a few select Brazilians, was short-lived. Emperor Pedro sent the army to close it down, and the legislative leaders were exiled. Pedro oversaw the writing of a constitution that consolidated almost all power with him. After years of rebellions and political instability, Pedro fled to Europe and left his five-year-old son as heir to the throne. Regents ruled for Pedro II until the political chaos caused Brazilian aristocrats to install him as emperor early and illegally, at age fifteen (the law required he be eighteen, but it was ignored).[30] Pedro II reigned for forty-nine years.

It was not until 1889 that the monarchy in Brazil fell after years of domestic unrest. Pressure mounted, for example, from internal reformers and also the British empire finally to end slavery. The population of some Brazilian provinces was as much as 66 percent slaves, and no other country in the New World enslaved more people than Brazil.[31] Four million slaves were captured, sold, and sent to Rio de Janeiro during the slave trade (ten times more than were sent to the United States).[32] Slaves could be thrown into burning furnaces, tortured with thumb screws, or forced to endure the *novena*, or nine days of whippings.[33] Slavery was finally abolished in 1888, but little was done to help the ex-slaves. Finally, in November 1889, military leaders led the coup that ended the empire. Monarchist resistance continued for several years, but nominally Brazil had become a republic, albeit one dominated by an oligarchy that could not hold open elections for fear of losing power.[34] Around the turn of the century, only 627,000 people in a nation of twenty-two million could vote.[35] In the early twentieth century, 85 percent of Brazil remained illiterate and only 5 percent of the adult population voted.[36]

In Asia at this time, China and Japan were preparing to go to war over Korea.[37] For centuries China had been ruled by the Qing dynasty (1644–1911), which steadily marched outward, conquering new lands.[38] Slavery was routine in China, with millions "permanently indentured at hard and filthy labor."[39] The emperor, the "Son of Heaven," exercised complete authority.[40] The peasantry, which constituted 80 percent of the population, was powerless; peasants survived on an acre or two of land and were subject to oppressive taxation.[41] Women were propertyless, seldom educated, and suffered through the brutalities of footbinding.[42] A literary inquisition rooted out books that threatened the regime, deviant authors were killed or banished, a censorate policed moral codes and searched for improprieties, and individuals had no rights.[43] In 1848 a rebellion in China tried to topple the Qing dynasty. The Taiping Rebellion, as it was called, was led by Hong Xiuquan, who tried to reduce illiteracy and slavery, promote greater access to land, and end female footbinding and prostitution. More than six hundred walled cities changed hands during the ensuing war, which was fought with pikes and swords and during which massacres were common.[44] As many as thirty million Chinese had died by the end of the war.[45]

The diminishing strength of imperial China during the late nineteenth century contributed to Japan's growing aggressiveness in the region. In 1868 the Meiji Restoration brought the end of military rule under the Tokugawa shogunate (1603–1867) and the return of rule by the emperor. The restoration was led by a faction of young samurai who sought to build a powerful army through, in part, the imposition of universal conscription.[46] The new army was designed to quell burgeoning peasant revolts and to break the ongoing resistance of older feudal clans.[47] The influence of Western ideas and demands for liberalization eventually caused the Meiji emperor to proclaim the Meiji Constitution in 1889, but it was written in secret by a few select oligarchs.[48] These oligarchs and the military and allied bureaucrats would still control the country, and the overall basis of Japanese government was grounded in the deification of the emperor.[49] Only 1 percent of the population could vote in the first Meiji era election.[50] A state religion was also imposed.[51] Despite some loosening of social hierarchies, various forms of bondage and pariahdom persisted, and a harsh prison system took root.[52] Schools were designed to "create subjects useful for the state."[53] Most Japanese people were heavily taxed peasants, and the "history of the Japanese peasantry during the Meiji period is a pathetic record of the most abysmal squalor punctuated by frequent incidence of disastrous crop failures and mass starvation."[54] Peasants labored under a "tyrannical ruling class which exercised virtually total control over their daily lives."[55] War with China finally came over a prostrate Korea, and upstart Japan's victory over a weakened Chinese dynasty sparked intense rivalries in the region, which devolved into endless carnage for the next half-century.[56]

If the cases of Russia, Brazil, China, and Japan fail to convey the stark differences between their history and development in the U.S. Midwest during the same era, consider France and Britain, two nations tightly woven into the traditional telling of early American history. After marching all over Europe, the armies of revolutionary France were finally defeated, the country was pinned back into its traditional borders, and the monarchy was restored during the early nineteenth century. Frenchmen were not allowed to vote unless they paid 300 francs a year in taxes, and they could not run for office unless they paid 1,000 francs in taxes.[57] In 1831 the voting requirement was lowered to 200 francs, but this allowed only some 250,000 Frenchmen out of an adult male population of nine million to vote.[58] It was not until 1848 that France granted full voting rights to men over age twenty-one, a change that increased the total number of voters from 246,000 to ten million, the first time a major European state had granted universal male suffrage.[59] Soon after, however, France returned to imperial rule with the rise of Louis Napoleon Bonaparte, who embraced laws again restricting suffrage, press freedoms, and political assembly.[60] Working with the military, Louis Napoleon seized complete power, abolished the National Assembly, declared himself emperor, and either killed resisters or exiled them to Algeria.[61]

Even in England, home to the Magna Carta and Parliament and the birthplace of modern republicanism, democratic development stalled. About seventy families dominated English politics.[62] The House of Commons in the early nineteenth century remained a "landed preserve."[63] It was difficult for democrats to navigate the *"thick* character of England: the symbolism of the Crown, the strength of the landed classes, the centrality of an established church, the desire of the bourgeoisie (or its sons) to join the gentry, the weight of the Establishment, and the lure of titles and honors—the basic fact that England was a society in which a hereditary social order dominated the political and economic orders."[64] Democratic development came slow. In 1832 the Reform Bill modified some rotten election boroughs, which had allowed the perpetuation of aristocratic rule, but the number of eligible voters in England and Wales grew only from 435,000 people to 657,000, and thus the gentry and nobility maintained control.[65] By the late 1860s, only one million of the seven million adult men in England and Wales could vote. The Reform Act of 1867 doubled this number to two million. The Third Reform Act in 1884 added another six million people to the electorate.[66]

Although looking outside the United States is wise for comparative purposes, internal regional comparisons are also revealing. The country, as

Frederick Jackson Turner once explained, was a nation of distinct regions.[67] The South was always considered an internal Other, for example, a place of widely diverging ideas and customs.[68] When "Yankees traveled south or southerners traveled north (or when foreign visitors visited North America), they never failed to emphasize the most obvious differences between" between American regions.[69] The South was seen as violent, hedonistic, indolent, and racist compared to the sober, persevering, tolerant, and energetic regions to the north.[70] The norms embraced by the planter elite of the South contrasted starkly with the "pragmatic rationalism so conspicuous a part of a Franklin-esque Yankeedom."[71] An "ideology of literacy," as James McPherson called it, prevailed in the Midwest, where schools and colleges were ubiquitous and a bourgeois culture of uplift and reform predominated.[72] Southern literacy rates were comparatively much lower. A martial culture of honor and hierarchy also prevailed in the South.[73] For southerners, the practice of "dueling could and did become intertwined with their prideful search for a regional cultural identity distinct from and superior to that of the self-righteous and hostile North."[74] Southern honor was the "keystone of the slaveholding south's morality."[75] This contrasted to the Midwest, where slavery was prohibited and a growing group of reformers and activist ministers attempted to undermine and abolish it, unlike in the South, where slavery found ecclesiastic justification.[76] Slavery made the entire course of southern economic development distinct.[77] The intense defense of slavery and the deepening of southern separatism triggered a bloody civil war fought along sectional lines, leaving the South to contend with a legacy of "frustration and failure" and entangled in a "mystique of prideful 'difference,' identity, and defensiveness."[78] The contrasting regions were, as one southerner said, "entirely separated by climate, by morals, by religion, and by estimates so totally opposite to all that constitutes honor, truth, and manliness, that they cannot longer exist under the same government." The contrast between the open society and free-labor ideology of the Midwest and the norms of the Slave Power was, one Ohio congressman said, the difference "between systems, between civilizations."[79]

Consider South Carolina. In the 1600s the English king granted lands in the Province of Carolina to English lords in exchange for their fealty in domestic conflicts. English planters from Barbados then brought plantation agriculture to Carolina along with African slaves, who soon became a majority of the population.[80] In comparison with other parts of the future

United States, there is ample reason that South Carolina is seen as "infamously different with its Barbadian cultural hearth and its slave majority."[81] The presence of loyalists and those devoted to the English king made South Carolina a particularly bloody battleground during the American Revolution. After independence, prominent South Carolinians like John C. Calhoun persistently resisted integration into the United States and defended the southern slave system; the breach finally came when South Carolina led the secession of the southern region of the country.[82] After the war, as midwestern states were liberalizing their voting laws and passing nondiscrimination and open-voting statutes, South Carolina governors like "Pitchfork Ben" Tillman were rewriting constitutional provisions to disenfranchise blacks.[83] During the later civil rights era, South Carolina was the first state to challenge the constitutionality of the Voting Rights Act, in 1966 (Chief Justice Earl Warren used the discriminatory remarks of figures like Tillman when writing his decision about the law).[84] All this contributed to the South Carolinian Wilbur Cash's finding that "there exists among us . . . a profound conviction that the South is another land, sharply differentiated from the rest of the American nation, and exhibiting within itself a remarkable homogeneity."[85]

If the distinctions between the South and the Midwest are stark, the distinctions between the Midwest and New England are less dramatic, but certainly present. One cannot dismiss the importance of the flow of New Englanders across the burned-over district of upstate New York and through the Erie Canal to points in the Midwest, where they often obtained positions of authority.[86] But they also blended into other migration streams and made the Midwest highly complex and pluralistic. Frontier conditions also had the effect of eroding older patterns of privilege and deference. The economic power of the urban East also give rise to long-standing tensions with the emerging Midwest. As historians have emphasized in recent years, some Mid-Atlantic and New England states also had a legacy of slavery from their colonial years that was not transmitted to the Northwest Territory in any significant way.[87] Thus the more democratic and pluralistic Midwest could be contrasted to the more aristocratic and monochromatic Northeast for much of the nineteenth century, although it is important not to exaggerate these differences. Some of the founders of the American republic saw the Midwest as a place where the remaining obstacles to a properly functioning American republicanism could be overcome.[88] If the Midwest remains closer to the unique dissenting tradition in New England than other regions of the United States, especially its religious idealism, its culture of thrift and uplift, its civic strengths, and its yeoman traditions, this also helps to highlight the Midwest's major differences from other parts of the world, including old monarchical Britain, from which New Englanders revolted.

All this points to a more specific purpose for this book. Only with a wide global perspective can one see the democratic development of the Midwest properly and realize how far advanced the region was vis-à-vis the rest of the world. In the Midwest there was a zealous commitment to educating the masses so that reason and learning could underpin democratic governance. This included college education. Old World social hierarchies and privileges were broken down in the Midwest, fostering a democratic culture. Most people in other places were landless peasants, whereas in the Midwest most people were fee-simple land-owning yeoman farmers. Most people elsewhere had no guaranteed civil rights, unlike the citizens of the constitutional polities of the Midwest. People actively voted in the Midwest. Religious freedom prevailed. A pragmatic and entrepreneurial spirit undergirded the culture. This is why an Ohio orator could reasonably say during the early nineteenth century that Ohio, the first of the midwestern states to emerge during the early republic and a model for those that followed, was the "truest democracy which had yet existed."[89] When the midwestern regionalist writer William Gallagher said in 1850 that the region was a grand "Experiment in Humanity" where the "freest forms of social development" in the world could be found, it was not puffery.[90] He was objectively and comparatively correct. The emergent midwestern civilization, Gallagher said, could one day enable its citizens to realize "their real dignity and importance in the social scale, by proclaiming to them that they are neither slaves nor nonentities, but true men and women," which was saying a lot in the world of 1850.[91] Gallagher's focus on the exceptional democratic character of the Midwest underscores why it is past time for a new look at a region whose history has been lost to the American imagination. It is a history we need now to remind us of our ideals and how many battles we have already won.

A few thoughts should be shared about the organization of this book. Instead of the few pages above, I could have spent a hundred pages explaining the comparative historical position of the Midwest, especially given its importance to the grounding of this book. Or I could have devoted long chapters in the pages that follow to explaining civic clubs in the Midwest or the details of midwestern units serving in the Civil War or the various fronts of temperance campaigns or the dozens of writers who took up midwestern regionalism. Each one of the chapters contained herein could have gone on for five hundred pages. Though I find the stories of small-town Elks lodges and the community and civic energy they represent endlessly fascinating, as an author one simply cannot expect a reader to endure the amount of description necessary to convey the ubiquity and density of the world of fraternal lodges, church committees, and community groups in the midwestern culture of "joining." "Life is short," the intellectual historian James Kloppenberg wisely notes, "and our books are often already too long."[92] Short treatments of important matters must suffice because too long of a slog would cause us to lose good people by the side of the trail, but it must be remembered that the world of churches and lodges and community picnics constituted the social realm where most midwesterners lived for most of the period discussed in this book.

So too the world of farming. For much of the period covered in these pages the vast bulk of midwesterners were farmers or engaged in economic activities related to farming. Although it is generally not wise to subject a reader to dozens of pages of detailed descriptions of nineteenth-century agriculture, one must not forget the centrality of farming to the Midwest for most of its history. All this is to say that one of the problems of midwestern history is that so much of it is hiding in plain sight, obscured by the fish-recognizing-water problem described by the midwesterner David Foster Wallace during a commencement address at Kenyon College in Ohio.[93] Much of the midwestern experience involves the rhythms of agrarian and small-town life— what Van Doren thought was so dull—and so it gets lost in the din as we all chase more entertaining distractions. In the end, a historian has to draw lines and set limits and construct parameters; what to put in, what to cut, what to shorten, what to emphasize are the central problems of historical narration. I want people to read this book and not give up, so I tried to keep the story moving. I do try, however, to provide copious notes so that readers, fellow historians in particular, can follow the trail of sources used to make my arguments and seek greater detail if they so choose. I hope some of them will pick up a shovel and lend a hand and help the effort to dig out the Midwest's lost history.

Although I try to condense major aspects of midwestern history, this is not the case for the story of African Americans in the Midwest, which is the subject of chapter 4. This story, however, should be read with the proper proportions in mind. In 1850, for example, there were 400,000 people in Michigan, but only 2,500 African Americans, only a fraction of a percent of the total population.[94] Despite these low numbers, the story of African Americans is especially important to American history overall and to the dialogue of our present era, so it receives extra attention. This book focuses on the majority of midwesterners during the nineteenth century and notes many of their achievements; still, I want to emphasize, once again, that not everyone, especially African Americans, succeeded or thrived in the Midwest, especially during the early decades of the region. Although their focus lies beyond the scope of this study, I highlight some important works that readers should consider on this front if they want to read further. The most timely book is from the longtime Indiana University historian James Madison, who recently published his study on the Ku Klux Klan in Indiana during the 1920s.[95] Kevin Boyle's study of race relations in Detroit during the 1920s is also important.[96] The stories of the race riot in Chicago after World War I and the race riot and ensuing racial crisis in Detroit during World War II must also be considered.[97] The story of regional distinctions between the Midwest and the South can also be analyzed by way of the many books on the African American Great Migration to midwestern cities, both large and small.[98] Also of particular interest is work on Malcolm X's boyhood in Omaha and Lansing.[99] All of these topics are suggestive and underscore the need, at some later date, to take the topics tackled in this volume beyond the nineteenth century and far deeper into the twentieth.

The handling of other people and topics should also be briefly noted. The advances of women in the Midwest is a major subject of this book, which stands to reason. Attention to the history of women in the region cannot fairly be called disproportionately large because they constitute half the population. Less attention, however, is given to Native Americans, but much of the history discussed here takes place after the crucial midwestern Indian wars of the 1790s. There is also a massive historiography of midwestern Native American history to consult, representing the impressive work product of scores of scholars over the past forty years. The many battles and experiences of midwestern troops during the Civil War are not addressed in detail, but the impact of the war on regional identity is certainly discussed. The economic history of the Midwest is also not afforded significant attention, even though the region had grown into an economic powerhouse by the end of the nineteenth century. All of these topics, in even more granular detail, could and should be books themselves, but the goal here was to create a "lumping" book, where a big picture is sketched, and not a "splitting" book, where micro-stories that deviate from the big picture are told. More precisely, I aim to be a "moderate" lumper in this book, to use the term of the historian Jack Hexter, explaining the main currents of midwestern history while certainly acknowledging those elements that do not fit the pattern (which is not to say that these exceptional, divergent, or subaltern elements are any less important).[100] Sketching the big picture is "one of the historian's best controls for forays into the particular," notes Robert Dawidoff, and once that big picture comes into view I hope it helps spark more study of smaller-scale subsets of midwestern history.[101]

By focusing on the experience of the large bulk of midwesterners and the majoritarian culture, I am deviating from a now-popular scholarly approach. Some people argue that "social justice demands that those with the most social capital, such as scholars, have a responsibility to give voice to the least powerful by cultivating a standpoint that centers marginalized experiences and interests."[102] In contrast to such an approach, this book is more broadly focused on the history that most midwesterners lived through. It avoids "bagelization," as one scholar dubs it, or the tendency to focus on the perimeters of society, leaving the center empty and unaccounted for.[103] More specifically, the aim of this book is to stay focused on the growth of democratic institutions and the development of a robust civic culture in the Midwest, the formation of a coherent identity for the region, the social advances of underprivileged groups such as African Americans and women, and the spirit of democratic involvement and the enthusiasm for reform that enveloped all of the above. There is much to admire in some of the broad patterns of nineteenth-century midwestern development, and they are recognized—in contravention of the tendency, as the president of the College of St. Thomas in St. Paul once cautioned, to surrender to the "human fascination with calamity" or the lure of the "narrative of misfortune"—as central features of the Good Country.[104]

The time frame of this book, what historians call periodization, also requires explanation. The story largely begins with the organization of Ohio about 1800, with necessary allusions to the earlier adoption of the Northwest Ordinance by the Continental Congress, the law that served as the foundational charter for the Midwest and guided its development. The book ends with the era roughly before the beginning of World War I, around 1900. The period in between includes the key stages of democratic development in the Midwest, the emergence of a grounded democratic culture, and the sharpening of a specifically midwestern identity, particularly during the 1850s, out of a space that in earlier decades some saw as generically western. By the late nineteenth century, Peak Midwest had been achieved and the Midwestern Moment had arrived, but by the era of World War I the Midwest had begun to enter a new phase owing to international developments, industrialization, urbanization, migration, technology, and other factors such as the rise of a central administrative state, professionalization, mass culture, and global wars. The Midwestern Moment, the era of regional ascendance from roughly the Civil War to World War I, was passing and the high standing of the Midwest—once seen as the "warm center of the world," in the words of the Minnesotan F. Scott Fitzgerald—began to lose its centrality to American life.[105] The era of World War I and its aftermath—a time, the Nebraskan Willa Cather said, when the "world broke in two"—must await a future volume. By the post–World War I era, the American version of Victorianism, which is central to the story of the Midwest told in this volume, had "lost its cultural hegemony," as the historian Daniel Walker Howe has said, so what came after requires a new way of thinking about the world.[106]

A comment on nomenclature is also in order. As indicated by the name given to the founding charter of the Midwest, the Northwest Ordinance, the region was first dubbed the Northwest, or the region to the west of the original colonies that was above the Ohio River and distinct from the South. As Americans moved farther west, the region became the Old Northwest to distinguish it from a later Northwest encompassing the Dakotas and then an even later Pacific Northwest. As recent research has shown, the region we now know as the Midwest started to become known as the Middle West as early as the 1850s, distinguishing it from the Far West. During this same period, the region's steady divergence from the American South proceeded apace and was dramatically sharpened by the Civil War. Later, in an act of abbreviation around the time the twentieth century arrived, the term "Midwest" came into usage and is still the common term used today. For the sake of clarity and simplicity, I use "Midwest" frequently in this book unless an old source is being quoted. But for aficionados of historiography and linguistic etymology, I wanted to point out early on the transition between regional monikers and how that matter is handled in this volume.

Most writing, even nonfiction history, is connected to some personal experience, and this book is no exception. About the time that Hefner's parents were finishing college in Nebraska my maternal grandfather, a fine Irishman named Richard Barry, was moving from his boyhood farm in Johnson County, Iowa (he lived near the high-sounding town of Oxford, no less), to find his own farm in eastern South Dakota. His ancestors had come over during the Great Hunger, settled in Nebraska, served in the Union Army during the Civil War, and ended up back in Iowa. My paternal great-grandfather, Ferdinand Lauck, had migrated from Mecklenburg province in eastern Germany to Dakota Territory during the 1880s. The Barrys and Laucks ended up farming near the towns of Winfred and Junius in Lake County, South Dakota, and my parents, Dale Lauck and Patricia Barry, met one day when the Lauck threshing crew was harvesting wheat on a farm owned by a Barry relative. My parents, Dale and Pat, were farming in Lake County when I was born. They had me when they were slightly older than the norm, so I had a good sense of their worlds and an older, agrarian, and small-town Midwest. It was not perfect place, of course, but it always seemed to be populated with decent people who cared about each other and worked hard. This world, I came to find out, was not understood by many of the intellectuals, writers, professors, and cultural arbiters I came to know in the wider world. I wrote this book in hopes of opening the truths of this old world to them and, I hope, to many others.

CHAPTER 1

"A FREE AND UNRESTRICTED MODE OF LIFE"

PLANTING DEMOCRACY IN THE MIDWEST

During the summer of 1787, at the same time that the famed delegates to the convention in Philadelphia met to craft a constitution, the Continental Congress met in New York City in relative obscurity. In New York that summer the war-weary Congress busied itself writing the Northwest Ordinance, a statute designed to govern the territory of the future Midwest, which had recently been acquired from England during the Revolution. Uncertainty reigned in New York as the former Dutch colony turned British colonial stronghold looked to a new era of American governance. During the long Revolutionary War, New York City had been a garrison town, home to thousands of British troops and a hub of loyalist support for the crown. But a new era of thought and practice was at hand, marking a sharp break with monarchical Europe. The idealistic charter crafted that summer by the Continental Congress would tap ascendant republican thought, overcoming legacies of royalism and colonial submission and imperial domination, and yield a new and unique democratic order in the future Midwest, one unequaled in world history. A later senator from Ohio opined that the Ordinance was "coeval with the Constitution, born the same year, of the same parents, and baptized in the same good old republican church."[1] Historians have rightly proclaimed that the Ordinance "has no parallel in the history of other modern states."[2]

Most of life in the world that preceded the era of the American Revolution could only be described as oppressive, a condition too widely invoked in recent decades for situations anything but, at least in relative terms. In contrast to a common strand of current thinking, we once recognized the late eighteenth century as a critical demarcation point for the beginning of a new era of human freedom. In a classic treatment, R. R. Palmer poetically described the age of revolutions that brought new social forces to life, terror to France, and democracy to the young United States, or at least large parts of it.[3] At that point the "American republic was a lonely experiment in a world of monarchies."[4] This experiment triggered other exertions of independence and a long series of American replicas, many failed, around the world.[5] After the Revolution and the crafting of its foundational charters, the United States had "written golden pages in history, as attested by the individuals, groups, and countries that imitated it, envied it, were inspired by it in the ensuing two centuries."[6] It is approaching a half-century since Gordon S. Wood emphasized, as part of a once well-known but now neglected school of thought, that reformers in England and America tried to tap a classical vein of republican thought to constrain and overcome modern royalism.[7] Of all these developments in modern democracy, the most advanced and most enduring and perhaps the most forgotten is what unfolded in the American Midwest, where democratic idealism advanced the furthest.

Before plunging into an exploration of the formative era of the Midwest, it is essential to highlight some core components of life in the region that can be difficult to comprehend deep into the twenty-first century. Monarchy, royal privilege, and feudal social structures were once deeply entrenched in continental Europe and, in a diminished form, in England. Even though there had been some erosion of monarchical power in England over the centuries owing to the Magna Carta and Glorious Revolution, a class system and aristocracy still persisted. The English social structures that perpetuated the inferiority of most people to kings, masters, and fathers was planted in the American colonies, but there they began to shrink so far from the mother country. Out on the western frontiers of the American colonies they collapsed.[8] The Midwest saw the emergence of the first true Americans, or people not directly from Europe or heavily imprinted by European culture, unlike the East Coast, where, as Frederick Jackson Turner said, the "constant touch of this part of the country with the Old World prevented the modifying influences of the new environment from having their full effect."[9] Because American democracy tapped the thought of dissenters in Britain, it had "English roots," noted one historian, "but fertilized by nature's bounty in the Mississippi Valley, it has flowered there as it never did in Europe."[10] Unlike Europeans, the Americans did not have to "uproot ancient abuses," did not have "to topple a ruling class, to end feudalism, to wipe out the Infamy, to oust the Jesuits, to abolish the Inquisition."[11] Manasseh Cutler, the leader of the first major American settlement in Ohio, said that in the Midwest "there will be no wrong habits to combat and no inveterate systems to overturn—there will be no rubbish to remove before you lay the foundations."[12] The editor of the *Cincinnati Literary Gazette* opined that the people of Ohio were "little fettered by established habits" and not "disposed to consider hereditary prejudices and heirlooms which cannot be parted with."[13] Out in the Midwest people could be uniquely free, a condition they widely recognized and routinely celebrated. Such midwesterners as Abraham Lincoln were strong advocates of a basic education so a person could be an active citizen and would be "enabled to read the histories of his own and other countries, by which he may duly appreciate the value of our free institutions."[14]

Lincoln was proud of his nascent region because the early Midwest saw an erosion of long-standing rules of social deference and an entrenchment of egalitarianism.[15] Aristocratic privilege and the constraining "cake of custom" meant less to these young Americans in this new social order.[16] J. Hector St. John Crevecoeur emphasized that the Americans were much more egalitarian and that their "dictionary" was "short in words of dignity, and names of honor." "We have no princes, for whom we toil, starve, and bleed," he said.[17] After visiting places such as Michigan Territory, Crevecoeur described the emerging country as "devoid of the vestiges of hereditary rank and privilege."[18] In an early speech to the Ohio Historical Society, James Perkins, a young Cincinnati lawyer who was active in a literary society called the Semi-Colon Club and a debating society called The Inquisition, wrote that Ohio was "founded a nearly true democratic community" and absent a "feudal spirit."[19] In 1837, Ohio judge Timothy Walker, echoing Manasseh Cutler, pointed out that, because the Northwest Ordinance set forth the principles of a democratic society from the beginning, "no ancient rubbish had to be cleared away."[20] Aristocracy-preserving primogeniture, for example, which held landed estates together for the benefit of the first-born son, had been abolished in the Midwest.[21] Part of midwesterners' great disdain for the South was, suggested one editor, due to slavery's tendency to generate "aristocratic feeling, and to destroy the American sentiment of social equality." German immigrant to the Midwest Carl Schurz recognized the deep regional divide. In the South, he said, the "despotic spirit of slavery and mastership combined pervades their whole political life like a liquid poison." One Michigan congressman noted that the southern surveillance state attendant to slavery brought a "system of espionage . . . which would disgrace the despotism and darkness of the middle ages."[22]

All this is what Frederick Jackson Turner was referring to when he described the "shearing off" of ancient hierarchies and ancestral privileges in the frontier Midwest.[23] When young Louis Phillipe, later to become king of France, visited Ohio, a straight-shooting tavern owner told him that he had many royals visit his establishment. "Who were they?" asked the young duke. "We're all kings here," declared the proud Buckeye before he kicked the future king out for complaining.[24] In the emerging Midwest hired hands rejected the term "servant" and insisted on being called "help" and on eating with the family, not at a servants table.[25] A European traveler in Indiana noted that "the feeling of equality pervades this State so much, that people do not like to work for wages."[26] Family name and religious affiliation and political connections "counted for less in the unfolding society of the Old Northwest than in the more highly ordered and structured society of the East."[27] This reflected the "West's passionate, dogmatic trust in the common man."[28] One immigrant to Belleville, Illinois, exhausted by the feudal rules and bureaucratic corruption of Europe, praised his new home: "Here everything rests on natural, unartificial foundations."[29] This immigrant echoed Whitman, who, when he visited Kansas, emphasized that he loved the "newer garden of creation" in the Midwest, a place where European conventions and models were least influential and local spirit the strongest.[30] "It is in the Middle West," Turner concluded, "that society has formed on lines least like Europe. It is here, if anywhere, that American democracy will make a stand against a tendency to adjust to a European type."[31] In the Midwest, one observer said, "democracy stalks unchecked. No one puts on airs."[32]

Another key to understanding the early development of the American Midwest is the ubiquity of religion. Perhaps the first communal structure erected in every settlement in the Midwest was a Christian church. There would be so many churches in Lincoln, Nebraska, not far from where Hugh Hefner's parents landed, that it was known as "The Holy City."[33] Town names also proclaimed the region's Christian grounding: Antioch, Goshen, Eden, Hebron, Lebanon, Mount Olive, New Palestine, Palestine, Paradise, Sinai, St. Paul, St. Peter, Zion. On the bookshelves of new midwestern homes were books such as *The Gospel Plan, Lectures on the New Testament, Prayers Suitable for Children and Sunday Schools,* and *A Few Sighs from Hell; or, The Groans of a Damned Soul.*[34] Settlers sang "On Jordan's Banks I Stand," "Washed in the Blood," and "Amazing Grace."[35] Christian devotion united settlers of differing stripes who saw themselves entering an "Edenic wilderness, a new Arcadia," and their beliefs "went straight back to the Book of Genesis."[36] From the beginning, given the settlers' Christian ardor, "Protestant missionaries imagined that the Mississippi Valley was a future center of Christendom."[37] Christianity shaped personal and communal life, guided reform efforts, sparked commitment to civic endeavors, and permeated public affairs. The Illinois constitutional convention of 1818, for example, received petitions asking that the new constitution "declare the Scriptures the word of God and that the constitution be founded thereon," a not uncommon gesture in the early Midwest.[38]

The widespread exercise of Christian beliefs of various form had been made possible by the framers of the Northwest Ordinance. Conscious of centuries of savage sectarian warfare in Europe, the Ordinance guaranteed a new era of religious freedom in the Midwest. It had been the practice for kings and princes to impose a theocratic order on their states in Europe and elsewhere. Such mandates had fueled the religious wars of the seventeenth century, which killed millions of Europeans. In New England the Puritan church had also come to control its colonies, and an orthodox "New England Way" prevailed.[39] At the time of the Revolution, nine out of the thirteen colonies still fused church and state.[40] Into the 1830s, New Englanders had to pay taxes to support the Puritan Congregational church. New England's religious leaders worried that people on the frontier were too "impatient of the restraints of law, religion, and morality" and too resistant to taxes.[41] They rightly sensed that midwestern practices were different.

In the Midwest, the Northwest Ordinance guaranteed that Americans, for the first time, could worship how they saw fit, and the social pressure to conform was lessened.[42] In 1833 one minister found Ohio "to be a place where

24

freedom of thought prevails. I say things constantly with effect that if lisped in New England would be overborne at once by the dominant opinions."[43] But in his new home on the midwestern frontier ecclesiastical control was drastically diminished and a separation of church and state maintained.[44] The pressure to conform that might have arisen even in the absence of a state-controlled religion was greatly lessened by the wide diversity of religious life in the Midwest. New England Congregationalists moved into the region, to be sure, but so did backcountry Presbyterians, mid-Atlantic Quakers, Southern Episcopalians, and many emergent and new Christian sects, all part of what historians have described as the "utter fragmentation of Protestantism in the Old Northwest."[45] In addition, the great wave of immigration during the nineteenth century brought even greater diversity in the form of European Catholics, Lutherans, Jews, and others. The mixture of religions and ethnicities and regional influences ensured that no single group could dominate and that there would be "no deferential society in the Old Northwest."[46]

There was so much diversity in some early settlements in the Midwest and so few people and so much space that some settlers simply coalesced into a generic nondenominational Christianity that brought worshipers under one roof. Differences among Christian sects were often "submerged in the erection of a common chapel until each could build its own meeting house."[47] The result was the emergence of a "generalized religiosity" and an "American Civil Religion."[48] In the town of Naples, Illinois, a settlement of three hundred people with "persons from nearly every state in the Union," there emerged a necessary and practical "interdenominational cooperation in both religious and educational matters." In 1835 the settlement of Kenosha, Wisconsin, built a community school that was available without charge to any congregation that wanted to worship there, and it "thus became a powerful focus of communal feeling despite the sectarian loyalties that persisted in the newly planted town." In towns like Naples or Kenosha, one historian noted, the "number of Methodists, Baptists, Presbyterians, or Episcopalians was insufficient for any group to develop a separate denominational culture," and as a result common schools were by nature highly intermixed by faith. In Racine, Wisconsin, cooperation also prevailed. The school doubled as a church where some religious services and Sunday school were held. When some Catholics complained about this use of public property, the settlers built a large church that all denominations could use, and thus "a nonsectarian school gave birth to a nondenominational church" and a "settlement" began the transformation into a "community."[49]

Community boosting and market-oriented entrepreneurs also tamped down religious frictions, creating a "fundamental tolerance" and a "built-in attitude of placation."[50] Midwestern ministers also tended to emphasize a regional flexibility and their learning at "brush college," as opposed to formal eastern schools of theology, and allied themselves with the Methodist minister Peter Cartwright, who said people "wanted a preacher that could mount a stump, a block, or old log, or stand in the bed of a wagon, and without note or manuscript, quote, expound, and apply the word of God to the hearts and consciences of the people."[51] All told, "theological and ecclesiastical fences" broke down, Christians "accommodated unprecedented diversities," and a "civic and universal" "pan-Protestant ideology" emerged that was so universal it also appealed to Jews and Catholics.[52] A Wisconsin-based scholar used this era of newly arriving ethnic groups to craft the theory of American democratic pluralism.[53]

All of this had been made possible by the Northwest Ordinance, the first article of which guaranteed the free exercise of one's religion.[54] The Ordinance then proceeded to set forth the rules for a new democratic order in the Midwest. The second article codified a long list of rights: habeas corpus, trial by jury, proportionate representation, bail, the presumption of innocence, a prohibition on cruel punishments, and property and contract rights. One historian opined that article 2 "reads like a checklist of republican virtues, with precedent going back all the way to the Magna Carta of 1215."[55] The third article required a focus on education in the new region because, as it asserted, "religion, morality, and knowledge" were "necessary to good government and the happiness of mankind." The Ordinance generously provided for the establishment of new democratic states in the Midwest on an equal footing with existing states as part of what one historian called an "unbelievably liberal colonial system."[56] Most important, article 6 of the Ordinance banned slavery. As Daniel Webster observed, article 6 "fixed forever the character of the population in the vast regions northwest of the Ohio, by excluding from them involuntary servitude," and "impressed on the soil itself, while it was yet a wilderness, an incapacity to sustain any other than freemen."[57] Of the major founding documents—the Constitution, the Declaration, and the Northwest Ordinance—the Ordinance has been seen as the most authentically

American, the most grounded in American experiences, and the most geared to the proper development of western lands.[58] The Ordinance gave a unique cast to the Midwest and thus became the "first act of self-definition" for the region.[59] The ban on slavery in particular engendered a sense of the Midwest "as a section with a distinct character that linked free institutions to economic development."[60] Given the previous "history of empires and slavery in the North American interior," the historian John Craig Hammond explains, "the ultimate exclusion of slavery from the old Northwest was exceptional."[61]

All of the ideals underlying the Ordinance were at work as the constitutional order of the Midwest began to take shape. In 1802, in the first of several critical democratic moments that would be repeated in other midwestern states, Ohioans elected thirty-five delegates to write a constitution. Participation was strong—in Hamilton County, home to Cincinnati, ninety-four candidates ran for ten delegate slots.[62] The campaigns to become delegates were "democratic, competitive, and played out in newspapers, broadsides, and stump speeches."[63] After the fall harvest, the delegates met in Chillicothe along the Scioto River to do their work, which took inspiration from the ideals of the American Revolution and followed the model for governance set forth in the Northwest Ordinance. That November delegates "overwhelmingly voted to exclude slavery and involuntary servitude from Ohio."[64] The new state charter afforded the most power to a two-house legislature in order to erode the standing of the executive (Ohioans were tired of colonial governors appointed by the central government in Washington exercising excessive authority).[65] Article 8 set forth a robust bill of rights that forbid slavery, ensured the free exercise of religion, banned debtor's prisons, promoted free speech and assembly and democratic governance, and guaranteed that "no hereditary emoluments, privileges or honors shall ever be granted or conferred by this State." Although there was debate over certain ideological points, the historian Andrew Cayton explained, the "most impressive thing about the settlement of Ohio was how quickly the frontier period passed, how rapidly men resolved their differences into a relatively stable society fully integrated into the larger Atlantic world." They had built a new social order based on a government limited in its authority, a high degree of autonomy for individuals, and a largely unregulated economy in which "no legally established institutions—no aristocracy, church, or army—exercised extraordinary power."[66]

In short order, the other budding states north of the Ohio River followed suit and even borrowed some of Ohio's constitutional work product. In May 1816, settlers in Indiana voted to select delegates to a convention to write a constitution for the future state. The next month forty-three delegates, mostly farmers plus a few preachers and lawyers, assembled at Corydon, the territorial capital, in a new stone courthouse and began their eighteen-day deliberations (William Henry Harrison named the town after the young shepherd in his favorite song, "The Pastoral Elegy": "Can you boast of a shepherd so fair / So gentle, so modest, and kind / His easy and elegant air / And the graces that shone in his mind!"[67] Because of the intense heat, delegates often met outside under a tree that became known as the Constitution Elm.[68] Most important, pro-slavery forces were defeated at the convention. In fact, the final constitution condemned slavery as grounded in "usurpation and tyranny" and formally prohibited the document from ever being amended to allow for the introduction of slavery or involuntary servitude.[69] Article 1 of the constitution also set forth a strong bill of rights. One editor celebrated the "solemn decorum, the high sense of manly freedom, and the acuteness of political discussion, which animated the assembly in this infantine state of society."[70]

Two years later, in July 1818, people in Illinois voted to select delegates to a constitutional convention. In the old French village of Kaskaskia, thirty-three elected delegates assembled, and by the end of August a constitution had been crafted after twenty-one days of work.[71] It banned slavery, except that those who were slaves prior to the adoption of the constitution would remain slaves; their children, however, would be born free. One anti-slavery advocate wrote, "I would rather see our rich meadows and fertile woodlands inhabited alone by the wild beasts and birds of the air, than that they should ever echo the sound of the slave driver's scourge, or resound with the cries of the oppressed African."[72] The Illinois constitution embraced the midwestern ideal of "living in a democratic society that was not dominated by a so-called superior class at the top and unsoundly based upon an enslaved laboring class at the bottom."[73] The charter also required that money from public land sales be directed into education, including the construction of a college or university.[74]

The southern portions of the three original states of the Midwest grew with the help of water transport on the Ohio River and began to fill with people; soon after, the northern parts of the region also began to develop and embrace even more democratic practices than their preceding midwestern brethren. In 1835 settlers in Michigan voted to form a new polity, and the Wolverine State, after settling a boundary dispute with Ohio over the future of Toledo and a successful but wintry "Frostbitten Convention" of eighty-two constitutional delegates in Ann Arbor, was admitted to the Union in 1837.[75] Thereafter Iowa entered the Union in 1846, Wisconsin in 1848, and Minnesota in 1858, and so followed the recognition and celebration of these democratic achievements.[76] All of these midwestern constitutions were crafted after the Revolution during an age of growing democratic and egalitarian commitments and an intensifying "culture of constitutionalism," when the "special aura around the notion of a constitution" took hold.[77]

The new constitutions of the Midwest established the framework for democratic life in the region and active voting soon followed. In 1802, Ohio gave unconditional voting rights to white males, "who are compelled to labor on the roads of their respective townships or counties," but since all adult males were obliged to work on the roads everyone won the franchise (by one vote, delegates at the Ohio constitutional convention failed to extend the suffrage to African Americans).[78] In 1816, the new Indiana constitution provided for universal manhood suffrage for whites absent any help with the roads or any conditions whatsoever, as did Illinois.[79] Michigan soon followed, again with unrestricted white male suffrage.[80] So followed Wisconsin, Minnesota, Iowa, and Nebraska.

The broad franchise in the Midwest contrasted starkly with other regions. In New York City suffrage was limited to those who paid rent of $25 a year or more. In South Carolina a white man could vote if he lived in the state for two years, but he could vote only for congressmen and for the state's lower house.[81] In the old South several such obstacles to voting persisted: in many states people could not vote for governor or for county officials; some voters' ballots counted for more than other voters'; into the 1820s, Virginia still required voters to own property (twenty-five acres with a 12 by 12 foot house, or fifty acres of unsettled land).[82] Many states required voters to have paid taxes, including New Hampshire, Delaware, Massachusetts, Rhode Island, Pennsylvania, Georgia, Connecticut, New York, and North Carolina.[83] Taxpaying requirements were not dropped until much later in several states: Mississippi (1832), Tennessee (1834), New Jersey (1844), Connecticut (1845), and Louisiana (1845). Taxpaying requirements were actively retained via decisions made in Pennsylvania (1838), New Hampshire (1851), and Massachusetts (1851). Despite its modern reputation for progressivism, there was no universal manhood suffrage in Massachusetts until 1891.[84] "Paupers" were also banned from voting in New Hampshire (1792), South Carolina (1810), Maine (1819), Massachusetts (1821), Virginia (1829), Delaware (1831), Rhode Island (1842), and New Jersey (1844).[85] Older eastern states, in short, became democratic much more slowly than the new midwestern states.[86]

Midwesterners were not shy about using their robust suffrage rights. Two-thirds of voters cast ballots in Ohio for the election of delegates for the 1802 constitutional convention and for the 1803 congressional election.[87] Early Ohio strongly encouraged voting, in part through the use of secret ballots, and came to be seen as having "an unrestricted and universal elective franchise."[88] Early general elections for state legislature and Congress in Ohio saw over 70 percent turnout at a time when communications and travel were not simple matters.[89] Elections for governor in Ohio during the 1820s generated turnout on the level of 60–70 percent.[90] The most dedicated historian of early Ohio political history concluded that the "political system in Ohio was thoroughly democratized by the early years of the nineteenth century."[91]

Town halls and meeting houses and civic activities in general supported and gave shape to democratic life in the emerging midwestern states. Civic passions could also be found in arguments over which towns would serve as the county seat.[92] Later came more ornate state capitals to host democratic debate and lawmaking. The civic culture that emerged in the Midwest by midcentury was on full display in Illinois when Senator Stephen Douglas, after being greeted by a half-mile-long procession, joined Abraham Lincoln, who was met by a similar throng and bands and speeches, for a three-hour debate in Quincy.[93]

The formal statutes, constitutions, voting laws, candidate debates, and elections were sustained by the development of a democratic culture in the Midwest. Older codes of deference eroded in the region, an egalitarianism prevailed, and the republican ideology that fueled the American Revolution found its most fertile ground. Midwestern republicanism meant an accessibility to public officials that was "unlike the East, where magistrates, military officers, and politicians were held in awe." Judges, lawyers, military leaders, and government officials in the Midwest, on the other hand, were also tavern keepers and farmers. One traveler commented, "It no doubt seems singular to the English reader, to hear of judges and captains keeping taverns . . . but it is very common in this republican country."[94] The image of the midwestern common man burst into national politics in 1840 when William Henry Harrison of Indiana and Ohio defeated the New Yorker Martin Van Buren for president. Harrison was portrayed as a log cabin–dwelling midwesterner who defended the region while Van Buren sprinkled eau de cologne on his whiskers and had gold spoons at his table, foretelling a future of midwestern populism and regionalist sentiments.[95] As the song went:

Oh, how, tell me how does your buckeye cabin go?
It goes against the spoilsman, for well its builders know
It was Harrison who fought for the cabins long ago.[96]

Soon followed Lincoln's more iconic bootstrap story (one historian recently deemed Lincoln "a real, indeed a typical, self-made man of his age"), the rough-hewn efficiency of the leather goods clerk Ulysses S. Grant, and wide access to James Garfield (who went from canal worker on the Cleveland-Akron run to president) during his original front-porch campaign.[97]

Midwestern democratic culture, in addition to its celebration of the common man, was leavened by the diverse mix of peoples in the Midwest, which prevented any one sociocultural group from dominating midwestern states. In addition to the mixture of Christian religions in the Midwest, the adherents of those religions came from different regions and subregions of the country. By 1850, Ohio had a more diverse population than any other state in the country.[98] The first major influence in the southern Midwest was immigration from the upland South over the Ohio River.[99] But then Yankees came across on the Erie Canal route; in the spring of 1832, a thousand Yankees a day passed through Buffalo on their way to the Midwest.[100] Yankees brought their white church spires and village greens to the Western Reserve of northeast Ohio and created a "New Connecticut"—settlers from Plymouth, Norwalk, and Greenwich founded Plymouth, Norwalk, and Greenwich, Ohio.[101]

Yankees used clotheslines, launched dairies and built strong barns, and had tidy farms; southerners went another direction.[102] In a common formulation highlighting a subregional north-south divide in the Midwest, the historian Walter Havighurst noted the frictions between the southerners and Yankees in Indiana: "Western Yankees regarded Hoosiers as ignorant and shiftless, while Hoosiers considered the Yankees sly and grasping."[103] Stephen Douglas liked to needle Lincoln for shading his slavery views based on whether he was speaking in southern or northern Illinois, or, in other words, speaking to the southern- or Yankee-oriented parts of the state.[104] Mixed in with the Yankees and southerners were the remaining pockets of French influence, new English settlers, German immigrants, and Quakers from the mid-Atlantic states. In the 1840s the Irish rolled in from the "hungry counties of Ireland," where a quarter of Erin would perish from famine, and they were soon digging the canals and building the railroads of the Midwest.[105] When visiting the Midwest, Emerson commented on the "poor Irishman, the wheelbarrow is his country."[106] But the Irish were soon active in midwestern urban politics and winning mayorships there. Then came a wave of Scandinavian immigrants, who became particularly prominent in the western parts of the Midwest, especially Minnesota and the Dakotas. In 1882, Knute Nelson of Minnesota, the son of an unmarried domestic servant, became the first Norwegian elected to Congress and went on to become the "Grand Old Man" of the "Grand Old Party."[107] Later, as the twentieth century dawned, came many Poles, Jews, and other eastern European immigrants to burgeoning midwestern cities, adding to the "ethnological layer-cake."[108]

As suggested by the career of Knute Nelson and others, many immigrants recognized the openness of midwestern political life in ways that old-stock Americans at times did not. One early immigrant to the Midwest commented on the motivations for moving to a new region and cited the escape of onerous taxes, providing for one's family, fear of arbitrary government punishment, and simply the "propensity for a free and unrestricted mode of life."[109] The German refugees of the revolutions of 1848 understood these new freedoms particularly well and were eager to embrace real democratic politics in the United States and escape monarchical Europe.[110] One German immigrant who had fought "German despotism" at home proudly embraced his new freedoms in Kansas.[111] Such immigrant enthusiasm for civic life, especially among newly arrived Germans, could be seen during the visit of Louis Kossuth in 1852, when the famed Hungarian democrat made several stops in the region. In Columbus, Ohio, he was escorted to the state capital by a German artillery company, a German marching band, the Turnverein club, German butchers on horseback, and a chorus.[112] After stops in Cleveland and Cincinnati, Kossuth was "impressed by the German-American zeal for political participation."[113] The legislatures of Indiana and Ohio adopted pro-Kossuth resolutions, and in Hamilton, Ohio, citizens offered him five hundred muskets for his battle against European tyranny.[114] After his visit to Ohio, Kossuth boarded a special riverboat, the *Wisconsin,* for a trip down the Ohio River to Indiana, where he was met by thousands of well-wishers in Madison, then boarded the "Kossuth Special" north to Indianapolis, where upon arrival he spoke to a crowd and contrasted Europe and the United States. The latter offered freedom, he said, whereas in the former, under arrogant despots, "twenty centuries of blood have watered the red-hot chains, and still the fetters are not broken." He was received by both houses of the Indiana legislature and then addressed the Association of Friends of Hungary at the Masonic Temple, praising the free press while touting Hungary's record of defending Christian civilization and constitutionalism.[115] Kossuth saw the Midwest as the "territorial paradise of the oppressed German and Irish peasant[s]," who were enjoying the "most democratic and equal society on earth."[116] The Hungarian pursuing democratic ideals in corrupt Europe was so popular in the Midwest that settlers in Iowa named a county after him, and Kossuth asked Iowans to aid the democratic cause in Hungary.[117] Southerners, meanwhile, were appalled at the attraction of abolitionists to Kossuth and feared his message of democratic reform and his calls for interventions to aid democratic movements.[118] Ohio GOP senator Benjamin Wade relished the discomfort Kossuth caused southerners: "Every speech he makes is the best kind of Abolition lecture. This is felt keenly by our Southern brethren."[119]

The liberties enjoyed by the new immigrants extended beyond politics to economic life. Gustav Unonius, a Swedish immigrant to the Midwest, remarked on the "unlimited freedom" of the region, including in the trades: "A man who today is a mason may tomorrow be a doctor, the next day a cobbler."[120] The Swedish immigrant's amazement at the employment options available to him in the Midwest in contrast to the Old World highlights how the market orientation of the Midwest fostered an open democratic culture. He praised the midwestern economy for its freedoms and noted the many jobs that settlers did in comparison to the old country, where restrictive "Swedish guild-ordinances" controlled economic life.[121] A German immigrant praised the "free and happy land" he had moved to and was proud to report to his brother back home, "I am my own boss."[122] Old World and colonial strictures on who could form a business and make profits were absent in the Midwest. Max Weber noted that "no medieval antecedents or complicating institutional heritage [served] to mitigate the impact of the Protestant ethic on American economic development."[123] A kingly obsession with glory and a noble's fixation on honor were absent.[124] Midwestern egalitarianism "reflected the traditional republican aversion to aristocracy, but was combined here with a celebration of industry, enterprise, and development."[125]

In addition to opening up society and the business system, market mores reinforced the moral teachings of Christian/Victorian culture. Much of the literature of moral uplift and striving during the early nineteenth century "read like an endless sermon on the importance of the bourgeois habits of industry, temperance, honesty, health, and especially moderation."[126] Merchants on small-town main streets eagerly pursued moral training and the ideal of industriousness.[127] The famed bourgeois virtues governed the market system and were adopted by young entrepreneurs.[128] The industrious clerks who embraced moral improvement in the East thought of moving to the midwestern frontier to start their own businesses so they could be owners, and many of them did.[129] Yankee businessmen thrived and some, like Marshall Field, Walter Newberry, Philip Armour, and Gustavus Swift, went on to earn great wealth.[130] When Emerson lectured in Illinois he noted the common efforts toward material gain and interests in the land market and "prices, & sections, & quarter sections of swamp lands."[131] In this world of open markets and land sales and free labor, people held a lot of different jobs. One observer of early Ohio noted that a midwestern "doctor returns from his rounds . . . feeds his pigs; and yet his skill as a physician is not doubted on that account. Nor is the sentence of the magistrate . . . esteemed less wise or impartial, even by the losing party of his wrangling disputants, because Cincinnatus-like, he is called from the plough/tail to the bench of justice."[132]

The image of the midwestern magistrate toggling between his courtroom and his pig farm points to the agrarian grounding of the Midwest. Although an assessment of the Midwest's market proclivities must obviously include main-street merchants, the market was certainly at work in the rural Midwest too. Until the coming of the twentieth century the Midwest was dominated by small farms, and agrarian sentiments prevailed. The purchasing of land and equipment, the selling of land after its value grew, and the marketing of surplus grains and livestock drew on farmers' business acumen and bourgeois virtues and relied on the hard work of farming—and it did so in a distinct rural form.[133] Hard work could yield a good living in the new country. One observer in Indiana counseled the poor back East, "ye poor starving wretches of our blind and horrible alleys and loathsome cellars," to come to the Midwest and "find corn and pork and turkey and squirrels and opossums and deer to eat! . . . Go, squalid slaves! beg an axe—put out—make tracks for the tall timber."[134] Farmers were proud to own their own plots of land, which was rare in the Old World.[135] New immigrants, who had been peasants in Europe, eagerly acquired land and praised the fertility of the Midwest: Ohio soils were "truly astounding"; Illinois soils were "inexhaustively productive"; Minnesota had a rich "fat black mull"; Iowa had "from five to twenty feet of rich black earth" stretched "as flat as a board without a single stone near it"; in Nebraska thousands of acres were available "with no stones or stumps to hinder the cultivator's plow."[136]

The new Midwest saw a marriage of fertile valleys and the ideology of republican labor and a bounteous progeny. In a speech to the Wisconsin state fair, Lincoln praised farmers' work ethic, their striving, and their constant practical education in "soils, seeds, and seasons—hedges, ditches, and fences, draining, drouths, and irrigation—plowing, hoeing, and harrowing—reaping, mowing, and threshing."[137] Midwesterners rejected the "idea that a man cannot be a true gentleman and labor with his hands" and saw such a belief as a "dead and dishonored dogma."[138] As long as this new society remained populated by striving and independent yeoman farmers embracing education and pragmatism, "oppression" by "crowned-kings, money-kings, and land-kings" would be impossible.[139] When he became president, with southern resistance gone, Lincoln greatly advanced the cause of yeoman agriculture in the Midwest by signing the Homestead Act, opening up thousands of new farms to young and entrepreneurial midwestern farmers, and the Land-Grant College Act, creating colleges geared to agrarian concerns.[140]

Farmers were eager to attend country churches and support rural one-room schools, which were central fonts of midwestern culture and morality.[141] Rural families embraced and perpetuated the moral training and ideology of work popular in the Midwest at large and often voiced concern about young folk moving to cities and becoming entangled in urban vice.[142] Farm journals, which sold widely, including *Wallace's Farmer* in Iowa, published articles about moral training with titles such as "Getting the Boy Started Right."[143] In a common construction, *Wallace's* compared the virtues of country life to bad cities, which "bred sin, corruption, and sloth, especially through the use of alcohol and tobacco."[144] Some rural folk viewed the city with dread and "saw young men and women drifting into cheap dance halls, saloons, and even brothels for entertainment."[145] Young country boys were consistently warned about the city and its confidence men and painted women.[146] Success manuals of the era "praised the values of rural life, expressed contempt for all that was alien and urban, and generally seemed to try to keep the boys home on the farm."[147] The songbook of the Grange, a farm organization launched by a Minnesotan during the 1860s, included melodies such as "Stay on the Farm" and "The Happy Peasant."[148] In the Midwest, a frequent target of concern was Chicago.[149] Part of the response included the emergence of institutes, lyceums, and libraries that "would provide highly mobile young men of the urban centers, isolated from traditional institutional frameworks of morality, the means for maintaining character in a disorienting environment."[150]

The prevalence of agrarian culture in the Midwest also created a tight link to nature. From the earliest days of settlement midwesterners were immersed in a world of rivers, forests, soils, and weather. Tree clearing, the planting of fruit trees and crops, the worship of corn ("This glorious plant, transmitted by the alchemy of God"), and land preparation in general were common in the Midwest (the *Drainage Journal* was founded in Indianapolis).[151] This fit the Victorian embrace of hard work and the celebration of the outdoors and explained the depictions of scenic rivers, farms, duck hunting and fishing, and other rural images on midwestern parlor walls.[152] The agrarian sensibility also included nature tours and jaunts to scenic destinations.[153] The embrace of nature and parks and recreation on the Midwest's copious lakes was directly linked to the Victorian praise of nature's "morally therapeutic effect."[154] Liberty Hyde Bailey, who was raised on a midwestern farm, went to a country school, and attended a youthful Michigan State College, was a strong advocate of studying nature in schools along with geography and urged young people to travel and see more of the natural world.[155] Because of the advocacy by Bailey and others who preached the appreciation of nature, many famous naturalists emerged from the Midwest.[156] The study of natural science and history also thrived (in part due to the emphasis on science education in midwestern schools and the attraction to scientific study more generally).[157] Arbor Day, invented in Nebraska, led to programs to beautify schools and the broader landscape with new trees and to connect students to agriculture.[158] Fishing and hunting were also commonplace. One business manager in Minnesota said that hunting was his "chief source of amusement and recreation . . . not to speak of its beneficial effect on my health."[159]

Farmers were also active in politics and community life. Participation in local affairs fostered the growth of "township freedom" and training for basic political activities, as Tocqueville recognized: "The institutions of a township are to freedom what primary schools are to science."[160] Cooperation among farmers yielded a culture of neighborliness, communal joining, and "visiting."[161] Cooperative efforts extended from cabin building to logrolling (working together to clear a piece of land of trees and roll out the logs—the origin of the political term) to barn raising to harvesting.[162] Another venture was cornhusking, for which "neighbors came from miles around to make a frolic of hard labor" with roast pork and spirits.[163] Community came in the form of games, weddings, barbecues, rifle matches, exhibitions, shivarees, and fence-building and firewood-fetching operations.[164] Country fairs were common.[165]

If cultures are measured by their iconography, it follows that midwestern communities built palaces of corn to be centers of civic life.[166] Scholars have also noted that "every militia muster, every cabin-raising, scow-launching, shooting match, and logrolling was in itself a political assembly where leading figures of the neighborhood made speeches, read certificates, and contended for votes."[167] Beyond socializing and local politics, farmers used their community connections and organizing skills to form important farmer advocacy groups. In Wisconsin, for example, the Wisconsin State Agricultural Society emerged in 1851, and the Wisconsin Dairymen's Association and the Wisconsin State Grange were both formed in 1872.[168] The Midwest became the headquarters or active area of support for farmers' movements in the nineteenth century, including the Grange, the Farmers' Alliance, and the Populist parties and many smaller efforts.[169]

As the twentieth century arrived and urbanization and industrialization transformed the nation, various reformers tried to preserve the rural midwestern tradition of yeoman democracy. This included efforts to limit the power of railroads, to restrict monopoly power, and generally to improve rural living conditions.[170] There were many precedents for the latter, but it formally began when articulated by Theodore Roosevelt in 1907 in a speech in Lansing, Michigan, that began the Country Life Movement.[171] Country Lifers wanted to preserve the culture of rural life and "hoped that country people could content themselves with the virtues of simple living."[172] The 4-H organization, founded in Springfield, Ohio, catered to farm children and emerged from the Country Life drive.[173] Political leaders like William Hoard of Wisconsin and Henry Wallace of Iowa were advocates for the "uplift" and improvement of rural schools. Country Lifers also hoped to "infuse a love of the countryside" into rural schools' practical curricula. During this era Ray Stannard Baker, writing as David Grayson, became a prominent novelist by pushing themes related to the goodness of rural life in novels such as *Adventures in Contentment* (1906) and *Three Acres and Liberty* (1907).[174] Even as farming and rural life became less a fixture of midwestern day-to-day life, formal agrarian thought and pro-farmer public policy remained prominent. Nevertheless, the arrival of a conscious effort to save the rural Midwest was also a sign that its dominance was fading.[175]

The agrarian way of life and communal strengths that reformers were trying to save were part of the rich civic heritage in the Midwest that extended beyond the country to the small towns of the region. The first level of civic life in a midwestern town stemmed from Christian churches, which frequently hosted dinners, lectures, meetings on social issues, spelling bees, Sunday schools, and other such meetings.[176] School boards, agricultural societies, and committees to build churches, schools, and even colleges were also common, as were various voluntary associations, service clubs, and fraternal organizations, whose lodges were ubiquitous. These included the Masons, the Odd Fellows, the Grand Army of the Republic (for Union war veterans), the Knights of Pythias, Ancient Order of United Workmen, Moose clubs, and related service organizations like Rotary, Kiwanis, and Lions, which were very popular.[177] Rotary and Lions were founded in Chicago, Kiwanis in Detroit, and a related organization, the Gideons (who placed Bibles in hotel rooms), was launched in Janesville, Wisconsin.[178] The Midwest, with Illinois at its center, was considered the "heartland of the service club movement."[179] In a typical example of the merger of fraternal clubs and political culture, when Lincoln spoke in Indianapolis in 1859 after debating, once again, Stephen Douglas, this time throughout Ohio instead of Illinois, he spoke at the Masonic Hall, a common place of civic activity.[180]

Most towns also had locally specific organizations, often focused on advancing the arts in some form.[181] Jacksonville, Illinois, thought of as the "Athens of the Middle West" for its civic culture and colleges, boasted such groups as the Ladies' Education Society, the Club, the Literary Union, and the Jacksonville Sorosis.[182] The latter was formed by five Jacksonville women for the purpose of studying literature, science, and current events, and its first president—in a sign of the diversity of civic and educational clubs available—was also a member of the Ladies' Education Society, the Jacksonville Art Association, the Women's Christian Association, the Morgan County Historical Society, the Microscopical Society, the Horticulture Society, American Akademe, and the Household Science Club.[183] Muncie, Indiana, was home to the Literary Society, the Ethical Society, the Ladies Matinee Musicale, the Municipal Choir, and the Apollo, where members read papers such as "Madonna in Art" and "True Idea of Inspiration."[184]

Discussion and debate topics tackled by clubs and literary societies could range from mundane matters such as street lights to complex philosophical questions.[185] A young Scottish immigrant to Cincinnati named Alexander Kinmont established a private school and served as a minister in a Swedenborgian church and was in high demand as a speaker, in part because of his series of lectures in the late 1830s that became the book *The Natural History of Man, and the Rise and Progress of Philosophy* (1839).[186] Farther south, the lively St. Louis Philosophical Society was led by German immigrants. One of the members of this group, William Torrey Harris, wrote an article about Herbert Spencer that was rejected by the prominent journal *North American Review*. Harris and his fellow midwesterners believed that the article was rejected because of eastern snobbery against the provinces, so they launched their own journal to publish their own work, the *Journal of Speculative Philosophy*.[187] It became the first regularly published English-language journal of philosophy. Another contributor to the journal was Hiram Jones, who led the Plato Club in Jacksonville, Illinois, which was similar to philosophical societies in other cities such as Quincy and Chicago.[188] Jacksonville, Decatur, Bloomington, and Quincy remained outposts of Platonic thought; Hegel reigned in Terra Haute and St. Louis.[189]

The embrace of philosophy and the arts in the Midwest went in many directions. After the Civil War the region saw much investment in cultural institutions such as large performance halls, opera houses, libraries, theaters, symphony halls, parks, and art museums.[190] The public halls hosted bigger lectures, exhibitions, celebrations, and theater productions.[191] Touring companies put on dramas that criticized "demon rum" through productions such as *The Drunkard* and exposed slavery via *Uncle Tom's Cabin* but also offered more highbrow productions such as *Faust, Beckett,* and various works of Shakespeare.[192] In 1866, Kansas Citians enjoyed plays such as *Lucretia Borgia, Macbeth, Othello, Camille, Ingomar, Deborah,* and *East Lynne.*[193] Opera houses spread widely and were seen as the "crowning achievement in the community's social and cultural life, symbolic of civilization in the most exalted sense."[194] At the Crete, Nebraska, opera house the Crete Dramatic Club, an arm of the Independent Order of Good Templars, performed *Othello, Romeo and Juliet,* and *Faust.*[195] Other audiences enjoyed *Ben-Hur, The Count of Monte Cristo,* and *The Last Days of Pompeii.*[196] In Minnesota, both local thespians and touring companies could use the Duluth Grand Opera House, the Philharmonic Hall in Winona, Breen's Opera in Moorhead, the Opera House in St. Cloud, the Grand Opera House in Minneapolis, Erreson's Hall in Crookston, Brown's Theater Comique of Minneapolis, and Peake's Opera in Wadena.[197]

Public sculpture also became more common, with frequent displays of work by midwestern artists such as Lorado Taft.[198] Minnesota erected statues to Henrik Ibsen, Henry Wadsworth Longfellow, and Christoph Friedrich von Schiller.[199] Public murals were popular and were prominently displayed in places such as the Iowa and Kansas capitals.[200] An archipelago of midwestern art institutes and museums also emerged.[201] One historian discovered that Muncie, which he first thought of as an average and "nondescript American town," had an "artistic movement replete with a composer of epic poems, a painter of large, oil-based likenesses, several artistic clubs, an art school, and several monumental works of architecture."[202]

Much of this building and expansion was driven by prominent charities, generous individuals, and general civic commitment.[203] The death of the Chicagoan Charles Hutchinson, a banker and Board of Trade member, was a reminder of the depth of civic obligation felt by leading citizens. He had been the founder of the Art Institute; president of the Chicago Orphan Asylum; a board member for Hull House, the Presbyterian Hospital, and the Old People's Home; the treasurer of the University of Chicago; and a member of the Chicago Club, the Caxton and Literary clubs, and the Cliff Dwellers (another literary club).[204] Or consider William Ogden, who sat on the boards of the Chicago Historical Society, the University of Chicago, Rush Medical College, the Chicago Orphan Asylum, the Erring Women's Refuge, and the Astronomical Society.[205] Similarly, Walter Loomis Newberry, a Chicago businessman active in civic affairs who would serve as president of the Chicago Historical Society and acting mayor, set aside funds in his will for the creation of a free public library.[206] The result was a princely bequest of over $2 million, which the leaders of the Newberry Library used as they "self-consciously attempted to build the greatest research library in America."[207] These individuals represented an ideal of "civic stewardship" that was common in the cities and towns of the Midwest and undergirded thousands of charitable causes and community endeavors.[208] Midwestern elites saw civic and cultural stewardship as a duty.

Civic spiritedness birthed many visible and still-familiar cultural institutions in the nineteenth-century Midwest, yet there was a deeper language to the civic tradition in the region that dated back centuries. Beyond the common culture of Christianity there was a shared English heritage, generating frequent invocations of the history of Anglo-Saxon liberties, their loss under the Norman yoke, their restoration with the Magna Carta, the rise of Parliament, and the crucial role of the rule of law and Blackstone's *Commentaries* in giving life to the law.[209] In a sign of the appeal of this tradition, when Emerson lectured in the Midwest his topic was often "England and English Character."[210] The works of the Scottish bard Robert Burns, in another measure of British influence, were ubiquitous, and several towns named themselves Waverly.[211] Acts of town naming and the resulting nomenclature capture the Anglo influence: Albion, Andover, Byron, Cambridge, Cromwell, Dorchester, Gibraltar, Gladstone, Hastings, Kent, Manchester, Monmouth, Oxford, Tennyson, Trafalgar, Waterloo, Windsor. Midwestern public discourse prominently included the minority republican currents coursing through England during the eighteenth century that fully flowered among the American revolutionaries.

This American republicanism was steeped in the classical tradition of Greece and Rome, which provided the reference points, analogies, warnings, and actual architecture for public life. Public figures in the Midwest embraced classical history, as the American founders had done.[212] Midwestern colleges taught Greek and Latin and midwestern city names bore the classical imprint: Arcadia, Argos, Athens, Carthage, Cicero, Cincinnati, Clio, Delphos, Indianapolis, Ithaca, Minneapolis, New Athens, Seneca, Sparta, Virgil, Xenia. An elementary school in Muncie, Indiana, placed the Hellenistic sculpture

Laocoon and His Two Sons in the rotunda, alongside statues of Minerva, Venus, and Mercury.[213] In a highly typical example of a popular allusion in political speech, when J. Sterling Morton, the father of Arbor Day, spoke at Nebraska's state fair in 1859, he recalled that early Nebraska legislators called upon the "wisdom and sagacity of Solon and Lycurgus."[214] The embrace of a combined English heritage and classical history can be seen in the first reading lists of Chautauqua, which was widespread in the Midwest: John Richard Green, *Short History of the English People;* J. P. Mahaffy, *Old Greek Life;* Stopford Brooke, *English Literature;* Augusta Larned, *Old Tales Retold from Grecian Mythology.*[215] The first year of the four-year Chautauqua reading cycle focused on English culture, the second year Rome, the third year Greece, and the final year Europe in general.[216]

For the youthful midwestern states, the most immediate institutional reference point was not the Athenian assembly or the original Magna Carta but the Northwest Ordinance. Public opinion held that that the principles of the Ordinance "were the ripe fruit of many centuries of Anglo-Saxon civilization."[217] The early Ohio historian Caleb Atwater said that the Ordinance "was justly considered as the Magna Charta of Ohio, and all of the states northwest of the Ohio river."[218] The historian Milo Quaife saw the Ordinance as on par with the Constitution, the Quebec Act, and "Magna Charta, extorted from reluctant King John at Runnymede seven hundred years ago."[219] Others similarly saw the Ordinance as the "Magna Carta of the West" and the culmination of centuries of political development.[220] One Ohio judge opined that the Ordinance "approaches as nearly to absolute perfection as anything to be found in the legislation of mankind; for after the experience of fifty years it would perhaps be impossible to alter without marring it."[221] The idealism of the Ordinance was tapped by later midwesterners such as the founders of the GOP who embraced the battle cry "Free Soil, Free Labor, Free Speech, Free Men" and made it the "political credo of the Northwest."[222] A town in Kansas took the history of English liberty and republicanism so seriously that it named itself Runnymede.[223]

These allusions to English history and the classical tradition constituted one pillar of the common culture that formed in the Midwest. It was a common culture that included American writers like Emerson, Henry Wadsworth Longfellow, and John Greenleaf Whittier and then expanded to include strong and new midwestern voices such as James Whitcomb Riley.

The parameters of this common culture were further established by Christian sermons, biblical parables, Victorian norms, agrarian rhythms, an emergent American nationalism, and an increasingly evident regional consciousness. The material side of this common culture was anchored by the typical midwestern farm house and small-town main street. The natural setting was hill, dale, and prairie and a life cycle of a wintry grind, planting and tending, and harvest labor. All of these were the mainstays of midwestern daily life, discourse, and culture and provided the essential references and icons of the region and era.

As revealed by the valorization of the Ordinance and the appetite for maintaining the iconography of the region's common culture, memorialization and the embrace of historical symbolism came fast in the Midwest. The first formal settlement there, for example, came at Marietta, which was settled by New Englanders who sailed down the Ohio River on a ship suggestively named the *Mayflower*. The town was named after the French queen who aided the American revolutionaries. The settlers of Marietta set the pattern, organizing a church, a school, and a town common and setting aside three acres for the market, after which followed a gristmill, a windmill, a militia, and greater recognition of the town's place in the stream of history and its role in the formation of historical memory.[224] On the town's centenary, in a typical peroration, the Ohio-born President Rutherford Hayes praised Marietta and its founders for their service with President Washington during the war.[225] When Massachusetts senator George Hoar spoke at the centennial of the Northwest Ordinance, he praised Marietta as "another Plymouth."[226] The event reinforced the centrality of the Revolution for midwestern civic leaders and demonstrated the tapping of images of the American Revolution throughout the century. The governor of the Northwest Territory had named the largest town in the territory Cincinnati to recognize the society of Revolutionary War heroes who founded the country and saw George Washington as a modern Cincinnatus, an allusion to the Roman farmer who was called in from his fields and plough to save the republic.[227]

Throughout the early nineteenth century, midwesterners continued to highlight the critical work of the political architects of the region, including Nathan Dane and Thomas Jefferson, who were seen as blocking slavery in the Northwest Territory and planting free institutions in the region.[228] In 1825, in an emblematic moment, the legislature of Illinois voted for a bill naming eight Illinois counties after heroes of the Revolution: Adams, Hancock, Warren, Mercer, Henry, Putnam, Knox, and Schuyler.[229] In a reflection of the importance of the Revolutionary War, English history, and classicism to early midwestern political culture, the county seats of Warren, Henry, and Hancock counties were named Monmouth, Cambridge, and Carthage.[230]

Although the well-known heroes of the Revolution were widely venerated, the embrace of Marietta and its history was part of a cresting wave of recognition of key events *in the region* that deepened its memory of its own history. These were the seeds of a stronger midwestern regional identity that would emerge throughout the century. George Rogers Clark, for example, was recognized for seizing the territory that would become the Midwest from the British during the Revolutionary War.[231] Later followed a classical-style monument to Clark in Vincennes, Indiana. Other early embraces of historical memory include the recognition of General Anthony Wayne and his military victories in the Midwest, which led to the naming of Wayne County (Detroit), Michigan, and Fort Wayne, Indiana, as well as institutions such as Wayne State University.[232] The Sons of the American Revolution chapter in Toledo, Ohio, built a monument to Wayne formally dedicated at the Commodore Oliver Hazard Perry Hotel in a speech given by the secretary of war, an Iowan.[233] As suggested by the name of the hotel hosting the Wayne monument dedication, Commodore Perry's victories on Lake Erie during the War of 1812 were frequently celebrated, especially in northern Ohio.

The recognition of military leaders of early battles in the Midwest should not imply the neglect of others. Native American leaders, for example, were often recognized.[234] So too were common pioneers and farmers who settled the Midwest. The sculptor Lorado Taft, born in Elmwood, Illinois, in 1860, later created the statue *The Pioneers* for his hometown and dedicated it "To the Pioneers who bridged the streams, subdued the soil, and founded a state."[235] At the dedication of the statue, Taft's brother-in-law, the regionalist writer Hamlin Garland, delivered a dedication address titled "The Westward March of the Pioneer."[236] In another example, civic leaders in Vandalia, Illinois, erected the *Madonna of the Trail* statue to honor the sacrifices of women pioneers; ten thousand spectators enjoyed a parade, a pageant, and the songs "My Soul Doth Magnify the Lord" and "Illinois" as the statue was dedicated.[237] Perhaps the culmination of this spirit was the vast number of memorials to World War I soldiers and doughboys just as the Midwestern Moment was peaking and American soldiers helped save democracy in Europe.[238]

During the latter half of the nineteenth century, Lincoln and the Civil War became major foci of midwestern memorialization projects. Many towns and counties named themselves after Lincoln.[239] In 1874, Illinoisan Ulysses S. Grant dedicated the Lincoln statue in Springfield, and fifty-seven years later the Iowa-born president Herbert Hoover returned to rededicate it in front of sixty thousand people, who heard renditions of "Swing Low Sweet Chariot" and "Illinois."[240] In 1904 the small village of Bunker Hill in Illinois erected a 40 foot statue to Lincoln that featured a woman inscribing "With charity toward all and malice toward none" on the side.[241] In 1912 in Lincoln, Nebraska, ten thousand people gathered for the dedication of Daniel Chester French's bronze sculpture of Lincoln. Former Nebraska congressman and presidential candidate William Jennings Bryan spoke at the event, and Civil War veterans gave a spirited rendition of "Marching through Georgia."[242] In a similar ceremony repeated scores of times around the Midwest, Minnesota units of the Grand Army of the Republic presented a statue of Lincoln to the city of Minneapolis, one that featured the now-martyred president at the time of the Lincoln-Douglas debates. Three thousand people watched as the American Legion Auxiliary Glee Club sang "Where Are the Boys of the Old Brigade?" and the governor of Minnesota recounted that his state, which totaled 172,000 people at the time of the Civil War, sent 22,000 men, 13 percent of the state's population, to join the Union Army.[243] Lorado Taft again contributed works such as *Lincoln, the Young Lawyer* in Urbana, *Lincoln-Douglas Debate* in Quincy, a U.S. Grant monument in Kansas, and a Civil War monument in Winchester, Indiana.[244]

In addition to recognizing Lincoln, Taft also sculpted the Student Veteran Memorial in Hillsdale, Michigan.[245] The memorial was a sign of the reverence not simply for Lincoln but for common soldiers of the Civil War and for lesser-known generals who served the Union cause. It was a sentiment tapped when President Grant went to Des Moines in 1875 and said that the "perpetuation of our free institutions" depended on recalling the sacrifices of ordinary Union soldiers: "Let their heroism and sacrifice be ever green in our memory."[246] The famed Grant Park in Chicago would soon be named for this son of Illinois and hero of the war, but it was just as typical that frontline Union soldiers would be recognized (as would the lives of emancipated slaves).[247] In 1902, Indianapolis dedicated a towering monument to the common soldiers of the Union (in a sign of budding regionalism, it also included smaller memorials to prominent figures in Indiana and midwestern history).[248] Between 1885 and 1918, 150 Civil War monuments were built in Kansas (90 percent of the total memorials built to the Union cause in the state), and they mostly honored the common Union solider.[249] Now-forgotten commanders also received their due. In 1917, for example, the town of McPherson, Kansas, commissioned an Ohio sculptor to craft a statue of its namesake, General James Birdseye McPherson (originally from Clyde, Ohio). Dedication day started with every bell in the city ringing forty-eight times (for each state in the Union) and the blowing of every steam whistle, and the ceremony drew in forty-five thousand people for speeches, music, troop drills, and a pageant.[250]

The McPherson monument was purposely unveiled on the Fourth of July, the biggest civic celebration of the year in midwestern towns.[251] In 1839, when Iowa City celebrated its first Fourth of July, the flag flew from an oak tree on capital square, one hundred settlers gathered for a meal (which included a hidden barrel of Cincinnati whiskey and a tin cup tucked into the back of a wagon), the Declaration of Independence was read along with other speeches and toasts, and firecrackers and pyrotechnics went off as smithies hammered anvils piled with gun powder.[252] In 1862 the speaker for the July 4th event in Plainview, Minnesota, was met on the road by marshals in uniform and escorted by two hundred men to the event, where four thousand Minnesotans were consuming chicken, beef, pies, cakes, strawberries, and lemonade and enjoying horse races, trotting matches, cavalry performances, and speeches. The speaker's wife recalled the scene: "cannon booming, band playing, mob cheering, fire crackers whizzing."[253]

If the Fourth of July deepened the memory of the American founding in general, other activities reinforced the specific story of the Midwest. The Grand Army of the Republic, founded in Illinois in 1866, reminded the public of the sacrifices of midwestern soldiers during the Civil War and planted them deep in the regional consciousness.[254] Memories of the founding of a town or the settlement of an area of countryside were also recorded and celebrated by a growing number of active old settlers' associations, whose events often attracted sizeable crowds.[255] When Walt Whitman spoke to the Old Settlers of Kansas in Bismarck Grove in 1879, thirty thousand people attended.[256] Midwestern colleges, from their origins, also stressed historical studies.[257] By the end of the nineteenth-century, midwestern historical societies were also organized and became an integral part of a wider movement to promote a broader awareness of the region's history.[258] In a typical display of this desire for history, the Ohioan James Garfield gave a lecture to the newly formed Geauga County Historical Society about the settlement of the Northwest Territory.[259] The midwestern history movement included the creation of state history journals, the launch of the Mississippi Valley Historical Association at a meeting in Lincoln, Nebraska, and the emergence of an active group of "prairie historians" focused on studying the history of the Midwest.[260] Other scholars active in the Midwest during the later nineteenth century were sure to emphasize the importance of writing history that was accessible to most citizens and connected to their experiences.[261] One advocate of historical studies and civic education from Illinois reminded the Ohio Valley Historical Association, meeting in Marietta, that it "is a valuable lesson to learn that the homely things of everyday life, the familiar facts of local environment, have truths for us as significant as those of far-away places and remote times."[262]

A related phenomenon was the growth of historical pageants, often sponsored by state historical societies, which highlighted the history of a town or state and contributed to regional identity formation.[263] Pageants were seen as the "expression of the community soul" in which "*place* is the hero."[264] The purpose of the pageant was to "revive or to maintain the memory of the past and to arouse and promote civic healthfulness." Pageant organizers placed a strong emphasis on using local talent and keeping the presentations clean, which is why pageants were considered superior to the more risqué traveling theater. The historical episodes that were the focus of the pageants were developed using what could be "found in the town and private archives of the locality."[265] By teaching regional history these pageants planted seeds of identity and fostered rootedness and a dedication to communal life. The chairman of the committee that organized the "Pageant and Masque of Saint Louis" in 1914 believed that "out of the beauty of art . . . will spring an aroused civic pride and love of home that will develop a sense of community obligation and mutual co-operation."[266]

Many of the pageants and public celebrations in the Midwest were advertised in and reported on in newspapers, which kept citizens engaged in the affairs of the town and the public sphere lively. Newspapers in the Midwest were commonplace.[267] As early as 1824, forty-eight of the nation's 598 newspapers were printed in Ohio.[268] By 1840, only three years after statehood, there were thirty-eight active newspapers in Michigan (as many as there were in all the colonies during the Revolution).[269] The new major newspapers in the Midwest such as the *Chicago Evening Post* (1865), *Inter-Ocean* (1872), *Chicago Daily News* (1875), and *Indianapolis News* (1869) were widely read and circulated.[270] So too the *Chicago Tribune,* the *Omaha World Herald,* and the *St. Paul Globe.*[271] Figures such as Eugene Field, a prominent Chicago columnist, emerged as widely read public intellectuals.[272] A young man from Lansing, Michigan, Ray Stannard Baker, also got his start writing for the Chicago newspapers before going on to a prominent career as a reformer, historian, and diplomat.[273] After his youth in Illinois, Ernest Hemingway started writing while a reporter at the *Kansas City Star.*[274] By 1889 there were 733 daily and weekly newspapers in Kansas, more per capita than any other state.[275] Because of all the newspapers and the improving transportation system, news literally traveled fast. By 1893 the morning Chicago newspapers reached Osage, Iowa, on the 3:47 afternoon train (instead of having to wait for the late-night Winona passenger train).[276] The newspapers in the Midwest and their wide distribution spoke to the democratic impulses of the region and the demise of central authorities' control over public discourse, as did the ever-active grassroots politicking and energetic public sphere in the region; the papers would become key elements of the region's democratic culture.

The active public sphere, robust civic life, newspaper culture, and participatory politics of the Midwest led to an active reform movement. In the early decades, this took the form of basic infrastructure improvements such as roads, canals, and railroads (which was unlike the South: "Nothing of any resemblance to this occurred in Alabama or Mississippi").[277] It also included active Christians seeking reforms designed to promote morality and was largely driven by the representatives of the rural Protestant culture that predominated in the Midwest.[278] These reforms included temperance, promoting education, ending slavery, educating women, and healthy living. The president of Oberlin College in Ohio proclaimed that the "true Christian reformer" was a "universal reformer, seeking the correction of all evils," which at Oberlin stretched from aggressive abolitionism to women's education to the peace movement to temperance to personal hygiene to anti-gluttony teachings.[279] In Battle Creek, Michigan, reforming Adventists established a sanitarium, hospital, and Kellogg's foods, then later set up a college in Lincoln, Nebraska.[280] Samuel S. McClure and other alumni of the *Knox Student* newspaper at Knox College in Illinois founded and ran *McClure's Magazine* as a reform publication.[281] Many private charities were founded, and prominent medical and research institutions such as the Mayo Clinic, Cleveland Clinic, Menninger Clinic in Topeka, and pharmaceutical firm Eli Lilly emerged from the reform and social improvement ethos.

Outside of the private sphere, midwestern legislators also voted to create institutions to aid the blind, the mentally ill, homeless, poor, and other downtrodden groups.[282] When visiting Indianapolis while on the active midwestern lecture circuit, Emerson was impressed with Indiana's state blind asylum and, upon hearing that the ninety-five students there enjoyed "poetical recitations," proceeded to regale them with a Sir Walter Scott ballad.[283] Indiana's eagerness to host a Scott-invoking Emerson certainly highlighted some of the fruits of the civic reform movement in the Midwest, but the embrace of a prominent intellectual also spoke to the prevalence of literary life and the depth of the democratic culture that had developed in the nineteenth-century Midwest.

From the beginning of the nineteenth century, various factors and institutions caused the development of this democratic culture in the Midwest. The legal charter for the region yielded freestanding sovereign states that ensured the rights of citizens and contributed to the steady erosion of various forms of aristocratic privilege persisting elsewhere around the world. A mixture of Christian denominations instilled a basic morality but also fostered a degree of pluralism and toleration and theological freedom not present in other polities dominated by one religious sect. Elections with robust turnout came early to the Midwest, as did votes for delegations to attend constitutional conventions to draft organic charters for the emerging midwestern states, all of which would include detailed bills of rights. These democratic documents were reinforced by a culture held open by settlers from varying regions and ethnic groups who embraced egalitarian norms and eagerly sought to participate in democratic life and an economic system open to all comers. Economic life was animated by principles of moral uplift and gain, which often took the form of clearing land and building a farm through sweaty but virtuous labor. When the work day was done, midwesterners often turned to a social life defined by local clubs, fraternal lodges, opera halls, and farm organizations and a civic life shaped by libraries, charities, historical societies, and churches. When they entered the political realm, their rhetoric included references to Athens and Rome and the Magna Carta and the triumphs of the American Revolution and a recognition that all these precedents contributed to a robust democratic life in a new and emergent land.

CHAPTER 2

"MOULDED FOR GOOD"

THE GROWTH OF A COMMON
DEMOCRATIC CULTURE
IN THE MIDWEST

The rise of midwestern democracy was not simply a matter of newspaper editorials, statutes, parades, and voting. The broader political and civic culture of the Midwest was undergirded by a powerful system of social ethics, moral training, republican mores, and democratic institutions. The culture that came to predominate in the rural areas and small towns of the nineteenth-century Midwest—despite tales of uncouth adventurers and frontiersmen in the early days of settlement and various dissenting voices in later years—was a tempered Victorianism adjusted to frontier conditions and American pragmatism. This common midwestern culture blended the traditions of Christianity; a midwesternized Victorian ethos of improvement, self-help, and striving; free-labor (anti-slavery) ideology; a reverence for physical work; the bourgeois virtues of prudence and temperance; and educational aspiration, optimism, democratic openness, republicanism, and meritocracy together to create productive citizens and a region of uplift and ambition. The result was a society where Christianity, republican law and order, market culture, civic obligation, and a midwestern-modified gentility of manner largely prevailed.[1]

The foundation of this culture was Christianity.[2] Family prayers and Bible readings in Christian homes, it was believed, would help produce virtuous and hardworking young people.[3] Bibles and other Christian symbols were always present in a properly structured household, and many believed, as a young woman in Worthington, Ohio, wrote in her diary, that the Christian home should be "a little heaven on earth."[4] Right Christian belief would bring protection. As an Illinois man instructed, "Put on the armor of God, that ye may be able to stand against the wiles of the Devil."[5] Christian devotion also took the form of hymn singing. In B. B. Hotchkin's book *Manliness for Young Men* (1864) the family sang a hymn praising the soul-making power of the Lord: "When in the slippery paths of youth / With headless steps I ran / Thine arm, unseen, conveyed me safe / And led me up [to be] a man."[6] It was a practice that Methodist Lucy Hayes, born in Chillicothe, Ohio, took to the White House, where she led the singing of hymns.[7] Adam Holm, a young preacher who had immigrated from Scotland to Minnesota and been trained at Epworth Seminary in Dubuque, Iowa, finally settled in Dodge City and worked to bolster the moral standards of the community through hymn singing, sermons, and personal proselytizing. He saw the "preacher, the teacher, and the newspaper man, the irresistible trinity of modern civilization, all contributing more or less to the advancement of our city and the development of a higher tone in morals and religion."[8]

Part of saving one's soul and being "a man of God" involved hard work and demonstrating one's "usefulness" to society and thereby rising in one's social standing. A young lawyer in Ohio said that a "man of moderate abilities, by close application . . . may rise above those of the brightest genius." A young Illinois salesman and abolitionist said that a man should use "every hour to advantage. When we use our time with economy we can accomplish anything."[9] This was the culture of striving embraced by another Illinoisan, named Abraham Lincoln, who counseled his law partner, "The way for a young man to rise is to improve himself every way he can."[10] Such sentiments caused Lucy Hayes's husband Rutherford B. to start a journal while at Kenyon College in Ohio so he could keep track of his self-improvement: "By keeping a diary in which to record my thoughts, desires, and resolves, I expect to promote stability of character," he wrote, and "if I commit to writing all of my resolves, I shall be more careful not to make them hastily, and when they are made I shall be more anxious to keep them."[11] A father in Illinois sent his son who was away at school a copy of *Princes of Persia* to read and advised him to "quarrel with no one, avoid meddling with the disputes of others, unless with a view to promote an accommodation; and though I would wish you to support the dignity of a youth, be neither mean nor arrogant."[12] All this fit the mood of the young and meritocratic Midwest, with its "unfettered opportunity for all" and "careers open to talent."[13] At the Muncie, Indiana, high school, where students had to take four years of Latin, graduates were coached with the Latin dictum *Palman qui meruit ferat:* "The reward belongs to him who has earned it."[14] Unlike the aristocratic and slave-oriented South or effete Europe, young people were reminded, the Midwest celebrated the working man earning his way by the sweat of his brow.[15]

A common form of advancement and self-improvement was book reading. By the time of the Civil War, over 90 percent of midwesterners could read and most middle-class families owned books; on the Ohio frontier during the antebellum era more than 50 percent of families above the level of median wealth owned three or more books, which were in high demand.[16] Ohio printers released nearly 600 books and broadsides by 1820, Indiana 601 by 1835, and Illinois 474 by 1840.[17] By the later nineteenth century the largest concentration of subscription book publishers was in the Midwest, mostly based in Cincinnati, Indianapolis, St. Louis, and Kansas City, which were all "practical locations from which to dispatch agents into the surrounding countryside."[18] Of particular note is the highly influential Bobbs-Merrill company in Indianapolis, which published many books about the Midwest, and the publishers in Cincinnati, which was the "recognized capital of the western book trade."[19] In short order, as many as a million books a year were published in Cincinnati, including *Carrs Sermons, Paradise Lost, Modern Chivalry,* and *Seneca's Morals.*[20] Before the Civil War, Cincinnati was home to six major publishers, forty-three bookstores, and nearly four thousand print publications.[21] The books published by these companies included a "heavy dose of Christian moralism" and were premised on self-improvement via reading.[22] The late nineteenth-century Victorian era was "a time when improving one's mind by reading and participating in group programs was considered the responsibility of all right-thinking Christian people of good will."[23] Common conduct and character books focused on "citizenship, duty, democracy, work, building, conquest, honor, reputation, morals, manners, integrity" and especially manhood.[24]

Book reading fostered a broader book culture, including thousands of book clubs, literary societies, and book exchange systems.[25] When one English traveler arrived in St. Louis in 1822, he met "several gentlemen" who had not only read all of Walter Scott's early Waverly novels "but even the last one, the *Fortunes of Nigel,* which had only been published a short time before I left England."[26] Lord Byron was impressed to hear of his popularity in the Midwest: "These are the first tidings that have ever sounded like *Fame* to my ears—to be redde on the banks of the Ohio."[27] Because so many people read books, authors were well known and a topic of everyday conversation. When William Dean Howells was visiting Representative James A. Garfield in Hiram, Ohio, in the late 1860s, Garfield ran around to all his neighbors yelling, "Come over here! He's telling about Holmes and Longfellow and Lowell and Whittier!"[28]

Books were common in the home.[29] Growing up in Wisconsin, Hamlin Garland learned from his "bookish" paternal grandmother "to love the poems of Whittier and Longfellow," and his maternal grandfather was an "intensive reader of the Old Testament."[30] Garland loved his extra reading time in the winter, when he would eagerly consume piles of newspapers and such books as Walter Scott's *Ivanhoe*, Jane Porter's *Scottish Chiefs*, Emerson Bennett's *The Female Spy* (about the Civil War), and Milton's *Paradise Lost*.[31] In Minnesota, Henry Sibley was reading William Prescott's *Ferdinand and Isabella* and *Conquest of Mexico*, Henry Hallam's *Middle Ages*, and Adolphe Thiers's *French Revolution*.[32] The writer Herbert Quick developed his taste for literature by reading novels during his Iowa boyhood. Iowa farm families like the Garlands and Quicks actively read Dickens and enjoyed subscriptions to *Frank Leslie's Illustrated Weekly, Godey's Lady's Book*, the *Eclectic Magazine of Foreign Literature*, and *Harper's Weekly*.[33] Nebraska literary clubs read *Spartacus to the Gladiators, Little Orphan Annie*, and *Whistling in Heaven*, and Nebraska farm houses had Dante, Dickens, Scott, and Thackeray readily at hand.[34] One Indiana woman who moved to Nebraska to buy farmland and teach school had von Ranke's *The Lives of the Popes*, the five-volume *History of the Reformation*, and Redpath's *History of the United States* on her shelves (she also read *Harpers* along with the *Des Moines Register* and the *Cincinnati Enquirer*).[35] The shelves of the Pound family in Nebraska included Kingsley's *Greek Heroes*, Macaulay's *History of England*, Hawthorne's *Tanglewood Tales*, and Froissart's *Chronicles* (a history of the Hundred Years' War).[36]

Pictures of famous writers were hung on the walls of midwestern homes, including those of William Cullen Bryant, Henry Wadsworth Longfellow, John Milton, and John Ruskin. Many homes put up the lithograph *Our Great Authors: A Literary Party at the Home of Washington Irving*, which features

Holmes, Emerson, Lowell, Longfellow, Irving, Bryant, Cooper, and Whittier chatting beneath a bust of Shakespeare.[37] When the catalogs of Chicago's Montgomery Ward store began circulating, they brought in many more books to midwestern homes, including practical books on scientific farming, Bibles, shooting and hunting books, leather-bound copies of Dante's *Inferno,* Milton's *Paradise Lost,* and Tennyson's *Idylls of the King,* and various works of George Eliot, Nathaniel Hawthorne, and Harriet Beecher Stowe.[38]

Libraries were foundational to this culture of books. In early Ames County, Ohio, local leaders, believing in the "many beneficial effects" of libraries and viewing them as a "source of rational entertainment and instruction," agreed to trap and hunt during the winter and use the pelt proceeds to buy books. In 1804 they took their $70 in earnings to Boston and bought fifty-one books to launch what they dubbed the Coonskin Library.[39] Early Ohio libraries followed in Belpre, Dayton, New Town, Wooster, Poland, Zanesville, Lebanon, and other towns.[40] Libraries in the Midwest at first were smaller private and community associations but later were common public projects.[41] The Midwest would later see the building of more Carnegie libraries than any other region.[42]

On the impact of all these libraries, consider the Osage Public Library in Garland's hometown, so named after the early developer Orin Sage, who made a donation to create the institution. The top book choice by Osage's library patrons was James A. Froude's *History of England,* and others in the top twenty included George Eliot (*Daniel Deronda*), Thackeray (his book *The Virginians,* about young men who fight with General Wolfe at Quebec and then join the American Revolution), Lew Wallace (the Hoosier author of *Ben-Hur*), and Thomas Talmage (for his book *Series of Sermons*). The library's most popular author, Pansy, wrote stories with a Christian message for young people that parents engaged in moral training appreciated. The distinction of having the greatest number of varied titles in the library belonged to William Taylor Adams, who wrote novels for young people focused on soldiers (pro-Union, naturally), sailors, and adventurers in Europe, Africa, and the Far East that some adults worried were too sensational (these concerns were allayed by his writing motto: "First God, then country, then friends"). Overall, the most popular authors in the library after Pansy were Harriet Beecher Stowe, William Dean Howells, George Eliot, James Fenimore Cooper, Hans Christian Anderson, Charles Dickens, Edward Eggleston, and Walter Scott.

Although Horatio Alger is not on this list, "his books nonetheless enjoyed a constant and steady demand" as they "glorified masculine ideals of rationality, strength, enterprise, and courage." In the 1920s intellectuals would start to mock Alger, but well into the 1890s his books "still reflected a middle-class reform mentality that resonated in the rhetoric of Osage newspapers and pulpits." Another extremely popular author was clergyman E. P. Roe, who published an 1872 bestseller about a hero of the Chicago fire of 1871 (*Barriers Burned Away*), then a pro-Union book about the Civil War era focused on a striving young woman (*An Original Belle*), and then a book about the temptations of the city and the greatness of rural life (*Driven Back to Eden*).[43] The library also carried serious science periodicals such as *Scientific American* and *Popular Science Monthly* (and books by Charles Darwin) and also the *North American Review, Review of Reviews, McClure's, Cosmopolitan,* and three Osage town newspapers along with the *Chicago Daily Record*.[44]

Or consider the library in Muncie, Indiana, a town where reading "was central to the lives" of the town's residents. In classic Victorian fashion, the Muncie library board "saw reading as an essential tool for moral improvement" and "upward mobility." They preferred reading in "which Christian moralism took center stage," along with history, classic tales, and lighter fare. Prior to the construction of a new library building, the town had a circulating library run by a Union Army veteran who also served as the town postmaster. The books he circulated included Gibbon's *Decline and Fall of the Roman Empire,* Macaulay's *History of England,* and Plutarch's *Lives,* along with various works by Shakespeare, Washington Irving, Ruskin, Dickens, and Samuel Johnson.

In 1875 a new public library opened in the City Building of Muncie. It "operated within the Christian ethos that characterized the entire community," embraced an "informally religious character," and carried many Christian books. When it opened, the library held over two thousand books along with some periodicals. The board of the new library promoted "moral uplift," acted as "moral guardians" in terms of what books would be available, and maintained an "ongoing concern with providing moral guidance through its collection, particularly for children." This new library was filled with the works of Thomas Hardy, Dickens, Twain, Jules Verne, Lew Wallace, Milton, Louisa May Alcott, the complete works of Shakespeare, the poetry of Robert Browning, Henry Wadsworth Longfellow, and Lord Byron, many works on

Christianity, and many government publications.[45] Works by Horatio Alger, Harriet Beecher Stowe's *Uncle Tom's Cabin,* Anna Sewell's *Black Beauty,* and Frances Hodgson Burnett's *Little Lord Fauntleroy* were, the librarian reported, "constantly off the shelves in the hands of Readers." Alger books were checked out a "staggering" number of times, and there was a constant and "insatiable demand for books by Alger" and the boys' adventure books of Harry Castlemon (the penname of Union Navy veteran Charles Fosdick). Also popular was G. A. Henty's *By Pike and Dyke: A Tale of the Rise of the Dutch Republic.*

The Muncie library expanded with money from Andrew Carnegie, who funded 1,689 new libraries, 768 of them in the Midwest (156 in Indiana). Carnegie saw his libraries as "temples of civic learning" that promoted democratic ideas and citizenship and were, he said, "cradles of democracy." With additional money the number of authors on the library shelves expanded with new voices and additional works from repeat performers: Dickens, Robert Louis Stevenson, Jane Austen, the Bronte sisters, Shakespeare, Victor Hugo, Alexander Dumas, Goethe, Austen, Scott, Tennyson, Emerson, Hawthorne, Thoreau, Lowell, Oliver Wendell Holmes Sr., James Whitcomb Riley, Henry James, and William Dean Howells. The library also carried *Harper's, Atlantic Monthly, Century Illustrated, London Graphic, Scientific American, North American Review, Scribner's, Fortnightly Review,* and many local and regional newspapers. Through this culture of literacy the citizens of Muncie, especially the younger generation, could develop a "sense of moral discrimination," as the Muncie librarian said, and they could be "moulded for good."[46]

In addition to the general works of fiction and history common to midwestern homes and libraries, other prominent types of books that emerged were success manuals, which were bought by millions of Americans, especially in rural areas and small towns. These books emphasized that, with the "diligent application of virtues such as honesty, frugality, industry, reliability, and loyalty, buttressed by the force of character and true manhood," anyone could rise and succeed—themes that were replicated in the sermons, speeches, commencement addresses, newspaper articles, and pamphlets that dominated the culture. The authors of these books captured the "pulse of those in the American heartland" (the books were not popular in the South, in part because they often depicted scenes of glorious victory by Union forces during the Civil War) who embraced striving and sought upward mobility and economic success. In keeping with the times, University of Chicago rhetoric and English professor William Mathews wrote a series of self-help articles for the *Chicago Tribune* in 1871 that became his popular book *Getting On in the World, or Hints on Success in Life* (1873). His works were published and widely consumed in Chicago, Cleveland, Indianapolis, and other midwestern locales.[47] When giving his inaugural address at the University of Minnesota in 1869, president William Watts Folwell, the author of a multivolume history of Minnesota, similarly stressed how concentrated striving could lead to professional success: "So long as there is open to young men the prospect of a name and a home, of a high social position to be won with clean hands and unsoiled garments by headwork," these young men would seek to move up, strive, and perhaps become professionals.[48]

The book culture of the Midwest was supported by a robust speaking circuit. Going to lectures, which were often designed to focus on practical and "useful" themes and geared toward general audiences, was especially popular with the "young and ambitious" who were "pursuing mental and moral self-improvement."[49] Lectures were also "serious and moral" and provided a "tool for achieving a broad though difficult-to-measure goal of 'rise,' 'betterment,' 'fame,' or 'success.'"[50] Skilled oratory and the practiced eloquence of traveling lecturers undergirded the prominent "lyceum and lecturing movement in the midwestern United States" and impressed young and eager audiences.[51] Lyceum lectures, fitting the time and place, were to be "patriotic, non-partisan, educationally democratic, benevolent, and Christian."[52] "Nearly every town had its own lyceum by the mid-1830s," explains Mary Kupiec Cayton, including Cincinnati (1830), Cleveland (1832), Columbus (1835), and Indianapolis (1836).[53] The first of Michigan's more than thirty-five lyceums was launched by a territorial judge in 1818, and it actively debated women's suffrage, slavery, aiding democratic patriots in South America, whether Napoleon succeeded more through his own genius or fortuitous circumstances (the former proposition prevailed by a vote of 10–6), and weighty issues such as whether Detroit should limit the number of dogs within the city limits.[54] Within a few years of the settlement of Rock Creek, Illinois, there emerged the Philo Polemic and Literary Society, the Tyro Polemic Society, and the Polemical Society on Rock Creek.[55] Davenport, Iowa, set up its lyceum in 1839, only three years after the city was chartered.[56] Northfield, Minnesota, organized its lyceum, replete with a literary magazine, two years after the town was founded.[57] Henry Ward Beecher's famous "Lectures to Young Men" was originally delivered to the Young Men's Lyceum in Indianapolis.[58] Beecher was a frequent lecture circuit speaker, as were many other abolitionists.[59] In 1838 the Springfield Young Men's Lyceum gave Abraham Lincoln the stage for him to analyze the murder of the abolitionist Elijah Lovejoy.[60] As a young man on the rise in Illinois, Lincoln had been quick to join self-improvement groups and debating societies and the local lyceum.[61] Sylvester Graham was hired to be a professor of natural philosophy at Lane Theological Seminary in Ohio after students heard his "Lectures to Young Men on Chastity" there.[62] To give audiences a different flavor, the Association of Western Literary Societies hired P. T. Barnum to tour and lecture in Ohio, Illinois, Indiana, Wisconsin, Iowa, and Missouri (in addition to arranging more standard speakers such as Beecher, Frederick Douglass, Wendell Phillips, William Lloyd Garrison, Clara Barton, Carl Schurz, Anna E. Dickinson, Horace Mann, Horace Greeley, Oliver Wendell Holmes, James Russell Lowell, Henry David Thoreau, and Ralph Waldo Emerson).[63]

When Emerson toured the Midwest his audiences were literary societies, Young Men's Societies, and Young Men's Mercantile Libraries, which were populated by young men, often from farms in the Midwest, who had read advice manuals counseling them about the "formation and maintenance of character and the path to social acceptability in their new environment" and the "cultivation of an internalized system of morality."[64] Emerson focused on "self-culture" and saw the "main enterprise of the world" as the "upbuilding of man," the perfect theme for the young and ambitious Midwest.[65] During an Indianapolis lecture, for example, he emphasized people's capacity for wisdom and growth.[66] "Emerson seemed to his listeners to be merely passing along practical advice on practical subjects—the epitome of self-culture," notes the historian Mary Kupiec Cayton.[67] In St. Paul, where he arrived after a −20 degree open sleigh ride, Emerson emphasized that "common sense is always right, has the presence of all wit, all learning. It milks the cow, chops the wood, plants, hoes, reaps, and ministers to the necessities of the race."[68] Emerson's focus on manhood and self-reliance had a major "influence on the cohort of men who produced success manuals" popular in the Midwest.[69] In another measure of Emerson's influence, the striving future president Rutherford B. Hayes was a member of the Cincinnati Literary Club and heard Emerson when he came to give a widely praised lecture there.[70]

Emerson gave his last lecture in Chicago in 1871, just as the Chautauqua movement was launching.[71] Chautauqua was founded in 1874 to train Sunday school teachers and then broadened into a lecture circuit where speakers emphasized self-improvement, education, and Christianity.[72] Chautauqua grounds often featured big top tents, canopies, classical columns, pediments, pavilions, and assorted august buildings.[73] Chautauqua represented rural and small-town values, uplift, a commitment to education and personal and social improvement; it "represented the people who had avidly supported Abraham Lincoln and Union" and elected midwestern Republican presidents from Lincoln to Hoover.[74] Chautauqua Week was a major event in a midwestern town and featured tent meetings, flags and banners, sermons, lectures, book discussions, and the singing of "Onward Christian Soldiers."[75] The Chautauqua in Crete, Nebraska, held over ten days each summer, championed the "Victorian values of self-restraint (e.g., temperance) and self-improvement"; included days sponsored by the Union veterans of the Grand Army of the Republic and the Woman's Christian Temperance Union; featured a "Blackstone Hall" (named after the famous English jurist) that hosted lectures on Milton, Goethe, and Shakespeare; and offered popcorn, lemonade, and ice cream to children.[76]

Outside of formal Chautauqua events the literary lecture circuit was also robust. Frequent literary club speakers included Booker T. Washington, Susan B. Anthony, Emerson, and Lew Wallace.[77] Wallace was emblematic of this culture. An Indiana native, he served as a general in the Civil War, then came home to write books, including the famed *Ben-Hur: A Tale of the Christ* (1880), and settle into his Crawfordsville estate with a picturesque library.[78] Mark Twain was also a frequent and popular speaker in the Midwest. He noted after a talk to the YMCA in Indianapolis that he spoke to a "perfectly jammed house, just as I have had all the time out here."[79]

The depth of the book and lecture culture of the Midwest by the end of the nineteenth century can be witnessed in a tour by the Ohio-born writer William Dean Howells. In 1899, Howells's extensive tour began in Ypsilanti and included stops at the Detroit Home and Day School; the Twentieth Century Club and the Central Music Hall in Chicago; the YMCA in Evanston; Grinnell College and Drake University in Iowa; the English Literature Club of Lincoln, Nebraska; and the Ladies' Literary Club of Marion, Kansas. In an indication of his regional imagination and preferences, Howells refused to book stops farther west than Kansas.[80] In Topeka, after a lecture titled "Novels," Howells was reminded of the centrality of Christianity to the Midwest when he recognized regional authors such as Hamlin Garland and William Allen White but failed to mention Charles Sheldon, a Topeka minister who was sitting in the front row and whose Jesus-focused novel *In His Steps* (1897) had sold fifty million copies.[81] Such a faux pas did not limit his appeal, however. When Howells hit Indianapolis for a lecture his audience totaled 1,200, and the assembled "Hoosiers regarded Howells' appearance as the cultural if not the social event of the season."[82]

Howells was escorted by the Indiana novelist Booth Tarkington and hosted by Tarkington's sister Ovid Butler Jameson, who, according to the *Indianapolis News,* ran a "virtual salon for prominent figures of the literary, theatrical and civic culture world."[83] Tarkington himself was widely known for his novels and as a defender of the Midwest.[84] Howells was entering an Indiana world infused with great and recognized literary talent: Lew Wallace (whose *Ben-Hur* had sold 1.2 million copies), Charles Major (whose *When Knighthood Was in Flower* sold one million copies), Meredith Nicholson, Gene Stratton Porter, Mary Hartwell Catherwood, Maurice Thompson, Edward Eggleston, Tarkington, Theodore Dreiser, and the famed James Whitcomb Riley. When Riley later died in 1916, in a sign of his literary prominence more than thirty-five thousand Hoosiers came out in Indianapolis to view the casket of the fallen midwestern bard.[85]

The culture of uplift and striving that drove book consumption and powered the lecture circuit started early by virtue of the schools. Like most institutions in the Midwest, the schools were heavily Christian. As the historian of education Paul Theobald has noted, the genesis of education in the region "was overwhelmingly a religious affair."[86] Education leaders thought that through the common schools the Midwest would be "imbued with republican virtues" and that the "region would be appropriately Christianized."[87] When the state teachers' association was established in Illinois during the 1830s, the organizer Theron Baldwin said: "We wish to see the school house & church go up side by side & the land filled with Christian teachers as well as preachers [who are] vital to the highest interests of these states" and will ensure "that *universal education* be taken up as a great *Christian enterprise.*"[88] The first state superintendent of schools in Illinois, Newton Bateman, called public schools the "noblest legacy bequeathed by Christian learning to the nation and the age."[89] The many subjects taught in the schools organized in Indiana, including history, English, rhetoric, and Latin, were designed to shape students and help society "advance towards a higher civilization and a Christian culture."[90] Proponents of education sought to build a system of education "based firmly on religion and traditional morality" and were part of a "wider antebellum Protestant crusade to forge a Christian nation."[91] Since educators were highly conscious of the culture they were building, they were acutely aware of the need for cultural "transmission" by way of teacher training, normal schools, and books such as Horace Bushnell's *Christian Nurture* (1847).[92]

The molding of young Christians and good citizens was required, many thought, to make the American experiment work. Education leaders believed that "republican government, resting on public opinion, would survive only with an enlightened citizenry."[93] Teachers were "fired by the idealistic belief that universal public education could lead to self-betterment."[94] This required a moral education from the schools that school administrators and teachers thought should be "character factories dedicated to the production of Christian leaders."[95] Education was about "character building," and schools were part of a "character-training movement" that stressed basic virtues such as promptness, thrift, and industry.[96] Young Abraham Lincoln in Illinois saw education as the pathway to "morality, sobriety, enterprise and industry."[97] Students were taught that a man "must patiently abide his time . . . not in listless idleness, not in listless pastime, but in constant, steady cheerful endeavor, always willing, fulfilling his task."[98] Educators opposed "wishy-washy morality. The rules were clear: NEVER DRINK; NEVER SMOKE; WORK HARD; OBEY AUTHORITY."[99]

Falling into a life of crime or poverty was, education advocates believed, a sign of weak character.[100] Properly trained students would echo the warnings of adults about idleness: "The men them boys become, will sit in the Bar room while their families are left in dark cellars to starve."[101] Teachers and parents sought to create an environment that would "enrich the life by lifting up the soul to higher and purer ideas" while protecting the child's "mind from vice, to keep him away from evil associations, to check the beginnings of evil, to starve out wrong tendencies, and nip in the bud every undesirable emotion."[102] The focus on hard work and opposition to vice led to the introduction of temperance lessons into the schools. By the 1890s, "all the states of the Midwest required that some portion of the school day should be given to the study of the evils of alcohol."[103] Not just adults understood the importance of schools to the young republic. One Ohio girl praised her school's critical function: "To promote the cause of liberty, we must promote the cause of intelligence. Let those, then, who mourn over the popular commotions which sometimes agitate our country, do everything in their power to lengthen the cords and strengthen the power of the common school."[104]

In keeping with the strong book and literary culture of the Midwest, the schools emphasized reading. The assistant principal in Osage, Iowa, said teachers should "mold the taste of the child" toward the best books; a "taste for good reading opens for us a foretaste of Heaven," and books provide models for "moral character . . . the love of beauty, goodness and truth . . . a sense of duty and honor."[105] A large part of a school day focused on spelling, writing, diction, reading, and, to be sure, the reading of important books.[106] In his one-room school in Iowa, Hamlin Garland was introduced to the "poems of Scott, Byron, Southey, Wordsworth, and a long line of English masters" and Shakespeare too.[107] At an Indiana high school where, after completing Shakespeare, the senior class was required to read *Paradise Lost,* one senior quoted Ruskin: "Bread of flour is good, but there is bread sweet as honey, if we would eat it, in a good book."[108] The reading list for middle school pupils in turn-of-the-century Minnesota included "Evangeline" by Henry Wadsworth Longfellow, *Stories of Dickens, Adventures of a Deerslayer* by James Fenimore Cooper, *Captains Courageous* by Rudyard Kipling, *Knickerbocker's History of New York* by Washington Irving, *Treasure Island* by Robert Louis Stevenson, and *Harold, Last of Saxon Kings* by Edward Bulwer Lytton (children's reading was reinforced by adults who were reading Chaucer and Tennyson for their Chautauqua classes).[109] Texts also included moral philosophy, politics, and religion (typically of a Protestant bent). The last part of the school day was usually reserved for history and geography and lectures on topics such as the American Revolution.[110] History texts often took note of American democratic achievements and northern military victories in the Civil War because of the strong influence of Union veterans and the Grand Army of the Republic.[111]

In midwestern education the McGuffey Reader, created by Ohio-born William Holmes McGuffey while a professor at Miami University in Oxford, Ohio, was ubiquitous. McGuffey Readers were first compiled and published in Cincinnati in 1836 for use in Indiana and Ohio and were widely used in midwestern states such as Iowa until the end of the nineteenth century.[112] The series of six McGuffey Readers dominated the field of school readers—122 million copies were published.[113] These readers generally "mirrored the values" of "home, neighborhood, and country store."[114] A quarter of the readers' content was Christian in the early editions, and much of the rest of the content focused on moral stories and teachings.[115] McGuffey promoted the reading of "good" books that would inspire readers with "love of what is right and useful"; he believed that "next to the fear of God implanted in the heart . . . nothing is a better safeguard to character, than the love of good books. They are the handmaids of virtue and religion," whereas "bad books are the public fountains of vice."[116] McGuffey said reading was "a decided healthful and moral influence" and that "constant and open moralizing" would lead to the molding of good character.[117] He believed that "character is more valuable than knowledge and a taste for pure and ennobling literature is a safeguard for the young that cannot be safely ignored."[118] His readers fit perfectly the needs of midwestern parents and introduced students to the "best writing in the English language."[119]

The broad-based and democratic education system in the Midwest was unique to the region. The importance of schools was codified from the earliest days of the Midwest because the Northwest Ordinance had required a commitment to education. Congressional land sales stipulated that a section of each township be set aside for schools.[120] The Indiana constitutional convention of 1816 voted to include requirements for education, mandating that funds derived from land sales be used exclusively for the "purpose of promoting the interest of Literature, and the sciences, and for the support of seminaries and public schools"; additionally, laws were to be passed for the encouragement of "intellectual, Scientific, and agricultural improvement" and the "promotion and improvement of arts, sciences, commerce, manufactures, and natural history."[121] These Indiana provisions were seen as "liberal beyond their day."[122] Widespread education in Illinois started with the free school law of 1825, which held that a "virtuous and enlightened" "free people" must understand their "rights and liberties" by way of the "improvement and cultivation of the intellectual energies" of the state's citizens.[123] Michigan lawmakers changed the process of public land distribution and gave land directly to the state (instead of local districts) to develop an education system and created a state superintendent of education to oversee schools.[124]

Michigan law required that "every township containing fifty inhabitants or householders shall employ a schoolmaster of good morals to teach children to read and write . . . as well as arithmetic, orthography [spelling], and decent behavior," and log cabin schools sprouted up all over the state.[125] All of these early public schools, true to their region, were heavily focused on Christian teaching, moral instruction, and combatting social evils.[126]

The early public schools in the region were bolstered by private academies. Between 1803 and 1850 in Ohio, the state chartered 170 denominational seminaries and high schools.[127] They were also called "institutes," "societies," and "lyceums," but the most common term was "academy."[128] Indiana saw the emergence of Madison Academy, Hanover Academy, the Red Brick Academy, Cambridge Academy, and many others, as did other midwestern states. These included the once well-known Howe's Academy in Mt. Pleasant, Iowa, and the Cedar Valley Academy in Osage, Iowa, the latter producing Hamlin Garland. Howe's Academy seniors took courses in logic, Latin, Greek, trigonometry, philosophy, political economy, and theology; juniors took courses in geometry, Greek, rhetoric, history, astronomy, literature, botany, and zoology. Hamlin Garland remembered Cedar Valley Seminary's library having Scott, Dickens, and Thackeray on its shelves. Cedar Valley Seminary also had one of the first gymnasiums west of the Mississippi River and developed sports programs to promote character formation; it also built a program of organized debate for oratorical training. By the turn of the century there were at least two dozen academies in operation in Iowa.[129]

The commitment to education in the Midwest yielded strong results. By "1850 more than half of the school-aged children in the Northwest were attending school, and by the outbreak of the Civil War almost all white children, and a surprising number of black children, received some public education in the region."[130] Education continually improved by way of more teacher training in normal schools (teacher colleges), greater taxpayer support and public textbook distribution, the hiring of more superintendents and other expert administrators, and more compulsory schooling.[131] In keeping with an emphasis on usefulness and midwestern pragmatism, courses were added to the curriculum focusing on practical skills and studies related to farming.[132] In short order 90 percent of school-age kids in the Midwest went to school.[133] Iowa, Nebraska, and Kansas saw enrollment of over 90 percent of school-age children by the end of the nineteenth century and "led the entire nation at that date."[134] By the end of the nineteenth century, six thousand schoolhouses dotted the Nebraska prairie, mostly wood frame but also sod, log, and brick, and these structures were often the center of communal life.[135] An early settler in Prairie View, Kansas, described "a small white-painted building which was not only the schoolhouse, but the center—educational, social, dramatic, political, and religious—of a pioneer community of the prairie region of the West."[136] Kansas schools, where high school debate first took root by way of ideas imported from Wisconsin, also trained children for public speaking and civic life.[137] These new rhetorical skills developed in debate undoubtedly helped many of the young people in the ascendant and entrepreneurial Midwest, but even more practical training was available. Schools would add classes like woodworking and foundry practice, and manual training for sewing and carpentry became more common.[138] In calling for such practical courses an editor in Toledo said, "Knowledge unapplied is worse than useless. It is grain uncut and unthreshed."[139]

By the time of World War I, the number of country schools was the highest it would ever be.[140] The more than one hundred thousand country schools in the Midwest by the turn of the century constituted more than half of such schools in the entire country and "produced the most literate people in the nation."[141] As the region urbanized, more complex school systems also emerged. A typical urban school in the Midwest became increasingly sophisticated and ornate over time and was seen as a "cathedral of culture."[142] The "Gary plan" for urban education, which emerged from Gary, Indiana, offered a broad curriculum and a "full range of educational experiences."[143] Cleveland also became an early city to adopt an organized educational plan, and in 1895 the National Educational Association "endorsed an urban school plan based largely on the Cleveland system."[144] In 1897, St. Louis adopted it, and several other cities followed.[145] Whether the early one-room schools or later, larger, more urban schools, developments in the Midwest contrasted to the East, where elite private schools remained more influential, and to the South, where education lagged and segregation prevailed.[146] On the eve of the Civil War, southern states offered ten days of public school per white child (African Americans received close to zero), whereas fifty days of school were offered in the Midwest.[147]

The Midwest also excelled in the realm of college education, which flourished in the region. Founders of midwestern towns "had hardly erected shelters for themselves and for their households before they were thinking of a college," a noble aspiration linked to the "growing belief in the destiny of the great Northwest."[148] By the time of the Civil War there were over one hundred colleges in the Midwest, mostly denominational.[149] These colleges again reinforced the central role of Christianity in the region while also embracing a combination of traditional subjects of study leavened with topics that spoke to midwestern pragmatism. Colleges in the Midwest were thus a critical part of what historian Kenneth Wheeler calls the region's "culture of usefulness."[150] In 1860 there were twenty colleges in Ohio, more than in any other state (Massachusetts had four, by way of comparison, and South Carolina refused to charter private colleges until the 1850s).[151] Ohio colleges often required students to perform manual labor to pay for college, a key midwestern variation in higher education (in the South military drills were emphasized, and in the Northeast gymnastics was emphasized).[152] Knox College in Illinois, for example, was originally chartered as Knox Manual Labor College.[153] Wheeler notes that, "while some college students carried firearms on the parade ground and others dangled from rings and bars, Old Northwest students swung axes, turned the lathe, and milked the cows."

College leaders in the Midwest consistently emphasized building regionally unique institutions that embraced the virtue of physical labor, emphasized usefulness and practicality (a bit less Latin, a bit more farming), and broke free from the eastern "oligarchy" prevailing in American intellectual and economic life.[154] The president of Miami University in Ohio, created in 1809, saw his college as one for busy farmers to attend and thus combined Christianity and the classics with science, math, and land surveying to advance the cause of usefulness.[155] At what would become Michigan State University, students cleared forestland and worked on the college farm, learning tree pruning and the laying of drain tile.[156] The University of Michigan, in addition to traditional scholarship, added an emphasis on practicality in the form of programs in engineering, mining, pharmacy, dentistry, law, and medicine, courses increasingly taught by professors born and raised in the region.[157] When the midwestern-led GOP pushed through the Land Grant College Act during the Civil War (the southerners previously blocking the bill were then out of Congress), it specifically catered to farmers and workers and emphasized practicality and the creation of free, independent, and industrious citizens.[158] The regent of Illinois Industrial University (later the

University of Illinois) said his school would "demonstrate that the highest culture is compatible with the active pursuit of industry."[159] In 1910, Frederick Jackson Turner of the University of Wisconsin gave the commencement address at Indiana University, praising the "State Universities of the Middle West" for combining traditional learning and new work in practical science for a new age of the "test tube and microscope" to transcend the region's "axe and rifle" era.[160] This "union of vocational and college work," Turner continued, proceeded from the anti-aristocratic and pragmatic natures of the "democratic states of the Middle West."[161]

Into the 1860s and 1870s many religious colleges continued to form in the Midwest.[162] This included, perhaps most important, the new University of Chicago in 1891, which was formed out of a failing Baptist college with donations from John D. Rockefeller. The university emphasized the strength of its faculty and practical social science research, especially in Chicago, and was "both peculiarly Midwestern and anchored in the liberal Protestant religious culture" of the era.[163] An emphasis on practicality and solving local and regional problems by relying on local experts undergirded the pursuit of the "Wisconsin idea" in Madison, which was in part inspired by the regionally oriented Turner.[164]

By the end of the nineteenth century a "distinctive Midwestern educational spirit" had emerged, and "utility became a rallying cry in a regional rebellion" that contrasted an "effete" East with a Midwest grounded in "action, practicality, realism, and progress." The attitude was personified by Ohio-born James Canfield, who turned down three years of study in Europe to work on the railroad in Minnesota and Iowa, then became a professor at the University of Kansas, later president of the University of Nebraska (1891–95), and then president of Ohio State University (1895–1900).[165]

The usefulness of midwestern colleges included an emphasis on Christianity. Charles Grandison Finney, once he joined the faculty at Oberlin College in Ohio, instructed believers "to aim at being useful in the highest degree possible," including "usefulness in religion."[166] The result was a great proliferation of churches and church-affiliated colleges. Yankee immigrants, for example, brought Bibles and Webster spellers and a zeal for colleges, resulting in the creation of Miami University, Ohio University, Western Reserve College, Wabash College, Marietta College, Oberlin College, Shurtleff College, Illinois College, Knox College, Wittenberg College, and Beloit College.[167]

Marilynne Robinson has observed that colleges with "strong religious affiliations and reformist social agendas proliferated through the Middle West, little intellectual communities that put into practice their belief in educating women, in forbidding the use of alcohol, in expediting the escape of fugitives from slavery, in enlarging the influence of religious revivalism."[168] Most college presidents were Christian ministers.[169] Lane Theological Seminary in Cincinnati was a prominent center for the training of these ministers. Oberlin College was founded to train "Christian crusaders" and, as one founder said, to become the "burning and shining light which shall lead on to the Millennium."[170] Professors at Ohio colleges conducted chapel services, preached sermons, led prayer meetings, organized revivals, and generally "watched over the religious life of students."[171] A math professor at the University of Minnesota would begin his classes with a prayer.[172] From 1844 to 1862, according to one report, the denominational colleges of the Midwest had witnessed ten thousand conversions stemming from revivals, many of which took place at Wabash, Illinois, Marietta, and Knox colleges.[173]

Midwestern colleges made religious training, Christian leadership, and daily Bible study a central part of campus life. The president of Hanover College in Indiana said these were necessary to make the "wise and the good" the "constant companions" of students, and his college required attendance at daily prayer, Sunday morning worship, and Sunday Bible exercises. Eureka College in Illinois also required daily "historical, geographical, chronological, ethical and literary" studies of the Bible. Knox College had daily devotionals and lectures on religion; Asbury DePauw called students to prayer at sunrise; Western Reserve students held twice-a-day devotions in the college chapel; and Antioch students attended two Sunday services.[174] College presidents, in their dual role as ministers, frequently led these services.[175] Presidents John Bascom and James Burrill Angell of the University of Wisconsin and the University of Michigan first considered the ministry for their careers, and Angell opposed Sunday theater in Ann Arbor and protested the abolition of scriptural readings at trustee meetings.[176] Henry Tappan, president at the University of Michigan before Angell, lectured on the "Evidences of the Christian Religion," and his successor, Erastus Otis Haven, delivered six hundred sermons during his six-year presidency.[177] At the University of Minnesota students attended chapel at 8:00 each morning to hear a Bible reading and say a prayer, and the services were conducted by a faculty member.[178] At Ohio State University the first four presidents enforced daily compulsory chapel.[179] Twice-daily chapel services, enforced by monitors, were mandatory until 1871 at the University of Michigan, where president Angell thought the "Christian spirit" should "shape and color the life of the university."[180] At the University of Wisconsin, daily chapel was compulsory and often supplemented by morning and evening prayers.[181] Beloit College in Wisconsin published the poem "Beloit," later set to music, which captured the Christian mission of midwestern colleges:

As Jehovah's great prophet took chrism of
The priest,—
Where the Rock is softly flowing,
To its ocean bridal going,
And Beloit, in emerald glowing,
Faith's loyal fortress stands.[182]

At Western Reserve College they wrote a hymn for the laying of the college cornerstone in 1826:

May Christian soldiers here be reared
To fight the battles of the Lord,
To win with souls the glorious prize
The great reward beyond the skies.[183]

The Christianity of midwestern colleges meant character building. Manasseh Cutler, the principal founder of Marietta, Ohio, pushed for the creation of a new college in Athens, which in 1804 became Ohio University and in 1839 brought in William McGuffey as its president (hiring him away from Cincinnati College), just as he was beginning his career of promoting character education and development. At Miami University the "curriculum emphasized both the Bible and the classics, good morality, good manners, and good literature."[184] The inaugural address of the first president of Western Reserve College in Hudson, Ohio, made clear that the goal of his school was moral instruction: "The glory of God requires us to make the elevation of our moral nature our constant aim—our unwearied endeavor in the work of education."[185] Moral teaching and reflection were designed, as one sermon at Mount Union

College in Alliance, Ohio, emphasized, to prevent the soul from going "adrift without a rudder, sail, or compass, upon an ocean of doubts and darkness."[186]

College presidents saw their role as instilling good character in students. For President Angell of the University of Michigan, "society is always just what its members make it by their character; nothing more, nothing less." The person of strong character, one cultural historian of the era explains, "stood for power, permanence, and fortitude," and "strong character transcended fickle public opinion and fleeting public repute." The "person of character was in control" and "paced life properly, heard the true rhythm of the universe; and chose the real over the illusory, the natural over the artificial. He demonstrated such judiciousness, discretion, equanimity, and balance that right and wrong became clear to him, duty defined, and worldly matters set straight, perhaps for a lifetime."[187] Presidents Angell, William Watts Folwell of the University of Minnesota, and John Bascom of the University of Wisconsin all focused on the importance of character development and raising the young person with an eye toward creating good Christian republican citizens.[188] "It's all in the bringing up," Folwell said.[189]

This emphasis was often channeled into religious organizations. Professor Richard T. Ely of the University of Wisconsin promoted the idea of having various denominations build educational centers, guild halls, and chapels on campuses of state colleges so that, he said, there would be "more adequate provision made for moral training."[190] President Charles Van Hise of Wisconsin agreed with Ely and "urged the leaders of each denomination in Wisconsin to install a student pastor at Madison and to construct near the campus a building to serve as a center for religious study and a home for safeguarding and advancing the character of students of their faith."[191] The highly successful YMCA, which first started in 1858 at the University of Michigan, embraced a similar mission and promoted a "Christian gospel of self-improvement, a gospel that also included the improvement of society."[192]

Moral instruction was also a key component of the ubiquitous college literary societies, scientific clubs, debating societies, college magazines, periodicals, and poetry clubs.[193] In her study of student societies at midwestern colleges, Rita Saslaw found that they were "formed with literary and moral self-improvement as their goal."[194] She focused on two "deeply religious" colleges, Western Reserve, founded in Hudson, Ohio, in 1826, and Oberlin, founded in 1834. Western Reserve, where 95 percent of its 384 students were in literary societies, embraced a classical education plan: "Oberlin followed Charles Grandison Finney's true revivalist spirit." Student groups focused on rhetorical and reading skills and "literary self-improvement [were] considered a direct means of moral self-improvement, and moral self-improvement was indeed the primary goal of the college and of life" (literary achievement was made possible in part because Oberlin boasted the largest college library in the country).

Students were part of the college establishment, so student societies did not promote direct action or protest, with the exception of the Oberlin Young Men's Anti-Slavery Society and the Agricultural and Horticultural Society of Oberlin. The Union Society at Oberlin College made clear in its constitution that it existed for the "cultivation of the moral and intellectual powers." Students at Miami College in Ohio formed societies "to promote morality, friendship and good feeling amongst us."[195] The Athenian Society and Philomethean Society at Indiana University promoted the "cultivation of manly and mannered practice."[196] Typical organizations at midwestern colleges included the Society of Natural History at Oberlin; the Handel Society at Western Reserve; the Atlantian Literati, Columbian Institute, and Western Literary Society at Wabash College; the various literary societies, debate clubs, and oratorical festivals at Illinois College; the Erodelphian Society at Monmouth College; the Zetagathian Literary Society at the University of Iowa; the Miltonian Society at Cornell College (Iowa); the Chrestomathian and Philogian societies at Iowa College (later Grinnell); and the rival literary and debating societies at the University of Minnesota, the Philomathian and the Delta Sigma.[197] Debating societies and debates between colleges were popular in Wisconsin and included traveling groups of students who would cheer on the debaters.[198] After the Civil War, in addition to these clubs and activities, more and more colleges built gymnasiums and embraced sports, especially baseball and football, and touted the benefit of sport for a society that "favored competitive persons with strong nerves, vigor, muscles, and a cool head."[199]

The focus on Christianity and the values of work and industry at midwestern colleges meant the adoption of moral codes. In 1833, when two followers of Charles Grandison Finney founded Oberlin College in northeast Ohio, they promoted healthy living and godliness and shunned worldly temptations: "Any alcoholic beverage was described as the devil's poison, and the smoke from tobacco as the fumes of hell."[200] President Charles Storrs of Western Reserve

College also focused on the "development of the whole man" and "avoiding foolish amusements." One student was kicked out of Western Reserve for having playing cards in his room and for "improper and ungentlemanly conduct in the Literary Society." It was a reminder that nineteenth-century colleges "were conservative institutions with the role of preserving the values of society for oncoming generations."[201] Presidents Folwell, Bascom, and Angell of Minnesota, Wisconsin, and Michigan supported temperance and were anti-tobacco.[202] Philander Chase, president of Kenyon College and Jubilee College (in Illinois), denied workers building the colleges "ardent spirits" because they would cause poor workmanship, profanity, quarreling, and accidents and deprive workers' families of needed income. Oberlin banned tobacco as did Antioch College, where president Horace Mann said, "It is not mere smoke, young men, which you see floating off in cloudy spirals, it is part of our souls; when your nerves become impregnated with tobacco, they can no longer execute your will." Asbury-DePauw forbid students from keeping horses lest they ride off into trouble and neglect their studies. Alton College had students live in the same building and eat at the same table as the professors and their families.[203] The student code at Ohio University banned the possession of indecent pictures, the singing of lascivious ballads, and "other gross immoralities," including the imbibing of "spiritous or fermented liquors" and visits to taverns and alehouses (except with permission of the faculty).[204] A circular for Smithson College in Indiana, in addition to explaining its regimen of Latin, Greek, ancient history, and readings of Tacitus, Cicero, and Herodotus, promised parents that the college would "be moral," provide "constant parental oversight" of students, require them to "attend church punctually," and allow "no immoral conduct or vicious habits."[205] In a sign of the prevailing winds, President Henry Tappan of the University of Michigan was criticized for serving wine at his house in the "European" manner.[206] The Michigan Methodist conference expected the college in Ann Arbor to "exercise a watchful care of the moral and religious character" of its students.[207]

The emphasis on moral teaching and practicality at midwestern colleges did not mean a neglect of traditional subjects. At the Midwest's first settlement in Marietta, Rufus Putnam called for the teaching of the classics at Muskingum Academy.[208] Ohio colleges more generally supported a curriculum of Greek and Roman history, ancient languages such as Greek and Latin, and moral philosophy to shape young people and highlight their

"awareness of self as a moral being made in the image of God."[209] At Western Reserve student entrance requirements included knowledge of Latin
and Greek, Virgil's *Aeneid* and *The Bucolics,* geography, English, and eight
selected orations of Cicero, along with testimonials of good character.[210] At
Illinois College in the 1870s students were still required to complete three
years of Latin and four years of Greek.[211] At the Illinois Female College in
Jacksonville (later MacMurray College), women read Cicero and Virgil in
Latin their sophomore year (during their junior and senior years their classes
included French, ancient and modern history, political economy, logic, natural philosophy, and astronomy).[212] A professor of Greek at Wabash College
in Indiana defended "classic learning, sturdy discipline, and sterling moral
culture" from those who would water down the curriculum.[213]

A loosening of the curriculum did occur, however. One prominent classics
professor who was born in Rushville, Illinois, and became head of the Latin
department at Indiana University wisely counseled his farm and small-town
students to focus on good citizenship and not "get so deeply immersed in
Latin and Greek as to forget that you are a nineteenth century American."[214]
Such views contributed to the creation of a curriculum that mixed medical, agricultural, and natural sciences with classicism, the study of Greek
and Latin, philosophy, rhetoric, English, and theology.[215] In Michigan, for
example, administrators were sure to mix agricultural and mechanical arts
with a classical curriculum.[216]

After the "denominational era" of college building in the Midwest came
the sprouting of various state colleges (Kansas in 1864, Wisconsin in 1866,
Illinois in 1867, Minnesota in 1868). The newer land grant institutions featured more science and agriculture, which fit with the existing pragmatism
of midwestern colleges and the economic mainstay of the region, and also
included the traditional classicism and continued the Christian tradition with
ministers as presidents, camp meetings, courses on Christianity, and departments of religion.[217]

Whatever the precise mix of emphases on campus, midwestern colleges
represented many of the forces that drove midwestern culture. Early midwestern colleges were founded by Christians who sought to promote moral
codes of behavior that would sustain midwestern republicanism. All told,
a common culture emerged that was defined by Christianity, agrarianism,
pragmatism, a republicanism infused with attention to the classics, and a

commitment to civics, lecture circuits, book learning, literacy, and schools that taught the great figures of American literature. All of this was increasingly done in a way that was regionally specific, as the rise of midwestern land grant colleges demonstrated, and served to forge a particular midwestern identity. By the end of the nineteenth century, this common culture of the Midwest had become widely accepted and deeply rooted.

This dominant midwestern culture was obviously neither welcoming to nor embraced by everyone, however. African Americans, for example, faced varying levels of exclusion and discrimination.[218] So too did women, although they often were guardians of this culture and sought reforms, such as suffrage, within its parameters.[219] In contrast to African Americans and white women, who largely immigrated to or were born in the Midwest during the 1800s, some Native Americans had lived in the region for several decades. During the 1600s, a major war ensued between the Iroquois tribes of the East and Huronia, and the refugees and "survivors of the Iroquois shatter zone" ended up in the future Midwest.[220] This war also forced the Algonquian tribes of the Ohio River valley and Great Lakes to move farther into the Midwest.[221] These population shifts left the Ohio Country as an open space for hunting.[222] As late as the 1680s, the Ohio Country and the territory north of Lake Erie, according to Elizabeth Mancke, "were depopulated, leaving them a vast and still volatile hunting grounds, with the Haudenosaunee [Iroquois] projecting control over them."[223] "The Iroquois wars of the seventeenth century depopulated the Ohio Valley," notes the historian Robert Owens, so "Northwest Indians simply could not point to centuries-long habitation in one area" when making future claims to places such as Ohio.[224] By the 1740s, however, remnants of various tribes had trickled into the Ohio Country, including the Shawnee, who settled, in part, on the Scioto River, and the Delaware, who settled near the Muskingum River.[225]

These newly settled tribes, along with some others farther west, became known as the "Ohio Indians" and would shape the prehistory of the Midwest.[226] Many of them became closely allied with French settlers around the Great Lakes through an elaborate trading system and aided the French in their extensive war in the Ohio Valley against the British and their allies the Iroquois.[227] After British victory in the Seven Years War, a series of battles, skirmishes, and massacres continued between the Algonquian tribes and British colonials on the western edges of British North America, a conflict that "is among the ugliest and most barbarous of anywhere in eighteenth-century America."[228] When the American colonials revolted against Britain, the king's tribal allies made war on the Americans and the bitterness generated by these battles persisted for decades.[229]

After the Revolution, the Americans attempted to establish sovereignty over the midwestern lands won from the British crown, and the new nation's first major military challenge became the Ohio Valley, where the British kept aiding and advising their Indian allies.[230] Congress thought that since the Native Americans in the region had allied with the British during the war they should cede these lands as "compensation for their actions in the Revolution," just as the British had ceded the Ohio Country and the entire Northwest to the Americans.[231] Despite American plans for the region after the Revolution, the British still occupied a series of forts south of the new Canadian-American border established by the treaty ending the war. "British authorities in Canada were happy to retain posts that gave them great influence over the Indians south of the Great Lakes, provided a buffer for Canada, and helped control the fur trade with American territory," according to the historian Reginald Horsman. Despite the postwar treaty ceding the Midwest, the British told their Indian allies to resist any American settlements north of the Ohio River.[232] The resulting Indian-American conflict saw the defeat of two American armies led by Josiah Harmar and Arthur St. Clair and finally ended in 1794 when American forces prevailed at the Battle of Fallen Timbers near Toledo, Ohio.[233] When some Great Lakes tribes again allied themselves with the British during the War of 1812, much of which was fought in the Midwest, American–Native American tensions again spiked.[234] The American Revolution, Karim Tiro explains, "did not really end in the Old Northwest until 1795, and conflict flared anew in 1810–1813."[235]

After the War of 1812, with the tribes defeated on the battlefield, an era of treaty making began slowly to diminish the active Native American presence in the Midwest through the creation of Indian reservations or the negotiated or coerced removal of Natives from the Midwest to lands farther west.[236] In 1825, for example, Lewis Cass, governor of Michigan Territory, successfully persuaded the Shawnee prophet Tenskwatawa to move west.[237] The Shawnee leader Black Hoof, who had fought with the Americans during the War of 1812 and remained on friendly terms, resisted moving, but after his death in 1831 many Shawnees followed Tenskwatawa west.[238]

Some Americans were not sympathetic to the plight of the Native Americans since they had been longtime enemies on the battlefield. Americans also tended to see the small number of Native Americans in a vast and fertile region as wasting the resources of the Midwest by not becoming farmers and organizing permanent villages.[239] Because some Native Americans were mobile, not engaged in farming, and non-Christian, they were at times denounced as savages in need of civilization.[240] In keeping with the culture of the Midwest, Indians were pushed to become farmers and Christians and to attend school and undergo the morality training expected of other youth in the Midwest—all steps that advocates of midwestern culture found perfectly normal but for many Native American leaders represented a domineering or even erasure of Indian modes of life.[241] The prospect of holding the line against the increasingly dominant culture looked increasingly grim to some of these leaders.[242]

The story of Native Americans in the Midwest was not entirely one of defeat and dispossession, however. Native Americans in the region continued to exhibit various levels of agency and find openings in social and civic arenas.[243] Historians have begun to "reject facile notions of tragedy, subordination, stasis, and victimology" and started to focus on continuing and active forms of Native American culture in the Midwest.[244] Some Native Americans accepted the dominant culture, including Leopold Pokagon, the leader of a Potawatomi band who embraced temperance and became a Christian.[245] The Pokagon example highlights how the priorities of the dominant culture, in this case anti-alcohol campaigns or Christian missionary work, could at times be embraced by Native Americans, who not infrequently turned toward the Americans and away from native traditionalists. More Sacs and Foxes followed Keokuk, who sought accommodation, than Black Hawk, who resisted and allied himself with the British.[246] Most of the Shawnees in early Ohio "remained neutral or supported the Americans."[247] In his recent study of the politics and diplomacy of the Maumee and Wabash River valleys, Patrick Bottiger also explains that "many of the Miamis were partial to the Americans."[248]

As suggested by these adaptations and compromises, midwesterners often accepted Native Americans. Although some would look on this as expropriation today, during the nineteenth century some settlers sought to honor the significance of Indian leaders by way of naming. This included states with Native American names such as Ohio, Michigan, Wisconsin, Kansas, the Dakotas, and Iowa. When traveling up the Mississippi in 1861, Henry David Thoreau's travel party companion, the son of Horace Mann, noted the bluff above and the town named for Sioux Chief Red Wing.[249] Many other midwestern towns also adopted Native American monikers: Calumet, Chetek, Chicago, Chillicothe, Cuyahoga Falls, Decorah, Escanaba, Ishpeming, Kalamazoo, Kenosha, Kokomo, Mackinac, Maquoketa, Omaha, Peoria, Pontiac, Sandusky, Sioux City, Sioux Falls. The prominent midwestern sculptor Lorado Taft, in another form of recognition, erected statues of Black Hawk and Chief Paduke. In Minnesota, statues of Hiawatha and Minnehaha were erected at Minnehaha Falls, and in other parts of the region Indian leaders Keokuk, Leatherlips, and others were similarly honored, and Indians were portrayed positively in various forms of popular culture.[250] "Throughout the nineteenth century," the historian John Higham once explained, "the Currier and Ives prints, which often treated blacks condescendingly, never demeaned or ridiculed Indians. They appeared always as dignified human beings with a legitimate life of their own."[251]

Native Americans in the Midwest were also afforded some voting rights long before women and African Americans. As early as 1824, some mixed-ancestry Native Americans were voting in the Midwest and playing a role in the increasingly robust democratic practices of the region.[252] In 1848 the first Wisconsin constitution afforded voting rights to Native Americans who had left tribal life and become "civilized."[253] The 1850 Michigan constitution also gave Indians the right to vote if they were not a member of a tribe, or were "detribalized" (at the same time, Michigan voters strongly rejected a referendum to adopt African American suffrage).[254]

Earlier Michigan laws had afforded Native Americans judicial rights and privileges and access to the court system and public schools.[255] In 1849 the Minnesota territorial house of representatives defeated a black suffrage bill (9–7) but passed a bill granting suffrage rights to "persons of a mixture of white and Indian blood" who "adopted the habits and customs of civilized men."[256] At the 1857 constitutional convention in Minnesota, suffrage was extended to mixed bloods (called the "French vote") and "civilized" Indians.[257] Because of these changes, at least five Native Americans served in the Wisconsin legislature and nine in the Minnesota legislature.[258] Periodically, Congress granted citizenship to Native Americans who cut their connections to their tribes.[259] In a reversal of this trend, in 1884 the U.S. Supreme Court found that a Nebraska man who had abandoned his tribal ties, assimilated, started farming, and spoke English was still not eligible to vote.[260] In 1917 a Minnesota court also ruled that Native Americans who had not assimilated were not eligible to vote.[261] Other Native Americans won the right to vote through the Dawes Act, which divided reservations into small farms to be owned by individual Native Americans, and through service in World War I.[262] Nearly two-thirds of Native American had become citizens and won the right to vote by the time a universal suffrage bill passed Congress in 1924.[263]

As the examples of advances in Native American voting rights indicate, the dominant culture did not treat Native Americans with unremitting hostility. Article 3 of the Northwest Ordinance, for example, set forth a tone of accommodation and was careful to assert that the "utmost good faith shall always be observed towards the Indians; their lands and property shall never be taken from them without their consent. . . . their property, rights, and liberty, they shall never be invaded or disturbed, unless in just and lawful wars authorized by Congress; but laws founded in justice and humanity, shall from time to time be made for preventing wrongs being done to them, and for preserving peace and friendship with them." Early midwestern leaders such as Judge James Varnum of the Ohio Company instructed others to treat Indians with "humanity and kindness," and Ohio territorial governor St. Clair wanted a "good Understanding with the Natives."[264]

This spirit of openness and fair dealing did not always prevail, of course, and the fate of some Native Americans in the Midwest is perhaps the grimmest chapter of midwestern history. A treaty with the Wyandots involved negotiation and consideration on both sides, for example, but the pain of removal was real. The Wyandots, a collection of refugees of the Iroquois wars from various tribes who settled in northern Ohio about 1800, signed their treaty in 1842. In exchange for 148,000 acres in Kansas, perpetual annuities, cancelation of their debts, travel expenses, and a new school, 674 Wyandots gave up their 109,000 acres near Sandusky.[265] They left Ohio for Kansas in 120 wagons and several buggies and with three hundred horses, beginning a sorrowful trek that several other midwestern tribes had already taken.[266] After much negotiation and delay, for another example, the Miamis signed a treaty in 1840 exchanging roughly 500,000 acres in Indiana for 500,000 acres in Kansas and the payment of their outstanding debts.[267] After the Miami chief's son and several subchiefs toured the Kansas reserve and found it satisfactory, 325 Miami were moved to Kansas in 1846.[268] Others, of course, were less taken with Kansas and, in particular, objected to the sparsity of trees, which had been plentiful back in the Great Lakes Midwest.[269]

Although such distant moves and the pain of dislocation are often seen as signs of the heartlessness of the dominant culture, there were also signs of mercy. Prior to removal, native leaders were often given an opportunity to tour and examine the lands to which they were moving. Indians were also moved to the arable lands of eastern Kansas so they had a chance to farm successfully and not sent farther west, beyond the 100th meridian, to the dry country where cultivation was arduous and risky.[270] Other tribes made strong cases for being allowed to stay where they were located and succeeded in resisting removal.[271] Christian missionaries to Indian reservations did, at times, try to proceed with a degree of charity and humility. President Grant thought he was striking a blow against corruption in the Indian agencies and advancing humanitarian goals when he afforded Christian churches the authority over reservations.[272] As terrible as these acculturation efforts sound to twenty-first-century ears, the outreach and reforms pursued during the nineteenth century were often done in good faith and in conformity with the norms of midwestern culture, which was widely viewed as democratic and progressive. That we may now look on these efforts to transform Native culture with great sadness and regret should not blind us to an accurate understanding of what nineteenth-century reformers and bureaucrats intended.

Another social group that struggled against midwestern norms was the Irish. During the 1840s, as the potato famine in Ireland worsened, more Irish immigrants decamped for the United States, where they sometimes met with hostility. The Irish were variously tarred as drunks, radicals, and Catholics with possible allegiances to Rome, not the American republic, and as general disruptors of the social order.[273] The dominant rural Protestant culture of the Midwest was particularly concerned with Catholic influence creeping into public schools.[274] The "Cincinnati Bible War" of the 1860s and earlier disputes, for example, were sparked by frictions between Catholics and Protestants over what portions and versions of the Bible would or could be read in school.[275] President Grant raised doubts about the separate Catholic school system during a speech in Des Moines in which he called for a "good common school education, unmixed with sectarian, pagan or atheistical tenets," and by "sectarian" he meant "Catholic."[276] In another sign of suspicions of Catholics, one question debated in the literary societies of Wabash College in Indiana was "Ought Congress to take any means to prevent the spread of Catholicism?"[277]

Because such questions hovered in the midwestern air, some Catholics, according to a study of a public library in Iowa, "undoubtedly felt themselves excluded on the basis of religion," and the library "may have seemed a place of moral danger" since its selections and culture were so Protestant.[278] Similar feelings animated Catholic students at the University of Wisconsin, who complained about the historian William Francis Allen "slandering" Catholics in his "Medieval Institutions" class.[279] In response to such slights, Catholics were keen to start their own parochial school systems and their own colleges. The latter included prominent institutions such as St. Louis University, founded in 1818; St. Xavier in Cincinnati, founded in 1831; Notre Dame in South Bend, Indiana, founded in 1842; and Marquette University in Milwaukee, founded in 1881.[280] At the same time that they matriculated at their own denomination's universities, Catholic students also worked to find a place at public colleges. At a Thanksgiving dinner for Catholic students in 1883 hosted by Mrs. John Melvin at the University of Wisconsin, Melvin suggested they start a society for the "study of Irish and Catholic history and literature," which they did and named it the "Melvin Club." This became the origin of Catholic Newman centers (after the English cardinal) on campus after it was renamed to be more generally recognizable. Catholic or Newman clubs then started at the University of Michigan (1889), Iowa (1901), Chicago (1902), Minnesota (1903), and Missouri (1903).[281]

It was in the political realm, however, that the Irish made the most progress. They often came to dominate Democratic machines in midwestern cities, which annoyed the Protestant Republican establishment and middle-class reformers who frequently tried to upend urban "boss rule."[282] If some Irish embraced the Victorian middle-class norms of the Midwest or became economically successful—or "lace curtain Irish"—they would become generally acceptable.[283]

An even larger immigrant group to the Midwest was the Germans, who were roughly half Catholic, depending on where they had lived in Germany. German Catholics, like the Irish, also supported separate institutions from the Protestant majority and earned the particular animus of temperance reformers, who denounced the German culture of beer. When Protestant women reform groups advocated female suffrage later in the nineteenth century, their greatest perceived foe was foreign immigrants, usually German and Irish, who thought, not wrongly, that the enfranchisement of women voters could lead to the passage of prohibition laws.[284] It also caused friction in local neighborhoods. The German immigrants of Chippewa County, Minnesota, for example, "voted that the Black Duck Lake Scandinavian Temperance Society should not be allowed to use the schoolhouse for their meetings" because they did not want to aid the cause of prohibition.[285]

Despite such frictions, Germans largely prospered in the nineteenth-century Midwest. If German immigrants opposed reformers' prohibition efforts, they were at the same time strong supporters of abolition and other reforms. Gustav Koerner, an immigrant from Frankfurt who became a lawyer and civic leader in Illinois, said, "Negro slavery is the only rope by which the devil holds the American people."[286] Another prominent German immigrant, Carl Christian Schurz, first immigrated to Wisconsin and became an active reformer and leader in the Republican Party and served as a Union general in the Civil War—"attacking the crudest form of that bondage of the individual which was forever his arch enemy"—before settling in Missouri and beginning a life of reform politics.[287] German immigrants to St. Louis, Indianapolis, Milwaukee, Cincinnati, and other midwestern cities established and supported orchestras, singing societies, newspapers, Turnverein associations and other gymnastics clubs, and other civic organizations.[288] Despite its record of success and achievement, the German Midwest was thoroughly disrupted during World War I by zealous supporters of the war, often in the form of wartime preparedness and security committees run by the midwestern Protestant establishment, who opposed the persistence of German-language newspapers and the teaching of German in the common schools.[289]

Non-Christian religious minorities could also, at times, feel alone, unwelcome, or worse. In her study of Osage, Iowa, Christine Pawley notes that, "apart from one Jewish family, one Spiritualist, and those few who listed their religion as 'none,' the population was entirely Christian," a situation that could leave Jews and others feeling isolated.[290] Agrarian activists sometimes invoked anti-Semitic themes, a claim Richard Hofstadter once made prominent. Later research, however, indicated that groups such as the Populists did not rely on anti-Semitic imagery any more than other social groups (Hofstadter's students, it was later discovered, strongly urged him not to make his unverified claims). "Populist antisemitism," the historian Robert Johnston notes, "seems to have paled in comparison to the upper-class antisemitism of the national elite."[291] The historian Oscar Handlin found that Populist views of Jews were not different from those of other groups extant during the 1890s and, in general, he found a "prevailing temper of tolerance."[292] The Populist orator and writer Ignatius Donnelly "certainly indulged in classic stereotypes," Johnston explains, "but he also went out of his way to condemn the historical persecution of the Jews." Given their critiques of the economic system, the Populists targeted bankers, but they especially focused on English bankers who had much influence on the American economy, and the "Populists almost always targeted these bankers, rather than the Jews."[293] In his study of the Populist standard-bearer William Jennings Bryan, Michael Kazin found that anti-Semitism "was quite rare" among Bryan supporters.[294] Even Hofstadter admitted in his consequential book on the reform era that a character in Donnelly's novel *Caesar's Column* noted the "terrible persecutions to which the Jews had been subjected for centuries."[295]

Contrary to Hofstadter's questionable claims, examples of toleration can be found throughout the historical record. Mildred Goldberg, for example, whose husband owned a clothing store, was a prominent and successful member of women's clubs in Monroe, Michigan.[296] A Mrs. Katz of the Shakespeare Club in Osage, Iowa, was "well-respected, holding leadership roles in the club and presenting papers on Judaism and on the international issues of concern to Jews."[297] Mr. Katz was also a member of the Osage Masons.[298] The Yale historian Robin Winks, who grew up in Indiana, recalled no anti-Semitism in the ranks of the Chautauqua circuit he traveled as a young man.[299]

Mormons faced more difficult circumstances. After the sect's founding in upstate New York in the 1830s, Mormons then moved west, first settling in Kirtland, Ohio, and finding unfriendly neighbors.[300] The midwestern-based Republican Party, in its first national platform, denounced "those twin relics of barbarism, polygamy and slavery," equating the GOP's hatred of slavery with Mormon religious practices.[301] The Mormons were later forced out of Missouri and then Nauvoo, Illinois, before settling at the edge of the Utah desert.[302]

The Mormons were perhaps particularly outside the mainstream, but their tale underscores the story of those who were less than fully a part of the dominant rhythms of midwestern life. Freethinkers, or atheists, might also have encountered turbulence in the Midwest, but prominent ones such as Robert Ingersoll seem to have excelled in civic affairs. Other observers were "impressed by the tolerance that prevailed in Cincinnati in the spring of 1829 when the orthodox Rev. Alexander Campbell and the freethinking Robert Owen publicly debated their respective convictions."[303] Some early midwesterners who did not put down roots and participate in communal life were dismissed as peripatetic vagabonds, squatters, and "white savages."[304] In later years, those who were economically unsuccessful might end up as itinerant farm workers, sometimes dubbed tramps or hoboes.[305]

Although many immigrants succeeded in the Midwest and welcomed the ability to own and hoe their own land, some surely bristled at the expectations of assimilation. Others found little to love in the Midwest and did not stay long. Some visitors to the Midwest, especially, it seems, those from England, were critical of the crudeness of conditions and said so; "Trolloping" (a term derived from the snooty British traveler Frances Trollope) "became a favorite practice and, in fact, still is in certain circles."[306] Trollope and others unfairly criticized the Midwest for something it was not, complaining that the banks of the Ohio River did not include "occasionally a ruined abbey, or feudal castle, to mix the romance of real life with that of nature."[307] She wanted more aristocrats and fewer common people who, she thought, were uncultured and crude. There was a rowdy crowd and gamblers and such in the region, noted the Nebraska-born historian Merle Curti, but "this element was very small," mostly the "noisy activities of a few characters" such as canal men and river boatmen; the Midwest in general "had a wholesome respect for order and in reality established it quickly."[308] There were many "fine, genuinely cultured people," another historian noted, to "offset the unpleasant types."[309] As the Midwest began to populate with more immigrants from New England, the mid-Atlantic states, and northern Europe, another social group, southern migrants, mostly in the lower latitudes of Ohio, Indiana, and Illinois, became more marginal and were variously dubbed "suckers," "Hoosiers," "butternuts," and other derisive terms.[310] Their alienation sharpened as the Civil War approached and regional tensions mounted, and as the defining parameters and identity of the Midwest took shape.

Although southerners and other groups may at times have bristled at the dominant culture of the Midwest, they also embraced it, in varying degrees, as it became more deeply entrenched throughout the century. By 1900 a common midwestern culture prevailed that was grounded in a highly developed American republicanism, Christian moralism, an ethic of character development and improvement, and a commitment to uplift, striving, and work. A familiar scene in this culture might be farmers sitting down after a long day of labor to read the *Des Moines Register,* a success manual, or a copy of Macaulay's *History of England* borrowed from one of the many local libraries. Perhaps on the weekend a farmer's family went to enjoy the county fair, to hear a lyceum lecturer, or to the various programs under the big tents of the annual Chautauqua. On Monday the farm kids would have walked to the country school, where they might read Wordsworth and tales about moral strength and fortitude. Perhaps, in the future, these children might matriculate at one of the dozens of Christian colleges in the Midwest, where they would receive more moral training, greater exposure to the classics of the Western tradition, and perhaps some mechanical training in agriculture or engineering. The culture of democratic advancements, open politics, literacy and learning, economic self-determination, and ordered freedom would fundamentally shape the Midwest, setting the place apart and giving rise to an emergent form of regional identity.

CHAPTER 3

"THE ATTITUDE OF
A SECTION ITSELF"

THE FORMATION OF MIDWESTERN
REGIONAL IDENTITY

While World War II was raging, a group of scholars in the Midwest gathered to think about their region. English professor Howard Troyer, the chairman of the Committee on Faculty Lectures at Lawrence College in Appleton, Wisconsin, assembled an impressive roster of thinkers to come to campus and opine about the Midwest. By the time of the war, Troyer could assert without equivocation or doubt that various American regions had taken root: the Deep South, the Desert Southwest, the Far West of California, the Pacific Northwest, New England, the Eastern Atlantic states, and the Midwest.[1] At the same time as the Wisconsin conference, another prominent historian could confidently say that the people of the "region are conscious of an identity of interests, and of a common outlook upon life, which give to the Old Northwest an individuality as distinct as that possessed by the people of New England, or of the Old South."[2] During the war, when the governor of Iowa was organizing a regional meeting related to economic planning, he invited representatives from the twelve states that were widely thought of as constituting the Midwest.[3]

Although diminished somewhat since the World War II era by faster communications, mass culture, the global economy, the internet, and other various cosmopolitanisms, Troyer's regional designations still persist and are meaningful sources of identity. The origins of regional consciousness and the emergence of the Midwest as an obvious and identifiable region can be found in the early nineteenth century in the decades after the adoption of the

Northwest Ordinance. Crucial steps in the formation of the region include an early north/south split between the western lands on either side of the Ohio River, subsequent social and political frictions between these regions, the hardening of regional lines during the Civil War era, and the blossoming of various modes of midwestern regional culture and thought premised on a separation from the East.

From the beginning of the republic people began to see and talk about the Midwest as a place that was unique and separate. The Northwest Ordinance of 1787 was passed to govern the area north of the Ohio River, and the Southwest Ordinance of 1790 specifically set forth that it was to govern the area south of the river. When Ohioans wrote their first constitution in 1802, they demarcated the beginnings of the Midwest by declaring their state's legitimacy based on the congressional enabling act governing the area "northwest of the river Ohio." When de Tocqueville descended the river he noted that the Kentucky side was sparsely populated by idle people and its environs slave-oriented and that the Ohio side was humming with activity and was where "man appears to be in the enjoyment of that wealth and contentment which is the reward of labor."[4] The Ohioan Thomas Ewing, foster father of William Tecumseh Sherman, said that labor "is held honorable by all on one side of the line because it is the vocation of freemen—degrading in the eyes of some on the other side because it is the task of slaves."[5] De Tocqueville and Ewing were highlighting social conditions that made the Midwest and the South different and would contribute to a growing awareness of midwestern uniqueness and shape a process of regional identity formation. Historians have followed suit and agreed that from the earliest days of the republic there could be seen a distinct line in the newly settled regions between slave areas and "the free West."[6]

Before assessing the deep divide between the Midwest and the South, however, it is important to note the Midwest's separation from and remaining connections to the Northeast. From the time of the colonial era there had been frictions between the more populated and more powerful coastal regions and the "backcountry."[7] From the "beginning East and West have shown a sectional attitude," said Frederick Jackson Turner, and the "interior of the colonies on the Atlantic was disrespectful of the coast, and the coast looked down upon the upland folk."[8] The sense of marginality in the backcountry and the fear of being dominated by eastern capital, culture, and political power would persist and grow throughout the nineteenth century and after. A rough line separating the real and imagined East from the Midwest developed around the eastern boundary of Ohio.[9] There began a new territory that emerged after the Revolution, distinct from the original American colonies. This is not to imply a complete break with the Northeast, however. Many midwesterners came from the Northeast, maintained financial ties to eastern cities, and sent their children to prominent colleges in the East. New England, in particular, played an important role in the early years of midwestern settlement. But the East, especially as time passed, was still considered a separate culture and space, a center to the peripheral Midwest, albeit one that drew in, Gatsby-like, the sons and daughters of the interior heartland. During the latter half of the nineteenth century the dominance of the East would increasingly meet resistance in the Midwest, which began to assert its own identity and support regionalist artists and writers attuned to the interests and rhythms of their own region.

During the first half of the nineteenth century the starkest regional divergence existed between the Midwest and the South. If the talented children of the Midwest went off to a distant college, it was usually in New England or New York, not the South, which was often seen as a foreign country, a land of alien institutions. The historian Eric Foner explains that the "whole mentality and flavor of southern life . . . seemed antithetical to the North. Instead of progress, the South represented decadence, instead of enterprise, laziness. . . . To those with visions of a steadily growing nation, slavery was an intolerable hindrance to national achievement." In contrast to the vigorous, democratic, and entrepreneurial Midwest, one Wisconsinite, in a typical formulation, saw southerners as a "set of cowards, full of gasconade, and bad liquor, brought up to abuse negroes and despise the north, too lazy to work; they are not above living on the unrewarded labor of others." In contrast to the Midwest, said one Ohio congressman, the South "builds up no middle class of intelligent farmers, artisans, and mechanics, who constitute the real strength, who make the real wealth, and are justly the pride and glory of the free states."[10] Four million slaves were held in bondage in the South by the time of the Civil War, whereas the Northwest Ordinance had banned slavery in the Midwest. When the Civil War finally came, one of the first reasons cited by Mississippi in its statement of secession was the "hostility" to slavery "manifested in the well-known Ordinance of 1787, in regard to the

Northwestern Territory [i.e., the Midwest]."[11] The iconic defender of the Old South and the "evil genius of the Slave Power," Senator John C. Calhoun of South Carolina, routinely denounced the Northwest Ordinance as a "sin" against the South.[12]

Slavery existed at the top of a list of differences that divided the regions into separate cultural spheres. In the South, the Cavalier culture stemming from the region's first immigrants prevailed. The aristocratic pro-crown and Church of England immigrants of the early southern colonies contrasted with the more varied culture of the Midwest made up of anti-crown dissidents such as the Puritans, the Quakers of Pennsylvania, and upland nonslaveholding Scotch-Irish southerners.[13] The southern culture of honor, dueling, militarism, and violence contrasted with the more democratic and entrepreneurial Midwest.[14] One Georgia editor said he was "sickened" by the "free society" of the Midwest and its "conglomeration of greasy mechanics, filthy operatives, small-fisted farmers, and moon-struck theorists" who were "hardly fit for association with a southern gentlemen's body servant."[15] The South was hierarchical and rural; the "planter ideal stressed values and practices that were frankly old world and sometimes even feudal in origin and tone" and even included "medieval joustings."[16] Self-improvement, uplift, and literacy, meanwhile, were prized in the Midwest, and the South's medieval fantasies dismissed. The reform movements and improvement plans of the Midwest "aroused both contempt and fear in the South," in part because abolitionism was fused into them, but also because the South remained generally suspicious of "progress" and wedded to reaction.[17] The distinction could be seen in the realm of education. By 1870, nearly 80 percent of midwestern children attended school, whereas 29 percent of southern kids did.[18] Regional tensions shaped education policy, since many southerners associated common schools with meddling reformers and hostile abolitionists.[19]

The states of the southern frontier that were settled during the early nineteenth century such as Alabama, Mississippi, and Tennessee "drew their values, not from the commercializing and industrializing East, but from the rural, slave society of the Southern seaboard states" such as South Carolina. Cotton came to dominate southern culture, and 75 percent of cotton was produced by slave labor.[20] One visitor to the South called it a region where "people live in cotton houses and ride in cotton carriages. They buy cotton, sell cotton, think cotton, eat cotton, drink cotton, and dream cotton. They marry cotton wives, and unto them are born cotton children."[21] This cotton South remained decidedly rural; by 1850 there were more cities over three thousand people in Illinois and Indiana alone than in all the nine states of the solid South below Kentucky and Virginia. Illinois and Indiana also had more capital invested in manufacturing than all the seven states of the Deep South combined. The South felt that it was losing ground in relative terms to the North, and this "awareness of minority status stimulated the southern sense of solidarity, apartness, and defensiveness, and caused the elaboration of the perennial southern political doctrines of states' rights."[22]

The belief among southerners that they were losing power corresponded to growing frustration in the Midwest with continued southern control over national institutions and thus growing animosity between the regions. The intense "regional unity" of the southern states gave rise to growing concerns about what came to be called the Slave Power.[23] Despite criticism from historians about the extreme rhetoric employed during this era, the historian Bertram Wyatt-Brown emphasized that "there indeed *was* a Slave Power, sustained by the monolithic southern response to external (and even internal) criticism."[24] An Ohio newspaper noted that slave interests were part of a "deliberate plot . . . to sustain the slavery of this country . . . and to extend it over almost illimitable regions."[25] Midwesterners such as Joshua Giddings of Ohio often enumerated the sins of the Slave Power, including trying to invade Kansas Territory and extend slavery into the Southwest.[26] The Cincinnati *Daily Commercial* confidently opined, "There is such a thing as the SLAVE POWER. It has marched over and annihilated the boundaries of the states." A typical Whig convention in Michigan denounced the "undying efforts of the Slave power for political supremacy," and other midwesterners actively led the resistance to "our southern masters." The Irish and Germans, the most prominent immigrant groups in the Midwest at midcentury, believed that the Slave Power was a threat to their new civil liberties and access to citizenship; Germans, in particular, became a strongly anti-slavery voting bloc.[27] Irish and German immigrants, aware of the region's rates of illiteracy and general backwardness, "avoided the benighted South."[28] Anti-slavery attitudes among German immigrants were particularly salient since the Midwest had become the heartland of German immigration and by far the most German region in the country.[29] Midwestern distinctiveness was also sharpened by criticisms of the Slave Power of the South because it was often linked to the financial power of the Northeast.[30] In an allusion to Massachusetts linen factories, for example, slaveowners and industrialists were linked together as "the Lords of the Lash and the Lords of the Loom."[31]

Given these deep regional differences, sectional frictions steadily mounted throughout the first half of the nineteenth century and manifested themselves in political squabbles and, finally, in a shooting war. In 1820 the particular issue at hand was the future of Missouri. Tensions were momentarily halted by the Missouri Compromise, which banned the institution of slavery anywhere north of Missouri's southern boundary.[32] This decision contributed to a growing north-south divide by holding slavery below a certain geographic line. Regional tensions were also caused by tariffs, which were favored by midwestern congressmen and commercial interests and bitterly opposed by southern cotton planters, who wanted more open trade to sell their fiber to Europe. South Carolina leaders denounced the "Tariff of Abominations" and threatened to "nullify" federal tariff laws during the early 1830s.

The latter half of the decade also saw a rapid increase in the amount of abolitionist activity, much of it springing from places such as Oberlin College and Lane Theological Seminary in Ohio; Galesburg, Illinois ("the chief city of the Abolitionists in Illinois," according to a St. Louis newspaper); midwestern Quaker enclaves; and various evangelical churches and colleges around the Midwest.[33] The annexation of Texas and the war with Mexico during the 1840s were spurred on by southerners seeking more lands below the Missouri Compromise line that might allow the extension of slavery and greater slave state influence in Washington. Midwestern congressmen such as Abraham Lincoln, on the other hand, opposed the war in Mexico because it would strengthen the Slave Power.[34] The Wilmot Proviso, which anti-slavery legislators tried to attach to Mexican War legislation, sought to block extension of slavery to new territories and did so by using the exact same Northwest Ordinance language that banned slavery (during the famed Webster-Hayne debates of the 1830s, Webster also invoked the ordinance's ban on slavery).[35] The proviso caused great and ongoing regional tensions—during his one term in Congress Lincoln said he voted on versions of the proviso upwards of forty times—but was always defeated by southerners voting along strict sectional lines.[36] The more the South prevailed in the political battles of the first half of the nineteenth century, the more the North denounced the tentacles of the Slave Power for controlling the federal government.

The regions also diverged beyond the particular issue of slavery. In the South, large plantations dominated agriculture, and cotton was increasingly king during the antebellum era; in the Midwest, yeoman farming was the rule and diversified farms were the norm as midwestern agriculture expanded westward. Midwestern farms mixed wheat, corn, cattle, pigs, chickens, dairy, gardens, orchards, and a variety of economic pursuits. In the South, the planter class dominated politics, and millions of people were excluded from the political process; in contrast, the ideology of the common man prevailed in midwestern politics, and suffrage rights expanded throughout the nineteenth century. The Midwest, already home to a mix of peoples from various regions, also became home, starting in the 1840s, to a rich mix of new immigrants from Ireland, Germany, Scandinavia, and other places; the South remained largely unaffected by immigration, and its existing English/Scotch-Irish ethnic patterns prevailed. Educational levels were much higher in the Midwest and colleges more widespread. The Midwest also remained home to a wider mix of religions than the South.[37] In a sign of midwestern openness and theological diversity, many utopian societies were also founded in the Midwest; they largely avoided the South (only two of the over one hundred utopian communities established by reformers during the nineteenth century were located in the South).[38] A harbinger during the 1840s of what was to come, the religions that did transcend region began to divide over slavery, leading to the creation of Southern Baptists, the Methodist Episcopal Church South, a southern wing of Presbyterians, and other sectional religious entities.[39]

A regional split along religious lines was nearly inevitable given the South's defense of slavery and the growth of a forceful anti-slavery movement in the Midwest led by Protestant reformers.[40] When discussing abolitionism, the historian John Higham noted the "peculiar evangelical ferment of the Midwest," which alienated the emergent region from the slave-dominated South.[41] Ohio, with its long border with a southern slave state, became a land to which escaping slaves fled and in which the abolitionist movement gained momentum.[42] Kentucky slaveowners called it the "Ohio problem."[43] As early as 1817, the newspaper *Philanthropist* began publishing in Mt. Pleasant and became the first newspaper in the country to champion the abolition of slavery.[44]

By 1838 more than three hundred anti-slavery societies had been organized in Ohio, an abolitionist press network was established, especially in Cincinnati and the eastern regions of the state, and activists had organized (including a young John Brown, who was growing up near Akron).[45] Oberlin, Ohio, became known as the town that sparked the Civil War because of its intense abolitionist movement.[46] People from Oberlin, for example, rescued a slave from slave catchers in the famous Oberlin-Wellington Rescue that inflamed southern slaveowners. Letters signed by "Many a Buckeye" in Marietta denounced the "invasion of Ohio" when slave hunters from Virginia abducted runaway slaves along with white Ohioans trying to help them flee.[47] Ohio governor Salmon P. Chase also fought slave hunters and worked consistently to advance African American freedoms in his state.[48] Kentuckians like Henry Clay constantly complained about slaves slipping across the river into Ohio.[49] When aggressive fugitive slave legislation favorable to slaveowners was passed by Congress, the citizens of Trumbull County, Ohio, responded by passing more than a dozen resolutions attacking the "greatly aggravated aggression of the slave power on our rights as citizens of a free state" and pledged, "We will not, under any circumstances, render obedience [to it]."[50] Another Buckeye said, "I have never seen such intense excitement pervade this community as now exists against the Fugitive Slaw Law."[51]

Women in Ohio and around the Midwest were an especially strong force and avoided the divisive battles that weakened abolitionism in the Northeast as they developed their own regional movement.[52] Ohio senator Benjamin Wade was fiercely abolitionist and despised the southern aristocracy.[53] A young college professor in Ohio and soon to be Union general named James Garfield also denounced the "aristocratic privilege" of the South and opposed any concessions to the Slave Power.[54] Losing a war to the South, according to one private in the 2nd Ohio Cavalry, would be a victory of "Monarchs, Kings and Aristocrats" and "Old World" despotism.[55] One Ohio congressman introduced a resolution that was construed as calling for abolition (which Democrats allowed a vote on in order to highlight, as they saw it, Republican extremism), and more than half of House Republicans, including the party leaders from Iowa and Ohio, voted for it.[56] Ohio Republican congressman Joshua Giddings warred against slavery, and Buckeye congressman John Bingham ultimately crafted the key provisions of the Fourteenth Amendment requiring equal application of the laws.[57] Giddings also brought fellow midwesterner Abraham Lincoln to the cause.[58] The anti-slavery work of all these Buckeyes was bolstered by ministers such as Theodore Dwight Weld and others who "helped give Ohio the largest number of antislavery societies in the nation."[59]

Given Ohio's oversized influence in the region as the first midwestern state, its greater population (in 1840, Ohio cast more electoral votes than Indiana, Illinois, and Michigan combined), and the tendency of its young men to move west into newer states, its anti-slavery efforts redounded throughout the Midwest.[60] Throughout the 1850s, Ohio and the broader Midwest hosted widely attended meetings of the Northwestern Christian Anti-Slavery Conventions in Chicago, Cincinnati, Columbus, and other cities and moved additional Christian congregations in the direction of abolitionism.[61] During election season, in some midwestern counties the abolitionist Liberty Party even won majorities.[62] Because of Ohio and the welling anti-slavery movement in the region, the Midwest, as Marilynne Robinson concluded, "became a bulwark against the spread of the slave economy."[63]

The Midwest-South rupture finally came in the 1850s. To begin the decade, tensions flared over the issue of California. The Compromise of 1850 allowed California into the Union as a free state, but it also granted Utah and New Mexico the right to decide whether to be slave or free, an expression of the popular sovereignty ideas advanced by Michigan Democratic senator Lewis Cass and Illinois Democratic senator Stephen Douglas. This dashed the hopes of anti-slavery activists who sought to block slavery in the territories just as it had been formally blocked from the Midwest by the Northwest Ordinance.

Perhaps more explosive was the inclusion, as part of the compromise, of the Fugitive Slave Act. These measures, passed along "strikingly sectional" lines, were deeply unpopular in the increasingly anti-slavery Midwest.[64] They meant the addition of two more potential slave states to the Union and also that the police powers of the federal government and unwilling local officials would be harnessed to capture slaves who escaped over the Ohio River to freedom.[65] Such escapes were featured in the wildly successful novel *Uncle Tom's Cabin,* written by Harriet Beecher Stowe, based on her time in Cincinnati when her husband taught at Lane Theological Seminary (originally intended as an "anti-slavery fort") and as she embraced local civic affairs, including the activities of the Cincinnati Semi-Colon Club and its stable of regionalists.[66] The book sold millions of copies and caused Ohio

towns to debate where Eliza might have traversed the icy river.[67] Throughout the 1850s abolitionists in the Midwest would actively resist efforts to
recapture runaway slaves, and southerners would in turn routinely denounce
abolitionist hotbeds and the Midwest's active underground railroad network
whose lantern-lit paths routinely helped slaves escape.[68] One Indiana man,
for example, guided some two thousand fugitive slaves to freedom between
1826 and 1846.[69] Midwestern states such as Michigan and Ohio also passed
personal liberty laws designed to frustrate southern usage of the Fugitive
Slave Act, and the Wisconsin Supreme Court freed an abolitionist for rescuing slaves and even declared the fugitive law unconstitutional.[70]

The final spark that would ignite the Civil War came over the issue of
the territories of Kansas and Nebraska. Democrats such as Senator Stephen
Douglas of Illinois, in order to promote the building of a transcontinental
railroad beginning in the Midwest, sought to push Kansas and Nebraska
toward statehood to prepare the area for surveying and railroad construction, and his plan was a lock to win solid southern support. The resulting
Kansas-Nebraska Act of 1854, following the principle of popular sovereignty, allowed the new Kansas and Nebraska territories to choose to be free
or slave in a space where slavery, by virtue of the long-standing Missouri
Compromise, was supposed to be forbidden.[71] When Iowa joined the Union
in 1846, for example, it joined as a free state without quarrel since it had been
part of the Louisiana Purchase and thus subject to the anti-slavery rules of
the Missouri Compromise. But after passage of the Nebraska bill, as it was
then known, in a vote divided by section, upending the Missouri Compromise, such procedures provided no clarity. Senator Benjamin Wade of Ohio
denounced the Nebraska bill as a "declaration of war on the institutions of
the North, a deliberate sectional movement by the South for political power,
without regard for justice or consequences." Future Ohio governor Salmon P.
Chase saw the Nebraska bill as a product of the Slave Power and "part and
parcel of an atrocious plot" to create a "dreary region of despotism, inhabited
by masters and slaves."[72] The *Daily Cleveland Herald* deemed the bill the
"sum of all villainies."[73] Slavery in Nebraska territory, said the governor of
Iowa, would mean "unthrift and sparseness, stand-still and decay." Everything was at stake, declared William Seward, and the "people of the northwest" and how their region developed would determine if the nation would
be free or slave.[74] A young lawyer in Springfield, Illinois, named Lincoln

"assumed leadership of the anti-Nebraska men" and spoke out against the Nebraska bill as a betrayal of the legacy of the Northwest Ordinance, which, Lincoln emphasized, had banished slavery from the Midwest and made the region prosperous.[75] If the Midwest's Northwest Ordinance could have been extended to Nebraska territory, said Salmon Chase of Ohio, the region would enjoy "freedom not serfdom; freeholds not tenancies; democracy not despotism; education not ignorance . . . progress, not stagnation or retrogression."[76]

Soon after passage of the Nebraska bill, pro-slavery Missourians and anti-slavery forces from the Midwest and Northeast poured into Kansas and battled over control of the future state. The law triggered a "sectional race to establish political hegemony in Kansas."[77] The result was "Bleeding Kansas"—the burning of Lawrence by pro-slavery forces, other various outrages by Missouri ruffians, John Brown abolitionists' murder of five slaveowners, an influx of anti-slavery evangelical activists, and the death of some two hundred people.[78] The Nebraska bill split deep along party lines. Every midwestern Whig voted against it, almost every southern Whig voted in favor, and southern Democrats overwhelmingly favored the measure. Ohio senator Benjamin Wade thought the bill would destroy the republic and saw a corresponding total eclipse of the sun as a sign of the coming end.[79] One historian called the bill the "most explosive piece of legislation ever passed by a U.S. Congress."[80]

The Kansas-Nebraska Act caused a rapid chain reaction in American politics. Anti-slavery opponents of the bill quickly organized themselves and spurred the rapid rise of a major new political party in the Midwest.[81] People opposed to the spread of slavery immediately formed the new Republican Party in places like Ripon, Wisconsin, Crawfordsville, Iowa, and Jackson, Michigan. In the latter town various people and factions famously gathered in a grove of oak trees to forge their new anti–Nebraska bill party.[82] The new Michigan Republican Party that resulted adopted a platform denouncing slavery as a "relic of barbarism" and the "slaveholding oligarchs of the South" for their "schemes of aristocracy," and it vowed to "cooperate and be known as Republicans until the contest" against the feudal South "be terminated."[83] By midsummer anti–Nebraska bill conventions had convened and organized new state Republican parties "throughout the Middle West."[84] The GOP, one historian noted, became the "first willfully sectional party in American history."[85] The lighting-quick rise of the Republicans led to the

Democrats losing sixty-six House seats in 1854 (the number of Democrats dropped from ninety-one to twenty-five—only seven Democrats who voted for the Nebraska bill survived).[86] The splintered Whig Party expired and the Midwest-based GOP was born of its remnants plus assorted free soilers, abolitionists, and others.

The prime directive of the Midwest-centered GOP was the upending of the southern Slave Power.[87] The Republican Party commonly discussed the need to end slavery and to reconstruct the South's backward institutions and culture completely.[88] In 1856 the upstart Republicans nominated the famed pathfinder John C. Frémont for president, who promptly declared his support for a free Kansas and his opposition to the enforcement of the Fugitive Slave Law and ran under the banner "Free Soil, Free Men, and Fremont." The national Republican platform, echoing the early Michigan platform, deemed slavery a "relic of barbarism."[89] That fall Frémont carried Iowa, Wisconsin, Michigan, and Ohio, a harbinger of the coming GOP domination of the Midwest. Southerners routinely attacked Frémont as anti-slavery, and he lost every state in the solidly Democratic South.

Soon after the 1856 election came the holdings of *Dred Scott v. Sanford* (1857), a case with decidedly midwestern origins. Dred Scott was a slave in Missouri who was taken to Illinois and then to Fort Snelling in Wisconsin Territory, or what would become the state of Minnesota. In order to gain his freedom, abolitionist lawyers in St. Louis brought suit on behalf of Scott upon his return to Missouri and argued that he had been taken to free areas of the Midwest where slavery was prohibited. Once a person stayed in free territory, they argued, slaveowners forfeited rights to that person by virtue of the "once free, always free doctrine."[90] Prior to the Scott case, more than 40 percent of the slaves who had brought such lawsuits prevailed.[91] In the end, a southerner-dominated Supreme Court stunned the country by ruling that Scott, as a slave, had no standing to bring a suit. It further argued that the long-standing Missouri Compromise, which had prohibited slavery from the states of the Louisiana Purchase above the southern boundary of Missouri, was unconstitutional. The Court also ruled that the Northwest Ordinance, the foundational charter of the Midwest, could not grant either freedom or citizenship to Scott. The *Dred Scott* case was a major blow to the Midwest's ban on slavery and accompanying case law and a major defeat for midwestern abolitionists who had been aiding the escapes of southern slaves for years. The Court's assault on the Northwest Ordinance, in particular, "outraged Abraham Lincoln and other Midwesterners" and brought regional warfare a step closer.[92]

The potential spread of slavery into Kansas and Nebraska, the harassment of slaves seeking freedom in the Midwest by southern slave catchers, and the repudiation of the Midwest's foundational Northwest Ordinance all fueled regional tensions and drove the Midwest and South further apart. Southerners raged about slaves who escaped across the Ohio River into the Midwest and the network of abolitionists who helped them, not to mention the rhetoric of the aggressively anti-slavery and midwestern-based GOP, which, given its irrelevance in the South, had no reason to placate its southern members as the Whig Party had done.[93] Midwesterners fumed over the attacks on the Northwest Ordinance and their frustrated vision for a free-soil West and their hopes for the creation of new lands for yeomen farming. Midwestern political leaders turned to the person who had done the most to challenge Douglas, the man responsible for the hated Kansas-Nebraska Act. In 1858, Abraham Lincoln had debated Douglas and challenged his policies all over Illinois, but the state legislature (which then chose U.S. senators) still sent Douglas back to Washington. Lincoln's fame had grown, however, as indicated by his reprise of all of his anti-Nebraska arguments throughout the politically critical state of Ohio in 1859, and he had become the leader of a new anti-slavery party based in the Midwest that was not afraid to challenge the southern Slave Power.[94]

Lincoln's growing prominence in Republican circles and his continued opposition to the Kansas-Nebraska law were great strengths for the midwestern rail-splitter as the GOP assembled for its national convention in 1860 in Chicago (the rail-splitter imagery stemmed from the 1859 Illinois state Republican convention in Decatur, where two of the three thousand rails Lincoln had split as a young man were presented to him).[95] In the end, after outmaneuvering figures such as Ohio governor Salmon P. Chase and Missouri congressman Edward Bates, Lincoln won the nomination as a symbol of midwestern free-labor ideology and a vigorous opponent of the spread of slavery farther west. The young Republican Party would go on to win its first presidential race in 1860 with the anti-slavery Lincoln at the top of the ticket. It was the beginning of the "Lincoln cult" and the origins of the first iconic midwestern figure, a common man from the center of the country who would reflect and solidify his region's identity.[96]

The presidential race was decided along clear regional lines. Lincoln won all the midwestern states then in the Union (Kansas, Nebraska, and the Dakotas were still in the territorial stage) and was universally opposed in the Democratic South (Lincoln received 1 percent of the vote in Virginia and was not even allowed on the ballot in many southern states). Soon after the anti-slavery Republican was declared the winner of the presidential race, southerners started clamoring for secession, and war quickly came. A *Chicago Tribune* opinion writer spoke for many when he blamed the war on the "arrogant assumptions of the Slavery Oligarchy."[97]

Minnesota, where Lincoln won 64 percent of the vote, was the first to send military units to aid the cause in the form of the First Minnesota Volunteers, one of hundreds of midwestern units that would march off to fight for Mr. Lincoln.[98] In a sign of the coming sacrifices soon to be made, the Minnesota regiment would endure an 82 percent casualty rate at the battle of Gettysburg.[99] In Lincoln's home state of Illinois the governor declared, "Our people will wade through seas of blood before they will see a single star or solitary stripe erased from the glorious flag of our Union."[100]

Over half of the Union's troops would come from the Midwest, even though the region constituted only a quarter of the country's population.[101] The original five midwestern states sent nearly a million soldiers to war for the Union, and the Midwest provided nearly all of Lincoln's generals and most of his cabinet.[102] Ohio alone produced sixty-four Union generals.[103] Midwestern towns were emptied of fighting-age men. Hillsdale College in Michigan saw its entire student body march off to war, along with a quarter of the men in Michigan.[104] Lawrence College in Wisconsin was also quick to "declare itself for the Union" via speeches by the school president and other dignitaries. Lawrence professors raised companies to fight, the entire class of 1864 went to war, and the college provided a "steadfast wall of blue."[105] These large Union armies led by Ohio generals were fed by midwestern farms, which provided nearly 80 percent of the Union's wheat, corn, and oats; at the same time, New England's agricultural production shrank.[106]

The Ohio and Mississippi River valleys proved to be the crucial theaters of the war for the Union cause. The former GOP presidential nominee John C. Frémont was first given command of the Department of the West, and he organized the Western army and even issued an early emancipation proclamation, but he generally proved to be a weak commander. His most important decision was the appointment of the Illinoisan U.S. Grant, initially the commander of the Twenty-first Illinois regiment, as commander of the critical city of Cairo, Illinois, down where the Ohio and Mississippi Rivers meet.[107] Grant, who had been running a leather goods store in Galena, Illinois, began marching on and capturing Confederate forts and generally securing Kentucky and Tennessee while the Union armies in the East continually stumbled. At a pivotal moment of his advance, Grant was joined by General Don Carlos Buell, a son of Ohio and Indiana, at an encampment on the Tennessee River near a little church named Shiloh. Grant's new underling, General William Tecumseh Sherman, an Ohioan who had succeeded Grant as commander of the District of Cairo, also joined Grant's army as a division commander. In the bloodiest battle of the war to date—with more casualties than the Revolutionary, 1812, and Mexican wars combined—midwestern troops delivered the first major victory for the Union cause. Regiments from Illinois, Michigan, Wisconsin, Missouri, and, most important, Iowa, blunted rebel attacks with a "Hornet's Nest" of bullets at the famed Sunken Road until Grant could organize a counterattack.[108] The victory of Grant's troops over units from Alabama, Mississippi, Arkansas, Louisiana, and Tennessee, in a show of midwestern force over the renegade South, led to Union control of the Mississippi River valley and ultimately secured the Western theater for Lincoln.[109] After Vicksburg and other victories, Lincoln called Grant to Washington to replace the latest of his flailing eastern generals, who kept suffering defeats and risking a successful Confederate invasion of the North. Lincoln gave Grant command of all the Union armies and set Sherman loose to burn the South.

Campaigns such as Shiloh gave definitive shape to midwestern identity. The Union cause at Shiloh was led by midwesterners who commanded specifically midwestern units. The Union Army of the Tennessee would go on to celebrate its victories and toast their memories for many years to come. At a meeting of the Society of the Army of the Tennessee in Des Moines in 1875, President Grant praised his fellow midwestern soldiers for all the sacrifices they made to save the nation's "free republican institutions" from the southern threat.[110] Midwestern soldiers who fought through the South were appalled by the conditions there, such as the high levels of poverty and illiteracy. One soldier from the Eighty-sixth Ohio wrote home while marching through the South: "Citizens are very ignorant. they can't read nor write."[111]

They also remembered being greeted with hostility by southern civilians.[112] Ending slavery in the South—which they saw as a "blight" that "withered all it touched"—was often on their mind. John Campbell of the Fifth Iowa wrote in his diary, "I believe that duty to my country and my *God*, bid me assist in crushing this wicked rebellion against our government, which rebellious men have instigated . . . to secure the extension of that blighting curse—*slavery*—o'er our fair land." A soldier in the Fifty-third Indiana said, "More I see of slavery in all its enormity the more I am satisfied that it is a curse to our country. . . . Outside the towns in the South the people are a century behind the free states." An Illinois farm boy, proud of the "youngest and brightest nation of all the earth," vowed to never bow to southern "traters and forsake the graves of our fathers."[113]

Such emotions and experiences did not soon fade, and remembering their fallen comrades in the Union Army became an important aspect of midwestern life carried on via endless patriotic ceremonies, encampments, lodge meetings, and political rallies. Prominent regional voices also emerged from this era to keep memories of the war alive, including Ambrose Bierce, who served in the Ninth Indiana at Shiloh. Lew Wallace, the prominent Indiana writer and author of *Ben-Hur*, also served as a Union general at Shiloh (and the deftness of his response to rebel attacks continued to be debated for years).[114]

Off the battlefield and in a new South-less Congress, the Republican agenda proceeded unobstructed. No longer would the southern "gag rule" block discussion of anti-slavery petitions.[115] For years, southern lawmakers had also blocked free-soil midwesterners from passing a homestead law that would provide small farms to Americans in exchange for five years of labor and farm improvements. Southerners had blocked the legislation because it was antithetical to the slave-based agriculture of the southern model and because it extended midwestern yeoman farming westward.[116] In 1862, after years of being stymied, the bill passed, resulting in the creation of tens of thousands of new farms in Iowa, Minnesota, Nebraska, Dakota Territory, and other states and territories.[117] Congress also passed land grant legislation in 1862 creating agricultural colleges, legislation that had been advocated by Jonathan Baldwin Turner of Illinois College since the 1830s and underscored the midwestern commitment to pragmatism, free labor, and agrarianism.[118] Southerners rightly saw the law as an attempt to promote small-scale, decentralized farming—that is, an effort to undermine plantation agriculture—and overwhelmingly voted against it when it was considered in Congress before southern legislators bolted.[119] During the debate Iowa Republican congressman James Harlan denounced southerners for their hostility to free-labor ideology and saluted the "man who labors and sweats for his own bread."[120]

Federal banking legislation that had been blocked for years by southern Democrats of the Jacksonian persuasion also passed, along with an income tax, and the first paper money was issued by the federal government. Without the presence of southerners, congressional leaders such as Benjamin Wade and James Ashley, both Republicans from Ohio, could craft legislation creating new territories that strictly banned slavery.[121] During the debate over one such bill, Representative Ashley of Toledo argued that the "slave barons of the South" had premised their attack on the Union on protecting an evil institution, and thus the "logic of events tells me unmistakably that slavery must die." Wade, chairman of the Senate Committee on Territories, similarly saw the legislation as an attack on the Slave Power.[122]

The absence of southerners from Congress meant that Republican leaders in Washington could formally abolish slavery. During the war, congressmen Ashley of Ohio and James F. Wilson of Iowa pushed for an amendment to the Constitution that would permanently abolish the peculiar southern institution. Their efforts were taken up by John B. Henderson of Missouri and the chairman of the Senate Judiciary Committee, Lyman Trumbull of Illinois. The Judiciary Committee used the language of the Northwest Ordinance to craft what would become the Thirteenth Amendment to the Constitution. Republicans strongly supported passage of the measure in votes during 1864; Democrats opposed it. During the 1864 election season the GOP added passage of the Thirteenth Amendment to its party platform, and Lincoln endorsed the measure and made it a top legislative priority. House Speaker Schuyler Colfax of Indiana guided the measure to final passage by a two-thirds vote in January 1865, with all Republicans voting yes and fifty-six Democrats voting no.[123] Lincoln's Illinois became the first state to ratify the amendment, on February 1, 1865. After the quick action by the Illinois legislature, the *Chicago Daily Tribune* wrote, "Probably Illinois will prove to be the first State to ratify this second Magna Carta of human liberty. Glory be to God."[124] The Fourteenth Amendment, making African Americans citizens and neutralizing the hated *Dred Scott* decision, and the Fifteenth Amendment, mandating African American suffrage, soon followed. Republican efforts to maintain African American voting rights in the South persisted for decades, and southern efforts at disfranchisement mounted and finally prevailed by the 1890s.[125]

The heightened sectional conflict of the 1850s and then the Civil War killed the remnants of unity still lingering from an earlier era in the American West. The slaughter at Shiloh and a hundred other places drove home the deep divisions between the Midwest and the South, and the memories kindled in hundreds of midwestern Grand Army of the Republic lodges maintained the regional animosities. The South also mattered less economically to the Midwest. During the first decades of the nineteenth century, much of the Midwest's trade flowed down the Ohio River to the Mississippi and on down to New Orleans, giving the early Midwest a partial southern economic connection.[126] But with the building of the Erie Canal and other smaller midwestern canals, the greater use of the Great Lakes for commerce, and the coming of a dense railroad network in the Midwest, the region's economic orientation changed from the South to the Northeast.[127] In 1850 the Midwest sent the bulk of its corn down the Ohio River to the South and sent quadruple the amount of pork to the South as it did to the East; by 1860, after expanding midwestern and eastern railroads became integrated, the Midwest was sending quadruple the amount of corn to the East that it sent to the South and six times the amount of pork.[128]

Through the middle decades of the century, the regions were also becoming more deeply divided by economic policy. The Midwest and the North in general favored tariffs to protect their burgeoning industrial sectors. So began a movement for "home manufactures" that declared that the region must choose "either to be in a state of dependence, with foreign manufactures, or be independent, clothed in homespun, the products of our own labor."[129] The South, meanwhile, sought more open trade to sell its growing cotton stores. By the time of the Civil War, southern cotton constituted two-thirds of American exports.[130] Most of the grains and meat produced on midwestern farms was consumed domestically, so foreign trade was less of a concern in the region. The Midwest and South were also divided over improvements such as canals and bridges and Great Lakes harbors, which midwestern legislators eagerly sought in order to spur economic traffic.[131] Midwesterners thought such improvements boosted economic development, but the South opposed giving greater authority to the central government and feared the loss to Great Lakes shipping of goods that once flowed by river to the South. All these factors diminished a once generic "West" in favor of a clear division between the Midwest and the South.[132] In a sign of the regional reorientation, the number of midwestern newspapers that once had "Western" in the title dropped from fifty in the early decades of the nineteenth century to fifteen in 1840 to one in 1860. The Ohio River had become a stark dividing line between the Midwest and South.[133]

The first postwar presidential election did little to lessen regional political tensions. The Union war commander who finally pulverized Confederate armies and unleashed Sherman on the South was selected as the GOP presidential nominee at the national convention in Chicago. In the fall of 1868, Lincoln's midwestern hammer, Ulysses S. Grant, won every midwestern state. Grant did the same in 1872. Ohio congressman and governor and former Union general Rutherford B. Hayes won the GOP nomination at the Cincinnati convention in 1876 and went on to win every midwestern state except Indiana and win the presidency over New Yorker Samuel Tilden. In 1880, the GOP convention in Chicago nominated Ohio congressman James Garfield, a Union war general who had served at the critical battle of Shiloh. Garfield won every midwestern state except border state Missouri and lost every southern state. After a narrow defeat in the 1884 presidential election with an eastern candidate, Republicans again turned to a midwestern standard-bearer. In 1888 in Chicago, the GOP chose Benjamin Harrison, a former Indiana senator and Union war general, and he went on to win every midwestern state except Missouri and lose every southern state. In 1896, Ohio governor William McKinley, yet another Union war veteran, was selected as the GOP candidate at the national convention in St. Louis and rolled to the presidency, winning the core states of the Midwest. In 1900, McKinley won every midwestern state except Missouri and lost every southern state.[134]

Throughout all of these postwar elections in which midwestern Republican candidates ran for president, not one of them won a southern state. The South remained an impenetrable Democratic bastion. When these Republican presidential candidates were on the hustings they frequently "waved the bloody shirt," reminding voters that the South had rebelled and tried to break up the Union, and these reminders became a prominent part of midwestern political culture. For four decades after the Civil War, waving the bloody shirt "remained relatively effective, especially in the Middle West."[135] Prominent midwestern speakers gave blistering anti-South speeches that reminded audiences of all the sins of the Confederacy.[136] Brand Whitlock, the journalist and future mayor of Toledo, remembered that he often heard the "bloody shirters' harangues against the South" as a young man.[137] One question debated in the literary societies of Wabash College in Indiana was "Should the government of the U.S. execute all Rebels above the rank of Brigadier General? Should the returning rebels be represented in Congress?"[138] In earlier years the literary societies of the Midwest constantly debated questions such as "Can Congress Abolish Slavery in the United States Without Infringing the Constitution?"[139] Emerson's lecture tours focused on the Midwest because he was an abolitionist and not welcome in the South, which he viewed with a "special scorn"; similarly, when Harriet Beecher Stowe lectured, her stops were Toledo, Detroit, Terre Haute, Springfield and Bloomington (Illinois), Dayton, Columbus, Cincinnati, and Chicago, not destinations in the South.[140] "In Emerson's view," one historian noted, "more than northern armies had triumphed in 1865; the middle-class culture in the North had proved itself both superior to and more durable than the aristocratic culture in the South."[141]

Midwestern political leaders, many of them Union war veterans, did not hesitate to remind voters which region rebelled and threatened the Union. Major-General John "Black Jack" Logan, a future U.S. senator from Illinois, established the Grand Army of the Republic in Illinois for Union war veterans, and it consistently waved the bloody shirt and became known as "The Grand Army of the Republican Party."[142] Senator Zachariah Chandler of Michigan denounced a Democratic newspaper for trying to "beat Grant" and quickly reminded audiences of Fort Donelson and Shiloh and the "bloody chasm" that separated Michiganders from the South. When running for president in 1876, Rutherford B. Hayes of Ohio embraced the Republican plank demanding the "permanent pacification of the Southern section of the country." Hayes told his campaign managers how effective it was in midwestern politics to bash the South, and how motivated voters were by the "dread of a solid South, rebel rule, etc etc." When Benjamin Harrison was running for governor of Indiana, when James Garfield of Ohio was running for president, even when young Robert LaFollette was running for district attorney in Dane County, Wisconsin, they all waved the bloody shirt and attacked the South. Governor Joseph Foraker of Ohio, when running for reelection in 1887, won praise for dramatically refusing to return captured southern battle flags; at his renomination convention delegates waved Foraker badges emblazoned with his vow "No rebel flags will be surrendered while I am Governor!"

When the Grand Army of the Republic held its National Encampment in Columbus, Ohio, in 1888 and Democratic presidential candidate Grover Cleveland did not attend, he was criticized for snubbing the Union veterans and mockingly asked why he did not send a substitute (Cleveland failed to serve during the war and instead hired a substitute).[143] During a heated debate over the Democratic House's choice of a doorkeeper, the *Chicago Tribune* denounced the "Confederate element in the Democratic party" for snubbing a Union war veteran (and former U.S. senator from Minnesota and Illinois) in favor a former rebel, and southerners derided such bloody shirt tactics and the GOP's "malignity for the South."[144] Republican senator Angus Cameron of Wisconsin saw this controversy in broader terms and warned voters about the power of the "solid South" and the dangers of a nation governed by the "ex-Confederate politicians and the Democratic leaders of the South . . . [who] flung her . . . into the arms of a civil war" that was "a contest . . . of the powers of darkness against the powers of light, of ancient barbarism against modern civilization; of despotism founded . . . on the slavery of a black race against a free republic."[145]

While midwesterners were branding southerners as treasonous and the Midwest deviated dramatically away from the South, there also grew a self-conscious regionalism often directed at separating the Midwest from the feared hegemony of the East. These forces could be detected in the beginnings of the Midwest, of course. The Northwest Ordinance signaled that the Midwest would be separate and new and hold the dreams of those founders who sought to overcome the remnants of colonialism in the East.[146] Early administrators from the East sent to govern the emergent Midwest were constant sources of frustration and viewed as colonial overlords dating from the time Arthur St. Clair governed the Northwest Territory. The Appalachian mountain chain also served as a symbolic as well as a very real dividing line between the Midwest and the East for many years. Senator Rufus King of New York said in 1786 that "nature has severed the two countries by a vast and extensive chain of mountains, interest and convenience will keep them separate, and the feeble policy of our disjointed Government will not be able to unite them." Migrants into the Midwest, Frederick Jackson Turner noted, "when they crossed the Alleghanies became self-conscious and even rebellious against the rule of the East."[147] Widening the separation, in the 1820s and 1830s, just as abolitionism was intensifying in the Midwest and frictions with the South were growing, midwestern regionalist voices were becoming louder and better organized. These voices were reacting against an eastern domination of American intellectual and cultural life, and a "resentment against eastern publishers and periodicals" was building toward a "literary declaration of independence."[148] States in the West, concluded the *Western Journal* of St. Louis in 1851, were tired of being seen as "Provinces of the East" and were seeking their own identity.[149]

Several prominent midwestern regionalist champions emerged in the early nineteenth century. Daniel Drake of Cincinnati, a physician dubbed "the Franklin of the West," had a curiosity that led him beyond medicine to the natural history of the Midwest. He also promoted regional literature, new libraries, and medical research and the creation of an early museum of natural history for the region. Drake's published works included books on early Ohio and the geography of the region as well as much nature writing.[150] In 1815, Timothy Flint joined Drake and settled in Cincinnati and, in 1827, began publishing the *Western Monthly Review*.[151] Flint also wrote books such as *Recollections of the Last Ten Years* (1826) and *A Condensed Geography and History of the Western States* (1828), which became some of the earliest works about the region.[152] After his service in the War of 1812, James Hall also went west, ultimately founding the *Illinois Monthly* in 1830 in Vandalia, Illinois.[153] Hall generally sought to place "specimens of western talent, enterprise, and intelligence before the public."[154] He published an account of the geography and way of life in Ohio titled *Letters from the West* (1828). The *Hesperian: Or, Western Monthly Magazine,* was founded by William Gallagher in Columbus and similarly sought to "publish original works from the ablest pens of the Ohio Valley."[155] Gallagher followed his early efforts by publishing *Selections from the Poetical Literature of the West* (1841), the first ever compilation of midwestern poetry.[156] The first collection of prose was Hall's *Western Souvenir* (1828).[157] Another emerging regional publication was William Turner Coggeshall's Ohio-based *Genius of the West: A Magazine of Western Literature,* whose editor was a strong leader of the regionalist cause.[158] Just before the Civil War, Coggeshall would publish another anthology of midwestern poetry featuring one hundred poets.[159] Other regional publications from the era included the *Cincinnati Mirror, Centinel of the*

North-Western Territory, and *Western Spy and Literary Cadet* out of Cincinnati; the *Western Literary Magazine* out of Columbus; *Chicago Magazine;* and the *Western Journal and Civilian* out of St. Louis; several of these had a significant number of subscribers.[160]

All of these publications were designed to foster a regional culture independent of the East. As James Hall saw it, the democratic settlers of the midwestern frontier did not appreciate being "patronized or high-hatted" by easterners and were seeking their own distinct culture.[161] Timothy Flint was weary of the eastern rejection of midwestern writing: "One, who has not seen can not know, with what a curl of the lip, and crook of the nose an Atlantic reviewer contemplates the idea of a work written west of the Allegheny mountains."[162] Benjamin Drake (the brother of Daniel) advised his region to stop being "indebted to foreign pens and foreign genius" and generate its own authors and intellectuals.[163] A true "Republic of letters," Coggeshall said, must be a "confederacy of individualities" that included the voices of the Midwest.[164] All the efforts of these budding regionalists were directed at establishing "a kind of intellectual independence of the old regions" of the East.[165] One Sandusky editor told the Sandusky Athenaeum to skip eastern speakers and bring in local talent because the midwestern population had "made its mark in the pulpit, at the bar, in the lecture room"; the regional speaking circuit should avoid the "broken down, hackney-horse lecturer from the East."[166] At the laying of the cornerstone of the building Old Middle on the campus of Beloit College, a minister from Beaver Dam, Wisconsin, said people in his state "could not and would not rely on the East for education": "The western people [were] a peculiar people and [needed] an education conformed to their position and circumstances" that was "practical," "expanded, liberal and democratic," and a break from the "diseased monotony and fastidious refinement" of eastern colleges.[167]

A need to understand the basic history of the Midwest was a prime aspect of the regionalist project, and regionalists saw historical awareness as a "civic duty."[168] Vandalia, Illinois, for example, wasted no time creating civic institutions such as its Antiquarian and Historical Society, launched in 1827.[169] Cincinnati saw the early creation of a history museum.[170] The Historical Society of Michigan started in 1828, the Indiana Historical Society in 1830, and the Wisconsin State Historical Society in 1846. When the Ohio Historical Society was formed, its organizers stated, with classical flourish, that its purpose was to "collect the materials of history, a copious store, from which some future Tacitus or Gibbon may weave the strong and elegant web of historical narrative." The historians of the new region were not mere apologists or compilers. They "were not uncritical" of the Midwest, notes Terry Barnhart in his studies of early midwestern intellectual history. "History," said the regionalist Timothy Flint, must be "sternly impartial, and strictly true," and anything that fails these tests "has no claim to that sacred title, however exalted it may be in point of style."

Apropos of a balanced history, the early midwestern historians, despite later claims to the contrary, did not neglect Native Americans. Although not written in a form that would be acceptable in the twenty-first century, the research was substantial and often quite respectful and sympathetic. The purposes of the Historical Society of Michigan included discovering and preserving the "aboriginal history of the Country of the Lakes, and of the Territory of Michigan in particular."[171] The story of the mound builders was especially important to these historians and reflected their understanding of the fullness of historical time and the Midwest's place in it.[172] Increase Lapham in Wisconsin, for example, took an intense interest in mound building and its history and went on to write a great deal about the state's ancient history, including *The Antiquities of Wisconsin* (1855).[173] More recent Native American history was also not ignored. Benjamin Drake wrote books such as *The Life and Adventures of Black Hawk* (1838) and *Life of Tecumseh, and of His Brother the Prophet* (1841). Henry Schoolcraft, a cofounder of the Historical Society of Michigan, understood the plight of the Native Americans and did much to advance the early study of the region's tribes in his widely read reports and books and thus gave rise to American ethnology.[174] When William Cullen Bryant visited his brothers in Illinois it yielded his classic poem "The Prairies," which mostly focused on the mound builders.[175] The first book of the prominent Indiana historian Jacob Piatt Dunn was about the mistreatment of Native Americans.[176] Frederick Jackson Turner's dissertation focused on the Native American fur trade.[177]

Of related interest and of similar importance to many regionalists was the natural history of the Midwest. "The prehistoric past of the West fascinated men with a bent for scientific inquiry," noted Merle Curti in his study of American intellectual history. Museums of natural history sprang up around the Midwest, including an impressive institution promoted by Daniel Drake in Cincinnati, which was quickly joined by a rival museum. Caleb Atwater was a Williams College graduate who moved to Circleville, Ohio, and became a Presbyterian minister who embraced the cause of building a school system in Ohio and also delved into natural history. After years of investigating the region's burial mounds and geology and contributing to the American Antiquarian Society, Atwater published *A Description of the Antiquities Discovered in the State of Ohio and Other Western States* (1833). Other prominent midwestern geologists emerged in subsequent years.[178]

Linked to interest in the natural history of the Midwest was the appreciation of the natural wonder of the region, which was pervasive in regionalist writing. Gallagher, for example, sought recognition for the "great and varied natural resources" of the Midwest.[179] In 1855 the journal *Genius of the West* instructed midwestern intellectuals to merge the region's "unbounded sense of freedom" and its "release from conventionalities" with a "communion with the magnificence of boundless forests, prairies, streams and lakes."[180] Timothy Flint regretted that some could not enjoy the "breeze of the beautiful Ohio" river and were stuck "in the dark dens of the city."[181] Midwestern literature would dismiss the formal models and topics of British writing, preferring "Nature's magnificent repose" to "affectation or parlor prettiness, waxwork niceties, and milliner-like conceits."[182] All this preceded the coming of a prominent generation of midwestern naturalists such as John Muir, John Wesley Powell, Aldo Leopold, and Frederick Jackson Turner.[183]

A more popular and less formal version of regional identity emerged from the folktale tradition. The sentimental and "mawkish legends of the West" were commonly circulated by writers and regionalists such as Timothy Flint and James Hall.[184] One widely known figure was Mike Fink, "king of keelboaters," who guided boats down the Ohio River but also worked on smaller rivers such as the Great Miami and the Maumee.[185] John Chapman, better known as Johnny Appleseed, became known for his planting of apple trees in the early stages of the settlement of Ohio (he also "scattered religious tracts in pioneer cabins").[186] The north woods of Minnesota and Wisconsin also became better known because of the exploits of Paul Bunyan and his blue ox Babe, along with the ferocious beast called the Hodag, and the prairies of Iowa and Nebraska better known because of the legend of Febold Feboldson.[187] Folk music spread in the form of gospel hymns, traditional ballads, boatmen's songs, and tunes such as "The Michigan Emigrant's Song," the

"Western Trappers' Camp Song," "The Gallant Old Backwoodsman," and "The Minne Sota Song."[188]

Folktales about midwestern fertility sprouted; Iowa soil was so fertile that a crowbar stuck in the ground yielded a crop of nails overnight; fields were so productive that they produced one hundred bushels of corn when cultivated and seventy-five when not.[189] Henry Wadsworth Longfellow gathered some ideas from the books of midwestern explorer Henry Rowe Schoolcraft, and it became the country's first epic poem, "The Song of Hiawatha," set in the Midwest. Longfellow, a critic of the South and friend of abolitionist Charles Sumner, emphasized the importance of union in his story and of Hiawatha's efforts to bring together various factions, a narrative that served to further divide the pro-Union North from the rebellious South.[190] A Hoosier also created the "Raggedy Ann" stories.[191] A folk art tradition started that would last until the present.[192] Practical midwestern folk sayings caught on ("don't chew the cabbage twice"; "don't know beans from buckshot") and so did folk music and festivals that were often linked to new immigrant groups to the Midwest.[193] Midwestern Polka would come from this tradition.[194]

The most common form of cultural regionalism, literature, similarly flowered.[195] The goal of the midwestern regionalists, Terry Barnhart has explained, was to produce a "literature and history that would declare its intellectual and cultural independence from the literary establishment in the northeastern United States."[196] Poets and novelists, Caleb Atwater thought, had spent too much time focusing on elites and had "employed themselves in placing on the very front of the stage, the warriors, the kings, the nobles, the rich, the proud, the haughty, standing on stilts or in buckskins, while the common people were seated, out of our sight, behind them."[197] It was time that the frontier's "homespun democracy," as the historian Merle Curti called it, was "reflected in a distinctive literature." In this new literature for an emerging region, James Hall emphasized, "where everything should be measured by its usefulness," writers should focus on productive labors and industry and social advances in their stories.[198] By the time of the Civil War, the writers of the Midwest had already produced a sizable body of work.[199] So too had midwestern artists.[200]

Most fundamental to the new literary consciousness of the emerging Midwest was the recognition of the region's democratic achievements. Midwestern civilization, William Gallagher emphasized, would enable its people to realize "their real dignity and importance in the social scale, by proclaiming to them that they are neither slaves nor nonentities, but true men and women."[201] Gallagher's remarks, which were made to the Historical and Philosophical Society of Ohio, highlighted how midwestern citizens were distinct from the peasants of Europe and Asia and the slaves of the South. During the planning for the first major midwestern settlement in Ohio, Mannaseh Cutler emphasized the clean slate offered by the Midwest that could prove to be a "wide model" for the world. All his work to promote regional writing, Daniel Drake said, should reflect the advances of the region's "liberal political and social institutions." Midwestern democracy, declared the editor of the *Cincinnati Daily Gazette,* was "untrammeled with the prejudices and superstitions of old." The historian Terry Barnhart noted the widely held view that the Midwest was a "sanctuary of freedom." The settlers "made numerous distinctions and generalizations about the region as compared to societies they regarded as less open, less republican in character, less heterogenous, and less representative of America as a whole."[202]

The emergence of regionalist thought in the antebellum Midwest and the continually escalating tensions with the South had ushered in a new phase of midwestern identity formation by the 1850s. By this decade people living in the old Northwest Territory "began to think of themselves as different. They were not part of the South, the East, or the Far West or the mountains and plains."[203] During this decade, as Andrew Offenburger has explained, the term "Middle West" came into use.[204] After the Mexican-American War of 1846–48 and the acquisition of a vast territory extending to the Pacific Ocean, what would become the Midwest was no longer the western edge of the country. When railroads were planned for construction to the far west, what was once west became the middle of the country, or midwestern, and the term "Midwest" began showing up on railroad maps.[205] As the divide with the South expanded, what was once considered the general "West" also split into a free West and a southern-oriented region. With the deepening of the Midwest's agrarian sympathies and the rise of abolitionism in the region, midwesterners "could hardly picture their Eden populated by fellow humans held in bondage" and thus "they divorced the lands of the Southwest from their Garden, which they confined now to the Upper Mississippi Valley."[206] With the coming of the war it became customary to "omit the southern part of the Mississippi Valley and to write about a Middle West that lies between the

Canadian boundary and the Ohio River and extends westward a greater or less distance beyond the Mississippi River," and this usage became sanctioned by dictionaries, government reports, the census, and conventional wisdom.[207] A well-defined Midwest, one separate from the South and distinct from what we now see as the West—the land beyond the 100th meridian—was emerging.[208]

The new Midwest was economically strong and, by 1870, had a greater population than New England and the Mid-Atlantic states combined and was becoming the nation's agricultural and industrial heartland.[209] The region had matured from its "embryonic state" and was rooted and stable and capable of fostering the production of enduring art.[210] It was the kind of regional identity that emerges "wherever people live together long enough to enclose their daily experience in a skein of common memories."[211] By the later 1800s the term "Middle West" "was firmly entrenched and began to appear regularly in capitalized form."[212] As Frederick Jackson Turner explained, the Midwest "took the attitude of a section itself," asserting its identity alongside the Northeast and Old South.[213]

In addition to a clear regional identity and moniker there arose a successful and recognized regionalist literature. Some critics held that prior to the Civil War the Midwest had "produced no Melville, no Hawthorne, no Whitman, no Emerson," but some intellectual infrastructure in the form of regional magazines had been established. In the years after the war the payoff came in the form of ascendant writers who "were not freakish flowerings from barren ground" but "products of western soil, prepared for four decades by industrious and forgotten literary pioneers."[214] William Dean Howells, even though he went east, had a deep grounding in Ohio and believed in the decentralization of culture and recognized the rising influence of "the Great Middle West."[215] One of his first works was a campaign biography of the first midwestern Republican president, Abraham Lincoln, who gave him the Venice consulship, and he proudly served as a true blue Ohio Republican, not averse to hoisting the bloody shirt and sharply rejecting the "unrepentant but reconciled rebel leaders who tried to destroy us as a people."[216] James Whitcomb Riley of Indiana was also universally known during the late nineteenth century and cut a wide swath for midwestern writers.[217] When the Indiana Club convened in Chicago in 1902, it could celebrate the several regional authors of the Hoosier state, including Riley and the vocal defender of the Midwest, Booth Tarkington.[218] Regionalist literary groups such as the

Society of Midland Authors in Chicago also became prominent.[219] These were signs that a fully formed midwestern identity with midwestern voices had been achieved. By the late nineteenth century, after decades of intensifying regional differentiation, a "once vague and variously labeled landscape" had become a "distinct and powerful place" known as the Midwest.[220]

The regionalist historian Michael Steiner points to several regional artists and intellectuals who led the effort to entrench midwestern identity. He calls them the "master architects of American regional theory and practice" who were active in the 1890s and early 1900s."[221] Wisconsin's Frank Lloyd Wright, for example, criticized the continued use of European design and the slavish dependence on the East and advanced an "organic architecture that seemed to grow from the prairies, woods, and rolling hills of his native region."[222] Wright listened to his mother's injunction: "Keep close to the earth, boy: in that lies strength."[223] Hamlin Garland, a son of Wisconsin and Iowa who had also lived in Dakota Territory, made the case for regionalism in the literary realm. Garland demanded, as a lecture in 1893 made clear, "The Literary Emancipation of the West." He thought inland writers and critics too often "wait for the judgment of the East, of London." Garland rightly believed that a new corpus of work would come from the "mingling seas of men in the vast interior of America." Garland proclaimed the cultural liberation of the Midwest from eastern domination in his manifesto *Crumbling Idols* (1894), which describes the rise of midwestern writing and other arts and proclaims that the "literary supremacy of the East is passing away." The book was specifically written in a manner that "challenged eastern cultural supremacy."[224]

Garland's lecture on midwestern literary independence, delivered at the famed Chicago World's Fair of 1893, was accompanied by the historian Frederick Jackson Turner's address celebrating midwestern frontier independence from the East.[225] Turner followed his address by spending decades outlining and describing the varied regions of the United States.[226] He called on the American republic to be a "nobler structure," one in which each region "will find its place as a fit room in a worthy house."[227] Turner drew on his memories of a midwestern upbringing to advance a vision of his region "as a matrix of cultural diversity and bulwark against the leveling forces of mass culture."[228] Other prominent midwestern authors followed in the wake of Garland and Turner.[229] The number of regionalist writers became so prevalent in the Midwest's biggest city by the turn of the century that their combined work was dubbed the Chicago Renaissance.[230]

With these more prominent voices came more regional publications to amplify their work. In 1872, *Kansas Magazine* was launched as a counterweight to the Boston-based *Atlantic Monthly* and to promote a "Midwestern identity distinct from that of cultural centers in the East."[231] In 1883, *Northwest Magazine* started in Minneapolis and, in 1891, *Reedy's Mirror* started in Missouri and would become a frequent outlet for emerging midwestern writers such as Edgar Lee Masters and Vachel Lindsay.[232] In 1894 in Iowa, the *Midland Monthly* was launched by Johnson Brigham, and it would publish authors such as Garland and Octave Thanet.[233] In 1915, after the *Midland Monthly* had expired, a young midwesterner named John T. Frederick started the *Midland* in Iowa City to give another home to midwestern writers and to "counterbalance the eastern bias in publishing" and the "literary despotism" of New York.[234] He started by highlighting the many Iowa authors celebrated at a "homecoming" event in 1914.[235]

During the Chicago years of the *Dial* (1880–1918), when it was edited by Union veteran Francis Fisher Brown, it was the "leading critical review in the Midwest."[236] In the same period Chicago also witnessed the launch of *Poetry—A Magazine of Verse* (1912), and Margaret Anderson, originally from Indianapolis and a graduate of the Western College for Women in Oxford, Ohio, launched the *Little Review* (1913).[237] In subsequent years other regional literary journals would come on the scene such as *Prairie Schooner* in Nebraska.[238] Formal literary magazines were aided by powerful newspapers in the region such as the *Chicago Daily News,* which employed such writers as Ben Hecht and supported book review editors, among them Henry Blackman Sell and Harry Hansen.[239] Historical societies also became much more sophisticated and often published journals setting forth the histories of midwestern states.[240] On a parallel track and in a strong signal of regional orientation, cultural awareness, and midwestern business savvy, the Meredith family of Des Moines launched the magazines *Successful Farming* in 1902 and *Better Homes and Gardens* in 1922.[241] Meredith's publications were joined by a panoply of midwestern farm newspapers and journals.[242] Perhaps more than formal literary reviews, such publications entrenched the key components of midwestern regional identity by focusing on farming, small towns, and communal life.

The burst of literary energy in the Midwest brought a new era of regional culture, and it did so in a particularly midwestern fashion. Midwestern writers contrasted their work with the drawing room daintiness of the Northeast and embraced realism, or what one historian called "the candid and the salty."[243] William Dean Howells of Ohio first pioneered the genre, and Theodore Dreiser of Indiana followed suit. Most famously, perhaps, Dreiser's *Sister Carrie* (1900) told the tale of one young Wisconsin woman's descent into poverty and vice in Chicago.[244] Mark Twain's novels and his speeches on the midwestern speaking circuit were popular because he was "unpolished, unrestrained, and unabashedly defiant of the genteel East."[245] The Chicago novelist Henry B. Fuller carried on this tradition and was praised by none other than H. L. Mencken for being "the first American novelist to get away from the moony old spinsters of New England and depict the actual human beings of America."[246] By 1920, Mencken thought "four-fifths of the real literature of America" came out of a two-hundred-mile radius of Chicago.[247] Mencken also praised the novelist Ruth Suckow, a Grinnell College student-turned-novelist who focused her work on rural Iowa, though not with the cynical cruelty of a Mencken.[248] From Nebraska, Beth Streeter Aldrich offered a balanced portrait of life on the midwestern prairie.[249] Willa Cather, who learned Latin and read classics at the University of Nebraska during this era, became the voice of the homesteading experience, along with Ole Rolvaag, who attended St. Olaf College in Minnesota and wrote about Norwegian immigrant farmers.[250]

Accompanying and bolstering the wave of regionalist writers was a series of new and influential structures designed to support midwestern culture. This included the organization of symphony orchestras in St. Louis (1880), Chicago (1891), Cincinnati (1894), Detroit (1914), and Cleveland (1915).[251] The building of the Chicago Auditorium (1890), with its smooth exterior designed by Chicago architects Dankmar Adler and Louis Sullivan and interior designed by Frank Lloyd Wright, created what Wright called "the greatest room for opera in the world." In 1891, the Chicago Symphony Orchestra welcomed the famed German conductor Theodore Thomas to the Auditorium, where he shared his love of music and developed and promoted new composers from the region.[252] In 1904, Thomas moved to yet another new home for the Chicago Symphony Orchestra on Michigan Avenue.

Support for music was accompanied by support for the pictorial arts in the form of new institutions such as the Gallery of Fine Art in Columbus (1878), the Art Institute of Chicago (1879), the St. Louis School and Museum of Fine Art (1879), the Minneapolis Institute of Art (1883), the John Herron Museum in Indianapolis (1883), the Detroit Institute of Arts (1885), and the Kansas City Art Institute (1885), all of which embraced an anti-eastern regionalist spirit and promoted a democratic art scene accessible to the general public.[253] These were accompanied by the emergence of midwestern artists who organized clubs, colonies, and exhibitions, focused on traditional artistic ideals such as truth and beauty and capturing regional scenes on canvas. They developed a "distinctive regional identity" in part by resisting European fads (students at the Art Institute of Chicago would burn an effigy of Henri Matisse in a display of protest).[254] In a sign of their regional inclinations, some of these artists painted murals specifically highlighting midwestern iconography.[255] A wave of art museums followed.[256] Many sculptures were simultaneously created for midwestern parks.[257] The park designs were elaborate and included impressive landscape architecture.[258] From his home in Wisconsin, Jens Jensen advocated public parks and gardens grounded in midwestern flora. He was "fiercely proud of midwestern culture and values," "railed against the use of imported plants and formal styles," and saw the New York–dominated American Society of Landscape Architects as an "eastern klick" and a "bunch of deadbeats."[259] Ossian Cole Simonds of Michigan similarly argued that the "beauty of the Midwest's natural environment could be conveyed through designed landscapes, incorporating native plants and natural features."[260]

The wave of new sculpture, art museums, and park building gave shape and form to midwestern cities. Much of this building was linked to the "City Beautiful" movement, which helped mold impressive new cities for an emerging region.[261] More monuments to civic and intellectual endeavor soon followed. Major libraries were built in many midwestern cities, for example, including Chicago. The Chicago Public Library, launched in earnest in 1873 with the gift of seven thousand books from England made after the Great Chicago Fire, grew to house two hundred thousand books and spread to six branches by 1893.[262] In 1885 the Newberry Library was opened, and then in 1897 the Crerar Library was launched by the owner of the Joliet Steel Company (it looked down on "dirty French novels" and "works of questionable moral tone").[263] The construction boom included imposing historical society buildings in Ohio (1914) and Minnesota (1918). The latter building was dedicated in an elaborate ceremony at which Frederick Jackson Turner was the keynote speaker.[264] Other intricate and classical buildings dating to this era included state capitols such Wisconsin's in Madison, which was launched in 1906 and featured murals of Wisconsin, marble columns, and sculptures denoting Faith, Strength, Knowledge, and Prosperity.[265] Nebraska's capitol in Lincoln, launched in 1919, included a 400 foot tower with *The Sower* on top, a paean to the agrarian ideal, and "The Salvation of the State is Watchfulness in the Citizen" carved over an entrance flanked by the motto "Wisdom Justice Power Mercy: Constant Guardians of the Law."[266]

The numerous colleges in the region became larger and more sophisticated, and in 1892 the University of Chicago opened under the guidance of Ohio-born and -raised William Rainey Harper, who began hiring the greatest academic minds in the country (he paid $7,000 a year, in contrast to Princeton, which paid $3,500). The building boom and surging civic pride crested with the Chicago World's Fair in 1893. The voice of the regionalist revolt, Hamlin Garland, wrote to his poor farming parents back in South Dakota: "Sell the cook stove if necessary and come. You *must* see this fair" (twenty-seven million people agreed and attended).[267]

By the turn of the twentieth century the region had reached Peak Midwest. The many successful businesses of the region were fueling the region's many creative ventures, which were more and more geared toward the discovery and reinforcement of midwestern regional identity.[268] The term "Middle West," then the abbreviated "Midwest," was widely in use.[269] In 1920 major publications were describing midwestern literary genres, however wrongly, and discussing the wave of midwestern regionalist writing.[270] For generations, midwestern presidents sat in the White House, including, during the early twentieth century, William McKinley, William Howard Taft, and Warren Harding of Ohio and Herbert Hoover of Iowa. During this era midwesterners "dominate[d] American culture and politics," concluded the historian Richard White.[271] Powerful large-circulation midwestern newspapers shaped public discourse. The Midwest sat at the "warm center of the world," according to the Minnesotan F. Scott Fitzgerald.

This was an era before ubiquitous mass media and before regionalism was increasingly submerged by a powerful national culture produced on the coasts. It was before the coming of a powerful central state, when states and regions were more autonomous.[272] This was when the American Midwest led a regional resistance to the nation's full-fledged dive into international politics. Midwesterners led that resistance by highlighting their long history of democratic achievements and civic progress while differentiating themselves from the slave South and the aristocratic East and corrupt Europe. They could rightly boast a long history of progress, region building, and democratic gains. But this grand story also had a dark side.

"ALSO A SEAMY SIDE TO CERTAIN PHASES OF THE HISTORY OF THE VALLEY"

RACIAL FAILURES AND ADVANCES IN THE GOOD COUNTRY

In June 1833, some slave catchers from Kentucky landed in Detroit. They represented all the horrors of the South that many Black people in Ohio and Michigan had fled or were trying to escape, even to the point of killing their children to avoid their return to a life of slavery in Kentucky.[1] During this particular month the human prey of the slave catchers was Thornton and Ruth Blackburn, who had fled bondage in the bluegrass south of the Ohio River. They had left the day before Independence Day in 1831 and crossed the river to Jeffersonville, Indiana, and then traveled to Cincinnati, then north to Sandusky and finally to Detroit, where they settled.[2] After they were apprehended by slave catchers, the Blackburns were locked in the county jail, then given a court hearing on their fate. When they could not show evidence of their free status, a judge ordered them handed over to the slave catchers under provisions of the Fugitive Slave Act of 1793. But locals came to their aid. A visitor to Ruth's cell switched clothes with her and she escaped the jail in disguise.[3] The next day Thornton was to be taken by cart down to the river where the steamboat *Ohio* waited to take the slave hunters and Thornton back to the South. Instead, as Thornton was leaving the jail, African American protestors rushed the sheriff, and Thornton escaped and later joined Ruth across the river in Canada. The jail was set alight and the sheriff died from his injuries, which caused some whites in Detroit to call for greater control of the city's African American population. The mayor demanded Blacks who could not prove their free status leave the city, but few did. A committee formed to study the incident warned of alleged threats by protesters to burn the city and advised that Blacks adhere to a 9:00 P.M. curfew and be banned from landing boats on the river. The committee also called for the enforcement of racial codes designed to control African Americans.[4]

As this Detroit story demonstrates, the American Midwest also had a dark side, despite all its achievements and successes. For several decades, the primary thrust of American historiography has been to catalogue such failings, not just in the Midwest but in the country at large. There has been much merit in this work and it should be digested fully by everyone seeking to understand the American past. But this body of work also needs to be balanced against what happened that is valuable to remember and with due respect afforded to those who did good. In the principle of proportionality can be found a useful prism to view the American Midwest and to judge its history. The good and decent in the region, in other words, should be weighed against the wicked and the profane. Indiana University historian William O. Lynch, a native of Carroll County, Indiana, and an editor of the *Indiana Magazine of History,* observed on the eve of World War II that "probably no part of the world has produced more sturdy and worthy citizens in proportion to population" than the Midwest. "Of able leaders, of great men and women in every field of endeavor, there has come from its farms, villages, and cities a fairly steady supply." But, he said, "there is also a seamy side to certain phases of the history of the Valley."[5]

That side of the Midwest is explored in this chapter in order to place the achievements of the Midwest in proper perspective. "The historian always has the obligation to be appreciative as well as critical," said one fair-minded historian of the Midwest, and that double-sided and complex goal is the burden of this chapter.[6] The specific charge is to explain the sufferings of African Americans in the early Midwest and, over time, the quite sizable advancements that were made in African American civil rights in the region by the end of the nineteenth century. The point is not to resuscitate the "North Star Legend"—the belief in perfect racial harmony outside of the South—but to weigh all the evidence, being sure to chronicle the Midwest's many racial failings, but also to recognize signs of progress in the region.[7]

As underscored by the Blackburn incident and in keeping with much recent thinking about modern America, the Midwest's greatest failing occurred in the arena of race relations. Although slavery was banned by the Northwest Ordinance and Blacks would ultimately win many freedoms and build some successful communities in the Midwest, they faced serious overt racism during the beginning stages of midwestern history. In early Ohio, for example, African American rights were, in the end, limited, but the debate was robust and the advocates for African Americans nearly prevailed on some critical issues. The thirty-five delegates elected (including by African American voters) to the first Ohio constitutional convention gathered in Chillicothe in 1802.[8] They voted unanimously to ban slavery and, by a vote of 21–12, outlawed indentured servitude, which was sometimes used to disguise conditions proximate to slavery.[9] The ban on indentured servitude was a victory for those delegates favoring African American rights such as Ephraim Cutler and Rufus Putnam, the New Englanders who founded Marietta. By a vote of 20–13, the convention later added a provision specifying that labor contracts for African Americans could not be made outside of the state and could not be longer than one year, a provision designed to protect African Americans from abusive forms of indentured servitude and seen as a "second statement emphasizing the prohibition of slavery in any form, especially for blacks."

The strongly worded provisions banning slavery and indentured servitude ensured that de facto forms of bondage did not arise, as they did in other states. In another early decision, delegates voted 19–15 for a constitutional provision stating that "all male negroes and mulattoes now residing in the territory shall be entitled to the right of suffrage." Then delegates voted 19–16 to preclude African Americans from public offices but later repealed this restriction by a vote of 17–16. Three days before the adjournment of the convention, the delegates reconsidered the earlier decision to grant voting rights to African Americans. Delegates voted 17–17 to repeal African American voting rights, a tie broken by the president of the convention in favor of repealing the voting rights provision adopted earlier.

Despite the ultimate setbacks, one historian rightfully noted the "degree of persistence the pro-negro delegates exerted in their efforts to give equal voting rights to all qualified males in the state."[10] The framers also did not place racial restrictions on jury and militia service, giving testimony in court, and immigration to Ohio in the constitution. The ban on African American voting made clear, however, that Blacks were to be excluded from the political system. One historian concluded that "Ohio's founding fathers intended to permit blacks to reside in the state and enjoy the protection of its laws, but to have no part in governing."[11] The constitutional convention, according to the treatment authored by the founder of the Association for the Study of African American Life and published in the first issue of the *Journal of Negro History*, "simply left Negroes out of the pale of the newly organized body politic."[12]

After the state constitution was written and Ohio became a state, its new legislature began operating and was more willing to restrict African American freedoms than the delegates to the constitutional convention had done. The strong presence of southerners in early Ohio, especially migrants from Virginia and Kentucky, suggested the direction that racial law making would take in the state.[13] In 1804 and 1807, Ohio legislators adopted "black laws," state statutes limiting Black freedoms in particular ways.[14] The 1804 law required Blacks to show papers indicating they were not escaped slaves and to register with county clerks.[15] Any whites hiring unregistered Blacks were subject to $50 fines. To protect free Blacks, attempts to kidnap them were made punishable by $1,000 fines, half of which would be paid to an informer (creating strong incentives to protect free Black neighbors), or by up to ten years in prison or ten years hard labor (harboring a fugitive slave, by comparison, was punishable only with a $10–$50 fine).[16]

The 1807 law banned Blacks from testifying against whites in court.[17] It also required Blacks to find two sureties to offer a bond of $500 to ensure good behavior and to guarantee, the authors argued, that county poor farms would not be overburdened.[18] The foremost historian of these laws has found that they were "rarely enforced," that few Blacks registered, and that those who did "were able to confirm their free status and perhaps use that registration to protect their liberty."[19] If Blacks were fugitive slaves they "simply did not register and, with few exceptions, were left alone." The laws certainly did not stop African American immigration to Ohio. The number of Blacks in Ohio grew from 337 in 1800 to 36,000 by 1860. Other black laws limited the right of African Americans in Ohio to serve on juries and to join the state militia and limited their access to schools and poorhouses.[20]

In Indiana, the situation was slightly more complex than in Ohio. In Indiana slavery carried over from the French colonial era and the preexisting

French slaves were not set free upon statehood. As a result, there were still 190 slaves in the state in 1820. Most of the slaves in Indiana were in Knox County, the location of the old French settlement of Vincennes. Upon statehood in 1816, Indiana's new constitution formally banned slavery and indentured servitude and, in a unique twist, made the constitution's anti-slavery provisions unamendable. As result, many slaveholders left Indiana. Court decisions also undermined slavery by making clear that slaves were set free by the 1816 constitution. By 1830 there were only three slaves officially left in Indiana. Although the vestiges of slavery slowly disappeared, some slaves were, in a legal ruse, converted to indentured servants. The Indiana state legislature also passed some black laws during early statehood. These laws denied Blacks the right to vote, the right to testify against whites in court, and the right to serve in the militia; additionally, they required Blacks to prove their free status.[21]

In Illinois the racial issues were much more complex given the region's earlier history and its deeper French imprint. When the United States took control of the Illinois Country during the Revolution, it was heavily French owing to the persistence of the institutions of New France and in particular French people in enclaves such as Kaskaskia and Cahokia. These French settlers embraced feudal practices and held slaves. When Britain took control of the Mississippi River valley in 1763 after the fall of New France, the French settlements totaled three thousand people, including nine hundred African American slaves, but about half of this group left the Illinois Country after the war to avoid becoming British subjects. Of the sixteen hundred French settlers who remained, six hundred were African American slaves. At the time of the American Revolution, half of Kaskaskia's population of one thousand was African American.[22]

Prior to English control, slaves had been subject to the laws of Louis XIV, which were adopted in 1734 to regulate slavery in Louisiana, which included the Illinois Country. After the British takeover, the French inhabitants "were allowed to retain all the rights, including the holding of slaves, which they had held under their French king." After the American takeover of the future Midwest after the Revolution, the Northwest Ordinance was adopted and banned slavery. The governor of the Northwest Territory, Arthur St. Clair, declared to the French slaveholders that the Ordinance's slavery ban prevented the introduction of new slaves but "did not affect previously acquired slave property."[23] Overall, however, the Ordinance's ban on slavery revealed the "American indifference to the concerns of the French inhabitants," and this caused many French slaveowners to decamp to the Spanish-held and slavery-friendly Missouri country.[24] The persistence of French slavery is important to recognize because, as John Craig Hammond has recently noted, "historians tend to neglect the presence, persistence, and significance of the slavery and empires that predated the expansion of the United States into the continental interior." Too many historians fail to recognize the "French and Spanish origins of slavery in the Mississippi Valley."[25]

Under the American regime, Illinois soon achieved statehood. The Illinois constitution of 1818, in compliance with the Northwest Ordinance, banned slavery. But it banned slaves who might "hereafter" enter the territory only, a weaker provision than the Indiana constitutional ban, which simply banned slavery. The Illinois ban on indentured servitude also included potential loopholes. The constitution allowed slaves to be brought into Illinois to labor, for up to one year, in the "salt works near Shawnee-town" in southern Illinois, but this provision expired in 1825. Because of the new constitution's evasion of the precise fate of existing slaves in Illinois, the question would linger. Not until 1845 would the Illinois Supreme Court specifically declare that children born to slaves in Illinois after the passage of the Northwest Ordinance were free. The Illinois constitution of 1847 then completely eliminated slavery. Because of the various restrictions on slavery, the number of slaves in Illinois remained low, especially relative to the South. By way of comparison, Kentucky was home to 127,000 slaves in 1820 compared to 917 in Illinois. The official number of slaves in Illinois dropped to 747 by 1830 and to 331 a decade later.[26]

Illinois also adopted its own set of black laws, modeled after the French Code Noir, denying citizenship to African Americans, requiring Blacks to show a certificate of freedom to live in the state, banning Blacks from testifying against whites in court, and preventing tavern owners from selling alcohol to slaves. Illinois's black laws required African Americans to prove their free status and allowed overseers of the poor to remove indigent Blacks from their towns. Former slaves were required to hold a $1,000 bond as a guaranty against becoming an expensive charge to a particular county. In addition to the black laws, forms of indentured servitude continued to ensnare some Blacks during the early years of statehood, while others were proficient at using the legal process and other openings and ambiguities in an unpopular system to win their freedom.[27]

The toleration and perpetuation of slavery, the adoption of black laws, and the continuation of indentured servitude can be directly traced to the early population of Illinois, which was largely southern.[28] It was also due to the shape of Illinois, which jutted down deep into the South, far past the northernmost points of Kentucky, Virginia, and Missouri and nearly to Tennessee. Cairo, Illinois, was farther south than Richmond, Virginia.[29] The early settlers of Illinois, many from the more heavily peopled Kentucky, attempted during the early years of statehood to legalize slavery formally. In 1823 pro-slavery southerners in the legislature, via shady machinations, were able to pass a measure to force a vote on a referendum for calling a constitutional convention to consider changing the young state's constitution to allow slavery. The debate over slavery was intense and many citizens joined in on one side or the other. Opponents of slavery, who were growing in strength with the settlement of the central parts of the state, relied on the legacy of the American Revolution, the Northwest Ordinance, and American republicanism to advance their cause; the proponents of the convention were reticent to embrace slavery openly because of its obvious betrayal of egalitarian principles.[30]

The prospect of formally institutionalizing slavery in Illinois and bolstering southern control of the state sparked a strong and influential anti-slavery movement.[31] New immigrants such as the Englishman Morris Birkbek, who organized a settlement in Edwards County, extolled the virtues of his new American freedoms and denounced slavery as a "leprosy" and "a foul blotch" that would besmirch a new and emerging republican polity.[32] The hero of the anti-slavery cause was Governor Edward Coles, a former Virginian who had set his slaves free (the pronouncement had come on a flatboat in the middle of the Ohio River), embraced the anti-slavery cause, sought repeal of the black laws, and asked the legislature to "take steps to liberate the French slaves."[33] Through an intense campaign of sermons, newspaper editorials, and pamphleteering led in part by new anti-slavery societies and energized evangelicals in the state, the pro-slavery effort was defeated and the call to revise the 1818 constitution rejected by a vote of 6,640–4,972 (57–43 percent), in an election that saw nearly 80 percent turnout.[34] The vote fell on regional lines. The southern counties of Illinois such as Alexander, home to Cairo, and

Gallatin, home to the salt works of Shawneetown, and those home to the old French slave-holding towns of Cahokia, Kaskaskia, and Vandalia (St. Clair, Randolph, and Fayette counties) heavily favored the slavery forces; central Illinois counties such as Morgan, home to the Jacksonville Yankees, and Sangamon, home to Springfield, voted heavily against slavery.[35]

Michigan would become home to many northern-oriented settlers, especially Yankees, but during its early history it was home to French slaveowners, similar to Indiana and Illinois. A French commandant reported the presence of slaves in Detroit in 1701, owned by both the French and Native Americans.[36] The first slaves in Detroit were captured in the South by Native Americans and sold to French settlers.[37] Other slaves were Native Americans who were captured by rival tribes and sold to the French.[38] In 1765, two years after the transfer of French control of Detroit to the British after the French and Indian War, there were sixty slaves in Detroit; by 1796, when the British officially withdrew from Detroit in favor the Americans as a result of the American Revolution, there were three hundred slaves in Detroit (out of a population of 2,200).[39] Because of American governance and new restrictions on slavery under the Northwest Ordinance, many British slaveowners in Detroit moved to Canada and many Canadian slaves tried to escape to Detroit.[40]

Because of the small number of slaves and the mores of French Catholic culture, slavery in early Michigan in comparison to the South has been described as "always decidedly smaller and less brutal," and its demise seemed nigh. In an early decision of the supreme court of Michigan Territory, the colorful judge Augustus Elias Brevoort Woodward ruled that some slaves held by a British woman had to remain slaves under the postwar U.S.--U.K treaty, which protected British property, but he did so unwillingly and, in a hopeful sign, openly denounced slavery and said any remaining slaves who were subject to the jurisdiction of the Northwest Ordinance should be set free.[41] In 1835, Michiganders wrote a constitution with the expectation of statehood and—after the state of Ohio, the territory of Michigan, and Congress finished haggling over the fate of Toledo—Michigan finally became a state in January 1836.[42] The constitution banned slavery but also limited voting to white males after a lengthy debate and a vote (63–17) to defeat Black suffrage. During the territorial era, Michigan was governed by black laws that required proof of one's free status, and after statehood, Michigan state statutes banned interracial marriages and limited militia service to whites.

Race riots, including the 1833 Blackburn riot in Detroit, also occurred, and state referenda to allow Black suffrage failed.[43] In a major contrast to Ohio, Indiana, and Illinois, however, the new state of Michigan did not adopt black laws governing residency and requiring surety bonds.[44]

The moderating effects of Catholicism and Yankee abolitionism that shaped early Michigan were not present in early Iowa, which was farther south and west than Michigan and oriented toward Missouri and southern Illinois. When Iowa became a state in 1846 it was heavily southern, and the passage of black laws was therefore almost inevitable.[45] During its territorial days Iowa had adopted laws requiring surety bonds and prohibiting African Americans from voting, serving in the militia, testifying against whites in court, marrying whites, and receiving public education.[46] At the same time, the territorial legislature also made the kidnapping of Blacks punishable by hard labor and authorized fines of up to $100 against sheriffs and jailers who illegally imprisoned Blacks.[47] During the convention held to draft an Iowa constitution in 1844 there was a "flurry of discussion" over granting Black suffrage, as there was about excluding Blacks from Iowa, but both ideas were killed.[48] In the end, the Iowa constitution drafted in 1844 blocked Black suffrage, and this ban was retained in the 1846 constitution that became operational with statehood. The 1846 Iowa constitution also barred Blacks from serving in the legislature or militia.

The politics of Iowa would soon change, however. By 1854 a new, non-southerner governor (the first two Iowa governors were from Virginia and Kentucky) was elected, primarily because of the growing number of northern/midwestern settlers in Iowa and in a reaction to the new federal Fugitive Slave Law and the Nebraska bill.[49] Governor James Grimes, originally from New Hampshire, wrote to Salmon Chase that the southern part of Iowa was still pro-slavery but that he thought he could win a majority of Iowans over to "free principles" because the growing population of the northern part of his state would "be to Iowa politically what the Western Reserve is to Ohio."[50] Although Iowa was trending in the direction of abolitionists, a referendum on Black suffrage still went down to heavy defeat in 1857.[51]

Farther north the anti-Black attitudes were less extreme. Wisconsin became a state in 1848, and as in other midwestern states its constitution banned slavery. But unlike earlier states to emerge from the Northwest Ordinance, Wisconsin did not adopt black laws.[52] The Wisconsin constitution, however, did follow other midwestern states and deny Black suffrage, but only after an extensive debate and vigorous lobbying by proponents of Black suffrage during conventions in 1846 and 1848.[53] One delegate to the 1848 convention said that Black suffrage "stirred up a great deal of excitement" and produced "much additional discord," so the issue was left to the legislature to handle.[54] Minnesota became a state in 1858 and banned slavery in its constitution and, like Wisconsin, did not adopt black laws.[55] Neither Minnesota nor Wisconsin ever banned interracial marriage.[56] Unlike other midwestern states, the states of the upper Midwest also never denied Blacks the right to testify against whites in court.[57]

Despite areas of the region that were less restrictive, life for many African Americans in the Midwest remained oppressive in the early nineteenth century. In 1829 a white mob angry about labor competition from Blacks entered a Black neighborhood in Cincinnati and demanded the residents leave. Cincinnati officials, citing the residency requirements of the black laws, ordered noncompliant Blacks out in thirty days.[58] More than twelve hundred Blacks left Cincinnati for Canada, and some of those who stayed behind had their homes and businesses ransacked by whites.[59] In 1836 more Blacks were forced to leave Cincinnati when social tensions erupted after a Black boy prevailed over a white boy in a neighborhood fight.[60] In 1841 a fight between Irish immigrants and Blacks escalated to the point where a white mob broke into the offices of an abolitionist newspaper and threw the printing press into the Ohio River, then stole a cannon from the local militia and fired shells into a Black neighborhood.[61]

Whites sympathetic to African Americans were also targeted. Theodore Weld was preaching abolitionism in Circleville, Ohio, in the 1830s when a rock came through a window and clocked him on the head (the blow was not enough to prevent him from finishing his sermon, although he was dizzy for a few days).[62] Others were not so lucky. In 1837 the abolitionist editor Elijah Lovejoy was killed in Alton, Illinois, by an anti-abolitionist mob and his press destroyed and thrown, piece by piece, into the river.[63] Although Illinois, especially its southern half, was often hostile to Blacks, Indiana remained known as the "most Negrophobic state in the North" because of its heavy southern orientation and resulting racial tensions.[64] In 1843, for example, Frederick Douglass was assaulted during a speech in Pendleton, Indiana.[65] Although indentured servitude was formally banned in Indiana in keeping with the requirements of the Northwest Ordinance, the remaining French slaveholders in Vincennes found loopholes for avoiding compliance. Indiana's black laws remained on the books, few efforts were made to aid fugitive slaves, Blacks were banned from schools, and interracial marriage was banned, a step other midwestern states did not take. In 1851 Indiana went further and amended its constitution to ban free Blacks from entering the state, and that same year the Iowa legislature passed a statute barring Blacks from the state.[66] In 1853 Illinois, which was also heavily southern and once a home to slave-holding French settlers, also adopted a law forbidding free Blacks from entering the state, and it was upheld by the state supreme court. During the same era, southern states such as South Carolina and Arkansas either passed laws expelling free Blacks or heavily pressured free Blacks to leave, which partially explains midwestern fears of increased Black migration.[67]

To fight back against the remaining vestiges of slavery and newer forms of racial oppression, reformers had a powerful weapon. For opponents of slavery in the region, the historic charter for the Midwest, the Northwest Ordinance, was critical to their organizing, rhetoric, and ultimate success. The Ordinance's Article 6 ban on slavery was clearly based on New England demands and similar to Jefferson's earlier efforts, along with veterans of the Continental army, to ban slavery in the territories. Nathan Dane, a delegate to the Continental Congress from Massachusetts (and namesake of Dane County, Wisconsin), and Manasseh Cutler of Marietta settlement fame pushed hard for the ban on slavery in the Northwest Territory.[68] The ban on slavery in the Midwest took on a life of its own and became iconic and legendary and fought for as matter of regional pride. From the beginning of the development of the early Midwest, orators and legislators highlighted the freedoms of the region and contrasted them to the persistence of servility in the South.[69] Lincoln, in a speech in Cincinnati in 1859, declared that it was the Ordinance that "made the difference" and kept slavery south of the Ohio River.[70] Important groups of settlers in the Midwest such as anti-slavery New Englanders, Pennsylvania Quakers, and Continental army officers also maintained their opposition to slavery (in stark contrast to the settlers of French New Orleans and Spanish Missouri), upheld the legacy of the Ordinance, and kept the region free. "In the history of empires and slavery in the North American interior," the historian John Craig Hammond explains, "the ultimate exclusion of slavery from the old Northwest was exceptional."[71]

By the 1830s, champions of the Northwest Ordinance, emergent abolitionists, and other reformers were making their presence felt in midwestern
politics and winning more battles for racial equality.[72] While mob violence
and threats severely shut down abolitionist work in the East, the "abolitionists' educating and institution-building, their preaching and publishing and
propagandizing, were unrivaled in the Middle West, virtually unanswered,
except by mobs, whose excesses they had learned to exploit to excite public
sympathy." Because of the energies of the Great Awakening and the leadership of Lyman Beecher and his family, Marilynne Robinson has explained,
there was a "cultural colonization of the Middle West by abolitionists."[73] Tiya
Miles has explained that a "regional bias" that highlighted New England and
slighted the Midwest has caused historians to miss the critical role of the
Midwest in abolitionism.[74] Some observers argued that the construction of
the Erie Canal, which brought Yankees from New England and upstate New
York into the northern Midwest, was more responsible for the end of slavery
than loud eastern abolitionists like William Lloyd Garrison.[75]

The abolitionists of Ohio were particularly intense and well organized.[76]
In 1834 key abolitionists such as Theodore Weld and James Gillespie Birney,
inspired by the evangelical leader Charles Grandison Finney, launched the
Ohio Anti-Slavery Society, which became active throughout the state.[77]
Evangelicals, Quakers, free Blacks, Western Reserve Yankees, German
immigrants, and others embraced the "flaming moral zeal of Theodore Weld
and others in the thirties," launched newspapers, and "laid the foundations
of the antislavery movement."[78] Lane Theological Seminary in Cincinnati
opened in 1832, and in 1834 Theodore Weld led a mass conversion of its
students to abolitionism. Because of their abolitionist activism in a city on
the border with the South, the students were forced out and so they formed
Oberlin College in northeast Ohio, which became a "hotbed of antislavery
activity."[79] Oberlin welcomed its first Black students in 1835 and became
"a nursery for abolitionism."[80] Weld taught the "abolition school" at Oberlin and then sent his followers out to preach around Ohio. They organized
many societies, including one with four thousand members, and soon Birney
founded the abolitionist newspaper in Cincinnati called the *Philanthropist.*

In 1858 the discernable results of sermonizing and editorializing
were on display as a group of students, Oberlin faculty, abolitionists, and
free Blacks rescued a fugitive slave in the town of Wellington, Ohio. The

Oberlin-Wellington Rescue led to the indictment of thirty-seven abolitionists and a habeas corpus dispute that went to the Ohio Supreme Court. Chief Justice Joseph Swan ruined his political career in Ohio by not supporting the writ, and Justice Jacob Brinkerhoff, a founder of the Ohio GOP, gladly challenged the 1850 Fugitive Slave Law and went on to great political success, proving the "potency of antislavery and Black rights in Ohio."[81] Because of such actions, as the historian Nicole Etcheson has explained, "Ohio gained a reputation as hostile territory for masters attempting to recover their fugitives."[82] Ohio colleges besides Oberlin also aided the abolitionist cause. As early as 1828, Ohio University in Athens graduated its first Black student, who had started life as a slave in Alabama. Another product of Ohio University and Oberlin, 1832 graduate Edward James Roye, went on to become the president of Liberia. Antioch and Wilberforce would also provide higher education to Blacks in Ohio.[83] Western Reserve College was "moderately antislavery" and its doors were formally open to Blacks, and Miami University similarly aided the anti-slavery cause.[84] Eastern donors often worried that midwestern colleges were becoming too radically abolitionist.[85]

Abolitionist efforts quickly spread beyond Ohio. In Michigan, abolitionists and managers of the Underground Railroad ran schools for Blacks and aided fugitive slaves in defiance of apprehension statutes, and the state became known for the "consistency and brazenness with which citizens flaunted the law."[86] The new Liberty Party and its Ann Arbor–based newspaper *Signal of Liberty,* the Colored Vigilant Committee in Detroit, and Michigan's Colored Citizens conventions pressured the legislature to bolster Black rights.[87] Christian colleges in Michigan, like those in Ohio, were also centers of abolitionist activities, as they were in Illinois.[88] Knox College was the first college in Illinois to award a college degree to a Black man, and its students would command Black troops during the Civil War and free many slaves.[89] Illinois College, its president Edward Beecher (son of Lyman Beecher, brother of Henry Ward Beecher, sister of Harriet Beecher), and its all–New England faculty also became a "thorn in the side of a slavery district," and "antislavery sentiment flowed from the college literary societies, oratorical festivals and commencement addresses."[90] After the murder of Elijah Lovejoy in Alton its faculty took strong anti-slavery positions, causing some southern sympathizers to threaten professors with a "hemp cord . . . or a messenger of lead, or a bowie knife."[91] Pro-southern Democratic newspapers called out Illinois College as "the fountain and hot-bed of ultra abolition-ism."[92] In league with Illinois College was the Mission Institute, founded in Yankee-heavy Quincy, Illinois (with main streets named Maine, Hampshire, Vermont, and York), to agitate against slavery in neighboring Missouri.[93]

In Wisconsin, in a typical example, a newspaper editor in Trempealeau County "took a firm, uncompromising abolitionist position, criticized race prejudice and tried to explain its base, and argued vigorously for Negro suf-frage."[94] In 1843 the Iowa Anti-Slavery Society was formed and its allies organized an "exceptionally vigorous civil rights movement" that was heav-ily Christian and would transform the political culture of Iowa.[95] Iowa Con-gregationalist minister Asa Turner, who had been radicalized by the lynching of the abolitionist martyr Elijah Lovejoy in Illinois, told a congregant that "slavery is a cancer eating out the life of our body politic. There is no rem-edy for it but the knife. . . . The nation may bleed to death, but it is our only hope."[96] One of their first victories was the repeal of the Iowa Black exclusion law in 1860 after it had been on the books for less than a decade.[97] In Min-nesota, abolitionists were active under the energetic leadership of Jane Grey Swisshelm and Reverend Henry M. Nichols.[98] In an 1857 sermon, Nichols predicted an ultimate victory against southern sin: "The stain spots on our political purity will all be removed. The black gangrene upon our southern limbs will be entirely healed. Slavery shall die; its death knell shall come, because, God reigns."[99] Even in Indiana, recent scholarship has emphasized, the "smothering racism interpretation" has gone too far and missed impor-tant abolitionist activity in the state.[100]

Because of abolitionist activism at colleges and the work of anti-slavery societies, and because of supportive state officials and electorates, mid-western states often frustrated southerners' efforts to recapture their slaves. Midwestern courts and grand juries frequently undermined the efforts of southern slave catchers. The various statutes, lawsuits, legal opinions, jury decisions, elections, and other forms of activism indicate that on the "issue of basic protections for free blacks and fugitive slaves the 'prevailing opinion' favored due process."[101] Numerous slaves, with the help of abolitionist law-yers, sued and won their freedom by arguing that they had passed through a free state and were therefore liberated.[102]

In a sign of popular support for their activities, many abolitionists also won popular elections when seeking office. Byron Paine, the attorney who defended the abolitionists charged with freeing the slave Joshua Glover in Racine, went on to win election to the Wisconsin Supreme Court.[103] The Ohio abolitionist leader Salmon P. Chase was elected to the Cincinnati city council and as a U.S. senator and governor multiple times and was a well-known architect of arguments against Black oppression.[104] The anti-slavery activist Lyman Trumbull was elected to the U.S. Senate from Illinois and so too was Judge Benjamin Wade in Ohio after declaring from the bench that he would never enforce the fugitive slave law.[105] Lincoln said in his debate with Douglas in Quincy that, although he did not see Blacks as exact physical equals of whites, he believed "there is no reason in the world why the negro is not entitled to all the rights enumerated in the Declaration of Independence—the right of life, liberty and the pursuit of happiness. I hold that he is as much entitled to these as the white man."[106] The voters in the increasingly prominent midwestern GOP, the historian Eric Foner concluded, recognized Black humanity.[107] After three political cycles of aggressively advocating Black rights, Lincoln and the GOP swept the Midwest during the 1860 presidential election.

Because of abolitionist energies and the legacy of the Northwest Ordinance and despite a regressive early history, the Midwest could point to signs of racial progress that were grounded in the democratic practices of the region. As the historian Stephen Middleton has noted, the "political and legal culture that created the Black Laws also created a constitutional system under which the principles for a movement against them would sprout." Ohio, because of its early development in the region and large population (including over half the Blacks in the Midwest), proved to be a key leader on racial issues. Both the Northwest Ordinance and the Ohio constitution had banned slavery. Ohio allowed a Black press to operate and disputes between Blacks and whites to be heard in court and supported limited Black education; Ohioans also were strongly opposed to the kidnapping of Blacks.[108] From the beginning of statehood, Ohio had strong laws designed to stop this "nefarious and inhuman practice," and these laws were strengthened multiple times in subsequent decades. As early as 1817, Ohio courts were ruling that any slaves who were brought through Ohio by their masters were automatically free, a ruling later buttressed by a state statute requiring the same.[109] Ohio, in short, rejected comity, or the legal principle undergirding the doctrine that one state should respect another state's laws.[110]

In 1856 the Ohio Supreme Court again reaffirmed that slaves became free the moment they entered Ohio.[111] In 1846 an Ohio governor fought hard to win the freedom of a Kentucky slave who had lived in Columbus and thus should have been free, despite his later return to Kentucky.[112] In 1857, Ohio also passed three new personal liberty laws to prevent the kidnapping of Blacks, including one that closed Ohio's jails to slave catchers, and also codified the judicial rule that any slaves brought into Ohio were automatically free.[113] The passage of personal liberty laws in Ohio and elsewhere was the "most radical, persistent, and effective of the abolitionist strategies against the slavery interests in antebellum America" and the "abolitionists' most tangible victory in their battles for securing the freedom of blacks and at the same time for challenging slaveholders' rights over slaves."[114] By the 1850s, according to one historian, Ohio was a "relatively safe haven for southern blacks seeking a refuge from slavery." All these actions justify a broader "Midwest against slavery" narrative and undermine the notion of static oppression in the region.[115]

Reformers were filing petitions to repeal Ohio's black laws as early as 1829, and in 1837 Ohio's first Black state convention, attended by two hundred Black leaders, similarly called for the repeal of the state's black laws. Along with the emergence of active abolitionists in the 1830s, the stage was set for a "virtual civil rights revolution" in Ohio.[116] In 1839, Ohio created a complicated system for returning fugitive slaves that involved court hearings and judicial review, a process that significantly slowed the work of slave catchers. In 1844 prominent Whig newspapers in Ohio were calling for the repeal of the black laws, and in 1845 Whigs were able to pass a bill in the state senate repealing the ban on Blacks testifying against whites in court (it failed in the house 30–23).[117] In 1846 in the Ohio legislature, a select committee considered the repeal of the black laws and concluded that they were "contrary to the letter of the constitution, and should therefore be repealed without delay." That same year the Whig candidate for governor, William Bebb, campaigned for modifying the black laws and was given great support by the anti-slavery leader Salmon Chase. In a December 1848 convention, Ohio's Free Soilers, led by Chase, called for repeal of the black laws and, using their new leverage in the legislature, they largely succeeded.[118]

In 1849, House Bill 52 passed the house 52–10 and the senate 23–11, with especially heavy support from the anti-slavery Western Reserve.[119] House

Bill 52 repealed the ban on Blacks testifying against whites, abolished the surety bond requirement, and allowed Blacks to settle freely in Ohio without proof of their status. Blacks could now vote in school board elections in locations where segregated African American schools were operating (an earlier Ohio Supreme Court decision had also extended voting rights to Blacks of mixed ancestry who were more than "half white"). In 1853 another Ohio law mandated that counties provide education to Blacks, allowing localities to choose whether to segregate or integrate, and some chose the latter.[120]

Progress also came in Illinois. The statewide vote in the 1820s to call a convention to allow slavery failed by a wide margin, after all, and other racial restrictions slowly diminished in subsequent years. In 1836 the Illinois Supreme Court held that all indenture agreements that did not rigidly follow the procedures set forth in statute and in the constitution were null and void and the indentures set free. By 1841 the court had ruled that the sale of indentures was illegal.[121] Throughout the 1840s, Illinois courts eroded slave-oriented practices, indentures, and forms of involuntary servitude, and in 1845 an Illinois Supreme Court case made clear that the slaves of the old French settlers were to be set free.[122] In 1850 the Chicago Common Council instructed citizens and police officers paid by the council not to cooperate in the capture of fugitive slaves, and Chicago became known as hostile to slave-catchers. In 1855 the legislature passed a law to aid Illinois Blacks who had been kidnapped, and this law strengthened an earlier but weaker law passed in 1825. Although Illinois did prohibit Black immigration during the 1850s, as did Indiana and Iowa, the enforcement was "sporadic and lax." By 1865, after a series of twists and turns, all the black laws of Illinois were repealed and Blacks were allowed to testify against whites in court.[123]

After the Illinois legislature repealed the black laws along party lines (Republicans supporting repeal, Democrats opposing), celebrations were held across the state, including one in Springfield where Blacks orchestrated a sixty-two-gun salute in Springfield, one shot for each member of the state house and senate who voted to terminate the black laws.[124] John Jones, an African American tailor in Chicago, fired off his own cannon to celebrate the victory and was honored in Springfield "by being chosen to ignite the cannon fuse symbolically ending the black laws."[125]

There were also signs of racial progress in Michigan. Judge Augustus Elias Brevoort Woodward was finally able to use his aversion to slavery in a prominent case, ruling against a Canadian citizen seeking return of his slaves who had escaped across the river to Detroit; he set free two young African Americans by relying, in part, on the Northwest Ordinance. The condemnatory judicial rulings coupled with a large in-migration of anti-slavery Yankees would soon extinguish the final remnants of slavery in Michigan Territory (the 1830 census recorded only one slave in the territory), and Detroit would become an active stop on the Underground Railroad.[126] In 1837, when Michigan became a state, it did not adopt black laws governing residency as had more southern midwestern states such as Ohio, Indiana, and Illinois. In 1847 a Michigan trial court ruled that certain people of mixed-race origins could vote.[127] In a well-known 1848 case, slave-catchers from Kentucky attempted to snatch Adam and Sarah Crosswhite and their five children, a Black family in Marshall, Michigan, but were rebuffed by a biracial crowd; the crowd's actions were overlooked by a jury appalled by slavery and the efforts of the slave-catchers were frustrated.[128] In 1855, Michigan adopted a strong personal liberty law that prohibited Michigan officials from assisting federal marshals in the apprehension of runaway slaves, required county attorneys to defend slaves, banned the use of county jails to detain slaves, and made clear that any slaves passing through Michigan were automatically set free.[129] That same year Blacks were given the right to vote in school district elections.[130]

In 1866 the Michigan Supreme Court ruled that people who were less than half Black could vote. Although seen as progressive for the time, the decision was based on the observance of physical characteristics such as nose shape and was rightly mocked by a dissenting justice who questioned how such arbitrary judgments could be made: "If this be the correct rule, we had better have the constitution amended, with all speed, so as to authorize the election or appointment of nose pullers or nose inspectors to attend to the election polls."[131] All things considered, Michigan's racial policy by the 1850s "was relatively liberal for the antebellum United States," and the state became known for its "racial equalitarianism."[132] The historian Roy Finkenbine noted that "Michigan acquired a reputation among antebellum Americans—Black and white, slave and free—as a beacon of liberty on the Great Lakes."[133]

Northern midwestern states such as Wisconsin and Minnesota, which had better records on race than other midwestern states to begin with, also saw much racial progress, as did, farther south, Iowa, which rapidly caught up. Wisconsin, for example, passed a strong personal liberty law. In keeping with this law, Wisconsin activists were animated by the Sherman Booth case, in which an abolitionist was imprisoned for blocking the return of a fugitive slave and the Wisconsin Supreme Court used the opportunity to set free the abolitionist and to declare the Fugitive Slave Act unconstitutional.[134] When overruled by the southern-controlled Taney U.S. Supreme Court, the Wisconsin Supreme Court refused to acknowledge the decision. After the chief justice of the Wisconsin court dissented from the anti-slavery decision, abolitionists organized against him and, in a sign of their political power, he was defeated in the next judicial election.[135] The Wisconsin Supreme Court was the highest court in the country to assault slavery on constitutional grounds.[136]

African Americans also won some victories in Minnesota.[137] In 1860, even after *Dred Scott*, the Minnesota constitution was used as the basis for freeing a slave who was brought to Lake Harriet and said she wanted to be free, a desire local abolitionists quickly seized upon, initiating a successful lawsuit to win her freedom. In the 1880s, Minneapolis even hired a Black police officer, and soon after St. Paul followed suit and then organized a Black fire company. Many Blacks owned homes in St. Paul, and the neighborhoods were not particularly segregated by race.[138] In Iowa the first decision rendered by the state supreme court applied the Northwest Ordinance and held that a slave who traveled to the state was automatically free. In 1856, Iowa ended its ban on Blacks testifying in court. The new 1857 Iowa constitution also permitted Black schools if they were segregated. In 1860, Iowa repealed its Black exclusion law.[139]

Progress was also made in the realm of education, one of the most sensitive social and political subjects in all of American history. As early as the 1820s there were halting efforts to promote Black education in Ohio, and some schools allowed Black children to join white students in the classroom. In Ohio Black children were excluded from the public school system created in 1821, then in 1829 a law provided for the public education of Black children, but in 1831 noncompliance led to this law's repealed. The 1831 law, however, did allow for integrated education, unlike the 1829 law, and the use of tax money collected from African Americans for Black schools.[140] As a result, various programs to educate Black children in Ohio gained traction. For example, various Black education projects, sometimes run by African Americans and sometimes run by officials at Lane Seminary or other whites, gained ground in Cincinnati. The result was the creation of several Black academies and a high school where students were taught by accomplished Black teachers.[141] Black schools, run by reformers and abolitionists, were also operational in towns such as Chillicothe, Circleville, Columbus, Dayton, and Zanesville. By 1840 there were schools for African American children in every Ohio city.[142] On the Western Reserve Blacks were sometimes welcomed into public schools, and in Cleveland (once dubbed "Negro Heaven") in the 1840s an integrationist school board put all students together, even assigning Black teachers to mixed-race classrooms.[143]

By the 1830s there was evidence of Black and white kids attending school together in at least two Ohio counties, and by the 1840s there was general recognition that Black and white children were attending school together in various locations. In 1849 the Ohio legislature passed a law requiring school districts to educate Blacks and specifically authorized integrated education if no parents objected, ratifying the existing school practices in Cleveland, Norwalk, Oberlin, Sandusky, Xenia, and other towns.[144] This legislation also reaffirmed the right of Blacks to use the taxes they paid to the state to establish schools for Black kids if they chose.[145] In Cincinnati, because of the size and sophistication of its Black-run school system, the city's Blacks fought for and won passage of a state law creating the separate Black Board of Directors to run Cincinnati's Black schools using public funds.[146] In 1853, Ohio passed a state law mandating funding for Black education.[147] By 1850, 25 percent of Black children in Ohio were attending school, and by 1860 the figure was 40 percent.

In 1860 more Black children were being educated in Ohio than in the entirety of the American South, where it was often illegal to provide them schooling. In 1860 a greater percentage of Black children attended school in Ohio than in large eastern states such as Pennsylvania, New Jersey, and New York (Ohio also had a greater percentage of Black children in school than there were *white* children in school in Virginia, Tennessee, Florida, Louisiana, and Arkansas).[148] One study found 121 Black schools in Ohio by 1865, and another found that 25 percent of Ohio schools were integrated by that same date.[149] In Toledo in 1871, after some petitions from African American parents and the election of some new members of the school board, the new board just voted to integrate the city's schools because of "good conscience and economic good sense" and the pride of terminating "another relic of slave days."[150] In 1876 the Ohio Supreme Court officially ruled against school segregation and integrated the Ohio school system. After high school in Ohio Blacks could also attend integrated colleges such as Oberlin College or African American colleges such as Wilberforce University.[151] In the mid-nineteenth century, 5–8 percent of Oberlin's graduates were Black. In 1887 the Ohio legislature followed the Ohio Supreme Court and formally banned segregated schools by a vote of 59–13 and 24–7 (some of the strongest resistance to the legislation came from Cincinnati's Black teachers, who wanted to preserve their Black-run school system).[152]

Michigan also saw progress in the education of Black youth. In the 1830s, Detroit created "colored schools," and in 1841 the state legislature appropriated money to fund a separate Black school district in Detroit, where most of the Blacks in Michigan lived.[153] Blacks could also attend the Raisin Institute, run by the abolitionist Laura Haviland in southeastern Michigan, which was a manual labor school for Black children.[154] In Michigan by 1846, integrated schools were possible by local option, resulting in mixed education in Ann Arbor, Cass County, and throughout most of southwest Michigan. The Michigan legislature also passed a statute in 1855 affording Blacks the right to vote in school board races. During the 1850s Black school attendance in Michigan quintupled. By 1860, 46 percent of school-age Blacks attended school in Michigan. A greater percentage of Black children attended school in Michigan than did white children in ten southern slave states. By 1867 most of Michigan's schools were integrated, and the major exceptions were cities such as Detroit and Jackson. Prominent Republican leaders fought to finish school integration. In 1867 former Michigan governor Austin Blair filed a lawsuit to require the school district in Jackson to allow Black students, a lawsuit made moot two months later when the Michigan legislature passed a law to abolish school segregation.[155] More specifically, Michigan passed laws in both 1867 and 1871 guaranteeing equal access to schools and banning separate schools based on race. School officials in Detroit dragged their feet on desegregation by questioning whether the statewide school equality statute applied to them because of a special Detroit education statute passed earlier, but the courts rejected this argument.[156] In 1869 the Michigan Supreme Court made abundantly clear that Michigan schools were not to be segregated.[157]

Education for Blacks was also available in Iowa. As early as 1850 (when there were only 265 Blacks in Iowa) some African American children in

Iowa were attending white schools despite laws against it. The 1857 Iowa constitution required that "all the youth of the state" receive an education but did not require integrated schools. In 1858 the Iowa legislature required that school boards provide separate schools for Blacks unless the public schools already were allowing Black attendance, which some were.[158] In abolitionist Grinnell, a fugitive slave girl was welcomed into the public school in 1859 (the same year that John Brown came through town, along with twelve slaves from Missouri he was taking to Canada, and met with Senator J. B. Grinnell, transforming the senator's front parlor into a "temporary arsenal of rifles, swords, pistols, and ammunition").[159]

The education system that emerged in Iowa was based on the Mann Report of 1856, as in Horace Mann, the famed educator and president of Antioch College in Ohio. By 1860, 36 percent of school-age Blacks attended school in Iowa and 63 percent of Black adults were literate.[160] After the Civil War, the prominent African American community leader Alexander Clark sent his daughter to the white school in Muscatine, and when she was turned away he brought suit and won. Iowa's constitution required that common schools be open to all, and the Iowa Supreme Court held that this meant the free and integrated education of African Americans.[161] That ruling also meant that the state had eliminated the possibility of a "separate but equal" doctrine in Iowa twenty years before the U.S. Supreme Court created it in *Plessy v. Ferguson.*[162] The Iowa decision was based on the application of Iowa state law and decided before the adoption of the federal Fourteenth Amendment; it became the "first successful school desegregation case in U.S. history."[163] Soon all Iowa schools were open to all children. Alexander Clark Jr. would graduate from the integrated Muscatine High School and became the first Black graduate of the University of Iowa law school, and his father Alexander Clark Sr. would soon follow (and later become U.S. ambassador to Liberia).[164]

Racial exclusion in education declined throughout the region. Overall in the Midwest "integrated education could be found in parts of most states, while everywhere else Blacks were at least offered segregated education."[165] In 1850 over 70 percent of Black people in Milwaukee were literate and also owned "moderate amounts of property."[166] By 1860, 23 percent of school-age Blacks attended school in Illinois and 29 percent in Wisconsin.[167] African American children could attend Chicago schools until 1863, when a city ordinance disallowed integrated schools but required separate schools for Black children. Then in 1865 Chicago's schools were again desegregated. The 1870 Illinois constitution required a free public school system in which "all children of this State shall receive a good common school education." An 1874 law again required equal education and adopted fines to ensure compliance.[168]

In Kansas during the Civil War era Blacks received educations via private schools, freedmen's schools, and contraband schools. In 1868 the Kansas legislature passed a law allowing either separate or integrated schools, and in 1879 it passed a law allowing segregated elementary schools but banning segregated high schools.[169] In 1867 in Nebraska, during the final session of the territorial legislature, a bill was passed deleting "white" from the school code and removing a requirement that school districts maintain separate Black schools, but the territorial governor vetoed it.[170] Most governance was left to local districts; Omaha, among others, kept its schools "public and free to all children" of the city, and schools were integrated by 1872. In Lincoln, Nebraska, the schools were not segregated and the school district cooperated with local Blacks. Nebraska City maintained a separate Black school until 1879, when it was closed and the Black pupils joined the main school.[171]

Advances in education were welcome, but the sine qua non to all those seeking advances in African American rights in the Midwest was progress on Black suffrage, which happened in practice before it became a wider public issue. "Throughout the upper mid-west," one historian noted, "there is evidence that blacks voted in many elections without challenge."[172] Consider Ohio and Michigan. In the realm of voting and other civic rules, Ohio courts ruled as early as 1831 that certain mixed-race people were considered eligible voters. By the 1850s Blacks were voting on the Western Reserve, in Greene County, and in Cleveland, regardless of state law.[173] In 1855 a Black man named John Mercer Langston was elected a town clerk in Lorain County, Ohio, and he became the first Black admitted to the Ohio bar (he was the grandfather of Langston Hughes).[174] By 1860, Ohio Blacks could vote for school boards for Black schools. When he ran for governor of Ohio in 1867, Rutherford B. Hayes ran on an aggressively pro–Black suffrage platform and against the "brutal tendencies of the rebel states."[175]

In Michigan, Blacks could vote in all school board elections after the legislature passed a new law in 1855. As early as the 1830s Blacks voted at times in Detroit, Lapeer County, and Monroe. Local officials in Detroit openly allowed free Blacks to vote by the 1850s. In Cass County by the 1850s there were numerous Black farmers, so the state allowed all property owners, including Blacks, to vote in school board elections and in bond votes on public debt.[176] On adoption of the Fifteenth Amendment in 1870, Blacks in Ohio and Michigan could officially vote in all elections.[177] In 1867, Nebraska adopted Black suffrage as part of the congressional requirements for admission as a new state, and other midwestern states, some by popular vote, adopted Black suffrage at about the same time.[178]

In Iowa in 1865 the politically dominant GOP endorsed Black suffrage by a 513–242 party convention vote, and Republicans won strong victories in the subsequent elections.[179] At the GOP convention endorsing Black suffrage, Iowa congressman Hiram Price called on his party to "do right" by the "colored men" who were "loyal and true to the Government in the days of its greatest peril," to vote for suffrage, and to "have the satisfaction of wiping out the last vestige of the black code that has long been a disgrace to our State."[180] That same year, seven hundred veterans of the Iowa Black Civil War unit, the Sixtieth U.S. Infantry Colored Regiment, met in Davenport and also petitioned for suffrage.[181] The movement was buoyed by nearly eighty thousand Iowa Civil War veterans, one-ninth of the state's overall population of seven hundred thousand, some of whom were more willing to support suffrage after what they had seen in the South. In 1866, Republicans in the Iowa legislature voted (69–16 in the house and 38–7 in the senate) to put Black suffrage on the ballot and, in accordance with the procedures for constitutional revision, did so again in 1868 by a larger margin (72–18, 40–7).[182]

In the fall of 1868, GOP presidential candidate Ulysses S. Grant asked Iowa, which he called a "bright radical star" for the Union, to "be the first State to carry impartial suffrage through unfalteringly."[183] Iowa responded with a strong 57 percent vote in favor of Black suffrage. The 1868 vote also eliminated the racial aspects of the census enumeration and allowed Blacks to join the Iowa militia.[184] In 1875, Grant visited a meeting of the Army of the Tennessee in Des Moines and said Iowans must "labor to add all needful guarantees for the more perfect security of Free Thought, Free Speech, a Free Press, Pure Morals, Unfettered Religious Sentiment and of Equal Right and Privileges to all men irrespective of Nationality, Color or Religion."[185] Grant's strong record on race impressed many, and Iowa responded to his call.[186] An 1880 referendum in Iowa to open the general assembly to Black membership passed with 64 percent of the vote. The 1880 vote eliminated the last racially discriminatory provisions in the Iowa constitution.[187]

Blacks in Wisconsin also won the right to vote. In 1835 the Black cook Joe Oliver voted in a county election in Milwaukee in a sign of what was to come. Wisconsin Territory called a constitutional convention in 1846, and David Giddings (a relative of the Ohio abolitionist Joshua Giddings) moved to allow Black suffrage, but he received only thirteen supporting votes.[188] Lack of support for the constitution from abolitionists who wanted Black suffrage contributed to the defeat of the 1846 constitution at the polls. By a vote of 55–49 at the 1846 constitutional convention, supporters of Black suffrage were able to secure a separate referendum on Black suffrage that fall, but it was defeated 14,615–7,664.

After the defeat of the 1846 constitution at the polls, Wisconsinites tried again in 1847 to write a constitution at a smaller constitutional convention, and Black-rights sympathizers again sought Black suffrage. In 1846 their efforts had been defeated 14–125, but a year later, in a smaller conclave, they were defeated by the closer margin of 29–69.[189] Ultimately the 1847 constitutional convention adopted language providing for suffrage for white men and "persons of Indian blood" and gave the legislature the power to grant suffrage to "persons not herein enumerated" if it was agreed to by popular vote.[190] This constitution was ratified by Wisconsinites in March 1848 and soon thereafter the new state legislature "provided for the submission to the people of a law extending the elective franchise to persons of African blood." In 1849, Wisconsin voted 5,265–4,075 (56–44 percent) to grant Black suffrage.[191] In 1866 the Wisconsin Supreme Court recognized and applied the law, making Wisconsin the first midwestern state to grant Black suffrage.[192]

In 1849 legislators in Minnesota Territory made a strong effort to win suffrage for Blacks (the measure failed 9–7 in the territorial house of representatives). Although the new state of Minnesota had not passed black laws, the absence of Black suffrage rights limited Blacks' ability to serve on juries and run for office, which were contingent on being eligible to vote. After the rise of a strong Republican Party in 1855 and after Minnesota became a state in 1858, the issue of Black suffrage returned. The GOP had pledged to stand for the "abolition of slavery, temperance, and the commitment to stand up to southern hegemony" and, as a GOP platform plank read, "No civil disabilities on account of color or religious opinion"—in other words, support for the extension of civil rights to Blacks. Although Republicans wanted to insert Black suffrage into the constitution created in 1857, they deferred action in favor of a separate popular vote to ensure safe acceptance of the constitution. Union success in the war, a well-organized abolitionist lobby, and strong GOP control of the Minnesota legislature ultimately led to passage of a bill, putting Black suffrage on the 1865 ballot (it passed the house 31–8 and the senate 16–4). Democratic Party leaders and newspapers attacked the GOP relentlessly as pro-Black, pro-miscegenation, and pro–racial amalgamation, and the referendum failed, but the vote was close, 14,651–12,138 (54–46 percent). After an overwhelming GOP vote in the legislature, Black suffrage was again placed on the fall 1867 ballot. Some voting glitches undermined GOP votes for the measure, contributing to its defeat by only 1,298 votes (2 percent). The Republican legislature tried again in 1868; one GOP congressional candidate said, "I would rather be defeated a dozen times over than have the suffrage amendment lost." This time it passed by nine thousand votes, winning in forty of the forty-one GOP counties and losing in nine of the ten Democratic counties.[193]

The several attempts to pass Black suffrage laws in Minnesota speak to the doggedness of the midwestern GOP on the voting rights front and its willingness to suffer political reversals when advancing the cause. Historians have recognized the "consistency with which the Republicans pushed the suffrage issue in the face of hostile voters and the impotency of the small black vote" and rightly attributed the persistence to "moral idealism."[194] Advocating Black suffrage certainly hurt the GOP politically more than it helped, but the party kept supporting voting rights and other advancements for African Americans.[195] On the key votes for Black-rights legislation in 1866, 92 percent of U.S. House Republicans and 84 percent of U.S. Senate Republicans voted in favor, and Republican state legislators collectively voted to ratify the Fifteenth Amendment, securing voting rights, 1,826–20.

In addition to suffrage, Republicans in Congress voted consistently throughout the 1850s and 1860s for "measures designed to improve the treatment of the Negro as a slave as well as to protect his civil and political rights."[196] In contrast to the midwestern GOP's strong advocacy of Black suffrage and ultimate success in Wisconsin, Iowa, and Minnesota, defeats in other regions were common. In 1865, Connecticut had voted down Black suffrage with 55 percent of the vote, and in 1868 New York voted it down with 53 percent. Between 1865 and 1870, negro suffrage referenda failed in fourteen northern states. One of the reasons for advocating the federal Fifteenth Amendment was to circumvent the problem of state suffrage referenda failing regularly.[197] The electoral victories for Black suffrage in 1868 in Iowa and Minnesota "gave an important fillip to the movement for a Fifteenth Amendment."[198]

The Fifteenth Amendment (guaranteeing voting rights) was ratified by all midwestern states; ratification failed in Kentucky, Delaware, Tennessee, Maryland, California, and New York, and the southern states were forced to adopt it.[199] In Michigan in 1869, for example, the bill to ratify the Fifteenth Amendment passed the state senate 25–4 and the house 68–24 on strictly party line votes and then was adopted by voters in the fall of 1870 by a tight margin of 54,105–50,598.[200] On March 31, 1870, Detroit Blacks celebrated President Grant's endorsement of the Fifteenth Amendment and marchers carried banners with portraits of prominent GOP leaders and a banner reading "The Republican Party Made Us Free." On April 7, 1870, in Detroit a large festival was held to celebrate the ratification of the constitutional amendment—a cannon was fired at 10 A.M., commencing a parade that included a hundred Black schoolboys, revelers holding up portraits of Grant and Lincoln, fifty members of the Youths' Mental Improvement Club, and fifty members of the 102nd United States Colored Infantry. They all proceeded to the Detroit Opera House, where President Grant's proclamation on the ratification was read aloud, followed by a long poem by the Black "bard of the Maumee," George DeBaptiste Bell, who addressed the hall's overflowing audience, which was a third white. With his French background, Bell may have been especially moved that all vestiges of the old French slave system of Michigan were swept away and particularly appreciated George Clemenceau's statement: "With the ratification of the Fifteenth Amendment the American revolution was over."[201]

Black suffrage meant the rise of a whole new era of Black politics and politicians in the Midwest. John W. E. Thomas, for example, was born in Mobile, Alabama, became an Illinois teacher, and was elected to the Illinois house from Chicago in 1876. The first two Black state house members in Ohio were George Washington Williams of Cincinnati (1880–81) and John P. Green of Cleveland (1882–83).[202] Frank Wheaton, a graduate of the University of

Minnesota law school, was elected to the Minnesota legislature in 1898 in a white district.[203] Even in deep southern Illinois Blacks made political gains.[204] A Black minister in Batavia warned fellow Blacks not to fall for Democratic campaign promises because, in a reference to the recent death of a local Black, Democrats had drunk the "blood of one poor colored man within the past two weeks."[205] When solidifying the Black vote in late nineteenth-century Detroit, Republicans recalled the "Democratic riot of 1863, in which a mob of Democrats hunted down and murdered the friends and relatives of the very colored men whose votes they now unblushingly seek."[206] In states like Ohio where the political parties were often closely balanced, parties had to court the Black vote.[207] When Republican governor Joseph B. Foraker was seeking office in the 1880s, for example, he eagerly courted the Black vote.[208] According to Foraker, the "Negro vote was so large that it was not only important but an essential factor in our considerations. It would not be possible for the Republican party to carry the state if that vote should be arrayed against us."[209]

During this same era, as midwestern Blacks were exercising their voting rights and running for and even winning elective offices, legislatures were also reinforcing the place of African Americans in midwestern life with the passage of additional legal protections. After the Civil War, several midwestern states passed sweeping civil rights laws and state courts enforced them, a legislative movement and a judicial history largely forgotten today.[210] In 1874, Kansas passed a law prohibiting businesses from discriminating on the basis of race, color, or previous condition of servitude.[211] In 1884, Ohio passed an equal rights act guaranteeing the right to use public facilities and repealed all remaining remnants of the state's black laws. Because of several major advances in Ohio after the war, the historian Stephen Middleton has opined, "African Americans in Ohio had much to celebrate" as the century drew to a close.[212]

In Iowa in 1884 the state legislature passed an act guaranteeing equal access to hotels, public transportation, theaters, and other places of amusement. In 1892 the legislature added restaurants, bathhouses, and "other places where refreshments are served." With these actions, the historian Dorothy Schwieder concluded, Iowans had made "their state one of the most progressive in civil equality for blacks."[213] Even before the passage of these state laws and before the national Civil Rights Act of 1875, the Iowa Supreme Court, in a case involving accommodations on a steamboat traveling from

Keokuk to Quincy, Illinois, had ruled that no differential treatment between the races was allowed. The court ruled that treating Blacks differently on steamboats was a "gross injustice," a "positive wickedness," and "intended to inflict oppression and wrong." The practices of the steamboat operator, the court continued, were based on a "prejudice, be it proclaimed to the honor of our people, that is fast giving way to nobler sentiments, and, it is hoped, will soon be entombed with its parent, slavery."[214]

In 1885, a year after adoption of the Ohio and Iowa laws, Minnesota, Nebraska, and Illinois also passed civil rights laws. They were similar to the Michigan civil rights act, also adopted in 1885, which guaranteed "full and equal privileges of inns, restaurants, eating houses, barber shops, public conveyances and theaters" to people of all races.[215] In 1883 the Michigan legislature had also repealed the state's miscegenation law (at the same time, in a decision highlighting regional distinctions, Alabama's law making intermarriage a felony was upheld by the U.S. Supreme Court).[216] In 1893, Michigan passed another statute to ban life insurance companies from considering race when determining insurance rates. In a case involving a restaurant, the Michigan Supreme Court made clear that "in Michigan there must be and is an absolute, unconditional equality of white and colored before the law. The white man can have no rights or privileges under the law that are denied to the black man." Said the court, "It is not for the courts to cater to or temporize with a prejudice which is not only not human, but unreasonable." The opinion, written by Justice Allen Morse, a Union veteran who lost an arm at Missionary Ridge, held that the "humane and enlightened judgment of our people has decided—although it cost blood and treasure to do so—that the negro is a man; a freeman; a citizen; and entitled to equal rights before the law with the white man."[217] In 1895, Wisconsin Republicans also passed a law punishing racial discrimination in restaurants and other public places and made violations punishable by fines up to $100 and six months in prison.[218] The passage of these statutes and their enforcement across the Midwest led to a period of hopefulness and racial integration in midwestern cities such as Chicago while southern states were adopting sweeping laws to impose rigid Jim Crow segregation.[219]

Advancements in suffrage rights, the adoption of new civil rights protections, and electoral victories were all impressive; still, the most tangible sign of success for African Americans was their efforts to escape southern slavery and build new communities in the Midwest throughout the nineteenth century. Despite black laws and other obstacles, Black migration out of the South and into the Midwest persisted. Illinois, which was second only to Indiana among the midwestern states in its hostility to Black migrants, saw a 40 percent increase in its Black population in the decade prior to the Civil War. Other large increases in other states during that decade "suggest that the anti-black laws of Ohio, Indiana, and Illinois had relatively little impact on black migration." With the exception of Indiana, the most southern state in the Midwest, the "midwestern states had continuous and impressive growth in their black populations." By 1860, Ohio, Michigan, Wisconsin, Minnesota, and Iowa allowed unrestricted immigration of free Blacks.[220] These migrants often built successful midwestern communities around prosperous farming operations that tapped and fed the agrarian ideology of the region.[221] Black migrants were, according to a recent study, "able to carve out spaces in the rural Old Northwest where astonishing levels of equality were possible."[222] In the 1830s, after encountering hostility within the city, some Cincinnati Blacks left for Mercer County, Ohio, and acquired 30,000 acres of land to farm.[223] The Black community of Salem, Ohio, grew to thirty families by the 1830s, and the community was quick to build a church and a school and organize a temperance society.[224]

In a parallel example, New Philadelphia, Illinois, was organized in 1836 and became the earliest town in the country to be planned and organized by an African American. Its founder was Frank McWorter, a Kentucky slave who had bought his freedom and dubbed himself "Free Frank."[225] Jean Baptiste Point du Sable, an African American who built a home at the mouth of the Chicago River in 1779 and later a trading post and became known as the founder of Chicago, also developed 800 acres near Peoria.[226] In part because of the success of the Cass County Black settlement in the southwest corner of Michigan, southern Blacks looked to the Midwest as a "haven from slavery and Negrophobia."[227] Several other Black settlements in Michigan were launched in Allegan, Calhoun, Kalamazoo, and Van Buren counties.[228] The town of Covert, Michigan, in Van Buren County was a particularly successful Black settlement, as was Monroe, halfway between Toledo and Detroit.[229] So too was Buxton, Iowa, where many Blacks moved to establish a community and mine coal, and Todd County, Minnesota, which focused on farming.[230] After the Civil War, many Blacks also moved to Kansas, becoming the famous Exodusters.[231] As the historian Nell Irvin Painter noted, "Kansas was no Canaan, but it was a far cry from Mississippi and Louisiana."[232] Just to the north in Nebraska, African Americans also moved in and started farming.[233]

As suggested by their desire to buy and own land and become farmers who sold goods for the market, the social progress among African Americans in the Midwest was in part due to their embrace of the economic life of the region and its market-oriented middle-class culture of striving. The Black bourgeoisie adhered to the same norms—grounded in Christian ethics, hard work, Victorian mores, and a market orientation—as the bulk of the Midwest residents. Black leaders in Ohio pushed "moral and social uplift through self-help and greater racial pride," often by way of black churches.[234] A convention of African American leaders in Ohio in 1852 proclaimed their "belief in the value of hard work, thrift, education, morality, religion, and family."[235] Ohio African American leader W. O. Bowles said his race needed "a manly independence to be secured by the accumulation of wealth, the improvement of morals, the development of intellect and the courageous support and exaltation of our race institutions."[236] In Cincinnati, Blacks also built churches, opened businesses, and bought land and generally endeavored to "embrace every opportunity to rise."[237] Blacks in Detroit worked hard to build Black institutions, but their foremost priority was the organization of churches, which also served as schools and political meeting places. They succeeded to such an extent that some thought Black Detroit was "over-churched." They also launched literary societies and specific groups such as the Detroit Study Club, which examined "the lives of English and American poets." An 1843 survey by the Colored Vigilant Committee of Detroit listed a young men's society, a debating club, a reading room, a library, and a temperance organization, which all met in churches, plus over twenty benevolent and self-improvement clubs in the city.[238]

Such clubs and fraternal organizations directed their efforts in support of temperance, Sunday schools, revivalism, prison reform, free public schools and industrial education, abolition, and Black and women's suffrage. At the 1843 "state colored convention" in Michigan, Blacks advocated education, both civil and religious, temperance, and more moral reform societies. They adopted resolutions promoting farming and the mechanical arts that asserted that "indolence is the parent of vice." In a reference to democratic advances in the Midwest that drew contrasts with Europe and the American South, the convention resolved to "wage war against tyranny in every form, whether emanating from a crowned head abroad, or an overbearing aristocracy at home."[239] When the veterans of Iowa's Black Civil War units met in 1865, their petition asked Blacks to pursue "education, industry, and thrift that would certainly be rewarded with increasing intelligence and wealth" and counseled Blacks "to abstain from the use of intoxicating drink."[240] In Kansas, Black leaders advocated "self-help," "uplift," the embrace of the "Horatio Alger myth," and "racial solidarity."[241] Chicago would become a home of Black entrepreneurship.[242]

The Black middle-class culture of uplift was often channeled through fraternal organizations and newspapers. Michigan Blacks, for example, started twenty-three chapters of the Masons and Odd Fellows and joined the Knights Templar, Knights of Pythias, Shriners, True Reformers, Brothers of Friendship, Negro Elks, United Brothers of Friendship, Good Samaritans, and women's auxiliaries.[243] In St. Paul, Blacks were highly active in Black Masonic lodges, other fraternal orders, and the Robert Banks Literary Society.[244] In Iowa City Blacks formed Ethiopian Lodge No. 1 of the Independent Order of Good Templars.[245] In Nebraska, Prince Hall Masonry was popular, as it was in other midwestern states.[246] Even in southern Indiana, Black Masons donned their regalia and marched through the city of Madison on the Ohio River to celebrate the British West Indies' Emancipation Day.[247] Chicago became home to more unique organizations such as the Sionelli (Illinois in reverse) Adelphi Social Club, the Grand Pacific Club, the Danabegy Club, and the Hannibal Guards.[248] Female Black benevolent societies also followed Christianity and focused on "stressing good character and good works" and "banding together to help those who wanted to help themselves," and Black women's clubs were popular.[249] All these societies and clubs "were intended to improve the race—spiritually, morally, and physically," and yielded support for organizations such as the Christian Industrial Club, an uplift entity designed to help young African American women.[250] Combining uplift with triumphalism over the wicked South, some Black veterans of the Civil War formed Grand Army of the Republic lodges, including two, in Dayton and Indianapolis, named for Martin Delany, the first African American officer in the Union Army.[251]

The middle-class norms of Black civic life were reinforced in the Black press. In Minnesota, for example, the aptly named John Quincy Adams

edited the *Western Appeal,* later to become the *Appeal* (to "lessen its identifi-
cation exclusively with the Midwest"), in part to "encourage self-respect and
dignity among blacks," especially among the "literate, cohesive, and stable
community of successful businessmen" of Minneapolis and St. Paul.[252]
Raised in Fond du Lac, Wisconsin, and Yellow Springs, Ohio, and a graduate of Oberlin College, Adams became "one of the most influential Afro-
Americans in the Upper Midwest." Adams urged individual striving and
schooling because "education and wealth are the lever and fulcrum that will
remove all obstacles" to equality and civil rights.[253] The goals of Black newspapers such as the *Appeal,* the Chicago *Conservator,* the *Cleveland Gazette,*
the Urbana *Informer,* the *Detroit Plaindealer,* the *Indianapolis Freeman,* the
Indianapolis *Leader,* the *Indianapolis World,* the Logansport *Visitor,* and the
Springfield *Informer* were the "advancement of literacy, racial enlightenment, and moral and social betterment."[254] When Robert Abbott's famous
Defender was launched in Chicago in 1905, it joined five Black newspapers
already publishing in the city. All of these "midwestern African-American
newspapers created a powerful nexus of communication among black communities" and circulated and reinforced ideas of uplift and striving. As cities
grew in the late nineteenth century and rural Black settlements were less
prevalent, there was even more "assimilation of White middle class norms
by an aspiring Black bourgeoisie."[255]

African Americans in the Midwest made enormous strides during the
nineteenth century, benefiting from growing calls and movements for racial
equality and witnessing a veritable civil rights revolution. Nevertheless, the
story inevitably returns to where it began. The Detroit race riot of 1833 was
not a singular episode of racial terror. Acts of anti-Black terror followed in
Decatur, Akron, Springfield (Ohio and Illinois), East St. Louis, Chicago,
Omaha, and other smaller and forgotten places.[256] These race riots and other
acts of racial violence tended to be concentrated in the southern Midwest,
near the Ohio River and within the Confederate pale, but not always.[257] Short
of race riots, hostility to Blacks could be found in the form of exclusion
efforts, resistance to civil rights laws, and opposition to integration, especially in the southern tier of the Midwest and in the region's "Butternut"
enclaves where the Union war effort was dismissed as a waste of blood and
treasure.[258] These were the sentiments that sparked off another anti-Black
riot in Detroit in 1863, led by Irish immigrants who saw little need to join a

war effort to help Black slaves.[259] But precisely because of this intense resistance in certain areas, the degree of overall racial progress in the Midwest is especially impressive. Although the Midwest fell far short of twentieth-first-century ideals of racial harmony during its early decades and various attempts were made to restrict African American migration to the region, the arc of racial progress in the Midwest bent decidedly upward and there was a "clear trend in the direction of granting greater legal rights and protections to free blacks."[260] As important as racial progress was to many reform-minded midwesterners, they also had other causes in mind.

CHAPTER 5

"NOTHING ELSE QUITE
LIKE IT IN THE WORLD"

THE MIDWEST AND THE AGE
OF MILD REFORM

One of the many young Republican political leaders in the Midwest who pushed hard for African American suffrage and civil rights was Ignatius Donnelly, who had moved to Minnesota in 1856. He was a devotee of Abraham Lincoln and, when the Civil War came and Governor Alexander Ramsey was away in Washington, Lieutenant Governor Donnelly took command and signed the proclamation of April 16, 1861, that called for Minnesota volunteers to put down the rebellion.[1] Soon thousands of Minnesotans were marching off to fight the American South under orders from their Illinois commander-in-chief. In the "darkest hour" of the young republic, Donnelly said, Lincoln was "faithfully resigned to the task before him. . . . In all the history of mankind no man, save Christ himself, ever carried a more unbearable burden of forgiveness written upon every line in his sad face."[2]

Donnelly did not stop with supporting the Union, Lincoln, the GOP, and the cause of African American freedom. The war era was just the beginning of his lifetime of work to promote broader reforms. Because the vast majority of midwesterners were farmers, these reforms included such matters as regulating the cost of shipping grain, but they also included broader issues such as temperance, women's suffrage, the adoption of the Australian ballot, anti-corruption measures, and the problem of monopoly in general. As Donnelly demonstrates, the decades after the Civil War in the Midwest saw robust reform drives in manifold directions. Donnelly sought, he said, to "erect a banner around which the swarming hosts of reform could rally."[3]

These reform efforts underscored the democratic practices and energies, traditions, and civic culture that had taken hold in the Midwest. They could lead to solid progress, as the advances in African American civil rights described in the previous chapter indicate and as the story of women's rights told in this chapter shows. In other realms the reforms advanced either made little progress or would not be looked on favorably today. All told, the midwestern reform era highlighted the strength of the democratic institutions that had been planted in the Midwest, their mature functioning, and a region willing to consider and adopt incremental, but not radical, reforms to make their region better. Drives for reform, in keeping with the culture of the region, were often led by Christians or grounded in Christian teachings, premised on social uplift, geared toward farmers, organized via the dense network of civic institutions in the Midwest, and generally concerned with the forces that distorted the republican order they had worked so hard to build.

Consistent with the heavy agrarian orientation of the Midwest and the region's respect for uplift through education, a great emphasis was placed on college education, especially a form related to the interests of farmers. The result was the passage of the land grant education plan through Congress during the war, when southerners were not present to block its progress.[4] Soon followed the creation of an archipelago of future research institutions around the Midwest that would become Ohio State University, Michigan State University, Iowa State University, and their sister institutions. The cause of education was also embraced by Oliver Kelley, a Minnesota farmer known for his skill at mechanical innovations and experimenting with new crops. Kelley drew on his deep involvement in the Masons and in 1867 launched a new farm organization titled the Patrons of Husbandry, also known as the Grange.[5] The original plan was to promote education among farmers and provide recreational and social opportunities in rural areas.[6] Speaking of the Grange, Elizabeth Sanders notes that the "first large social movement of the post-Civil War era was directed toward the education of farmers."[7]

The Grange was organized into different levels and units and subunits, similar to the Masons or other fraternal lodges, and held meetings and scheduled lectures in Grange halls and hosted socials they called "feasts." The Grange, which allowed women to join on an equal footing with men, became the "largest, strongest, and most impactful social movement of its time." The Grange was most prevalent in the Midwest, which was home to half the

Grange's members. After intense organizational efforts in Iowa, Wisconsin, Illinois, Nebraska, Kansas, and Indiana in 1873–74, the number of Grange organizations and halls reached twenty-three thousand and the Grange's membership totaled 750,000. In 1873, Ignatius Donnelly became the chief lecturer for the Minnesota Grange.[8]

In 1876 the Grange decided that, in addition to social and educational functions, seeking "desirable legislation was acceptable." Grangers sought better schools and free textbooks and additional technical training for farmers. But, most important, the Grange soon became linked to the biggest concern of the midwestern farmer in the postwar years, the power of the railroads.[9] The railroads represented a major disruption in the pattern of life in the Midwest, which had seen much of its trade oriented toward rivers and lakes and flatboats and ships. The railroad proved to be a much faster and more efficient form of transportation, and towns frequently competed to woo a rail line. But once the lines were built and a transportation network was established, the railroads possessed enormous power to set freight rates for farmers, who saw them as arbitrary and unfair. As Donnelly pointed out, it cost as much to ship wheat from Minneapolis to Milwaukee as it did from Milwaukee to Liverpool.[10] As a result, farmers began to organize, often through the Grange, to limit the economic power of railroads. Illinois, Minnesota, Iowa, and Wisconsin would all pass laws regulating railroad rates long before Congress passed the national Interstate Commerce Act of 1887. The pressure for national action came mostly from midwestern farmers. In 1874 an Iowa congressman became the first sponsor of a federal railroad regulation bill, one that gained its greatest support from strong Grange areas.[11]

Before national action took place, however, reform happened in midwestern states. Concerns about railroad rates had caused delegates to the Illinois constitutional convention of 1870 to add a provision to the state's charter requiring legislative action to address the railroad problem. In 1871 the Illinois legislature passed a rate law for railroads and grain elevators and created a state rail commission. After the state supreme court struck down the law, Illinois legislators passed another in 1873.[12] In Minnesota, legislators passed laws in 1871 and 1874 that fixed rates and created a railroad commissioner. In Iowa in 1873, Grangers worked with members of the Anti-Monopoly Party to pass regulations on freight and passenger rates.[13] In Wisconsin in 1874 farmer advocates also passed the Potter Law, which set maximum rates on shipping freight and transporting passengers and created a commission to oversee railroad regulations.[14] When the Wisconsin GOP convened in Milwaukee in 1873, "virtually the entire party platform was devoted to some phase of the railroad question"; the railroad regulation law that was passed was a "reform measure largely the work of the Republican Party and designed to placate the angry farmers of Wisconsin."[15]

Ohio also passed a rate-setting bill, although its enforcement provisions were weak, and Michigan created the position of rail commissioner to supervise the railroads. "All over the nation," explained one historian, "attention turned toward the Middle West, for never before in the United States had corporations of any kind been subjected to such restrictive and specific legislation as that passed by midwestern lawmakers." This legislation, directed at the most powerful economic entities in American life, was adopted because of pressure from politically organized farmers in midwestern states. In 1873, in a typical example, the Northwest Farmers' Convention met in Chicago and called for more action on railroad rates, better credit terms, and more regulation of monopolies; the result was new railroad laws in Illinois and other midwestern states.[16]

The "Granger laws" regulating railroads ultimately made their way to the U.S. Supreme Court. In 1877, in *Munn v. Illinois,* the Supreme Court respected the "continuity of Anglo-Saxon law" dating to the time of William and Mary and held that, although in most cases a "man may fix what price he pleases," this rule can be modified in monopolistic circumstances involving public goods.[17] The *Munn* opinion was written by Justice Morrison Remick Waite, who had been a Republican lawyer in Toledo and an Ohio state senator and was appointed to the Court by President Grant (snide easterners dismissed the Toledo lawyer: "Mr. Waite stands in the front-rank of second-rate lawyers").[18] Waite drew on the public interest doctrine announced by Sir Matthew Hale, the lord chief justice of England in the 1600s. The Court noted the legality of previous price regulations in England related to ferries, common carriers, bakers, millers, and wharfingers when ruling that the grain warehouse firm of Munn and Scott in Chicago could be subject to the new Granger law. The concerns of midwestern yeoman farmers about the power of the emergent railroads had advanced from local grousing to editorializing to organizing in Grange halls to stump speeches to legislative lobbying to new state statutes to litigation in the highest court in the land to a legal victory for reformers. As Russell Nye concluded, "Grangerism was the earliest form of Midwestern progressivism," a multilayered movement of reformers active in the region during the late nineteenth century.[19]

Farmers also responded by using their organizational abilities to set up cooperative buying firms. These new cooperatives focused on consumer goods and also larger items such as farm implements. Because of farmer buying power, Montgomery Ward and Company in Chicago specifically targeted farmers for business. Farmers also sold cooperatively. In 1872 in Iowa, one-third of the grain elevators and warehouses were owned by Grangers. Grangers also went into milling, the cream business, and even insurance.[20] Oliver Kelley thought farmer marketing cooperatives would cut out the middleman, undermine the monopoly power of big business, and earn farmers more money. Later the Northern Alliance organized discount buying efforts such as the "Economy Club," which narrowed the costs of the middlemen and saved farmers 20–60 percent on goods. Farmers in Iowa organized to manufacture barbed wire to avoid paying the prices of the barbed wire trust. They also built fifty-three grain elevators and warehouses, organized dozens of cooperative stores, and assisted in the trade of machinery, wagons, lumber, and other products. In Indiana and Illinois the Farmers' Mutual Benefit Association successfully pooled its members' grain and sold it directly to avoid middlemen. By the turn of the century, Minnesota, Iowa, and Wisconsin ranked first, second, and third in the number of farmer cooperatives in the country.[21] All of these efforts spoke to the strength of social and civic networks among midwestern farmers and to their organizational abilities.

The underlying concern for most agrarian reformers was that the great and unique democratic institutions that had been built in the Midwest were being eroded by the power and influence of large-scale corporations. In 1873 a farmers' convention held in Springfield, Illinois, denounced monopolies as "detrimental to the public prosperity, corrupt in their management, and *dangerous to republican institutions.*"[22] In signs of reformers' awareness of midwestern democratic progress in a world of authoritarianism, Mary Lease of Kansas (of "raise more hell and less corn" fame) saw the great danger as the coming of "Russian despotism," and in Donnelly's fiction Americans help free persecuted Russians by making them literate.[23] An 1880 farmers convention in Chicago criticized the monopoly power of railroads as "corrupting to our politics, a hindrance to free and impartial legislation, and a menace to the very safety of our republican institutions."[24]

The railroads stood for the problem of monopoly, that is, the growing concentration of industrial firms which, farmers feared, stymied competition and warped democratic practices. In the 1850s, for examples, there had been two hundred companies making farm machinery, thousands of oil companies, and 450 coal companies. But these older, decentralized business sectors vanished. By 1900, two hundred firms were handling half of the nation's business. Leading the pack was John D. Rockefeller, who moved to Cleveland after the Civil War and began refining oil; by 1870 his firm was the largest in the Midwest (Rockefeller's Standard Oil trust lasted until 1892, when the Ohio courts broke it up and it moved to New Jersey). The specific concern of midwestern farmers was the railroads and the power they possessed. They often won favor, for example, by widely distributing free passes to ride the railroad to politicians, editors, lobbyists, judges, and others they wanted to influence. Railroads also spent copiously on lobbying (the La Crosse and Milwaukee Railroad spent $872,000 on political influence during one year in the 1870s).

The power of the railroads was also enhanced by their land holdings. In Iowa, the railroads received land grants larger than the states of Rhode Island and Connecticut combined, and in Minnesota they received more land than the size of two Massachusetts. In Nebraska the railroads received lands that more than totaled the size of New Hampshire. Because of their influence, many farmers argued, railroads were able to dodge their fair share of taxes. In Illinois, for example, the railroads were capitalized at $42,450 a mile but taxed at $7,800 a mile. Because of the growth of large corporations and new lobbying techniques from railroads and other large-scale entities, reformers feared that the "old-style democracy was gone, or was going fast."[25]

Another aspect of the monopoly problem was concern over the "money power": currency issues, debt, and the power of eastern bankers, a set of issues that further divided the Midwest from the East Coast and deepened midwestern regional consciousness.[26] One direct trigger of these concerns was the federal government's decision to stop using greenbacks, which started during the economically difficult years of the Civil War, and return to linking money directly to gold. The soft-vs.-hard money debate over what role this played in the depression of 1873 took on a deeply "sectional character," and quickly the "issue opposed midwesterners to northeasterners."[27] The Wall Street plutocrats and monopolists, Donnelly said, "rule the nation more despotically than under the old pro-slavery regime" of the South.[28] To increase their voting power on the money question, thereby heightening sectional tensions, midwestern congressmen pushed a bill to reapportion the House before the 1870 election instead of waiting until 1872 (after the 1870 census, the Midwest would become the most populous region of the country, with more House members than any other region). When a soft-money bill passed in the 1873/74 Congress, midwesterners voted for it and easterners against it.[29]

Beyond the legislative wrangling, the money debate altered the postwar political dynamics in the Midwest. The greenback issue brought Civil War general James Baird Weaver of Iowa into politics along with "Roaring Bill" Allen of Ohio, "Blue Jeans" Williams of Indiana, Edward Allis of Wisconsin, and Ignatius Donnelly of Minnesota.[30] In 1878 the soft-money advocates even supported the creation of the new Greenback-Labor Party, which was formally launched by eight hundred delegates meeting in Toledo.[31] That fall, Greenbackers won a million votes and put fifteen men in Congress, including Weaver, who left the Republican fold, organized Greenback clubs, and won a U.S. House seat in southeastern Iowa.[32] In 1880 the Greenbackers ran Weaver for president, and he received three hundred thousand votes.

In the 1870s, farmer "alliances" also began organizing, including the early components of what would become the Northwestern Alliance in the Midwest. In 1880, Milton George, the Ohio-born farmer-turned-editor of the *Western Rural,* organized the first local alliance in Chicago, where his newspaper was based. Within a year a thousand locals had been organized and four state organizations built in Wisconsin, Iowa, Nebraska, and Kansas. By 1882, using his Grange experience as a model, George had helped organize eight midwestern states, two hundred more local alliances, and one hundred thousand farmer members.[33]

Like many midwestern civic organizations and the Grange before it, the Northwestern Alliance, better known as the Northern Alliance, embraced Christianity and organized by way of thousands of lectures, dinners, libraries, newspapers, meetings, picnics, and educational seminars.[34] In 1882 the Northern Alliance created a seal and published a song book for local meetings featuring rural ballads. George counseled working through the caucuses and conventions of the existing political parties and not starting a third party. The

Northern Alliance, based in the offices of George's *Western Rural*, focused on the monopoly problem, including a school textbook trust, and issues such as insurance costs, fair taxation, and of course the railroads.

The Northern Alliance of the later 1880s, after George's influence had diminished and people like Donnelly became more active, began to become more politically engaged. After organizing the alliances and emphasizing the avoidance of partisan politics for years, Donnelly said that remaining nonpolitical was like manufacturing a gun "that will do everything but shoot." After many meetings and conventions and debates, the varied forces of agrarian reform decided to run third-party candidates in 1892 and set July 4th in Omaha of that year as the date and place of choosing a national slate by the symbolically precise number of 1,776 delegates.[35]

As American farmers organized in the late nineteenth century it was easy to detect differences between the South, the West, and the borderlands of the plains and the western Midwest, on the one hand, and the core of the Midwest on the other. Most famously, when the Northern Alliance, based in the Midwest, and the Southern Alliance, organized in Texas, met in St. Louis in 1889, they could not agree to merge because of their differences.[36] The Southern Alliance had secret rituals and would be more radical, more militant, more connected to the Knights of Labor, and more racist.[37] It banned Blacks, for example, and openly opposed national laws designed to protect the voting rights of southern Blacks, including the force bill of 1890, which was advocated by midwestern senators such as John Spooner of Wisconsin and relentlessly opposed by southerners in Congress.[38] The Northern Alliance was based in Chicago and was more loosely organized and nonsecret, found its "strength chiefly in the Middle West," was "older and milder," welcomed Blacks, and remained officially nonpartisan, though in reality it worked through the regionally dominant Republican Party.[39] Hovering over any negotiations between midwestern and southern farmers, of course, was "continuing sectional prejudice." The many Union Civil War veterans who tended to lead midwestern farm organizations were less than enthused about joining an entity that would be majority southern. One midwestern editor saw the Southern Alliance as too much of a "rebel yell."[40]

The regional differences could be seen in what the contrasting farm organizations advocated. Midwestern farmers were focused on the binder-twine trust because they grew wheat, which was bound by twine, whereas the southern group focused on the bagging or jute trust, since they grew cotton and stored it in bags. The Southern Alliance also pushed the "sub-treasury plan" for government ownership of warehouses and corresponding crop loans, which many midwestern farmers opposed. The regional alliances also fought over synthetic foods. Midwestern farmers, who often ran dairy operations and sold butter, despised oleomargarine, which southern farmers liked because it used cottonseed oil. Midwestern congressmen supported the regulation and taxation of oleomargarine; southerners in Congress "fought it bitterly as unconstitutional, as economic discrimination and as interference with cheap food for consumers and labor classes." Similarly, midwestern farm advocates strongly opposed "compound lard" because it undermined the market for hog lard, a common product of midwestern corn/hog farms. Midwestern farmers denounced "counterfeit lard," and Iowa congressman Edwin Conger, a Union war veteran representing the nation's leading hog state, became the champion of national legislation regulating and taxing compound lard. The result was bitter regional fights in Congress over the Conger lard bill.

Such fights only deepened regional divisions between a more-radical Southern Alliance and the midwestern organization, whose members were more prosperous, more conservative, and more willing to work within the existing political structure. The Midwest, once the "territorial heart of the Granger movement," was less supportive of the later Populist third-party movement because, as one historian noted, the "agrarians of this section wanted reform but not revolution." Milton George, leader of the Northern Alliance, would stick with the GOP during the crucial 1896 election, as would the core of the Midwest, and limit the "Bryan West to the hinterland beyond Iowa and Minnesota."[41]

Although the midwesterners were less radical than the southerners and more staid in their politics, it does not mean they failed to seek basic and meaningful reforms. In Iowa, for example, the Farmers Alliance success-fully banned price fixing, fought compound lard, reduced legal interest from 10 percent down to 8 percent, pushed for more experimental farming at Iowa State College, and outlawed free rail passes. In Nebraska, reformers would pass laws mandating the Australian ballot, providing for free school books, and regulating insurance companies. In Dakota Territory during the 1880s, farmers drew deeply on the republican traditions of the Midwest to forge a new constitution and two new states that embraced moderate reforms addressing the power of railroads.

The various midwestern state Granger laws ultimately inspired Congress to pass the Interstate Commerce Act of 1887. The first chair of the ICC was Thomas Cooley, a Michigan Supreme Court justice and founding faculty member of the University of Michigan Law School. In 1884, Cooley had retired from the law school and turned to the railroad issue full time, vowing to address the growth and abuse of monopoly power.[42] Pressures from midwestern farmers also led to the passage of a powerful federal law restricting trusts and controlling monopolies, which was pushed through by Senator John Sherman of Ohio, the brother of the triumphant Union general of the Civil War.[43] In support of the Sherman Antitrust Act, Senator Sherman said his countrymen should not be controlled by "a few men sitting at their council board in the city of New York" and saw a tight combination or monopoly as a "kingly prerogative, inconsistent with our form of government."[44] None of these actions were radical, but instead geared toward promoting existing republican institutions, constraining new forms of inflated economic power, and perpetuating small-town and agrarian life. It was all part of what Richard Hofstadter called the "genial reforms of Progressivism" or, more specifically, what Stanley Solvick once called the "mild progressivism" of the Midwest.[45]

The Interstate Commerce Act and the Sherman Antitrust Act are still recognized by the historically minded; smaller-scale but still important reforms were also enacted but seldom remembered today. Agrarian reformers remained attuned to the remoteness of some farming regions and the need for postal access, a matter particularly important to young people who left the farms in the Midwest where they grew up to move farther west. The Ohioan John McLean had done much to make the postal system much stronger.[46] In the later part of the nineteenth century, reformers often focused on rural free delivery of the mail.[47] RFD started with a $10,000 appropriation to launch the program advocated by Republican U.S. senator Philetus Sawyer of Oshkosh, Wisconsin.[48] Improved country mail service was often connected to the importance of improving rural roads so that mail could be delivered and farmers could market their products more efficiently.[49] Better roads and more mail also connected remote farms. The Grange opined, "Bad roads spell ISOLATION for the American farmer in giant letters which reach across the continent from ocean to ocean."[50]

Many midwestern GOPers and civic leaders also pushed hard for pensions for disabled Civil War veterans or the widows of Union soldiers killed in action.[51] The final drive for legislation took place in the wake of Shiloh and was led by Lincoln's commissioner of pensions (a newspaper editor from Ohio), his attorney general (from St. Louis), and his secretary of the interior (from Indiana).[52] Midwesterners also worked to end the long-running "spoils" system, the practice of political victors appointing their allies to the full list of government offices. Senator George H. Pendleton of Ohio pushed through the Pendleton Civil Service Act of 1883, outlawing mandatory campaign contributions by government workers and creating entrance exams for civil service jobs; midwesterners who opposed the legislation were largely defeated for reelection.[53] Passage of the legislation was due in no small part to the 1881 assassination of the popular midwestern president James Garfield, an Ohio Republican and Civil War veteran, by a disgruntled seeker of spoils.[54]

In the 1890s some agrarian activists decided to join the third-party Populists, but this movement was weak in the core of the Midwest and, instead, incremental agrarian reforms tended to be advanced through other channels. In keeping with the farm protest of recent years, the 1892 Omaha platform of the Populists written by Ignatius Donnelly bashed monopolies and the money power and did so in the language of Christian moralism.[55] That fall, the Populist nominee James Weaver of Iowa won five states, including Kansas and North Dakota, and the Populists won two Senate seats and eleven House seats. In 1896 at the Democratic convention in Chicago, party leaders nominated William Jennings Bryan of Nebraska and wisely adopted a silver plank to draw in Populist support. The Populist convention in St. Louis then endorsed Bryan because of the silver plank and thus, in Richard Hofstadter's estimation, "committed suicide."[56]

Populists lost their own identity and were further weakened by fusion with the Democrats, but they had never been strong in the central Midwest. Historians have noted populism's "failure to gain a following in the farmbelt states of the old Northwest that only ten or fifteen years before had been leading centers of disaffection."[57] There was more support for the Populists closer to the 100th meridian in the Great Plains borderlands, but the "situation was different in the States of the Old Northwest," which "had long since ceased to exhibit symptoms of rural unrest."[58] In 1896, Bryan of Nebraska won only the western and plains sections of the Midwest and lost Iowa,

Illinois, Wisconsin, Minnesota, Michigan, Indiana, Ohio, and even North Dakota, which all remained loyal to the traditional midwestern GOP and voted for William McKinley of Ohio. By way of the traditional party system, midwestern agrarians sought modest reforms such as encouraging farmer cooperatives, making marketing improvements, elevating the Department of Agriculture to a cabinet-level agency (in 1889), creating the Bureau of Markets within the USDA, training farmers to be better bookkeepers and to understand soils and nitrogen, and building a system of county agents and experiment stations to promote the use of the latest science and technology.[59] Even many populist ideas, which were sometimes thought radical, "proved in later years to be either harmless or useful."[60] The reform-minded Midwest and its agrarian culture would produce many young intellectuals and professors who shaped rural and farm policy during the early twentieth century.[61]

At one of the several conventions where agrarian protests and other reforms were discussed—this one in Cincinnati in 1891—Ignatius Donnelly regretted that all the reform ideas in the air did not make it into the platform being debated. He singled out women's suffrage in particular.[62] The only group in the Midwest larger than farmers seeking positive political reforms was women. During the several attempts to expand suffrage to include Blacks in previous decades, the cause of women's suffrage had been mentioned. Some cynical politicos had attempted to link Black and women's suffrage in order to undermine them both.[63] Despite these ploys and other attempts to exploit the lingering patterns of patriarchy and outright mockery (one Chicagoan told Jane Addams to visit the slum and induce a man "to sell you his pecker and balls" so she could be a man and have "the privilege of casting a vote"), by the end of the century midwestern women could lay claim to several social and political advances that outpaced other regions.[64] They often won these advances working through the most basic and fundamental institutions of midwestern life—Christianity and its various churches and the civic order of clubs and social groups. The network of women's civic and social clubs was dense and politically effective.[65] Perhaps no other group in the Midwest was able to use the region's Victorian middle-class culture of uplift and joining more effectively to advance their cause than women.

Most fundamental to the organizational power of midwestern women was the Christian church, which was often staffed and made operational by women in towns and surrounding farming regions. In the Episcopal church

in Northfield, Minnesota, for example, women were "active, central partici-
pants" and largely managed the church. The Ladies Social Circle, in particular, organized and ran the church (in a frontier reversal of gender norms,
men could join as honorary members of the Circle but could not vote, hold
office, or run meetings, and they had to pay double the dues). The women
of the church also raised the money necessary for the church to function,
and they controlled church spending.[66] A study of Lutheran churches in Ann
Arbor, Michigan, found that "those most involved in the churches were the
women."[67] Women active in Christian churches were also at the center of
social groups, temperance organizations, and suffrage drives. So too a deep
Christian "religious faith permeated the worldview of Populist women" and
the women in other farm groups.[68]

Beyond Christian churches and affiliated groups and auxiliaries, women
were also active in nondenominational civic organizations and clubs, which,
given the culture of the Midwest, were naturally focused on uplift and self-
improvement but were also often connected to broader reform efforts.[69] The
number of women's clubs that could be found throughout the towns and cities of the Midwest was "astounding."[70] In Jackson, Michigan, for example,
there were twenty active women's clubs.[71] In Red Oak, Iowa, the women's
Monday Club had seventy-five members from various religious denominations, including four women who were doctors, women who owned businesses, and the editor of one of the local newspapers.[72] In Decatur, Illinois,
the women's study club was highly active and made up, one member
recalled, "of women who would seek culture and be steadfast in the pursuit
of it. When once within the magic circle, they are assimilated and bound
together by friendship and loyalty." In Chicago, the Fortnightly Club's purpose was "to enlarge the mental horizon as well as the knowledge of our
members."[73] In Wyoming, Illinois, some women worked with their Mason
husbands to form the Order of the Eastern Star to promote "greater sociability."[74] The Clio Club of Hastings, Minnesota, studied and wrote papers about
ancient Greek history in keeping with the classical interests of the era. The
Carpe Diem Club of Findlay, Ohio, was more modern, focusing its studies
on France and the court of Louis XIV.

Other groups included the Ladies' Education Association of Jacksonville, Illinois, the Ladies Library Association of Kalamazoo, Michigan,
and the Minerva Club of New Harmony, Indiana.[75] In Osage, Iowa, women

organized such groups as the Women's Relief Corps (a GAR auxiliary), the Ladies of the Maccabees, and the Rebekahs (an auxiliary to the Masonic offshoot the Ancient Order of the Eastern Star).[76] Osage's most prestigious women's groups were the Shakespearean Women's Club (which considered but then rejected the admission of men) and the Woman's Christian Temperance Union, along with several other "reading circles."[77] In Indianola, Iowa, women could choose from the Indianola Business and Professional Women's Club, the Shakespeare Club, the Monday Club, the Garden Club, the Eastern Star, and many church aid societies.[78] In Muncie, Indiana, women were particularly active in the Woman's Club and, more generally, were known to be active readers and joiners. Other options for Muncie women included the Pegasus Poetry Club, a branch of the National League of American Penwomen, and the Muncie Art Students' League.[79] The latter organization highlights the importance of art to midwestern women and the emergence of local artist guilds, sketch clubs, and art expositions.[80] Many women's clubs promoted art, both its creative production and the collection of the work of regional artists.[81]

Although women's clubs were often town-oriented, women were also involved in rural and farmer organizations.[82] To recruit women, the Grange had given the pagan goddesses Demeter, Pomona, Ceres, and others prominent places in their rituals.[83] The idea caught on. Farm women near Grimes, Iowa, for example, formed the Daughters of Ceres in 1898.[84] Luna Kellie of Nebraska was an elected state officer of the Nebraska Alliance and embraced the agrarian mission and the causes of "religion and morality, civic duty, education, and women's equality."[85] Some midwestern women's clubs focused on lectures and developing speaking skills. The prominent speaker Lucia Griffin emerged from Knoxville, Iowa, for example, where she learned the "Protestant ethic of thrift, piety and hard work" from her family and used it to become a prominent orator.[86] Above the local level were state federations that brought women's clubs together for conventions and meetings, including for African American women.[87] In 1873 the Association for the Advancement of Women was formed, and in 1877 it held a regional conference in Cleveland, which a thousand women attended (there were no AAW chapters in the South until 1879).[88]

Many midwestern club women focused on reading and sharing books and the affairs of the local library. One wag captured it this way: "Iowa! I have always heard that that is where the women read next year's books though they may wear last year's hats."[89] Two out of every three library patrons in Osage, Iowa, were women, and 69 percent of the books were checked out by women or girls. The "typical" Osage Public Library user "was a young, middle-class woman who attended one of the British-origin Protestant churches."[90] Most of the book borrowers at the Muncie library were also women, especially white-collar women who "consumed in large quantities the romantic, sentimental, and domestic fiction that circulated widely in the late Victorian era" and included authors such as Booth Tarkington and Louisa May Alcott. Muncie women had a heavy preference for fiction and stories, but there was also a "steady, if comparatively modest demand for classics," prominent American writers like William Dean Howells and Mark Twain, and social and political books.[91]

Women certainly had many female writers to read. Many of them read the Bronte sisters, Louisa May Alcott, and Harriet Beecher Stowe. Women's literature was not hard to find given that in 1871 "women were writing almost three-fourths of all novels published."[92] One particularly popular kind of book was Martha Finley's Elsie Dinsmore series.[93] Finley grew up in Ohio and lived in South Bend, Indiana, and her religiously themed novels "were well represented in the corpus of books read by young girls in the turn-of-the-century Midwest." Girls were particularly drawn to Louisa May Alcott, who put women at the center of her stories and who also supported women's rights and suffrage, themes also at work in her fiction. Women's influence over book reading and literary consumption was also linked to their role in library affairs. When the Board of Library Trustees was set up in Osage, Iowa, in 1895 to govern the library, for example, it numbered four women and five men. Women often used their influence to uphold the social codes of the Midwest; they had great influence over which books a library carried and often directed readers to "fiction in which Christian moralism took center stage."[94] Women were part of a social "civilizing function" and hewed to a "genteel standard." [95] At the time, there was a growing concern about mass culture and, in particular, salacious books often directed at women.[96] Censorship was not common, however, and most libraries did stock the "immoral" books to meet demand for them.[97] People outside the dominant Protestant middle class also frequently used midwestern libraries.[98]

Women's role in midwestern book culture was fostered by their educational attainments, which were many. Unlike some cultures, even to this day, young girls in the Midwest were highly educated. Early elementary education for girls and their coeducation with boys "established a foundation for the progressive development of equality," noted one historian.[99] The Nebraska education superintendent argued that the ubiquitous and coeducational midwestern schools were "free from the prejudices which grow up amid old associations, that are peculiar to long settled and unchanging communities."[100] The importance of educating girls equally with boys and to educate them together was never contested.[101] It was in the Midwest that New England ideals "and the inclusion of women within those ideals after the American Revolution took root to form a national system of schooling that was open to girls and boys alike."[102] These young women often performed very well. Many more girls graduated from Muncie High School, for example, than did boys.[103]

Private academies were also open to midwestern girls. These included the Steubenville Female Seminary, the Oxford Female Academy, and the Lake Erie Female Seminary in Ohio and the Rockford Female Academy in Illinois (attended by Jane Addams) along with another in the always-intellectual Jacksonville, Illinois. The young women at Oxford Female Academy were assigned such books as Goldsmith's *History of Greece and Rome,* Whelpley's *Compendium of Ancient and Modern History,* Blair's *Lectures on Rhetoric,* Colburn's *Mental Arithmetic,* Brun's *Geography,* Davies's *Algebra,* and Goodrich's *History of the United States.* Several female academies flourished in Cincinnati, and in April 1830 the *Western Monthly Review* reported that eleven gold medals were awarded at the commencement ceremonies of Cincinnati Female College for proficiency in Latin, Greek, French, mathematics, music, and painting.[104] In 1841 the Milwaukee Female Academy was created (it taught Latin and Greek), and in 1851 Lucy Parsons launched the Milwaukee Normal Institute and High School (which became Milwaukee Female College).[105] Howe's Academy in Iowa was "aggressively co-educational" and busy at "turning out male and female teachers for the common schools of southeast Iowa."[106]

As the Howe's emphasis indicates, many young women went on to become teachers, who became the backbone of intellectual growth in the Midwest.[107] As many as 35 percent of employed women in Iowa, Nebraska, and Kansas in the 1880s worked as teachers. These teachers "brought to the schoolhouses the moral, ethical life-styles demanded by their communities and espoused in the *McGuffey's Readers*" and were "inspired by an idealistic belief in universal public education as the means of improvement for children, for themselves, and for the community at large."[108] The Ladies Society for the Promotion of Education in the West also sought to send in "competent female teachers, of unquestionable piety" to teach in the Midwest.[109]

The education of midwestern girls did not end with high school. Women's club work in Jacksonville, Illinois, for example, included the formation of the Ladies' Association for Educating Females, which, as part of its mission, paid for girls to go to Illinois College.[110] Many private seminaries in the Midwest would also grow into colleges, organized by Christian denominations, which were coeducational and strongly emphasized science, a practical curriculum, and the training of teachers for the thousands of midwestern schools.[111] In 1837, Oberlin in Ohio became the first college in the country to enroll women (the college trustees reported that coeducation cultivates "mind and manners, promotes real virtue, and corrects frivolities, irregularities, and follies common to youth").[112] By 1838 a quarter of Oberlin's students were female (at the same time 5–7 percent of the student body was African American). Oberlin's coeducational practices were first seen as "radical," but "within a decade the idea was spreading in the Midwest."[113] At Antioch College in Ohio in the 1850s, Horace Mann and others pushed to "admit women and Negroes on terms of equality with white men students." Mann announced that Antioch would recognize the "claims of the female sex to equal opportunities of education with the male" and this would "tend indirectly to elevate the character of women."[114]

All the denominational colleges in Michigan were open to women and were coeducational.[115] In 1851/52, for example, Hillsdale College granted degrees to eight women.[116] The Christian colleges in the Midwest that embraced coeducation in the 1840s and 1850s included Antioch, Central College, Downer, Hillsdale, Hiram, Heidelberg, Eureka, Earlham, Illinois Institute (later Wheaton), Iowa College, Iowa Wesleyan, Lincoln, Lombard, Muskingum, Otterbein, Urbana, Baldwin, Lawrence, Mt. Union, Adrian, Lawrence, Franklin, Plainsfield (later North Central), Ripon, Upper Iowa, and Western College (later Leander Clark College, then absorbed into Coe College).[117] The original University of Chicago was coeducational at its creation in 1873, as was its later reincarnation.[118] One study found that before the Civil War most of the coeducational colleges in the country were in the

Midwest (there was only one in New England, and "southerners had a preference for single-sex education").[119] Coeducation brought with it women's activities, clubs, sports, and other events. At Monmouth College in Illinois, for example, women's literary and oratory clubs were popular. In 1857, eighteen Monmouth women founded the Amateurs des Belles Lettres (ABL) with the motto *Droit et Avant* ("Right and Forward").[120] Women's oratory topics included "Edinburgh after Flodden" (about the great battle of 1513), "Labor," and "Has Our Nation Been Surrounded with Circumstances Favorable to the Growth of Literature, as Other Nations?"[121]

Collegiate coeducation, concluded the historian of higher education Kenneth Wheeler, "was a product of the Old Northwest," where it "flourished."[122] It thrived because coeducation fit the culture of the Midwest much better than it did other regions, where it lagged behind. Private Christian coeducational colleges in the Midwest embraced the idea of "Real Women," who were "full-blooded, capable, practical, and rational" and rejected the dainty notions of eastern drawing room women.[123] The many Christian denominations in the Midwest also "tended to be less conservative than those in the East" and more open to pragmatic and reform-oriented practices such as coeducation.[124] The greater number of colleges in the Midwest, the diversity of church-affiliated colleges, the lack of concern about the gaze of eastern traditionalists, the openness fostered by the "rural heterogeneity" of the Midwest, and a focus on practically drawing together all human talent fostered midwestern coeducation.[125] Speaking to the issue of pragmatism and empirical results, the president of Oberlin and, later, Adrian College in Michigan found that twice as many men failed college courses as women. President James Angell of the University of Michigan concluded that "women are on the average the better students."[126] Midwestern college leaders also recognized that it was more practical to have one set of buildings for all their students instead of expensively maintaining two, one for women and one for men.[127]

These decisions made the Midwest decidedly different from the South and the Northeast. Coeducational options were not available in New England and the South, "where women attended single-sex colleges, most of which taught a curriculum centered upon the ornamental or genteel."[128] "Southern colleges and universities were among the most vehement opponents of coeducation" well into the twentieth century.[129] The strong "chivalric ideal" at work in the South meant an "exaggerated deference for [women's] delicacy and innocence," and as a result the "women's rights movement which gained attention in the North in the 1850s found no echo in the South."[130] College education for women in the Midwest also "took a form quite different from what was happening in the East," where women's higher education followed a "separatist" model. The creation of Vassar (1861), Wellesley (1875), and Smith (1875), for example, meant separate institutions for women and not inclusion in the broader system of collegiate education. But these northeastern women's colleges were "anomalies," notes Gail Griffin, and not part of a broader network of colleges anything close to that built up in the Midwest. By the end of the Civil War era, Griffin explains, the "higher education of women had made little progress except in the Middle West."[131] Midwestern colleges were contrasted with "eastern institutions [known] for their conservative and more rigid restrictions on social interactions." Even land grant institutions in the South and East strongly resisted coeducation.[132] The historian Doris Malkmus, who studied the rapid adoption of coeducation in Iowa and highlights the phenomenon as a midwestern "innovation," also explains that "coeducation spread *from* the colleges of Iowa and the Midwest across the nation in the years after the Civil War."[133]

The coeducation ideal that found a home at midwestern private colleges was quickly embraced by midwestern state colleges. The University of Iowa became the first coeducational state university in the country. In 1856, Iowa's first class of students numbered eighty-three men and forty-one women, and many of these students became teachers (in 1861, debating societies and literary and science clubs for women were created).[134] In 1863 the University of Wisconsin admitted its first female student, and by the end of that war-burdened year the number of women enrolled at the college (180) was nearly equal to the number of men (181).[135] By 1869, six women had earned their bachelor's degree from Wisconsin.[136] In 1837, Michigan had made plans for a "female department" in its university's charter, but the legislature did not appropriate the necessary funds.[137] Women were finally admitted into the University of Michigan in 1870 when the board of regents adopted a new policy. That fall thirty-four women entered the university (eleven entered the literary department, three the pharmacy department, eighteen the medical department, and two the law department).[138]

In ascending order, the midwestern state universities that led the way for the entire country to coeducation were first Iowa then Wisconsin, Kansas,

Indiana, Minnesota, Missouri, and Michigan (California came next and was the "only one beyond the boundaries of the Midwest" in the first group of coeducational colleges).[139] Sarah Parke Morrison, after teaching at Glendale Female College and Western Female Seminary, both in Ohio, became the first female student at Indiana University (IU) in 1867.[140] The *Evansville Indiana* newspaper reported: "Ladies are admitted to College classes on the same terms as males" (and further noted that "tuition is free for all").[141] After that first lonely fall semester as the only female student at Indiana, Morrison was joined by a dozen more women in the spring, and by 1874 she had been named an adjunct professor of English Literature at IU and later became a popular lecturer, temperance advocate, and poet. In an indication of the new avenues available to Morrison, women at IU could join the Hesperian Literary Society, the Edgeworthalean Society, and the Independent Society.[142]

In Iowa it was college women who formed the first literary societies.[143] At what would become the University of Iowa and the University of Northern Iowa, women formed the Erodelphian Literary Society, the Hesperian Literary Society, the Aonian Literary Society, the Athena Society, the Margaret Fuller Ossoli Society, the Shakespearean Circle, the Homerian Society, and the Chrestomathian Literary Society. In a nod to midwestern regional writers, women at the University of Iowa also formed the Hamlin Garland and Octave Thanet societies. In Nebraska, the Palladian Society held mixed-gender debates over resolutions such as "The liquor trade should be abolished" (the woman in this debate was also an editor on the *Hesperian,* the Palladian's literary journal). At Wisconsin, one literary society did not invite women to participate but another "was distinguished for courtesy in inviting the young women to the meetings."[144]

Women's activities at midwestern colleges extended to sports. One of the earliest programs of physical education for college women began in 1879 at the University of Nebraska when a professor of military science began giving young women close-order drill.[145] Soon followed instruction for Nebraska women in calisthenics, gymnastics, fencing, basketball, tennis, and hockey, much of it in a gymnasium named for General Grant.[146] Nebraska produced the scholar-athlete Louise Pound, who mastered tennis (winning several women's championships and nearly winning the men's tournaments too) and golf (she was the Nebraska state champion); she also earned a Ph.D. in literature from the University of Heidelberg in Germany and then became a professor at Nebraska, teaching Old English, Middle English, and literature and promoting the study of American folklore (publishing such books as *Nebraska Folklore*) and embracing a "thoroughgoing regional optimism."[147] In 1896, when basketball was first introduced to the Nebraska gymnasium, Pound became (naturally) a master at the sport, leading her team to victory over the University of Minnesota in front of five thousand fans.[148] As the sport of basketball took off in the 1890s in Wisconsin, college women's teams were often organized before men's.[149]

Coeducation spoke to midwestern pragmatism and regional uniqueness. "Midwestern sex roles were flexible," notes the historian Kristin Mapel Bloomberg, and midwestern agrarian life meant equal participation in many forms of work and community life.[150] Children in the frontier Midwest "freed themselves from many of the gender constraints of eastern society."[151] The mixed peoples of the Midwest, including foreign immigrants, "were less concerned with middle-class Yankee ideals of sex separation."[152] James Angell, president of the University of Michigan, dismissed the Northeast's paltry efforts at coeducation and saw midwestern advances as products of the "true spirit of robust frontier democracy."[153] The historian Julie Roy Jeffrey found the "evidence connecting coeducation to the freedom of the West" strong.[154] There were simply "fewer entrenched traditions and established bastions of power" to block the adoption of coeducation in the Midwest, which, at the "heart of the continent," became the "real heart of the revolution" in coeducation.[155] "Coeducation," one historian noted, "was almost unknown in the east."[156] The "older and established all-male institutions" of the East refused to admit women and, when they were later forced to, "did so with resentment and prejudice against new female students."[157]

Bloomberg argues that "coeducation was both a midwestern innovation and an authentic expression of midwestern values."[158] Midwestern colleges were the first in the world to practice coeducation.[159] By the time of the Civil War, women attending college was not a practice "except in the Middle West."[160] Coeducation, Bloomberg concludes, was a "hallmark of Midwestern values that rejected constraining Eastern cultural roles and promoted a democratic form of egalitarianism."[161] This included a greater emphasis on pragmatism and instruction in practical skills.[162] Once gains were made, they were not given back. When a new Wisconsin president from the East tried to force women into a separate college or school (similar to the structure at Harvard and Columbia), it went very poorly and was reversed.[163] What remained starkly true was the regional nature of collegiate coeducation. In 1873, of the 8,141 women who attended coeducational colleges or universities, 70 percent were in the Midwest and only 1 percent were in New England or the Mid-Atlantic states.[164] By the end of the nineteenth century, when only 28 percent of northeastern colleges were coeducational, nearly 90 percent of midwestern colleges were.[165]

The educational advances of midwestern women speak to broader advances in the region and the erosion of the line that separated the spheres of men and women. The newspaper editor Jane Swisshelm, for example, who was based in St. Cloud, Minnesota, was publicly active and worked and wrote to advance abolition and women's suffrage. She personifies the "blurring of gender distinctions" on the midwestern frontier and shows that "gender roles were less rigid" there.[166] So too did Rosa Hudspeth, who moved from Iowa to Nebraska to become a newspaper editor and novelist.[167] So too does the story of Elizabeth Scott, from Morton, Illinois, and Alice Fish, of Colfax, Iowa, who settled on the Nebraska frontier. Together they formed a farming and ranching partnership near Brewster, Nebraska, enjoying much freedom and becoming enmeshed in midwestern culture by avidly supporting Chautauqua, their Congregational church, and the local chapter of the Homes for the Friendless (a charity for unwed mothers).[168] This world of active women included not uncommon figures such as Esther Griffin White, who wore short skirts, joined the National Association for the Advancement of Colored People, played golf, and was a newspaperwoman (the Hoosier writer Meredith Nicholson counseled her to "tame the young mustang of your style").[169] Midwestern women would put their progress and demands on display at major events such as the Chicago World's Fair, where, for example, Sarah Ann Hackett Stevenson, a physician and president of the Chicago Woman's Club, called for female doctors to be integrated more fully into the general world of medicine.[170] These and other examples underscore how women openly questioned gender assumptions and spoke out for equal rights.[171]

This extended to rural life. The spheres of women and men on midwestern farms, the most common form of life in the region, were hardly separate. Women were heavily involved in all aspects of the farming operation.[172] Linked to the world of farms and property were changes in the fundamental law of the region, benefiting women. The Northwest Ordinance, for example, had abolished primogeniture, which was common in England and the colonies. As a result, an intestate death would lead to the equal distribution of a person's property, including to daughters, instead of solely to the eldest son.[173] Wisconsin, Kansas, and other states also passed laws ensuring that women could own property and that it would not become the husband's upon marriage.[174] One Indianapolis court watcher who saw many divorces commented on the "recently acquired freedom and independence of the new woman" (he suggested more midwestern thrift as a method to avoid divorces, which he saw as largely disputes over money).[175] A study of courts in Illinois found that wives were routinely successful when they sought a divorce.[176] These instances of women's agency underscored the erosion of patriarchy and other traditional European hierarchies on the frontier. In frontier Indiana, a woman asked who her master was responded, "In this country there is no mistresses nor masters; I guess I am a woman citizen."[177]

Midwestern women, often armed with college degrees, organized through clubs, and bolstered by the more open culture of the region, sought a wide variety of reforms. Early on this included fighting for the anti-slavery cause, often in conjunction with men.[178] When Iowa abolitionists formed their anti-slavery group in 1843, for example, participation in its operations was open to women.[179] When the war came, women were also active. Pro-Union women in Kansas actively resisted southern aggression and fought off border ruffians; the "tales of the Kansas civil war are replete with instances of women's heroism." When one rebel tried to inspect a woman's home in Kansas, she threw hot water in his face: "I have respect for the United States troops. You can search the house, but, as for this puke of a Missourian he shall not come in!"[180] Midwestern women were also heavily involved in civic clubs designed to support the Union cause and in institutions such as the Sanitary Commission, which aided veterans, widows, and orphans.[181] Annie Wittenmyer of Iowa, for example, embraced midwestern pragmatism and usefulness by helping to found the Keokuk Ladies Aid Society and the Iowa Orphan's Home and by serving as the Iowa state sanitary agent during the war.[182] She was on the march to Vicksburg during the war, setting up hospital kitchens, and with Sherman as he marched to the sea, and she earned the support of General Grant and others.[183]

The reform work of women and their clubs went far beyond the cause of abolition and the Union. One common cause was the building of community libraries.[184] The Iowa club women who worked on libraries, for example, had much success. The number of free libraries in the state jumped from four in 1895 to ninety-six by 1907. Women's clubs in midwestern towns pushed many other advances such as building parks and playgrounds, planting shade trees, policing weeds, and promoting nature areas and gardens; they led anti-smoking and anti-spitting campaigns and pushed broader social reforms such as abolishing child labor and adopting female suffrage. Campaigns under the banner of "Village Improvement" led to anti-litter efforts, beautification work, and the planting of much greenery.[185] The Ladies Association for Educating Females in Jacksonville, Illinois, focused its work on schooling for indigent girls and, because of their work, a "vast indirect influence [was] exerted in the educational life not only of Illinois but throughout the Middle West."[186] The Minneapolis Woman's Club, infused with "family ideals and the values of the Victorian middle-class home," stressed self-improvement, civic betterment, and projects such as the preservation of native wild flowers, school cleaning, and urban beautification. The longtime president of the MWC, Alice Ames Winter, preached a "zeal for betterment" as the "essence" of the organization, the "yeast that sets pulses to throbbing and happiness harnessing itself to good."[187] Women's organizations in Chicago advocated better garbage collection, fire prevention, improvements to the lake front, and improved housing.[188] The women's clubs of Battle Creek, Michigan, raised money to release squirrels into the city's parks. The Civic Improvement Society of Monroe, Michigan, was led by women and focused on beautifying streets and parks, preserving a cemetery, and improving sanitation.[189] Many of these Monroe women had earlier been involved in community clubs, church guilds, music societies, the Shakespeare Society, and the Friends in Council.[190] A prominent women's club in Quincy, Illinois, organized for "educational purposes," met to discuss William Lecky's *History of the Rise and Influence of the Spirit of Rationalism in Europe* (1865).[191] The Daughters of the American Revolution in Iowa adjusted to their regional circumstances and, instead of protecting Revolutionary War battle sites like their northeastern colleagues, focused on local causes.[192] The Iowa DAR, which alternated with the Ohio DAR as the largest state DAR group in the Midwest, was a "progressive organization" that focused on organizing settlement houses, ending child labor, reducing infant mortality, and teaching immigrants English and American history.[193]

The largest-scale and most intense social campaign of organized women in the Midwest was against alcohol. In one typical peroration, a Christian woman writing in the *Leavenworth Daily Commercial* in Kansas in March 1874 denounced men for failing to "cure the licentiousness of the age—to extirpate the curse of intemperance which prevails over the length and breadth of the land. I am ready, as the Israelites were, to call on the Lord and on all the Deborahs, Jaels and Judiths in the land, to march forth to battle, and to destroy root and branch this offspring of hell, this child of perdition. Let every woman take off a head, as Judith smote the head of Holofoornes. Let the women fight until there shall be nothing of old king alcohol but empty barrels, jugs and demijohns—a poor old dead carcass."[194]

As this call to arms indicates, the anti-alcohol protests of praying and singing women constituted an "assertion of religious authority," which was the foundation of prohibition drives. Although women protesters mostly "confined themselves to praying, singing, preaching, and signing petitions," two women in Leavenworth smashed up a saloon with axes and shouted, "[This is] how my husband acts when he comes home drunk from your whiskey!" Another Leavenworth woman denounced the weak men who could not avoid those "low places whose atmosphere reeks with liquor fumes, obscenity and blasphemy." Women in Fort Scott, Kansas, brought children to saloons to have the free lunch offered to attract customers in order to show that their "fathers' drinking literally took food out of the mouths of their children."[195] In Plano, Illinois, temperance women assaulted saloons with hatchets, hammers, and "various other weapons of destruction," and a "general smash of barrels, decanters, and bottles ensued" (the proprietors were relieved that protesters spared the billiard tables during the "fever heat").[196] In a more sedate but far more common approach, women in Muskegon, Michigan, donned white ribbons of temperance and pledged not to tempt men by serving them wine, cider, or other strong drink and declared their opposition to marrying men opposed to temperance.[197]

These prohibition protests in Kansas, Illinois, and Michigan were not unique. During the winter and spring of 1873 and 1874, women around the Midwest formed a crusade that organized marches on saloons, where they prayed for their closure. This mass women's march, totaling more than fifty-six thousand activists, led to protests at thousands of saloons, a "massive women's grassroots campaign" that was "concentrated in Ohio, Michigan,

Indiana, and Illinois."[198] These four midwestern states saw two-thirds of the anti-alcohol crusades of this era and supplied three-fourths of the crusaders.[199] This mass protest led to the creation of the Woman's Christian Temperance Union in Hillsboro, Ohio, in 1874, and soon its famous president, Francis Willard of Wisconsin (who grew up on a farm near Janesville), was scorching the liquor trade around the region with fiery Christian denunciations.[200] Willard, who left her job as dean of women at Northwestern University, promised a "war to the knight and the knife to the hilt."[201] The formation of the WCTU in Ohio corresponded with the "Ohio Movement" for prohibition, which broke out in southwestern Ohio and became known as the "Women's Whiskey War." It "sought by religious and moral fervor not only to destroy the drink demon and close the saloon but to induce the saloon keeper to sign the pledge and become converted."[202] In 1875, Annie Wittenmyer of Iowa, the first president of the WCTU, and her then assistant Willard worked with Senator Oliver Morton of Indiana to wheel thousands of temperance petitions onto the U.S. Senate floor tied up with blue ribbons.[203]

As the leadership of Wittenmyer, Willard, and Morton indicates, prohibition efforts became "particularly middle western," and the Midwest became the "center of temperance propaganda"; the movement in the Midwest became "much more important than any other section of the country."[204] The WCTU saw Chicago as the "temperance mecca of the continent."[205] From the headquarters in Evanston, Illinois, Willard and the WCTU, in midwestern pragmatic fashion and in keeping with the embrace of various reforms of this era, advocated a "Do Everything" strategy, stressing the need to allow local leaders to pursue all sorts of plans that worked in their area.[206] The WCTU's motto was "For God, and home, and everyland."[207] This air of social reform and Christian temperance would also cause the Congregational minister Howard Russell to launch the Anti-Saloon League in Ohio in 1895.[208]

The prohibition efforts of midwestern women further broadened the scope of their social and political activities. These women reformers "fully accepted the assumptions promoted by nineteenth-century roles that assigned virtue, nurture, and idealism to respectable Anglo-Protestant women," but they "rejected conventional divisions drawn between a feminine private sphere and a masculine public sphere that confined women's moral authority and power to the home." Women prohibitionists "crossed the lines drawn between public and private, inserted religious values into public political

debates, and promoted a larger role for women in politics and government."
In a sign of the direction of these organized efforts, when women in Kansas
formed a prohibition party the first platform plank they adopted was not temperance but women's suffrage (they also nominated a woman to run for state
superintendent of public instruction).[209]

Progress on political reform soon followed. Kansas prohibitionists won a
victory in 1880 when voters approved a ban on alcohol sales (not repealed
until 1948) and thus began a half-century of political battles within midwestern states over the use of alcohol—as well as social battles between
prohibitionists and bootleggers running Cherokee Red whiskey in Kansas
and Templeton rye in Iowa and sundry other local concoctions brewed up
around the region.[210] Kansas women also won the right to vote and run in
city elections in 1887 (and would win full suffrage in 1912).[211] As the Kansas suffrage victory indicates, midwestern temperance campaigns opened
the political world to women and would lead them to political equality by
way of their activism, which included basic civic advances such as making
women frequent and sought-after fixtures of the active lecture circuit.[212]

Although women would ultimately win full suffrage rights, there were several mostly forgotten steps along the way in which the Midwest led the nation
in the fight for women's political power and rights. In 1854, for example,
a woman was elected constable of Perry County, Illinois. In Missouri, the
law school at Washington University along with "other Midwestern schools
were the first to accept and graduate female students."[213] WU's first woman
law student, Lemma Barkeloo, was first refused admission by Harvard and
Columbia before applying to WU. Afterward she elected to stay in the Midwest because, she said, the people of the region "were generous and liberal in
their sentiments and she would be better sustained here than in the East." In
1870, Ada Miser Kepley became the nation's first female law school graduate when she completed her studies at the old University of Chicago, and
another UC student, Sarah Kilgore Wertman, transferred to the University of
Michigan and graduated from its law school in 1871.[214] In 1869 in Iowa, Belle
Mansfield became the first woman in the country officially admitted to a state
bar (although at least one other woman was already unofficially practicing
law in Iowa). This precedent caused seven women to apply to the bars of Iowa
and Illinois that year.[215] By contrast, women were not allowed into Columbia
University law school until 1929 and not into Harvard until 1950.[216]

During this same era, several Iowa women held the position of notary public, once a prominent official position in legal transactions, and other lower-level public offices, and this trend caught on throughout the Midwest. In Illinois in 1874, Myra Bradwell successfully fought for the right to be a notary public and a lawyer; the "same advances took decades to achieve in most other jurisdictions."[217] That same year the supreme court of Ohio ruled that women could serve as probate clerks and administer legal oaths.[218] Nellie G. Robinson of Ohio, who graduated from Cincinnati Law School in 1893 and became the first woman admitted to practice in Cincinnati's federal courts, successfully fought the battle over notary publics in that state.[219] Other women public officeholders followed. From the beginning of statehood in 1861 in Kansas, women had voted in school district elections.[220] In 1872, Ellen Webster was elected superintendent of schools in Harvey County, Kansas; four other Kansas women won similar county offices about the same time, and others won election as registers of deeds or were appointed notary publics.[221] In 1875, Elizabeth Cook was elected the county superintendent of schools in Warren County, Iowa.[222] That same year, Minnesota passed a law granting women the right to vote in school elections and to serve on school boards.[223] In 1887, in Argonia, Kansas, Susannah Medora Salter, a twenty-seven-year-old Ohio native and Kansas State graduate, became the first woman mayor in the country.[224] In Cottonwood, Kansas, voters chose a female mayor along with electing an entirely female city council. By 1900, more Kansas women had been elected to offices than in any other state. By 1912, seventy-five Kansas women had been elected to county offices other than school superintendent, and they were all chosen by an all-male electorate.[225]

In addition to the legal profession and public offices, women advanced in the field of medicine. The University of Michigan, for example, admitted women to its medical school during the 1870s; Harvard rejected such a move at the time. In Ohio, the number of women doctors jumped sharply from forty-two in 1870 to 451 by 1900.[226]

All of these advances would finally lead to women's suffrage, a cause greatly advanced by women who were products of midwestern coeducation and veterans of temperance campaigns. Dr. Anna Howard Shaw, for example, the president of the National Woman Suffrage Association, was a graduate of Albion College in Michigan. Her "sister in arms," Carrie Chapman Catt, born in Wisconsin, was an 1877 graduate of Iowa State College. The active suffragist Julia Nelson of Red Wing, Minnesota, was a graduate of Hamline University in St. Paul.[227] Many women advocating suffrage argued from a defense-of-the-home standpoint and "claimed that the ballot in the hands of women would defend families from corrupt and immoral forces" such as liquor. Women's commitment to protecting domestic life would mean their votes would be used to "uplift their homes, families, and communities."

When women finally prevailed, they did so by emphasizing their involvement in and defense of the civic order of the Midwest. They argued that their "stellar records of public service positioned them to fulfill the obligations of citizenship."[228] Early victories came when women were allowed to vote in school board elections in Kansas (1859), Michigan (1875), Illinois (1891), and Ohio (1894). In 1879, Dakota Territory made it legal for women to vote at school district meetings and then voted to allow them to serve as county superintendents of schools.[229] In 1885, Senator Thomas W. Palmer of Michigan, a "dyed-in-the-wool Republican" from the beginning of the GOP in 1854, gave the first major speech in favor of women's suffrage in the U.S. Senate.[230] In 1887 the governor of Kansas signed the Municipal Suffrage Law, giving women the right to vote in local government elections (which, in an era of local option votes on prohibition, meant a great deal). Michigan, Minnesota, Iowa, South Dakota, and Illinois granted women suffrage in school votes and municipal races, and Illinois and Minnesota would grant presidential suffrage before the Nineteenth Amendment passed.[231] Voters in South Dakota and Michigan passed women's suffrage measures in 1918, and the legislatures of Minnesota, North Dakota, Iowa, Indiana, Wisconsin, and Ohio passed presidential suffrage during their 1919 sessions (Nebraska did so in 1917).[232]

The historian Sara Egge explains that "no other region had this level of legislative activity in favor of the cause." When Congress passed the Nineteenth Amendment, half of the first fifteen states to ratify the amendment, often at great expense, were midwestern. The "civic responsibility argument set midwestern suffragists apart from their counterparts in other regions," and this argument fit with the mood of "patriotic service to community and country" that intensified during World War I. The Midwest "became the most pro-suffrage region" as the dispatch of troops to Europe approached. It was impressive, Egge emphasizes, "how rapidly and enthusiastically Midwesterners came to favor woman suffrage."[233] The South, by way of contrast, lagged considerably behind on women's suffrage rights. Whereas the WCTU in the Midwest was highly active in advocating women's suffrage, the WCTU in southern states, the historian Charles Postel has noted, "never came around to endorsing women's right to vote."[234]

The reforms pursued by midwestern women were often supported by a growing number of prominent reform mayors, some of whom became governors.[235] These included figures such as Hazen "Potato Patch" Pingree of Detroit, Samuel "Golden Rule" Jones and Brand Whitlock of Toledo, and Tom Johnson of Cleveland.[236] Pingree was a Union veteran who escaped from Andersonville prison, witnessed Lee's surrender at Appomattox, and then became a leather cutter and successful shoemaker in Detroit.[237] He became an active Republican and joined the right clubs, including the Michigan Club, which supported his run for mayor in 1889 against the corrupt Democratic machine in the city.[238] Pingree won 13,954–11,616 by promising clean government, efficiency, an improved sewer system, new parks, better streetcars, and the paving of streets; he would win three more mayoral terms before successfully running for governor.[239] The Black Ohio poet Paul Laurence Dunbar wrote a poem for Pingree:

Who takes out pavements rough and old
And makes them worthy to behold.
What patchers used to get from you
You pay to have your streets made new
For Pingree's at the city's head
We'll vote for him and vote for bread.[240]

Under Pingree's "potato patch plan," Detroit residents could grow vegetables on unused city property.[241]

Like Pingree in Detroit, the four-term mayor of Cleveland, Tom Johnson, was also an active reformer and was especially focused on improving street railway service.[242] Lincoln Steffens would call Johnson the "best mayor of the best governed city in America."[243] In Toledo, Mayor Jones was elected as a Republican reformer in 1897, and he focused on improving city parks, opening free kindergartens, and other reforms. He also instituted an eight-hour day for city workers (he was nicknamed "Golden Rule" because at his business he promised to pay workers a fair wage if they followed the Golden

Rule).[244] After Jones, Toledo elected Brand Whitlock, an Ohio preacher's son who was elected mayor four times and was also a novelist, lawyer, and journalist.[245] Some reformers also advocated changes in urban governance to lessen the power of political machines. Reformers in Iowa, for example, advanced the "Des Moines Plan" to adopt a commission form of city government, and it was copied in many other cities in the region.[246]

Some active reformers from this era went on to be elected governor.[247] In Illinois, John Peter Altgeld, who grew up on an Ohio farm and served in the Union Army, became a teacher and lawyer and a member of the Grange. After becoming active in reform circles in Chicago he rose through the political ranks and was elected governor in 1892. He promoted various reforms such as a civil service system, factory inspections, the adoption of anti-trust laws, and parole and probation for prisoners, and he protected workers who went out on strike.[248] Altgeld appointed the famed Florence Kelley, a veteran of Jane Addams's Hull House, as state factory inspector.[249] In Iowa, Albert Cummins, a veteran opponent of the barbed wire trust, was elected on a reform platform in 1901 and pursued the "Iowa Idea"—the pursuit of anti-trust actions combined with railroad regulation and the ending of tariff protections for monopolistic industries. Cummins ran as a Republican reformer because, as the saying went, Iowa "would go Democratic when hell went Methodist."[250] In South Dakota, Republican Governor Coe Crawford, an Iowa-born lawyer of deep Presbyterian faith, successfully reformed the campaign finance system and regulated lobbying.[251] In Indiana, Republican reformer James Franklin Hanly was elected governor as "the poor man's candidate" and, as a "teetotaling Methodist," he focused in particular on curbing saloons, gambling, and associated political corruption.[252]

Perhaps most famous, in Wisconsin, Robert La Follette Sr. was elected Dane County (Madison) state's attorney, congressman, and, after a few failed attempts, governor in 1900 as a progressive Republican reformer.[253] La Follette was influenced by the Grange movement, took counsel from President John Bascom at the University of Wisconsin, and generally sought to defend the interests of small farmers and small shopkeepers.[254] He advocated the regulation of the railroads, the repeal of railroad tax exemptions, and the adoption of the direct primary. La Follette's "Wisconsin Idea" was to draw on the University of Wisconsin's experts and scholars to run and advise progressive boards and commissions.[255] La Follette helped rekindle the railroad regulatory efforts of the Grange era of the 1870s and gave additional energy to the Public Service Commission.[256]

Reform mayors and governors were also aided by an emerging group of reform intellectuals. La Follette and the Wisconsin progressives had an "intellectual base" that included Bascom and Charles Van Hise, both presidents of the University of Wisconsin, and professors such as the economist Richard T. Ely, the sociologist Edward Ross, and John Commons, an Oberlin College graduate whose reform writings and economic analyses were widely absorbed.[257] In Illinois, Governor Altgeld was close to the lawyer Clarence Darrow and other Chicago reformers. In Kansas and around the Midwest, reformers often followed the writings of William Allen White, editor of the *Emporia Gazette*.[258] In Ohio, Washington Gladden, the longtime minister of the Columbus First Congregational Church, was active in intellectual circles and advocated workers' rights, religious toleration, and aid to the poor. Gladden's views were strongly shaped by Christian teachings and the emerging Social Gospel movement.[259] Oberlin College also launched the Institute of Christian Theology with Washington Gladden as its first president and hosted symposia featuring speakers such as Jane Addams and Clarence Darrow, both active in Chicago reform circles.[260] George Herron, who ministered to churches in Indiana, Iowa, and Minnesota, was also a highly active public intellectual, including a stint as professor of applied Christianity at Grinnell College in Iowa.[261] Intellectuals such as John Bascom and Richard Ely, like Gladden, were highly sympathetic to the more active Christian churches and those embracing the Social Gospel.[262] Using a version of the Social Gospel he deemed the "Civic Church," a "spiritual counterpart to the town meeting" that became the Civic Federation, William Stead sought to "drive the devil out of Chicago."[263] Stead, "imbued with a healthy dose of Victorian idealism," saw his Civic Church as the "intelligent and fraternal cooperation of all those who are in earnest about making men and things somewhat better than they are today."[264]

Some midwestern intellectuals revised the thinking of various fields of study in a manner that lessened older dogmas and opened the door to new views of society and methods of reform.[265] Midwestern fiction writers who embraced the genre of realism, some of whom also worked as journalists and "muckrakers," also contributed to this intellectual scene, as did some fantasy novelists, including Ignatius Donnelly.[266]

These thinkers and reformers were seeking to strengthen an existing social safety net that had been built up over earlier decades in the Midwest. The most visible and recent form of social support could be found in the settlement houses. Jane Addams, for example, started Hull House in 1889, making it the second settlement house in the country, and she focused on aiding the impoverished Nineteenth Ward of Chicago.[267] In a sign of her midwestern devotion to being useful, Addams prodded successful people to assist the society around them.[268] She and her fellow reformers also pointed to the social costs of alcohol. The large-scale plan of the WCTU to advocate temperance was often sincerely billed as an effort to stop working men from wasting precious income on drink and to devote their time and money to their families.[269] The WCTU saw alcoholism as a "malady of the mind," which required Christian devotion to overcome, and also as a medical problem, which required public health efforts to address.[270] In addition to the manifold women's temperance efforts there were many general prohibition drives and those led by men pushing other men to care for their families and abandon alcohol. Billy Sunday, for example, was an Iowa orphan who made it to the Chicago Whitestockings as a baseball player. He married a Chicagoan, began preaching at the Chicago YMCA, and was soon stumping the Midwest and denouncing alcohol and gambling, which "sent thousands of souls to hell."[271] Efforts were also made to cure men of the drink habit. In Lincoln, Nebraska, for example, the Garten Institute was created to cure alcoholics. Patients were allowed to drink as much liquor as they wanted, then were injected with medicine that produced a "terrible nausea like seasickness which resulted in a horrible dislike for even the smell of any kind of liquor."[272]

At the local level, and with less fanfare than the public campaigns against alcohol, various forms of poor relief were available for those on the "wrong side of the tracks" or who were done in by the latest turn of the business cycle. Women in Monroe, Michigan, for example, ran local charities to aid the downtrodden, but, in keeping with temperance efforts, focused on the "deserving poor"—those who avoided alcohol (aid seekers with too many dogs were also at risk of being judged as having "Turkish tastes" and thus undeserving).[273] Other forms of private aid were also available and, given the strength of civic institutions in the Midwest, they were substantial.[274] The WCTU in Chicago pushed for assistance to young children and sought to "dot the city over with free kindergartens," a reform also embraced by

Mayor Jones in Toledo.[275] In Lincoln, Nebraska, Springfield, Illinois, and other cities there existed a Home for the Friendless.[276] Unwed mothers were also given aid.[277]

In addition to private relief and assistance organizations, midwestern states funded a variety of social institutions. The first Indiana constitution, for example, made clear that the state must establish farms and asylums for the aged, infirm, and indigent.[278] Other states followed suit.[279] Sanatoriums for those suffering from tuberculosis and other maladies were established.[280] Efforts were also made to assist children with whooping cough, measles, scarlet fever, and other diseases.[281] In most local areas there was also a poorhouse, or, in rural areas, a poor farm, where families whose luck had run out could find food and shelter in exchange for farm work.[282] Facilities for the mentally ill were created.[283] So were homes for orphans.[284] Efforts to aid orphans were often focused on "moral uplift, restoring traditional values, preparing underprivileged people for roles as democratic citizens, and recapturing a sense of community and individual responsibility."[285] States also ran reform schools and "industrial schools" for wayward children.[286] From 1875 to 1920, seventeen hundred young women were sent to the Industrial School for Girls in Wisconsin (the legislature had outlawed sending children to the county poorhouse in 1875). Of that group, 10 percent were sent there after enduring some form of parental abuse, but others were there because of "delinquent" behavior such as hanging out in pool halls and keeping "bad company."[287] Although far from ideal, such institutions did provide a system for rescuing abused children from their situations.

All told, midwestern states constructed a substantive safety net long before the twentieth-century debates over a federal welfare state. By the time of the Civil War, the state of Ohio had created four "insane asylums," a penitentiary, a reform school for boys (a girls reform school and a medium-security reform school for boys were in the works), an institution for the "idiotic," a "deaf and dumb asylum," a soldiers' home, and a home for the orphans of soldiers and sailors.[288]

The work of settlement houses, local charities, and state aid programs in part speaks to reformers' focus on the problems associated with a new and changing nonagrarian Midwest and the effects of industrialism and modern urban life. The new urban-industrial order and its corresponding social tensions could be seen most clearly in Chicago, which exploded in size in the late nineteenth century. During the various strikes around the nation in 1877, for example, workers in Chicago protested throughout the city, denouncing the aristocratic privilege of monopolist "big bugs" and demanding higher wages and an eight-hour work day. To appeal to the large number of Union war veterans, labor leaders said they sought to "level the capitalists in the same way that the Southern slaveholders had recently been leveled."[289] The famous Haymarket Affair of 1886 in Chicago ended with seven policemen dead because of an anarchist bomb, an episode that did little to aid the cause of labor (and weighed down Governor Altgeld, who pardoned the anarchists).[290] In the northern reaches of the Midwest, iron and copper mines at times became sites of labor strife.[291] In 1894 workers at the Pullman railway car plant in Illinois protested after a wage cut.[292] George Pullman, who had created a company-run city with many worker amenities and was seen as a kind of utopian reformer in his own right, dismissed the workers' protests, so they went out on strike.[293] The labor action made the president of the American Railway Union, Eugene Debs of Terre Haute, Indiana, a national figure who would go on to run for president five times in the early twentieth century.[294] It also boosted the support of Governor Altgeld among workers, since he was sympathetic to their cause. Another reformer made a name for himself in 1894 when Jacob Coxey, a veteran Greenbacker and quarry owner from Massillon, Ohio, marched an "army"—also called the Commonweal of Christ—to Washington, D.C., to protest in favor of publics works programs and jobs.[295]

These protests and industrial strife were signs of a new and distinct political economy that was coming to the twentieth-century Midwest which, in its early stages, sparked some labor-oriented reforms. In 1867, Illinois passed a law creating an eight-hour day, which suffered from loopholes but also became the basis for reform demands in other places. In part because of a desire to address working conditions that caused strikes, but more generally to promote social reform idealistically, evangelical churches and other reform groups also sought pro-labor policies. Some farm activists cooperated with labor. Various women's clubs, the WCTU, and other groups also worked against child labor. The WCTU was "especially concerned with the fate of girls and women condemned to the convict labor system that prevailed in much of the South and beyond." In 1901, Jane Addams founded the Juvenile Protective Association to oppose child labor. Workers' compensation laws were adopted. Urban workers and labor groups also supported reform candidates for mayor and other city offices.[296] Some urban reformers embraced socialism, and some socialists won mayorships. Beginning around 1910, for example, socialists were politically strong in Milwaukee.[297] The most widely circulated socialist newspaper was published in Kansas. [298] The socialist Eugene Debs of Indiana, denouncing "crowns and castes" and economic oligarchs, won 6 percent of the vote (nearly 900,000 votes) in the 1912 presidential election (he also ran in 1900, 1904, 1908).[299] In 1910 there were more Socialist Party members in Ohio, Illinois, and Wisconsin than in New York and Pennsylvania combined.[300]

In the main, however, reform in the nineteenth-century Midwest was not radical.[301] Reformers came from many walks of life, drew on midwestern political culture, and often cooperated in the pursuit of straightforward reforms such as civil service protections, scientific agriculture, conservation, tax reform, adoption of the Australian ballot and direct primaries, abolishing child labor, fighting corruption, and other nonradical reforms such as improving roads.[302] Reformers certainly supported abolition and improving civil rights for African Americans, as noted in chapter 4, and saw abolitionism as part of a wider reforming impulse. The Michigan abolitionist Laura Smith Haviland wrote in her book that she supported "all reforms" that would "cleanse the muddy waters" of American life and improve society.[303] This included several steps forward for women in the realm of education and political action. As indicated by the advances for women, the reformers active in the Midwest before 1900 won a fair number of victories through the democratic process in contests with stand-patters and entrenched officials and those who resisted reforms for various and not necessarily nefarious reasons.[304]

Since most of the midwestern reformers saw their society as advanced and democratic, most were not fueled by utopian dreams or radical ideas. The supposed muckraker and Chicago writer Ray Stannard Baker, speaking of his fellow reformers and writers, believed they were "far more eager to understand and make sure than to dream of utopias. . . . We 'muckraked' not because we hated our world but because we loved it. We were not hopeless, we were not cynical, we were not bitter."[305] The midwestern reform project was not a class protest, concluded Russell Nye in his history of the movement, "nor a struggle of labor against capital in the Marxian sense." "The Midwest's spirit of protest is simply its own, compounded out of its geography, its culture, its economic and social history. There is nothing else quite like it in the world," Nye concluded. Reforms in the region were a "thoroughly indigenous compound of various elements in Midwestern history," "moderate rather than revolutionary," geared toward "practical solutions," and "aimed at planned experimentation rather than disintegration and upheaval."[306] Socialism was not a strong movement and populism, despite the grand claims of some, tended to be most active on the western edges of the Midwest; in any case, far from being radical, Populists were mostly followers of Jefferson and Lincoln and drew on the American tradition of republicanism.[307]

After the turn of the century a new set of circumstances would emerge in the Midwest. Too much of the European "Old World" was creeping into the twentieth-century Midwest, a character in a novel by the Chicago writer Henry Fuller worried—a world of concentrated power, anti-democratic thought, and industrialism, with its "resultant noise, waste, stenches, stains, dangers, explosions."[308] In 1894 the Ohio-born William Dean Howells commented that the familiar "free fight" for life and achievement and striving in the old days of the Midwest was fading into a clash between big impersonal forces of economic power and politics. The Omaha platform of the Populists, drafted by Ignatius Donnelly, worried about the country "degenerating into European conditions." Although the historian Richard Hofstadter was famously wrong about various aspects of this era, including the nature of agrarian reform, he was largely correct that the reform impulse came from those who inhabited an older nineteenth-century world dominated by the centrality of Christianity, personal character, small farms, small businesses, main streets, and old-style professions—a distinct order, one that existed before the coming of a different age, one of large-scale government, mega-corporations, global entanglements, and mass media.[309] This new era was under way by the coming of World War I, and what it ushered in for the American Midwest is another multilayered topic in need of exploration. But our focus today is the era that came before and why it behooves us to remember its virtues.

CONCLUSION

FINDING VIRTUE IN
THE GOOD COUNTRY

As the curtain fell on the nineteenth century, yet another son of the Midwest sat in the White House. William McKinley, elected president in 1896 and again in 1900, was born in Niles, Ohio, in 1843, the seventh of nine children of Nancy and William McKinley Sr. After a boyhood move to Poland, Ohio, about twenty miles to the southeast, McKinley matriculated at Poland Seminary, the town's academy, or high school, an institution ubiquitous in the well-educated Midwest. At the three-story brick school McKinley became the first president of the Everett Literary and Debating Society (named after the prominent orator and U.S. senator Edward Everett) and read books, supplementing his studies at home, where his mother had stocked the family library with Hume's *History of England* and Gibbon's *Decline and Fall of the Roman Empire*.[1] McKinley was well mannered and a good student. Like others of his generation and region, McKinley thought achievement came with "self-help and industry" and he "accepted the basic ideas that flavored the era, believing that application, industry, caution, and conciliation brought success in life."[2] The McKinleys were devoted Christians and staunch abolitionists. Specifically, they were Methodists and, even to some people in the late nineteenth century, William Jr.'s "deeply felt religious views seem[ed] old-fashioned," but he tried to uphold the morality of his family tradition (he did not want to be photographed while smoking, for example, "lest he set a bad example for young people," a practice that some found "prudish and ultra-Victorian in retrospect").[3] When the war came, he naturally fought for the Union, serving in the Twenty-third Ohio Infantry under the command of his fellow Buckeye and future president Rutherford B. Hayes. He saw the face of battle at Antietam and in the Shenandoah Valley. McKinley fought with many other men from Ohio, the anchor state of the Midwest—the state supplying more troops to the Union per capita than any other.[4]

After the war, McKinley earned his law license and settled in Canton, Ohio, and joined the Grand Army of the Republic lodge, the Loyal Legion, the Masons, the YMCA, and the Knights of Pythias and was appointed superintendent of the Sunday school at the Methodist church.[5] He entered Ohio politics and ultimately became the last in a long line of midwestern Union war veterans to serve as president of the United States.[6] While in the White House, McKinley, like Hayes, was a moderate reformer, took his good offices seriously, and was thought a hail fellow well met and a decent man from the Good Country.

McKinley's presidency (1897–1901) is also properly seen as representing the end of an era and the coming of a new age.[7] His death by an anarchist's bullet in 1901 signaled the coming of new radicalisms and a blood-soaked twentieth century.[8] What comes after McKinley tends to interest historians much more than what came before, and his public service and the time and place he represented no longer stir the blood. His time in office is seen as "monotonously similar to those of preceding Republican administrations," which were also led by Union men from the Midwest.[9] The Southern writer Thomas Wolfe dismissed them as forgettable old men, "lost Americans," whose "gravely vacant and bewhiskered faces mixed, melted, swam together in the sea-depths of a past intangible, immeasurable, and unknowable as the buried city of Persepolis."[10] The leader of the famed New York Intellectuals, Richard Hofstadter, dismissed them as "famous in American annals chiefly for their obscurity," about whom "not much need be said."[11]

The monotony of McKinley and his bearded fellows from the Midwest is rather the point of this book and, with all apologies to Richard Hofstadter, I think much more needs to be said about them and their home and era. Although historians and much of the public have not displayed much interest in the nineteenth-century Midwest, a land and epoch too often dismissed as inconsequential if it is thought of at all, it is time for a second look. There is much worth remembering behind the beards. A fresh review of the facts placed in proper perspective reveals that the American Midwest was the most democratic place in the world as it took shape in the nineteenth century. It adopted state constitutions, written in open conventions, that were highly democratic, guaranteed a wide range of civil rights, and provided for a wide suffrage. In the Midwest rigid social hierarchies broke down. Feudal institutions and land baronies, still common throughout most of the world, were recognizably absent. For most of the nineteenth century most midwesterners were farmers who prospered on the fertile lands of the region and lived in rough equality with their neighbors. The Iowa-born and -raised sociologist Carl Taylor said there "has never before been anything in the world like the rural culture of the corn belt, where farmers have attained the highest level of living . . . in the world for 'dirt farmers.'"[12] The social stratification common to Europe, the Old South, and most of the world did not prevail there. As Jess Gilbert concluded in a recent study, the "late nineteenth-century rural Midwest was substantially a one-class society."[13] Many of these egalitarian-oriented young rural midwesterners marched off to fight a bitter sectional war and to battle the forces of oppression and aristocracy that threatened the entire republic; in the process, their own regional attachments and sense of identity deepened.

As the century went on, midwesterners steadily extended the franchise in various forms to Native Americans, Blacks, and women. Drawing on deep reservoirs of Christian belief, republicanism, civic commitment, and their own democratic experience, many sought reforms to preserve the agrarian way of life, undermine economic monopolies, upend disruptive social forces such as alcohol, and generally improve the lives of their fellows via modest and incremental reforms pursued through democratic means. The region was united by a common culture or civil religion grounded in the ideals of the Revolution, free-labor beliefs, Victorian norms, entrepreneurial ideals, love for the republic, and democratic egalitarianism. As another bewhiskered midwestern president, Benjamin Harrison—Ohio-born, Union colonel of an Indiana regiment, graduate of Presbyterian Miami University in Ohio, opponent of racial servitude, Hoosier U.S. senator, GOP stalwart—said to a reunion of Union veterans in 1890, progress must be measured "not only in . . . material things which are great, but . . . also in those qualities of mind and heart, in morality, in the love of order, in sobriety, in respect for the law, in a God-fearing disposition among the people, in love for our country, in all these high and spiritual things."[14] Harrison called for "pure homes and God-fearing, order-loving fathers and mothers" to rear their children in "abodes of order, cleanliness, piety, and intelligence," for the "triumph of pluck and thrift over hard and discouraging conditions," and for the instillation of the virtues of "self-sacrifice, love, and willingness to give ourselves for others."[15]

To be sure, the Midwest failed on various fronts. Racism and black laws, especially during the early decades of the nineteenth century, will forever tarnish the Midwest's reputation. So too will ongoing patriarchal social patterns and mistreatment of Native Americans. We must remember the Detroit race riots, the removal of the Shawnees, the many times that civically minded women seeking the right to vote were rebuffed, and other instances in the train of abuses that mar the region's history. These sins are critical to recall when attempting to understand the Midwest, and they must be seriously weighed when passing judgment on the region, as this book has attempted to do.[16] For those who would sanitize the American past and overlook the nation's failings, these sections of the book are particularly important.

Less important, but still part of the typical indictment of the Midwest, is the "Hefner complaint": there were too many nosey neighbors, fun-hating Methodists, and priggish WCTU regulators of social life. Marilynne Robinson summarizes the caricature and names the villains: "gloomy religious fanatics who hate life."[17] Or, as historians have summarized the condition, the nineteenth century was "stuffy, hidebound, repressed, and old-fashioned."[18]

Although it is true that midwesterners tried to instill virtue in the young and promote public morality and that there existed a widely agreed upon culture, it was rarely harsh or austere or forced on the noncompliant. The review of the record for this book found relatively few instances of violence or punitive social repercussions for deviations from accepted moral codes. All of this is difficult to measure, of course, but the cases of obvious repression seem low. This was a region, after all, that prided itself in breaking down aristocratic norms and celebrating the common man and the openness of a new society. Parents and the clergy obviously sought a clean culture and defended standards of decency, as they saw them at the time. Nevertheless, the evidence of extremism is thin. A detailed study of the public library in Muncie, Indiana, found that a wide variety of books were made available and did not find evidence of social control or censorship or of outside forces trying to subvert the book choices of the library board.[19] The library, home to twelve thousand books in 1902, was managed and run by women who were generally interested in promoting reading and not excessively moralistic or censorious.[20] A study of the library in Osage, Iowa, found that the book selection committee similarly gave "library users what they wanted."[21] These library patrons in Iowa and Indiana, instead of opting solely for polite and agreeable fare, often chose to read the gritty realism of popular midwestern authors such as William Dean Howells, Hamlin Garland, and Theodore Dreiser. Speakers invited to midwestern platforms included the at times ribald Mark Twain and even the edgy Oscar Wilde. Dissenting religious groups, with the stark exception of the Mormons, and utopian reformers found a home in the Midwest.[22] One historian linked this openness to the "joyous pantheism of the frontier" and noted a strain of religious skepticism and the vague religiosity of figures such as Lincoln and Twain.[23] Scientific research and science education were celebrated, the anti-Bryan shibboleths of "Inherit the Wind" notwithstanding. Women were increasingly expanding their social and civic sphere and running for and winning political offices and finally succeeding at winning general suffrage rights. This was not medieval Spain—dissent was entirely possible if one chose. This social looseness is what worried the heads of more tightly organized eastern churches. A region this big and politically stable and diverse and anti-slavery, "thickly strewn with colleges and universities and with a long history of relative wealth," Marilynne Robinson protests, is no simple "backwater or cultural desert."[24]

If sweeping judgments about a specific region across a century of history seem unwieldy, consider a particular and critical example. Consider Carl Van Doren, who did more than any one person to create the image of the Midwest as a stultifying and repressive hinterland and to plant it deep in the scholarly imagination as a standard category of cultural and historical analysis. He pronounced his "revolt from the village" thesis in 1921 from high in the intellectual hierarchy in New York, where he was a Columbia University English professor and the literary editor of the increasingly radical magazine the *Nation*.[25] Van Doren claimed that, at long last, a smart group of budding midwestern writers were rebelling against the repression and coarseness of midwestern life.

Despite his bold arguments and their longevity in the groves of academe, Van Doren's claims in his revolt thesis were wrong, as attested to by his own recollections, which substantiate the descriptions of the nineteenth-century Midwest advanced in this book. In 1885, during the same era that Hugh Hefner's parents were born in Nebraska, Carl Van Doren was born on a farm near Hope, Illinois, where his ancestors had settled after migrating from Pennsylvania to near Sandusky, Ohio, then to Decatur and then to Hope. In the original manuscript for his memoir, Van Doren describes an idyllic and "happy childhood" with loving parents. His farmhouse, set among maples, cedars, and elms, was literally surrounded by a white picket fence (to keep the sheep from eating the lilacs and asparagus). Hope had a community church (where his grandparents had organized the Sunday school), an elementary school, a blacksmith shop, and a couple stores and was surrounded by cornfields and bathed in panoramic sunsets at dusk. Most people in Van Doren's church in Hope were "easy going" and joined the "sober club for the encouragement of good behavior," and the "congregation's whole creed" was abbreviated into a motto and printed on the wall behind the pulpit: "Christian Character is the Test of Fellowship." "To be honest and decent in daily affairs was all that was required of any member" of Hope's church, Van Doren remembered, "and that was required rather by the general community than by the church alone."[26]

Education, sociability, and comity were prized in Hope. At school Van Doren and his classmates studied reading, grammar, writing, spelling, arithmetic, geography, physiology, algebra, ancient history, and American history; they played rounders, handy-over, prisoner's base, and I spy and went ice skating. He and his brother rode their pony to neighboring towns for spelling bees. He practiced for oratory contests while milking cows. The first book he owned was John Richard Green's *History of the English People* (in four volumes), which he won in a contest at age nine: "Its chapters on the dim Anglo-Saxons stand up in my memory like old photographs." He also read Shakespeare's *The Tempest,* Scott's *Ivanhoe,* Bunyan's *Pilgrim's Progress,* Defoe's *Robinson Crusoe,* Bulwer-Lytton's *The Last Days of Pompeii,* Swift's *Gulliver's Travels,* Longfellow's *The Song of Hiawatha* and "Evangeline," and Wallace's *Ben-Hur* along with works of Hawthorne, Plutarch, Gibbon, Whittier, Dickens, Thackeray, Twain, Washington Irving, James Fenimore Cooper, and James Whitcomb Riley ("who belonged to Indiana but might have been writing about us") and less lofty titles such as the *Compleat Angler.*

The big event every year was the Fourth of July, along with the more sedate Old Settlers' Day, and these celebrations included picnics with roast chicken, pickled beets, deviled eggs, biscuits, apple jelly, stewed pears, and lots of pies. The Fourth included speeches, bunting, fireworks, baseball games, and "sly courting." Most everyone was a Republican and the local hero was Representative "Uncle Joe" Cannon, the famed GOP Speaker of the House of this era and a frequent orator on local hustings. Hope and its rural environs "had been almost classless" and defined by a "feeling of fraternity" and a "sense of neighborliness," Van Doren concluded. The "classic pattern" in Van Doren's rural Illinois world was to "work, save money, buy property, and hold a stake in the social enterprise." "Feuds seldom lasted," abusive husbands were shunned, adultery was "rare," and wives often thought of sex as "family duty," which failed to meet modern standards of pleasure and liberation, certainly, but was also not oppressive. Most people were similar, there were not wide social gaps or divisions, extremes "in vices or even in virtues" were not common, and a sense of "normality" enveloped the town.[27]

During high school in neighboring Urbana, Van Doren said he became "bored" and "turned quickly to rebellion," "felt a need for change," and decided he wanted to become a writer. Instead of being involved in high school affairs and other social activities, he became a "self-conscious spectator." He embraced "snobbishness." Noting the "instinct of children to rebel," Van Doren, in an act of self-diagnosis, noted that even "if they have no reason for it they invent them." In college at the University of Illinois, a "black melancholy" came over him. So too did a desire to become a "brilliant poet," to move to New York and live a private life, and generally to follow the "instinct that draws a young provincial to his capital." When he went to New York and told people he had a "happy childhood," he recalled, "many of them [were] envious, more of them skeptical," because it had become so common to "abuse families." Among the thinking classes of New York, Van Doren explained, an "unhappy childhood is rated as an asset. . . . Without saying how he suffered as a child, who can hint how sensitive he is? Who can prove he is original now without recalling that he was rebellious then? On that lewd scapegoat, the family, its members heap their sins." The trend was to be unhappy, and the smart move was to denounce the fogies who said otherwise.

At the *Nation,* Van Doren vowed to fight the "conservative resistance to the new books" of the era and to stake out strong positions and "take the side of life" over the old and stodgy.[28] He created the "revolt from the village" construct to highlight the divide between the old/bad and the new/good, and he saw the purported revolt as driven by "revenge" against his elders and "written out of hatred" for their dreary world.[29] "Dullness had come to be the villain," Van Doren exclaimed, "as sin had once been."[30] The truth of his experience back in the village of Hope paid no dividends in New York.

The purpose here is not to condemn a young Carl Van Doren for his youthful ambitions, posturing, and distortions. But it is to pinpoint the greatest contributor to the creation and perpetuation of the myth that a whole swath of writers concluded that their midwestern hometowns were hellish places and to highlight the important revelation that, after a deeper look, even the greatest propagator of the anti-midwestern turn in scholarly and popular culture understood, testified to, and believed in the virtues of the Good Country.

Because of Van Doren and an assorted group of writers and intellectuals and years of scholarly neglect, we lost sight of the Midwest and what it was. If it is true that the amount of social repression has been greatly exaggerated by Hefner, Van Doren, Hofstadter, and others who have shaped our view of the past, then it is time to adjust the dominant narrative of American history that has emerged in recent years. The democratic advances of the Midwest must be more properly weighed and considered in light of the global events and political conditions of the era. If one focuses specifically on democracy as a category of historical analysis, there is much for the Midwest to brag about, but we do not hear much of it. The energies of historians in recent decades have been placed elsewhere, and this has made it difficult to recapture the past as it was lived. As Louise Stevenson has noted, the present-day emphasis on "race, class, and gender, commanded no privileged space" back during the height of nineteenth-century American Victorian culture. She cautions that the people of that era "understood the world differently than we do." She believes that "some historians distort the past by imposing categories on its people and institutions" and warns against "scholars looking back with present-centrism and labelling people of historically distant cultures as narrow-minded, hypocritical, sectarian, paranoid, or inauthentic performers."[31] Marilynne Robinson warns against the constant reliance on "small and dreary determinisms" that deny agency, narrow our ability to detect free-will moral choices, and exclude from consideration factors and motivations related to transcendent beliefs such as Christianity.[32]

Judged on their own terms and not ours, midwesterners generally sought to build a constitutional order based on Christian and republican principles and Victorian morality, and they generally succeeded. This "culture was committed to the mission of teaching men how to behave," and the record is replete with examples of midwesterners doing such every day.[33] The Cincinnati newspaper *Liberty Hall*, for example, edited by the Congregational preacher John W. Browne, sought articles from its readers about farming, biography, science, poetry, religion, patriotism, and especially "moral and instructive essays" that would shape the culture, guide behavior, and instill virtue.[34] In Iowa the *Osage News* reprinted a sermon calling on those involved in print culture to protect all souls in their community: "Printers of all Christendom, editors, reporters, compositers, pressmen, publishers and readers of that which is printed, resolve that you will not write, set up, edit, issue or read anything that debases body, mind or soul."[35] This mission was also carried on in the thousands of midwestern book clubs and literary societies. The Union Literary Society created in Wichita in 1872, which became the Wichita Liberal Fraternity in 1873, had as its purpose to study the classics, hold spelling bees, organize fairs, and generally advance "high moral standards and encourage free thought and self-culture."[36]

The focus on moral instruction in the Midwest broadly worked. One woman who was a product of a one-room schoolhouse in Indiana later recalled that "cheating, lying, and stealing were not done; we considered them sins. Christian ethics were respected even by those who were not Christian."[37] Prominent school problems included petty misdemeanors such as students whispering to each other and using too much paper.[38] This is to say that behavior issues in schools, a revealing window into the broader culture, were minor.[39] Well-ordered schools were part of a larger social system that was bolstered by a strong civic culture, a common culture of books and reading, and a spirit of idealism and reform. In our own period of decay—an era of callow tweets, sensationalism, celebrity worship, extreme loneliness, and mass and manufactured and purposeful distraction, all of which is unleashing rampant anxiety and depression and devouring our young—this old culture deserves a second look and not our condescension.[40]

This reconsideration might make us think of what Van Doren called "normality," an appeal to a central set of basic American norms and the tenets of the nation's civil religion. We need greater attention to our public discourse and more informed debate and a greater dedication to knowing civics and American history, and we should denounce efforts to tear down statues of Ulysses S. Grant and expunge the name Abraham Lincoln from our schools.[41]

Grant and Lincoln were sons of the Good Country who did the right thing and deserve a prominent place in the common culture of the United States. They should not be cast into the abyss in a mindless crusade against icons of the past through uninformed hostility to symbols of an older culture. If not a "return to normalcy," to borrow the phrase of an Ohio-born president trying to settle the passions and paroxysms of the World War I era, we need an exercise in remembering those sound and decent parts of the Good Country that dampened hysteria and promoted calm, including figures such as Grant and Lincoln. What I am suggesting is a remembrance of a particular and grounded interior American normalcy that prevailed in the nineteenth-century Midwest, not a repressive or scary war on deviancy that some conjure when a nod to better days is suggested. We would do well to remember that old order because, despite the fog of disrepute that has blinded us to a proper appreciation of the Midwest, most people from the region praised their "home as a place of beauty, friendship, joy, harmony, and peace."[42] The supposed "rebels and renegades," Malcolm Cowley once wrote, missed the "complete picture" of the American past, especially the "smiling parts, the broad farmlands, the big Sunday dinners after coming home from church."[43] The historian of the Midwest and the early republic Andrew Cayton, who left us far too early, just as the effort to revive midwestern history was beginning, fondly recalled his childhood in Ohio and the "basic values associated with that world: family, respectability, mutual respect, integrity, what my mother used to call character."[44] These are the virtues of the Good Country worth remembering and reviving.

In addition to judging nineteenth-century midwesterners by standards they would understand, weighing the broad context of their lived experiences, and remembering their virtues, we should take their sense of place and region seriously. Midwesterners saw their region as different from the aristocratic Northeast and the feudal South. This pride of place and sense of identity fostered a healthy desire to resist outside domination. As the Nebraska writer Mari Sandoz once said, midwesterners often objected to the "intellectual and cultural dictatorship" of the "Atlantic seaboard" that was "foisted upon us the day the first malcontent crossed the Alleghenies."[45] There was, many midwesterners felt, a "distinct condescension towards people who lived west of Buffalo" or even just west of Manhattan, which generated a smart ditty: "The Western States have Buffalos to slight 'em / Buffalos, Manhattans; and so ad infinitum."[46]

CONCLUSION

These feelings only deepened over the course of the nineteenth century and led to a robust regionalist movement that spawned many journals, books, declarations of independence, and other noble efforts to preserve some regional autonomy.[47] The problem persists, of course, and remains a part of the "almost universal disdain felt by the populated, industrialized, moneyed, and sophisticated part of any nation for its provinces, its hinterland—the disdain of the Parisian for the rest of France, of the Prussian for the south of Germany, or the Londoner for Scotland or Ireland or the north of England."[48] The journalist Tom Brokaw, who was born and raised in South Dakota and retired just as this book was coming together, said that American news production was "much, much too wedded to the East Coast and West Coast only" and counseled reporters to see the interior of the country.[49] The common view in the middle of the country that it is disregarded and mocked by the coastal news industry and commentariat is one of the persistent fissures in American life that will continue to spark discord until it is properly addressed. One simple method of doing so is to invest resources in the research and publication of midwestern history and to pass along the knowledge of this field to future leaders who, we hope, will be genuinely interested in supporting a vigorous American pluralism that includes the Midwest.

It is time to fill the massive hole in the middle of American history. This book is my attempt to make sense of the big fleshy core of midwestern life during the region's first century. There is much more to say, to be sure, and I urge lots of people to jump in and hope for the conversation to get rolling on a large scale, ideally abetted by a few more institutional supports. I am not claiming that what is covered herein are the only parts of the Midwest worth studying. We can surely agree that the main currents of midwestern history have been neglected without triggering another exercise in "mapping the fault lines between privilege and resentment and fighting over who is part of the elite and who is entitled to victim status," in the weary warning of the critic A. O. Scott, seemingly exhausted by decades of culture war posturing.[50]

Part of Scott's frustration is the neglect—or outright attempt at erasure—of older and wiser voices like Wallace Stegner, who grew up in Iowa and earned his Ph.D. at the University of Iowa before heading west. Stegner offered a warning from those from another time, from the "squares," about the values and virtues that can still be found in the forgotten, the abused, and the cast off. Stegner recognized the coercive cultural power of New York, with its concentration of publishing and media and hipness, leaving entire regions neglected. In response, he tried to create space for the people and places who were "so unfashionable as to be practically voiceless." Stegner wanted us to remember the lost interior places and the niches of American life where "they breed more meliorists than nihilists, and they encourage booster clubs, culture clubs, and reform movements more commonly than the despair, decadence, masochism, sadism, self-pity, anger" and other emotions and forces common to literary and intellectual life.[51] Surely we can recognize the neglect of the old Midwest and see its virtues *and also* research and recognize those who were once not a prominent part of the midwestern story, thereby bringing some symmetry and proportionality to the whole affair, avoiding either/or history and round upon round of denunciations and reprisals, and simply work hard to imagine and capture the full story of the region.

To achieve this goal and fully to understand the Midwest and the reasons midwesterners resisted coastal scorn and neglect, we must be willing to set aside our prejudices, the kind set forth at the beginning of this book and that continue to linger in the culture as so many snide asides, dismissive stereotypes, and journalistic safari-like expeditions into the dark interior of the American continent (or rejections of entire states, such as the dean at the University of Missouri, who deemed the state's residents "bumpkins, hicks, and illiterates who lived in Hooterville").[52] For too long, any views not sufficiently critical of the Midwest have been castigated as rose-colored and nostalgic. But the evidence shows that many midwesterners and other observers were not blinded by myth, but in fact had views that were rooted in reality and the lived experience of millions of people in the region.[53] Those who looked fondly on the Midwest were not guilty of false nostalgia, or of believing in something imaginary or disconnected from truth; instead, they embraced a genuine nostalgia, a love of a home that seemed increasingly distant, and endured feelings of sickness about what had been lost, or "soul-nausea—what results when the things we hold dearest are trampled and desecrated."[54]

People who were reared in this culture issued warnings about its passing that deserve to be heard. West of where Van Doren was born in 1885, Gustav Niebuhr had arrived in 1881, "a German immigrant destined for life in the Midwest."[55] Niebuhr and his children lived Christian lives in small towns in Missouri and Illinois and "learned to think of hope and power as the special promises of these open spaces."[56] During the early twentieth century, while a minister in Michigan, the family's famous son Reinhold Niebuhr worried about the evaporation of the "roseate hopes of the previous century"—the "century of hope"—and the diminution of Christian culture, the disconnection from the natural world, the coming of technological dependence, the erosion of republican norms, and the worship of utopian schemes over pragmatic problem solving.[57] Niebuhr worried about the old midwestern world that was slipping away. So too did the young and precocious Christopher Lasch in Omaha, who followed Niebuhr's thought. After a long intellectual journey, Lasch came to see the consequences of losing the small-scale, agrarian, and ordered moral world of the Midwest. Lasch argued that the attack by intellectuals on the provinces and the American interior "left no alternative to nostalgia except a cosmopolitanism wholly contemptuous" of large parts of the country.[58] The claims of progress and the touting of the miracles of technology and the promise of the liberation of the self from communal forms of life were oversold, Lasch thought, and have left us longing for better times and more worthy places.

Near the completion of this book my thinking about its rationale came full circle by way of another interview by Terry Gross on National Public Radio. This time Gross was interviewing the writer Tim O'Brien on her show *Fresh Air* and discussing his new book about fatherhood. In addition to pressing O'Brien aggressively to quit smoking, Gross questioned how O'Brien's father, a Brooklyn native, ended up in the small town of Worthington, Minnesota. Gross assumed, without hesitation, that O'Brien's father was unhappy because he was "stuck in this small farming town away from Brooklyn," which meant a "deprivation that you can't fulfill your dreams."[59] Gross displayed little regard for those who might have found small-town Minnesota or the broader Midwest quite amenable, and thus she embodies the dominant mode of thought among intellectuals that needs to be questioned.

We need new thinking to escape this box, and we are not without hope. The critic Rita Felski, in a lonely dissent against the norm, may serve as the thin edge of the wedge that will pry open some space for a fresh approach. Felski calls attachment to places and people and art a form of "stickiness" that few intellectuals can comprehend when the "language de jour is one of dislocating, disorienting, demystifying." Felski, as if rebutting Gross's jab at small-town Minnesota, says the "fear of stickiness is the fear of being stuck in place," "as if the condition of being-attached were an inherent weakness or defect, as if ties served only as restraints and limits." She makes room for "sticky sentiment," the love of home or pride of place that nineteenth-century midwesterners felt, and endorses a "course correction" in American letters away from our entrenched intellectual tendencies and toward an ability "to value the experience of being bound, in ways that cut aslant the modern prizing of unrestricted agency and freedom."[60] In this context, the voices of the squares of the Midwest deserve to be resurrected and heard again and their lost history recovered. This act of recovery could be a hopeful signal to us all in this moment of democratic peril and doubt. Maybe, if the signal is bright enough, Terry Gross will even see it flickering out in the dark interior hinterlands of the republic.

A revival of civic engagement, more grounded forms of education, republican idealism, moral training for citizenship, a respect for the common culture of old, and a devotion to a balanced history that helps us see their collective value seem in order. The old Midwest could be a reservoir of idealism and hope if we knew its history. Revealed truths can have power. Maybe this knowledge will bolster our spirits, provide a light, and help guide us out of the current darkness and loneliness and cynicism.

NOTES

INTRODUCTION

1. "Hugh Hefner on Early 'Playboy' and Changing America's Values," Fresh Air broadcast, National Public Radio, September 28, 2017, rebroadcasting Terry Gross telephone interview of Hugh Hefner from the Playboy Mansion in 1999.

2. Michael O'Connor, "Omaha Playboy Club, Hugh Hefner's Parents Tie the Late Magazine Founder to Nebraska," *Omaha World-Herald*, September 29, 2017.

3. In 1963, Bogue thought that "city-reared and urban-oriented historians [had] come increasingly to dominate our profession" and that interest in the history of rural life was passing. Allan G. Bogue, *From Prairie to Corn Belt: Farming on the Illinois and Iowa Prairies in the Nineteenth Century* (Chicago: University of Chicago Press, 1963), preface, n.p. Bogue spent much of his early career "trying to understand the agricultural history of the Midwestern prairie states and the grasslands immediately beyond." Bogue, *The Farm on North Talbot Road* (Lincoln: University of Nebraska Press, 2001), xii. Bogue says, "I was born a Midwesterner because southwestern Ontario is essentially Midwestern in its natural environment—farther west than Ohio, farther south than much of Minnesota and Wisconsin." Lauck, "The Last Prairie Historian: An Interview with Professor Allan G. Bogue, Historian of the American Midwest," *Middle West Review* 1, no. 1 (Fall 2014), 95.

4. Bogue to Lasch, November 27, 1962, and Lasch to Bogue, December 20, 1962, in Lasch Papers, University of Rochester Libraries.

5. Blake Bailey, *Philip Roth: The Biography* (New York: W. W. Norton, 2021), 203 (frog-marched). In contrast to Roth's derisive treatment, the Iowa regionalist Ruth Suckow noted the communal nature of midwestern football games. Suckow, "The Folk Idea in American Life," *Scribner's Magazine* 88 (September 1930), 250.

6. Philip Roth, "Iowa: A Very Far Country Indeed," *Esquire* 63, no. 6 (December 1962); Barry Gross, "In Another Country: The Revolt from the Village," *MidAmerica* 4 (1977), 102–3. While at Iowa, Roth was trapped in a marriage to a deeply troubled woman who was from a broken home in Michigan and whom he had met while teaching at the University of Chicago in the 1950s. Roth recalled this wife as a "dispossessed refugee from a sociological background" in the Midwest and as someone "adrift" and "resentfully alienated from her Michigan upbringing." He thought that "rooted most deeply in this pictorial embodiment of American Nordic rootedness was her hatred for her past and her fear of the future." Philip Roth, *The Facts: A Novelist's Autobiography* (New York: Farrar, Straus and Giroux, 1988), 82–83. Roth explored the woman's behavior by way of the character "Lucy Nelson" in the novel

When She Was Good (New York: Random House, 1967). See Claudia Roth Pierpont, *Roth Unbound: A Writer and His Books* (New York: Farrar, Strauss and Giroux, 2013), 35–52; Roth, *Facts*, 143–46 (noting that his wife's harsh tales of growing up in Michigan were greatly exaggerated); Adam Mars-Jones, "In the Egosphere," *London Review of Books*, January 23, 2014; Bailey, *Philip Roth*, 176 (casting doubt on Roth's wife's Michigan experience). Roth's novel *Letting Go* (New York: Random House, 1962) was also set in Iowa City. For a comparison of this work by Roth and Sinclair Lewis's famous character, see James B. Carothers, "Midwestern Civilization and Its Discontents: Lewis's Carol Kennicott and Roth's Lucy Nelson," *Midwestern Miscellany* 9 (1981), 21–30. Roth's disdain for an older Midwestern isolationism is also evident in his later novel *The Plot against America* (New York: Houghton Mifflin, 2004), in which the isolationists defeat Roosevelt in 1940. During his years at Iowa, Roth was famously called to account for his unconventional and sarcastic writings by the broader Jewish community. See David Remnick, "Into the Clear: Philip Roth Puts Turbulence in Its Place," *New Yorker*, May 8, 2000. Because of the controversy, during his Iowa years Roth purposely "tried to stay away from" his more famous work on the Jewish-American experience. Adam Kirsch, "When He Was Good; The Reverence for Philip Roth—and the Irony of It," *New Republic*, December 30, 2013/January 6, 2014. My request for an interview of Roth about his Iowa years was rejected. Jessica Henderson (Roth's agent) to author, December 10, 2013 and February 26, 2014.

7. Bailey, *Philip Roth*, 199.

8. For access to available sources and for an academic approach to this search for balance, see Jon K. Lauck, "Soft, Democratic, and Universalist: In Search of the Main Currents of Traditional Midwestern Identity and a Grand Historiographic Synthesis," *Middle West Review* 6, nos. 1–2 (Fall/Spring 2019–2020), 63–133.

9. Eric Miller, *Hope in a Scattering Time: A Life of Christopher Lasch* (Grand Rapids, MI: William B. Eerdmans, 2010), 168.

10. Carl Van Doren, "Contemporary American Novelists X. The Revolt from the Village: 1920," *Nation* 113, no. 2936 (October 12, 1921, Fall Book Supplement).

11. Georg Brandes, *Impressions of Russia* (New York: Thomas Y. Crowell, 1966 [1889]).

12. Jurgen Osterhammel, *The Transformation of the World: A Global History of the Nineteenth Century* (Princeton, NJ: Princeton University Press, 2014), xvii.

13. Romeyn Taylor, "Chinese Hierarchy in Comparative Perspective," *Journal of Asian Studies* 48, no. 3 (August 1989), 490.

14. Peter Kolchin, "Comparing American History," *Reviews in American History* 10, no. 4 (December 1982), 76 (quotation); Carl N. Degler, "Comparative History," *Journal of Southern History* 34, no. 3 (August 1968), 425.

15. George Wilson Pierson, *Tocqueville in America* (Gloucester, MA: Peter Smith, 1969), 271.

16. Michael McGerr, "The Price of the 'New Transnational History,'" *American Historical Review* 96, no. 4 (October 1991), 1056–67 (arguing against the growing opposition to highlighting national differences by way of comparative history).

17. Brandes, *Impressions of Russia*, 32 (features), 36 (will and submission), 37, 38–39; Joseph S. Roucek, "Education in Czarist Russia," *History of Education Journal* 9, no. 2 (Winter 1958), 42.

18. See Nancy Shields Kollmann, *Honor Bound: State and Society in Early Modern Russia* (Ithaca, NY: Cornell University Press, 2016), 203–31; Peter Waldron, *Governing Tsarist Russia* (New York: Palgrave Macmillan, 2007), 15–16.

19. Sidney Harcave, *Years of the Golden Cockerel: The Last Romanov Years, 1814–1917* (New York: Macmillan , 1968), 251–59.

20. Waldron, *Governing Tsarist Russia*, 51–53.

21. Anatole G. Mazour, *The First Russian Revolution, 1825* (Stanford, CA: Stanford University Press, 1937), 2.

22. Hugh Stetson-Watson, *The Russian Empire, 1801–1917* (New York: Oxford University Press, 1967), 21–26.

23. Lazar Volin, "The Russian Peasant and Serfdom," *Agricultural History* 17, no. 1 (January 1943), 43, 45–46. On the similarities of serfdom and slavery, see Peter Kolchin, *Unfree Labor: American Slavery and Russian Serfdom* (Cambridge, MA: Harvard University Press, 1987).

24. Sidney Monas, *The Third Section: Police and Society in Russia under Nicolas I* (Cambridge, MA: Harvard University Press, 1961).

25. John D. Klier, *Russians, Jews, and the Pogroms of 1881–1882* (Cambridge: Cambridge University Press, 2011); John Klier and Shlomo Lanbroza, eds., *Pogroms: Anti-Jewish Violence in Modern Russian History* (Cambridge: Cambridge University Press, 1992).

26. Adam Giesinger, *From Catherine to Khrushchev: The Story of Russia's Germans* (Winnipeg, SK: Marian Press, 1974); Fred C. Koch, *The Volga Germans: In Russia and the Americas, from 1763 to the Present* (University Park: Pennsylvania State University Press, 1977); Timothy J. Kloberdanz, "The Volga Germans in Old Russia and in Western North America: Their Changing World View," *Anthropological Quarterly* 48, no. 4 (October 1975), 209–22.

27. At the same time I found the Brandes book, I was reading and reviewing a new biography of Susan Sontag. Given the angle of my review, the Sontag book's author, Benjamin Moser, strongly urged me to consider the history of Brazil, where he often lived. See Lauck, "Notes on Deep America," *Local Culture: A Journal of the Front Porch Republic* 3, no. 1 (Spring 2021), 68–73.

28. E. Bradford Burns, *A History of Brazil*, 3rd ed. (New York: Columbia University Press, 1993), 64, 74. Burns, who became a preeminent expert on the history of Brazil while a longtime professor at the University of California, Los Angeles, was originally an Iowan. For his last book he returned home and wrote a magisterial history of the regionalist movement in Iowa. Burns, *Kinship with the Land: Regionalist Thought in Iowa, 1894–1942* (Iowa City: University of Iowa Press, 1996). Allan Carlson points to Burns's book as one of the three crucial books in the revival of midwestern history. Carslon, "The Midwest: A Place With a History and a Future," *Front Porch Republic*, January 1, 2020.

29. Leslie Bethell, *Brazil: Essays on History and Politics* (London: School of Advanced Study, University of London, Institute of Latin American Studies, 2018), 149.

30. Burns, *History of Brazil*, 82–83, 89–90, 122–23, 128–29, 138–39.

31. Leslie B. Rout Jr., "Race and Slavery in Brazil," *Wilson Quarterly* 1, no. 1 (Autumn 1976), 73, 76.

32. Nicolas Bourcier, "Brazil Comes to Terms with Its Slave Trading Past," *Guardian*, October 23, 2012.

33. Rout, "Race and Slavery," 83.

34. Rex A. Hudson, *Brazil: A Country Study* (Washington, DC: Federal Research Division, Library of Congress, 1998), 56.

35. Hudson, *Brazil*, 56; Bethell, *Brazil*, 149–50. See also Richard Graham, *Patronage and Politics in Nineteenth-Century Brazil* (Stanford, CA: Stanford University Press, 1990).

36. Bethell, *Brazil*, 151–53.

37. *The Cambridge History of China*, vol. 2, John K. Fairbank and Kwang-Ching Liu, eds. (Cambridge: Cambridge University Press, 1980), 101–4.

38. Peter C. Perdue, *China Marches West: The Qing Conquest of Central Eurasia* (Cambridge. MA: Harvard University Press, 2005).

39. Pamela K. Crossley, *A Translucent Mirror: History and Identity in Qing Imperial Ideology* (Berkeley: University of California Press, 1999), 181.

40. Ranbir Vohra, *China's Path to Modernization: A Historical Review from 1800 to the Present* (Englewood Cliffs, NJ: Prentice-Hall, 1987), 12.

41. Vohra, *China's Path to Modernization*, 15, 18–19. See also Anders Hansson, *Chinese Outcasts: Discrimination and Emancipation in Late Imperial China* (Leiden: E. J. Brill, 1996).

42. John King Fairbank, *China: A New History* (Cambridge, MA: Harvard University Press, 1992), 173–75. Fairbank, similar to Burns, was a product of Sioux Falls, South Dakota. Burns and Fairbank are part of a group of cosmopolitan midwesterners who came to write about the world, the most famous of which was once John Clark Ridpath. Frederick Witzig, "The Perils and Promise of Midwestern Studies," *Studies in Midwestern History* 1, no. 2 (March 2015), 19–23. See also Lauck, "Soft, Democratic, and Universalist," 106, n. 98.

43. Vohra, *China's Path to Modernization*, 11, 13, 18.

44. Fairbank, *China*, 209.

45. Temma Kaplan, *Democracy: A World History* (New York: Oxford University Press, 2015), 56.

46. Harry D. Harootunian, "The Progress of Japan and the Samurai Class, 1868–1882," *Pacific Historical Review* 28, no. 3 (August 1959), 255–66.

47. Hyman Kublin, "The 'Modern' Army of Early Meiji Japan," *Far Eastern Quarterly* 9, no. 1 (November 1949), 22.

48. Peter Duus, *The Rise of Modern Japan* (Boston: Houghton Mifflin, 1976), 113–14; Alistair D. Swale, *The Meiji Restoration: Monarchism, Mass Communication, and Conservative Revolution* (New York: Palgrave Macmillan, 2009).

49. George M. Beckman, *The Making of the Meiji Constitution: The Oligarchs and the Constitutional Development of Japan, 1868–1891* (Lawrence: University of Kansas Press, 1957).

50. Andrew Gordon, *A Modern History of Japan: From Tokugawa Times to the Present* (New York: Oxford University Press, 2003), 93; Ian Buruma, *Inventing Japan, 1853–1964* (New York: Modern Library, 2003), 38.

51. Helen Hardacre, *Shinto and the State, 1868–1988* (Princeton, NJ: Princeton University Press, 1991); Fumiko Fukase-Indergard and Michael Indergard,

"Religious Nationalism and the Making of the Modern Japanese State," *Theory and Society* 37, no. 4 (August 2008), 343–74.

52. Daniel V. Botsman, "Freedom without Slavery? 'Coolies,' Prostitutes, and Outcastes in Meiji Japan's 'Emancipation Moment,'" *American Historical Review* 116, no. 5 (December 2011), 1325–26; J. E. Thomas, *Modern Japan: A Social History since 1868* (London: Longman, 1996), 73–82; Thomas Nelson, "Slavery in Medieval Japan," *Monumenta Nipponica* 59, no. 4 (2004), 474–79; Daniel V. Botsman, *Punishment and Power in the Making of Modern Japan* (Princeton. NJ: Princeton University Press, 2004).

53. Fukase-Indergard and Indergard, "Religious Nationalism," 363.

54. Andre G. Kuczewski, review of Mikiso Hane, *Peasants, Rebels, and Outcasts: The Underside of Modern Japan* (New York: Pantheon Books, 1982), in *Journal of Social History* 18, no. 1 (Autumn 1984), 125.

55. Kuczewski, review, 125.

56. Fairbank, *China*, 221.

57. *The History of France, from the Earliest Period to the Present Time*, vol. 1 (London: John Cassell, Strand, and Ludgate-Hill, 1852), 30.

58. Priscilla Robertson, *Revolutions of 1848: A Social History* (Princeton, NJ: Princeton University Press, 1952), 15.

59. Christopher Hobson, *The Rise of Democracy: Revolution, War and Transformation in International Politics since 1776* (Edinburgh: Edinburgh University Press, 2015), 128–29.

60. Gordon Wright, *France in Modern Times: 1760 to the Present* (Chicago: Rand McNally, 1960), 178. For a focus on comparisons between French and American democratic development from an essential comparative scholar, see Jean-Claude Lamberti, *Tocqueville and the Two Democracies* (Cambridge, MA: Harvard University Press, 1989).

61. Andre Maurois, *A History of France* (New York: Farrar, Straus and Cudahy, 1948), 417–19; Wright, *France in Modern Times*, 182; Stacey Renee Davis, "Turning French Convicts into Colonists: The Second Empire's Political Prisoners in Algeria, 1852–1858," *French Colonial History* 2 (2002), 93–113.

62. Frederick C. Dietz, *A Political and Social History of England* (New York: Macmillan, 1935), 493.

63. S. G. Checkland, *The Rise of Industrial Society in England, 1815–1885* (London: Longmans, 1964), 325.

64. Daniel Bell, "'American Exceptionalism' Revisited: The Role of Civil Society," *Public Interest* 95 (Spring 1989), 48.

65. David Harris Wilson, *A History of England* (New York: Holt, Rinehart and Winston, 1967), 643–44; John A. Phillips and Charles Wetherell, "The Great Reform Act in 1832 and the Political Modernization of England," *American Historical Review* 100, no. 2 (April 1995), 413–14. The Great Reform Act of 1832 increased the percentage of people who could vote in England only from 13 to 18 percent. Donald Ratcliffe, "The Right to Vote and the Rise of Democracy, 1787–1828," *Journal of the Early Republic* 33, no. 2 (Summer 2013), 221. Another figure puts the percentage of the population who could vote in England in 1800 at 3.1 percent. John A. Phillips, "Popular Politics in Unreformed England," *Journal of Modern History* 52, no. 4 (December 1980), 600.

66. Hobson, *Rise of Democracy*, 133. See generally Ian Machin, *The Rise of Democracy in Britain, 1830–1918* (New York: Palgrave, 2001).

67. Frederick Jackson Turner, *The Significance of Sections in American History* (New York: Henry Holt, 1932); Michael C. Steiner, "The Significance of Turner's Sectional Thesis," *Western Historical Quarterly* 10, no. 4 (October 1979), 437–66.

68. Orville Vernon Burton, "The South as 'Other,' the Southerner as 'Stranger,'" *Journal of Southern History* 79, no. 1 (February 2013), 7–50; Sheldon Hackney, "The South as a Counterculture," *American Scholar* 42 (Spring 1973), 283–93; David R. Jansson, "Internal Orientalism in America: W. J. Cash's *The Mind of the South* and the Spatial Construction of American National Identity," *Political Geography* 22, no. 3 (2003), 293–316; John Richard Allen, *The First South* (Baton Rouge: Louisiana State University Press, 1961).

69. R. Blakeslee Gilpin, "The Other Side of the World: Battling the Exceptional South," *Early English Literature* 52, no. 2 (2017), 446 (quotation); Steven Hahn, "Honor and Patriarchy in the Old South," *American Quarterly* 36, no. 1 (Spring 1984), 145; Jamie Winders, "Imperfectly Imperial: Northern Travel Writers in the Postbellum U.S. South, 1865–1880," *Annals of the Association of American Geographers* 95, no. 2 (June 2005), 391–410; Thomas D. Clark, ed., *Travels in the New South: A Bibliography*, 2 vols. (Norman: University of Oklahoma Press, 1962).

70. Jansson, "Internal Orientalism in America," 294, 308; Fred Hobson, "The Savage South: An Inquiry into the Origins, Endurance, and Presumed Demise of an Image," *Virginia Quarterly Review* 61, no. 3 (Summer 1985), 377–95; Elliott J. Gorn, "'Gouge and Bite, Pull Hair and Scratch': The Social Significance of Fighting in the Southern Backcountry," *American Historical Review* 90, no. 1 (February 1985), 18–43. On the intensity of regional tensions, see David Brion Davis, *The Slave Power Conspiracy and the Paranoid Style* (Baton Rouge: Louisiana State University Press, 1970).

71. William H. Pease, "The Saints and Sinners of Bertram Wyatt-Brown," *Reviews in American History* 15, no. 2 (June 1987), 180. Research has "presented the slaveholders as sincere and impassioned opponents of liberal capitalism whose social ideals were closer to those of antibourgeois European conservatives than to those of Yankee advocates of progress and reform." George M. Frederickson, "From Exceptionalism to Variability: Recent Developments in Cross-National Comparative History," *Journal of American History* 82, no. 2 (September 1995), 597 (discussing Eugene D. Genovese, *The World the Slaveholders Made: Two Essays in Interpretation* [New York: Pantheon, 1969]). This is not to deny that any market forces were at work in the South, but simply to highlight differing regional attitudes and cultures.

72. James M. McPherson, "Antebellum Southern Exceptionalism: A New Look at an Old Question," *Civil War History* 50, no. 4 (December 2004), 430.

73. Bertram Wyatt-Brown, *Southern Honor: Ethics and Behavior in the Old South* (New York: Oxford University Press, 1982); Edward R. Crowther, "Holy Honor: Sacred and Secular in the Old South," *Journal of Southern History* 58, no. 4 (November 1992), 619–36; Edward L. Ayers, *Vengeance and Justice: Crime and Punishment in the 19th Century American South* (New York: Oxford University Press, 1984); Kees Gispen, ed., *What Made the South Different?* (Jackson: University Press of Mississippi, 1990); Orlando Patterson, "The Code of Honor in the Old

South," *Reviews in American History* 12, no. 1 (March 1984), 24–30; John Hope Franklin, *The Militant South, 1800–1861* (Cambridge, MA: Harvard University Press, 1956).

74. Shearer Davis Bowman, "Honor and Martialism in the U.S. South and Prussian East Elbia during the Mid-Nineteenth Century," in Gispen, *What Made the South Different?*, 23.

75. Bertram Wyatt-Brown, *Yankee Saints and Southern Sinners* (Baton Rouge: Louisiana State University Press, 1985), vii.

76. Michael Snay, "American Thought and Southern Distinctiveness: The Southern Clergy and the Sanctification of Slavery," *Civil War History* 35, no. 4 (December 1989), 311–28; Donald G. Mathews, *Religion in the Old South* (Chicago: University of Chicago Press, 1977); Elizabeth Fox-Genovese and Eugene D. Genovese, "The Divine Sanction of Social Order: Religious Foundations of the Southern Slaveholders' World View," *Journal of the American Academy of Religion* 55, no. 2 (Summer 1987), 211–33; J. Brent Morris, *Oberlin, Hotbed of Abolitionism: College, Community, and the Fight for Freedom and Equality in Antebellum America* (Chapel Hill: University of North Carolina Press, 2014); John R. McKivigan, "The Christian Anti-Slavery Convention Movement of the Northwest," *Old Northwest* 5, no. 4 (Winter 1979–1980), 345–66; Stacey M. Robertson, *Hearts Beating for Liberty: Women Abolitionists in the Old Northwest* (Chapel Hill: University of North Carolina Press, 2010); James Connor, "The Antislavery Movement in Iowa," part 2, *Annals of Iowa* 40, no. 6 (Fall 1970), 450–79; Oleta Prinsloo, "'The Abolitionist Factory': Northeastern Religion, David Nelson, and the Mission Institute near Quincy, Illinois, 1836–184," *Journal of the Illinois State Historical Society* 105, no. 1 (Spring 2012), 36–68; Gunja SenGupta, "Servants for Freedom: Christian Abolitionists in Territorial Kansas, 1854–1858," *Kansas History* 16, no. 3 (Autumn 1993), 200–213; Jeanne Gillespie McDonald, "Edward Beecher and the Anti-Slavery Movement in Illinois," *Journal of the Illinois State Historical Society* 105, no. 1 (Spring 2012), 9–35; Douglas Montagna, "Ohio, Evangelical Religion, and the Merging of the Antislavery Movement: Joshua R. Giddings, Salmon P. Chase, and Their Remarkable Crusades against Slavery," *Studies in Midwestern History* 5, no. 1 (2019), 1–35.

77. Peter Temin, "Free Land and Federalism: American Economic Exceptionalism," in Byron E. Schafer, ed., *Is America Different? A New Look at American Exceptionalism* (Oxford: Oxford University Press, 1991), 79–81; John D. Barnhart, *Valley of Democracy: The Frontier versus the Plantation in the Ohio Valley, 1775–1818* (Lincoln: University of Nebraska Press, 1953), 3–19.

78. C. Vann Woodward, *The Burden of Southern History* (Baton Rouge: Louisiana State University, 1960), 190–191 (first quotation); Robert Penn Warren, *The Legacy of the Civil War: Meditations on the Centennial* (New York: Random House, 1961), 14 (second quotation); Gaines M. Foster, *Ghosts of the Confederacy: Defeat, the Lost Cause, and the Emergence of the New South, 1865 to 1913* (New York: Oxford University Press, 1987). On the growth of southern separatism or nationalism, see Avery O. Craven, *The Growth of Southern Nationalism, 1848–1861* (Baton Rouge: Louisiana State University Press, 1953); Drew Gilpin Faust, *The Creation of Confederate Nationalism: Ideology and Identity in the Civil War South* (Baton Rouge: Louisiana State University Press, 1988); John McCardell, *The Idea*

of a Southern Nation: Southern Nationalists and Southern Nationalism, 1830–1860 (New York: W. W. Norton, 1979).

79. McPherson, "Antebellum Southern Exceptionalism," 422 (climate and systems).

80. Larry E. Hudson Jr., *To Have and to Hold: Slave Work and Family Life in Antebellum South Carolina* (Athens: University of Georgia Press, 1997).

81. Catherine Armstrong, *Landscape and Identity in North America's Southern Colonies from 1660 to 1745* (Surrey: Ashgate, 2013), 11.

82. On southern nationalism in South Carolina, see Manisha Sinha, *The Counter-revolution of Slavery: Politics and Ideology in Antebellum South Carolina* (Chapel Hill: University of North Carolina Press, 2000), and Paul D. H. Quigley, "'That History Is Truly the Life of Nations': History and Southern Nationalism in Antebellum South Carolina," *South Carolina Historical Magazine* 106, no. 1 (January 2005), 7–33.

83. See Stephen Kantrowitz, *Ben Tillman and the Reconstruction of White Supremacy* (Chapel Hill: University of North Carolina Press, 2000); Burton, "South as 'Other,'" 15.

84. Burton, "South as 'Other,'" 40. See South Carolina v. Katzenbach, 383 US 301 (1966).

85. W. J. Cash, *The Mind of the South* (New York: Doubleday, 1954), 11.

86. Susan Gray, *The Yankee West: Community Life on the Michigan Frontier* (Chapel Hill: University of North Carolina Press, 1996); David Hackett Fischer, *Albion's Seed: Four British Folkways in America* (New York: Oxford University Press, 1989); John C. Hudson, "Yankeeland in the Middle West," *Journal of Geography* 85, no. 5 (September 1986), 195–200; David Maldwyn Ellis, "The Yankee Invasion of New York, 1783–1850," *New York History* 32, no. 1 (1951), 3–17.

87. On this legacy, see Jonathan Daniel Wells, *The Kidnapping Club: Wall Street, Slavery, and Resistance on the Eve of the Civil War* (New York: Bold Type Books, 2020). On the abolition of slavery in New England and Pennsylvania during the Revolution and in New York (1799) and New Jersey (1804), see the classic treatment by Arthur Zilversmit, *The First Emancipation: The Abolition of Slavery in the North* (Chicago: University of Chicago Press, 1967).

88. Gleaves Whitney, "The Upper Midwest as the Second Promised Land," in Jon K. Lauck, Joe Hogan, and Gleaves Whitney, eds., *Finding a New Midwestern History* (Lincoln: University of Nebraska Press, 2018), 281–302.

89. James H. Perkins, "Discourse before the Ohio Historical Society," *Transactions of the Ohio Historical and Philosophical Society* 1 (1836), 298.

90. Terry A. Barnhart, "'A Common Feeling': Regional Identity and Historical Consciousness in the Old Northwest, 1820–1860," *Michigan Historical Review* 29, no. 1 (Spring 2003), 48–49.

91. Barnhart, "'Common Feeling,'" 49.

92. James T. Kloppenberg, "In Retrospect: Morton White's *Social Thought in America*," *Reviews in American History* 15, no. 3 (September 1987), 518.

93. Wallace: "There are these two young fish swimming along, and they happen to meet an older fish swimming the other way, who nods at them and says, 'Morning, boys, how's the water?' And the two young fish swim on for a bit, and then

eventually one of them looks over at the other and goes, 'What the hell is water?'" Wallace, "This is Water," Kenyon College, May 21, 2005.

94. To be precise, African Americans were 0.006 percent of the population of Michigan in 1850. Minnesota and Illinois were also 0.006 percent; Iowa 0.001 percent; Ohio and Indiana 0.01 percent; Wisconsin 0.002 percent; and Missouri, a borderland slave state, 13 percent. Campbell Gibson and Kay Jung, *Historical Census Statistics on Population Totals by Race, 1790 to 1990*, Population Division Working Paper No. 56 (Washington, DC: U.S. Census Bureau, September 2002), Tables 28, 29, 30, 37, 38, 40, 50, 64

95. James H. Madison, *The Ku Klux Klan in the Heartland* (Bloomington: Indiana University Press, 2020).

96. Kevin Boyle, *Arc of Justice: A Saga of Race, Civil Rights, and Murder in the Jazz Age* (New York: Henry Holt, 2001).

97. William M. Tuttle Jr., *Race Riot: Chicago in the Red Summer of 1919* (Urbana: University of Illinois Press, 1996); Kevin Boyle, "The Ruins of Detroit: Exploring the Urban Crisis in the Motor City," *Michigan Historical Review* 27, no. 1 (Spring 2001), 109–27.

98. Jon K. Lauck, "'I'm a Rootless Man': Richard Wright and the Limits of Midwestern Regionalism," *MidAmerica* 44 (2017), 78–95. On the Great Migration and smaller Midwestern cities, see the special issue of *Middle West Review* 7, no. 2 (Spring 2021).

99. Joseph Hogan, "Malcolm X in Michigan," *Middle West Review* 3, no. 2 (Spring 2017), 137–42.

100. J. H. Hexter, *On Historians: Reappraisals of Some of the Masters of Modern History* (Cambridge, MA: Harvard University Press, 1979), 241–42.

101. Robert Dawidoff, "*The Growth of American Thought:* A Reconsideration," *Reviews in American History* 14, no. 3 (September 1986), 475 (quotation), 474 (arguing that the historical profession "has lost its bearings in specialization").

102. Ashley Glassburn, "Settler Standpoints," *William and Mary Quarterly* 76, no. 3 (July 2019), 399. The point here is to promote scholarly comity and a diversity of viewpoints and not to yield to the currently dominant paradigm of historical writing or to demand that all scholarship be done the same. Let a thousand flowers bloom.

103. Because of the "bagelization" of the academy, "nearly all of the action has occurred at the perimeter for such a long time that we now have a difficult time even conceiving its center"; the "focus on aberrant or eccentric spaces" has created a "centerless field in which all the intellectual chewing goes on at the edges." Jeff Allred, "Situating Normal: Questions of Centrality in American Studies," *American Literary History* 25, no. 2 (Summer 2013), 441 (discussing American studies). Drew Cayton once observed that, "in general, historians tend these days to want to aggrandize those who lost at the expense of those who won and to imagine that the world might be better if the outcome had been reversed." Andrew R. L. Cayton, "The Meanings of the Wars for the Great Lakes," in David Curtis Skaggs and Larry L. Nelson, eds., *The Sixty Years' War for the Great Lakes, 1754–1814* (East Lansing: Michigan State University Press, 2001), 379.

104. James P. Shannon, "Bishop Ireland's Connemara Experiment," *Minnesota History* 35, no. 5 (March 1957), 205.

105. Jon K. Lauck, *From Warm Center to Ragged Edge: The Erosion of Midwestern Literary and Historical Regionalism, 1920–1965* (Iowa City: University of Iowa Press, 2017).

106. Daniel Walker Howe, "Victorian Culture in America," in Howe, ed., *Victorian America* (Philadelphia: University of Pennsylvania Press, 1976), 28.

CHAPTER 1

1. Senator Thomas Corwin speech, July 24, 1848, Isaac Strohm, ed., *Speeches of Thomas Corwin, with a Sketch of His Life* (Dayton, OH: W. F. Comly, 1859), 406.

2. James M. Banner Jr., "The Charter of Federal Colonialism," *Reviews in American History* 16, no. 2 (June 1988), 205.

3. R. R. Palmer, *The Age of Democratic Revolutions: The Political History of Europe and America, 1760–1800* (Princeton, NJ: Princeton University Press, 1959).

4. Robert Kelley, *The Cultural Pattern in American Politics: The First Century* (Lanham, MD: University Press of America, 1979), 109.

5. David Armitage, *The Declaration of Independence: A Global History* (Cambridge, MA: Harvard University Press, 2007); Palmer, *Age of Democratic Revolutions*, 239–82.

6. Donald W. Treadgold, *Freedom: A History* (New York: New York University Press, 1990), 212.

7. Gordon Wood, *The Radicalism of the American Revolution* (New York: Vintage, 1991).

8. James H. Kettner, *The Development of American Citizenship, 1608–1870* (Chapel Hill: University of North Carolina Press, 1978).

9. Frederick Jackson Turner, "Western State-Making in the Revolutionary Era," *American Historical Review* vol. 1, no. 1 (October 1895), 70.

10. William F. Raney, "The People of the Land," in *The Culture of the Middle West* (Appleton, WI: Lawrence College Press, 1944), 24.

11. Henry Steele Commager, *The Empire of Reason: How Europe Imagined and America Realized the Enlightenment* (New York: Doubleday, 1978), 265 (quotation); Ray Allen Billington, *Land of Savagery, Land of Promise: The European Image of the American Frontier in the Nineteenth Century* (New York: W. W. Norton, 1981), 241–61.

12. Frederick Jackson Turner, "The Significance of the Section in American History," *Wisconsin Magazine of History* 8, no. 3 (March 1925), 263.

13. Merle Curti, *The Growth of American Thought* (New York: Harper and Brothers, 1943), 264.

14. Paul E. Belting, "The Development of the Free Public High School in Illinois to 1860," *Journal of the Illinois State Historical Society* 11, no. 4 (January 1919), 468.

15. James E. Davis, "'New Aspects of Men and New Forms of Society': The Old Northwest, 1790–1820," *Journal of the Illinois State Historical Society* 69, no. 3 (August 1976), 164–66; J. R. Pole, "Historians and the Problem of Early American

Democracy," *American Historical Review* 67, no. 3 (April 1962), 629; Andrew R. L. Cayton, *The Frontier Republic: Ideology and Politics in the Ohio Country, 1780–1825* (Kent, OH: Kent State University Press, 1986), xi; George M. Frederickson, *The Inner Civil War: Northern Intellectuals and the Crisis of the Union* (Urbana: University of Illinois Press, 1965), 8–9; John Higham, *From Boundlessness to Consolidation: The Transformation of American Culture, 1848–1860* (Ann Arbor, MI: William L. Clements Library, 1969), 6.

16. David Spring, "Walter Bagehot and Deference," *American Historical Review* 81, no. 3 (June 1976), 526.

17. J. Crevecoeur, *Letters from an American Farmer* (New York: Dolphin Books, n.d.), 46–48.

18. John V. Jezierski, "A Fortnight in the Wilds: Alexis de Tocqueville, Michigan, and the *Democracy*, 1831," *Michigan History* 64, no. 3 (May/June 1980), 29.

19. James H. Perkins, "Discourse before the Ohio Historical Society," *Transactions of the Ohio Historical and Philosophical Society* 1 (1836), 282; Robert C. Vitz, "The Troubled Life of James Handasyd Perkins," *Queen City Heritage* 53, no. 3 (Fall 1995), 42, 43–44 (noting that Perkins was also the editor of *The Western Messenger*, the first president of the Cincinnati Historical Society, and actively involved in the Cincinnati Law Library, Ohio Mechanics Institute, Cincinnati Astronomical Society, and Western Academy of Natural Science).

20. Peter S. Onuf, "The Northwest Ordinance and Regional Identity," *Wisconsin Magazine of History* 72, no. 4 (Summer 1989), 298.

21. Dan Elbert Clark, *The Middle West in American History* (New York: Thomas Y. Crowell, 1937), 176; John A. Lupton, "Inheriting the Earth: The Law of Succession," in Daniel W. Stowell, ed., *In Tender Consideration: Women, Families, and the Law in Abraham Lincoln's Illinois* (Urbana: University of Illinois Press, 2002), 104 (explaining that "English laws placed many encumbrances on the land to sustain an aristocracy").

22. Eric Foner, *Free Soil, Free Labor, Free Men: The Ideology of the Republican Party before the Civil War* (New York: Oxford University Press, 1970), 64 (feeling, despotic, and espionage). See generally Joseph H. Mahaffey, "Carl Schurz's Letters from the South," *Georgia Historical Quarterly* 35, no. 3 (September 1951), 222–57.

23. Frederick Jackson Turner, *The Frontier in American History* (New York: H. Holt, 1920), 293.

24. Walter Havighurst, *The Heartland: Ohio, Indiana, Illinois* (New York: Harper and Row, 1956), 176. See also Donald J. Ratcliffe, "The Changing Political World of Thomas Worthington," in Andrew R. L. Cayton and Stuart D. Hobbs, eds., *The Center of a Great Empire: The Ohio Country in the Early American Republic* (Athens: Ohio University Press, 2005), 36–61, and Cushing Strout, *The American Image of the Old World* (New York: Harper and Row, 1963).

25. Davis, "'New Aspects,'" 164, 166.

26. Frederick Trautmann, "Kossuth in Indiana," *Indiana Magazine of History* 63, no. 4 (December 1967), 308. See also James Shortridge, "The Emergence of 'Middle West' as an American Regional Label," *Annals of the Association of American Geographers* 74, no. 2 (1984), 214.

27. Davis, "'New Aspects,'" 169.

28. Henry May, "Political Ideas in the Middle West," in *Culture of the Middle West*, 29 (quotation); William E. Lingelbach, "Foreward," in Jeannette P. Nichols and James G. Randall, eds., *Democracy in the Middle West, 1840–1940* (New York: D. Appleton-Century, 1941), vii.

29. Helmut Hirsch, "Theodor Erasmus Hilgard, Ambassador of Americanism," *Journal of the Illinois State Historical Society* 37, no. 2 (June 1944), 164–72.

30. Robert R. Hubach, "Walt Whitman in Kansas," *Kansas Historical Quarterly* 10, no. 2 (May 1941), 150–54 (quotation); Kenyon Gradert, "Walt Whitman's Heartland Romance," in Jon K. Lauck, ed., *The Making of the Midwest: Essays on the Formation of Midwestern Identity, 1787–1900* (Hastings, NE: Hastings College Press, 2020), 101–13.

31. Turner quoted in Daniel Bell, "The End of American Exceptionalism," *Public Interest* 41 (Fall 1975), 208, 209 (noting the "observations of European travelers, applauding or appalled, as they observed the free-and-easy ways of Midwestern Americans, the unwillingness to 'doff one's cap' or use the deferential 'sir'").

32. Rollin Lynde Hartt, "Middle-Westerners and That Sort of People," *Century Magazine* 93 (1916), 173.

33. Robert Cochran, *Louise Pound: Scholar, Athlete, Feminist Pioneer* (Lincoln: University of Nebraska Press, 2009), 8.

34. Clara Martin Baker, "Books in a Pioneer Household," *Journal of the Illinois State Historical Society* 32, no. 3 (September 1939), 261–87.

35. Edward Everett Dale, "Culture on the American Frontier," *Nebraska History* 26, no. 2 (April–June 1945), 81.

36. Bruce Cumings, *Dominion from Sea to Sea: Pacific Ascendancy and American Power* (Chicago: University of Chicago Press, 2010), 14.

37. Barton E. Price, "The Protestant Imagination and the Making of the Midwest as America's Heartland," in Lauck, *Making of the Midwest*, 85. See also T. Scott Miyakawa, *Protestants and Pioneers: Individualism and Conformity on the American Frontier* (Chicago: University of Chicago Press, 1964).

38. R. Carlyle Buley, *The Old Northwest: Pioneer Period, 1815–1840*, vol. 1 (Indianapolis: Indiana Historical Society, 1950), 87.

39. Alan Simpson, *Puritanism in Old and New England* (Chicago: University of Chicago Press, 1955), 22–25.

40. Treadgold, *Freedom*, 211–12. See also Chris Beneke and Christopher S. Grenda, eds., *The First Prejudice: Religious Tolerance and Intolerance in Early America* (Philadelphia: University of Pennsylvania Press, 2011), and Steven Waldman, *Sacred Liberty: America's Long, Bloody, and Ongoing Struggle for Religious Freedom* (New York: HarperCollins, 2019).

41. Rush Welter, "The Frontier West as Image of American Society: Conservative Attitudes before the Civil War," *Mississippi Valley Historical Review* 46, no. 4 (March 1960), 595.

42. Paul Finkelman, "The Northwest Ordinance: A Constitution for an Empire of Liberty," in *Pathways to the Old Northwest: An Observance of the Bicentennial of the Northwest Ordinance* (Indianapolis: Indiana Historical Society, 1988), 7.

43. Kenneth H. Wheeler, "How Colleges Shaped a Public Culture of Usefulness," in Cayton and Hobbs, *Center of a Great Empire*, 107.

44. Louis B. Wright, *Culture on the Moving Frontier* (Bloomington: Indiana University Press, 1955), 90.

45. Andrew R. L. Cayton and Peter Onuf, *The Midwest and the Nation: Rethinking the History of an American Region* (Bloomington: Indiana University Press, 1990), 48.

46. Davis, "'New Aspects,'" 168 (quotation); J. G. Randall, "Remarks by the Chairman," in Nichols and Randall, *Democracy in the Middle West*, 7; Havighurst, *Heartland*, 160–61; Avery Craven, "The Advance of Civilization into the Middle West in the Period of Settlement," in Dixon Ryan Fox, ed., *Sources of Culture in the Middle West: Backgrounds versus Frontier* (New York: Russell and Russell, 1964 [1934]), 46; R. Douglas Hurt, *The Ohio Frontier: Crucible of the Old Northwest, 1720–1830* (Bloomington: Indiana University Press, 1998), 284–314.

47. Stanley Elkins and Eric McKitrick, "A Meaning for Turner's Frontier: Part I: Democracy in the Old Northwest," *Political Science Quarterly* 69, no. 3 (September 1954), 332.

48. C. Robert Haywood, *Victorian West: Class and Culture in Kansas Cattle Towns* (Lawrence: University Press of Kansas, 1991), 91.

49. Timothy L. Smith, "Protestant Schooling and American Nationality, 1800–1850," *Journal of American History* 53, no. 4 (March 1967), 688 (powerful and insufficient), 689 (nonsectarian).

50. Elkins and McKitrick, "Meaning for Turner's Frontier," 348–49.

51. Sidney E. Mead, "In Search of God," in John J. Murray, ed., *The Heritage of the Middle West* (Norman: University of Oklahoma Press, 1958), 160.

52. John Higham, "Hanging Together: Divergent Unities in American History," *Journal of American History* 61, no. 1 (June 1974), 12–13.

53. Michael C. Steiner, *Horace M. Kallen in the Heartland: The Midwestern Roots of American Pluralism* (Lawrence: University Press of Kansas, 2020). See also Ralph Janis, "Ethnic Mixture and the Persistence of Cultural Pluralism in the Church Communities in Detroit, 1880–1940," *Mid-America* 61, no. 2 (April–July 1979), 99–106.

54. See Jason S. Lantzer, "Forging God's Country: The Northwest Territorial Ordinance, the Second Great Awakening, and the Midwestern Vision for America," in Lauck, *Making of the Midwest*, 17–23.

55. Phillip R. Shriver, "Freedom's Proving Ground: The Heritage of the Northwest Ordinance," *Wisconsin Magazine of History* 72, no. 2 (Winter 1988/1989), 129.

56. Ray A. Billington, "The Historians of the Northwest Ordinance," *Journal of the Illinois State Historical Society* 40, no. 4 (December 1947), 397.

57. Daniel Webster, *The Works of Daniel Webster* (Boston: Little, Brown, 1851), 3, 264 (speech given January 20, 1830).

58. Onuf, "Northwest Ordinance," 303.

59. Terry A. Barnhart, "An Emerging Voice: The Origins of Regional Identity and Mission in the Old Northwest," in Lauck, *Making of the Midwest*, 1.

60. Banner, "Charter of Federal Colonialism," 208.

61. John Craig Hammond, "Slavery, Settlement, and Empire: The Expansion and Growth of Slavery in the Interior of the North American Continent, 1770–1820," *Journal of the Early Republic* 32, no. 2 (Summer 2012), 203.

62. Elkins and McKitrick, "Meaning for Turner's Frontier," 335.

63. John Craig Hammond, "'The Most Free of the Free States': Politics, Slavery, Race, and Regional Identity in Early Ohio, 1790–1820," *Ohio History* 121 (2014), 42.

64. Hammond, "'Most Free of the Free States,'" 43.

65. Clark, *Middle West in American History*, 183; Cayton, *Frontier Republic*, 77.

66. Cayton, *Frontier Republic*, x (impressive), 110 (legally).

67. "Corydon's Absence: A Pastoral Elegy," *Weekly Magazine or Edinburgh Amusement* (June 30, 1774), 17–18; Havighurst, *Heartland*, 158; James H. Madison, "Extending Liberty Westward: The Northwest Ordinance of 1787," *OAH Magazine of History* 2, no. 4 (Fall 1987), 17. On the prestatehood era, see John D. Barnhart, "The Democratization of Indiana Territory," *Indiana Magazine of History* 43, no. 1 (March 1947), 1–22.

68. Buley, *Old Northwest*, vol. 1, 69.

69. 1816 Indiana Constitution, article 8.

70. Quoted in *Philanthropist* (Ohio), June 28, 1816 and cited in Buley, *Old Northwest*, vol. 1, 70.

71. Richard V. Carpenter and J. W. Kitchell, "The Illinois Constitution of 1818," *Journal of the Illinois State Historical Society* 6, no. 3 (October 1913), 328.

72. Agis, *Illinois Intelligencer* (Kaskaskia), July 1, 1818, quoted in Buley, *Old Northwest*, vol. 1, 83.

73. *Valley of Democracy*, 214.

74. Buley, *Old Northwest*, vol. 1, 81.

75. Roger L. Rosentreter, "Michigan's Quest for Statehood, 1832–1837," in Richard J. Hathaway, *Michigan: Visions of Our Past* (East Lansing: Michigan State University Press, 1989), 83, 91.

76. J.C.P., "The Celebration of the Fiftieth Anniversary of the Adoption of the Constitution of the State of Iowa," *Annals of Iowa* 8, no. 1 (1907), 62–65.

77. Joyce Appleby, "The American Heritage: The Heirs and the Disinherited," *Journal of American History* 74, no. 3 (December 1987), 800.

78. 1802 Ohio Constitution, Art. IV, sec. 5; Helen M. Thurston, "The 1802 Constitutional Convention and Status of the Negro," *Ohio History* 81, no. 1 (Winter 1972), 23; Donald Ratcliffe, "The Right to Vote and the Rise of Democracy, 1787–1828," *Journal of the Early Republic* 33, no. 2 (Summer 2013), 238. A large county delegation composed of migrants from Virginia was "largely responsible for the convention's decision to deny voting rights to African Americans." Hammond, "'Most Free of the Free States,'" 43. Ohio briefly had a modest taxpaying requirement for voters, but this was dropped by other midwestern states as state creation efforts moved west.

79. John D. Barnhart, "Sources of Indiana's First Constitution," *Indiana Magazine of History* 39, no. 1 (March 1943), 55.

80. Rosentreter, "Michigan's Quest for Statehood," 83, 91.

81. Ratcliffe, "Right to Vote," 238.

82. Ratcliffe, "Right to Vote," 252.

83. Robert J. Steinfeld, "Property and Suffrage in the Early American Republic," *Stanford Law Review* 41, no. 2 (January 1989), 354, n. 59. Steinfeld recognizes that "the new Western states" often dropped restrictions on voting, but this is properly seen as new midwestern states.

84. Ratcliffe, "Right to Vote," 253, n. 67.

85. Steinfeld, "Property and Suffrage in the Early American Republic," 335.

86. See Dixon Ryan Fox, *The Decline of Aristocracy in the Politics of New York, 1801–1840* (New York: Columbia University, 1919), and Harvey Strum, "Property Qualifications and Voting Behavior in New York, 1807–1816," *Journal of the Early Republic* 1, no. 4 (Winter 1981), 347–71.

87. Donald J. Ratcliffe, "Voter Turnout in Early Ohio," *Journal of the Early Republic* 7, no. 3 (Autumn 1987), 231. Ratcliffe explains that part of the reason voter participation grew during early Ohio statehood was the end of the Northwest Ordinance's requirement that voters own 50 acres freehold or town lots of equivalent value.

88. Ratcliffe, "Voter Turnout in Early Ohio," 234.

89. Donald Ratcliffe, "The Experience of Revolution and the Beginnings of Party Politics in Ohio, 1776–1816," *Ohio History* 85 (1976), 186–230.

90. Ratcliffe, "Voter Turnout in Early Ohio," 237.

91. Donald J. Ratcliffe, *Party Spirit in a Frontier Republic: Democratic Politics in Ohio, 1793–1821* (Columbus: Ohio State University Press, 1998), 12. For examples of the lively aspects of early Ohio politics, see Emil Pocock, "Popular Roots of Jacksonian Democracy: The Case of Dayton, Ohio, 1815–1830," *Journal of the Early Republic* 9, no. 4 (Winter 1989), 489–515.

92. Elkins and McKitrick, "Meaning for Turner's Frontier," 345; Ernest V. Shockley, "County Seats and County Seat Wars in Indiana," *Indiana Magazine of History* 10, no. 1 (March 1914), 1–5; Henry F. Mason, "County Seat Controversies in Southwestern Kansas," *Kansas Historical Quarterly* 2, no. 1 (February 1933), 45–65. See also Tom Schmiedler, "Civic Geometry: Frontier Forms of Minnesota's County Seats," *Minnesota History* 57, no. 7 (Fall 2001), 330–45.

93. Thomas J. Brown, "The Age of Ambition in Quincy, Illinois," *Journal of the Illinois State Historical Society* 75, no. 4 (Winter 1982), 242–62. On the forgotten campaigns the following year, see Harry V. Jaffa and Robert W. Johannsen, eds., *In the Name of the People: Speeches and Writings of Lincoln and Douglas in the Ohio Campaign of 1859* (Columbus: Ohio State University Press, 1959).

94. Davis, "'New Aspects,'" 166 (awe and doubt).

95. Henry May, "Political Ideas in the Middle West," in *Culture of the Middle West*, 31. On the famed log cabins, see Donald A. Hutslar, *The Architecture of Migration: Log Construction in the Ohio Country, 1750–1850* (Athens: Ohio University Press, 1986).

96. Meredith Nicholson, *The Valley of Democracy* (New York: Charles Scribner's Sons, 1919), 191.

97. Kenneth J. Winkle, "Abraham Lincoln: Self-Made Man," *Journal of the Abraham Lincoln Association* 21, no. 2 (Summer 2000), 4; Robert N. Bellah, "Civil Religion in America," *Daedalus* 96, no. 1 (Winter 1967), 9 (on Lincoln as a centerpiece of American civil religion); Jeffrey Normand Bourdon, "Germans, Jubilee

Singers, and Axe Men: James A. Garfield and the Original Front-Porch Campaign for the Presidency," *Ohio History* 121 (2014), 112–29; Hendrik Booraem, *The Road to Respectability: James A. Garfield and His World, 1844–1852* (Lewisburg, PA: Bucknell University Press, 1988).

98. Hubert G. H. Wilhelm and Allen G. Noble, "Ohio's Settlement Landscape," in Leonard Peacefull, ed., *A Geography of Ohio* (Kent, OH: Kent State University Press, 1996), 80–109.

99. John D. Barnhart, "The Southern Influence in the Formation of Ohio," *Journal of Southern History* 3, no. 1 (February 1937), 28–42; John D. Barnhart, "Sources of Southern Migration into the Old Northwest," *Mississippi Valley Historical Review* 22, no. 1 (June 1935), 49–62; John D. Barnhart, "Southern Contributions to the Social Order of the Old Northwest," *North Carolina Historical Review* 17, no. 3 (July 1940), 237–48.

100. Gregory Rose, "South Central Michigan's Yankees," *Michigan History* 70, no. 2 (March/April 1986), 32–39; Havighurst, *Heartland*, 151; Kelley, *Cultural Pattern in American Politics*, 98.

101. Thomas J. Schlereth, "The New England Presence on the Midwest Landscape," *Old Northwest* 9, no. 2 (Spring 1983), 128–42; Havighurst, *Heartland*, 153; Richard Lyle Power, "The Crusade to Extend Yankee Culture, 1820–1865," *New England Quarterly* 13, no. 4 (December 1940), 638–53.

102. Havighurst, *Heartland*, 155; Foner, *Free Soil, Free Labor*, 48–50. See also Susan E. Gray, *The Yankee West: Community Life on the Michigan Frontier* (Chapel Hill: University of North Carolina Press, 1996).

103. Havighurst, *Heartland*, 152. See also Frank I. Herriott, "The Transfusion of Political Ideas and Institutions in Iowa," *Annals of Iowa* 6, no. 1 (1903), 46–54; James Z. Schwartz, *Conflict on the Michigan Frontier: Yankee and Borderland Cultures, 1815–1840* (DeKalb: Northern Illinois University Press, 2009); Douglas K. Meyer, *Making the Heartland Quilt: A Geographical History of Settlement and Migration in Early-Nineteenth-Century Illinois* (Carbondale: Southern Illinois University Press, 2000); and Nicole Etcheson, "The Making of Midwesterners: The Fletcher Family in Indiana," in Lauck, *Making of the Midwest*, 115–28.

104. Hermann R. Muelder, "'The Moral Lights around Us,'" *Journal of the Illinois State Historical Society* 52, no. 2 (Summer 1959), 248–49.

105. Havighurst, *Heartland*, 167; Eileen McMahon, "The Irish Midwest," manuscript submitted to Oxford University Press for inclusion in John K. Lauck, ed., "The Oxford Handbook of Midwestern History."

106. Havighurst, *Heartland*, 167.

107. Millard L. Gieske and Steve J. Keillor, *Norwegian Yankee: Knute Nelson and the Failure of American Politics* (Northfield, MN: Norwegian-American Historical Association, 1995).

108. Hartt, "Middle-Westerners," 171.

109. Settler Johann David Schoepf quoted in Davis, "'New Aspects,'" 164.

110. Merle Curti, "The Impact of the Revolutions of 1848 on American Thought," *Proceedings of the American Philosophical Society* 93, no. 3 (June 1949), 209–15; Carl Frederick Wittke, *Refugees of Revolution: The German Forty-Eighters*

in America (Philadelphia: University of Pennsylvania Press, 1952); Adolf Eduard Zucker, *The Forty-Eighters: Political Refugees of the German Revolution of 1848* (New York: Columbia University Press, 1950); Daniel Bell, "American Exceptionalism Revisited," *Public Interest* 95 (Spring 1989), 49 (noting,"Marx was constantly warning the German radicals not to go to the United States" because the "democratic and egalitarian atmosphere" would undermine socialist beliefs). See also Marcus Lee Hansen, *The Immigrant in American History* (Cambridge, MA: Harvard University Press, 1940); Billington, *Land of Savagery*.

111. Eric Dudley, "Remembering and Forgetting: The Memorialization of General James Birdseye McPherson in McPherson, Kansas," *Kansas History* 36, no. 4 (Winter 2013/2014), 265.

112. Havighurst, *Heartland*, 178. For an earlier example of a prominent visitor enlivening civic life, see C. B. Galbreath, "Lafayette's Visit to Ohio Valley States," *Ohio Archaeological and Historical Quarterly* 29, no. 3 (July 1920), 163–266.

113. Havighurst, *Heartland*, 178.

114. Frederick Trautmann, "Kossuth in Indiana," *Indiana Magazine of History* 63, no. 4 (December 1967), 299–301. See John W. Oliver, "Louis Kossuth's Appeal to the Middle West," *Mississippi Valley Historical Review* 14, no. 4 (March 1928), 481–95.

115. Trautmann, "Kossuth in Indiana," 305 (centuries), 306.

116. Kossuth quoted in Henry Clyde Hubbart, "Regionalism and Democracy in the Middle West, 1840–1865," in Nichols and Randall, *Democracy in the Middle West*, 49.

117. "Kossuth Asked Iowa to Help Cause," *Annals of Iowa* 29, no. 1 (Summer 1947), 56.

118. Michael A. Morrison, "American Reaction to European Revolutions, 1848–1852: Sectionalism, Memory, and the Revolutionary Heritage," *Civil War History* 49, no. 2 (June 2003), 113; Richard H. Sewell, *A House Divided: Sectionalism and Civil War, 1848–1865* (Baltimore, MD: Johns Hopkins University Press, 1988), 37.

119. Sewell, *House Divided*, 38.

120. Davis, "'New Aspects,'" 171.

121. Davis, "'New Aspects,'" 168.

122. Stephen J. Tonsor, "'I Am My Own Boss'—A German Immigrant Writes from Illinois," *Journal of the Illinois State Historical Society* 54, no. 4 (Winter 1961), 392–404.

123. Max Weber, *The Protestant Ethic and the Spirit of Capitalism* (New York: Scribner, 1935), 55–56.

124. Ralph Lerner, "Commerce and Character: The Anglo-American as New-Model Man," *William and Mary Quarterly* 36, no. 1 (January 1979), 5.

125. Onuf, "Northwest Ordinance," 295.

126. Burton J. Bledstein, *The Culture of Professionalism: The Middle Class and the Development of Higher Education in America* (New York: W. W. Norton, 1978), 219; John W. Meyer, David Tyack, Joane Nagel, and Audri Gordon, "Public Education as Nation-Building in America: Enrollments and Bureaucratization in the American States, 1870–1930," *American Journal of Sociology* 85, no. 3 (November 1979), 599.

127. Mary Kupiec Cayton, "The Making of an American Prophet: Emerson, His Audiences, and the Rise of the Culture Industry in Nineteenth-Century America," *American Historical Review* 92, no. 3 (June 1987), 606.

128. Deirdre McCloskey, *Bourgeois Virtue: Ethics for an Age of Commerce* (Chicago: University of Chicago Press, 2007).

129. Thomas Augst, *The Clerk's Tale: Young Men and Moral Life in Nineteenth-Century America* (Chicago: University of Chicago Press, 2003), 6; Jocelyn Wills, *Boosters, Hustlers, and Speculators: Entrepreneurial Culture and the Rise of Minneapolis and St. Paul, 1849–1883* (St. Paul: Minnesota Historical Society Press, 2005); Jeffrey S. Adler, *Yankee Merchants and the Making of the Urban West: The Rise and Fall of Antebellum St. Louis* (New York: Cambridge University Press, 1991); Les Valentine, "Boosting 'Omaha the Market Town': The 1906 Trade Excursion across Northern Kansas," *Kansas History* 15, no. 2 (Summer 1992), 82–96. On Nebraska origins and the bootstrap story of the creator of Hallmark Cards, see L. Robert Puschendorf, "The Halls of Hallmark: The Nebraska Years," *Nebraska History* 89, no. 3 (Fall 2008), 2–13.

130. Havighurst, *Heartland*, 156.

131. Donald F. Tingley, "Ralph Waldo Emerson on the Illinois Lecture Circuit," *Journal of the Illinois State Historical Society* 64, no. 2 (Summer 1971), 198. Aristocratic European observers often complained about the middle-class focus on gain. See Daniel Walker Howe, *What Hath God Wrought: The Transformation of America, 1815–1848* (New York: Oxford University Press, 2007), 310; Robert C. Nesbit, "Making a Living in Wisconsin, 1873–1893," *Wisconsin Magazine of History* 69, no. 4 (Summer 1986), 251.

132. Davis, "'New Aspects,'" 167–68.

133. Ginette Aley, "Grist, Grit, and Rural Society in the Early Nineteenth Century Midwest: Insight Gleaned from Grain," *Ohio Valley History* 5, no. 2 (Summer 2005), 3–5; Jeremy Atack and Fred Bateman, "Self-Sufficiency and the Marketable Surplus in the Rural North, 1860," *Agricultural History* 58, no. 3 (July 1984), 296–313; Sean Hartnett, "The Land Market on the Wisconsin Frontier: An Examination of Land Ownership Processes in Turtle and LaPrairie Townships, 1839–1890," *Agricultural History* 65, no. 4 (Autumn 1991), 38–77; Pamela Riney Kehrberg, "Child Labor on Nebraska Farms, 1870–1920," *Nebraska History* 82, no. 1 (Spring 2001), 2–10. Notwithstanding his generally anti-farmer views, Richard Hofstadter was right to emphasize the market orientation of farmers. Richard Hofstadter, *The Age of Reform: From Bryan to FDR* (New York: Vintage Books, 1955), 39–59.

134. Joseph Schafer, "Beginnings of Civilization in the Old Northwest: The Ordinance of 1787," *Wisconsin Magazine of History* 21, no. 2 (December 1937), 224.

135. Mark W. Friedberger, "Handing Down the Home Place," *Annals of Iowa* 47, no. 6 (Fall 1984), 518–36.

136. Billington, *Land of Savagery*, 231–32.

137. Joseph Schafer, ed., "Lincoln's 1859 Address at Milwaukee," *Wisconsin Magazine of History* 10, no. 3 (March 1927), 256.

138. James E. Potter, "'The Prairie Plow Was at Work': J. Sterling Morton's 1859 Address on Nebraska Agriculture," *Nebraska History* 84, no. 4 (Winter 2003), 212.

139. Schafer, "Lincoln's 1859 Address," 257. See also Marcia Noe, "The Innocent Midwest and the New Midwestern Pastoral," in Lauck, *Making of the Midwest*,
37–52, and Robert T. Rhode, "The Persistence of Place: Alice Cary's Authentic
Rural Settings," *Ohio Valley History* 7, no. 1 (Spring 2007), 47–59.

140. Richard Edwards, Jacob K. Friefeld, and Rebecca S. Wingo, *Homesteading
the Plains: Toward a New History* (Lincoln: University of Nebraska Press, 2017);
Homer E. Socolofsky, "Success and Failure in Nebraska Homesteading," *Agricultural History* 42, no. 2 (April 1968), 103–8.

141. The average Midwestern farm was 250 acres, a great contrast to the landed
estates of Europe and the tidewater plantations of the South. Elkins and McKitrick, "Meaning for Turner's Frontier," 336. See also Mary Hurlbut Cordier, "Prairie
Schoolwomen, Mid-1850s to 1920s, in Iowa, Kansas, and Nebraska," *Great Plains
Quarterly* 8, no. 2 (Spring 1988), 102–19.

142. Morton and Lucia White, *The Intellectual versus the City: From Thomas
Jefferson to Frank Lloyd Wright* (Cambridge, MA: Harvard University Press,
1962); Pamela Riney-Kehrberg, "'But What Kind of Work Do the Rest of You
Do?': Child Labor on Nebraska Farms, 1870–1920," *Nebraska History* 82, no. 1
(Spring 2001), 2–10.

143. Christine Pawley, *Reading on the Middle Border: The Culture of Print
in Late-Nineteenth-Century Osage, Iowa* (Amherst: University of Massachusetts
Press, 2010), 189–90; John J. Fry, "'Good Farming-Clear Thinking-Right Living':
Midwestern Farm Newspapers, Social Reform, and Rural Readers in the Early
Twentieth Century," *Agricultural History* 78, no. 1 (Winter 2004), 34–49; Paula M.
Nelson, "'Everything I Want Is Here!': The *Dakota Farmer's* Rural Ideal, 1884–
1934," *South Dakota History* 22, no. 2 (Summer 1992), 105–35.

144. Pawley, *Reading on the Middle Border*, 191 (quoting Pawley).

145. Wayne E. Fuller, "Changing Concepts of the Country School as a Community Center in the Midwest," *Agricultural History* 58, no. 3 (July 1984), 425.

146. Karen Halttunen, *Confidence Men and Painted Women: A Study of Middle-
Class Culture in America, 1830–1870* (New Haven, CT: Yale University Press,
1982), 3; Margaret L. Woodward, "The Northwestern Farmer, 1868–1876: A Tale of
Paradox," *Agricultural History* 37, no. 3 (July 1963), 137–38.

147. Judy Hilkey, *Character Is Capital: Success Manuals and Manhood in
Gilded Age America* (Chapel Hill: University of North Carolina Press, 1997), 23.

148. Pawley, *Reading on the Middle Border*, 191.

149. Timothy B. Spears, *Chicago Dreaming: Midwesterners and the City, 1871–
1919* (Chicago: University of Chicago Press, 2005); Dennis B. Downey, "William
Stead and Chicago: A Victorian Jeremiah in the Windy City," *Mid-America* 68, no.
3 (October 1986), 153–66. The rise of prostitution and venereal disease in cities led
to the creation of the "social hygiene" movement, and its first outpost was Chicago.
Jeffrey P. Moran, "'Modernism Gone Mad': Sex Education Comes to Chicago,
1913," *Journal of American History* 83, no. 2 (September 1986), 482.

150. Cayton, "Making of an American Prophet," 605–6.

151. Richard J. Oglesby, "Tribute to Corn," *Journal of the Illinois State Historical Society* 4, no. 3 (October 1911), 341 (quotation); Richard Lyle Power, "Settlers

on Corn Belt Soil," *Indiana Magazine of History* 49, no. 2 (June 1953), 161–72; Havighurst, *Heartland*, 146; "'State Song,' 'Corn Song,' and 'Iowa—Beautiful Land,'" *Annals of Iowa* 16, no. 1 (Summer 1927), 52–57; Cynthia Clampitt, *Midwest Maize: How Corn Shaped the U.S. Heartland* (Urbana: University of Illinois Press, 2015), 173–86.

152. Louise L. Stevenson, *The Victorian Homefront: American Thought and Culture, 1860–1880* (Ithaca, NY: Cornell University Press, 1991), 6.

153. Theodore C. Blegen, "The 'Fashionable Tour' on the Upper Mississippi," *Minnesota History* 20, no. 4 (December 1939), 377–96 (describing the nature tours on the river); Curtis C. Roseman and Elizabeth M. Roseman, eds., *Grand Excursions on the Upper Mississippi River: Places, Landscapes, and Regional Identity after 1854* (Iowa City: University of Iowa Press, 2004); Stephen J. Keillor, *Grand Excursion: Antebellum America Discovers the Upper Mississippi* (Afton, MN: Afton Historical Society Press, 2004); Aaron Shapiro, *The Lure of the North Woods: Cultivating Tourism in the Upper Midwest* (Minneapolis: University of Minnesota Press, 2013); Rebecca A. Buller, "Intersections of Place, Time, and Entertainment in Nebraska's Hidden Paradise," *Nebraska History* 92, no. 2 (Summer 2011), 82–95; John Fraser Hart, "Resort Areas in Wisconsin," *Geographic Review* 74, no. 2 (April 1984), 192–217.

154. Stevenson, *Victorian Homefront*, 60; David C. Smith, *City of Parks: The Story of Minneapolis Parks* (Minneapolis: University of Minnesota Press, 2008); L. H. Pammel, "The Arbor Day, Park and Conservation Movements in Iowa," *Annals of Iowa* 17, no. 4 (Spring 1930), 270–313.

155. Wayne E. Fuller, "Making Better Farmers: The Study of Agriculture in Midwestern Country Schools, 1900–1923," *Agricultural History* 60, no. 2 (Spring 1986), 156; David Thomas, "A Fortnight in Michigan's Forests," *Michigan History* 72, no. 4 (July/August 1988), 36–47; John Linstrom and Daniel Rinn, "Agrarian 'Naturism': Liberty Hyde Bailey and the Michigan Frontier," in Joseph Hogan, Jon K. Lauck, Paul Murphy, Andrew Seal, and Gleaves Whitney, eds., *The Sower and the Seer: Perspectives on the Intellectual History of the American Midwest* (Madison: Wisconsin Historical Society Press, 2021), 140–60; Paul Theobald, *Call School: Rural Education in the Midwest to 1918* (Carbondale: Southern Illinois University Press, 1995), 161; Stevenson, *Victorian Homefront*, 34–35.

156. M. M. Quaife, "Increase Allen Lapham, Father of Forest Conservation," *Wisconsin Magazine of History* 5, no. 1 (September 1921), 104–8; William H. Tishler, ed., *Jens Jensen: Writings Inspired by Nature* (Madison: Wisconsin Historical Society Press, 2012); Wallace Stegner, *Beyond the 100th Meridian* (Boston: Houghton, Mifflin, 1954); Walter Brookfield Hendrickson, *David Dale Owen: Pioneer Geologist of the Middle West* (Indianapolis: Indiana Historical Bureau, 1943); Susan L. Flader and J. Baird Callicott, eds., *The River of the Mother of God and Other Essays by Aldo Leopold* (Madison: University of Wisconsin Press, 1991); Sue Leaf, *A Love Affair with Birds: The Life of Thomas Sadler Roberts* (Minneapolis: University of Minnesota Press, 2013); Annette Gallagher, "Citizen of the Nation: John Fletcher Lacey, Conservationist," *Annals of Iowa* 46, no. 1 (Summer 1981), 9–24; Ronald S. Vasile, "The Early Career of Robert Kennicott, Illinois' Pioneering Naturalist," *Illinois Historical Journal* 87, no. 3 (Autumn 1994), 150–70; Linnie

Marsh Wolfe, *Son of the Wilderness: The Life of John Muir* (New York: Alfred A. Knopf, 1945); Sigurd Olson, *The Lonely Land* (New York: Alfred A. Knopf, 1961); William Cronon, "Landscape and Home: Environmental Traditions in Wisconsin," *Wisconsin Magazine of History* 74, no. 2 (Winter 1990–91), 93.

157. On the creation of many midwestern scientific societies such as the Natural History Association of Wisconsin, the Grand Rapids Lyceum of Natural History, and the Chicago Academy of Sciences, see Walter B. Hendrickson, "Science and Culture in the American Middle West," *Isis* 64, no. 3 (September 1973), 329. See also Victoria E. M. Cain, "From Specimens to Stereopticons: The Persistence of the Davenport Academy of Natural Sciences and the Emergence of Scientific Education, 1868–1910," *Annals of Iowa* 68, no. 1 (Winter 2009), 1–36; Maurice M. Vance, *Charles Richard Van Hise: Scientist Progressive* (Madison: State Historical Society of Wisconsin, 1960); Sue Leaf, *Minnesota's Geologist: The Life of Newton Horace Winchell* (Minneapolis: University of Minnesota Press, 2020); Harold F. Mayfield, "Edward Lincoln Moseley, Naturalist and Teacher, 1865–1948," *Northwest Ohio Quarterly* 56, no. 1 (Winter 1984), 3–17; Walter B. Hendrickson, "Science and Culture in Nineteenth Century Michigan," *Michigan History* 57, no. 2 (Summer 1973), 140–50; Stephen Goldfarb, "Science and Democracy: A History of the Cincinnati Observatory, 1842–1872," *Ohio History Journal* 78, no. 3 (Summer 1969), 172–78.

158. Theobald, *Call School*, 161; Merrill Fabry, "This Is Why Arbor Day Is a Thing," *Time*, April 28, 2017.

159. Rotundo, "Body and Soul," 29.

160. Ted V. McAllister, "The Tocqueville Problem and the Nature of American Conservatism," *Anamnesis* 1, no. 1 (2011), 72 (township freedom), 74 (Tocqueville).

161. Edward Everett Dale, "The Social Homesteader," *Nebraska History* 25, no. 3 (1944), 158; Nathan Sanderson, "More Than a Potluck: Shared Meals and Community-Building in Rural Nebraska at the Turn of the Twentieth Century," *Nebraska History* 89, no. 3 (2008), 120–31.

162. Elkins and McKitrick, "Meaning for Turner's Frontier, 331; Allen G. Noble and Hubert G. H. Wilhelm, eds., *Barns of the Midwest* (Athens: Ohio University Press, 1995).

163. Malcolm J. Rohrbough, *The Trans-Appalachian Frontier: People, Societies, and Institutions, 1775–1850* (New York: Oxford University Press, 1978), 145.

164. Schafer, "Beginnings of Civilization," 224; Gary Koerselman, "The Quest for Community in Rural Iowa: Neighborhood Life in Early Middleburg History," *Annals of Iowa* 41, no. 5 (Summer 1972), 1007.

165. Chris Rasmussen, "Progress and Catastrophe: Public History at the Iowa State Fair, 1854–1946," *Annals of Iowa* 63, no. 4 (Fall 2004), 357–89; Richard Gaskell, *The Missouri State Fair: Images of a Midwestern Tradition* (Columbia: University of Missouri Press, 2000); Chris Rasmussen, "'Fairs Here Have Become a Sort of Holiday': Agriculture and Amusements at Iowa's County Fairs, 1838–1925," *Annals of Iowa* 58, no. 1 (Winter 1999), 1–26.

166. Sarah Laskow, "The Forgotten Midwest Craze for Building Palaces Out of Grain," *Atlas Obscura*, November 21, 2015; Dorothy Schwieder and Patricia Swanson, "The Sioux City Corn Palaces," *Annals of Iowa* 41, no. 8 (Spring 1973), 1209–27; David Erpestad and David Wood, *Building South Dakota: A Historical*

Survey of the State's Architecture to 1945 (Pierre: South Dakota State Historical Society, 1997), 198–202; Rod Evans, *Palaces on the Prairie* (Fargo: North Dakota Institute for Regional Studies, 2009).

167. Elkins and McKitrick, "Meaning for Turner's Frontier," 336.

168. Gerald Prescott, "Wisconsin Farm Leaders in the Gilded Age," *Agricultural History* 44, no. 2 (April 1970), 184. See also Robert Leslie Jones, "A History of Local Agricultural Societies in Ohio to 1865," *Ohio Archaeological and Historical Quarterly* 52, no. 2 (April–June 1943), 120–40.

169. May, "Political Ideas in the Middle West," 25; Roy Vernon Scott, "The Rise of the Farmers' Mutual Benefit Association in Illinois, 1883–1891," *Agricultural History* 32, no. 1 (January 1958), 44; George Cerny, "Cooperation in the Midwest in the Granger Era, 1869–1875," *Agricultural History* 37, no. 4 (October 1963), 187–93; Fred Trump, *The Grange in Michigan: An Agricultural History of Michigan over the Past 90 Years* (Grand Rapids: The Author, 1963). See also chapter 5 of this volume.

170. See chapter 5 of this volume.

171. Scott J. Peters and Paul A. Morgan, "The Country Life Commission: Reconsidering a Milestone in American Agricultural History," *Agricultural History* 78, no. 3 (Summer 2004), 289–316; Theobald, *Call School*, 165.

172. Theobald, *Call School*, 167.

173. Clayton S. Ellsworth, "The Coming of Rural Consolidated Schools to the Ohio Valley, 1892–1912," *Agricultural History* 30, no. 3 (July 1956), 122; Theobald, *Call School*, 171.

174. Theobald, *Call School*, 161–62 (uplift), 174 (infuse), 165. See also Wheeler McMillen, ed., *Harvest: An Anthology of Farm Writing* (New York: Appleton-Century, 1964).

175. David B. Danbom, "Romantic Agrarianism in Twentieth-Century America," *Agricultural History* 65, no. 4 (Fall 1991), 1–12.

176. Stevenson, *Victorian Homefront*, 50, xxxii; Trygve R. Tholfsen, "The Intellectual Origins of Mid-Victorian Stability," *Political Science Quarterly* 86, no. 1 (March 1971), 63; John Tomsich, *A Genteel Endeavor: American Culture and Politics in the Gilded Age* (Stanford, CA: Stanford University Press, 1971), 14.

177. Don H. Doyle, "The Social Functions of Voluntary Associations in a Nineteenth-Century American Town," *Social Science History* 1, no. 3 (Spring 1977), 340–41; Pawley, *Reading on the Middle Border*, 139.

178. Ferenc M. Szasz, "The Stress on 'Character and Service' in Progressive America," *Mid-America* 63, no. 3 (October 1981), 150–51.

179. Jeffrey A. Charles, *Service Clubs in American Society: Rotary, Kiwanis, and Lions* (Urbana: University of Illinois Press, 1993), 5; Mark C. Carnes, "Middle-Class Men and the Solace of Fraternal Ritual," in Mark C. Carnes and Clyde Griffin, eds., *Meanings for Manhood: Constructions of Masculinity in Victorian America* (Chicago: University of Chicago Press, 1990), 38; Stevenson, *Victorian Homefront*, 52.

180. George S. Cottman, "Lincoln in Indianapolis," *Indiana Magazine of History* 24, no. 1 (March 1928), 1.

181. See chapter 5.

182. Charles H. Rammelkamp, "Four Historic Societies of Jacksonville, Illinois," *Journal of the Illinois State Historical Society* 18, no. 1 (April 1925), 195.

183. Phebe D. Bassett, "The Jacksonville Sorosis Organized: Founding November 30th, 1868," *Journal of the Illinois State Historical Society* 18, no. 1 (April 1925), 209–12.

184. Andrew P. Yox, "Lost World of Art: Middletown, USA, 1865–1914," *Mid-America* 83, no. 2 (Summer 2001), 106, 118.

185. For a Kansas example, see James C. Malin, "Kansas Philosophers, 1871: T. B. Taylor, Joel Moody, and Edward Schiller," *Kansas Historical Quarterly* 24, no. 2 (Summer 1958), 168–71.

186. Joseph L. Blau, "Food for Middle Western Thought," in Murray, *Heritage of the Middle West*, 190.

187. Blau, "Food for Middle Western Thought," 192–93.

188. Paul Russell Anderson, "Hiram K. Jones and Philosophy in Jacksonville," *Journal of the Illinois State Historical Society* 34, no. 1 (March 1941), 478–520; Blau, "Food for Middle Western Thought," 194–95.

189. Paul Russell Anderson, "Quincy, an Outpost of Philosophy," *Journal of the Illinois State Historical Society* 34, no. 1 (March 1941), 50–83.

190. William H. Tishler, ed., *Midwestern Landscape Architecture* (Urbana: University of Illinois Press, 2000); Michael J. Harkins, "George Washington Lininger: Pioneer Merchant and Art Patron," *Nebraska History* 52, no. 4 (Winter 1971), 346–57; Judith Zivanovic, "Touring Melodramas and Midwest Frontier Values," *Heritage of the Great Plains* 23 (Spring 1990), 18; Richard L. Poole, "Boosting Culture in the Gilded Age: Sioux City Theater, 1870–1904," *Annals of Iowa* 50, no. 2 (Fall 1989), 130–57; Eva Draegert, "Cultural History of Indianapolis: The Theater, 1880–1890," *Indiana Magazine of History* 52, no. 1 (March 1956), 21–48; Stevenson, *Victorian Homefront*, 49; James C. Malin, "Theatre in Kansas, 1858–1868: Background for the Coming of the Lord Dramatic Company to Kansas, 1869," *Kansas Historical Quarterly* 23, no. 1 (Spring 1957), 10–13; Oliver B. Pollak, "Capitalism, Culture, and Philanthropy: Charles N. and Nettie Fowler Dietz of Omaha," *Nebraska History* 79, no. 1 (1998), 34–43; Nancy J. Volkman, "Landscape Architecture on the Prairie: The Work of H. W. S. Cleveland," *Kansas History* 10, no. 2 (Summer 1987), 89–110; Curti, *Growth of American Thought*, 282; Eva Draegert, "Cultural History of Indianapolis: Music, 1875–1890," *Indiana Magazine of History* 53, no. 3 (September 1957), 265–304.

191. Zivanovic, "Touring Melodramas," 18; James C. Malin, "Early Theatre at Fort Scott," *Kansas Historical Quarterly* 24, no. 1 (Spring 1958), 31–34; Eva Draegert, "The Theater in Indianapolis before 1880," *Indiana Magazine of History* 51, no. 2 (June 1955), 121–38; Harold E. Briggs, "Early Variety Theatres in the Trans-Mississippi West," *Mid-America* 34, no. 3 (July 1952), 188–201; Barbara Brice, "The Amateur Theatre in Iowa Life," *Mid-America* 31, no. 4 (October 1949), 248–57.

192. Zivanovic, "Touring Melodramas," 19–20.

193. Harold E. and Ernestine Briggs, "The Theatre in Early Kansas City," *Mid-America* 32, no. 2 (April 1950), 95.

194. Ronald L. Davis, "Opera Houses in Kansas, Nebraska, and the Dakotas: 1870–1920," *Great Plains Quarterly* 9, no. 1 (Winter 1989), 13 (quotation); Willa Cather, "The Incomparable Opera House," *Nebraska History* 49, no. 4 (1968), 372–78 (on the opera house in Red Cloud, Nebraska); Robert A. Schanke, "Fremont's Love Opera House," *Nebraska History* 55, no. 2 (1984), 220–53; Duane Fike, "The Table Rock Opera House, 1893–1900: A Small-Town Community Theater," *Nebraska History* 58, no. 2 (1977), 149–74; Harlan F. Jennings, "Grand Opera in Nebraska in the 1890s," *Opera Quarterly* 11, no. 2 (June 1995), 2–13; Harlan F. Jennings, "Grand Opera in Kansas in the 19th Century," *Kansas History* 3, no. 2 (Summer 1980), 67–69.

195. Douglas O. Street, "Band's Opera House, the Cultural Hub of Crete, 1877–1900," *Nebraska History* 60, no. 1 (Spring 1979), 67; Miriam Stanley Carleton-Squires, "Music of Pioneer Days in Nebraska," *Nebraska History* 20, no. 3 (Summer 1939), 41. A University of Nebraska professor also made the major finds that advanced the study of Shakespeare. J. W. Robinson, "Shakespeare and Nebraska: Charles William Wallace, 1865–1932, and the 'Great Index of the World,'" *Nebraska History* 60, no. 1 (Spring 1979), 1–20.

196. Davis, "Opera Houses," 22–23.

197. Andrew F. Jensen, "Two Decades of Trouping in Minneasota, 1865–85," *Minnesota History* 28, no. 2 (June 1947), 97–99; L.A., "Early Drama in Minneapolis," *Minnesota History Bulletin* 5, no. 1 (February 1923), 43–45.

198. Ada Bartlett Taft, *Lorado Taft: Sculptor and Citizen* (Greensboro, NC: M.T. Smith, 1946); Timothy J. Garvey, *Public Sculptor: Lorado Taft and the Beautification of Chicago* (Urbana: University of Illinois Press, 1988); Timothy J. Garvey, "Conferring Status: Lorado Taft's Portraits of an Artistic Community," *Illinois Historical Journal* 78, no. 3 (Autumn 1985), 162–78.

199. Moira F. Harris, "Worthy of Their Own Aspiration: Minnesota's Literary Tradition in Sculpture," *Minnesota History* 55, no. 8 (Winter 1997/1998), 369.

200. Bailey Van Hook, *The Virgin and the Dynamo: Public Murals in American Architecture, 1893–1917* (Athens: Ohio University Press, 2003).

201. Christa Adams, "'Splendid and Remarkable Progress in the Midwest: Assessing the Emergence and Social Impact of Regional Art Museums, 1875–1925," *Middle West Review* 7, no. 1 (Fall 2020), 85–92; Wendy Greenhouse, "'More Beauty and Less of Ugliness': Conservative Painting in Chicago, 1890–1929," in Kent Smith, Susan C. Larsen, Wendy Greenhouse, and Susan Weiniger, eds., *Chicago Painting, 1895–1945: The Bridges Collection* (Springfield: University of Illinois Press with Illinois State Museum, 2004), 24 (describing the Institute as a "magnet for aspiring artists from throughout the vast middle section of the United States"), 25 (noting that the Institute saw itself as a "storehouse, a university, and a general exchange for art for the whole middle west"); Dennis N. Mihelich, "George Joslyn: America's First Media Mogul," *Nebraska History* 82, no. 1 (2001), 26 (Joslyn, the Omaha art benefactor, made a fortune by "creating a virtual monopoly in the auxiliary printing business, supplying standardized, preprinted news to more than 12,000 newspapers"); Joel S. Dryer, "The First Art Exhibition in Chicago," *Journal of the Illinois State Historical Society* 99, no. 1 (Spring/Summer 2006), 28–45; Jo L. Wetherilt Behrens, "'Painting the Town': How Merchants Marketed the Visual Arts

to Nineteenth-Century Omahans," *Nebraska History* 92, no. 1 (2011), 14–39. See also chapter 3 of this volume.

202. Yox, "Lost World of Art," 118 (also noting that a later era "consigned Victorian refinement to a lost world").

203. Kenneth L. Kusmer, "The Functions of Organized Charity in the Progressive Era: Chicago as a Case Study," *Journal of American History* 60, no. 3 (December 1973), 657–78; K. David Hanzlick, *Benevolence, Moral Reform, Equality: Women's Activism in Kansas City, 1870–1940* (Columbia: University of Missouri Press, 2018).

204. "Charles L. Hutchinson, 1854–1924, Founder of the Art Institute, Chicago Dies," *Journal of the Illinois State Historical Society* 17, no. 4 (January 1925), 761–62.

205. Kathleen D. McCarthy, *Noblesse Oblige: Charity and Cultural Philanthropy in Chicago, 1849–1929* (Chicago: University of Chicago Press, 1982), 58.

206. Paul Finkelman, "Class and Culture in Late Nineteenth-Century Chicago: The Founding of the Newberry Library," *American Studies* 16, no. 1 (Spring 1975), 6.

207. Finkelman, "Class and Culture," 6; Arthur Plotnik, "A New Home and New Life for Treasures of the Newberry," *American Libraries* 13, no. 1 (January 1982), 50.

208. McCarthy, *Noblesse Oblige*, ix. See also Kathleen D. McCarthy, *American Creed: Philanthropy and the Rise of Civil Society, 1700–1865* (Chicago: University of Chicago Press, 2003) (noting the regional distinctions between a more charitable North and a less generous South).

209. Forrest McDonald, *Novus Ordo Seclorum: The Intellectual Origins of the Constitution* (Lawrence: University Press of Kansas, 1985), 76–77; Bernard Bailyn, *The Ideological Origins of the American Revolution* (Cambridge, MA: Harvard University Press, 1967), 31, 66–67; Gordon S. Wood, *The Creation of the American Republic, 1776–1787* (New York: W. W. Norton, 1969), 30–31; H. Trevor Colbourn, *The Lamp of Experience: Whig History and the Intellectual Origins of the American Revolution* (New York: W. W. Norton, 1965), 7–8. Although the invocation of Anglo-Saxon history often related to the unique evolution of English liberties in comparison to other European states, such references could also indulge forms of ethno-chauvinism or racism. See Richard Hofstadter, *Social Darwinism in American Thought* (Philadelphia: University of Pennsylvania Press, 1955), 170–92, and John Higham, *Strangers in the Land: Patterns of American Nativism, 1860–1925* (New Brunswick, NJ: Rutgers University Press, 1963). Anti-British sentiment was strong during and after the Revolution and during conflicts such as the War of 1812, was strong in the north during the Civil War when the South was attempting to coax English intervention on the southern side, and was present in some forms of populism, but by the end of the nineteenth century a rapprochement was beginning. See Lionel M. Gelber, *The Rise of Anglo-American Friendship: A Study in World Politics, 1898–1906* (New York: Oxford University Press, 1938).

210. Tingley, "Ralph Waldo Emerson," 196. He later wrote *English Traits.*

211. "The Centennial Anniversary of the Birth of Robert Burns, Celebrated in Springfield, January 25, 1859," *Journal of the Illinois State Historical Society* 17, nos. 1/2 (April–July 1924), 205–10.

212. McDonald, *Novus Ordo Seclorum*, 67; Bailyn, *Ideological Origins*, 24–25; Colbourn, *Lamp of Experience*, 21–25.

213. Yox, "Lost World of Art," 107.

214. Potter, "'The Prairie Plow Was at Work,'" 208.

215. Harrison John Thornton, "Chautauqua and the Midwest," *Wisconsin Magazine of History* 33, no. 2 (December 1949), 157.

216. James P. Eckman, "Promoting an Ideology of Culture: The Chautauqua Literacy and Scientific Circles in Nebraska, 1878–1900," *Nebraska History* 73, no. 1 (Spring 1992), 19.

217. Billington, "Historians of the Northwest Ordinance," 409 (quoting B. A. Hinsdale, *The Old Northwest* [New York: Townsend MacCoun, 1888]).

218. Onuf, "Northwest Ordinance," 299.

219. Milo M. Quaife, "The Significance of the Ordinance of 1787," *Journal of the Illinois State Historical Society* 30, no. 4 (January 1938), 416. See also Denis P. Duffey, "The Northwest Ordinance as a Constitutional Document," *Columbia Law Review* 95, no. 4 (May 1995), 929–68.

220. R. Douglas Hurt, "Historians and the Northwest Ordinance," *Western Historical Quarterly* 20, no. 3 (August 1989), 263.

221. Theodore C. Pease, "The Ordinance of 1787," *Mississippi Valley Historical Review* 25, no. 2 (September 1938), 172.

222. Finkelman, "The Northwest Ordinance," in *Pathways to the Old Northwest*, 15.

223. Nyle H. Miller, "An English Runnymede in Kansas," *Kansas Historical Quarterly* 42, no. 1 (Spring 1975), 22–24.

224. Malcolm J. Rohrbough, *The Trans-Appalachian Frontier: People, Societies, and Institutions, 1775–1850* (New York: Oxford University Press, 1978), 66; Andrew R. L. Cayton, "'A Quiet Independence': The Western Vision of the Ohio Company," *Ohio History* 90, no. 1 (Winter 1981), 5–20.

225. Wright, *Culture on the Moving Frontier*, 92.

226. Onuf, "Northwest Ordinance," 293.

227. William Henry Venable, "Cincinnati—A Civic Ode," *Ohio Archaeological and Historical Society Publications* 17, no. 1 (January 1908), 80–87.

228. Onuf, "Northwest Ordinance," 293–304.

229. "The Naming of a Group of Eight Illinois Counties Created at the Same Time," *Journal of the Illinois State Historical Society* 25, nos. 1/2 (April–July 1932), 120.

230. "Naming of a Group of Eight Illinois Counties," 122.

231. H. W. Olendenin, "Dedication of George Rogers Clark Monument, at Quincy Illinois," *Journal of the Illinois State Historical Society* 2, no. 2 (July 1909), 65–67; W. O. Thompson, "Significance of Memorials," *Ohio Archaeological and Historical Society Publications* 33, no. 3 (July–October 1924), 477–80 (lecture at the commemoration of the Rogers statue in Clark County, Ohio, in 1924). See also Milo M. Quaife, ed., *The Capture of Old Vincennes* (Indianapolis: Bobbs-Merrill, 1927), Ross F. Lockridge, *George Rogers Clark: Pioneer Hero of the Old Northwest* (Chicago: World Book, 1927), and William R. Nester, *George Rogers Clark: "I Glory in War"* (Norman: University of Oklahoma Press, 2012).

232. Paul David Nelson, *Anthony Wayne: Soldier of the Early Republic* (Bloomington: Indiana University Press, 1985).

233. James W. Good, "Ohio's Monument to General Anthony Wayne Unveiled," *Ohio Archaeological and Historical Society Publications* 39, no. 1 (January 1930), 4–8.

234. See chapter 2.

235. R. E. Hieronymous, "Lorado Taft's Pioneer Group at Elmwood," *Journal of the Illinois State Historical Society* 21, no. 2 (July 1928), 253–59.

236. Hieronymous, "Lorado Taft's Pioneer Group," 257.

237. Bess D. Moss, "Statue of the Madonna of the Trail Unveiled at Vandalia," *Journal of the Illinois State Historical Society* 21, no. 4 (January 1929), 534–40. See also Cynthia Prescott, *Pioneer Mother Monuments: Constructing Cultural Memory* (Norman: University of Oklahoma Press, 2019).

238. Edward Pluth, "To Honor the Soldier Dead: The Todd County World War I Monument," *Minnesota History* 66, no. 3 (Fall 2018), 118–31; Steven Trout, "Forgotten Reminders: Kansas World War I Memorials," *Kansas History* 29, no. 3 (Autumn 2006), 200–215; Joseph T. Stuart, "North Dakota and the Cultural History of the Great War," *North Dakota History* 83, no. 2 (Winter 2018), 3–17; Susan Wefald, "Remembering 'Our Boys': North Dakota's World War I Monuments and Memorials, 1918–1941," *North Dakota History* 83, no. 1 (Summer 2018), 20–35.

239. Raymond N. Dooley, "Lincoln and His Namesake Town," *Journal of the Illinois State Historical Society* 52, no. 1 (Spring 1959), 130 (noting that "twenty communities, hundreds of schools, thousands of streets and possibly ten thousand business enterprises bear the name Lincoln").

240. "Rededication of Lincoln Monument: Hoover Urges Nation to Rededicate Itself to the Ideals of Lincoln," *Journal of the Illinois State Historical Society* 24, no. 2 (July 1931), 333–39.

241. "Lincoln Statue: Bunker Hill, Macoupin County, Illinois," *Journal of the Illinois State Historical Society* 22, no. 3 (October 1929), 490.

242. James E. Potter, "Dedicating Nebraska's Lincoln Memorial, 1912," *Nebraska History* 89, no. 4 (2008), 222–23.

243. "Lincoln's Statue Unveiled at G.A.R. Ceremony, Minneapolis, Monday, May 26, 1930," *Journal of the Illinois State Historical Society* 23, no. 3 (October 1930), 517–19. For Nebraska's GAR memorials, see Richard Evans Keyes, "The Great Fraternity: Nebraska's Grand Army of the Republic, 1867–1920" (MA thesis, University of Nebraska-Omaha, 1997), 256–81.

244. "Lorado Taft's Statue of Lincoln Unveiled at Urbana, Illinois, July 3, 1927," *Journal of the Illinois State Historical Society* 20, no. 2 (July 1927), 240–42.

245. "Lorado Taft's Statue of Lincoln," 240–42.

246. "President Grant's Des Moines Address," *Annals of Iowa* 3, no. 2 (1897), 138.

247. William C. Lowe, "'A Grand and Patriotic Pilgrimage': The Iowa Civil War Monuments Dedication Tour of 1906," *Annals of Iowa* 69, no. 1 (Winter 2010), 1–50; Leslie A. Schwalm, "Emancipation Day Celebrations: The Commemoration of Slavery and Freedom in Iowa," *Annals of Iowa* 62, no. 3 (July 2003), 291–332.

248. John Bodnar, "Commemorative Activity in Twentieth-Century Indianapolis: The Invention of Civic Traditions," *Indiana Magazine of History* 87, no. 1 (March 1991), 4–5.

249. Randall M. Thies, "Civil War Valor in Concrete: David A. Lester and the Kinsley Civil War Monument," *Kansas History* 22, no. 3 (Autumn 1999), 169–70.

250. Dudley, "Remembering and Forgetting," 251–68.

251. William Oliver, "Celebrating the Fourth of July," *Journal of the Illinois State Historical Society* 35, no. 2 (June 1942), 187–88; Cora Dolbee, "The Fourth of July in Early Kansas, 1858–1861," *Kansas Historical Quarterly* 11, no. 2 (May 1942), 130–35; Adam Criblez, *Parading Patriotism: Independence Day Celebrations in the Urban Midwest, 1826–1876* (DeKalb: Northern Illinois University Press, 2013).

252. Edith Webber, "Early Fourth of July Celebrations," *Annals of Iowa* 36, no. 5 (Summer 1962), 374.

253. "A Country Fourth of July in Minnesota, 1862," *Minnesota History* 38, no. 2 (June 1962), 72–73.

254. Edward Noyes, "The Ohio G.A.R. and Politics from 1866 to 1900," *Ohio Archaeological and Historical Quarterly* 55, no. 2 (April–June 1946), 79; Hosea W. Rood, "The Grand Army of the Republic," *Wisconsin Magazine of History* 6, no. 4 (June 1923), 403–13; Frank H. Heck, *The Civil War Veteran in Minnesota Life and Politics* (Oxford, OH: Mississippi Valley Press, 1941); "Proposed Grand Army Corridor," *Annals of Iowa* 12, no. 3 (1915), 233–34; Frank H. Heck, "The Grand Army of the Republic in Minnesota, 1866–80," *Minnesota History* 16, no. 4 (December 1935), 427–44; Kyle S. Sinisi, "Veterans as Political Activists: The Kansas Grand Army of the Republic, 1880–1893," *Kansas History* 14, no. 2 (Summer 1991), 89–99; Charles M. Correll, "Some Aspects of the History of the G.A.R. in Kansas," *Kansas Historical Quarterly* 19, no. 1 (February 1951), 63–67; Nicholas W. Sacco, "The Grand Army of the Republic, the Indianapolis 500, and the Struggle for Memorial Day in Indiana, 1868–1923," *Indiana Magazine of History* 111, no. 4 (December 2015), 349–63; Stuart McConnell, *Glorious Contentment: The Grand Army of the Republic, 1865–1900* (Chapel Hill: University of North Carolina Press, 1992); Mary R. Dearing, *Veterans in Politics: The Story of the G.A.R.* (Baton Rouge: Louisiana State University Press, 1952).

255. Ora A. Clement, "Native Sons and Daughters of Nebraska," *Nebraska History* 25, no. 4 (1944), 271–78; Martha Tucker Morris, "The Society of Indiana Pioneers," *Indiana Magazine of History* 35, no. 4 (December 1939), 400–402; Benjamin G. Leighton, "Minnesota History and the Schools: Pioneer Reunions in St. Louis County," *Minnesota History* 25, no. 2 (June 1944), 158–64; "Sangamon County Old Settlers Reunion, New Berlin, August 28, 1912," *Journal of the Illinois State Historical Society* 5, no. 3 (October 1912), 409–15; "Old Settlers of Macoupin Met August 15, 1912," *Journal of the Illinois State Historical Society* 5, no. 3 (October 1912), 416; Marilyn Wendler, "A Look Back at the Roots of the Maumee Valley Historical Society," *Northwest Ohio History* 83, no. 2 (Spring 2016), 75–94.

256. Hubach, "Walt Whitman in Kansas," 150.

257. Sherman B. Barnes, "Learning and Piety in Ohio Colleges, 1865–1900," *Ohio History Journal* 69, no. 4 (October 1960), 348.

258. Meredith B. Colket Jr., "The Western Reserve Historical Society," *Ohio History Journal* 72, no. 2 (April 1963), 140–49; "Death of Dr. Reuben Gold Thwaites," *Journal of the Illinois State Historical Society* 6, no. 3 (October 1913), 473.

259. Allan Peskin, "James A. Garfield, Historian," *Historian* 43, no. 4 (August 1981), 488, 485 (noting that Garfield, when president of Western Reserve Eclectic Institute, introduced an American history course that he taught and considered introducing a bill in Congress making it compulsory for students to study American history), 489 (explaining that Garfield saw the South as "feudal," racist, and in need of an overall restructuring).

260. Jon K. Lauck, "The Prairie Historians and the Foundations of Midwestern History," *Annals of Iowa* 71, no. 2 (Spring 2012), 137–73.

261. Jacob Piatt Dunn, "Duty of the State to Its History," *Indiana Magazine of History* 6, no. 4 (December 1910), 137–43; Oliver Knight, "Claude G. Bowers, Historian," *Indiana Magazine of History* 52, no. 3 (September 1956), 247–68; James A. Rawley, "Edward Eggleston: Historian," *Indiana Magazine of History* 40, no. 4 (December 1944), 341–52; Frederick E. Witzig, "The Perils and Promise of Midwestern Studies," *Studies in Midwestern History* 1, no. 2 (March 2015), 19–24; Chris Smith, "A Plea for a New Appreciation of Popular History: John Clark Ridpath, a Case Study," *Indiana Magazine of History* 77, no. 3 (September 1981), 205–30; Nevin O. Winter, "What We Owe to the Past," *Ohio Archaeological and Historical Society Publications* 31, no. 1 (January 1922), 31–37.

262. Arthur W. Dunn, "The Civic Value of Local History," *Indiana Magazine of History* 4, no. 4 (December 1908), 172 (speech delivered to the OVHA on November 29, 1908).

263. "Indiana Pageants," *Indiana Magazine of History* 12, no. 3 (September 1916), 281. See also Nancy Berlage, *Memory, Modernity, and the Uses of the Past in Rural America* (Lincoln: University of Nebraska Press, 2022); Berlage, "The Uses of the Past: Public Memory and Farm Historical Pageantry," Midwestern History Association, Annual Conference, Grand Rapids, MI (June 2017); Berlage, "Farm Historical Pageantry, Gender, and Region, 1910–1930," Agricultural History Society, Annual Conference, Grand Rapids, MI (June 2017).

264. George McReynolds, "The Centennial Pageant for Indiana: Suggestions for Its Performance," *Indiana Magazine of History* 11, no. 3 (September 1915), 248–52 (italics added).

265. McReynolds, "Centennial Pageant for Indiana," 249 (revive), 250 (found).

266. McReynolds, "Centennial Pageant for Indiana," 249. The father of the Indiana novelist Ross Lockridge was well known for his work on pageants. He also wrote the book *George Rogers Clark*. For other examples, see Don Stubbs, "Pageant of the Past," *Minnesota History* 30, no. 4 (December 1949), 343–62; Fred S. Nichols, "A Township Pageants Its Progress," *Journal of the Illinois State Historical Society* 22, no. 4 (January 1930), 641–48; S. D. McKenney, "DAR Sponsor Pageant 'The Discovery of Illinois,'" *Journal of the Illinois State Historical Society* 20, no. 2 (July 1927), 255–57.

267. George W. Purcell, "A Survey of Early Newspapers in the Middle Western States," *Indiana Magazine of History* 20, no. 4 (December 1924), 347.

268. Wyman W. Parker, "Printing in Gambier, Ohio, 1829–1884," *Ohio History Journal* 62, no. 1 (January 1953), 55.

269. Frank Boles, "Michigan Newspapers: A Two-Hundred-Year Review," *Michigan Historical Review* 36, no. 1 (Spring 2010), 34; Bailyn, *Ideological Origins*, 1.

270. Allan Nevins, *The Emergence of Modern America, 1865–1878* (New York: Macmillan, 1927), 241.

271. Herbert Y. Weber, "The Story of the *St. Paul Globe*," *Minnesota History* 39, no. 8 (Winter 1965), 327–34; Wallace Brown, "George I. Miller and the Boosting of Omaha," *Nebraska History* 50, no. 3 (1969), 276–91.

272. Lewis O. Saum, *Eugene Field and His Age* (Lincoln: University of Nebraska Press, 2001).

273. John E. Semonche, *Ray Stannard Baker: A Quest for Democracy in Modern America, 1870–1918* (Chapel Hill: University of North Carolina Press, 1969).

274. Matthew J. Bruccoli, ed., *Earnest Hemingway, Cub Reporter: Kansas City Star Stories* (Pittsburgh, PA: University of Pittsburgh Press, 1970).

275. Don W. Wilson, "Barbed Words on the Frontier: Early Kansas Newspaper Editors," *Kansas History* 1, no. 3 (Autumn 1978), 147–49.

276. Pawley, *Reading on the Middle Border*, 29.

277. Elkins and McKitrick, "Meaning for Turner's Frontier," 347; Harry N. Scheiber, "The Ohio Canal Movement, 1820–1825," *Ohio Historical Quarterly* 69, no. 3 (1960), 231–59; John Lauritz Larson, *Internal Improvement: National Public Works and the Promise of Popular Government in the Early United States* (Chapel Hill: University of North Carolina Press, 2001).

278. Wayne E. Fuller, "The Rural Roots of the Progressive Leaders," *Agricultural History* 42, no. 1 (January 1968), 1–14. On the emergence of "organic intellectuals" out of the Midwest who sought to preserve and support midwestern rural life via various state actions in the early twentieth century, see Jess Gilbert, *Planning Democracy: Agrarian Intellectuals and the Intended New Deal* (New Haven, CT: Yale University Press, 2015).

279. Robert Samuel Fletcher, "Bread and Doctrine at Oberlin," *Ohio Archaeological and Historical Quarterly* 49, no. 1 (January 1940), 58–59.

280. Everett Dick, "The Founding of Union College, 1890–1900," *Nebraska History* 60, no. 3 (Fall 1979), 447–70. See Brian C. Wilson, *Dr. John Harvey Kellogg and the Religion of Biologic Living* (Bloomington: Indiana University Press, 2014).

281. See Herman R. Muelder, *Missionaries and Muckrakers: The First Hundred Years of Knox College* (Champaign: University of Illinois Press, 1984).

282. See chapter 5.

283. Lynda Beltz, "Emerson's Lecture in Indianapolis," *Indiana Magazine of History* 60, no. 3 (September 1964), 273; Frederick E. Schortemeier, "Indianapolis Newspaper Accounts of Ralph Waldo Emerson," *Indiana Magazine of History* 49, no. 3 (September 1953), 307–8.

CHAPTER 2

1. Cayton and Onuf, *Midwest and the Nation*; Timothy R. Mahoney, *Provincial Lives: Middle-Class Experience in the Antebellum Middle West* (New York: Cambridge University Press, 1999).

2. Daniel Walker Howe, "Victorian Culture in America," in Howe, *Victorian America*, 21.

3. Colleen McDannell, *The Christian Home in Victorian America, 1840–1900* (Bloomington: Indiana University Press, 1986), 4, 17, 21, 48, 79.

4. Stevenson, *Victorian Homefront*, 8–9. See also Richard W. E. Perrin, "Wisconsin's Victorian Houses: Architectural Reflections of Society in Transition," *Wisconsin Magazine of History* 45, no. 4 (Summer 1962), 290–95.

5. E. Anthony Rotundo, "Body and Soul: Changing Ideas of American Middle-Class Manhood, 1770–1920," *Journal of Social History* 16, no. 4 (Summer 1983), 26.

6. McDannell, *Christian Home*, 82.

7. Stevenson, *Victorian Homefront*, 11.

8. Haywood, *Victorian West*, 90.

9. Rotundo, "Body and Soul," 24–25 (quotations).

10. Winkle, "Abraham Lincoln," 16; John G. Cawelti, *Apostles of the Self-Made Man: Changing Concepts of Success in America* (Chicago: University of Chicago Press, 1965), 40 (explaining that in the "dramatic story of Abraham Lincoln's rise from rail-splitter to President, from poverty and obscurity to savior of the union, the ideal of the self-made man found its greatest epic"), 96. See also McCarthy, *Noblesse Oblige*, 77.

11. Wyman P. Parker, "President Hayes's Graduation Speeches," *Ohio History Journal* 63, no. 2 (April 1954), 135; Rotundo, "Body and Soul," 25.

12. "Letter from a Father to His Son at School" and "Letter from a Youth at School to His Father," *Journal of the Illinois State Historical Society* 33, no. 2 (June 1940), 239–40.

13. Elkins and McKitrick, "Meaning for Turner's Frontier," 349.

14. Frank Felsenstein and James J. Connolly, *What Middletown Read: Print Culture in American Small City* (Amherst: University of Massachusetts Press, 2015), 155.

15. Oscar B. Chamberlain, "'To Provide a Great Seal': Interpreting the Wisconsin State Seal as an Example of Antebellum Political Culture," *Agricultural History* 87, no. 1 (Winter 2013), 66 (noting that "no southern [state] seal portrays an act of labor"); Graham A. Peck, *Making an Antislavery Nation: Lincoln, Douglas, and the Battle over Freedom* (Urbana: University of Illinois Press, 2017), 29.

16. Howard H. Peckham, "Books and Reading on the Ohio Valley Frontier," *Mississippi Valley Historical Review* 44, no. 4 (March 1958), 649–63; Stevenson, *Victorian Homefront*, 30.

17. Peckham, "Books and Reading," 653.

18. Hilkey, *Character Is Capital*, 23; Parker, "Printing in Gambier," 55.

19. Mauck Brammer, "Winthrop B. Smith: Creator of the Eclectic Educational Series," *Ohio History* 80, no. 1 (Winter 1971), 45 (quotation); Eva Draegert, "Cultural History of Indianapolis: Literature, 1875–1890," *Indiana Magazine of History* 52, no. 3 (September 1956), 344–46; Jack O'Bar, "The Old Merrill Bookstore: Its Indianapolis Background and History and Its Relationship to the Bobbs-Merrill Company," *Journal of Library History* 20, no. 4 (Fall 1985), 408–26; Henry Hyde Hubbart, *The Older Middle West, 1840–1880: Its Social, Economic and Political*

Life and Sectional Tendencies before, during and after the Civil War (New York: D. Appleton-Century, 1936), 55; James J. Connolly, "Print Culture in the Midwest," manuscript submitted to Oxford University Press for inclusion in Lauck, "The Oxford Handbook of Midwestern History"; James J. Connolly, "Reading Regionalism in the Midwest: Evidence from 'What Middletown Read' Data," *Middle West Review* 7, no. 1 (Fall 2020), 69–76.

20. Hubbart, *Older Middle West*, 55; David D. Anderson, "The Queen City and a New Literature," *MidAmerica* 4 (1977), 8 (explaining that Cincinnati "supported a flourishing publishing industry that not merely published the McGuffey readers, the papers, and the journals, but in the papers and journals was sending the work of dozens of Ohio poets out to the rest of the area and country"); Walter Sutton, "Cincinnati as a Frontier Publishing and Book Trade Center, 1796–1830," *Ohio History Journal* 56, no. 2 (April 1947), 120.

21. Stuart A. Stiffler, "The Social Library Comes to Cincinnati and the Old Northwest," *Ohio Valley History* 17, no. 4 (Winter 2017), 5; Walter Sutton, *The Western Book Trade: Cincinnati as a Nineteenth-Century Publishing and Book-Trade Center* (Columbus: Ohio State University Press, 1961); Sutton, "Cincinnati as a Frontier Publishing and Book Trade Centre," 142–43.

22. Felsenstein and Connolly, *What Middletown Read*, 107; Stiffler, "Social Library," 4–13.

23. Haywood, *Victorian West*, 113; Felsenstein and Connolly, *What Middletown Read*, 140.

24. Augst, *Clerk's Tale*, 4, and noting Warren Susman, *Culture as History: The Transformation of American Society in the Twentieth Century* (New York: Pantheon, 1984), 273–74.

25. Pawley, *Reading on the Middle Border*, 3, 28, 45; Augst, *Clerk's Tale*, 4–5; Felsenstein and Connolly, *What Middletown Read*, 102; Bayrd Still, "Evidences of the 'Higher Life' on the Frontier: As Illustrated in the History of Cultural Matters in Chicago, 1830–1850," *Journal of the Illinois State Historical Society* 28, no. 2 (July 1935), 93; Louis L. Tucker, "The Semi-Colon Club of Cincinnati," *Ohio History Journal* 73, no. 1 (Winter 1964), 13–26; Lorin C. Halberstadt, "The Terre Haute Literary Club, 1881–1931," *Indiana Magazine of History* 27, no. 4 (December 1931), 317–25.

26. Peckham, "Books and Reading," 653.

27. Rowland E. Prothero, ed., *The Works of Lord Byron: Letters and Journals*, vol. 2 (London: John Murray, 1922), 360.

28. Nevins, *Emergence of Modern America*, 230.

29. Stevenson, *Victorian Homefront*, 23.

30. Pawley, *Reading on the Middle Border*, 9.

31. Pawley, *Reading on the Middle Border*, 12; Peckham, "Books and Reading," 661; Stevenson, *Victorian Homefront*, 33.

32. Theodore C. Blegen, "Henry H. Sibley, Pioneer Culture and Frontier Author," *Minnesota History* 15, no. 4 (December 1934), 383.

33. Stevenson, *Victorian Homefront*, 34, 40, 43.

34. Edward Everett Dale, "The Frontier Literary Society," *Nebraska History* 31, no. 3 (September 1950), 167–82; Dale, "Culture on the American Frontier," 87.

35. Cordier, "Prairie Schoolwomen," 112–13.

36. Cochran, *Louise Pound*, 19.

37. Stevenson, *Victorian Homefront*, 6, 24.

38. Pawley, *Reading on the Middle Border*, 33.

39. Peckham, "Books and Reading," 655; Sarah J. Cutler, "The Coonskin Library," *Ohio Archaeological and Historical Quarterly* 26, no. 1 (January 1917), 58–77. See also W. T. Norton, "Early Libraries in Illinois," *Journal of the Illinois State Historical Society* 6, no. 1 (July 1913), 246–51.

40. Peckham, "Books and Reading," 656, 657 (describing the social library movement as "contagious throughout the Ohio Valley" in which "libraries spread like a rash").

41. Weigand A. Wiegand, "'To Diffuse Useful Knowledge and Correct Moral Principles': Social Libraries in the Old Northwest, 1800–1850," in Paul H. Mattingly and Edward W. Stevens Jr., eds., *"Schools and the Means of Education Shall Forever Be Encouraged": A History of Education in the Old Northwest* (Athens: Ohio University Libraries, 1987), 85–95. Between 1803 and 1853, Ohio granted charters to 173 social library companies. The Vincennes Library Company in Indiana, for example, loaned copies of Milton, Pope, Homer, and many works of history, travel, law, philosophy, and poetry. Weigand, "To Diffuse," 89–90; J. Robert Constantine, "The Vincennes Library Company: A Cultural Institution in Pioneer Indiana," *Indiana Magazine of History* 61, no. 4 (December 1965), 305–89; Philip A. Kalisch, "High Culture on the Frontier: The Omaha Library Association," *Nebraska History* 52, no. 4 (1971), 410–17; Kristin Mapel Bloomberg, "'How Shall We Make Beatrice Grow!': Clara Berwick Colby and the Beatrice Public Library Association in the 1870s," *Nebraska History* 92, no. 4 (2011), 170–83; John W. Fritch and David M. Hovde, "Library Programs in Indiana in the 1850s," *Indiana Magazine of History* 111, no. 4 (December 2015), 422–53; "Iowa Library Legislation of 1894," *Annals of Iowa* 1, no. 6 (1894), 497–98; Hortense B. C. Gibson, "Wichita and Her Public Libraries," *Kansas Historical Quarterly* 6, no. 4 (November 1937), 387–93; Curti, *Growth of American Thought*, 271, 279.

42. Eira Tansey, "Branches from the Baron: Cincinnati's Carnegie Libraries," *Ohio Valley History* 16, no. 1 (Spring 2016), 46; John M. Witt, *The Carnegie Libraries of Iowa* (Washington, MO: Robidoux Books, 2003). See also Mary Cochran Grimes, "Books for Nebraska: Roy and Aileen Cochran and the Nebraska Public Library Commission," *Nebraska History* 78, no. 3 (1997), 102–9.

43. Pawley, *Reading on the Middle Border*, 27, 92, 80–81 (motto), 95–96, 101 (reflected, demand, and glorified), 101–3; Cawelti, *Apostles of the Self-Made Man*, 131–34 (noting the theme of overcoming obstacles to self-improvement in *Barriers Burned Away*). An inventory of the library's holdings in the late 1870s showed that 42 percent of its books were fiction. Of the nonfiction books in the collection, 43 percent of the books were history, 18 percent science, and 14 percent literature. Pawley, *Reading on the Middle Border*, 80.

44. Pawley, *Reading on the Middle Border*, 87–88.

45. Pawley, *Reading on the Middle Border*, 87–88.

46. Felsenstein and Connolly, *What Middletown Read*, 135 (central), 141 (tool), 131 (moralism), 40, 43, 44 (ethos, informally), 46–49 (uplift, guardians, concern),

49–53, 48 (constantly), 108 (insatiable), 114, 115, 144, 54, 62–63, 63 (temples), 89, 205, 91–93, 163 (sense, moulded). This study did not find Oscar Wilde or Walk Whitman to be available, perhaps because they were considered "obnoxious." Felsenstein and Connolly, *What Middletown Read*, 49. Experts thought that literary books "had great influence over the moral development of young people." Stevenson, *Victorian Homefront*, 37.

47. Hilkey, *Character Is Capital*, 5 (diligent), 13, 7 (pulse), 28, 21–22.

48. Bledstein, *Culture of Professionalism*, 33.

49. Stewart Winger, "High Priests of Nature: The Origins of Illinois State Normal 'University' in the Antebellum Lyceum," *Journal of the Illinois State Historical Society* 101, no. 2 (Summer 2008), 132–33; Stevenson, *Victorian Homefront*, 56 (young, pursuing).

50. Donald M. Scott, "The Popular Lecture and the Creation of a Public Mind in Mid-Nineteenth-Century America," *Journal of American History* 66, no. 4 (March 1980), 793, 795. See also Judith Spraul-Schmidt, "Exhibiting the Changing World through the Ohio Mechanics Institute: From Annual Fairs and Exhibitions to Grand Expositions, 1838–1888," *Ohio Valley History* 5, no. 1 (Spring 2005), 37–46.

51. Howe, "Victorian Culture in America," 24; Calvin W. Gower, "Lectures, Lyceums, and Libraries in Early Kansas, 1854–1864," *Kansas Historical Quarterly* 36, no. 2 (Summer 1970), 175–82; Cayton, "Making of an American Prophet," 604 (quotation); Edward W. Stevens Jr., "Science, Culture, and Morality: Educating Adults in the Early Nineteenth Century," in Mattingly and Stevens, *"Schools and the Means of Education,"* 69; Curti, *Growth of American Thought*, 280.

52. Leslie H. Meeks, "The Lyceum in the Early West," *Indiana Magazine of History* 29, no. 2 (June 1933), 88.

53. Cayton, "Making of an American Prophet," 604. Between 1831 and 1845, sixty lyceums were chartered in Ohio. Stevens, "Science, Culture, and Morality," 70; Still, "Evidences of the 'Higher Life,'" 94; Lucille Clifton, "The Early Theater in Columbus, Ohio, 1820–1840," *Ohio History Journal* 62, no. 3 (July 1953), 234. See generally Tom F. Wright, ed., *The Cosmopolitan Lyceum: Lecture Culture and the Globe in Nineteenth-Century America* (Amherst: University of Massachusetts Press, 2013).

54. Richard L. Weaver, "Prelude to an Institution: What Woodward Hath Wrought," *Michigan History* 59, no. 1 (1970), 29–43; Cawelti, *Apostles of the Self-Made Man*, 89–90 (explaining that the ambitious Corsican was often invoked as an example of a self-made man). Later, the women of Monroe, Michigan, also took up the issue of "wandering dogs." Joanna V. Brace, "The Power of Porch Talks: The Civic Improvement Society of Monroe, Michigan, 1901 to 1914," *Michigan Historical Review* 27, no. 2 (Fall 2001), 19.

55. R. E. Bone, R. S. Bone, and L. B. Wynn, "Rock Creek Lyceum," *Journal of the Illinois State Historical Society* 19, nos. 1/2 (April–July, 1926), 63–76.

56. Scott, "Popular Lecture," 791. The Lyceum in Ripon, Wisconsin, became Ripon College. Samuel M. Pedrick, "Early History of Ripon College, 1850–1864," *Wisconsin Magazine of History* 8, no. 1 (September 1924), 22.

57. Joan R. Gundersen, "The Local Parish as a Female Institution: The Experience of All Saints Episcopal Church in Frontier Minnesota," *Church History* 55, no. 3 (September 1986), 310–11.

58. Scott, "Popular Lecture," 799.

59. Stevenson, *Victorian Homefront*, 56.

60. Thomas F. Schwartz, "The Springfield Lyceums and Lincoln's 1838 Speech," *Illinois Historical Journal* 83, no. 1 (Spring 1990), 45–49; Scott, "Popular Lecture," 798.

61. Winkle, "Abraham Lincoln," 12.

62. Scott, "Popular Lecture," 799.

63. John Neufeld, "The Associated Western Literary Societies in the Midwest," *Michigan History* 51, no. 2 (Summer 1967), 161; Tingley, "Ralph Waldo Emerson," 194; Meeks, "Lyceum in the Early West," 88; Stevenson, *Victorian Homefront*, 56.

64. Cayton, "Making of an American Prophet," 605, 606 ("An example of mercantile leadership in cultural affairs that I take to be fairly typical in the Midwest was the organization of the St. Louis Mercantile Library Association, the organization that sponsored Emerson's visit in 1852"). See also Meeks, "Lyceum in the Early West," 90, and Robert R. Hubach, "Nineteenth-Century Literary Visitors to the Hoosier State: A Chapter in American Cultural History," *Indiana Magazine of History* 45, no. 1 (March 1949), 44–46.

65. Frederickson, *Inner Civil War*, 11; Cawelti, *Apostles of the Self-Made Man*, 87. Emerson's praise of farming also made him an ideal fit for the Midwest. Douglas C. Stenerson, "Emerson and the Agrarian Tradition," *Journal of the History of Ideas* 14, no. 1 (January 1953), 95–115.

66. Beltz, "Emerson's Lecture in Indianapolis," 276.

67. Cayton, "Making of an American Prophet," 610.

68. Hubert H. Hoeltje, "Ralph Waldo Emerson in Minnesota," *Minnesota History* 11, no. 2 (January 1930), 156.

69. Hilkey, *Character Is Capital*, 162.

70. Cayton, "Making of an American Prophet," 610; Stevenson, *Victorian Homefront*, 57.

71. Cayton, "Making of an American Prophet," 617; James P. Eckman, "Culture as Entertainment: The Circuit Chautauqua in Nebraska, 1904–1924," *Nebraska History* 75, no. 3 (1994), 245 (on the "marriage of lyceum and Chautauqua" because of the "genius of Keith Vawter of Cedar Rapids, Iowa, an executive of the Redpath Bureau of Chicago").

72. Nevins, *Emergence of Modern America*, 239–40; Andrew C. Rieser, *The Chautauqua Moment: Protestants, Progressives, and the Culture of Modern Liberalism* (New York: Columbia University Press, 2003); Szasz, "Stress," 145.

73. Stevenson, *Victorian Homefront*, 158.

74. Peter Feinman, "Chautauqua America," *American Interest* 5, no. 5 (May/June 2010), 83.

75. Melvin H. Miller, "Grass Roots Chautauqua in Michigan," *Michigan History* 52, no. 4 (December 1968), 299–309; Julie R. Nelson, "A Subtle Revolution: The Chautauqua Literary and Scientific Circle in Rural Midwestern Towns," *Agricultural*

History 70, no. 4 (Fall 1996), 653–71; Thornton, "Chautauqua and the Midwest," 152–63; Evert M. Winks, "Recollections of a Dead Art: The Traveling Chautauqua," *Indiana Magazine of History* 54, no. 1 (March 1958), 41–48 (noting, inter alia, that the only resistance to Chautauqua came in the South); Thomas J. Schlereth, "Chautauqua: A Middle Landscape of the Middle Class," *Old Northwest* 12, no. 3 (Fall 1986), 265–78; James M. Miller, "The Spiritual Force in Early Western Culture," *Ohio Archaeological and Historical Quarterly* 49, no. 3 (July 1940), 261–68; F. W. Brinkerhoff, "The Ottawa Chautauqua Assembly," *Kansas Historical Quarterly* 27, no. 4 (Winter 1961), 457–68; W. Stitt Robinson, "Chautauqua: Then and Now," *Kansas History* 22, no. 2 (Summer 1999), 132–41; Feinman, "Chautauqua America," 87; James M. Conlin, "The Merom Bluff Chautauqua," *Indiana Magazine of History* 36, no. 1 (March 1940), 23–28. See also Arthur S. Meyers, "'A Sturdy Core of Thinking, Fact Seeking Citizens': The Open Forum Movement and Public Learning in Terre Haute and Hammond, Indiana, in the 1920s," *Indiana Magazine of History* 99, no. 4 (September 1995), 225–40.

76. James P. Eckman, "Respectable Leisure: The Crete Chautauqua, 1882–1897," *Nebraska History* 69, no. 1 (1988), 19–29.

77. Oneita Fisher, "Literary Societies," *Annals of Iowa* 38, no. 7 (Winter 1967), 531; Hubach, "Nineteenth-Century Literary Visitors," 39–50.

78. Jon Solomon, *Ben-Hur: The Original Blockbuster* (Edinburgh: Edinburgh University Press, 2016), 19–101.

79. Paul Fatout, "Mark Twain Lectures in Indiana," *Indiana Magazine of History* 46, no. 4 (December 1950), 365.

80. Harrison T. Meserole, "The Dean in Person: Howells' Lecture Tour," *Western Humanities Review* 10 (Autumn 1956), 337–40.

81. Meserole, "Dean in Person," 344. The novel later inspired the What Would Jesus Do movement.

82. Robert Rowlette, "In 'The Silken Arms of the Aristocracy': William Dean Howells' Lecture in Indianapolis, 1899," *Indiana Magazine of History* 69, no. 4 (December 1973), 300. In another indication of the size of the crowds for such events, Howells drew fifteen hundred people in Emporia, a town of eight thousand. Meserole, "Dean in Person," 345.

83. Rowlette, "In 'The Silken Arms of the Aristocracy,'" 307 (quoting the newspaper).

84. Jeremy Beer, "Midlander: Booth Tarkington's Defense of the Midwest," in Jon K. Lauck, ed., *The Midwestern Moment: The Forgotten World of Early Twentieth-Century Midwestern Regionalism, 1880–1940* (Hastings, NE: Hastings College Press, 2017), 35–53; Jeremy Beer, "The Magnificent Tarkington," *Claremont Review of Books* (November 14, 2019).

85. John E. Miller, "The Funeral of Beloved Hoosier Poet, James Whitcomb Riley," *Studies in Midwestern History* 2, no. 6 (2016), 70–78.

86. Theobald, *Call School*, 25; David Tyack, "The Kingdom of God and the Common School: Protestant Ministers and the Educational Awakening in the West," *Harvard Educational Review* 36, no. 4 (Fall 1966), 447–48, 454 (noting that in the "Midwest missionaries developed a pattern of founding schools which they later adapted to other frontiers"); Bernard Mandel, "Religion and the Public Schools

of Ohio," *Ohio Archaeological and Historical Quarterly* 58, no. 2 (April 1949), 185–88; James C. Carper, "A Common Faith for the Common School? Religion and Education in Kansas, 1861–1900," *Mid-America* 60, no. 3 (October 1978), 147–62.

87. Theobald, *Call School*, 17.

88. Smith, "Protestant Schooling," 691 (italics in original).

89. Smith, "Protestant Schooling," 694.

90. Felsenstein and Connolly, *What Middletown Read*, 154 (quotation); Beth Sylvester Edwards, "Hoosier Schoolmaster, 1920–1940: A Case Study in Rural Elementary Education in South Central Indiana," *Indiana Magazine of History* 93, no. 3 (September 1997), 248.

91. Mary McDougall Gordon, "Patriots and Christians: A Reassessment of Nineteenth-Century School Reformers," *Journal of Social History* 11, no. 4 (Summer 1978), 554–55.

92. Howe, "Victorian Culture in America," 25.

93. Gordon, "Patriots and Christians," 556 (quotation); Lee Soltow and Edward Stevens, *The Rise of Literacy and the Common School in the United States: A Socioeconomic Analysis to 1870* (Chicago: University of Chicago Press, 1981)(on the effectiveness of small schools at reducing illiteracy and promoting social mobility).

94. Cordier, "Prairie Schoolwomen," 102.

95. Gordon, "Patriots and Christians," 557.

96. Carl F. Kaestle, "Social Change, Discipline, and the Common School in Early Nineteenth-Century America," *Journal of Interdisciplinary History* 19, no. 1 (Summer 1978), 4, 6 (quotations); Carroll Engelhardt, "Schools and Character: Educational Reform and Industrial Virtue in Iowa, 1890–1930," *Annals of Iowa* 47, no. 7 (Winter 1985), 618–36; Paula J. A. McNally, "Character Education in Rural Illinois: The One-Room Schools of Macoupin County, 1909–1947," *Journal of the Illinois State Historical Society* 96, no. 4 (Winter 2003/2004), 347–67; Erica R. Hamilton, "Looking from the Outside In: Preparation for Democratic Citizenship in a 1925 Michigan High-School Yearbook," *Michigan Historical Review* 38, no. 2 (Fall 2012), 91–105; Carroll Engelhardt, "Citizenship Training and Community Civics in Iowa Schools: Modern Methods for Traditional Ends, 1876–1928," *Mid-America* 65, no. 2 (April-July 1983), 55–69; Janet A. Miller, "Urban Education and the New City: Cincinnati's Elementary Schools, 1870–1914," *Ohio History* 88, no. 2 (Spring 1979), 155.

97. Belting, "Development of the Free Public High School," 468.

98. David B. Tyack, "The Tribe and the Common School: Community Control in Rural Education," *American Quarterly* 24, no. 1 (March 1972), 9; Christina Kotchemidova, "From Good Cheer to 'Drive-by Smiling': A Social History of Cheerfulness," *Journal of Social History* 39, no. 1 (Autumn 2005), 12 (noting that a corollary to uplift was the Victorian ideal of cheerfulness), 8 (explaining that the "emotion of sadness is rooted in passive behavior and is inversely related to the idea of self-help").

99. Tyack, "Tribe and the Common School," 9.

100. Kaestle, "Social Change," 6.

101. Tyack, "Tribe and the Common School," 9.

102. Engelhardt, "Schools and Character," 623.

103. Theobald, *Call School*, 81 (quotation); Pawley, *Reading on the Middle Border*, 53.
104. Stevenson, *Victorian Homefront*, 78.
105. Pawley, *Reading on the Middle Border*, 49, 39.
106. Theobald, *Call School*, 107; Tyack, "Tribe and the Common School," 10.
107. Pawley, *Reading on the Middle Border*, 13.
108. Felsenstein and Connolly, *What Middletown Read*, 157, 165.
109. Eckman, "Promoting an Ideology of Culture, 18; Annie Holmquist, "Middle School Reading Lists 100 Years Ago v. Today," *Intellectual Takeout*, July 19, 2016, www.intellectualtakeout.org/blog/middle-school-reading-lists-100-years-ago-vs -today.
110. Theobald, *Call School*, 107, 117–18.
111. Pawley, *Reading on the Middle Border*, 53, citing McConnell, *Glorious Contentment*, 224–28.
112. Brammer, "Winthrop B. Smith," 45–59 (describing the Ohio-based publisher of the McGuffey readers); David D. Anderson, *Ohio in Fact and Fiction: Further Essays on the Ohio Experience* (East Lansing: Michigan State University Press, 2006), 27–30; Pawley, *Reading on the Middle Border*, 13.
113. Paul S. Anderson, "McGuffey vs. the Moderns in Character Training," *Phi Delta Kappan* 38, no. 2 (November 1956), 53; Richard David Mosier, *Making the American Mind: Social and Moral Ideas in the McGuffey Readers* (New York: Russell and Russell, 1965), 168; Theobald, *Call School*, 108; Szasz, "Stress and 'Character and Service,'" 145.
114. Smith, "Protestant Schooling," 695 (quotation); Paul Glad, *The Trumpet Soundeth: William Jennings Bryan and His Democracy, 1896–1912* (Lincoln: University of Nebraska Press, 1960), 9–14.
115. Mandel, "Religion and the Public Schools of Ohio," 188; D. A. Saunders, "Social Ideas in McGuffey Readers," *Public Opinion Quarterly* 5, no. 4 (Winter 1941), 579–89.
116. Ruth Miller Elson, "American Schoolbooks and 'Culture' in the Nineteenth Century," *Mississippi Valley Historical Review* 46, no. 3 (December 1959), 422.
117. Pawley, *Reading on the Middle Border*, 53.
118. Henry Hobart Vail, *A History of the McGuffey Readers* (Cleveland: no publisher, 1910), 64–65.
119. Wayne Fuller, *The Old Country School* (Chicago: University of Chicago Press, 1982), 17.
120. Wright, *Culture on the Moving Frontier*, 90. On the origins of the first American kindergartens in places such as Marietta, Ohio, and Watertown, Wisconsin, see Josephine E. Phillips, "The Infant School That Grew Up," *Ohio Archaeological and Historical Quarterly* 47, no. 1 (January 1958), 59.
121. As soon as feasible a system of education was to be established "ascending in a regular gradation, from township schools to a state university, wherein tuition [should] be gratis, and equally open to all." Buley, *Old Northwest*, vol. 1, 73.
122. Buley, *Old Northwest* vol. 1, 74 (quotation); Otho Lionel Newman, "Development of the Common Schools of Indiana to 1851," *Indiana Magazine of History* 22, no. 3 (September 1926), 229–40.

123. John Pulliam, "Changing Attitudes toward Free Public Schools in Illinois, 1825–1860," *History of Education Quarterly* 7, no. 2 (Summer 1967), 191–92 (quotations); James E. Herget, "Democracy Revisited: The Law and School Districts in Illinois," *Journal of the Illinois State Historical Society* 72, no. 2 (May 1979), 132–34.

124. Rosentreter, "Michigan's Quest for Statehood," 84; Schafer, "Beginnings of Civilization," 232.

125. Justin L. Kestenbaum, "Modernizing Michigan: Political and Social Trends, 1836–1866," in Hathaway, *Michigan: Visions of Our Past*, 121.

126. Pulliam, "Changing Attitudes," 202–3.

127. Mandel, "Religion and the Public Schools of Ohio," 187; Ivan M. Tribe, "Rise and Decline of Private Academies in Albany, Ohio," *Ohio History Journal* 78, no. 3 (Summer 1969), 188–201.

128. Robert E. Belding, "Academies and Iowa's Frontier Life," *Annals of Iowa* 44, no. 5 (Summer 1978), 336; Willis Dunbar, "Public versus Private Control of Higher Education in Michigan, 1817–1855," *Mississippi Valley Historical Review* 22, no. 3 (December 1935), 390, 392–93.

129. John Hardin Thomas, "The Academies of Indiana," *Indiana Magazine of History* 10, no. 4 (December 1914), 331–38; Belding, "Academies and Iowa's Frontier Life," 345, 348, 352–55; Pawley, *Reading on the Middle Border*, 42. See also Forest C. Ensign, "The Era of Private Academies," *Palimpsest* 27, no. 3 (March 1946), 75–85.

130. Finkelman, "Northwest Ordinance," 11.

131. Carl E. Kaestle, "The Development of Common School Systems in the States of the Old Northwest," in Mattingly and Stevens, *"Schools and the Means of Education,"* 31–43; Charles E. Peterson Jr., "The Common School Advocate: Molder of the Public Mind," *Journal of the Illinois State Historical Society* 57, 3 (Autumn 1964), 261–69; Belting, "Development of the Free Public High School," 467–565; Joseph Schafer, "Genesis of Wisconsin's Free High School System," *Wisconsin Magazine of History* 10, no. 2 (December 1926), 123–49; Kathryn Kish Sklar, "Female Teachers: 'Firm Pillars' of the West," in Mattingly and Stevens, *"Schools and the Means of Education,"* 61 (noting that there were sixteen normal schools in Ohio, Indiana, Illinois, and Michigan by 1890).

132. Randolph C. Downes, "The People's Schools: Popular Foundations of Toledo's Public School System," *Northwest Ohio Quarterly* 29, no. 1 (1957), 17; Smith, "Protestant Schooling," 682; Felsenstein and Connolly, *What Middletown Read*, 160; Theobald, *Call School*, 160–61; Howe, "Victorian Culture in America," 23; Fuller, "Making Better Farmers," 154–68.

133. Stevenson, *Victorian Homefront*, 72.

134. Albert Fishlow, "Levels of Nineteenth-Century American Investment in Education," *Journal of Economic History* 26, no. 4 (December 1966), 428.

135. Richard E. Dudley, "Nebraska Public School Education, 1890–1910," *Nebraska History* 54, no. 1 (1973), 66. See generally Andrew Gulliford, *America's Country Schools* (Washington, DC: Preservation Press, 1984).

136. Tyack, "Tribe and the Common School," 5.

137. Most public schools in Kansas offered debate classes for credit, which was not a practice in the Northeast, West, and South. The Kansas debate program was

launched by a Kansan who admired the Wisconsin extension system. Claudia J. Keenan, "'Not as an End in Itself': The Development of Debate in Kansas High Schools," *Kansas History* 28, no. 2 (Summer 2005), 84–93.

138. Felsenstein and Connolly, *What Middletown Read*, 160.

139. Downes, "People's Schools," 17.

140. Theobald, *Call School*, 177.

141. Fuller, "Making Better Farmers," 154; David Tyack, "Forming Schools, Farming States: Education in a Nation of Republics," in Mattingly and Stevens, *"Schools and the Means of Education,"* 24 (noting that the early "non-system" of education in the Midwest "produced relatively high levels of literacy and school attendance"); Cordier, "Prairie Schoolwomen," 107–8.

142. William W. Cutler III, "Cathedral of Culture: The Schoolhouse in American Educational Thought and Practice since 1820," *History of Education Quarterly* 29, no. 1 (Spring 1989), 1–40.

143. Cutler, "Cathedral of Culture," 11.

144. Ronald M. Johnson, "Politics and Pedagogy: The 1892 Cleveland School Reform," *Ohio History* 84, no. 4 (Autumn 1975), 197. This was a Civic Federation and clergy-led effort seeking "greater morality in government." Johnson, "Politics and Pedagogy," 200.

145. Johnson, "Politics and Pedagogy," 197.

146. Raleigh A. Suarez, "Chronicle of a Failure: Public Education in Antebellum Louisiana," *Louisiana History* 12, no. 2 (Spring 1971), 109–22; Kaestle, "Development of Common School Systems," 33–37, 41 (emphasizing that the common schools in the Midwest were not a duplication of eastern schools and that reformers often pointed to Prussian schools as models).

147. Meyer et al., "Public Education as Nation-Building," 600.

148. Samuel Plantz, "Lawrence College," *Wisconsin Magazine of History* 6, no. 2 (December 1922), 145.

149. By the time of the Civil War there were twenty colleges in Ohio and fourteen in Indiana, and by 1868 there were twenty-one colleges in Illinois. Between 1838 and 1850, fifty academies, colleges, and universities were incorporated in Iowa. Ringenberg, "Church Colleges," 316; Russell M. Storey, "The Rise of the Denominational College," *Ohio Archaeological and Historical Society Publications* 25, no. 1 (January 1916), 52–58; E. Kidd Lockard, "The Influence of New England in Denominational Colleges in the Northwest, 1830–1860," *Ohio Archaeological and Historical Quarterly* 53, no. 1 (January–March 1944), 2; Herriott, "Transfusion of Political Ideas," 54; Earle D. Ross, "Religious Influences in the Development of State Colleges and Universities," *Indiana Magazine of History* 46, no. 4 (December 1950), 347–48; James Findlay, "Agency, Denominations and the Western Colleges, 1830–1860: Some Connections between Evangelicalism and American Higher Education," *Church History* 50, no. 1 (March 1981), 64 (noting the "special relationships which existed between the small colleges of the Midwest and the evangelical Protestant churches during the middle decades of the nineteenth century"); Lantzer, "Forging God's Country," 25.

150. Wheeler, "How Colleges Shaped," 105.

151. Wheeler, "How Colleges Shaped," 106–7; Wright, *Culture on the Moving Frontier*, 101; John William Oliver Jr., James A. Hodges, and James H. O'Donnell,

eds., *Cradles of Conscience: Ohio's Independent Colleges and Universities* (Kent, OH: Kent State University Press, 2003). In Ohio, "almost every town of consequence" had a college. Ralph Taylor, "The Formation of the Eclectic School in Cincinnati," *Ohio Archaeological and Historical Quarterly* 51, no. 4 (October–December 1942), 279. In contrast to Ohio, in Michigan the state legislature slowed the development of denominational colleges until 1855 to assist the growth of the state university in Ann Arbor (with the exceptions of allowing the creation of Marshall College, St. Phillip's College, St. Mark's College, and Hillsdale College). William C. Ringenberg, "Church Colleges vs. State University," *Michigan History* 55, no. 4 (Winter 1971), 312; Willis Dunbar, "Year of Decision on Michigan's Educational Policy: 1855," *Michigan History* 39, no. 2 (December 1955), 445–60. For a time, Michigan thought of using a Prussian-style top-down state-run university system, but this was abandoned in 1855. Ringenberg, "Church Colleges," 314.

152. Wheeler, "How Colleges Shaped," 109–12; Lockard, "Influence of New England," 12 (noting the creation of "manual labor departments providing farms and shops where [Midwestern college] students might earn part of their expenses"); Ross, "Religious Influences," 354; Fletcher, "Bread and Doctrine at Oberlin," 59; Paul Goodman, "The Manual Labor Movement and the Origins of Abolitionism," *Journal of the Early Republic* 13, no. 3 (Fall 1993), 355–88.

153. Richard S. Taylor, "Western Colleges as 'Securities of Intelligence & Virtue': The Towne-Eddy Report of 1846," *Old Northwest* 7, no. 1 (Spring 1981), 44.

154. Wheeler, "How Colleges Shaped," 112 (cows), 106–9 (oligarchy); Robert K. Richardson, "'Yale of the West': A Study of Academic Sectionalism," *Wisconsin Magazine of History* 36, no. 4 (Summer 1953), 260; Dunbar, "Public versus Private Control," 397; William J. McGill, "The Belated Founding of Alma College: Presbyterians and Higher Education in Michigan, 1833–1886," *Michigan History* 57, no. 3 (June 1973), 94; Edward A. Goedeken, "An Academic Controversy at Iowa State Agricultural College, 1890–1891," *Annals of Iowa* 45, no. 2 (Fall 1979), 110–22; Earle D. Ross, *Democracy's College: The Land-Grant Movement in the Formative Stage* (Ames: Iowa State College Press, 1942), 86–99; Doris Malkmus, "Origins of Coeducation in Iowa," *Annals of Iowa* 58, no. 2 (Spring 1999), 180.

155. Wright, *Culture on the Moving Frontier*, 105; James Rodabaugh, "Robert Hamilton Bishop, Pioneer Educator," *Ohio History Journal* 44, no. 1 (January 1935), 92–102.

156. Jurgen Herbst, "The Development of Public Universities in the Old Northwest," in Mattingly and Stevens, *"Schools and the Means of Education,"* 121; Dunbar, "Public versus Private Control," 402.

157. Alan Creutz, "The Prussian System and Practical Training," *Michigan History* 65, no. 1 (January/February, 1981), 32–39; Laurence R. Veysey, *The Emergence of the American University* (Chicago: University of Chicago Press, 1965), 100. See also Oliver B. Pollak, "Looking for 'Wide-Awake' Young People: Business Colleges in Nebraska, 1873–1950," *Nebraska History* 90, no. 1 (Winter 2009), 42–50.

158. Alan I. Marcus, "If All the World Were Mechanics and Farmers: Democracy and the Formative Years of Land-Grant Colleges in America," *Ohio Valley History* 5, no. 1 (Spring 2005), 23–36; John Y. Simon, "The Politics of the Morrill Act," *Agricultural History* 37, no. 2 (1963), 103–4; Roger L. Williams, *The Origins of Federal*

Support for Higher Education: George W. Atherton and the Land-Grant College Movement (University Park: Pennsylvania State University Press, 1991).

159. Stevenson, *Victorian Homefront*, 110 (quotation); Harry E. Kersey Jr., *John Milton Gregory and the University of Illinois* (Urbana: University of Illinois Press, 1968); George W. Smith, "The Old Illinois Agricultural College," *Journal of the Illinois State Historical Society* 5, no. 4 (January 1913), 475–80; Jackson E. Towne, "President Draper Gets a College of Agriculture in Spite of Himself," *Agricultural History* 36, no. 4 (October 1962), 207–12. See also Thomas R. Walsh, "Charles E. Bessey and the Transformation of the Industrial College," *Nebraska History* 52, no. 4 (1971), 383–409.

160. Turner's address, "Pioneer Ideals and the State University," is reprinted in Martin Ridge, "Frederick Jackson Turner at Indiana University," *Indiana Magazine of History* 89, no. 3 (September 1993), 225. On the study of farming at Turner's university, see E. L. Luther, "Farmers' Institutes in Wisconsin, 1885–1933," *Wisconsin Magazine of History* 30, no. 1 (September 1946), 59–68. See also Allan Nevins, *The State Universities and Democracy* (Urbana: University of Illinois Press, 1962); Roy V. Scott, "Early Agricultural Education in Minnesota: The Institute Phase," *Agricultural History* 37, no. 1 (January 1963), 21–34.

161. Ridge, "Frederick Jackson Turner at Indiana University," 225.

162. Keith L. Sprunger, "'Old Main' at Kansas Colleges: Splendor, Survival, and Loss," *Kansas History* 38, no. 3 (Autumn 2015), 164–79 (discussing ten colleges in Kansas); Ann L. Wilhite, "Cities and Colleges in the Promised Land: Territorial Nebraska, 1854–1867," *Nebraska History* 67, no. 4 (1986), 327–71 (discussing Nebraska colleges).

163. John W. Boyer, *The University of Chicago: A History* (Chicago: University of Chicago Press, 2015), 65 (quotation); Edgar J. Goodspeed, "The Old University of Chicago in 1867," *Journal of the Illinois State Historical Society* 3, no. 2 (July 1910), 52–57; Stevenson, *Victorian Homefront*, 114; Richard J. Storr, *Harper's University: The Beginnings* (Chicago: University of Chicago Press, 1966). The first president of Chicago was William Rainey Harper, who was born in New Concord, Ohio, attended Muskingum College in Ohio, and taught at Denison University in Ohio. Harper was active in Chautauqua and a Bible scholar. Thornton, "Chautauqua and the Midwest," 160–61. On Harper, Chautauqua, and the University of Chicago, see Joseph E. Gould, *The Chautauqua Movement* (New York: State University of New York, 1961).

164. Vernon Carstensen, "The Origin and Early Development of the Wisconsin Idea," *Wisconsin Magazine of History* 39, no. 3 (Spring 1956), 181–88; Veysey, *Emergence of the American University*, 105, 110.

165. Veysey, *Emergence of the American University*, 109 (distinctive, utility, effete, action), 111; LaVon Mary Gappa, "Chancellor James Hulme Canfield: His Impact on the University of Nebraska, 1891–1895," *Nebraska History* 66, no. 4 (1985), 392–410.

166. Wheeler, "How Colleges Shaped," 114. See also Marilynne Robinson, *When I Was a Child I Read Books: Essays* (New York: Farrar, Straus and Giroux, 2012), 166 (noting the college's "organized efforts at social betterment" and its "old language about moral advancement").

167. Havighurst, *Heartland*, 155–56; Craven, "Advance of Civilization into the Middle West," 58; Wright, *Culture on the Moving Frontier*, 108; Curti, *Growth of American Thought*, 273; John Frederick Bell, "When Regulation Was Religious: College Philanthropy, Antislavery Politics, and Accreditation in the Mid-Nineteenth Century West," *History of Education Quarterly* 57, no. 1 (February 2017), 68–93.

168. Marilynne Robinson, *The Death of Adam: Essays on Modern Thought* (New York: Picador, 2014), 140.

169. Taylor, "Western Colleges as 'Securities of Intelligence & Virtue,'" 41.

170. Fletcher, "Bread and Doctrine at Oberlin," 58.

171. Barnes, "Learning and Piety," 329.

172. Ross, "Religious Influences," 354.

173. Daniel T. Johnson, "Financing the Western Colleges, 1844–1862," *Journal of the Illinois State Historical Society* 65, no. 1 (Spring 1972), 52–53.

174. Lockard, "Influence of New England," 9 (wise, constant, historical), 10.

175. Barnes, "Learning and Piety," 330.

176. Bledstein, *Culture of Professionalism*, 200.

177. Ringenberg, "Church Colleges," 307.

178. William E. Leonard, "Early College Silhouettes," *Minnesota History* 16, no. 2 (June 1935), 180.

179. Barnes, "Learning and Piety," 330.

180. Ringenberg, "Church Colleges," 307; Veysey, *Emergence of the American University*, 101 (quotations).

181. Kristin Mapel Bloomberg, "'Let Us Not Look Regretfully on the Past': Clara Bewick Colby and Midwestern Women's Early Coeducation at the University of Wisconsin," *Middle West Review* 8, no. 1 (Fall 2021).

182. Richardson, "'Yale of the West,'" 282. On the civic centrality of the college, see Helen L. D. Richardson, "A Century of Church and College in Beloit," *Wisconsin Magazine of History* 45, no. 4 (Summer 1962), 296–301, and Robert K. Richardson, "How Beloit Won Its College," *Wisconsin Magazine of History* 28, no. 3 (March 1945), 290–306.

183. Lawrence B. Goodheart, "Abolitionists as Academics: The Controversy at Western Reserve College, 1832–1833," *History of Education Quarterly* 22, no. 4 (Winter 1982), 422.

184. Wright, *Culture on the Moving Frontier*, 104, 105 (curriculum). Cutler told Congress he wanted one section in each township granted for education, both schools and colleges, before he would buy land in Ohio. Schafer, "Beginnings of Civilization," 214.

185. Goodheart, "Abolitionists as Academics," 423–24.

186. Barnes, "Learning and Piety," 332.

187. Bledstein, *Culture of Professionalism*, 134 (society, stood, strong), 147 (person, paced). See essays on moral training in *Transactions of the Annual Meeting of the Ohio College Association* (Toledo: Published by the Association, 1895).

188. John Bascom, "Books That Have Helped Me," *Forum* 3 (May 1886); Bledstein, *Culture of Professionalism*, 196.

189. Bledstein, *Culture of Professionalism*, 196.

190. John Whitney Evans, "The Newman Idea in Wisconsin, 1883–1920," *Wisconsin Magazine of History* 54, no. 3 (Spring 1971), 204.

191. Evans, "Newman Idea in Wisconsin," 204.

192. Bledstein, *Culture of Professionalism*, 258. A chapter was also started at the University of Virginia. For another example, in this case focused on Penn College in Oskaloosa, Iowa, see Dorothy E. Finnegan, "A Potent Influence: The YMCA and YWCA at Penn College, 1882–1920s," *Annals of Iowa* 65, no. 1 (Winter 2006), 1–34. See also Clifford Putney, "Character Building in the YMCA, 1880–1930," *Mid-America* 73, no. 1 (January 1991), 49–57. A related organization, the Boy Scouts of America, first started in Northfield, Minnesota, and was organized by the Chicago publisher William Boyce. Kurt Leichtle, "The Founding Triumvirate: Founding of the BSA and Creative Conflict," paper in author's possession; Leichtle to author, February 25, 2021. See also David Macleod, *Building Character in the American Boy: The Boy Scouts, YMCA, and Their Forerunners, 1870–1920* (Madison: University of Wisconsin Press, 1983), 146.

193. Bledstein, *Culture of Professionalism*, 251.

194. Rita S. Saslaw, "Student Societies in Nineteenth Century Ohio: Misconceptions and Realities," *Ohio History* 88, no. 2 (Spring 1979), 198.

195. Saslaw, "Student Societies," 200 (deeply), 207 (spirit), 202 (morality, self-improvement), 203 (cultivation), 205; John Mark Tucker, "Azariah Smith Root and Social Reform at Oberlin College," *Journal of Library History* 16, no. 2 (Spring 1981), 281.

196. Jesse J. Gant, "'Younger and More Irreconcilable': James Albert Woodburn's Undergraduate Orations at Indiana University, 1875–1876," *Indiana Magazine of History* 108, no. 2 (June 2012), 162.

197. L. R. Lind, "Early Literary Societies at Wabash College," *Indiana Magazine of History* 42, no. 2 (June 1946), 173–76; Lockard, "Influence of New England," 8; Lawrence Poston, "Classicist on the Middle Border," *Indiana Magazine of History* 90, no. 3 (September 1994), 253; Leonard, "Early College Silhouettes," 182; Loren P. Beth, "Monmouth Literary Societies," *Journal of the Illinois State Historical Society* 43, no. 2 (Summer 1950), 120–22; Saslaw, "Student Societies," 209; Michael S. Hevel, "Public Displays of Student Learning: The Role of Literary Societies in Early Iowa Higher Education," *Annals of Iowa* 70, no. 1 (Winter 2011), 1–2, 7; Fisher, "Literary Societies," 530; Lawrence Hall, "All Beginnings Are Difficult," *Michigan History* 70, no. 5 (September/October 1986), 43 (discussing such societies at Alma College in Michigan); Hubbart, *Older Middle West*, 71.

198. Ronald A. Smith, "Athletics in the Wisconsin State University System, 1867–1913," *Wisconsin Magazine of History* 55, no. 1 (Autumn 1971), 9–12. The main interest of male students was debating, and a debating society was formed the first year of the existence of Lawrence College in Wisconsin. Plantz, "Lawrence College," 159. On the Knox College literary societies that created a system of intercollegiate debate, see Muelder, *Missionaries and Muckrakers*, 15–16.

199. Bledstein, *Culture of Professionalism*, 255 (quotation), 257; Stevenson, *Victorian Homefront*, 113.

200. Wright, *Culture on the Moving Frontier*, 109.

201. Saslaw, "Student Societies," 208 (development, avoiding), 209 (improper), 198 (conservative).

202. Bledstein, *Culture of Professionalism*, 154–55.

203. Lockard, "Influence of New England," 11 (ardent, smoke), 12; George Allen Hubbell, "Horace Mann and Antioch College," *Ohio Archaeological and Historical Society Publications* 14, no. 1 (January 1905), 15–16.

204. Thomas N. Hoover, "The Beginnings of Higher Education in the Northwest Territory," *Ohio Archaeological and Historical Quarterly* 50, no. 3 (July–September 1941), 256.

205. Donald F. Carmony, ed., "Smithson College Circular, 1871," *Indiana Magazine of History* 53, no. 1 (March 1957), 75, 79–80.

206. Dunbar, "Public versus Private Control," 401.

207. Ronald A. Brunger, "Albion College: The Founding of a Frontier School," *Michigan History* 51, no. 2 (Summer 1967), 147.

208. Wright, *Culture on the Moving Frontier*, 103.

209. Barnes, "Learning and Piety," 331, 334, 338.

210. Lockard, "Influence of New England," 13.

211. Poston, "Classicist on the Middle Border," 253.

212. Clarence P. McClelland, "The Morning Star of Memory," *Journal of the Illinois State Historical Society* 40, no. 3 (1947), 261.

213. Lawrence W. Levine, "Clio, Canons, and Culture," *Journal of American History* 80, no. 3 (December 1993), 858.

214. Poston, "Classicist on the Middle Border," 254, 256.

215. Lockard, "Influence of New England," 6; Hubbart, *Older Middle West*, 70.

216. Dunbar, "Public versus Private Control," 386.

217. Ross, "Religious Influences," 350–54; Nevins, *Emergence of Modern America*, 272.

218. See chapter 4.

219. See chapter 5.

220. Richard White, *The Middle Ground: Indians, Empires, and Republics in the Great Lakes Region, 1650–1815* (New York: Cambridge University Press, 1991), 14.

221. Francis Jennings, *The Ambiguous Iroquois Empire: The Covenant Chain Confederation of Indian Tribes with English Colonies* (New York: W. W. Norton, 1984), 102; Hellen Hornbeck Tanner, ed., *Atlas of Great Lakes Indian History* (Norman: University of Oklahoma Press, 1987), 30.

222. Elizabeth Mancke, "The Ohio Country and Indigenous Geopolitics in Early Modern North America circa 1500–1760," *Ohio Valley History* 18, no. 1 (Spring 2018), 8–9, 14 (examining the Ohio Country and explaining "from a continental Indigenous perspective" that wars caused great "reverberations" by the 1600s, "leaving the region depopulated"), 16; White, *Middle Ground*, 11 (describing the Iroquois driving the Algonquin tribes as far west as northern Wisconsin, leaving "a huge area between the Ohio River and the northern shores of the Great Lakes emptied of inhabitants by the Iroquois"); Hurt, *Ohio Frontier*, 9 ("Essentially, Ohio remained unoccupied"); Allen W. Trelease, "The Iroquois and the Western Fur Trade: A Problem of Interpretation," *Mississippi Valley Historical Review* 49, no. 1 (June 1962),

36 (summarizing an older view of these conflicts and focusing on friction over the beaver trade); David Andrew Nichols, *Peoples of the Inland Sea: Native Americans and Newcomers in the Great Lakes Region, 1600–1870* (Athens: Ohio University Press, 2018), 30–31, 36; Jose Antonio Brandao, *"Your Fyre Shall Burn No More": Iroquois Policy toward New France and Its Native Allies to 1701* (Lincoln: University of Nebraska Press, 1997) (highlighting the multiple causes of warfare besides the beaver trade and tracking 465 Iroquois military engagements between 1603 and 1701). On the Iroquois generally, see Daniel E. Richter, *The Ordeal of the Longhouse: The Peoples of the Iroquois League in the Era of European Colonization* (Chapel Hill: University of North Carolina Press, 1992).

223. Mancke, "Ohio Country," 17 (quotation), 18–19 (noting the "vast tracks of territory to the south and north of Lake Erie that Haudenosaunee [Iroquois] warfare had depopulated during" the 1600s and explaining that, "within these enormous tracts of land, what remained depopulated in the early eighteenth century were lands that would become known as the Ohio Country"); Nichols, *Peoples of the Inland Sea*, 39.

224. Robert M. Owens, "Jeffersonian Benevolence on the Ground: The Indian Land Cession Treaties of William Henry Harrison," *Journal of the Early Republic* 22, no. 3 (Autumn 2002), 407.

225. Mancke, "Ohio Country," 20; Nichols, *Peoples of the Inland Sea*, 37. On these "Native Pioneers," see chapter 1 of the same name in Michael N. McConnell, *A Country Between: The Upper Ohio Valley and Its Peoples, 1724–1774* (Lincoln: University of Nebraska Press, 1992).

226. Mancke, "Ohio Country," 20.

227. White, *Middle Ground*.

228. Richard R. Beeman, "The Varieties of Deference in Eighteenth-Century America," *Early American Studies* 3, no. 2 (Fall 2005), 333 (noting settler denunciations of a "litany of Indian depredations," including "their beating, scalping, skinning, boiling, and eating of white backcountry residents").

229. John P. Bowes, *Land Too Good for Indians: Northern Indian Removal* (Norman: University of Oklahoma Press, 2016), 18–21.

230. Reginald Horsman, "The Northwest Ordinance and the Shaping of an Expanding Republic," *Wisconsin Magazine of History* 73, no. 1 (Autumn 1989), 24; Lawrence A. Peskin, "Conspiratorial Anglophobia and the War of 1812," *Journal of American History* 98, no. 3 (December 2011), 656; Owens, "Jeffersonian Benevolence," 413 (noting that "British agents had encouraged Indian wars against white Americans"); J. Leitch Wright Jr., *Britain and the American Frontier, 1783–1815* (Athens: University of Georgia Press, 1975); Colin G. Calloway, "Beyond the Vortex of Violence: Indian-White Relations in the Ohio Country, 1783–1815," *Northwest Ohio Quarterly* 64, no. 1 (Winter 1992), 16–26 (making a plea for historians to understand the complexity of this era).

231. Horsman, "Northwest Ordinance and the Shaping," 24 (quotation); Daniel R. Griesmer, "'Better Our Circumstances': Settler Colonialism in Ohio during the 1780s," *Ohio History* 124, no. 1 (Spring 2017), 22 (explaining that the "United States government insisted that since the Natives sided with the British during the American Revolution, they had been on the losing side of the war and now had no

NOTES TO CHAPTER 2

right to try and claim any of the lands ceded to the United States in the Treaty of Paris"); Reginald Horsman, "American Indian Policy in the Old Northwest, 1783–1812," *William and Mary Quarterly* 18, no. 1 (January 1961), 36 (noting that the Americans told the Native Americans "that the land on which they lived had been ceded by Great Britain in the Treaty of Paris, and that as they had fought on the side of the British during the Revolution, they could justly be expelled to the north of the Great Lakes along with their allies," and that this "was justified as reparations for Indian hostility during the war"); Robert E. Berkhofer Jr., "Americans versus Indians: The Northwest Ordinance, Territory Making, and Native Americans," *Indiana Magazine of History* 84, no. 1 (March 1988), 95.

232. Horsman, "Northwest Ordinance and the Shaping," 26 (authorities); Robert M. Owens, *Red Dreams, White Nightmares: Pan-Indian Alliances in the Anglo-American Mind, 1763–1815* (Norman: University of Oklahoma Press, 2015); William Heath, *William Wells and the Struggle for the Old Northwest* (Norman: University of Oklahoma Press, 2015); Stephen Warren, *The Worlds the Shawnees Made: Migration and Violence in Early America* (Chapel Hill: University of North Carolina Press, 2014).

233. Colin Calloway, *A Victory with No Name: The Native American Defeat of the First American Army* (New York: Oxford University Press, 2015); Gregory Evans Dowd, *A Spirited Resistance: The North American Indian Struggle for Unity, 1745–1815* (Baltimore, MD: Johns Hopkins University Press, 1992).

234. In a combination of women's activism, civic engagement, and memorialization, the women of Monroe, Michigan, built a monument to the American settlers killed in the River Raisin massacre of 1813, in which eight hundred American "prisoners left unguarded were attacked and killed by Indians." Brace, "Power of Porch Talks," 7.

235. Karim M. Tiro, "New Narratives of the Conquest of the Ohio Country," *Journal of the Early Republic* 36, no. 3 (Fall 2016), 550.

236. Bowes, *Land Too Good for Indians*; Carl G. Klopfenstein, "The Removal of the Wyandots from Ohio," *Ohio Historical Quarterly* 66, no. 2 (April 1957), 119–36. This process has become known as "settler colonialism" in recent years. In contrast to colonialism, in which a foreign power controls a country for the purpose of extracting wealth and resources, settler colonialism involves the removal of a population and the settlement of a land with new people. Michael Witgen, "A Nation of Settlers: The Early American Republic and the Colonization of the Northwest Territory," *William and Mary Quarterly* 76, no. 3 (July 2019), 393. See also Horsman, "American Indian Policy," 44 (explaining, before the term became common, that the history of the Northwest was not precisely a case of settler colonialism because the Americans at times "advocated fair dealing with the Indians, impartial justice, reasonable trading practices, and strict regulation of the manner in which Indians lands might be obtained" and "teaching the Indians how to farm, to keep domesticated animals, and to build comfortable homes"); Griesmer, "'Bettering Our Circumstances,'" 24 (noting that "American settler colonialism was unique compared to other colonial powers throughout the world because of the willingness to negotiate treaties with Native groups"); Bowes, *Land Too Good for Indians*, 13 (explaining that the histories of the tribes in the Midwest "are in many ways too diverse to

discuss adequately in a single narrative"), 68 (quoting American officials saying that they could have simply taken native lands by force but they chose to negotiate); Allan Greer, "Settler Colonialism and Empire in Early America," *William and Mary Quarterly* 76, no. 3 (July 2019), 383–90 (noting various problems with settler colonial theory); Lorenzo Veracini, "'Settler Colonialism': Career of a Concept," *Journal of Imperial and Commonwealth History* 41, no. 2 (2013), 313–33 (discussing various forms of settler colonialism—"diehard colonialism," "hyper-colonialism," extraction colonialism—and tracing the concept to Australian and Algerian history).

237. Stephen Warren, "The Ohio Shawnees' Struggle against Removal, 1814–30," in R. David Edmunds, *Enduring Nations: Native Americans in the Midwest* (Urbana: University of Illinois Press, 2008), 86.

238. Warren, "Ohio Shawnees' Struggle," 75, 86.

239. Witgen, "Nation of Settlers," 391–92.

240. See Roy Harvey Pearce, *The Savages of America: A Study of the Indian and the Idea of Civilization* (Baltimore, MD: Johns Hopkins University Press, 1953).

241. Thomas Morgan, the commissioner of Indian affairs in charge of this education effort, was from Franklin, Indiana, and had served as a Union general in the Civil War and as commander of the Fourteenth United States Colored Infantry and later as the principal of the Nebraska State Normal School. Burton M. Smith, "Anti-Catholicism, Indian Education, and Thomas Jefferson Morgan, Commissioner of Indian Affairs," *Canadian Journal of History* 23, no. 2 (August 1988), 213; Frederick E. Hoxie, "Redefining Indian Education: Thomas J. Morgan's Program in Disarray," *Arizona and the West* 24, no. 1 (Spring 1982), 7 (noting the focus on moral reform and uplift, that "Morgan's reforms paralleled those taking place in school systems throughout the nation," and Morgan's "plan to integrate Indian children into public school districts adjoining reservations"); Thomas G. Andrews, "Turning the Tables on Assimilation: Oglala Lakotas and the Pine Ridge Day Schools, 1889–1920s," *Western Historical Quarterly* 33, no. 4 (Winter 2002), 410 (quotation), 411 (highlighting the focus on thrift, industry, character development, and "moral training to inculcate mainstream American values, particularly Protestant Christianity, Anglo-Saxon civility, and republican virtue"); Philip J. Deloria, "American Master Narratives and the Problem of Indian Citizenship in the Gilded Age and Progressive Era," *Journal of the Gilded Age and Progressive Era* 14, no. 1 (January 2015), 4 (noting that the conventional goals of the Society of American Indians were "personal freedom and personal advancement"); Warren, "Ohio Shawnees' Struggle," 72–73 (noting the opposition of male Shawnees to farming, which was seen as women's work). See also David Wallace Adams, *Education for Extinction: American Indians and the Boarding School Experience, 1875–1928* (Lawrence: University Press of Kansas, 1995); Brenda Child, *Boarding School Seasons: American Indian Families, 1900–1940* (Lincoln: University of Nebraska Press, 2000); and Bruce Rubenstein, "To Destroy a Culture: Indian Education in Michigan, 1855–1900," *Michigan History* 60, no. 2 (Summer 1976), 137–60.

242. In 1853 the commissioner of Indian affairs estimated the Native American population still in tribal relations in Minnesota to be about twenty-one thousand and about 8,500 in Wisconsin. Notably fewer lived in Indiana (perhaps three hundred) and Illinois (about two hundred), and there were "supposed to be few, if any,

in Michigan." All who once lived in Ohio were "now in Indian Territory, west." *The Seventh Census of the United States: 1850* (Washington, DC: Robert Armstrong, Public Printer, 1853), xciv. At the same time, the overall population of Ohio approached two million, with Indiana and Illinois one million each. A special thanks is due to the historian and demographer Dr. Greg Rose of Ohio State University at Marion for his assistance gathering this census data. For an earlier era, before removal, the historian Stephen Warren notes that in 1824 there were 2,350 Indians in Ohio and 11,500 in Indiana and Illinois combined. Warren, "Ohio Shawnees' Struggle," 76. Sami Lakomaki places fifteen hundred to two thousand Shawnees in the Ohio Country in about 1750. After some of this group moved west, this number dropped to about a thousand located near the mouth of the Maumee River. Sami Lakomaki, "'Our Line': The Shawnees, the United States, and Competing Borders on the Great Lakes 'Borderlands,' 1795–1832," *Journal of the Early Republic* 34, no. 4 (Winter 2014), 602.

243. See Michael Leonard Cox, "Isaac Walker and the Complexities of Midwestern Native American Identity," in Lauck, *Making of the Midwest*, 289–303.

244. Akim Reinhardt, "Indigenous Adaptations to Settler Colonialism," *Middle West Review* 5, no. 1 (Fall 2018), 152–53; Jeffrey Ostler and Nancy Shoemaker, "Settler Colonialism in Early American History: Introduction," *William and Mary Quarterly* 76, no. 3 (July 2019), 364 (arguing that "Indians did not give up their lands and identities easily, quickly, or entirely"). See also Theodore J. Karamanski, "Settler Colonial Strategies and Indigenous Resistance on the Great Lakes Lumber Frontier," *Middle West Review* 2, no. 2 (Spring 2016), 27–51.

245. Christopher Wetzel, *Gathering the Potawatomi Nation: Revitalization and Identity* (Norman: University of Oklahoma Press, 2015); John N. Low, *Imprints: The Pokagon Band of Potawatomi Indians and the City of Chicago* (East Lansing: Michigan State University Press, 2016).

246. Thomas J. Lappas, "'A Perfect Apollo': Keokuk and Sac Leadership during the Removal Era," in Daniel P. Barr, ed., *The Boundaries between Us: Natives and Newcomers along the Frontiers of the Old Northwest Territory, 1750–1850* (Kent, OH: Kent State University Press, 2006), 219–35; Thomas Burnell Colbert, "'The Hinge on Which All Affairs of the Sauk and Fox Indians Turn': Keokuk and the United States Government," in Edmunds, *Enduring Nations*, 54–71. On the shifting allegiances and complex identities of Native Americans in the early Midwest, see Donald H. Graff, "Three Men from Three Rivers: Navigating between Native and American Identity in the Old Northwest Territory," in Barr, *Boundaries between Us*, 143–56.

247. Of the thousand Shawnees in Ohio in 1800, about eight hundred "remained neutral or supported the Americans." R. David Edmunds, "Forgotten Allies: The Loyal Shawnees and the War of 1812," in Skaggs and Nelson, *Sixty Years' War*, 338.

248. Patrick Bottiger, *The Borderland of Fear: Vincennes, Prophetstown, and the Invasion of the Miami Homeland* (Lincoln: University of Nebraska Press, 2016), 8. See also Bradley J. Birzer, "Jean Baptiste Richardville: Miami Metis," in Edmunds, *Enduring Nations*, 94–108, and Harvey Lewis Carter, *The Life and Times of Little Turtle: First Sagamore of the Wabash* (Urbana: University of Illinois Press, 1987).

249. Evadene Burris Swanson, "The Manuscript Journal of Thoreau's Last Journey," *Minnesota History* 20, no. 2 (June 1939), 171.

250. Harris, "Worthy of Their Own Aspiration," 366; Edward Livingston Taylor, "Monuments to Historical Indian Chiefs," *Ohio Archaeological and Historical Society Publications* 9, no. 1 (July 1900), 1–31.

251. John Higham, "Integrating America: The Problem of Assimilation in the Nineteenth Century," *Journal of American Ethnic History* 1, no. 1 (Fall 1981), 10.

252. Jameson Sweet, "Native Suffrage: Race, Citizenship, and Dakota Indians in the Upper Midwest," *Journal of the Early Republic* 39, no. 1 (Spring 2019), 99, 100 (noting the "laxity of the racial hierarchy in the upper Midwest").

253. Sweet, "Native Suffrage," 102; Earl M. Maltz, "The Fourteenth Amendment and Native American Citizenship," *Constitutional Commentary* 17 (2000), 555–73 (noting the distinction between nontaxed Native Americans living under the authority of tribes and those who had left tribal life); Michael Smith, "The History of Indian Citizenship," *Great Plains Journal* 10, no. 1 (Fall 1970), 26 (explaining that the "general rule was that as long as the Indian maintained his tribal relationship, he was in effect a citizen of that tribe" and subject to "tribal customs and rules").

254. Edward J. Littlejohn, "Black before the Bar: A History of Slavery, Race Laws, and Cases in Detroit and Michigan," *Journal of Law in Society* 18, no. 1 (Spring 2018), 64; Ronald P. Formisano, "The Edge of Caste: Colored Suffrage in Michigan, 1827–1861," *Michigan History* 56, no. 1 (Spring 1972), 30; Sweet, "Native Suffrage," 102.

255. Caroline W. Thrun, "School Segregation in Michigan," *Michigan History* 38, no. 1 (March 1954), 13–15; Patrick J. Jung, "To Extend Fair and Impartial Justice to the Indian: Native Americans and the Additional Court of Michigan Territory, 1823–1836," *Michigan Law Review* 23, no. 2 (Fall 1997), 27 (explaining that "Indians quickly adopted strategies that allowed them to successfully achieve their goals" and that courts "extended relatively fair and impartial justice to Native peoples").

256. William D. Green, "Minnesota's Long Road to Black Suffrage, 1849–1868," *Minnesota History* 56, no. 2 (Summer 1998), 69; Michael Witgen, "Seeing Red: Race, Citizenship, and Indigeneity in the Old Northwest," *Journal of the Early Republic* 38, no. 4 (Winter 2018), 582 (noting that governments in the Northwest Territory "consistently recognized the mixed-race children of fur traders and Native women as citizens of the republic, even granting men the right to vote and hold public office").

257. Green, "Minnesota's Long Road," 73.

258. Sweet, "Native Suffrage," 103. In Dakota Territory some women were annoyed when Native Americans were extended the right to vote but women were not. Greg Rohlf, "Lorena King Fairbank and John King Fairbank: South Dakota Cosmopolitans," in Jon K. Lauck, ed., *Heartland River: A Cultural History of the Big Sioux River Valley* (Sioux Falls, SD: Center for Western Studies, 2021).

259. Jeannette Wolfley, "Jim Crow, Indian Style: The Disenfranchisement of Native Americans," *American Indian Law Review* 16, no. 1 (1991), 175.

260. Elk v. Wilkins, 112 U.S. 94 (1884).

261. Opsahl v. Johnson, 163 N.W. 988 (Minn. 1917) (finding that Native Americans who had voted in a county election on the legalization of liquor sales were ineligible, inter alia, because of lack of assimilation and not paying state taxes).

262. Willard Hughes Rollings, "Citizenship and Suffrage: The Native American Struggle for Civil Rights in the American West, 1830–1965," *Nevada Law Journal* 5, no. 1 (Fall 2004), 134.

263. Wolfley, "Jim Crow, Indian Style," 176 (finding that, "by 1924, nearly two-thirds of all Indians were granted citizenship by treaties or special and general statutes")

264. Barnhart, "Emerging Voice," 6, 10; Owens, "Jeffersonian Benevolence," 408 (noting that the Greenville Treaty of 1795 was signed by "ninety chiefs, mostly prominent leaders in their communities").

265. Hurt, *Ohio Frontier*, 2.

266. Hurt, *Ohio Frontier*, 2. The prairie Potawatomis sought removal to Kansas in exchange for annuities and other forms of payment, but disorganized government officials botched the travel plans. R. David Edmunds, "The Prairie Potawatomi Removal of 1833," *Indiana Magazine of History* 68, no. 3 (September 1972), 240–53.

267. Melissa Rinehart, "Miami Resistance and Resilience during the Removal Era," in Charles Beatty-Medina and Melissa Rinehart, eds., *Contested Territories: Native Americans and Non-Natives in the Lower Great Lakes, 1700–1850* (East Lansing: Michigan State University Press, 2012), 145, 153.

268. Bert Anson, "Chief Francis Lafontaine and the Miami Emigration from Indiana," *Indiana Magazine of History* 60, no. 3 (September 1964), 255, 262 (noting that the Miami chief Francis Lafontaine reported that the Miami people were "pleased with their new home" and "wanted a school operated by the Roman Catholic church").

269. Joseph T. Manzo, "Emigrant Indian Objections to Kansas Residence," *Kansas History* 4, no. 1 (Winter 1981), 247–54.

270. Francis Paul Prucha, "Indian Removal to the Great American Desert," *Indiana Magazine of History* 59, no. 4 (December 1963), 299–322.

271. Elizabeth Neumeyer, "Michigan Indians Battle against Removal," *Michigan History* 55, no. 6 (November 1971), 275–88.

272. On the Union war veteran and Iowa congressman William Vandever, a devout Presbyterian, and the call to treat reservations more humanely, see Douglas Firth Anderson, "'More Conscience Than Force': U.S. Indian Inspector William Vandever, Grant's Peace Policy, and Protestant Whiteness," *Journal of the Gilded Age and Progressive Era* 9, no. 2 (April 2010), 167–76. See also Robert H. Keller Jr., *American Protestantism and United State Indian Policy, 1869–82* (Lincoln: University of Nebraska Press, 1983), and R. Pierce Beaver, "The Churches and President Grant's Peace Policy," *Journal of Church and State* 4, no. 2 (November 1962), 174–90.

273. Eileen Muccino, "Irish Filibusters and Know Nothings in Cincinnati," *Ohio Valley History* 10, no. 3 (Fall 2010), 3–26; Jon K. Lauck, "'You Can't Mix Wheat and Potatoes in the Same Bin': Anti-Catholicism in Early Dakota," *South Dakota History* 38, no. 1 (Spring 2008), 1–46; Michael C. Coleman, "The Responses of American Indian Children and Irish Children to the School, 1850s–1920s: A Comparative Study in Cross-Cultural Education," *American Indian Quarterly* 23, nos. 3–4 (Summer–Autumn 1999), 83–112 (comparing Indian schools to schools in

England designed to assimilate the Irish, a practice not unrelated to the Irish experience in the United States); Smith, "Anti-Catholicism, Indian Education," 213–33 (noting that the head of Indian education was arguably more anti-Catholic/Irish than he was anti–Native American).

274. Theobald, *Call School*, 22–23, 27, 31. See generally Price, "Protestant Imagination," 85–100.

275. Margaret DePalma, "Religion in the Classroom: The Great Bible Wars in Nineteenth Century Cincinnati," *Ohio Valley History* 3, no. 3 (Fall 2003), 17–36; Robert Michaelson, "Common Schools, Common Religion? A Case Study in Church-State Relations, Cincinnati, 1869–1870," *Church History* 38, no. 2 (1969), 201–17; Harold M. Helfman, "The Cincinnati 'Bible War,' 1869–1870," *Ohio Historical Quarterly* 60, no. 4 (October 1951), 369–86.

276. "President Grant's Des Moines Address," 139. On Chicago's Catholic schools, see James W. Sanders, *The Education of an Urban Minority: Catholics in Chicago, 1833–1965* (New York: Oxford University Press, 1977).

277. Lind, "Early Literary Societies," 175.

278. Pawley, *Reading on the Middle Border*, 75.

279. Evans, "Newman Idea in Wisconsin," 205.

280. Storey, "Rise of the Denominational College," 56.

281. Evans, "Newman Idea in Wisconsin," 205–7 (study), 208.

282. For the reformers, Richard Hofstadter noted, the problem was that "the boss, particularly the Irish boss, who could see things from the immigrant's angle but could also manipulate the American environment, became a specialist in personal relations and personal loyalties." Hofstadter, *Age of Reform*, 184.

283. Richard D. Brown, "Modernization: A Victorian Climax," in Howe, *Victorian America*, 37.

284. Hofstadter, *Age of Reform*, 185; Laura McKee Hickman, "Thou Shalt Not Vote: Anti-Suffrage in Nebraska, 1914–1920," *Nebraska History* 80, no. 2 (Summer 1999), 56; Eileen L. McDonagh and H. Douglas Price, "Woman Suffrage in the Progressive Era: Patterns of Opposition and Support in Referenda Voting, 1910–1918," *American Political Science Review* vol. 79, no. 2 (June 1985), 418.

285. Theobald, *Call School*, 79.

286. Vaclav L. Benes, "Land of the Free," in Murray, *Heritage of the Middle West*, 137.

287. Carl Russell Fish, "Carl Schurz: The American," *Wisconsin Magazine of History* 12, no. 4 (June 1929), 346.

288. Benes, "Land of the Free," 136.

289. Petra DeWitt, *Degrees of Allegiance: Harassment and Loyalty in Missouri's German-American Community during World War I* (Athens: Ohio University Press, 2012); Paul J. Ramsey, "The War against German-American Culture: The Removal of German-Language Instruction from the Indianapolis Schools, 1917–1919," *Indiana Magazine of History* 98, no. 4 (December 2002), 286–303; Leola Allen, "Anti-German Sentiment in Iowa during World War I," *Annals of Iowa* 42, no. 6 (Fall 1974), 418–29; Patricia Michaelis, "Crisis of Loyalty: Examples of Anti-German Sentiment from Kansas Memory," *Kansas History* 40, no. 1 (Spring 2017), 20–29; La Vern J. Rippley, "Conflict in the Classroom: Anti-Germanism in

Minnesota Schools, 1917–19," *Minnesota History* 47, no. 5 (Spring 1981), 171–83; Frank Trommler, "The *Lusitania* Effect: America's Mobilization against Germany in World War I," *German Studies Review* 32, no. 2 (May 2009), 241–66.

290. Pawley, *Reading on the Middle Border*, 25.

291. Robert D. Johnston, *"The Age of Reform:* A Defense of Richard Hofstadter Fifty Years On," *Journal of the Gilded Age and Progressive Era* 6, no. 2 (April 2007), 131 (paled), 133; Norman Pollack, "The Myth of Populist Anti-Semitism," *American Historical Review* 68, no. 1 (October 1962), 1–21. In his intellectual history of the American historical profession, Peter Novick pointed to the contrast between the findings of Jewish scholars and historians from the Midwest and South. Johnston, *"Age of Reform,"* 129, n. 2, citing Peter Novick, *That Noble Dream: The "Objectivity Question" and the American Historical Profession* (Cambridge: Cambridge University Press, 1988), 339. See also Ronald R. Stockton, "McGuffey, Ford, Baldwin, and the Jews," *Michigan Historical Review* 35, no. 2 (Fall 2009), 85–96 (rebutting some historians' argument that Henry Ford's twentieth-century anti-Semitism stemmed from reading the McGuffey Readers).

292. Oscar Handlin, "Reconsidering the Populists," *Agricultural History* 39, no. 2 (April 1965), 68.

293. Johnston, *"Age of Reform,"* 131 (persecution), 133 (targeted); Jeffrey Ostler, "The Rhetoric of Conspiracy and the Formation of Kansas Populism," *Agricultural History* 69, no. 1 (Winter 1995), 1–27 (noting the prominence of anti-British rhetoric among Populists).

294. Johnston, *"Age of Reform,"* 134, n. 11, noting Kazin, *A Godly Hero: The Life of William Jennings Bryan* (New York: Alfred A. Knopf, 2006), 325–26, 272–73, 165–66, 204.

295. Hofstadter, *Age of Reform*, 79, n. 9. Hofstadter also argues that "Populist anti-Semitism was entirely verbal. It was a mode of expression, a rhetorical style, not a tactic or a program. It did not lead to exclusion laws, much less to riots or pogroms." Hofstadter, *Age of Reform*, 80. Hofstadter also noted that Carey McWilliams's book *A Mask for Privilege: Anti-Semitism in America* (Boston: Little, Brown and Company, 1948) "deals with early American anti-Semitism simply as an upperclass phenomenon." Hofstadter, *Age of Reform*, 81, n. 3.

296. Brace, "Power of Porch Talks," 8.

297. Karen Mason, "Women's Clubs of Iowa," *Annals of Iowa* 56, no. 1 (Winter 1997), 9–10. See also Michael J. Bell, "'True Israelites of America': The Story of the Jews of Iowa," *Annals of Iowa* 53, no. 2 (Winter 1994), 85–127.

298. Pawley, *Reading on the Middle Border*, 140. See also Scott Dalrymple, "Central Plains Entrepreneurs: The Rise and Fall of Goldsmith's Inc., 1878–2003," *Kansas History* 26, no. 4 (Winter 2003–2004), 238–51.

299. Winks, "Recollections of a Dead Art," 43. See also Joseph P. Schultz, ed., *Mid-America's Promise: A Profile of Kansas City Jewry* (Kansas City, MO: American Jewish Historical Society, 1982); Marc Lee Raphael, *Jews and Judaism in a Midwestern Community: Columbus, Ohio, 1840–1975* (Columbus: Ohio Historical Society, 1979); Dwight W. Hoover, "To Be a Jew in Middletown: A Muncie Oral History Project," *Indiana Magazine of History* 81, no. 2 (June 1985), 131–58; Linda Mack Schloff, *"And Prairie Dogs Weren't Kosher": Jewish Women in the Upper*

Midwest since 1855 (St. Paul: Minnesota Historical Society Press, 1996); Donald M. Douglas, "Forgotten Zions: Jewish Agricultural Colonies in Kansas in the 1880s," *Kansas History* 16, no. 2 (Summer 1993), 108–19; Hal K. Rothman, "Building Community: The Jews of Wichita 1860–1900," *Kansas Quarterly* 25, no. 2 (1994): 77–86; J. Sanford Rikoon, "The Jewish Agriculturalists' Aid Society of America: Philanthropy, Ethnicity, and Agriculture in the Heartland," *Agricultural History* 72, no. 1 (Winter 1988), 1–32; Nora Faires and Nancy Hanflik, *Jewish Life in the Industrial Promised Land, 1855–2005* (East Lansing: Michigan State University Press, 2005) (on Flint); Howe, "Victorian Culture in America," in Howe, *Victorian America*, 9 (noting that some Jews and Catholics embraced mainstream Victorian culture). For additional angles, see the special issue of *Middle West Review* on the Jewish Midwest (forthcoming).

300. Price, "Protestant Imagination," 91–93.

301. Rebecca Edwards, "Domesticity versus Manhood Rights: Republicans, Democrats, and 'Family Values' Politics, 1856–1896," in Meg Jacobs, William J. Novak, and Julian E. Zelizer, eds., *The Democratic Experiment: New Directions in American Political History* (Princeton, NJ: Princeton University Press, 2003), 178 (noting that "Republicans made vigorous use of federal power to eradicate plural marriage in the Church of Jesus Christ of Latter Day Saints").

302. Joseph Earl Arrington, "Destruction of the Mormon Temple at Nauvoo," *Journal of the Illinois State Historical Society* 40, no. 4 (December 1947), 417–18; Stephen C. LeSueur, *The 1838 Mormon War in Missouri* (Columbia: University of Missouri Press, 1990); John E. Hallwas and Roger D. Launius, *Cultures in Conflict: A Documentary History of the Mormon War in Illinois* (Logan: Utah State University Press, 1995); William G. Hartley, "Missouri's 1838 Extermination Order and the Mormons' Forced Removal to Illinois," *Mormon Historical Studies* 2, no. 1 (Spring 2001), 5–27; David Brion Davis, "Some Themes of Counter-Subversion: An Analysis of Anti-Masonic, Anti-Catholic, and Anti-Mormon Literature," *Mississippi Valley Historical Review* 47, no. 2 (September 1960), 205–24.

303. Curti, *Growth of American Thought*, 263; Hubbart, *Older Middle West*, 65.

304. Gregory H. Nobles, "Breaking into the Backcountry: New Approaches to the Early American Frontier, 1750–1800," *William and Mary Quarterly* 46, no. 4 (October 1989), 644 (explaining that "elite observers . . . saw an almost complete absence of 'civilized' behavior in the frontier; indeed, they made scarcely any distinction between white settlers and Indian 'savages'"); Beeman, "Varieties of Deference," 333.

305. Rebecca A. Shepherd, "Restless Americans: The Geographic Mobility of Farm Laborers in the Old Midwest, 1850–1870," *Ohio History Journal* 89, no. 1 (Winter 1980), 25–45; John C. Schneider, "Omaha Vagrants and the Character of Western Hobo Labor, 1887–1913," *Nebraska History* 63, no. 2 (Summer 1982), 255–72; David E. Schob, *Hired Hands and Plowboys: Farm Labor in the Midwest, 1815–60* (Urbana: University of Illinois Press, 1975); Nathan Tye, "Billy Clubs and Vagrancy Laws: Confronting the 'Plague of Hobos' in Nebraska, 1870s–1930," *Nebraska History* 99, no. 4 (Winter 2018), 208–23; Peter H. Argersinger and Jo Ann E. Argersinger, "The Machine Breakers: Farmworkers and Social Change in the Rural Midwest of the 1870s," *Agricultural History* 58, no. 3 (July 1984), 393–410;

Frank Tobias Higbie, *Indispensable Outcasts: Hobo Workers and Community in the American Midwest, 1880–1930* (Urbana: University of Illinois Press, 2003); Jerry Prout, *Coxey's Crusade for Jobs: Unemployment in the Gilded Age* (DeKalb: Northern Illinois University Press, 2016).

306. Hubbart, *Older Middle West*, 53 (quotation); Russell A. Griffin, "Notes and Documents: Mrs. Trollope and the Queen City," *Mississippi Valley Historical Review* 37, no. 2 (September 1950), 289–302; Havighurst, *Heartland*, 151; Curti, *Growth of American Thought*, 245. See also William S. Peterson, "Kipling's First Visit to Chicago," *Journal of the Illinois State Historical Society* 63, no. 3 (Autumn 1970), 290–301 (Kipling saw Chicago as smelly and money-grubbing). Oscar Wilde, for another example, did not go over in Indiana. Hubach, "Nineteenth-Century Literary Visitors," 46–47.

307. Hubach, "Nineteenth-Century Literary Visitors, 42.

308. Curti, *Growth of American Thought*, 291.

309. Schafer, "Beginnings of Civilization," 225.

310. On the southern element, see Christopher Phillips, *The Rivers Ran Backward: The Civil War and the Remaking of the American Middle Border* (New York: Oxford University Press, 2016).

CHAPTER 3

1. Howard Troyer, "Preface," in *Culture of the Middle West*, vi. Troyer had impeccable midwestern credentials. He was born in Indiana, attended Earlham College in Richmond, Indiana, and earned his Ph.D. from the University of Wisconsin, where he taught until joining Lawrence College. He then went on to serve as the dean of the liberal arts college at Cornell College in Mt. Vernon, Iowa, from 1957 to 1969.

2. Quaife, "Significance of the Ordinance of 1787," 415.

3. "Governors Revive Regional Issue," *Annals of Iowa* 25, no. 1 (Summer 1943), 80. Although the configuration can be traced to earlier decades, it is clear that these twelve states were considered the Midwest by about 1900. Shortridge, "Emergence of 'Middle West,'" 212.

4. Alexis de Toqueville, *Democracy in America*, 2 vols. (New York: Vintage, 1945), 1:376–77. See also Matthew Salafia, *Slavery's Borderland: Freedom and Bondage along the Ohio River* (Philadelphia: University of Pennsylvania Press, 2013).

5. Foner, *Free Soil, Free Labor*, 46.

6. Harry N. Scheiber, "On the Concepts of 'Regionalism' and 'Frontier,'" in Harry N. Scheiber, ed., *The Old Northwest: Studies in Regional History, 1787–1910* (Lincoln: University of Nebraska Press, 1969), viii (free), x; Patrick Griffin, "Reconsidering the Ideological Origins of Indian Removal: The Case of the Big Bottom 'Massacre,'" and Christopher Clark, "The Ohio Country in the Political Economy of Nation Building," in Cayton and Hobbs, *Center of a Great Empire*, 17 (explaining that the "Ohio River divided two distinct worlds"), 148, 152, 156.

7. Nobles, "Breaking into the Backcountry," 644–45, 648, 652–53; Eric Hinderaker and Peter C. Mancall, *At the Edge of Empire: The Backcountry in British North America* (Baltimore, MD: Johns Hopkins University Press, 2003); Mathew C. Ward,

Breaking the Backcountry: The Seven Years' War in Virginia and Pennsylvania, 1754–1765 (Pittsburgh, PA: University of Pittsburgh Press, 2003); Saul Cornell, "Aristocracy Assailed: The Ideology of Backcountry Anti-Federalism," *Journal of American History* 76, no. 4 (March 1990), 1148–72; William Hogeland, *The Whiskey Rebellion: George Washington, Alexander Hamilton, and the Frontier Rebels Who Challenged America's Newfound Sovereignty* (New York: Simon and Schuster, 2010).

8. Turner, "Significance of the Section," 258.

9. See Jon K. Lauck and Gleaves Whitney, eds., "East Meets (Mid)West: Essays on a Regional Borderland," book manuscript submitted to Kent State University Press.

10. Foner, *Free Soil, Free Labor*, 51 (mentality), 69 (cowards), 47–48 (builds).

11. See Mississippi's "A Declaration of the Immediate Causes which Induce and Justify Secession of the State of Mississippi from the Federal Union," January 9, 1861.

12. Merrill D. Peterson, *The Great Triumvirate: Webster, Clay, and Calhoun* (New York: Oxford University Press, 1987), 406; Lantzer, "Forging God's Country," 27 (sin).

13. Fischer, *Albion's Seed*.

14. McPherson, "Antebellum Southern Exceptionalism," 428–29; Wyatt-Brown, *Southern Honor*. See also Introduction, this volume.

15. McPherson, "Antebellum Southern Exceptionalism," 422.

16. Degler, "Two Cultures," 102 (quotations); Rollin G. Osterweis, *Romanticism and Nationalism in the Old South* (New Haven, CT: Yale University Press, 1949); Forrest A. Nabors, *From Oligarchy to Republicanism: The Great Task of Reconstruction* (Columbia: University of Missouri Press, 2018); Eugene D. Genovese, *The Political Economy of Slavery* (New York: Pantheon, 1965); David Bertelson, *The Lazy South* (New York: Oxford University Press, 1967); Allen C. Guelzo, *Fateful Lightning: A New History of the Civil War and Reconstruction* (New York: Oxford University Press, 2012), 23, 28; Peter O'Connor, *American Sectionalism in the British Mind, 1832–1863* (Baton Rouge: Louisiana State University Press, 2017), 58–59.

17. McPherson, "Antebellum Southern Exceptionalism," 430.

18. Meyer et al., "Public Education as Nation-Building," 597, 600.

19. Scott N. Morse, "'Knowledge Is Power': The Reverend Grosvenor Clarke Morse's Thoughts on Free Schools and the Republic during the Civil War," *Kansas History* 31, no. 1 (Spring 2008), 2.

20. Carl Degler, "The Two Cultures and the Civil War," in Stanley Coben and Lorman Ratner, eds., *The Development of an American Culture* (Englewood Cliffs, NJ: Prentice-Hall, 1970), 94 (drew), 96; James H. Soltow, "Cotton as Religion, Politics, Law, Economics and Art," *Agricultural History* 68, no. 2 (Spring 1994), 6–19.

21. Sewell, *House Divided*, 6.

22. David M. Potter, *The Impending Crisis, 1848–1861* (New York: Harper and Row, 1976), 33 (awareness); Degler, "Two Cultures," 98–99; McPherson, "Antebellum Southern Exceptionalism," 425; Fred Bateman and Thomas Weiss, *A Deplorable Scarcity: The Failure of Industrialization in the Slave Economy* (Chapel Hill: University of North Carolina Press, 1981).

23. Leonard L. Richards, *The Slave Power: The Free North and Southern Domination, 1780–1860* (Baton Rouge: Louisiana State University Press, 2000), 26 (quotation); William McDaid, "Kinsley S. Bingham and the Republican Ideology of Antislavery, 1847–1855," *Michigan Historical Review* 16, no. 2 (Fall 1990), 51; Brie Swenson Arnold, "'To Inflame the Mind of the North': Slavery Politics and the Sexualized Violence of Bleeding Kansas," *Kansas History* 38, no. 1 (Spring 2015), 22–24; Heather Cox Richardson, *To Make Men Free: A History of the Republican Party* (New York: Basic Books, 2014), 12–13. On the prominent Ohio governor, see also chapter 2, "Salmon P. Chase: The Constitution and the Slave Power," in Foner, *Free Soil, Free Labor*, 73–102.

24. Bertram Wyatt-Brown, review of David Brion Davis, *The Slave Power Conspiracy and the Paranoid Style* (Baton Rouge: Louisiana State University Press, 1969), *Journal of American History* 57, no. 2 (September 1970), 429 (emphasis in original). See also Matthew Karp, *This Vast Southern Empire: Slaveholders at the Helm of American Foreign Policy* (Cambridge, MA: Harvard University Press, 2016).

25. Russell B. Nye, "The Slave Power Conspiracy: 1830–1860," *Science and Society* 10, no. 3 (Summer 1946), 265.

26. Douglas A. Gamble, "Joshua Giddings and the Ohio Abolitionists: A Study in Radical Politics," *Ohio History* 88 (Winter 1979), 37–56; Nye, "Slave Power Conspiracy," 264; James Brewer Stewart, *Joshua R. Giddings and the Tactics of Radical Politics* (Cleveland, OH: Case Western Reserve University, 1970); Byron R. Long, "Joshua Reed Giddings: A Champion of Political Freedom," *Ohio Archaeological and Historical Society Publications* 28, no. 1 (January 1919), 1–8; Louis Filler, *The Crusade against Slavery, 1830–1860* (New York: Harper and Row, 1960), 103.

27. Nye, "Slave Power Conspiracy," 264 (*Daily Commercial*), 269; Ronald P. Formisano, *The Birth of Mass Political Parties: Michigan, 1827–1861* (Princeton, NJ: Princeton University Press, 1971), 244 (undying, masters).

28. Bledstein, *Culture of Professionalism*, 28.

29. Mischa Honek, "Abolitionists from the Other Shore: Radical German Immigrants and the Transnational Struggle to End American Slavery," *American Studies* 56, no. 2 (2011), 171–96; Alison Clark Efford, *German Immigrants, Race, and Citizenship in the Civil War Era* (New York: Cambridge University Press, 2013). For a prominent German Union army regiment, see Constantin Grebner, *We Were the Ninth: A History of the Ninth Regiment, Ohio Volunteer Infantry* (Kent, OH: Kent State University Press, 1987); Carl Wittke, "The Ninth Ohio Volunteers," *Ohio Archaeological and Historical Society Publications* 35, no. 2 (April 1926), 402–20; Andrew L. Slap, *The Doom of Reconstruction: The Liberal Republicans in the Civil War Era* (New York: Fordham University Press, 2006), xi.

30. See Gary B. Nash, "Slaves and Slaveowners in Colonial Philadelphia," *William and Mary Quarterly* 30, no. 2 (April 1973), 223–56.

31. Nye, "Slave Power Conspiracy," 264. On the linkage between New York financial interests and the southern cotton economy, see Wells, *Kidnapping Club*.

32. Sean Wilentz, "Jeffersonian Democracy and the Origins of Political Antislavery in the United States: The Missouri Crisis Revisited," *Journal of the Historical Society* 4, no. 3 (Fall 2004), 375–401. For an earlier divergence, see Andrew R. L. Cayton, "'Separate Interests' and the Nation-State: The Washington Administration

NOTES TO CHAPTER 3

and the Origins of Regionalism in the Trans-Appalachian West," *Journal of American History* 79, no. 1 (June 1992), 39–67.

33. Muelder, "'Moral Lights around Us,'" 251; Thomas D. Hamm, April Beckman, Marissa Florio, Kristi Giles, and Marie Hopper, "'A Great and Good People': Midwestern Quakers and the Struggle against Slavery," *Indiana Magazine of History* 100, no. 1 (March 2004), 3–25; Wilbur H. Siebert, "A Quaker Section of the Underground Railroad in Northern Ohio," *Ohio Archaeological and Historical Quarterly* 39, no. 3 (July 1930), 479–85. Many Quakers left the South because of slavery and became abolitionists in the Midwest, deepening the divide between the regions. Lantzer, "Forging God's Country," 21. Eastern donors became nervous because midwestern academics and reformers were so ardently abolitionist. Goodheart, "Abolitionists as Academics," 421–33.

34. Richard W. Etulain, "Abraham Lincoln: Political Founding Father of the American West," *Montana: The Magazine of Western History* 59, no. 2 (Summer 2009), 4.

35. Potter, *The Impending Crisis*, 21; Guelzo, *Fateful Lightning*, 64; Robert V. Remini, "The Northwest Ordinance of 1787: Bulwark of the Republic," *Indiana Magazine of History* 84, no. 1 (March 1988), 15. The Wilmot Proviso votes fell along regional lines. See also Peter S. Onuf, *Statehood and Union: A History of the Northwest Ordinance* (Bloomington: Indiana University Press), 144–45.

36. Sewell, *House Divided*, 24.

37. Jon Butler, "The Midwest's Spiritual Landscapes," in Lauck, Whitney, and Hogan, *Finding a New Midwestern History*, 196–210.

38. Degler, "Two Cultures," 98.

39. Donald G. Mathews, "The Methodist Schism of 1844 and the Popularization of Antislavery Sentiment," *Mid-America* 51, no. 1 (January 1968), 3–23; C. Bruce Staiger, "Abolitionism and the Presbyterian Schism of 1837–38," *Mississippi Valley Historical Review* 36, no. 3 (December 1949), 391–414; John R. McKivigan, *The War against Proslavery Religion: Abolitionism and the Northern Churches, 1830–1865* (Ithaca, NY: Cornell University Press, 1984); C. C. Goen, "Broken Churches, Broken Nation: Regional Religion and North-South Alienation in Antebellum America," *Church History* 52, no. 1 (March 1983), 21–35; Vernon Volpe, *Forlorn Hope of Freedom: The Liberty Party in the Old Northwest, 1838–1848* (Kent, OH: Kent State University Press, 1990); 19; Keith Harper, "Downwind from the New England Rat: John Taylor, Organized Missions, and the Regionalization of Religious Identity on the American Frontier," *Ohio Valley History* 9, no. 3 (Fall 2009), 25–42.

40. See Stanley Harold, *Gamaliel Bailey and Antislavery Union* (Kent, OH: Kent State University Press, 1986); Volpe, *Forlorn Hope;* Suzanne Cooper Guasco, *Confronting Slavery: Edward Coles and the Rise of Antislavery Politics in Nineteenth-Century America* (DeKalb: Northern Illinois University Press, 2013); Victor B. Howard, *Religion and the Radical Republican Movement, 1860–1870* (Lexington: University Press of Kentucky, 1990); Kate Everest Levi, "The Wisconsin Press and Slavery," *Wisconsin Magazine of History* 9, no. 4 (July 1962), 423–34; David W. Johnson, "Freesoilers for God: Kansas Newspaper Editors and the Antislavery Crusade," *Kansas History* 2, no. 2 (Summer 1979), 74–85.

41. John Higham, "The Rise of American Intellectual History," *American Historical Review* 56, no. 3 (April 1951), 466, discussing Gilbert Barnes, *The Antislavery Impulse, 1830–1844* (Washington: American Historical Association, 1933). On the popular resistance to slavery in the Midwest, see John Craig Hammond, *Slavery, Freedom, and Expansion in the Early American West* (Charlottesville: University of Virginia Press, 2007), 127–48.

42. Hurt, *Ohio Frontier*, 374. On the "geography of resistance," or physically escaping the South, see Cheryl Janifer LaRoche, *Free Black Communities and the Underground Railroad: The Geography of Resistance* (Urbana: University of Illinois Press, 2014), 87–102.

43. Middleton, *Black Laws*, 81.

44. Hurt, *Ohio Frontier*, 374.

45. Volpe, *Forlorn Hope*, 6–12; Robert Price, "The Ohio Anti-Slavery Convention of 1836," *Ohio Archaeological and Historical Society Publications* 45, no. 2 (April 1936), 173–85; Paul H. Boase, "Slavery and the Ohio Circuit Rider," *Ohio Historical Quarterly* 64, no. 2 (April 1955), 195–205; Mary Land, "John Brown's Ohio Environment," *Ohio Historical Quarterly* 57, no. 1 (January 1948), 24–30.

46. Nat Brandt, *The Town That Started the Civil War* (Syracuse, NY: Syracuse University Press, 1990); Wilbur Greeley Burroughs, "Oberlin's Part in the Slavery Conflict," *Ohio Archaeological and Historical Society Publications* 20, no. 3 (July 1911), 269–72; Barnes, *Anti-Slavery Impulse*, 76.

47. Kim M. Gruenwald, "Space and Place on the Early American Frontier: The Ohio Valley as a Region, 1790–1850," *Ohio Valley History* 4, no. 3 (Fall 2004), 44. On Michigan citizens' attacks on slave catchers, see Kestenbaum, "Modernizing Michigan," 123–24.

48. Gilbert Hobbs Barnes, *The Anti-Slavery Impulse, 1830–1844* (Washington, DC: American Historical Association, 1931), 74; Frederick J. Blue, *Salmon P. Chase: A Life in Politics* (Kent, OH: Kent State University Press, 1987).

49. Larry Gara, "The Fugitive Slave Law in the Eastern Ohio Valley," *Ohio History* 72, no. 2 (April 1963), 117.

50. Jonathan Daniel Wells, *Blind No More: African American Resistance, Free-Soil Politics, and the Coming of the Civil War* (Athens: University of Georgia Press, 2019), 74.

51. Wells, *Blind No More*, 75.

52. Robertson, *Hearts Beating for Liberty*.

53. Hans L. Trefousse, "The Motivation of a Radical Republican: Benjamin F. Wade," *Ohio History Journal* 73, no. 2 (Spring 1964), 64; Trefouse, *Benjamin Franklin Wade: Radical Republican from Ohio* (New York: Twayne, 1963). See also Harry Williams, "Benjamin F. Wade and the Atrocity Propaganda of the Civil War," *Ohio Historical Quarterly* 48, no. 1 (January 1939), 33–40.

54. Adam Goodheart, *1861: The Civil War Awakening* (New York: Knopf, 2011), 116.

55. James M. McPherson, *For Cause and Comrades: Why Men Fought in the Civil War* (New York: Oxford University Press, 1997), 113.

56. Mark J. Stegmaier, "An Ohio Republican Stirs Up the House: The Blake Resolution of 1860 and the Politics of the Sectional Crisis in Congress," *Ohio History* 116, no. 1 (January 2009), 62–87.

57. Robert P. Ludlum, "Joshua R. Giddings, Radical," *Mississippi Valley Historical Review* 23, no. 1 (June 1936), 49–60; Gerard N. Magliocca, *American Founding Son: John Bingham and the Invention of the Fourteenth Amendment* (New York: New York University Press, 2013), 39–65; McDaid, "Kinsley S. Bingham," 42–73; Paul Finkelman, "John Bingham and the Background to the Fourteenth Amendment," *Akron Law Review* 36, no. 4 (July 2015), 671–92; Paul Finkelman, "Race, Slavery, and Law in Antebellum Ohio," in Michael Les Benedict and John F. Winkler, eds., *The History of Ohio Law* (Athens: Ohio University Press, 2004), 750; Montagna, "Ohio, Evangelical Religion," 1–35; Corey Brooks, "Stoking the 'Abolition Fire in the Capitol': Liberty Party Lobbying and Antislavery in Congress," *Journal of the Early Republic* 33, no. 3 (Fall 2013), 525.

58. Francis P. Weisenburger, "Lincoln and His Ohio Friends," *Ohio History* 68, no. 3 (July 1959), 223; Elizabeth R. Varon, *Disunion! The Coming of the American Civil War, 1789–1859* (Chapel Hill: University of North Carolina Press, 2008), 280; Daniel J. Ryan, "Lincoln and Ohio," *Ohio Archaeological and Historical Society Publications* 32, no. 1 (January 1923), 7. See also Frederick J. Blue, "Friends of Freedom: Lincoln, Chase, and Wartime Racial Policy," *Ohio History* 102 (Summer/Autumn 1993), 85–97. In 1854 in Peoria, Lincoln gave a speech opposing the extension of slavery and citing the Northwest Ordinance as precedent for such a restriction. E. B. Smith, "Abraham Lincoln: Realist," *Wisconsin Magazine of History* 52, no. 2 (Winter 1968/69), 160.

59. Vernon L. Volpe, "Theodore Dwight Weld's Antislavery Mission in Ohio," *Ohio History Journal* 100 (Winter/Spring 1991), 6.

60. Volpe, *Forlorn Hope*, xix, 12.

61. McKivigan, "Christian Anti-Slavery Convention Movement," 345–65.

62. Volpe, *Forlorn Hope*, xvi. See also Joseph G. Rayback, "The Liberty Party Leaders of Ohio: Exponents of Antislavery Coalition," *Ohio Historical Quarterly* 57, no. 2 (April 1948), 165–75.

63. Robinson, *When I Was a Child*, 170.

64. Guelzo, *Fateful Lightning*, 66, 70; Sewell, *House Divided*, 26, 35 (strikingly).

65. The law overruled earlier court rulings that allowed local officials to ignore the demands of slave catchers and even prosecute them for kidnapping. Guelzo, *Fateful Lightning*, 72. See also W. Edward Farrison, "A Flight across Ohio: The Escape of William Wells Brown from Slavery," *Ohio Historical Quarterly* 61, no. 3 (July 1952), 272–80.

66. David S. Reynolds, *Mightier Than the Sword: Uncle Tom's Cabin and the Battle for America* (New York: W. W. Norton, 2011), 92–99; Guelzo, *Fateful Lightning*, 74; Hubbart, *Older Middle West*, 56; Robinson, *When I Was a Child*, 177.

67. Felix J. Koch, "Where Did Eliza Cross the Ohio?," *Ohio Archaeological and Historical Society Publications* 24, no. 4 (October 1915), 588.

68. Felix J. Koch, "Marking the Old 'Abolition Holes,'" *Ohio Archaeological and Historical Society Publications* 22, no. 2 (April 1913), 308–10; Lowell J. Soike, *Necessary Courage: Iowa's Underground Railroad in the Struggle against Slavery*

(Iowa City: University of Iowa Press, 2013); Wilbur H. Siebert, "The Underground Railroad in Ohio," *Ohio Archaeological and Historical Society Publications* 4 (January 1896), 44; Thomas J. Sheppard, "An Abolition Center," *Ohio Archaeological and Historical Society Publications* 19, no. 3 (1910), 265–66; John Patrick Morgans, *John Todd and the Underground Railroad: Biography of an Iowa Abolitionist* (Jefferson, NC: McFarland, 2006); Annetta C. Walsh, "Three Anti-Slavery Newspapers," *Ohio Archaeological and Historical Society Publications* 31, no. 2 (April 1922), 172–74; C. B. Galbreath, "Anti-Slavery Movement in Columbiana County," *Ohio Archaeological and Historical Society Publications* 30, no. 4 (October 1921), 355–57; Wilbur H. Siebert, "Beginnings of the Underground Railroad in Ohio," *Ohio Archaeological and Historical Quarterly* 56, no. 1 (1947), 70–72.

69. Lantzer, "Forging God's Country, 27.

70. Norman L. Rosenberg, "Personal Liberty Laws and Sectional Crisis: 1850–1861," *Civil War History* 17, no. 1 (March 1971), 25–44; Sewell, *House Divided*, 30.

71. In March 1853, in another manifestation of sectionalism and a move that could have prevented much bloodshed, all southern senators (except those from Missouri) had voted to block the creation of what is now Kansas as a free state. The bill had already passed the House of Representatives. Sewell, *House Divided*, 42.

72. Guelzo, *Fateful Lightning*, 77, 78 (declaration, parcel, dreary), 85; Sewell, *House Divided*, 44.

73. Greg Schneider, "The Midwest and the Development of the Republican Party," manuscript submitted to Oxford University Press for inclusion in Lauck, "The Oxford Handbook of Midwestern History."

74. Foner, *Free Soil, Free Labor*, 56 (unthrift), 55 (people). Marilynne Robinson echoes Seward, noting that without midwestern resistance to slavery "it is difficult to imagine how it would ever have been extirpated from the country as a whole." Robinson, *When I Was a Child*, 180.

75. Willard L. King and Allan Nevins, "The Constitution and the Declaration of Independence as Issues in the Lincoln-Douglas Debates," *Journal of the Illinois State Historical Society* 52, no. 1 (Spring 1959), 10; Etulain, "Abraham Lincoln," 4; Guelzo, *Fateful Lightning*, 88. On the democratic culture of Sangamon County and for a review of Lincoln's 5,200 cases, see Stacy Pratt McDermott, *The Jury in Lincoln's America* (Athens: Ohio University Press, 2012).

76. Foner, *Free Soil, Free Labor*, 56.

77. Michael Fellman, *Inside War: The Guerilla Conflict in Missouri during the American Civil War* (New York: Oxford University Press, 1989), 13.

78. SenGupta, "Servants for Freedom," 200–210.

79. Thomas Goodrich, *War to the Knife: Bleeding Kansas, 1854–1861* (Lincoln: University of Nebraska Press, 2004), 5. See also Stephen F. Maizlish, *The Triumph of Sectionalism: The Transformation of Ohio Politics, 1844–1856* (Kent, OH: Kent State University Press, 1983).

80. Mark E. Neely, *The Last Best Hope of Earth: Abraham Lincoln and the Promise of America* (Cambridge, MA: Harvard University Press, 1993), 32.

81. See Peck, *Making an Antislavery Nation*; Joel H. Silbey, "After 'The First Republican Victory': The Republican Party Comes to Congress, 1855–1856," *Journal of Interdisciplinary History* 20, no. 1 (Summer 1989), 4; Stephen Hansen, *The*

Making of the Third Party System: Voters and Parties in Illinois, 1850–1876 (Ann Arbor: UMI Research, 1980); James L. Huston, "The Illinois Political Realignment of 1844–1860: Revisiting the Analysis," *Journal of the Civil War Era* 1, no. 4 (December 2011), 507; Richard H. Sewell, *Ballots for Freedom: Antislavery Politics in the University States, 1837–1860* (New York: Oxford University Press, 1976); Allan Nevins, *The Emergence of Lincoln* (New York: Charles Scribner's Sons, 1950), 12, 27; Frederick J. Blue, "Chase and the Governorship: A Stepping Stone to the Presidency," *Ohio History* 90, no. 3 (Summer 1981), 197; Michael S. Green, *Freedom, Union, and Power: The Civil War Republican Party* (New York: Fordham University Press, 2004), 13; Michael A. Morrison, *Slavery and the American West: The Eclipse of Manifest Destiny and the Coming of the Civil War* (Chapel Hill: University of North Carolina Press, 1997); Earl Hess, *Liberty, Virtue, and Progress: Northerners and Their War for the Union* (New York: Fordham University Press, 1997).

82. "Gathering under the Oaks," *Ohio Archaeological and Historical Society Publications* 13, no. 4 (October 1904), 562. See also "Early History of the Republican Party in Ohio," *Ohio Archaeological and Historical Society Publications* 2, no. 2 (September 1888), 327–31.

83. Michael F. Holt, "Making and Mobilizing the Republican Party, 1854–1860," in Robert F. Engs and Randall M. Miller, eds., *The Birth of the Grand Old Party: The Republicans' First Generation* (Philadelphia: University of Pennsylvania Press, 2002), 29–30; William E. Gienapp, *The Origins of the Republican Party, 1852–1856* (New York: Oxford University Press, 1987), 104–5.

84. Sewell, *House Divided*, 49; Sewell, *Ballots for Freedom*, 264.

85. Frederickson, *Inner Civil War*, 49; Susan-Mary Grant, *North over South: Northern Nationalism and American Identity in the Antebellum Era* (Lawrence: University Press of Kansas, 2000), 5; Edwards, "Domesticity versus Manhood Rights," 176 (calling the GOP a "militantly sectional party").

86. Guelzo, *Fateful Lightning*, 86; Sewell, *House Divided*, 47.

87. Holt, "Making and Mobilizing the Republican Party," 43–44; Formisano, *Birth of Mass Political Parties*, 239–65.

88. Foner, *Free Soil, Free Labor*, 52.

89. Kenneth M. Stampp, *America in 1857: A Nation on the Brink* (New York: Oxford University Press, 1990), 135.

90. Robert Aitken, "Justice Benjamin Curtis and Dred Scott," *Litigation* 30, no. 1 (Fall 2003), 52.

91. Anne Twitty, *Before Dred Scott: Slavery and Legal Culture in the American Confluence, 1787–1857* (New York: Cambridge University Press, 2016), 21; Lea VanderVelde, *Redemption Songs: Suing for Freedom before Dred Scott* (New York: Oxford University Press, 2014).

92. Lantzer, "Forging God's Country," 28.

93. Keith P. Griffler, *River of Slavery, River of Freedom: African Americans and the Forging of the Underground Railroad in the Ohio Valley* (Lexington: University Press of Kentucky, 2004), 2; Richards, *Slave Power*, 3.

94. Graham Alexander Peck, "Abraham Lincoln and the Triumph of an Antislavery Nationalism," *Journal of the Abraham Lincoln Association* 28, no. 2 (2007), 1–27; Earl W. Wiley, "Behind Lincoln's Visit to Ohio in 1859," *Ohio State*

Archaeological and Historical Quarterly 60, no. 1 (January 1951), 28–35; Richards, *Slave Power*, 11–16.

95. M. P. Rindlaub, "More Recollections of Abraham Lincoln," *Wisconsin Magazine of History* 5, no. 3 (March 1922), 293; Charles Workman, "Tablet to Abraham Lincoln at Mansfield," *Ohio Archaeological and Historical Society Publications* 34, no. 4 (October 1925), 506; Mark A. Plummer, "Richard J. Oglesby, Lincoln's Rail-Splitter," *Illinois Historical Journal* 80, no. 1 (Spring 1987), 4; David Donald, "The Folklore Lincoln," *Journal of the Illinois State Historical Society* 40, no. 4 (December 1947), 383.

96. Donald, "Folklore Lincoln," 377; Ray Ginger, *Altgeld's America: The Lincoln Ideal versus Changing Realities* (New York: Funk and Wagnalls, 1958), 5.

97. Slap, *Doom of Reconstruction*, 61.

98. Anton Gag, Christian Heller, and Alexander Schwendlinger, "Minnesota and the Civil War," in Theodore C. Blegen, ed., *Minnesota: A History of the State* (Minneapolis: University of Minnesota Press, 1963), 239.

99. Richard Moe, *The Last Full Measure: The Life and Death of the First Minnesota Volunteers* (St. Paul: Minnesota Historical Society Press, 2001).

100. Engle, *Struggle for the Heartland*, 10.

101. Lanzter, "Forging God's Country," 29; Nicole Etcheson, "How the Midwest Won the Civil War," manuscript submitted to Oxford University Press for inclusion in Lauck, "The Oxford Handbook of Midwestern History."

102. Shriver, "Freedom's Proving Ground," 131; Onuf, "Northwest Ordinance," 293.

103. Etcheson, "How the Midwest Won the Civil War," __; Colonel W. L. Curry, "Ohio Generals and Field Officers in the Civil War," *Ohio Archaeological and Historical Quarterly* 23, no. 3 (1914), 306–11.

104. Kestenbaum, "Modernizing Michigan," 129.

105. Plantz, "Lawrence College," 160–61.

106. Etcheson, "How the Midwest Won," __.

107. Engle, *Struggle for the Heartland*, 19.

108. Donald F. Dosch, "The Hornets' Nest at Shiloh," *Tennessee Historical Quarterly* 37, no. 2 (Summer 1978), 176; Larry J. Daniel, *Shiloh: The Battle That Changed the Civil War* (New York: Simon and Schuster, 1997), 106.

109. Steven E. Woodworth, *Nothing but Victory: The Army of the Tennessee, 1861–1865* (New York: Vintage Books, 2005); Thomas Lawrence Connelly, *Army of the Heartland: The Army of Tennessee, 1861–1862* (Baton Rouge: Louisiana State University Press, 1967), 178. On the experiences of the only all-western brigade in the Eastern theater, see Alan T. Nolan, *The Iron Brigade: A Military History* (New York: Macmillan, 1961). The Second Wisconsin regiment of the Iron Brigade lost more soldiers in battle than any other regiment in the Union Army.

110. "President Grant's Des Moines Address," 138–39.

111. L. Bao Bui, "Letter Writing, Civilization, and Midwesterners," paper presented at Organization of American Historians conference, Sacramento, CA (2018).

112. Bell I. Wiley, "Southern Reaction to Federal Invasion," *Journal of Southern History* 16, no. 4 (November 1950), 491.

113. McPherson, *For Cause and Comrades*, 118 (blight, withered, enormity), 110 (youngest, traters); Woodworth, *Nothing but Victory*, 14 (believe). See also Joseph Allan Frank, *With Ballot and Bayonet: The Political Socialization of American Civil War Soldiers* (Athens: University of Georgia Press, 1998).

114. On the controversy over Wallace's response time to Grant's orders, see William M. Ferraro, "A Struggle for Respect: Lew Wallace's Relationships with Ulysses S. Grant and William Tecumseh Sherman," *Indiana Magazine of History* 104, no. 2 (June 2008), 125–52.

115. James M. McPherson, "The Fight against the Gag Rule: Joshua Leavitt and Antislavery Insurgency in the Whig Party, 1839–1842," *Journal of Negro History* 48, no. 3 (July 1963), 177–79; Sewell, *House Divided*, 20.

116. Roy Robbins, *Our Landed Heritage: The Public Domain, 1776–1936* (Princeton, NJ: Princeton University Press, 1942), 169, 175; George M. Stephenson, *The Political History of the Public Lands from 1840 to 1862* (Boston: Richard G. Badger, 1917), 169–70.

117. Edwards, Friefeld, and Wingo, *Homesteading the Plains*.

118. Donald R. Brown, "Jonathan Baldwin Turner and the Land-Grant Idea," *Journal of the Illinois State Historical Society* 55, no. 4 (Winter 1962), 370–84; Hubbart, *Older Middle West*, 70, 272; Simon, "Politics of the Morrill Act," 103–4; Williams, *Origins of Federal Support for Higher Education*; Stevenson, *Victorian Homefront*, 110 (quotation); Kersey, *John Milton Gregory*.

119. Sarah T. Phillips, "Antebellum Agricultural Reform, Republican Ideology, and Sectional Tension," *Agricultural History* 74, no. 4 (Autumn 2000), 820.

120. Phillips, "Antebellum Agricultural Reform," 821.

121. Deren Earl Kellogg, "'Slavery Must Die': Radical Republicans and the Creation of Arizona Territory," *Journal of Arizona History* 41, no. 3 (Autumn 2000), 267–88.

122. Kellogg, "'Slavery Must Die,'" 277 (logic), 279.

123. See James M. McPherson, "In Pursuit of Constitutional Abolitionism," in Alexander Tsesis, ed., *The Promises of Liberty: The History and Contemporary Relevance of the Thirteenth Amendment* (New York: Columbia University Press, 2010), 30–32.

124. *Chicago Daily Tribune*, February 2, 1865.

125. Xi Wang, *The Trial of Democracy: Black Suffrage and Northern Republicans, 1860–1910* (Athens: University of Georgia Press, 1997); J. Morgan Kousser, *The Shaping of Southern Politics: Suffrage Restriction and the Establishment of the One-Party South, 1880–1910* (New Haven, CT: Yale University Press, 1974); Michael Perman, "Redemption," in *The New Encyclopedia of Southern Culture*, vol. 10 (Chapel Hill: University of North Carolina Press, 2008), 273; LaWanda Cox and John H. Cox, "Negro Suffrage and Republican Politics: The Problem of Motivation in Reconstruction Historiography," *Journal of Southern History* 33, no. 3 (August 1967), 314.

126. Gruenwald, "Space and Place," 31–36.

127. McPherson, "Antebellum Southern Exceptionalism," 426; Stephen D. Engle, *Struggle for the Heartland: The Campaign from Fort Henry to Corinth* (Lincoln: University of Nebraska Press, 2001), 4, 6; Gruenwald, "Space and Place," 38–40.

128. Sewell, *House Divided*, 8. By the time of the war, the "Mississippi had practically ceased to compete with the lake, canal, and railroad routes eastward." Hubbart, *Older Middle West*, 74.

129. Harry N. Scheiber, "On the Concepts of 'Regionalism' and 'Frontier,'" in Scheiber, *Old Northwest*, xi.

130. Sewell, *House Divided*, 6.

131. On the debate over the Harbor and River Bill, which the South opposed, see Hubbart, *Older Middle West*, 21–27. See also Marc Egnal, "Explaining John Sherman: Leader of the Second American Revolution," *Ohio History* 114 (2007), 110.

132. See Phillips, *Rivers Ran Backward*. This also meant that a Kentucky considered western for much of its history became oriented to the South even though it never seceded and was a state of mixed loyalties during the war. Anthony Harkins, "Colonels, Hillbillies, and Fightin': Twentieth-Century Kentucky in the National Imagination," *Register of the Kentucky Historical Society* 113, nos. 2–3 (Spring/Summer 2015), 430; Anne E. Marshall, *Creating a Confederate Kentucky: The Lost Cause and Civil War Memory in a Border State* (Chapel Hill: University of North Carolina Press, 2013); Maryjean Wall, *How Kentucky Became Southern: A Tale of Outlaws, Horse Thieves, Gamblers, and Breeders* (Lexington: University Press of Kentucky, 2010); Matthew E. Stanley, *The Loyal West: Civil War and Reunion in Middle America* (Urbana: University of Illinois Press, 2017), 130–52.

133. Gruenwald, "Space and Place," 43–45. See also Kenneth H. Wheeler, "Higher Education in the Antebellum Ohio Valley: Slavery, Sectionalism, and the Erosion of Regional Identity," *Ohio Valley History* 8, no. 1 (Spring 2008), 1.

134. On the midwestern Civil War generals who became president, see James M. Perry, *Touched with Fire: Five Presidents and the Civil War Battles That Made Them* (New York: Public Affairs, 2003). See also Clifford H. Moore, "Ohio in National Politics, 1865–1896," *Ohio Archaeological and Historical Quarterly* 37, no. 2 (April 1928), 220–27; Ted Frantz, "When the Midwest Controlled the Presidency," in Lauck, *Making of the Midwest*, 143–56; June Drenning Holmquist, "Convention City: The Republicans in Minneapolis, 1892," *Minnesota History* 35, no. 2 (June 1956), 64.

135. Reinhard H. Luthin, "Waving the Bloody Shirt: Northern Political Tactics in Post–Civil War Times," *Georgia Review* 14, no. 1 (Spring 1960), 70; Jon K. Lauck, *Prairie Republic: The Political Culture of Dakota Territory, 1879–1889* (Norman: University of Oklahoma Press, 2010), 34–36, 68, 178; Richard N. Current, "The Politics of Reconstruction in Wisconsin, 1865–1873," *Wisconsin Magazine of History* 60, no. 2 (Winter 1976–77), 84. See also M. Keith Harris, *Across the Bloody Chasm: The Culture of Commemoration among Civil War Veterans* (Baton Rouge: Louisiana State University Press, 2014), chapter 2. On concerns about overuse of bloody shirt tactics by some in the GOP, see Stanley P. Hirshon, *Farewell to the Bloody Shirt: Northern Republicans and the Southern Negro, 1877–1893* (Bloomington: Indiana University Press, 1962).

136. Gant, "'Younger and More Irreconcilable,'" 147–85.

137. Luthin, "Waving the Bloody Shirt," 64. For a similar recollection, see Nicholson, *Valley of Democracy*, 192–93. The Ohioan William Dean Howells also had a character in his novel *The Rise of Silas Lapham* question whether Republicans

should "stop stirring up the Confederate brigadiers in Congress." Luthin, "Waving the Bloody Shirt," 71.

138. Lind, "Early Literary Societies," 175.

139. Fisher, "Literary Societies," 530.

140. Tingley, "Ralph Waldo Emerson," 192; Bledstein, *Culture of Professionalism*, 27; Grant, *North over South*, 50–52; E. Bruce Kirkham, "Harriet Beecher Stowe's Western Tour," *Old Northwest* 1, no. 1 (March 1975), 36.

141. Bledstein, *Culture of Professionalism*, 29 (quotation), 31.

142. Luthin, "Waving the Bloody Shirt," 65. See also McConnell, *Glorious Contentment*; Paul Taylor, *"The Most Complete Political Machine Ever Known": The North's Union Leagues in the American Civil War* (Kent, OH: Kent State University Press, 2018); Charles W. Calhoun, *Conceiving a New Republic: The Republican Party and the Southern Question, 1869–1900* (Lawrence: University Press of Kansas, 2006); and Richard H. Abbott, *The Republican Party and the South: 1855–1877: The First Southern Strategy* (Chapel Hill: University of North Carolina Press, 1986).

143. Luthin, "Waving the Bloody Shirt," 66 (beat, bloody), 67 (permanent, dread), 68–69, 70 (flags).

144. Ed Bradley, "The House, the Beast, and the Bloody Shirt: The Doorkeeper Controversy of 1878," *Journal of the Gilded Age and Progressive Era* 3, no. 1 (January 2004), 17, 25–26.

145. Bradley, "House, the Beast," 27.

146. Whitney, "Upper Midwest," 281–302.

147. Turner, "Significance of the Section," 260 (nature), 258 (crossed); Billington, "Historians of the Northwest Ordinance," 410–11.

148. David Donald and Frederick A. Palmer, "Toward a Western Literature, 1820–1860," *Mississippi Valley Historical Review* 35, no. 3 (December 1948), 415–16.

149. Turner, "Significance of the Section," 264.

150. Curti, *Growth of American Thought*, 279–80 (Franklin), 278.

151. James K. Folsom, *Timothy Flint* (New York: Twayne, 1964); Barnhart, "'Common Feeling,'" 42; Curti, *Growth of American Thought*, 276; Wright, *Culture on the Moving Frontier*, 120–21.

152. Philip Whitford and Kathryn Whitford, "An Evaluation of Timothy Flint's Observations on the Ohio and Mississippi Valleys," *Ecology* 41, no. 2 (April 1960), 391–93; Curti, *Growth of American Thought*, 276.

153. Hubbart, *Older Middle West*, 53; Curti, *Growth of American Thought*, 277. See John T. Flanagan, *James Hall: Literary Pioneer of the Ohio Valley* (Minneapolis: University of Minnesota Press, 1941); Randolph C. Randall, *James Hall: Spokesman of the New West* (Columbus: Ohio State University Press, 1964); John T. Flanagan, "James Hall, Pioneer Vandalia Editor and Publicist," *Journal of the Illinois State Historical Society* 48, no. 2 (Summer 1955), 119–36.

154. Arthur H. Hirsch, "Historical Values in the Mid-Century Literature of the Middle West," *Journal of the Illinois State Historical Society* 22, no. 3 (October 1929), 380; Barnhart, "'Common Feeling,'" 43.

155. James A. Tague, "William D. Gallagher, Champion of Western Literary Periodicals," *Ohio History Journal* 69, no. 3 (July 1960), 257–63; Barnhart, "'Common Feeling,'" 45.

156. John T. Flanagan, "Some Projects in Midwest Cultural History," *Indiana Magazine of History* 47, no. 3 (September 1951), 244; Hubbart, *Older Middle West*, 56.

157. Barnhart, "'Elegant and Useful Learning,'" 20.

158. William D. Andrews, "William T. Coggeshall: 'Booster' of Western Literature," *Ohio History Journal* 81, no. 3 (Summer 1972), 210–20; Donald and Palmer, "Toward a Western Literature," 416, 418; Barnhart, "'Common Feeling,'" 47.

159. William Turner Coggeshall, *The Poets and Poetry of the West* (Columbus, OH: Follett, Foster, 1860); Hubbart, *Older Middle West*, 57.

160. Hubbart, *Older Middle West*, 54; Donald and Palmer, "Toward a Western Literature," 422–23; Agnes M. Murray, "Early Literary Developments in Indiana," *Indiana Magazine of History* 36, no. 4 (December 1940), 327–33; Rhode, "Persistence of Place," 47–59; Robert D. Habich, *Transcendentalism and the Western Messenger: A History of the Magazine and Its Contributors, 1835–1841* (Cranbury, NJ: Fairleigh Dickinson University Press, 1985); M. M. Quaife, "Wisconsin's First Literary Magazine," *Wisconsin Magazine of History* 5, no. 1 (September 1921), 43–56; Clare Dowler, "John James Piatt, Representative Figure of a Momentous Period," *Ohio History Journal* 45, no. 1 (January 1936), 1–10; Anderson, "Queen City," 8; Wright, *Culture on the Moving Frontier*, 115; Roy P. Basler, "The Pioneering Period," *Centennial Review* 2 (1958), 121–22.

161. Curti, *Growth of American Thought*, 268.

162. Donald and Palmer, "Toward a Western Literature," 416

163. Barnhart, "'Common Feeling,'" 45.

164. Donald and Palmer, "Toward a Western Literature," 419.

165. Curti, *Growth of American Thought*, 278.

166. Stevens, "Science, Culture, and Morality," 71.

167. Richardson, "'Yale of the West,'" 258, 260.

168. Barnhart, "'Common Feeling,'" 59.

169. Terry A. Barnhart, "'Elegant and Useful Learning': The Antiquarian and Historical Society of Illinois, 1827–1829," *Journal of the Illinois State Historical Society* 95, no. 1 (Spring 2002), 7–32; Curti, *Growth of American Thought*, 286; Robert W. Johannsen, "History on the Illinois Frontier: Early Efforts to Preserve the State's Past," *Journal of the Illinois State Historical Society* 68, no. 2 (April 1975), 121–42.

170. M. H. Dunlop, "Curiosities Too Numerous to Mention: Early Regionalism and Cincinnati's Western Museum," *American Quarterly* 36, no. 4 (Autumn 1984), 524–48.

171. Barnhart, "'Common Feeling,'" 55–63, 62 (collect), 66 (uncritical, sternly, sacred), 56 (aboriginal).

172. Dunlop, "Curiosities Too Numerous to Mention," 527; Terry A. Barnhart, "A Dialectical Discourse: Constructing the Mound Builder Program," in Terry A. Barnhart, *American Antiquities: Revisiting the Origins of American Archaeology*

(Lincoln: University of Nebraska Press, 2015), 205; Barnhart, "'Elegant and Useful Learning,'" 16; Joshua Jeffers, "Colonizing the Indigenous Past: Settler-Colonial Place Making and the Ancient Landscape of the Early Midwest, 1775–1840," in Lauck, *Making of the Midwest*, 265–87.

173. Martha Bergland and Paul G. Hayes, *Studying Wisconsin: The Life of Increase Lapham* (Madison: Wisconsin Historical Society Press, 2014); Barnhart, "'Common Feeling,'" 63.

174. Richard G. Bremer, "Henry Rowe Schoolcraft: Explorer in the Mississippi Valley, 1818–1832," *Wisconsin Magazine of History* 66, no. 1 (Autumn 1982), 59; Barnhart, "'Common Feeling,'" 57–58; Taylor, "Monuments to Historical Indian Chiefs," 1–31 (calling for more monuments to Native Americans).

175. Keith Fynaardt, "The Spirit of Place as a Usable Past in William Cullen Bryant's 'The Prairies,'" *MidAmerica* 21 (1994), 50, 57, n. 2.

176. Dunn's first book was *Massacres in the Mountains: A History of the Indian Wars of the Far West, 1815–1875* (New York: Harper and Brothers, 1886). See Lana Ruegamer, "History, Politics, and the Active Life: Jacob Piatt Dunn, Progressive Historian," *Indiana Magazine of History* 81, no. 3 (September 1985), 265–69.

177. Ray A. Billington, "Young Fred Turner," *Wisconsin Magazine of History* 46, no. 1 (Autumn 1962), 46.

178. Curti, *Growth of American Thought*, 285 (prehistoric), 280, 277. See Leaf, *Minnesota's Geologist*.

179. Barnhart, "'Common Feeling,'" 48.

180. Hubbart, *Older Middle West*, 59–60.

181. Curti, *Growth of American Thought*, 288.

182. Benjamin T. Spencer, "A National Literature, 1837–1855," *American Literature* 8, no. 2 (May 1936), 126.

183. See Christian Knoeller, *Reimagining Environmental History: Ecological Memory in the Wake of Landscape Change* (Reno: University of Nevada Press, 2017).

184. Curti, *Growth of American Thought*, 265.

185. John T. Flanagan, "Morgan Neville: Early Western Chronicler," *Western Pennsylvania Historical Magazine* 21 (December 1938), 255–66 (describing the man who wrote about Fink); Walter Blair and Franklin J. Meine, *Half Horse, Half Alligator: The Growth of the Mike Fink Legend* (Chicago: University of Chicago Press, 1956); Benjamin A. Botkin, *A Treasury of Mississippi River Folklore: Stories, Ballads, Traditions, and Folkways of the Mid-American River Country* (New York: Crown, 1955); Michael R. Allen, *Western Rivermen, 1763–1861: Ohio and Mississippi Boatmen and the Myth of the Alligator Horse* (Baton Rouge: Louisiana State University Press, 1994); Leland D. Baldwin, *The Keelboat Age on Western Waters* (Pittsburgh: University of Pittsburgh Press, 1990).

186. Robert Price, *Johnny Appleseed: Man and Myth* (Bloomington: Indiana University Press, 1954); Curti, *Growth of American Thought*, 273.

187. Randall E. Rohe, "Place-Names: Relics of the Great Lakes Lumber Era," *Journal of Forest History* 28, no. 3 (July 1984), 127; Richard M. Dorson, *Bloodstoppers and Bearwalkers: Folk Traditions of the Upper Peninsula* (Cambridge, MA: Harvard University Press, 1952); Robert Gard and Elaine Reetz, eds., *The Trail of*

the Serpent: The Fox River Valley Lore and Legend (Madison: Wisconsin House, 1937); Wyman Walker, *Mythical Creatures of the North Country* (River Falls, WI: State University Press, 1969); Paul R. Beath, *Febold Feboldson: Tall Tales of the Great Plains* (Lincoln: University of Nebraska Press, 1948).

188. Bessie M. Stanchfield, "'The Beauty of the West': A Minnesota Ballad," *Minnesota History* 27, no. 3 (September 1946), 180; Curti, *Growth of American Thought*, 281; Franz Rickaby, ed., *Ballads and Songs of Shanty-Boy* (Cambridge, MA: Harvard University Press, 1926) (collecting songs from the lumberjacks of Michigan, Minnesota, and Wisconsin); Harry R. Stevens, "Folk Music on the Midwestern Frontier, 1788–1825," *Ohio History Quarterly* 57, no. 2 (April 1948), 126–46.

189. Billington, *Land of Savagery*, 233.

190. Nicholas A. Basbanes, *Cross of Snow: A Life of Henry Wadsworth Longfellow* (New York: Knopf, 2020).

191. Patricia Hall, *Johnny Gruelle: Creator of Raggedy Ann and Andy* (Gretna, LA: Pelican, 1993).

192. James P. Leary, *Threshing Days: The Farm Paintings of Lavern Kammerude* (Mount Horeb, WI: Wisconsin Folk Museum, 1992); Christopher Vondracek, "Artists of the Valley," in Lauck, *Heartland River*.

193. Frances M. Barbour, ed., *Proverbs and Proverbial Phrases of Illinois* (Carbondale: Southern Illinois University Press, 1965); George Kummer, "Specimens of Antebellum Buckeye Humor," *Ohio Historical Quarterly* 64, no. 4 (October 1955), 424–37; James P. Leary, *Folksongs of Another America: Field Recordings from the Upper Midwest, 1937–1946* (Madison: University of Wisconsin Press, 2015). See generally Frank R. Kramer, *Voices in the Valley: Mythmaking and Folk Belief in the Shaping of the Middle West* (Madison: University of Wisconsin Press, 1964). For a parallel track, see C. A. Norling, "'To Improve the Musical Taste, Capacity and Voices of Our People': The Rise of Public Art-Music Interests amidst the Rise and Fall of the Iowa State Normal Academy of Music, 1867–1871," in Lauck, *Making of the Midwest*, 231–48.

194. See James P. Leary, *Polkabilly: How the Goose Island Ramblers Redefined American Folk Music* (New York: Oxford University Press, 2006).

195. William H. Venable, *Beginnings of Literacy Culture in the Ohio Valley: Historical and Biographical Sketches* (Cincinnati, OH: Robert Clark, 1891); Venable, "Literary Periodicals of the Ohio Valley," *Ohio Archaeological and Historical Publications* 1 (June 1887), 198–202; Robert H. Wheeler, "The Literature of the Western Reserve," *Ohio History Journal* 100 (Summer/Autumn, 1991), 101–5; Logan Esarey, "The Literary Spirit among the Early Ohio Valley Settlers," *Mississippi Valley Historical Review* 5, no. 2 (September 1918), 143–57.

196. Barnhart, "'Common Feeling,'" 41–42.

197. Caleb Atwater, *The Writings of Caleb Atwater* (Columbus: published by the author, printed by Scott and Wright, 1833), 381. On Atwater's early promotion of the Midwest, see Shawn Selby, "'Industry, Enterprize and Energy': Caleb Atwater and the Meaning of Ohio," *Ohio History* 119 (2012), 101–18.

198. Curti, *Growth of American Thought*, 287 (homespun, reflected), 288 (usefulness).

199. See Ralph L. Rusk, *The Literature of the Middle West*, 2 vols. (New York: Columbia University Press, 1925).

200. Wendy J. Katz, "Creating a Western Heart: Art and Reform in Cincinnati's Antebellum Associations," *Ohio Valley History* 1, no. 3 (Fall 2001), 2–20; Julie Aronson, ed., *The Cincinnati Wing: The Story of Art in the Queen City* (Athens: Ohio University Press, 2003); Donald R. MacKenzie, "Early Ohio Painters: Cincinnati, 1830–1850," *Ohio History Journal* 73, no. 2 (Spring 1964), 111–32; Julie L'Enfant and Robert J. Paulson, "Anton Gag, Bohemian," *Minnesota History* 56, no. 7 (Fall 1999), 376–92; Kathleen M. Dillon, "Painters and Patrons: The Fine Arts in Cincinnati, 1820–1820," *Ohio History Journal* 96, no. 1 (Winter/Spring 1987), 7–32.

201. William Gallagher, *Facts and Conditions of Progress in the North-west: Being the Annual Discourse for 1850 before the Historical and Philosophical Society of Ohio* (Cincinnati, OH: H. W. Derby, 1850), 29.

202. Barnhart, "'Common Feeling,'" 49, n. 29 (wide), 44 (liberal, untrammeled), 48 (sanctuary), 66 (distinctions).

203. Martin Ridge, "How the Middle West Became America's Heartland," *Inland* 2 (1976), 13.

204. Andrew Offenburger, "U.S. Expansion and the Creation of the Middle West in the Nineteenth Century," manuscript submitted to Oxford University Press for inclusion in Lauck, "The Oxford Handbook of Midwestern History." Forty years ago, the geographer James Shortridge interpreted the term "Middle West" as applying to Kansas-Nebraska—that is, the place between the Northwest and Southwest on a north-south axis—and downplayed the east-west dynamic that Offenburger has found. Nevertheless, Shortridge agreed that the term "Middle West" was in wide use by about 1900 and applied to the traditional twelve-state understanding of the Midwest. Shortridge, "The Emergence of 'Middle West' as an American Regional Label," *Annals of the Association of American Geographers* 74, no. 2 (1984), 211–12.

205. Offenburger, "U.S. Expansion."

206. Ray Allen Billington, "The Garden of the World: Fact and Fiction," in Murray, *Heritage of the Middle West*, 29.

207. Raney, "People of the Land," 15.

208. Jon K. Lauck, ed., *The Interior Borderlands: Regional Identity in the Midwest and Great Plains* (Sioux Falls, SD: Center for Western Studies, 2019).

209. David R. Meyer, "Midwestern Industrialization and the American Manufacturing Belt in the Nineteenth Century," *Journal of Economic History* 49, no. 4 (December 1989), 925; Gregory S. Rose, "On the Path toward National Eminence: Economic Development in the Old Northwest, 1850–1860," in Lauck, *Making of the Midwest*, 157–81.

210. Wallace S. Baldinger, "The Middle West Builds a Home: Chicago as a Focus on the Arts," in *Culture of the Middle West*, 59.

211. Higham, "Hanging Together," 9 (quotation); Wayne Duerkes, "Travel Literature and Midwestern Identity: The Case of Illinois," in Lauck, *Making of the Midwest*, 53–54; Henrik Olav Mathiesen, "Belonging in the Midwest: Norwegian Americans and the Process of Attachment, ca. 1830–1860," *American Nineteenth Century* 15, no. 2 (2014), 119–46.

212. Offenburger, "U.S. Expansion."

213. Turner, "Significance of the Section," 262.

214. Donald and Palmer, "Toward a Western Literature," 427 (produced), 428 (freakish, products).

215. Michael C. Steiner, "Birth of the Midwest," in Jon K. Lauck, Gleaves Whitney, and Joseph Hogan, eds., *Finding a New Midwestern History* (Lincoln: University of Nebraska Press, 2018) 23, n. 31 (quotation); Alma J. Payne, "The Ohio World of William Dean Howells—Ever Distant, Ever Near," *Old Northwest* 10, no. 1 (Spring 1984), 127–37; Bev Hogue, "Forgotten Frontier: Literature of the Old Northwest," in Charles L. Crow, ed., *The Regional Literatures of America* (Malden, MA: Blackwell, 2003), 231–42.

216. Louis J. Budd, "Howells, the *Atlantic Monthly*, and Republicanism," *American Literature* 24, no. 2 (May 1952), 140, 142.

217. Richard Crowder, *Those Innocent Years: The Legacy and Inheritance of a Hero of the Victorian Era* (Indianapolis: Bobbs-Merrill, 1957).

218. Vincent P. DeSantis and Janet Brooks, eds., "George Cary Eggleston's Explanation for Indiana's Literary Achievements," *Indiana Magazine of History* 59, no. 1 (March 1963), 59–66; Arthur W. Schumaker, *A History of Indiana Literature* (Indianapolis: Indiana Historical Bureau, 1962); Beer, "Midlander," 35–53. See also James DeMuth, *Small Town Chicago: The Comic Perspective of Finley Peter Dunne* (Port Washington, NY: Kennikat Press, 1980).

219. Robert Loerzel, "'People Are Getting Tired of Broadway and Fifth Avenue': The Origins of the Society of Midland Authors," in Lauck, *Midwestern Moment*, 19–34.

220. Steiner, "Birth of the Midwest," 8.

221. Michael C. Steiner, "The Midwest and the Rise of American Regionalism, 1890–1915," *Middle West Review* 7, no. 1 (Fall 2020), 9–30.

222. Steiner, "Birth of the Midwest," 10 (quotation); H. Allen Brooks, *The Prairie School: Frank Lloyd Wright and His Midwest Contemporaries* (Toronto: University of Toronto Press, 1972); Richard W. E. Perrin, "Frank Lloyd Wright in Wisconsin: Prophet in His Own Country," *Wisconsin Magazine of History* 48, no. 1 (Autumn 1964), 32–47; H. Allen Brooks, ed., *Prairie School Architecture: Studies from "The Western Architect"* (Toronto: University of Toronto Press, 1975). See also John S. Garner, ed., *The Midwest in American Architecture* (Urbana: University of Illinois Press, 1991), and Thomas S. Hines, *Burnham of Chicago: Architect and Planner* (New York: Oxford University Press, 1974).

223. John Higham, "The Reorientation of American Culture in the 1890s," in John Weiss, ed., *The Origins of Modern Consciousness* (Detroit: Wayne State University, 1965), 43. See also David Van Zanten, "Chicago in Architectural History," *Studies in the History of Art* 35 (1990), 91–99.

224. Hamlin Garland, "Literary Emancipation of the West," *Forum* (October 1893), 163–66; Garland, *Crumbling Idols: Twelve Essays on Art Dealing Chiefly with Literature, Painting, and the Drama* (Chicago: Stone and Kimball, 1894), 11 (wait), 147 (supremacy); Steiner, "Birth of the Midwest," 13 (mingling); Keith Newlin, *Hamlin Garland: A Life* (Lincoln: University of Nebraska Press, 2008), 198 (challenged).

225. See Joseph Gustaitis, *Chicago's Greatest Year, 1893: The White City and the Birth of a Modern Metropolis* (Carbondale: Southern Illinois University Press, 2013).

226. See Donald G. Holtgrieve, "Frederick Jackson Turner as a Regionalist," *Professional Geographer* 26 (May 1974), 159–65; John E. Miller, "Frederick Jackson Turner and the Dream of Regional History," *Middle West Review* 1, no. 1 (Fall 2014), 1–9.

227. Steiner, "Birth of the Midwest," 15 (quotation); Steiner, "Regions, Regionalism, Place," in Joan Shelley Rubin and Scott Casper, eds., *Oxford Encyclopedia of American Cultural and Intellectual History*, vol. 2 (New York: Oxford University Press, 2013), 279–80; Frederick Jackson Turner, "The Place of the Ohio Valley in American History," *Ohio History Journal* 20, no. 3 (1911), 32–36.

228. Steiner, "Birth of the Midwest," 15.

229. Ann Massa, *Vachel Lindsay: Fieldworker for the American Dream* (Bloomington: Indiana University Press, 1970); Blake Nevius, *Robert Herrick: The Development of a Novelist* (Berkeley: University of California Press, 1962); Thomas Fox Averill, "Kansas Literature," *Kansas History* 25, no. 2 (Summer 2002), 144–65; E. K. Crews and Charles H. Chamberlin, "Illinois in Modern Literature," *Journal of the Illinois State Historical Society* 3, no. 2 (July 1910), 26–38; R. E. Banta, ed., *Indiana Authors and Their Books, 1816–1916: Biographical Sketches of Authors Who Published during the First Century of Indiana Statehood* (Crawfordsville, IN: Wabash College, 1949).

230. Bernard Duffey, *The Chicago Renaissance in American Letters* (East Lansing: Michigan State University Press, 1954); Vincent Starrett, *Born in a Bookshop: Chapters from the Chicago Renascence* (Norman: University of Oklahoma Press, 1965); James Albert Gazell, "The High Noon of Chicago's Bohemias," *Journal of the Illinois State Historical Society* 65, no. 1 (Spring 1972), 54–68; Dale Kramer, *Chicago Renaissance: The Literary Life in the Midwest* (New York: Appleton-Century, 1966); Hugh D. Duncan, *The Rise of Chicago as a Literary Center from 1885–1930* (Totowa, NJ: Bedminster Press, 1964); Donald F. Tingley, "The 'Robin's Egg Renaissance': Chicago and the Arts, 1910–1920," *Journal of the Illinois State Historical Society* 63, no. 1 (Spring 1970), 35–54.

231. Vanessa Steinroetter, "Walt Whitman in the Early Kansas Press," *Kansas History* 39, no. 3 (Summer 2016), 185–86.

232. Edgar C. Dunn, "Settlers' Periodical: Eugene Smalley and the *Northwest Magazine*," *Minnesota History* 33, no. 1 (Spring 1952), 29–34; Max J. Puzel, *The Man in the Mirror: William Marion Reedy and His Magazine* (Columbia: University of Missouri Press, 1998).

233. E. Bradford Burns, *Kinship with the Land: Regionalist Thought in Iowa, 1894–1942* (Iowa City: University of Iowa Press, 1996).

234. Tom Lutz, "The Cosmopolitan *Midland*," *American Periodicals* 15, no. 1 (2005), 75, 83 (quotations); Milton M. Reigelman, *The Midland: A Venture in Literary Regionalism* (Iowa City: University of Iowa Press, 1975).

235. James B. Weaver, "The Authors' Homecoming of 1914," *Midland* 1 (January 1915), 22–25.

236. Nicholas Joost, *"The Dial* in Transition: The End of the Browne Family's Control, 1913–1916," *Journal of the Illinois State Historical Society* 59, no. 3 (Autumn 1966), 272–73.

237. Gazell, "High Noon," 57.

238. Paul R. Stewart, *The Prairie Schooner Story: A Little Magazine's First Twenty-Five Years* (Lincoln: University of Nebraska Press, 1955); Tremaine McDowell, "Regionalism in American Literature," *Minnesota History* 20, no. 2 (June 1939), 114; John T. Flanagan, "Early Literary Periodicals in Minnesota," *Minnesota History* 26, no. 4 (December 1945), 293–311.

239. Richard Junger, *Becoming the Second City: Chicago's Mass News Media, 1833–1898* (Urbana: University of Illinois Press, 2010).

240. Ruegamer, "History, Politics, and the Active Life," 274–77; Ray Boomhower, *Jacob Piatt Dunn, Jr.: A Life in History and Politics, 1855–1924* (Indianapolis: Indiana Historical Society, 1997).

241. Carol Reuss, "Edwin T. Meredith: Founder of Better Homes & Gardens," *Annals of Iowa* 42, no. 8 (Spring 1975), 612.

242. John J. Fry, *The Farm Press, Reform, and Rural Change, 1895–1920* (New York: Routledge, 2005).

243. J. G. Randall, "Remarks By the Chairman," in Nichols and Randall, *Democracy in the Middle West*, 10 (quotation); Marcia Noe, "The Rise of Literary Realism and Regionalism in the Midwest," manuscript submitted to Oxford University Press for inclusion in Lauck, "The Oxford Handbook of Midwestern History"; David Pichaske, "Where Now 'Midwestern Literature'?" *Midwest Quarterly* 48, no. 1 (Autumn 2006), 107–10; Robert Cosgrove, "Realism: The Midwest's Contributions," *Old Northwest* 4, no. 4 (December 1978), 391–401.

244. Richard Lingeman, *Theodore Dreiser: At the Gates of the City, 1871–1907* (New York: G. P. Putnam's Sons, 1986). For other examples, see Clarence A. Brown, "Edward Eggleston as a Social Historian," *Journal of the Illinois State Historical Society* 54, no. 4 (Winter 1961), 405–18; Clyde E. Henson, "Joseph Kirkland's Novels," *Journal of the Illinois State Historical Society* 44, no. 2 (Summer 1951), 142–46; John T. Flanagan, "The Hoosier Schoolmaster in Minnesota," *Minnesota History* 18, no. 4 (December 1937), 347–70; James D. Stevenson Jr. and Randehl K. Stevenson, "John Milton Hay's Literary Influence," *Journal of the Illinois State Historical Society* 99, no. 1 (Spring/Summer 2006), 19–27.

245. Trygve Thoreson, "Mark Twain's Chicago," *Journal of the Illinois State Historical Society* 73, no. 4 (Winter 1980), 278.

246. Mencken quoted in John Hoffman, "The 'Upward Movement' in Illinois: Henry B. Fuller's Record of Cultural Progress, 1867–1917," *Journal of the Illinois State Historical Society* 76, no. 4 (Winter 1983), 260. See also Bernard R. Bowron Jr., *Henry B. Fuller of Chicago: The Ordeal of a Genteel Realist in Ungenteel America* (Westport, CT: Greenwood Press, 1974).

247. Mencken quoted in Pichaske, "Where Now," 111. See also Ronald Weber, *The Midwestern Ascendency in American Writing* (Bloomington: Indiana University Press, 1992).

248. Lauck, *From Warm Center to Ragged Edge*, 42.

249. Harl A. Dalstrom, "'Let Us Writer like Inspired Artists and Sell like Shrewd Yankees': Bess Streeter Aldrich's Early Twentieth-Century Middle West," in Lauck, *Midwestern Moment*, 55–70.

250. Robert L. Gale, "Willa Cather and the Usable Past," *Nebraska History* 42, no. 3 (September 1961), 183. For a related voice, see Bower Aly, "John G. Neihardt: Man, Poet, and Splendid Wayfarer," *Nebraska History* 55, no. 4 (Winter 1974), 573–79.

251. Karen Ahlquist, "Playing for the Big Time: Musicians, Concerts, and Reputation-Building in Cincinnati," *Journal of the Gilded Age and Progressive Era* 9, no. 2 (April 2010), 147; Joseph E. Holliday, "The Cincinnati Philharmonic and Hopkins Hall Orchestras, 1856–1868," *Bulletin of the Cincinnati Historical Society* 26 (April 1968), 158–73; Joseph E. Holliday, "Cincinnati Opera Festivals during the *Gilded* Age," *Bulletin of the Cincinnati Historical Society* 24 (April 1966), 130–49; Robert C. Vitz, *The Queen City and the Arts: Cultural Life in Nineteenth-Century Cincinnati* (Kent, OH: Kent State University Press, 1989); Janis White Dees, "Anna Schoen-Rene: Minnesota Musical Pioneer," *Minnesota History* 48, no. 8 (Winter 1983), 332–38. See also Michael J. Pfeifer, "The Symphonic Midwest: The Minneapolis Symphony Orchestra and Regionalist Identity, 1903–1922," in Lauck, *Midwestern Moment*, 101–12.

252. Ginger, *Altgeld's America*, 304–5 (greatest), 305–7.

253. Christa Adams, "'Splendid and Remarkable Progress' in the Midwest: Assessing the Emergence and Social Impact of Regional Art Museums, 1875–1925," *Middle West Review* 7, no. 1 (Fall 2020), 85–92. See also Adams, "Creating a Site of Midwestern Cosmopolitanism: Heterotopia, East Asian Art, and the Cleveland Museum of Art, 1914–1916," Lauck, ed., *Making of the Midwest*, 249–64.

254. Wendy Greenhouse, "'More Beauty and Less of Ugliness': Conservative Painting in Chicago, 1890–1929," in Kent Smith, Susan C. Larsen, Wendy Greenhouse, and Susan Weiniger, eds., *Chicago Painting, 1895–1945: The Bridges Collection* (Springfield, IL: University of Illinois Press with Illinois State Museum, 2004), 20 (regional), 24, 41, 43 ("Enhanced appreciation of Chicago's homegrown art as a refuge from foreign Modernist insanity added to familiar pleas for support of the city's own artists"), 48; Eva Draegert, "The Fine Arts in Indianapolis, 1875–1880," *Indiana Magazine of History* 50, no. 2 (June 1954), 107–8; Esther Mary Ayers, "Art in Southern Illinois, 1865–1914," *Journal of the Illinois State Historical Society* 36, no. 2 (June 1943), 164–89; William K. Alderfer, "The Artist Gustav Pfau," *Journal of the Illinois State Historical Society* 60, no. 4 (Winter 1967), 383–90; Craven, "Advance of Civilization into the Middle West," 64; Nancy Dustin, *William Louis Sonntag: Artist of the Ideal, 1822–1900* (Los Angeles: Goldfield Galleries, 1980); Wilbur D. Peat, *Pioneer Painters of Indiana* (Indianapolis: Art Association of Indianapolis, 1954); Mary Q. Burnett, *Art and Artists of Indiana* (New York: Century Company, 1921); Rachel S. Cordasco, "Tried by Fire: Susan Frackleton and the Arts and Crafts Movement in Wisconsin," *Wisconsin Magazine of History* 95, no. 4 (Summer 2012), 28–41.

255. Gregg R. Narber, *Murals of Iowa, 1886–2006* (Des Moines: The Iowan Books, 2010); Wallace S. Baldinger, "The Middle West Builds a Home: Chicago as a Focus on the Arts," in *Culture of the Middle West*, 59; H. Wayne Morgan, *Kenyon*

Cox, 1856–1919: A Life in American Art (Kent, OH: Kent State University Press, 1994)(Cox provided works for the state capitols in Iowa, Minnesota, and Wisconsin).
256. Adams, "'Splendid and Remarkable Progress,'" 85–92.
257. Tescia Ann Yonkers, "Sculptor Rudolph Evans: His Works on William Jennings Bryan and J. Sterling Morton," *Nebraska History* 65, no. 3 (Fall 1984), 395–410. See also Peter Bleed and Christopher M. Schoen, "The Lincoln Pottery Works: A Historical Perspective," *Nebraska History* 71, no. 1 (Spring 1990), 34–44 and Nancy E. Owen, "On the Road to Rockwood: Women's Art and Culture in Cincinnati, 1870–1890," *Ohio Valley History* 1, no. 1 (Winter 2001), 4–18.
258. Leonard K. Eaton, *Landscape Artist in America: The Life and Work of Jens Jensen* (Chicago: University of Chicago Press, 1964); Baldinger, "The Middle West Builds a Home," 66–68 (noting Jensen's masterpiece, Columbus Park in Chicago, and how Chicago's great parks were noticed by Ebeneezer Howard, who went on to write *Garden Cities of Tomorrow* (1902) and gave "rise to a sweeping revolution in modern city planning").
259. Tishler, *Midwestern Landscape Architecture*, 4 ("proud" and "railed" are the words of Tishler; "deadbeats" and "klick" [sic] are quotes from Jensen).
260. Julia Sniderman Bachrach, "Ossian Cole Simonds: Conservation Ethic in the Prairie Style," in Tishler, ed., *Midwestern Landscape Architecture*, 80.
261. Hines, *Burnham of Chicago*; Randall M. Thies, "Civil War Valor in Concrete: David A. Lester and the Kinsley Civil War Monument," *Kansas History* 22, no. 3 (Autumn 1999), 167 (describing the late 19th-century vogue for public sculpture and monuments as part of the "American Renaissance" from roughly 1876 to World War I, with the 1892–93 Columbian Exposition in Chicago as its "high point," which "ushered in the great age of public monuments and outdoor sculpture and served as a major impetus for the City Beautiful movement that advocated civic improvement through public artwork"). See William H. Wilson, *The City Beautiful Movement* (Baltimore: John Hopkins University Press, 1989) and Jeannine DeNobel Love, *Cleveland Architecture, 1890–1930: Building the City Beautiful* (East Lansing: Michigan State University Press, 2020).
262. Ginger, *Altgeld's America*, 307.
263. Kathleen D. McCarthy, *Noblesse Oblige: Charity and Cultural Philanthropy in Chicago, 1849–1929* (Chicago: University of Chicago Press, 1982), 152; Ginger, *Altgeld's America*, 307.
264. "Dedication of the Ohio State Archaeological and Historical Society Museum and Library Building," *Ohio History Journal* 23 (1914), 325–67.
265. John Zimm, "'Set like a Gem in the Clasp of Four Silver Lakes': The Wisconsin State Capitol at One Hundred," *Wisconsin Magazine of History* 100, no. 3 (Spring 2017), 30–39.
266. Orville H. Zabel, "History in Stone: The Story in Sculpture on the Exterior of the Nebraska Capitol," *Nebraska History* 62, no. 3 (Fall 1981), 285–89; Timothy J. Garvey, "Strength and Stability on the Middle Border: Lee Lawrie's Sculpture for the Nebraska State Capitol," *Nebraska History* 65, no. 2 (Summer 1984), 157–78. See also Marshal Damgaard, *The South Dakota State Capitol: The First Century* (Pierre: South Dakota State Historical Society Press, 2008).
267. Ginger, *Altgeld's America*, 308–9, 15–34, 21 (sell).

268. Many of these private institutions were funded by the Midwest's million-aires such as Newberry, Rockefeller, Ford, McCormick, Edison (born in Ohio), Post, Kellogg, and Armour. See Helen Lefkowitz Horowitz, *Culture and the City: Cultural Philanthropy in Chicago from the 1880s to 1917* (Lexington: University Press of Kentucky, 1976).

269. By 1900, the term "Middle West" was in wide use for the traditional twelve states of the region, and it was strongly associated with a cluster of cultural traits such as farming, thrift, humility, kindness, and character. "Belief in this cultural complex reached a peak about 1915." Shortridge, "Emergence of 'Middle West,'" 213. See also Steiner, "Birth of the Midwest," 7.

270. Jon K. Lauck, "The Myth of the 'Midwestern Revolt from the Village,'" *MidAmerica* 40 (2013), 39–85.

271. Richard White, *The Republic for Which It Stands: The United States during Reconstruction and the Gilded Age, 1865–1896* (New York: Oxford University Press, 2017), 16–19.

272. Rhodri Jeffreys-Jones and Bruce Collins, eds., *The Growth of Federal Power in American History* (DeKalb: Northern Illinois University Press, 1983).

CHAPTER 4

1. See Nikki M. Taylor, *Driven toward Madness: The Fugitive Slave Margaret Garner and Tragedy on the Ohio* (Athens: Ohio University Press, 2016). Taylor describes the story of the escaped slave Margaret Garner, which became the basis of Toni Morrison's novel *Beloved*.

2. Karolyn E. Smardz, "'There We Were in Darkness, Here We Are in Light': Kentucky Slaves and the Promised Land," in Craig Thompson Friend, ed., *The Buzzel About Kentuck: Settling the Promised Land* (Lexington: University Press of Kentucky, 1999), 248.

3. June Baber Woodson, "The Negro in Detroit," *Negro History Bulletin* 22, no. 4 (January 1959), 90.

4. David M. Katzman, *Before the Ghetto: Black Detroit in the Nineteenth Century* (Urbana: University of Illinois Press, 1973), 8–12. For more on the Blackburns, see Karolyn Smardz Frost, *I've Got a Home in Glory Land: A Lost Tale of the Underground Railroad* (New York: Farrar, Straus and Giroux, 2007).

5. William O. Lynch, "The Advance into the Middle West," in Nichols and Randall, *Democracy in the Middle West*, 39 (quotation); "Prof. Lynch to Retire," *Kokomo Tribune*, June 6, 1941. Lynch's chapter was originally delivered as a presidential address to the Mississippi Valley Historical Association in April 1939.

6. Hubbart, "Regionalism and Democracy," 47.

7. C. Vann Woodward, "The Antislavery Myth," *American Scholar* 31, no. 2 (Spring 1962), 316.

8. L. Diane Barnes, "'Only a Moral Power': African Americans, Reformers, and the Repeal of Ohio's Black Laws," *Ohio History* 124, no. 1 (Spring 2017), 10 (noting that "among the Ohio Territory citizens voting for delegates to the constitutional convention in October 1802 were a number of African American men"); Stephen

Middleton, *The Black Laws: Race and the Legal Process in Early Ohio* (Athens: Ohio University Press, 2005), 31–32.

9. Thurston, "The 1802 Constitutional Convention," 21; David A. Gerber, *Black Ohio and the Color Line, 1860–1915* (Urbana: University of Illinois Press, 1976), 3. Paul Finkelman explains that Ohio's "first constitution emphatically prohibited both slavery and long-term indentures for blacks [and] thus avoided the de jure and de facto bondage that later developed in Illinois and Indiana." Finkelman, "Race, Slavery, and Law," 750 (quotation), 752.

10. Thurston, "1802 Constitutional Convention," 21 (degree), 23–25, 26 (statement), 22 (entitled); Paul Finkelman, "The Strange Career of Race Discrimination in Antebellum Ohio," *Case Western Reserve Law Review* 55, no. 2 (2004), 376, 379; Middleton, *Black Laws*, 38.

11. Gerber, *Black Ohio*, 3 (fathers), 4; Middleton, *Black Laws*, 39.

12. C. G. Woodson, "The Negroes of Cincinnati Prior to the Civil War," *Journal of Negro History* 1, no. 1 (January 1916), 2.

13. Middleton, *Black Laws*, 19; Gerber, *Black Ohio*, 9; Barnhart, "Southern Influence," 28–42; J. Reuben Sheeler, "The Struggle of the Negro in Ohio for Freedom," *Journal of Negro History* 31, no. 2 (April 1946), 210; Gerber, *Black Ohio*, 9.

14. Frank U. Quillin, *The Color Line in Ohio: A History of Race Prejudice in a Typical Northern State* (Ann Arbor: George Wahr, 1913), 21–22; Middleton, *Black Laws*, 49–52; Woodson, "Negroes of Cincinnati," 2–3.

15. Sheeler, "Struggle of the Negro," 210; Barnes, "'Only a Moral Power,'" 11; Finkelman, "Strange Career," 382. Finkelman concluded that the registration process "was not terribly onerous" and not designed to exclude free blacks from the state, a step taken by most southern states by the 1830s, and that "registrations gave free blacks some protection from kidnapping by providing some proof of their free status." Finkelman, "Strange Career," 383–84.

16. Finkelman, "Strange Career," 382, 384, 395. Ohio also required that anyone seeking to capture a fugitive slave for return to the South must obtain a certificate of removal from a state judge. These anti-kidnapping provisions of state law were again strengthened in the 1830s. Finkelman, "Strange Career," 395.

17. Barnes, "'Only a Moral Power,'" 11.

18. Paul Finkelman, "The Legal Status of Free Blacks in the Antebellum Midwest," in Richard Sisson, Christian Zacher, and Andrew R. L. Cayton, eds., *The American Midwest: An Interpretative Encyclopedia* (Bloomington: Indiana University Press, 2007), 1556; Finkelman, "Strange Career," 377; "Race Hate in Early Ohio," *Negro History Bulletin* 10, no. 9 (June 1947), 204; Finkelman, "Prelude to the Fourteenth Amendment," 419, 431, 434 n. 116. The surety bond did not require the payment of $500. It "required that two freeholders in the community agree to pay up to five hundred dollars *if* the migrating black violated the terms of the law." Finkelman, "Strange Career," 385 (italics in original). With the bond requirement, "Ohioans merely introduced into midwestern law a precedent from Colonial New England, and their requirement of security for good behavior was simply a well known species of preventive justice known as 'surety of the peace.'" Robert R. Dykstra, "White Men, Black Laws: Territorial Iowans and Civil Rights, 1843–1883," *Annals of Iowa* 46, no. 6 (Fall 1982), 407. Paul Finkelman explains that the law

did not require anyone to actually post a cash bond. Rather, it required that two property owners agree to pay a penalty if the immigrant black became a pauper. If this occurred, the sureties had at least two other options before they had to pay this money to the overseers of the poor. If the sureties supported blacks who were "unable to support themselves," the bond would have been unnecessary. Similarly, if the impoverished black left the county, the bond would have been required because he would have been beyond the jurisdiction of the local overseers of the poor. . . . In practice, these restrictions were almost never enforced. The laws provided no enforcement mechanism.

No cases involving the enforcement of these laws could be found in Ohio, but if the state was "truly determined to limit its black population, the state's judges would have used these cases to question whether blacks had a right to be in the state." Indiana and Illinois also had few records of such cases. Finkelman, "Prelude to the Fourteenth Amendment," 436.

19. Paul Finkelman, "Legal Status of Free Blacks," 1556 (quotation). Historians agree that enforcement was minimal. Emil Pocock, review of Middleton, *The Black Laws*, in *Ohio Valley History* 6, no. 2 (Summer 2006), 65; Barnes, "'Only a Moral Power,'" 12; Finkelman, "Strange Career," 385–86; Middleton, *Black Laws*, 62–63; Gerber, *Black Ohio*, 14; "Race Hate," 204. But even "if sporadically employed, as such laws were, they importantly served slavery by giving the imprimatur of the state to racism. Reason might dictate the color prejudice was illogical, conscience that it was un-Christian, but the laws of the land proclaimed its legitimacy. Clearly, recognizing this, abolitionists urged black code repeal." Dykstra, "White Men, Black Laws," 412. Elsewhere, Dykstra draws an important distinction between "institutional" racism—that specifically set forth in statutory law—and "individual" and "cultural" racism—that based on personal or social attitudes. Robert R. Dykstra, "The Issue Squarely Met: Toward an Explanation of Iowans' Racial Attitudes, 1865–1868," *Annals of Iowa* 47, no. 5 (Summer 1984), 433, n. 6. Given the widespread existence and varying levels of racism in the nineteenth century, Dykstra calls for close analyses of varying contexts and distinctions between the "relatively enlightened and the wholly reactionary" racial views of various people and regions. Dykstra, "Issue Squarely Met," 436.

20. Finkelman, "Legal Status of Free Blacks," 1556 (simply); James H. Rodabaugh, "The Negro in Ohio," *Journal of Negro History* 31, no. 1 (January 1946), 18; Gerber, *Black Ohio*, 4; Sheeler, "Struggle of the Negro," 211; Finkelman, "Race, Slavery, and Law," 754–55.

21. Finkelman, "Legal Status of Free Blacks," 1555; Merrily Pierce, "Luke Decker and Slavery: His Cases with Bob and Anthony, 1817–1822," *Indiana Magazine of History* 85, no. 1 (March 1989), 35–37; Paul Finkelman, "Almost a Free State: The Indiana Constitution of 1816 and the Problem of Slavery," *Indiana Magazine of History* 111, no. 1 (March 2015), 77–79, 85–95; Finkelman, "Evading the Ordinance: The Persistence of Bondage in Indiana and Illinois," *Journal of the Early Republic* 9, no. 1 (Spring 1989), 40; State v. Lasselle, 1 Blackford (Indiana) 60 (1820); Sandra Boyd Williams, "The Indiana Supreme Court and the Struggle against Slavery," *Indiana Law Review* 30, no. 1 (1997), 306–8; McDonald, "Negro

in Indiana," 294; Barnes, "'Only a Moral Power,'" 12; Middleton, *Black Laws*, 59; Emma Lou Thornbrough, "Indiana and Fugitive Slave Legislation," *Indiana Magazine of History* 50, no. 3 (September 1954), 202–205.

22. Carl J. Ekberg, *The French Roots in the Illinois Country: The Mississippi Frontier in Colonial Times* (Urbana: University of Illinois Press, 1998); John W. Allen, "Slavery and Negro Servitude in Pope County, Illinois," *Journal of the Illinois State Historical Society* 42, no. 4 (December 1949), 412; Sigmund Diamond, "An Experiment in 'Feudalism': French Canada in the Seventeenth Century," *William and Mary Quarterly* 18, no. 1 (January 1961), 3–34; Earl E. McDonald, "The Negro in Indiana before 1881," *Indiana Magazine of History* 27, no. 4 (December 1931), 292; Robert Lucas and Arna Bontemps, "First, the French," in Brian Dolinar, ed., *The WPA Papers* (Urbana: University of Illinois Press, 2013), 2.

23. Arna Bontemps, "Slavery," in Dolinar, *WPA Papers*, 6 (allowed), 9 (previously). The *Ordonnance au sujet des Negres et ses Sauvages appeles Panis* of 1709 decreed that all black and Native American slaves were legally enslaved. David M. Katzman, "Black Slavery in Michigan," *Midcontinent American Studies Journal* 11, no. 2 (Fall 1970), 57. See generally James Simeone, *Democracy and Slavery in Frontier Illinois: The Bottomland Republic* (DeKalb: Northern Illinois University Press, 2000).

24. Hammond, "Slavery, Settlement, and Empire," 202; Finkelman, "Evading the Ordinance," 24; Elmer Gertz, "The Black Laws of Illinois," *Journal of the Illinois State Historical Society* 56, no. 3 (Autumn 1963), 458; Daniel Owen, "Circumvention of Article IV of the Ordinance of 1787," *Indiana Magazine of History* 36, no. 2 (June 1940), 111.

25. Hammond, "Slavery, Settlement, and Empire," 177 (neglect), 178 n. 3 (origins); Katzman, "Black Slavery in Michigan," 57 (noting, inter alia, that the practice of slavery among Native Americans was an "institution founded on the assumed right of the victor to sell captives taken in war," explaining the "French transplantation of feudalism" to New France and the colony's "turn to slavery," and noting that French settlers "regularly bought slaves from the Indians").

26. Finkelman, "Evading the Ordinance," 31, 46, 48; Allen, "Slavery and Negro Servitude," 411–23; John A. Jakle, "Salt on the Ohio Frontier, 1770–1820," *Annals of the Association of American Geographers* 59, no. 4 (December 1969), 707; Jarrot v. Jarrot, 2 Gilman (Illinois) 1 (1845); Richard J. Jensen, *Illinois: A History* (Urbana: University of Illinois Press, 1978), 4; Finkelman, "Legal Status of Free Blacks," 1555.

27. Bontemps, "Slavery," 9; Barnes, "'Only a Moral Power,'" 12; Gertz, "Black Laws of Illinois," 463, 467; M. Scott Heerman, "In a State of Slavery: Black Servitude in Illinois, 1800–1830," *Early American Studies* 14, no. 1 (Winter 2016), 118–19. Heerman also "challenges the idea that servitude simply recreated bondage and highlights the notion that it also offered African Americans a pathway closer toward freedom." Heerman, "State of Slavery," 118, n. 17.

28. Peck, *Making an Antislavery Nation*, 17–18; Paul Finkelman, "Slavery, the 'More Perfect Union,' and the Prairie State," *Illinois Historical Journal* 80, no. 4 (Winter 1987), 249–50; Gertz, "Black Laws of Illinois," 457; Meyer, *Making the Heartland Quilt*, 136–68; Barnhart, "Southern Influence," 348–78; Suzanne Cooper Guasco,

"'The Deadly Influence of Negro Capitalists': Southern Yeomen and Resistance to the Expansion of Slavery in Illinois," *Civil War History* 47, no. 1 (March 2001), 16.

29. Lulu Merle Johnson, "The Problem of Slavery in the Old Northwest, 1787–1858" (doctoral dissertation, University of Iowa, 1941), 81.

30. Peck, *Making an Antislavery Nation*, 17–19, 28–33; Adam Rowe, "The Republican Rhetoric of a Frontier Controversy: Newspapers in the Illinois Slavery Debate, 1823–1824," *Journal of the Early Republic* 31, no. 4 (Winter 2011), 683–92.

31. Merton Lynn Dillon, "The Antislavery Movement in Illinois: 1824–1835," in Scheiber, *Old Northwest*, 296–311; Guasco, *Confronting Slavery*.

32. Peck, *Making an Antislavery Nation*, 18–19; Rowe, "Republican Rhetoric," 685.

33. Onuf, *Statehood and Union*, 123 (quotation); Robert M. Sutton, "Edward Coles and the Constitutional Crisis in Illinois, 1822–24," *Journal of the Illinois State Historical Society* 82, no. 1 (Spring 1989), 33–46; Eudora Ramsay Richardson, "The Virginian Who Made Illinois a Free State," *Journal of the Illinois State Historical Society* 45, no. 1 (Spring 1952), 5–9; David Ress, *Governor Edward Coles and the Vote to Forbid Slavery in Illinois, 1823–1824* (Jefferson, NC: McFarland, 2006); Peck, *Making an Antislavery Nation*, 19; Rowe, "Republican Rhetoric," 680; Kurt Leichtle and Bruce Carveth, *Crusade against Slavery: Edward Coles, Pioneer of Freedom* (Edwardsville: Southern Illinois University Press, 2011); John Reda, *From Furs to Farms: The Transformation of the Mississippi Valley, 1762–1825* (DeKalb: Northern Illinois University Press, 2016), 137–41.

34. J. N. Gridley, "A Case under an Illinois Black Law," *Journal of the Illinois State Historical Society* 4, no. 4 (January 1912), 401; Dillon, "Antislavery Movement in Illinois," 296; Finkelman, "Evading the Ordinance," 49, n. 83; Peck, *Making an Antislavery Nation*, 28, 31; Theodore Calvin Pease, *The Frontier State, 1818–1848* (Urbana: University of Illinois Press, 1987 [1918]), 81. The 11,612 voters who turned out for the slavery vote dwarfed the 4,515 who turned out for the presidential election of 1824 a few months later. Peck, *Making an Antislavery Nation*, 31.

35. Peck, *Making an Antislavery Nation*, 32; Guasco, "'Deadly Influence,'" 26.

36. Littlejohn, "Black before the Bar," 19; Brett Rushforth, "'A Little Flesh We Offer You': The Origins of Indian Slavery in New France," *William and Mary Quarterly* 60, no. 4 (October 2003), 777–808; M. M. Quaife and Sidney Glazer, *Michigan: From Primitive Wilderness to Industrial Commonwealth* (New York: Prentice-Hall, 1948), 196.

37. Marilyn Hall Mitchell, "From Slavery to Shelley: Michigan's Ambivalent Response to Civil Rights," *Wayne Law Review* 26, no. 1 (November 1979), 2; Littlejohn, "Black before the Bar," 19; Formisano, "Edge of Caste," 21; Katzman, "Black Slavery in Michigan," 57.

38. Gregory Wigmore, "Before the Railroad: From Slavery to Freedom in the Canadian-American Borderland," *Journal of American History* 98, no. 2 (September 2011), 441; Katzman, "Black Slavery in Michigan," 57.

39. Littlejohn, "Black before the Bar," 22, 25; Katzman, "Black Slavery in Michigan," 61. Although the Treaty of Paris ended the American Revolution in 1783, Detroit was not officially transferred until 1796 under the terms of the Jay Treaty of

1794. Slaveowners tried to show that slaves were born during British rule and thus not eligible to be set free through the use of American law. Littlejohn, "Black before the Bar," 28.

40. Wigmore, "Before the Railroad," 438–39; Littlejohn, "Black before the Bar," 23; Mitchell, "From Slavery to Shelley," 3; Katzman, *Before the Ghetto*, 5 (noting that slavery in Canada persisted until 1833, when it was abolished in the British Empire).

41. Littlejohn, "Black before the Bar," 24 (decidedly), 33–44; Mitchell, "From Slavery to Shelley," 3; Denison v. Tucker, 1. St. Ct. Terr. Mich. 63 (1807); Edward J. Littlejohn, "Slaves, Judge Woodward, and the Supreme Court of the Michigan Territory," *Michigan Bar Journal* (July 2015), 22–25. For more on the case, see Tiya Miles, *The Dawn of Detroit: A Chronicle of Slavery and Freedom in the City of the Straits* (New York: New Press, 2017), 183.

42. Rosentreter, "Michigan's Quest for Statehood," 79–92.

43. Mitchell, "From Slavery to Shelley," 10; Formisano, "Edge of Caste," 21–23; Littlejohn, "Black before the Bar," 40–41; Willis F. Dunbar and William G. Shade, "The Black Man Gains the Vote: The Centennial of 'Impartial Suffrage' in Michigan," *Michigan History* 56, no. 1 (Spring 1972), 43; Littlejohn, "Black before the Bar," 44. Katzman, *Before the Ghetto*, 6–7. Littlejohn's study found the black laws of territorial Michigan to be "rarely enforced" and "unpopular and largely unenforced." Littlejohn, "Black before the Bar," 41, 47.

44. Roy E. Finkenbine, "A Beacon of Liberty on the Great Lakes: Race, Slavery, and the Law in Antebellum Michigan," in Paul Finkelman and Martin J. Hershock, eds., *The History of Michigan Law* (Athens: Ohio University Press, 2006), 85, 92; Paul Finkelman, "The Promise of Equality and the Limits of Law: From the Civil War to World War II," in Finkelman and Hershock, *History of Michigan Law*, 189 (explaining that, "unlike the states of the lower Midwest, which had laws requiring black migrants to register with local officials, after statehood Michigan did not attempt to limit black migration or to require any sort of registration system for African Americans entering the state"). The term "black laws" is used here to mean "specific codes directed at African Americans, especially those aimed at prohibiting or limiting black settlement within a state." On this definition and broader meanings, see Finkenbine, "Beacon of Liberty," 103–4, n. 1.

45. James Connor, "The Antislavery Movement in Iowa," *Annals of Iowa* 40, no. 5 (Summer 1970), 346; Joel H. Sibley, "Proslavery Sentiment in Iowa, 1833–1861," *Iowa Journal of History and Politics* 55, no. 4 (October 1957), 289–318; Dykstra, "White Men, Black Laws," 403.

46. Leola Bergmann, "The Negro in Iowa," *Iowa Journal of History and Politics* 46, no. 1 (January 1948), 9; Connor, "Antislavery Movement in Iowa," 354; Robert R. Dykstra, *Bright Radical Star: Black Freedom and White Supremacy on the Hawkeye Frontier* (Cambridge, MA: Harvard University Press, 1993); Dorothy Schwieder, *Iowa: The Middle Land* (Ames: Iowa State University Press, 1996), 68; James L. Hull, "Migration of Blacks to Iowa, 1820–1960," *Journal of Negro History* 66, no. 4 (Winter 1981/1982), 290–91.

47. Dykstra, "White Men, Black Laws," 409.

48. Bergman, "Negro in Iowa," 12 (quotation); Connor, "Antislavery Movement in Iowa," 357–58 (describing black suffrage at the 1844 convention as a "legitimate subject of debate" that was heard in a "surprisingly liberal spirit").

49. Louis Pelzer, "The Negro and Slavery in Iowa," *Iowa Journal of History and Politics* 2 (1904), 477–79; Joseph Frazier Wall, *Iowa: A Bicentennial History* (New York: W. W. Norton, 1978), 96–97; Connor, "Antislavery Movement in Iowa," 347–48; Sage, *History of Iowa*, 124–28; Robert Cook, "The Political Culture of Antebellum Iowa: An Overview," *Annals of Iowa* 52, no. 3 (Summer 1993), 239, 247.

50. F. I. Herriott, "Whence Came the Pioneers of Iowa?" *Annals of Iowa* 7, no. 5 (June 1906), 462 (quotation); Schwieder, *Iowa*, 72; Bergmann, "Negro in Iowa," 7.

51. G. Galin Berrier, "The Negro Suffrage Issue in Iowa, 1865–1868," *Annals of Iowa* 39, no. 4 (Spring 1968), 242.

52. Middleton, *Black Laws*, 58.

53. Ray A. Brown, "The Making of the Wisconsin Constitution," part 1, *Wisconsin Law Review* 1949, no. 4 (1949), 685–87; Brown, "The Making of the Wisconsin Constitution," part 2, *Wisconsin Law Review* 1952, no. 1 (1952), 43–45; Barnes, "'Only a Moral Power,'" 12. The adoption of the 1846 convention failed, 20,233–14,119, as did an accompanying referendum on black suffrage, 14,615–7,664. Leslie H. Fishel Jr., "Wisconsin and Negro Suffrage," *Wisconsin Magazine of History* 46, no. 3 (Spring 1963), 182–83.

54. Fishel, "Wisconsin and Negro Suffrage," 182.

55. Finkelman, "Prelude to the Fourteenth Amendment," 443. When discussing Michigan, Wisconsin, and Minnesota, Finkelman notes that "none of these far northern states ever discouraged blacks from moving to them after they entered the union." Finkelman, "Prelude to the Fourteenth Amendment," 449.

56. Finkelman, "Almost a Free State," 67, n. 13. Iowa repealed its anti-miscegenation law in 1851, Illinois in 1874, Michigan in 1883, and Ohio in 1887. Indiana did not repeal the law until 1965. Finkelman, "Almost a Free State," 67, n. 13.

57. Finkelman, "Legal Status of Free Blacks," 1557.

58. Middleton, *Black Laws*, 70–71; Barnes, *Anti-Slavery Impulse*, 70; Sheeler, "Struggle of the Negro," 213; Joan E. Cashin, "Black Families in the Old Northwest," *Journal of the Early Republic* 15, no. 3 (Autumn 1995), 452.

59. "Race Hate," 204; Middleton, *Black Laws*, 71; Woodson, "Negroes of Cincinnati," 7; Nikki Taylor, "Reconsidering the 'Forced' Exodus of 1829: Free Black Emigration from Cincinnati, Ohio to Wilberforce, Canada," *Journal of African American History* 87 (Summer 2002), 283–302 (emphasizing Cincinnati's blacks' decision to move on their own terms); Marilyn Baily, "From Cincinnati, Ohio to Wilberforce, Canada: A Note on Antebellum Colonization," *Journal of Negro History* 58, no. 4 (October 1973), 427–40. See generally See Nikki M. Taylor, *Frontiers of Freedom: Cincinnati's Black Community, 1802–1868* (Athens: Ohio University Press, 2005). See also Jaclyn N. Schultz, "In Search of Northern Freedom: Black History in Milwaukee and Southern Ontario, 1834–1864," *Wisconsin Magazine of History* 101, no. 1 (Autumn 2017), 51 (noting that many black Canadians "often related that they found the prejudice in Canada worse than what they'd experienced in the US free states"), and Karolyn Smardz Frost and Veta Smith Tucker, eds., *A*

Fluid Frontier: Slavery, Resistance, and the Underground Railroad in the Detroit River Borderland (Detroit: Wayne State University Press, 2016).

60. Middleton, *Black Laws*, 72; Sheeler, "Struggle of the Negro," 213; Eric Michael Rhodes, "Midwestern 'Mobocracy': The Emergence of Labor Politics and Racial Exclusion in Cincinnati and the Lower Midwest, 1829–1836," in Lauck, *Making of the Midwest*, 315–16.

61. Sheeler, "Struggle of the Negro," 213–14; Julie A. Mujic, "A Border Community's Unfulfilled Appeals: The Rise and Fall of the 1840s Anti-Abolitionist Movement in Cincinnati," *Ohio Valley History* 7, no. 2 (Summer 2007), 53–69. Sheeler concluded that the "greatest enemy to the Negro and his progress was the new immigrant groups, especially the Irish." Sheeler, "Struggle of the Negro," 226. See also Woodson, "Negroes of Cincinnati," 5, 13; Gerber, *Black Ohio*, 7; Katzman, *Black Ghetto*, 44, 101; Robert R. Dykstra and Harlan Hahn, "Northern Voters and Negro Suffrage: The Case of Iowa, 1868," *Public Opinion Quarterly* 32, no. 2 (Summer 1968), 202–15 (indicating that Irish and German areas were the most opposed to black suffrage during a key Iowa referendum).

62. Barnes, *Anti-Slavery Impulse, 1830–1844*, 81.

63. Merton L. Dillon, *Elijah P. Lovejoy: Abolitionist Editor* (Urbana: University of Illinois Press, 1961).

64. Finkelman, "Almost a Free State," 65. Finkelman, who has researched race and the early Midwest more than perhaps anyone, finds that the blanket argument that the antebellum North and the Midwest were hostile to blacks is wrong: "This thesis works for Indiana and Illinois, but is clearly not as viable for much of the rest of the North and even the Midwest." Finkelman, "Almost a Free State," 66, n. 4. Finkelman explains that "history illustrates that many scholars have been mistaken in believing that the North was overwhelmingly hostile to black rights at the end of the antebellum period." Finkelman, "Almost a Free State," 67, n. 13.

65. William S. McFeely, *Frederick Douglass* (New York: W. W. Norton, 1991), 108–12 (explaining that 130 supporters of Douglass were confronted by thirty hecklers and opponents).

66. Indiana Constitution (1851), § 13; Finkelman, "Almost a Free State," 65, 67; Berrier, "Negro Suffrage," 242 (noting that the Iowa exclusion act "was not enforced" and that the number of African Americans in Iowa tripled during the decade after the law passed). Because an antislavery editor refused to publish the law, it did not go into effect. Schwieder, *Iowa*, 86–87.

67. Nelson v. The People, 33 Ill. 390 (1864); Gertz, "Black Laws of Illinois," 472; Finkelman, "Almost a Free State," 68.

68. Schafer, "Beginnings of Civilization," 215; Sheeler, "Struggle of the Negro," 208; William Frederick Poole, *The Ordinance of 1787, and Dr. Manasseh Cutler as an Agent in Its Formation* (Cambridge, MA: Welch, Bigelow, 1876); Pease, "Ordinance of 1787," 167. The decision of southerners to not block the ban on slavery could have been for several factors: their perception that it would make extending slavery in the Southwest easier; the inclusion of a fugitive slave provision in the Ordinance; a belief that they should cut their losses in an era when the ideals of the Revolution could work against slavery; fear of economic competition; or other factors. See Paul Finkelman, "Slavery and the Northwest Ordinance: A Study in

Ambiguity," *Journal of the Early Republic* 6, no. 4 (Winter 1986), 350–54. On the praise for Dane during the early decades of the Midwest, see Onuf, "Northwest Ordinance," 300–301.

69. Onuf, "Northwest Ordinance," 294; Barnes, "'Only a Moral Power,'" 20. See generally Henry Louis Taylor, "The Northwest Ordinance and the Place of Ohio in African-American History," *Old Northwest* 14, no. 2 (June 1988), 131–44.

70. Lincoln, *The Collected Works of Abraham Lincoln*, 3 vols. (New Brunswick, NJ: Rutgers University Press, 1953–55), 454–57 (speech in Cincinnati in September 1959).

71. Hammond, "Slavery, Settlement, and Empire," 202, 203 (history, ultimate); Gerber, *Black Ohio*, 11; Finkelman, "Evading the Ordinance," 30.

72. Johnson, "Problem of Slavery in the Old Northwest," 138–85; McKivigan, "Christian Anti-Slavery Convention Movement," 345–65; Dana Elizabeth Weiner, *Race and Rights: Fighting Slavery and Prejudice in the Old Northwest, 1830–1870* (Ithaca, NY: Cornell University Press, 2015), 49–75.

73. Robinson, *Death of Adam*, 140–41 (propagandizing), 137 (colonization); Middleton, *Black Laws*, 123 (concluding that "Ohio abolitionists and social reformers were among the most energetic in the nation").

74. Tiya Miles, "'Shall Woman's Voice Be Hushed?': Laura Smith Haviland in Abolitionist Women's History," *Michigan Historical Review* 39, no. 2 (Fall 2013), 7.

75. Joseph Bougere, "Abolition," in Brian Dolinar, *Negro in Illinois: The WPA Papers* (Urbana: University of Illinois Press, 2013), 14.

76. Middleton, *Black Laws*, 75–108; Montagna, "Ohio, Evangelical Religion," 1–35.

77. Middleton, *Black Laws*, 81–82, 98–101; Eric J. Cardinal, "Antislavery Sentiment and Political Transformation in the 1850s: Portage County, Ohio," *Old Northwest* 1, no. 3 (September 1975), 223–38.

78. Hubbart, *Older Middle West*, 63; Gerber, *Black Ohio*, 11; Hamm et al., "'Great and Good People,'" 3–25; Howard H. Bell, "The National Negro Convention," *Ohio Historical Quarterly* 67, no. 4 (October 1958), 357–58; Lois K. Mathews, *The Expansion of New England* (Boston: Houghton Mifflin, 1909).

79. Finkelman, "Prelude to the Fourteenth Amendment," 426 (hotbed); Middleton, *Black Laws*, 82; Woodson, "Negroes of Cincinnati," 8; Harry Forrest Lupold, "Anti-Slavery Activities in a Western Reserve County," *Michigan History* 38, no. 7 (October/November 1975), 468–69; Burroughs, "Oberlin's Part," 269–72.

80. Lockard, "Influence of New England," 7; Barnes, *Anti-Slavery Impulse*, 76 (quotation); Middleton, *Black Laws*, 83; Gerber, *Black Ohio*, 12; Sheeler, "Struggle of the Negro," 215; Robert Samuel Fletcher, *History of Oberlin College from Its Foundation through the Civil War* (Oberlin, OH: Oberlin College, 1943), 533–35; Brandt, *Town That Started the Civil War*.

81. Barnes, *Anti-Slavery Impulse*, 77 (abolition), 83; Finkelman, "Prelude to the Fourteenth Amendment," 460, 461 (potency). On resistance to the Fugitive Slave Act in southwestern Ohio, see Stephen Middleton, "The Fugitive Slave Crisis in Cincinnati, 1850–1860: Resistance, Enforcement, and Black Refugees," *Journal of Negro History* 72, nos. 1–2 (Winter/Spring 1987), 20–32. In addition to the Western Reserve and Cincinnati, northwest Ohio also had an active abolitionist

group. See Marilyn W. Wendler, "Anti-Slavery Sentiment and the Underground Railroad in the Lower Maumee Valley," *Northwest Ohio Quarterly* 52, no. 2 (1980), 193–208.

82. Nicole Etcheson. Review of Middleton, Stephen, *The Black Laws: Race and the Legal Process in Early Ohio.* H-SHEAR, H-Net Reviews. August, 2006. www.h-net.org/reviews/showrev.php?id=12171, 2.

83. Gerber, *Black Ohio*, 11; Middleton, *Black Laws*, 83–84; Finkelman, "Strange Career," 394; Sheeler, "Struggle of the Negro," 218.

84. Lockard, "Influence of New England," 7 (quotation); James H. Rodabaugh, "Miami University, Calvinism, and the Anti-Slavery Movement," *Ohio Archaeological and Historical Quarterly* 48, no. 1 (January 1939), 70–73.

85. Taylor, "Western Colleges," 41–65.

86. Mitchell, "From Slavery to Shelley," 5 (quotation); Miles, "'Shall Woman's Voice Be Hushed?,'" 2–4; Merton L. Dillon, "Elizabeth Chandler and the Spread of Antislavery Sentiment to Michigan," *Michigan History* 39, no. 4 (September 1955), 481–94; Yvonne Tuchalski, "Erastus Hussey, Battle Creek Antislavery Activist," *Michigan History* 56, no. 1 (Spring 1972), 1–18; Wesley Norton, "The Methodist Episcopal Church in Michigan and the Politics of Slavery: 1850–1860," *Michigan History* 48, no. 3 (September 1964), 193–213; McDaid, "Kinsley S. Bingham," 42–73; John W. Quist, "'The Great Majority of Our Subscribers Are Farmers': The Michigan Abolitionist Constituency of the 1840s," *Journal of the Early Republic* 14, no. 3 (Autumn 1994), 325–58; Anthony Patrick Glesner, "Laura Haviland: Neglected Heroine of the Underground Railroad," *Michigan Historical Review* 21, no. 1 (Spring 1995), 19–48.

87. Formisano, "Edge of Caste," 24–25; Katzman, *Black Ghetto*, 35.

88. Dunbar, "Public versus Private Control," 402.

89. Muelder, *Missionaries and Muckrakers.* See also Merton L. Dillon, "Sources of Early Antislavery Thought in Illinois," *Journal of the Illinois State Historical Society* 50, no. 1 (Spring 1957), 36–50. On African American organizing, see Victoria L. Harrison, "We Are Here Assembled: Illinois Colored Conventions, 1853–1873," *Journal of the Illinois State Historical Society* 108, nos. 3–4 (Fall/Winter 2015), 322–46.

90. Lockard, "Influence of New England," 7–8 (quotations); Charles H. Rammelkamp, "The Reverberations of the Slavery Conflict in a Pioneer College," *Mississippi Valley Historical Review* 14, no. 4 (March 1928), 447–48; Jeanne Gillespie McDonald, "Edward Beecher and the Anti-Slavery Movement in Illinois," *Journal of the Illinois State Historical Society* 105, no. 1 (Spring 2012), 9–35; Bougere, "Abolition," in Dolinar, ed., *Negro in Illinois*, 18.

91. Lockard, "Influence of New England," 8 (quotation); 54–55. See also Jane Ann Moore and William F. Moore, *Owen Lovejoy and the Coalition for Equality: Clergy, African Americans, and Women United for Abolition* (Urbana: University of Illinois Press, 2020).

92. Lockard, "Influence of New England," 9 (quotation); Charles H. Rammelkamp, "Illinois College and the Anti-Slavery Movement," Transactions of the Illinois State Historical Society (Springfield, Illinois: Illinois State Journal Co., 1909), 192–203; Charles H. Rammelkamp, "The Reverberations of the Slavery

Conflict in a Pioneer College," *Mississippi Valley Historical Review* 14, no. 4 (March 1928), 447–61.

93. Prinsloo, "'Abolitionist Factory,'" 36–42. See also M. Scott Heerman, "'Reducing Free Men to Slavery': Black Kidnapping, the 'Slave Power,' and the Politics of Abolition in Antebellum Illinois, 1830–1860," *Journal of the Early Republic* 38, no. 2 (Summer 2018), 261–91, and Linda Jeanne Evans, "Abolitionism in the Illinois Churches, 1830–1865" (Ph.D. dissertation, Northwestern University 1981); Arna Bontemps, "Underground Railroad," in Dolinar, *Negro in Illinois*, 22–33.

94. Merle Curti, "Social Relationships in Trempealeau County," in Scheiber, *Old Northwest*, 99.

95. Dykstra, "White Men, Black Laws," 403 (quotation); Connor, "Antislavery Movement in Iowa," 343–76; Dykstra, *Bright Radical Star*, 126–92; Schwieder, *Iowa*, 69–70; Soike, *Necessary Courage*.

96. Dykstra, "White Men, Black Laws," 413.

97. Finkelman, "Slavery, the 'More Perfect Union,'" 260.

98. Frank Klement, "The Abolition Movement in Minnesota," *Minnesota History* 32, no. 1 (March 1951), 15–33; Kevin J. Golden, "The Independent Development of Civil Rights in Minnesota: 1849–1910," *William Mitchell Law Review* 17, no. 2 (1991), 451.

99. Charles W. Nichols, "Henry M. Nichols and Frontier Minnesota," *Minnesota History* 19, no. 3 (September 1938), 261.

100. Mark A. Furnish, "Black Hoosiers and the Formation of an Antislavery Stronghold in the Central Ohio Valley," *Ohio Valley History* 16, no. 3 (Fall 2016), 8–9 (quotation); Julia S. Conklin, "The Underground Railroad in Indiana," *Indiana Quarterly Magazine of History* 6, no. 2 (June 1910), 67–68.

101. Finkelman, "Prelude to the Fourteenth Amendment," 459, 463 (protections).

102. See Twitty, *Before Dred Scott* (finding that 40.2 percent of slave lawsuits in one Missouri court led to freedom), and VanderVelde, *Redemption Songs*.

103. Finkelman, "Prelude to the Fourteenth Amendment," 457; H. Robert Baker, *The Rescue of Joshua Glover: A Fugitive Slave, the Constitution, and the Coming of the Civil War* (Athens: Ohio University Press, 2006); Ruby West Jackson and Walter T. McDonald, *Finding Freedom: The Untold Story of Joshua Glover, Runaway Slave* (Madison: Wisconsin Historical Society Press, 2007).

104. Frank W. Hale, "Salmon Portland Chase: Rhetorician of Abolition," *Negro History Bulletin* 26, no. 5 (February 1963), 165–68; Finkelman, "Prelude to the Fourteenth Amendment," 428–29.

105. Finkelman, "Prelude to the Fourteenth Amendment," 458.

106. *The Collected Works of Abraham Lincoln* (New Brunswick, NJ: Rutgers University Press, 1953), 3, 249.

107. Foner, *Free Soil, Free Labor*, 261.

108. Middleton, *Black Laws*, 73 (sprout).

109. Finkelman, "Strange Career," 395–96 (nefarious), 396, 400–401. For a case involving Ohio abolitionists who in 1839 told Virginia slaves traveling through the state with their masters that they were free, see State v. Farr (1841) (not in an official

reporter); Finkelman, "Strange Career," 397; Finkelman, "Prelude to the Fourteenth Amendment," 447–48.

110. Finkelman, "Race, Slavery, and Law," 749.

111. Anderson v. Poindexter, 6 Ohio St. 622 (1856).

112. Finkelman, "Strange Career," 398 (describing Governor Mordecai Bartley's attempt to free the slave Jerry Phinney); Finkelman, "Prelude to the Fourteenth Amendment," 448.

113. Finkelman, "Strange Career," 378, 402; Finkelman, "Race, Slavery, and Law," 769–70.

114. Hyun Hur, "Radical Antislavery and Personal Liberty Laws in Antebellum Ohio, 1803–1857" (Ph.D. dissertation, University of Wisconsin-Madison, 2012), 7.

115. Finkelman, "Strange Career," 401 (relatively), 407 (against). Finkelman finds that interpretations that only highlight black oppression in the Midwest are "fundamentally wrong." Finkelman, "Strange Career," 373–74 (rejecting earlier works such as Leon F. Litwack, *North of Slavery: The Negro in the Free States* [Chicago: University of Chicago Press, 1961] and Eugene F. Berwanger, *The Frontier against Slavery: Western Anti-Negro Prejudice and the Slavery Extension Controversy* (Urbana: University of Illinois Press, 1967]), 407 (quotation). I first began my rethinking of my simple conception of these questions and recognizing the unique moment of racial progress during and after the Civil War after reading that the city pool in Lincoln, Nebraska, was desegregated until World War I. Jesse S. Ishikawa, "The Desegregation of the Lincoln Municipal Swimming Pool," *Nebraska History* 99, no. 3 (Fall 2018), 159 (noting that the Lincoln pool had been open to all races prior to the war but also that it was divided by gender). About the same time I noticed other statements that contradicted the grand narrative of race in nineteenth-century America. See Herman Murray Riley, "A History of Negro Elementary Education in Indianapolis," *Indiana Magazine of History* 26, no. 4 (December 1930), 288 ("Colored children were found in many public schools in common with white children").

116. Barnes, "'Only a Moral Power,'" 13; Middleton, *Black Laws*, 97, 104–5, 75 (virtual).

117. Finkelman, "Race, Slavery, and Law," 764; Leonard Erickson, "Politics and Repeal of Ohio's Black Laws, 1837–1849," *Ohio History* 82, nos. 3–4 (Summer/Autumn 1973), 156–57; Middleton, *Black Laws*, 128–29, 138.

118. Barnes, "'Only a Moral Power,'" 14 (contrary), 20; Erickson, "Politics and Repeal," 157.

119. Erickson, "Politics and Repeal," 171–72; Maizlish, *Triumph of Sectionalism*, 136; Middleton, *Black Laws*, 153–54; Gerber, *Black Ohio*, 5.

120. Barnes, "'Only a Moral Power,'" 20; Sheeler, "Struggle of the Negro," 222; Finkelman, "Strange Career," 377–78; Jeffries v. Ankeny, 11 Ohio 372 (1842). In other words, Ohio rejected the infamous "one-drop rule" applied by southern states. Jonathan L. Entin, "An Ohio Dilemma: Race, Equal Protection, and the Unfulfilled Promise of a State Bill of Rights," *Cleveland State Law Review* 51, no. 3 (2004), 396–400. Entin concluded that the Ohio Supreme Court "developed a jurisprudence that, although jarring to modern sensibilities, was in some respects surprisingly progressive for its time." Entin, "Ohio Dilemma," 396.

121. Gertz, "Black Laws of Illinois," 468–69.
122. Newton N. Newborn, "Judicial Decision Making and the End of Slavery in Illinois," *Journal of the Illinois State Historical Society* 98, nos. 1–2 (Spring/Summer 2005), 7–33; Finkelman, "Slavery, the 'More Perfect Union,'" 250 n. 4, 256; Jarrot v. Jarrot, 2 Gilman (Illinois) 1 (1845).
123. Finkelman, "Slavery, the 'More Perfect Union,'" 260–61, 267–68; Finkelman, "Prelude to the Fourteenth Amendment," 442 (sporadic); Gertz, "Black Laws of Illinois," 472; McPherson, *Struggle for Equality*, 236.
124. Roger D. Bridges, "Equality Deferred: Civil Rights for Illinois Blacks, 1865–1885," *Journal of the Illinois State Historical Society* 74, no. 2 (Summer 1981), 86–87; Charles A. Gliozzo, *John Jones and the Repeal of the Illinois Black Laws* (Duluth: University of Minnesota-Duluth, 1975), 10.
125. Bridges, "Equality Deferred," 87 (chosen); Gliozzo, *John Jones*, 10.
126. Littlejohn, "Black before the Bar," 34–38; Pattinson v. Whitaker, 1 Blume 385 (1807); Carol E. Mull, *The Underground Railroad in Michigan* (Jefferson, NC: McFarland, 2010).
127. Finkenbine, "Beacon of Liberty," 92; Finkelman, "Prelude to the Fourteenth Amendment," 428; Finkelman, "Hidden History," 381; Finkelman, "Promise of Equality," 189; Gordon v. Farrar, 2 Mich. (Doug.) 409 (1847); Mitchell, "From Slavery to Shelley," 14 (explaining that the plaintiff was awarded damages and that the "jury verdict was unusual in that blacks generally lost cases at the trial court level"). The Michigan Supreme Court ultimately ruled that election officials should decide if a vote was white. Formisano, "Edge of Caste," 28.
128. Giltner v. Gorham, 10 Fed. Cas. 424 (C.C.D. Mich. 1848).
129. Paul Moreno, "The *Workman* Case: Racial Equality in Nineteenth-Century Michigan," *Michigan Bar Journal* (December 2008)," 9 (deeming the law "stringent"); Littlejohn, "Black before the Bar," 47; Finkelman, "Promise of Equality," 189
130. Littlejohn, "Black before the Bar," 69.
131. People v. Dean, 14 Mich. 406, 438 (1866); Moreno, "*Workman* Case," 9; Katzman, *Black Ghetto*, 35–36.
132. Moreno, "*Workman* Case," 9 (liberal); Michael J. Pfeifer, "Lynching in Late-Nineteenth Century Michigan," in Michael J. Pfeifer, ed., *Lynching beyond Dixie: American Mob Violence outside the South* (Urbana: University of Illinois Press, 2013), 212 (egalitarianism); David G. Chardavoyne and Paul Moreno, *Michigan Supreme Court Historical Reference Guide* (East Lansing: Michigan State University Press, 2015), 158 (concluding that "Michigan had been among the most anti-slavery states in the Union, where abolitionists enjoyed relative safety and through which many fugitive slaves escaped to Canada via the Underground Railroad"); Finkelman, "Promise of Equality," 188–89.
133. Finkenbine, "Beacon of Liberty," 83.
134. Jeffrey Schmitt, "Rethinking *Ableman v. Booth* and States' Rights in Wisconsin," *Virginia Law Review* 93, no. 5 (September 2007), 1338; Ableman v. Booth, 21 How. 506 (1859); Joseph Schafer, "Stormy Days in Court—The Booth Case," *Wisconsin Magazine of History* 20, no. 1 (September 1936), 89–110; Finkelman, "Prelude to the Fourteenth Amendment," 448.

135. Francis J. Demet, "Massive Resistance and Negro Rights in Wisconsin," *Wisconsin Magazine of History* 43, no. 4 (Summer 1960), 288–89.

136. Schmitt, "Rethinking *Ableman v. Booth*," 1316; Jenni Parrish, "The Booth Cases: Final Step to the Civil War," *Willamette Law Review* 29 (1993), 237–78.

137. William D. Green, *Degrees of Freedom: The Origins of Civil Rights in Minnesota, 1865–1912* (Minneapolis: University of Minnesota Press, 2015).

138. E. Spangler, *The Negro in Minnesota* (Minneapolis: T. S. Denison, 1961), 29–30; Finkelman, "Prelude to the Fourteenth Amendment," 449; James F. Griffin, "Blacks in the St. Paul Police Department: An Eighty-Year Survey," *Minnesota History* 44, no. 7 (Fall 1975), 255. Golden, "Independent Development," 458.

139. Henry K. Peterson, "The First Decision Rendered by the Supreme Court of Iowa," *Annals of Iowa* 34, no. 4 (Spring 1958), 304–7; Connor, "Antislavery Movement in Iowa," part 2, 457–58; Berrier, "Negro Suffrage," 242–43; Finkelman, "Slavery, the 'More Perfect Union,'" 260, n. 39.

140. Finkelman, "Strange Career," 389–93; Barnes, "'Only a Moral Power,'" 12; David A. Gerber, "Education, Expediency, and Ideology: Race and Politics in the Desegregation of Ohio Public Schools in the Late 19th Century," *Journal of Ethnic Studies* 1, no. 1 (Fall 1973), 2. The 1829 statute also required that any school taxes collected from African Americans were to be used only "for the education of said black or mulatto persons." Finkelman, "Race, Slavery, and Law," 760. Finkelman explains that, by "exempting blacks from school taxes, the state in effect allowed blacks to finance their own schools with their own funds. Such schools were created in some parts of the state and could be organized around churches or other black institutions without any state supervision or intervention." Finkelman, "Race, Slavery, and Law," 761.

141. Woodson, "Negroes of Cincinnati," 7 (noting that by 1834 "many of the colored people were receiving systematic education"); Kabria Baumgartner, "Building the Future: White Women, Black Education, and Civic Inclusion in Antebellum Ohio," *Journal of the Early Republic* 37, no. 1 (Spring 2017), 123–24; Finkelman, "Race, Slavery, and Law," 749; Gerber, "Education, Expediency, and Ideology," 4 (by the 1850s this system was "catering to the needs of well over a thousand students and staffed by thirty Black teachers hired by Black administrators").

142. Sheeler, "Struggle of the Negro," 217; Baumgartner, "Building the Future," 129–34.

143. "The Negro in the Middle West," *Negro History Bulletin* 5, no. 8 (May 1942), 172, 189 (heaven); Gerber, *Black Ohio*, 13; Gerber, "Education, Expediency, and Ideology," 3, 15 (noting the "more tolerant racial atmosphere and the equalitarian traditions of the Western Reserve"); Finkelman, "Race, Slavery, and Law," 762.

144. Gerber, *Black Ohio*, 5; Finkelman, "Strange Career," 393; Sheeler, "Struggle of the Negro," 217; Finkelman, "Prelude to the Fourteenth Amendment," 469; Finkelman, "Almost a Free State," 16, n. 16; Finkelman, "Race, Slavery, and Law," 751; Leonard Erickson, "Toledo Desegregates, 1871," *Northwest Ohio Quarterly* 11 (1968), 8. See Kenneth L. Kusmer, *A Ghetto Takes Shape: Black Cleveland, 1870–1930* (Urbana: University of Illinois Press, 1976), 16–17.

145. Finkelman, "Strange Career," 377; Barnes, "'Only a Moral Power,'" 21; Finkelman, "Prelude to the Fourteenth Amendment," 469.

146. David Sandor, "'Black Is as Good a Color as White': The Harriet Beecher Stowe School and the Debate over Separate Schools in Cincinnati," *Ohio Valley History* 9, no. 2 (Summer 2009), 28; Nancy Bertaux and Michael Washington, "The 'Colored Schools' of Cincinnati and African American Community in Nineteenth-Century Cincinnati, 1849–1890," *Journal of Negro Education* 74, no. 1 (Winter 2005), 45; Gerber, "Education, Expediency, and Ideology," 4 (noting that "Black Cincinnatians had an unusual [for Ohio Blacks] opportunity to control their own educational affairs and to make their schools an object of community pride"). Peter Clark, the principal of the black high school, was a particularly prominent community leader. Gerber, "Education, Expediency, and Ideology," 4.

147. Finkelman, "Northwest Ordinance," 11.

148. Finkelman, "Strange Career," 390, 394; Finkelman, "Prelude to the Fourteenth Amendment," 470–71; Finkelman, "Legal Status of Free Blacks," 1555.

149. Gerber, "Education, Expediency, and Ideology," 3, 7; Katzman, *Black Ghetto*, 90, n. 19.

150. Erickson, "Toledo Desegregates, 1871," 10 (also noting that, "once the Board did act, there was no violent reaction to the ending of the educational color line," and that the "town did not seem to be particularly disturbed"). Blacks were also able to attend the Catholic schools in Toledo. Erickson, "Toledo Desegregates, 1871," 8.

151. Barnes, *Anti-Slavery Impulse*, 76. See also Lathardus Goggins, *Central State University: The First One Hundred Years, 1887–1987* (Kent, OH: Kent State University Press, 1988), and Adah Ward Randolph, "Building upon Cultural Capital: Thomas Jefferson Ferguson and the Albany Enterprise Academy in Southeast Ohio, 1863–1886," *Journal of African American History* 87 (Spring 2002), 182–95.

152. Gerber, "Education, Expediency, and Ideology," 3, 20–21. Gerber notes that many blacks opposed desegregation because of the loss of black teachers, black administrators, and freedom from harassment in white schools. Gerber, "Education, Expediency, and Ideology," 10–11, 15–16, 23.

153. Littlejohn, "Black before the Bar," 72; Katzman, *Black Ghetto*, 23; Moreno, "*Workman* Case," 9–10, 11 ("*Workman* confirmed the Court's antislavery and egalitarian disposition"); People ex rel. Joseph Workman v. The Board of Education of Detroit, 18 Mich. 400 (1869); William W. Stephenson Jr., "'For a True System of Free Schools Should Afford Equal Opportunities for All': Integration of the Detroit Public School System during the Period, 1839–1869," *Negro History Bulletin* 26, no. 1 (October 1962), 25; Thrun, "School Segregation in Michigan," 16–17.

154. Katzman, *Black Ghetto*, 16 (quotation); Miles, "'Shall Woman's Voice Be Hushed?'" 3; Glesner, "Laura Haviland," 28; Kestenbaum, "Modernizing Michigan," 123; Finkenbine, "Beacon of Liberty," 88.

155. Finkenbine, "Beacon of Liberty," 94; Finkelman, "Prelude to the Fourteenth Amendment," 428, 471, 474; Katzman, *Black Ghetto*, 35; Finkelman, "Legal Status of Free Blacks," 1555; Finkelman, "Hidden History," 385; Katzman, *Black Ghetto*, 50, 85.

156. Thrun, "School Segregation in Michigan," 8–10; Mitchell, "From Slavery to Shelley," 12; Katzman, *Black Ghetto*, 86.

157. People ex rel. Joseph Workman v. The Board of Education of Detroit, 18 Mich. 400 (1869); Littlejohn, "Black before the Bar," 72; Katzman, *Black Ghetto*, 23; Moreno, "*Workman* Case," 9–10, 11 ("*Workman* confirmed the Court's anti-slavery and egalitarian disposition"); Robin S. Peebles, "Fannie Richards and the Integration of the Detroit Public Schools," *Michigan History* 65, no. 1 (January/ February 1981), 30–31.

158. Schwieder, *Iowa*, 88; Arnie Cooper, "A Stony Road: Black Education in Iowa, 1838–1860," *Annals of Iowa* 48, no. 3 (Winter 1986), 120, 128 (youth); Frese, "From Emancipation to Equality," 84; Bergmann, "Negro in Iowa," 20.

159. Thomas A. Lucas, "Men Were Too Fiery for Much Talk: The Grinnell Anti-Abolitionist Riot of 1860," *Palimpsest* 68, no. 1 (1987), 14–20 (also explaining that a future addition of several adult black men who had escaped slavery caused much resistance in the town); George Mills, "The Crusade of John Brown," *Annals of Iowa* 35, no. 2 (Fall 1959), 103 (quotation).

160. Finkelman, "Prelude to the Fourteenth Amendment," 474; Cooper, "Stony Road," 129, 132.

161. Clark v. Board of Directors, 24 Iowa 266 (1968); Schwieder, *Iowa*, 85; Bergmann, "Negro in Iowa," 50; Paul Finkelman, "The Hidden History of Northern Civil Rights Law and the Villainous Supreme Court, 1875–1915," *University of Pittsburgh Law Review* 79 (2018), 373. The Court argued that African Americans could not be discriminated against just as schools could not "require the children of Irish parents to attend one school, and the children of German parents another; the children of catholic parents to attend one school, and the children of protestant parents another." Clark v. Board of Directors, at 275.

162. Wall, *Iowa*, 116; Dykstra, "Issue Squarely Met," 432.

163. Finkelman, "Hidden History," 374.

164. Frese, "From Emancipation to Equality," 85.

165. Finkelman, "Prelude to the Fourteenth Amendment," 463.

166. William J. Vollmar, "The Negro in a Midwest Frontier City: Milwaukee, 1835–70" (M.A. thesis, Marquette University, 1968), 24–25, 58.

167. Finkelman, "Prelude to the Fourteenth Amendment," 474.

168. McPherson, *Struggle for Equality*, 236; Arna Bontemps, "Rising," in Dolinar, *Negro in Illinois*, 61–62, 63 (good), 64. For a case of backsliding, see Shirley J. Portwood, "The Alton School Case and African American Community Consciousness, 1897–1908," *Illinois Historical Journal* 91, no. 1 (Spring 1998), 2–20.

169. James C. Carper, "The Popular Ideology of Segregated Schooling: Attitudes toward the Education of Blacks in Kansas, 1854–1900," *Kansas History* 1, no. 4 (Winter 1978), 255, 257, 262–63. For another case of backsliding, see David J. Peavler, "Drawing the Color Line in Kansas City: The Creation of Sumner High School," *Kansas History* 28, no. 3 (Autumn 2005), 190.

170. David J. Peavler Trowbridge, "'A Double Mixture': Equality and Economy in the Integration of Nebraska Schools, 1858–1883," *Nebraska History* 91, nos. 3–4 (Fall/Winter 2010), 138–39.

171. Trowbridge, "'Double Mixture,'" 143 (public), 144, 145, 147–50.

172. Finkelman, "Prelude to the Fourteenth Amendment," 478.

173. Gerber, *Black Ohio*, 8, 13; Finkelman, "Legal Status of Free Blacks," 1556.

174. Sheeler, "Struggle of the Negro," 215; William Cheek and Aimee Lee Cheek, *John Mercer Langston and the Fight for Black Freedom, 1829–65* (Urbana: University of Illinois Press, 1989). Langston is considered the first elected black official in the United States. Eric Foner, *Freedom's Lawmakers: A Directory of Black Officeholders during Reconstruction* (New York: Oxford University Press, 1996), 128. On Langston's brother, see Richard B. Sheridan, "Charles Henry Langston and the African American Struggle in Kansas," *Kansas History* 22, no. 4 (Winter 1999/2000), 268–83.

175. George Sinkler, "Race: Principles and Policy of Rutherford B. Hayes," *Ohio History Journal* 77, nos. 1–3 (Winter/Spring/Summer 1968), 149, 151 (brutal); Finkelman, "Prelude to the Fourteenth Amendment," 478; Finkelman, "Strange Career," 377.

176. Formisano, "Edge of Caste," 27; Finkelman, "Prelude to the Fourteenth Amendment," 478; Katzman, *Before the Ghetto*, 33, 35; Gerber, *Black Ohio*, 13; Finkelman, "Legal Status of Free Blacks," 1556.

177. In 1870, Michigan voters also passed amendments to the state constitution deleting the five times the word "white" was used, thus allowing black suffrage, service on juries and in the militia, and the holding of public office. Finkelman, "Hidden History," 387. "By 1871, well before the end of Reconstruction in the South, Michigan had integrated its schools and eliminated racial terminology in its constitution. Blacks were free to attend school with whites; black men could vote, serve in the militia, and be called for jury duty on the same basis as white men." Finkelman, "Hidden History," 388. In 1883, Michigan repeal its miscegenation law.

178. Green, "Minnesota's Long Road," 81.

179. Dykstra, "Issue Squarely Met," 444; Sage, *History of Iowa*, 174. The 1865 election "was fought largely on the sole issue of Negro suffrage," and the GOP prevailed. Berrier, "Negro Suffrage," 241.

180. Dykstra, "Issue Squarely Met," 444.

181. "Convention of Colored Soldiers," *Muscatine Journal*, November 18, 1865; Stephen J. Frese, "From Emancipation to Equality: Alexander Clark's Stand for Civil Rights in Iowa," *History Teacher* 40, no. 1 (November 2006), 83. On the regiment, see David Brodnax Sr., "'Will They Fight? Ask the Enemy': Iowa's African American Regiment in the Civil War," *Annals of Iowa* 66, no. 3 (Summer/Fall 2007), 266–92.

182. Berrier, "Negro Suffrage," 243–44, 257; Leslie H. Fishel Jr., "Northern Prejudice and Negro Suffrage, 1865–1870," *Journal of Negro History* 39, no. 1 (January 1954), 21–24.

183. Dykstra, *Bright Radical Star*, 227; Berrier, "Negro Suffrage," 258.

184. Wall, *Iowa*, 115; Sage, *History of Iowa*, 180.

185. "President Grant's Des Moines Address," 139.

186. Ron Chernow, *Grant* (New York: Penguin Press, 2017), xxii (concluding that Grant had the strongest record on racial equality of any president between Lincoln and LBJ). On President Garfield's racial progressivism, including his inaugural address in 1881, see Benjamin T. Arrington, *The Last Lincoln Republican: The Presidential Election of 1880* (Lawrence: University Press of Kansas, 2020), 31, 47, 145, 171.

187. Dykstra, "Issue Squarely Met," 432; Wall, *Iowa*, 115; Sage, *History of Iowa*, 181.

188. Vollmar, "Negro in a Midwest City," 2–3; Brown, "Making of the Wisconsin Constitution," part 1, 685; Frederic L. Paxson, "A Constitution of Democracy—Wisconsin, 1847," *Wisconsin Magazine of History* 2, no. 1 (June 1915), 14.

189. "Negro Suffrage and Woman's Rights in the Convention of 1846," *Wisconsin Magazine of History* 3, no. 2 (December 1919), 228; Bethel Saler, *The Settlers' Empire: Colonialism and State Formation in America's Old Northwest* (Philadelphia: University of Pennsylvania Press, 2015), 271; Brown, "Making of the Wisconsin Constitution," part 1, 687, and part 2, 44.

190. John Goadby Gregory, "Negro Suffrage in Wisconsin," *Transactions of the Wisconsin Academy of Sciences, Arts, and Letters* 11 (1896–97), 94–96. An earlier motion, which simply authorized the legislature to "admit colored persons to the right of suffrage," was defeated 35–34. Brown, "Making of the Wisconsin Constitution," part 2, 44; Fishel, "Wisconsin and Negro Suffrage," 184.

191. Gregory, "Negro Suffrage," 96 (provided), 97; Finkelman, "Prelude to the Fourteenth Amendment," 478; Brown, "Making of the Wisconsin Constitution," part 2, 44. Since this did not constitute a majority of all those voting, however, the measure was deemed to have failed. But later a GOP majority on the Wisconsin Supreme Court ruled that this was in error and that black suffrage was in fact the law. Gillespie v. Palmer, 20 Wis. 572 (1866); Gregory, "Negro Suffrage," 99–100; John O. Holzhueter, "Ezekiel Gillespie, Lost and Found," *Wisconsin Magazine of History* 60, no. 3 (Spring 1977), 178–84; Fishel, "Wisconsin and Negro Suffrage," 194–95; Current, "Politics of Reconstruction," 88. In the interim, two statewide votes on African American suffrage were held that failed 60 percent to 40 percent in 1857 and 54 percent to 46 percent in 1865. Gregory, "Negro Suffrage," 98.

192. Christy Clark-Pujara, "Contested: Black Suffrage in Early Wisconsin," *Wisconsin Magazine of History* 100, no. 4 (Summer 2017), 22–27. Between 1849 and 1866 there were other efforts to extend suffrage to African Americans. Fishel, "Wisconsin and Negro Suffrage," 185–88.

193. Green, "Minnesota's Long Road," 68–71, 71 (hegemony), 75 (disabilities), 71–81, 82 (defeated); Klement, "Abolition Movement in Minnesota," 15–33.

194. Dunbar and Shade, "Black Man Gains the Vote," 56 (consistency); Kenneth Stampp, *Era of Reconstruction*, 102 (idealism); Cox and Cox, "Negro Suffrage and Republican Politics," 313–14.

195. Current, "Politics of Reconstruction," 89; Michael Les Benedict, "Equality and Expediency in the Reconstruction Era," *Civil War History* 23, no. 4 (December 1977), 325, 331; Cox and Cox, "Negro Suffrage and Republican Politics," 319 (arguing that "Republican sponsorship of Negro suffrage meant flirtation with political disaster in the North").

196. Michael Les Benedict, "Racism and Equality in America," *Reviews in American History* 6, no. 1 (March 1978), 20, n. 3; Glenn M. Linden, "A Note on Negro Suffrage and Republican Politics," *Journal of Southern History* 36, no. 3 (August 1970), 419 (measures).

197. Robert R. Dykstra and Harland Hahn, "Northern Voters and Negro Suffrage: The Case of Iowa, 1868," *Public Opinion Quarterly* 32, no. 2 (Summer 1968), 203–5.

198. James M. McPherson, *The Struggle for Equality: Abolitionists and the Negro in the Civil War and Reconstruction* (Princeton, NJ: Princeton University Press, 1964), 424.

199. Silvana Siddali, "State Constitutions and the 15th Amendment: The Struggle for African American Constitutional Rights in the Northern Midwest," manuscript included in Jon K. Lauck and Gleaves Whitney, eds., "North Country: Essays on the Upper Midwestern Borderlands."

200. Dunbar and Shade, "Black Man Gains the Vote," 51, 54–55, 53 (noting that the referenda also abolished racial restrictions on militia service and apportionment).

201. Katzman, *Before the Ghetto*, 3–4, 176 (bard); Forrest G. Wood, *Black Scare: The Racist Response to Emancipation and Reconstruction* (Berkeley: University of California Press, 1968), 102 (Clemenceau).

202. David A. Jones, *From Slave to State Legislator: John W. E. Thomas, Illinois' First African American Lawmaker* (Carbondale: Southern Illinois University Press, 2012); Bridges, "Equality Deferred," 98; Gerber, "Education, Expediency, and Ideology," 16.

203. J. Clay Smith, "In the Shadow of *Plessy:* A Portrait of McCants Stewart, African-American Legal Pioneer," *Minnesota Law Review* 73 (1989), 500; Golden, "Independent Development," 461–62. Wheaton graduated from the University of Minnesota Law School in 1894, and McCants Stewart did in 1896. Stewart was in the Kent Debate Society, sheriff of the moot court, secretary of the senior class, and associate editor of the *Twin-City American*, a local black newspaper. When a Minneapolis restaurant would not serve McCants, several patrons who witnessed the event objected and testified for McCants when the Minneapolis city attorney's office prosecuted the restaurant owner for not serving him. A jury of twelve Minnesotans found the restaurant owner guilty. Smith, "In the Shadow of *Plessy*," 502. See also Paul D. Nelson, *Frederick L. McGhee: A Life on the Color Line, 1861–1912* (St. Paul: Minnesota Historical Society Press, 2002).

204. Christopher K. Hays, "The African American Struggle for Equality and Justice in Cairo, Illinois, 1865–1900," *Illinois Historical Journal* 90, no. 4 (Winter 1997), 274–75.

205. Bridges, "Equality Deferred," 98.

206. Katzman, *Black Ghetto*, 178.

207. Leslie H. Fishel Jr., "The Negro in Northern Politics, 1870–1900," *Mississippi Valley Historical Review* 42, no. 3 (December 1955), 472, 478, 480, 483; Gerber, "Education, Expediency, and Ideology," 17.

208. Percy E. Murray, "Harry C. Smith–Joseph B. Foraker Alliance: Coalition Politics in Ohio," *Journal of Negro History* 68, no. 2 (Spring 1983), 171–84.

209. Murray, "Harry C. Smith," 172; Robert Lionel Rowe, "State Response to the Civil Rights Issue, 1883–1885" (MA thesis, Portland State University, 1974), 27.

210. Finkelman, "Hidden History," 372–98 (focusing on jurisprudence in Iowa and Michigan).

211. Wallace F. Caldwell, "State Public Accommodations Laws, Fundamental Liberties and Enforcement Programs," *Washington Law Review* 40, no. 4 (1965), 843.

212. Middleton, *Black Laws*, 254, 260; Rowe, "State Response," 38–57. The burst of civil rights laws passed in the Midwest in the mid-1880s followed from

the U.S. Supreme Court striking down the national civil rights law passed during Reconstruction. Southern states did not pass state civil rights bills. U.S. v. Stanley, 109 U.S. 3 (1883); Rowe, "State Response," 25.

213. Schwieder, *Iowa*, 89 (refreshments, progressive); Rowe, "State Response," 112 (noting that "Iowa had long had a good reputation in civil rights matters").

214. Coger v. The North West, 37 Iowa 146 (1873), 153–54 (injustice, wickedness, oppression), 158 (prejudice); Finkelman, "Hidden History," 375; Dykstra, "Issue Squarely Met," 432.

215. On the Illinois law, see Elizabeth Dale, "'Social Equality Does Not Exist among Themselves, Nor among Us': Baylies vs. *Curry* and Civil Rights in Chicago, 1888," *Journal of American History* 102, no. 2 (April 1997), 313 (describing the "hopes for equality and integration" in late nineteenth-century Chicago); Gerber, *Black Ohio*, 47 (finding that "by the 1870s discrimination on trains and streetcars was a thing of the past in Ohio"); Thrun, "School Segregation in Michigan," 10–11 (full); Mitchell, "From Slavery to Shelley," 13; Rowe, "State Response," 80–81, 104, 112–19; Golden, "Independent Development," 456–57. Rowe found that Minnesota, Michigan, Iowa, and Nebraska "passed civil rights legislation with little apparent controversy, opposition, or even interest" and that the "lack of controversy may have been due to a general acceptance of the idea of integrated facilities." Rowe, "State Response," 118.

216. Mitchell, "From Slavery to Shelley," 13; Katzman, *Black Ghetto*, 91; Finkelman, "Hidden History," 389; Peter Wallenstein, *Tell the Court I Love My Wife: Race, Marriage, and Law—An American History* (New York: Palgrave Macmillan, 2002), 110–14.

217. Katzman, *Black Ghetto*, 91; Ferguson v. Gies, 82 Michigan 359, 366 (1890) (absolute, cater), 721 (humane).

218. Leslie H. Fishel Jr., "The Genesis of the First Wisconsin Civil Rights Act," *Wisconsin Magazine of History* 49, no. 4 (Summer 1966), 332. Fishel also noted "Wisconsin's outstanding record in the field of human rights." Fishel, "Wisconsin's First Civil Rights Act: A Research Query," *Wisconsin Magazine of History* 45, no. 3 (Spring 1962), 158.

219. Dale, "'Social Equality Does Not Exist among Themselves,'" 313; Valeria W. Weaver, "The Failure of Civil Rights, 1875–1883, and Its Repercussions," *Journal of Negro History* 54, no. 4 (October 1969), 370–71.

220. Finkelman, "Prelude to the Fourteenth Amendment," 442 (suggest), 443 (continuous), 446, 421.

221. See Stephen A. Vincent, *Southern Seed, Northern Soil: African-American Farm Communities in the Midwest, 1765–1900* (Bloomington: Indiana University Press, 1999).

222. Anna-Lisa Cox, *The Bone and Sinew of the Land: America's Forgotten Black Pioneers and the Struggle for Equality* (New York: PublicAffairs, 2018), 4. Cox maps 338 rural black settlements in the Midwest.

223. Woodson, "Negroes of Cincinnati," 8.

224. Middleton, *Black Laws*, 90. See also Jill E. Rowe, "Mixing It Up: Early African American Settlements in Northwestern Ohio," *Journal of Black Studies* 39, no. 6 (July 2009), 928–32.

225. Paul A. Schackel, "Remembering New Philadelphia," *Historical Archaeology* 44, no. 1 (2010), 7; Juliet E. K. Walker, *Free Frank: A Black Pioneer on the Antebellum Frontier* (Lexington: University Press of Kentucky, 1983). See also Sundiata Keita Cha-Jua, *America's First Black Town: Brooklyn, Illinois, 1830–1915* (Urbana: University of Illinois Press, 2000), and Dennis A. Buck, *From Slavery to Glory: African Americans Come to Aurora, Illinois 1850–1920* (Aurora, IL: Aurora Historical Society, 2005).

226. Lucas and Bontemps, "First, the French," 4.

227. Katzman, *Black Ghetto*, 13 (quotation); Finkelman, "Legal Status of Free Blacks," 1556 (noting that blacks in Cass County voted in elections); Roma Jones Stewart, "The Migration of Free People: Cass County's Black Settlers from North Carolina," *Michigan History* 71, no. 1 (January 1987), 34–38.

228. Littlejohn, "Black before the Bar," 50, n. 76.

229. Anna-Lisa Cox, "A Pocket of Freedom: Blacks in Covert, Michigan, in the Nineteenth Century," *Michigan Historical Review* 21, no. 1 (1995): 1–18; Anna-Lisa Cox, *A Stronger Kinship: One Town's Extraordinary Story of Hope and Faith* (Lincoln: University of Nebraska Press, 2006); James E. DeVries, *Race and Kinship in a Midwestern Town: The Black Experience in Monroe, Michigan, 1900–1915* (Urbana: University of Illinois Press, 1984).

230. Dorothy Schwieder, Joseph Hraba, and Elmer Schwieder, *Buxton: A Black Utopia in the Heartland* (Iowa City: University of Iowa Press, 2003); Richard M. Breaux, "'We Were All Mixed Together': Race, Schooling, and the Legacy of Black Teachers in Buxton, 1900–1920," *Annals of Iowa* 65, no. 4 (Fall 2006), 301–28; J. A. Swisher, "The Rise and Fall of Buxton," *Palimpsest* 26, no. 6 (June 1945), 179–92; Edward Pluth, "A 'Negro Colony' for Todd County," *Minnesota History* 61, no. 7 (Fall 2009), 312–24. On Wisconsin, see Jennifer Kirsten Stinson, "Becoming Black, White, and Indian in Wisconsin Farm Country, 1850s-1910s," *Middle West Review* 2, no. 2 (Spring 2016), 53–54.

231. Robert G. Athearn, *In Search of Canaan: Black Migration to Kansas, 1879–1880* (Lawrence: Regents Press of Kansas, 1978); Anne P. W. Hawkins, "Hoeing Their Own Row: Black Agriculture and the Agrarian Ideal in Kansas, 1880–1920," *Kansas History* 22, no. 3 (Autumn 1999), 200–213; Katie H. Armitage, "'Seeking a Home Where He Himself Is Free': African Americans Build a Community in Douglas County, Kansas," *Kansas History* 31, no. 3 (Autumn 2008), 154–75; Claire O'Brien, "'With One Mighty Pull': Interracial Town Boosting in Nicodemus, Kansas," *Great Plains Quarterly* 16, no. 2 (Spring 1996), 117–29; Charlotte Hinger, "'The Colored People Hold the Key': Abram Thompson Hall, Jr.'s Campaign to Organize Graham County," *Kansas History* 31, no. 1 (Spring 2008), 32–47; Charlotte Hinger, *Nicodemus: Post-Reconstruction Politics and Racial Justice in Western Kansas* (Norman: University of Oklahoma Press, 2016); Rusty Monhollon and Kristen Tegtmeier Oertel, "From Brown to Brown: A Century of Struggle for Equality in Kansas," *Kansas History* 27, nos. 1–2 (Spring/Summer 2004), 122–23.

232. Nell Irvin Painter, *Exodusters: Black Migration to Kansas after Reconstruction* (New York: W. W. Norton, 1976), 123. For another reminder of the sharp distinctions between the South and the Midwest, see Clarence Lang, "Locating the Civil Rights Movement: An Essay on the Deep South, Midwest, and Border South

in Black Freedom Studies," *Journal of Social History* 47, no. 2 (December 2013), 371–400.

233. Patrick Kennedy, "Nemaha County's African American Community," *Nebraska History* 82, no. 1 (Spring 2001), 11–25; Darold D. Wax, "Robert Ball Anderson, Ex-Slave, a Pioneer in Western Nebraska," *Nebraska History* 64, no. 2 (Summer 1983), 163–92.

234. Gerber, "Education, Expediency, and Ideology," 13 (quotation); James H. Madison, "Is There a Black Heartland? Questions of Place and Race in Midwestern History," in Gerald Early, ed., *Black Heartland: African American Life, the Middle West, and the Meaning of American Regionalism* (St. Louis, MO: Washington University, African and Afro-American Studies Program, 1997), 56; Jack S. Blocker Jr., "Building Networks: Cooperation and Communication among African Americans in the Urban Midwest, 1860–1910," *Indiana Magazine of History* 99, no. 4 (December 2003), 372–74 (on black churches); Gerber, *Black Ohio*, 20–21. See generally Cashin, "Black Families in the Old Northwest," 458; August Meier, *Negro Thought in America, 1880–1915* (Ann Arbor: University of Michigan Press, 1966), 165–66; and Kevin K. Gaines, *Uplifting the Race: Black Leadership, Politics, and Culture in the Twentieth Century* (Chapel Hill: University of North Carolina Press, 1996), 1–2.

235. Ann Clymer Bigelow, "Antebellum Ohio's Black Barbers in the Political Vanguard," *Ohio Valley History* 11, no. 2 (Summer 2011), 26; Gerber, *Black Ohio*, 22 (explaining black convention advocacy of "moral uplift through temperance, hard work, and religiosity"). The National Convention of Black Freemen held in Cleveland in 1848 was made up of mostly "self-made men" from the Midwest who were "printers, carpenters, blacksmiths, clergymen, barbers, grocers, tailors, editors, dentists, engineers, painters, and so on." Charles A. Gilozzo, "John Jones and the Black Convention Movement, 1848–1856," *Journal of Black Studies* 3, no. 2 (December 1972), 228. See also Paul Nelson, "National Afro-American Council Meeting, 1902," *MNOpedia*, April 10, 2014 (describing the St. Paul meeting of 1902 organized by Frederick McGhee).

236. Gerber, "Education, Expediency, and Ideology," 13; Finkelman, "Prelude to the Fourteenth Amendment," 477; Kusmer, *Ghetto Takes Shape*, 22 (noting that by 1850 24 percent of blacks in Cleveland owned real estate).

237. Woodson, "Negroes of Cincinnati," 8–12; Richard W. Pih, "Negro Self-Improvement Efforts in Ante-Bellum Cincinnati, 1836–1850," *Ohio History* 78, no. 3 (Summer 1969), 182–84 (on economic advances), 185 (noting the "several general uplift programs supported by black clergymen" and the Moral Reform Society of the Colored Citizens of Ohio, which called for the "suppression of intemperance, licentiousness, gambling, Sabbath-breaking, blasphemy, and all other vices").

238. Katzman, *Black Ghetto*, 18–19, 146 (overchurched), 153, 22 (lives).

239. Katzman, *Black Ghetto*, 32, 33 (indolence, wage). When rendering his decision in Workman v. Board of Education, Justice Thomas McIntyre Cooley emphasized the importance of integrated schools because integration could "level social distinctions and provide upward social mobility." Moreno, *"Workman* Case," 11 (quotation); Paul D. Carrington, "Deference to Democracy: Thomas Cooley and His Barnstorming Court," in Finkelman and Hershock, *History of Michigan Law*, 110–111.

240. Frese, "From Emancipation to Equality," 83.

241. Randall B. Woods, "After the Exodus: John Lewis Waller and the Black Elite, 1878–1900," *Kansas Historical Quarterly* 43, no. 2 (Summer 1977), 172. See also Philip R. Beard, "The Kansas Colored Literary and Business Academy: A White Effort at African American Education in Late-Nineteenth-Century Kansas," *Kansas History* 24, no. 3 (Autumn 2001), 200–217.

242. Christopher Robert Reed, *Knock at the Door of Opportunity: Black Migration to Chicago, 1900–1919* (Carbondale: Southern Illinois University Press, 2014) (emphasizing black economic achievements and striving); Robert E. Weems Jr., *The Merchant Prince of Black Chicago: Anthony Overton and the Building of a Financial Empire* (Urbana: University of Illinois Press, 2020). In addition to economic achievements, there were artistic advances. See Richard A. Courage and Christopher Robert Reed, eds., *Roots of the Black Chicago Renaissance: New Negro Writers, Artists, and Intellectuals, 1893–1930* (Urbana: University of Illinois Press, 2020). For criticism of deviation from middle-class norms, see Davarian L. Baldwin, *Chicago's New Negroes: Modernity, the Great Migration, and Black Urban Life* (Chapel Hill: University of North Carolina Press, 2007), 25–27.

243. Katzman, *Black Ghetto*, 147, 150. See also Blocker, "Building Networks," 374 (noting the forty-six black Mason halls in Ohio by 1900), and Gerber, *Black Ohio*, 20 (mentioning Xenia's Colored United Association, Columbus's Sons of Protection, and Cincinnati's Sons of Liberty and United Colored Association in Ohio).

244. Golden, "Independent Development," 458–59.

245. Bergmann, "Negro in Iowa," 49.

246. Dennis N. Mihelich, "The Origins of the Prince Hall Mason Grand Lodge of Nebraska," *Nebraska History* 76, no. 1 (Spring 1995), 10–21; Dennis N. Mihelich, "World War I, the Great Migration, and the Formation of the Grand Bodies of Prince Hall Masonry," *Nebraska History* 78, no. 1 (Spring 1997), 28–39; Blocker, "Building Networks," 374; Gerber, *Black Ohio*, 21. See also Jennifer Hildebrand, "The New Negro Movement in Lincoln, Nebraska," *Nebraska History* 91, nos. 3–4 (Fall/Winter 2010), 166–89.

247. Furnish, "Black Hoosiers," 6.

248. Arna Bontemps, "Social Life and Social Uplift," in Dolinar, *Negro in Illinois*, 165–66.

249. Katzman, *Black Ghetto*, 154; Knupfer, *Toward a Tenderer Humanity and a Nobler Womanhood: African American Women's Clubs in Turn-of-the-Century Chicago* (New York: New York University Press, 1996); Wanda A. Hendricks, *Gender, Race, and Politics in the Midwest: Black Club Women in Illinois* (Bloomington: Indiana University Press, 1998).

250. Katzman, *Black Ghetto*, 156.

251. Blocker, "Building Networks," 375; Nell Irvin Painter, "Martin R. Delany: Elitism and Black Nationalism," in Leon Litwack and August Meier, eds., *Black Leaders of the Nineteenth Century* (Urbana: University of Illinois Press, 1988), 149–71.

252. Golden, "Independent Development," 459 (encourage); David V. Taylor, "John Quincy Adams: St. Paul Editor and Black Leader," *Minnesota History* 43, no. 8 (Winter 1973), 288 (lessen), 283 (literate).

253. Taylor, "John Quincy Adams," 285, 288 (influential), 289 (fulcrum). Taylor views Adams as a "nominal 'Bookerite,'" that is, a supporter of the views of Booker T. Washington but also willing to seek political advances via various organizations. Taylor, "John Quincy Adams," 296.

254. Taylor, "John Quincy Adams," 283 (advancement), 284, 287; Blocker, "Building Networks," 381, 383; Michael Fultz, "'The Morning Cometh': African-American Periodicals, Education, and the Black Middle Class, 1900–1930,"*Journal of Negro History* 80, no. 3 (Summer 1995), 98 (explaining that black periodicals "forcefully advocated themes of self-help, character-building, social uplift, and race patronage and solidarity"). See also Henry G. LaBrie III, "James B. Morris Sr. and the *Iowa Bystander*," *Annals of Iowa* 42, no. 4 (Spring 1974), 314–22; Arnold Cooper, "'Protection to All, Discrimination to None': The *Parsons Weekly Blade*, 1892–1900," *Kansas History* 9, no. 2 (Summer 1986), 58–71; A. Gilbert Belles, "The Black Press in Illinois," *Journal of the Illinois State Historical Society* 68, no. 4 (September 1975), 344–52; Emma Lou Thornbrough, "American Negro Newspapers, 1880–1914," *Business History Review* 40, no. 4 (Winter 1966), 467–90.

255. Blocker, "Building Networks," 383 (nexus); Gerber, "Education, Expediency, and Ideology," 7 (assimilation); Allan H. Spear, *Black Chicago: The Making of a Negro Ghetto, 1890–1920* (Chicago: University of Chicago Press, 1967), 53–54.

256. Sundiata Keita Cha-Jua, "'The Cry of the Negro Should Not Be Remember the Maine, but Remember the Hanging of Bush': African American Responses to Lynching in Decatur, Illinois, 1893," in Pfeifer, *Lynching beyond Dixie*, 165–89; James L. Crouthamel, "The Springfield Race Riot of 1908," *Journal of Negro History* 45, no. 3 (July 1960), 164–81; Roberta Senechal, *The Sociogenesis of a Race Riot: Springfield, Illinois, in 1908* (Urbana: University of Illinois Press, 1990); Jack S. Blocker, "Race, Sex, and Riot: The Springfield, Ohio Race Riots of 1904 and 1906," in Pfeifer, *Lynching beyond Dixie*, 190–210; Felix L. Armfield, "Fire on the Prairies: The 1895 Spring Valley Race Riot," *Journal of Illinois History* 3, no. 3 (Autumn 2000), 185–200; Charles L. Lumpkins, *American Pogrom: The East St. Louis Race Riot and Black Politics* (Athens: Ohio University Press, 2008); "The Riot in Akron," *New York Times*, August 24, 1900; Orville D. Menard, "Lest We Forget: The Lynching of Will Brown, Omaha's 1919 Race Riot," *Nebraska History* 91, nos. 3–4 (Fall/Winter 2010), 152–64; Christopher P. Lehman, "Black Cloud: The Struggles of St. Cloud's African American Community, 1880–1920," *Minnesota History* 66, no. 6 (Summer 2019), 234–43. But see Gerber, *Black Ohio*, 15 (finding violence to be the "exception" and "little white resistance" to black settlements).

257. Gerber, *Black Ohio*, 10 (concluding that the "further one moved toward the banks of the Ohio, the more strictly were law and custom invoked to depress the Negro's status"); Brent M. S. Campney, *Hostile Heartland: Racism, Repression, and Resistance in the Midwest* (Urbana: University of Illinois Press, 2019).

258. See Phillips, *Rivers Ran Backward*; Emma Lou Thornbrough, "The Race Issue in Indiana Politics during the Civil War," *Indiana Magazine of History* 47, no. 2 (June 1951), 165–88; Thomas H. Smith, "Crawford County: A Study in Midwestern Copperheadism," *Ohio History Journal* 76, nos. 1–2 (Winter/Spring 1967), 33–53; Jacque Voegeli, "The Northwest and the Race Issue, 1861–1862," *Mississippi Valley Historical Review* 50, no. 2 (September 1963), 235–51.

259. John C. Schneider, "Detroit and the Problem of Disorder: The Riot of 1863," *Michigan History* 58 (Spring 1974), 5–24. See also John W. Oliver, "Draft Riots in Wisconsin during the Civil War," *Wisconsin Magazine of History* 2, no. 3 (March 1919), 334–37. One historian concluded that the 1863 race riot in Detroit "was the only major riot in the Midwest" during the war but noted some smaller incidents in St. Paul, Toledo, and Cincinnati. Katzman, *Black Ghetto*, 44. On the larger and more famous riots of New York City, see Adrian Cook, *The Armies of the Streets: The New York City Draft Riots of 1863* (Lexington: University Press of Kentucky, 1974).

260. Finkelman, "Prelude to the Fourteenth Amendment," 417.

CHAPTER 5

1. Moe, *Last Full Measure*.

2. Igantius Donnelly, *A Tribute to Abraham Lincoln*, 5 (no date, no publisher), cited in Martin Ridge, "Ignatius Donnelly: Minnesota Congressman, 1863–69," *Minnesota History* 36, no. 5 (March 1959), 174.

3. John D. Hicks, "The Birth of the Populist Party," *Minnesota History* 9, no. 3 (September 1928), 235.

4. See chapter 1.

5. William D. Barnes, "Oliver Hudson Kelley and the Genesis of the Grange: A Reappraisal," *Agricultural History* 41, no. 3 (July 1967), 229; Nye, *Midwestern Progressive Politics*, 45. Kelley discovered the term "Grange," an "archaic term for barn or granary," in *Webster's Unabridged*. Charles Postel, *Equality: An American Dilemma, 1866–1896* (New York: Farrar, Straus and Giroux, 2019), 40.

6. D. Sven Nordin, *Rich Harvest: A History of the Grange, 1867–1900* (Jackson: University Press of Mississippi, 1974).

7. Elizabeth Sanders, "The Midwest and Reform," manuscript submitted to Oxford University Press for inclusion in Lauck, "The Oxford Handbook of Mid-western History." On farmers and reform, see Elizabeth Sanders, *Roots of Reform: Farmers, Workers, and the American State, 1877–1917* (Chicago: University of Chicago Press, 1999).

8. Postel, *Equality*, 12 (largest), 19, 35; Nye, *Midwestern Progressive Politics*, 45–47, 69; Sanders, "Midwest and Reform," ___.

9. Nye, *Midwestern Progressive Politics*, 47 (desirable), 10; George H. Miller, *Railroads and the Granger Laws* (Madison: University of Wisconsin Press, 1971), 3–4 (explaining that Illinois, Iowa, Minnesota, and Wisconsin were the first states to address the railroad issue after the Civil War).

10. Herbert Hovenkamp, "Regulatory Conflict in the Gilded Age: Federalism and the Railroad Problem," *Yale Law Journal* 97, no. 6 (1988), 1057 (noting the issue of "price gouging on short hauls"); Postel, *Equality*, 61; Nye, *Midwestern Progressive Politics*, 38.

11. Sanders, "Midwest and Reform," ___.

12. William G. Ferris, "The Disgrace of Ira Munn," *Journal of the Illinois State Historical Society* 68, no. 3 (June 1975), 202; Nye, *Midwestern Progressive Politics*, 50; Postel, *Equality*, 65. See also Roy V. Scott, *The Agrarian Movement in Illinois, 1880–1896* (Urbana: University of Illinois Press, 1962).

13. John D. Hicks and John D. Barnhart, "The Farmers Alliance," *Mississippi Valley Historical Review* 6, no. 3 (July 1929), 260; Louis Bernard Schmidt, "The Farmers' Alliance," *Palimpsest* 31, no. 4 (April 1950), 137; Nye, *Midwestern Progressive Politics*, 51.

14. Robert S. Hunt, *Law and Locomotives: The Impact of the Railroad on Wisconsin Law in the Nineteenth Century* (Madison: State Historical Society of Wisconsin, 1958); Robert T. Daland, "Enactment of the Potter Law," *Wisconsin Magazine of History* 33, no. 1 (September 1949), 45–54; Stanley Caine, "Why Railroads Supported Regulation: The Case of Wisconsin, 1905–1910," *Business History Review* 44, no. 2 (Summer 1970), 179; Solon Justus Buck, *The Granger Movement: A Study of Agricultural Organization and Its Political, Economic, and Social Manifestations, 1870–1880* (Cambridge, MA: Harvard University Press, 1913), 183–84.

15. William L. Burton, "Wisconsin's First Railroad Commission: A Case Study in Apostasy," *Wisconsin Magazine of History* 45, no. 3 (Spring 1962), 191, 194.

16. Burton, 190 (attention); Nye, *Midwestern Progressive Politics*, 50.

17. F. Dumont Smith, "Decisive Battles of Constitutional Law: The Granger Cases," *American Bar Association Journal* 10, no. 5 (May 1924), 343 (Anglo-Saxon); Postel, *Equality*, 67; Munn v. Illinois, 94 U.S. 113 (1877).

18. *Nation*, January 22, 1874.

19. Nye, *Midwestern Progressive Politics*, 48.

20. Postel, *Equality*, 23; Nye, *Midwestern Progressive Politics*, 53–54; H. Roger Grant, *Self-Help in the 1890s Depression* (Ames: Iowa State University Press, 1983), 59–73; Larry Remele, "'God Helps Those Who Help Themselves': The Farmers Alliance and Dakota Statehood," *Montana: The Magazine of Western History* 37, no. 4 (Autumn 1987), 24.

21. Barns, "Oliver Hudson Kelley," 242; Roy V. Scott, "Milton George and the Farmers' Alliance Movement," *Mississippi Valley Historical Review* 45, no. 1 (June 1958), 104; Schmidt, "Farmers' Alliance," 136; Postel, *Equality*, 58. In a related reform, several labor exchanges were organized in Missouri and in cities such as Cincinnati, Toledo, and Akron. Grant, *Self-Help*, 47–52; Hicks and Barnhart, "Farmers Alliance," 269–70; Frank G. Swoboda, "Agricultural Cooperation in Wisconsin," *Wisconsin Magazine of History* 10, no. 2 (December 1926), 164–69.

22. Nye, *Midwestern Progressive Politics*, 42 (italics added).

23. Hofstadter, *Age of Reform*, 83, 85 (noting the power of comparisons between American democracy and autocratic Russia and fears of English interference in American affairs), 87.

24. Hicks and Barnhart, "Farmers Alliance," 256.

25. Nye, *Midwestern Progressive Politics*, 17–19, 36–39, 30 (old-style). See also Steven L. Piott, *The Anti-Monopoly Persuasion: Popular Resistance to the Rise of Big Business in the Midwest* (Westport, CT: Greenwood Press, 1985).

26. See generally Gretchen Ritter, *Goldbugs and Greenbacks: The Antimonopoly Tradition and the Politics of Finance in America, 1865–1896* (Cambridge: Cambridge University Press, 1997), and Walter T. K. Nugent, *The Money Question during Reconstruction* (New York: W. W. Norton, 1967).

27. Nicolas Barreyre, "The Politics of Economic Crises: The Panic of 1873, the End of Reconstruction, and the Realignment of American Politics," *Journal of the*

Gilded Age and Progressive Era 10, no. 4 (October 2011), 411, 412 (explaining that the "Midwest was identified as soft-money, and the Northeast as hard-money"); Jeffrey A. Frieden, *Currency Politics: The Political Economy of Exchange Rate Policy* (Princeton, NJ: Princeton University Press, 2015), 50. One contemporary account accurately noted that the "East, which is the chief object of Western and Southern hostility, includes the New England and Middle states, with New York as a centre." Frederick Emory Holmes, "The New Sectionalism," *Quarterly Journal of Economics* 10, no. 3 (April 1896), 269.

28. Irwin Unger, *The Greenback Era: The Social and Political History of American Finance, 1865–1879* (Princeton, NJ: Princeton University Press, 1964), 210.

29. Barreyre, "Politics of Economic Crises," 413–15. A prominent plan to redeem war bonds with paper money was also known as the "Ohio Idea." Barreyre, "Politics of Economic Crises," 412.

30. Nye, *Midwestern Progressive Politics*, 58; Richard M. Doolen, "'Brick' Pomeroy and the Greenback Clubs," *Journal of the Illinois State Historical Society* 65, no. 4 (Winter 1972), 434 (noting the "group of currency-reform editors in the Midwest that included Ignatius Donnelly of the St. Paul *Anti-Monopolist;* Thomas Buchanan of the *Indianapolis Sun;* and Robert Schilling of the Cleveland *Labor Advance*," along with Mark Pomeroy of Chicago). See also John D. Macoll, "Ezra A. Olleman: The Forgotten Man of Greenbackism, 1873–1876," *Indiana Magazine of History* 65, no. 3 (September 1969), 173–96. The People's Party's permanent national chairman, Herman Taubeneck, was from Illinois. Hofstadter, *Age of Reform*, 105. See also Jeannette P. Nichols, "Bryan's Benefactor: Coin Harvey and His World," *Ohio History Journal* 67, no. 4 (October 1958), 299–325.

31. Sanders, "Midwest and Reform," __.

32. Thomas Burnell Colbert, "Political Fusion in Iowa: The Election of James B. Weaver to Congress in 1878," *Arizona and the West* 20, no. 1 (Spring 1978), 25–27; Nye, *Midwestern Progressive Politics*, 58.

33. Scott, "Milton George," 90, 95–96, 98; Hicks and Barnhart, "Farmers Alliance," 255–58; Nye, *Midwestern Progressive Politics*, 58.

34. Robert A. McGuire, "Economic Causes of Late-Nineteenth Century Agrarian Unrest: New Evidence," *Journal of Economic History* 41, no. 4 (December 1981), 841; Nye, *Midwestern Progressive Politics*, 58; Joe Creech, *Righteous Indignation: Religion and the Populist Revolution* (Urbana: University of Illinois Press, 2006), 68–91.

35. Scott, "Milton George," 93–94, 96, 102, 105–9; Hicks and Barnhart, "Farmers Alliance," 259; Hicks, "Birth of the Populist Party," 225 (shoot), 244–45; Nye, *Midwestern Progressive Politics*, 76. Previous conventions included St. Louis in 1889, Ocala in 1890, Cincinnati and Indianapolis in 1891, Omaha and St. Louis and then Omaha in 1892.

36. Herman Clarence Nixon, "The Cleavage within the Farmers' Alliance Movement," *Mississippi Valley Historical Review* 15, no. 1 (June 1928), 22, 31; Hicks, "Birth of the Populist Party," 220–21, 224. For the sake of clarity in an area where titles are confusing, the Northern or Northwestern Alliance was formally known as the National Farmers' Alliance, and the Southern Alliance was known as the

National Farmers' Alliance and Industrial Union. Hicks and Barnhart, "Farmers Alliance," 255.

37. Hicks and Barnhart, "Farmers Alliance," 261–64, 266, 270; Nixon, "Cleavage within the Farmers' Alliance," 23; Hicks, "Birth of the Populist Party," 221; Nye, *Midwestern Progressive Politics*, 76. In a related regional schism, northern Populists supported women's suffrage and southern Populists did not. Gene Clanton, *Populism: The Humane Preference in America, 1890–1900* (Boston: Twayne, 1991), 141.

38. Nixon, "Cleavage within the Farmers' Alliance," 23; Scott, "Milton George," 107 (explaining that the leader of the Texas Alliance and a key organizer of the Southern Alliance, Charles W. Macune, said that merging with the Northern Alliance was not possible because it admitted blacks, and that Milton George agreed to pay the printing costs of the Colored Farmers' Alliance and Co-operative Union); Hicks, "Birth of the Populist Party," 221 (explaining that the "Southern Alliance drew the color line sharply, while the Northern Alliance ignored it"); Hicks and Barnhart, "Farmers Alliance," 264 (noting that in the Northern Alliance "colored persons were eligible to membership—a condition of affairs unthinkable in the South"). The 1888 GOP platform had promised to take action to improve the fairness of southern elections. Richard E. Welch Jr., "The Federal Elections Bill of 1890: Postscripts and Prelude," *Mississippi Valley Historical Review* 52, no. 3 (December 1965), 512–13. The 1890 elections bill passed the U.S. House entirely along party lines (Republicans in favor, Democrats opposed) and then was blocked in the Senate by a Democratic filibuster. Senator Spooner of Wisconsin "launched into a bloody-shirt tirade" against southern opposition, denouncing the race problem and unfair elections in Mississippi and other southern states. Thomas Adams Upchurch, *Legislating Racism: The Billion Dollar Congress and the Birth of Jim Crow* (Lexington: University Press of Kentucky, 2004), 153. See also Charles W. Calhoun, "Civil Religion and the Gilded Age Presidency: The Case of Benjamin Harrison," *Presidential Studies Quarterly* 23, no. 4 (Fall 1993), 658 (noting that GOP president Harrison considered the defeat of elections bill the "chief failure of his administration").

39. Nixon, "Cleavage within the Farmers' Alliance," 22–23; Hicks, "Birth of the Populist Party," 221; Hicks and Barnhart, "Farmers Alliance," 272 (noting that during the negotiations with the Southern Alliance the midwesterners "objected to the exclusion of negroes from membership"). Some non-Alliance midwestern publications also criticized the milder Northern Alliance for supporting what they considered unworkable schemes. Scott, "Milton George," 99–100.

40. Hicks and Barnhart, "Farmers Alliance," 274 (continuing, rebel).

41. Nixon, "Cleavage within the Farmers' Alliance," 24–25, 26 (fought), 26 n. 26 (explaining that "compound lard" was a term used to describe lard that combined vegetable oil, beef products, and hog lard as opposed to "pure hog lard"), 27–31, 33 (heart, agrarians, hinterland); Scott, "Milton George," 109; Hicks and Barnhart, "Farmers Alliance," 279.

42. Schmidt, "Farmers' Alliance," 138; Nye, *Midwestern Progressive Politics*, 65–66; Lauck, *Prairie Republic*; John Howard Brown, "The 'Railroad Problem' and the Interstate Commerce Act," *Review of Industrial Organization* 43, nos. 1–2

(August/September 2013), 10; Paul D. Carrington, "Law and Economics in the Creation of Federal Administrative Law: Thomas Cooley, Elder to the Republic," *Iowa Law Review* 83 (1998), 371–75.

43. Hans B. Thorelli, *The Federal Antitrust Policy: Origination of an American Tradition* (Baltimore, MD: Johns Hopkins University Press, 1955), 58–60; Herbert Hovenkamp, "Antitrust Policy after Chicago," *Michigan Law Review* 84, no. 2 (November 1985), 249–50; Robert H. Lande, "Wealth Transfers as the Original and Primary Concern of Anti-Trust: The Efficiency Interpretation Challenged," *Hastings Law Journal* 34 (1982), 82–83, 93–101; William Kolasky, "Senator John Sherman and the Origin of Antitrust," *Antitrust* 24, no. 1 (Fall 2009), 87. On the important but "largely ignored" life of Senator Sherman, see Gerald D. Nash, review of Nugent, *Money Question*, in *Civil War History* 14, no. 3 (September 1968), 274. Sherman was also a moderate on the currency question, leaning toward the soft-money midwestern farm interests, and would support silver in the form of the Sherman Silver Purchase Act. Unger, *Greenback Era*, 322–73.

44. Lande, "Wealth Transfers," 99, n. 136. The first use of the Sherman Act against railroads was the Northern Securities case, which broke up a trust governing three midwestern railroads: the Northern Pacific, the Great Northern, and the Chicago Burlington & Quincy. Simon Cordery, *The Iron Road in the Prairie State: The Story of Illinois Railroading* (Bloomington: Indiana University Press, 2016), 132.

45. Hofstadter, *Age of Reform*, 93 (genial); Stanley Solvick, "William Howard Taft and Cannonism," *Wisconsin Magazine of History* 48, no. 1 (Autumn 1964), 48 (mild).

46. Howe, *What Hath God Wrought*, 226; William H. Bergmann, "Delivering a Nation through the Mail: The Post Office in the Ohio Valley, 1789–1815," *Ohio Valley History* 8, no. 3 (Fall 2008), 1 (noting the growth of post offices, "especially in the Ohio Valley").

47. Wayne E. Fuller, *R.F.D.: The Changing Face of Rural America* (Bloomington: Indiana University Press, 1964), 177–98; Samuel Kernell and Michael McDonald, "Congress and America's Political Development: The Transformation of the Post Office from Patronage to Service," *American Journal of Political Science* 43, no. 3 (July 1999), 792–811; Christopher W. Wells, "The Changing Nature of Country Roads: Farmers, Reformers, and the Shifting Uses of Rural Space, 1880–1905," *Agricultural History* 80, no. 2 (Spring 2006), 153. Allan Bogue noted that "it was no accident that the region with the greatest concentration of [RFD] routes in 1912 was the Middle West, the great stronghold of rural Republicanism." Bogue review of Fuller, *R.F.D.*, *Indiana Magazine of History* 61, no. 1 (March 1965), 60.

48. Daniel P. Carpenter, *The Forging of Bureaucratic Autonomy: Reputations, Networks, and Policy Innovation in Executive Agencies, 1862–1928* (Princeton, NJ: Princeton University Press, 2001), 126–27.

49. Wayne E. Fuller, "Good Roads and Rural Free Delivery," *Mississippi Valley Historical Review* 42, no. 1 (June 1955), 67–83.

50. Fuller, "Good Roads," 76 (quotation) (also noting that the "good-roads movement sprang from agrarian roots").

51. Theda Skocpol, *Protecting Soldiers and Mothers: The Political Origins of Social Policy in the United States* (Cambridge, MA: Harvard University Press, 1992).

52. Megan J. McClintock, "Civil War Pensions and the Reconstruction of Union Families," *Journal of American History* 83, no. 2 (September 1996), 460–63. On the importance of communal connections justifying pensions, see Reid Mitchell, *The Vacant Chair: The Northern Soldier Leaves Home* (New York: Oxford University Press, 1993).

53. Sean M. Theriault, "Patronage, the Pendleton Act, and the Power of the People," *Journal of Politics* 65, no. 1 (2003), 57, 65 (arguing that public support "played a crucial role in securing passage of the Pendleton Act"); Ari Hoogenboom, *Outlawing the Spoils: A History of the Civil Service Reform Movement, 1865–1883* (Urbana: University of Illinois Press, 1968), 234; Joseph F. Katt, *Merit: The History of a Founding Ideal from the American Revolution to the Twenty-First Century* (Ithaca, NY: Cornell University Press, 2013), 198–99; Thomas S. Mach, *"Gentleman George" Hunt Pendleton: Party Politics and Ideological Identity in Nineteenth-Century America* (Kent, OH: Kent State University Press, 2007). No Senate Republicans and only eight of 118 House Republicans voted against the Pendleton Act. Democrats were divided. Theriault, "Patronage," 59–60.

54. Ari Hoogenboom, "The Pendleton Act and the Civil Service," *American Historical Review* 64, no. 2 (January 1959), 303; Hoogenboom, *Outlawing the Spoils*, 215.

55. Rhys H. Williams and Susan M. Alexander, "Religious Rhetoric in American Populism: Civil Religion as Movement Ideology," *Journal for the Scientific Study of Religion* 33, no. 1 (March 1994), 1–15.

56. Hofstadter, *Age of Reform*, 107. See also Jason Stacy, "Popucrats: Producerist Populism and the Formation of Midwestern Political Identity in the 1890s," in Lauck, *Making of the Midwest*, 379–92.

57. Benton H. Wilcox, "An Historical Definition of Northwestern Radicalism," *Mississippi Valley Historical Review* 26, no. 3 (December 1939), 382 (quotation); Hofstadter, *Age of Reform*, 99; Cooper, "Why Wisconsin?" 15; Chester McArthur Destler, "Consummation of a Labor-Populist Alliance in Illinois, 1894," *Mississippi Valley Historical Review* 27, no. 4 (March 1941), 592–94.

58. Chester McArthur Destler, "Agricultural Readjustment and Agrarian Unrest in Illinois, 1880–1896," *Agricultural History* 21, no. 2 (April 1947), 104.

59. Hofstadter, *Age of Reform*, 100, 111–14, 118, n. 9; Postel, *Equality*, 65; Nancy Berlage, *Farmers Helping Farmers: The Rise of the Farm and Home Bureaus, 1914–1935* (Baton Rouge: Louisiana State University, 2016); Christopher W. Shaw, "'Tired of Being Exploited': The Grassroots Origin of the Federal Farm Loan Act of 1916," *Agricultural History* 92, no. 4 (Fall 2018), 512–40.

60. Hofstadter, *Age of Reform*, 61.

61. See "Growing Agrarian Reformers in the Midwest: A Collective Biography," in Gilbert, *Planning Democracy*, 25–34, and Fuller, "Rural Roots of Progressive Leaders," 2–4.

62. Hicks, "Birth of the Populist Party," 234.

63. During the debate over adopting the Fifteenth Amendment in the Michigan legislature, some women's suffrage advocates argued that if blacks could vote then women should be able to vote too. During the debate in the Senate, Republican senator Bela Jenks of St. Clair moved to strike "male" from the resolution adopting

the Fifteenth Amendment, and it passed 15–11. GOP leaders thought this would jeopardize the statewide vote on the Amendment, so they reconsidered the motion and it failed 21–4, with the 4 dissenters being Democrats, who were trying to defeat ratification. In Minnesota, Democrats tried to delay black suffrage by amending the suffrage bill to add women so there would be more opposition (this failed 21–10 along party lines). Dunbar and Shade, "Black Man Gains the Vote," 53–54; Green, "Minnesota's Long Road to Black Suffrage, 78.

64. James J. Connolly, *An Elusive Unity: Urban Democracy and Machine Politics in Industrializing America* (Ithaca, NY: Cornell University Press, 2010), 115.

65. Sara Egge, *Woman Suffrage and Citizenship in the Midwest, 1870–1920* (Iowa City: University of Iowa Press, 2018).

66. Gundersen, "Local Parish as a Female Institution," 309 (active), 310–15.

67. Irene Haderle, "Women and Lay Activism: Aspects of Acculturation in the German Lutheran Churches of Ann Arbor, Michigan, 1870–1917," *Michigan Historical Review* 25, no. 1 (Spring 1999), 26–27.

68. Ann Vlock, "Justice, Not Charity: Luna Kellie and Great Plains Populist Reform, 1890–1901," *Great Plains Quarterly* 40, no. 3 (Summer 2020), 209. A non-Christian strain of thought and reform also existed in the Midwest. See Joanne Passet, "Yours for Liberty: Women and Freethought in Nineteenth-Century Iowa," *Annals of Iowa* 63, no. 2 (Spring 2004), 142 (noting that in 1893 "Iowa ranked second in the United States [after California] in membership in the Free-thought Federation").

69. Karen M. Mason, "Women's Clubs in Iowa," *Annals of Iowa* 56, no. 1 (Winter 1997), 2, 4–5; Cheryl Lyon-Jones, "'They Hoed the Corn,'" *Michigan History Magazine* 78 (July/August 1994), 36.

70. Mason, "Women's Clubs of Iowa," 3 (quotation); Hazel P. Buffum, "The Federation Grows," *Palimpsest* 34, no. 5 (May 1953), 222 (noting that the number of clubs in the Iowa Federation of Women's Clubs peaked at 931 by 1933); Kathleen L. Endres, *Akron's Better Half: Women's Clubs and the Humanization of the City, 1825–1925* (Akron, OH: University of Akron Press, 2006); Janice C. Steinschneider, *An Improved Woman: The Wisconsin Federation of Women's Clubs, 1895–1920* (Brooklyn, NY: Carlson, 1994); Anne Firor Scott, *Natural Allies: Women's Associations in American History* (Urbana: University of Illinois Press, 1991), 141–43 (on Chicago); Andrea Tuttle Kornbluh, *Lighting the Way . . . The Woman's City Club of Cincinnati, 1915–1965* (Cincinnati, OH: Woman's City Club, 1986); Genevieve G. McBride, *On Wisconsin Women: Working for Their Rights from Settlement to Suffrage* (Madison: University of Wisconsin Press, 1993); Jayne Morris-Crowther, *The Political Activities of Detroit Clubwomen in the 1920s: A Challenge and a Promise* (Detroit: Wayne State University Press, 2013); Catherine E. Rymph, *Republican Women: Feminism and Conservatism from Suffrage through the Rise of the New Right* (Chapel Hill: University of North Carolina Press, 2006).

71. Lyon-Jones, "'They Hoed the Corn,'" 36.

72. Peter Hoehnle, "Iowa Clubwomen Rise to World Stage: Dorothy Houghton and Ruth Sayre," *Iowa Heritage Illustrated* 83 (2002), 34.

73. Theodore Penny Martin, *The Sound of Our Own Voices: Women's Study Clubs, 1860–1910* (Boston: Beacon Press, 1987), 147 (circle), 1 (mental).

74. William R. Sandham, "The Origin of the Order of the Eastern Star," *Journal of the Illinois State Historical Society* 25, no. 3 (October 1932), 237–38.

75. Martin, *Sound of Our Own Voices*, 96–97; Sklar, "Female Teachers," 65.

76. Pawley, *Reading on the Middle Border*, 144. For more on Iowa, see Thomas J. Morain, *Prairie Grass Roots: An Iowa Small Town in the Early Twentieth Century* (Ames: Iowa State University Press, 1988), 88–108.

77. Christine Pawley, "'Not Wholly Self Culture': The Shakespearean Women's Club, Osage, Iowa, 1892–1920," *Annals of Iowa* 56, no. 1 (Winter 1997), 12–45; Mason, "Women's Clubs of Iowa," 9; Pawley, *Reading on the Middle Border*, 15, 28.

78. Hoehnle, "Iowa Clubwomen," 39.

79. Felsenstein and Connolly, *What Middletown Read*, 166, 102.

80. Sharon L. Kennedy, "Nebraska Women Artists, 1880–1950," *Nebraska History* 88, no. 3 (Fall 2007), 62–95. On a related activity, see Sue Studebaker, *Ohio Is My Dwelling Place: Schoolgirl Embroideries, 1800–1850* (Athens: Ohio University Press, 2002).

81. William M. Tsutsui and Marjorie Swann, "'Light the Beauty around You': The Art Collection of the Kansas Federation of Women's Clubs," *Kansas History* 26, no. 4 (Winter 2003/2004), 252–55. On the Decatur Art Club, see Martin, *Sound of Our Own Voices*, 59, 70. See generally Karen J. Blair, *The Torchbearers: Women and Their Amateur Arts Associations, 1890–1930* (Bloomington: Indiana University Press, 1994).

82. Donald B. Marti, "Woman's Work in the Grange: Mary Ann Mayo of Michigan, 1882–1903," *Agricultural History* 56, no. 2 (April 1982), 440–42 (also noting her focus on social uplift and involvement in Chautauqua); Mason, "Women's Clubs of Iowa," 10; Julie McDonald, *Ruth Buxton Sayre: First Lady of the Farm* (Ames: Iowa State University Press, 1980), 39–66; Hoehnle, "Iowa Clubwomen," 39–46; Donald B. Marti, "Sisters of the Grange: Rural Feminism in the Late Nineteenth Century," *Agricultural History* 58, no. 3 (July 1984), 255–56.

83. Postel, *Equality*, 38.

84. Mason, "Women's Clubs of Iowa," 10.

85. Vlock, "Justice, Not Charity," 208–9.

86. H. Roger Grant, "Lucia B. Griffin: Platform Speaker of the Lake Nineteenth Century," *Annals of Iowa* 42, no. 6 (Fall 1974), 462–67.

87. Marilyn Dell Brady, "Kansas Federation of Colored Women's Clubs, 1900–1930," *Kansas History* 9, no. 1 (Spring 1986), 19–30.

88. Stevenson, *Victorian Homefront*, 164–65.

89. Buffum, "Federation Grows," 226.

90. Pawley, *Reading on the Middle Border*, 69, 77.

91. Felsenstein and Connolly, *What Middletown Read*, 112, 118–19 (consumed), 109, 129 (steady).

92. Stevenson, *Victorian Homefront*, 35–36, 163 (three-fourths).

93. Pam Hardman, "The Steward of Her Soul: Elsie Dinsmore and the Training of the Victorian Child," *American Studies* 29, no. 2 (Fall 1988), 70 (describing this series as a "subtle protest against masculine authority").

94. Felsenstein and Connolly, *What Middletown Read*, 131 (moralism), 132, 146 (corpus); Pawley, *Reading on the Middle Border*, 68.

95. Tomsich, *Genteel Endeavor*, 15.
96. Dee Garrison, "Immoral Fiction in the Late Victorian Library," in Howe, *Victorian America*, 141.
97. Garrison, "Immoral Fiction," 144.
98. Pawley, *Reading on the Middle Border*, 77.
99. Cordier, "Prairie Schoolwomen," 108.
100. Quoted in Cordier, "Prairie Schoolwomen," 109.
101. Glenda Riley, *Frontierswomen: The Iowa Experience* (Ames: Iowa State University Press, 1981), 137.
102. Sklar, "Female Teachers," 57.
103. Felsenstein and Connolly, *What Middletown Read*, 157.
104. Wright, *Culture on the Moving Frontier*, 104; Sklar, "Female Teachers," 62; Jane Sherzer, "The Higher Education of Women in the Ohio Valley previous to 1840," *Ohio Archaeological and Historical Quarterly* 25, no. 1 (January 1916), 18.
105. Louise Phelps Kellogg, "The Origins of Milwaukee College," *Wisconsin Magazine of History* 9, no. 4 (July 1926), 389; Grace Norton Kieckhefer, "Milwaukee-Downer College Rediscovers Its Past," *Wisconsin Magazine of History* 34, no. 4 (Summer 1951), 211.
106. Belding, "Academies and Iowa's Frontier Life," 347–48.
107. Sklar, "Female Teachers," 57–67.
108. Cordier, "Prairie Schoolwomen," 107, 116.
109. Lockard, "Influence of New England," 5. Catherine Beecher was also actively in developing schools for midwestern girls. Kellogg, "Origins of Milwaukee College," 385. See also Polly Welts Kaufman, *Women Teachers on the Frontier* (New Haven, CT: Yale University Press, 1984).
110. Smith, "Protestant Schooling," 691. See also Margaret King Moore, "The Ladies' Association for Educating Females, 1833–1937," *Journal of the Illinois State Historical Society* 31, no. 2 (June 1938), 166–87, and Gayle Gullett, "A Contest over Meaning: Finding Gender, Class, and Race in Progressivism," *History of Education Quarterly* 33, no. 2 (Summer 1993), 235 (noting that "improving children's public education was the most ubiquitous of clubwomen's reforms").
111. Malkmus, "Origins of Coeducation," 162–96; Gail B. Griffin, "Emancipated Spirits: Women's Education and the American Midwest," *Change* 16, no. 1 (1984), 35; Andrea G. Radke-Moss, *Bright Epoch: Women and Coeducation in the American West* (Lincoln: University of Nebraska Press, 2008), 5–6.
112. Lori D. Ginzberg, "Women in an Evangelical Community: Oberlin, 1835–1850," *Ohio History Journal* 89, no. 1 (Winter 1980), 85 (quotation); Griffin, "Emancipated Spirits," 35; Frances J. Hosford, *Father Shipherd's Magna Charta: A Century of Coeducation in Oberlin* (Boston: Marshall Jones, 1937); Robert S. Fletcher, "Oberlin and Co-Education," *Ohio Archaeological and Historical Quarterly* 47, no. 1 (January 1938), 1 (explaining Oberlin's coeducation policies, its acceptance of African Americans, its vegetarian leanings, and also noting the college's active peace movement and that the "largest local chapter of the American Moral Reform Society in the West was at Oberlin"); Robert S. Fletcher, "The First Coeds," *American Scholar* 7, no. 1 (Winter 1938), 79 (explaining that the Oberlin

curricula for men and women were the same with the exception that women did not take Latin, Greek, and Hebrew).

113. Griffin, "Emancipated Spirits," 36. By 1899, Oberlin alone had graduated fifty-five black women. Mt. Holyoke, Wellesley, and Vassar combined had only graduated six. In 1890, 53 percent of Oberlin students were female. Griffin, "Emancipated Spirits," 40. See also Ronald W. Hogeland, "Coeducation of the Sexes at Oberlin College: A Study of Social Ideas in Mid-Nineteenth-Century America," *Journal of Social History* 6, no. 2 (Winter 1972/1973), 160–76.

114. Hubbart, *Older Middle West*, 71 (admit); Griffin, "Emancipated Spirits," 36 (Mann).

115. Dunbar, "Public versus Private Control," 402, 404.

116. Dunbar, "Public Versus Private Control," 400.

117. Wheeler, "How Colleges Shaped," 120, n. 18; Malkmus, "Origins of Coeducation," 178, n. 28, 191, n. 51; Helen R. Olin, *The Women of a State University: An Illustration of the Working of Coeducation in the Middle West* (New York: G. P. Putnam's Sons, 1909), 4. For an example of a women's college, see McClelland, "Morning Star of Memory,"255 (describing the creation of Illinois Conference Female College in 1855, which later became MacMurray College, and noting that it was "indigenous to the Middle West," not a replica of an eastern practice). See also Griffin, "Emancipated Spirits," 35 (noting Granville Female Seminary in Ohio, which became Shepardson College, which later merged with Denison University), and Dwight F. Clark, "A Forgotten Evanston Institution: The Northwestern Female College," *Journal of the Illinois State Historical Society* 35, no. 2 (June 1942), 115–32.

118. Griffin, "Emancipated Spirits," 35. See also Lynn D. Gordon, *Gender and Higher Education in the Progressive Era* (New Haven, CT: Yale University Press, 1990), 87 (discussing Alice Palmer, who held "the first full professorship at a coeducational university offered to a woman," plus seven additional women faculty, who gave "Chicago more female faculty than at any other contemporary coeducational institution"), 88 (describing Chicago as "a particularly progressive place for female students"). On women's colleges in Ohio such as Granville Female College, Female College, Ohio Wesleyan, Oxford Female College, and Western Female Seminary, see Renea Frey and Jacqueline Johnson, "From Social Grace to Social Power: Changing Nineteenth-Century Gender Norms in Leadership and Rhetorical Performance at Western College for Women," *Ohio History* 125, no. 1 (Spring 2018), 34.

119. Claudia Goldin and Lawrence F. Katz, "Putting the 'Co' in Education: Timing, Reasons, and Consequences of College Coeducation from 1835 to the Present," *Journal of Human Capital* 5, no. 4 (Winter 2011), 383.

120. Beth, "Monmouth Literary Societies," 122.

121. Beth, "Monmouth Literary Societies," 123.

122. Wheeler, "How Colleges Shaped," 106, 113.

123. Malkmus, "Origins of Coeducation," 182.

124. Griffin, "Emancipated Spirits," 36.

125. Wheeler, "How Colleges Shaped," 113–14.

126. Griffin, "Emancipated Spirits," 39 (quoting Angell).

127. Malkmus, "Origins of Coeducation," 168; Radke-Moss, *Women and Co-Education*, 5; Griffin, "Emancipated Spirits," 34.

128. Wheeler, "How Colleges Shaped," 113.

129. Amy Thompson McCandless, "Maintaining the Spirit and Tone of Robust Manliness: The Battle against Coeducation at Southern Colleges and Universities, 1890–1940," *NWSA Journal* 2 (1990), 199.

130. Degler, "Two Cultures," 102.

131. Griffin, "Emancipated Spirits," 33 (different, separatist), 34 (anomalies, progress); Stevenson, *Victorian Homefront*, 54; Bledstein, *Culture of Professionalism*, 118.

132. Radke-Moss, *Women and Co-Education*, 5 (rigid).

133. Malkmus, "Origins of Coeducation," 195–96 (italics added).

134. Wall, *Iowa*, 114; Robert E. Belding, "Iowa's Brave Model for Women's Education," *Annals of Iowa* vol. 43, no. 5 (Summer 1976), 342–43, 347 (quotation). In 1914, Benjamin Shambaugh launched a course on the "political and legal status of women." Belding, "Iowa's Brave Model," 348.

135. Olin, *Women of a State University*, 26, 31 (concluding that the Wisconsin regents were "uniformly favourable to coeducation both theoretically and practically considered"); Merle Curti and Vernon Carstensen, *The University of Wisconsin: A History, 1848–1925*, vol. 1 (Madison: University of Wisconsin Press, 1949), 201.

136. Bloomberg, "'Let Us Not Look Regretfully,'" __ (also noting that women at Wisconsin took the same courses and recited in courses with men, contrary to some previous interpretations).

137. Elizabeth M. Farrand, *History of the University of Michigan* (Ann Arbor: University of Michigan Press, 1885), 201.

138. Thrun, "School Segregation in Michigan," 16, 23. On what would become Western Michigan University, see Barbara Speas Havira, "Coeducation and Gender Differentiation in Teacher Training: Western State Normal School, 1904–1929," *Michigan Historical Review* 21, no. 1 (Spring 1995), 51 (explaining that "men and women were admitted under the same conditions, attended classes together, and met the same requirements" and that "equal numbers of women and men served on the faculty," but also noting persisting gender assumptions). See also a novel about one woman's experience at Michigan: Elisabeth Israels Perry and Jennifer Ann Price, eds., Olive San Louie Anderson, *An American Girl, and Her Four Years in a Boys' College* (Ann Arbor: University of Michigan Press, 2005 [1878]).

139. Belding, "Iowa's Brave Model," 347; Griffin, "Emancipated Spirits," 37. Iowa adopted coeducation in 1855, Kansas State in 1863, Wisconsin in 1863 (women were admitted to the Normal school in 1860), Indiana and Missouri in 1867, Iowa State and Ohio State in 1868, Kansas, Minnesota, and Nebraska in 1869. Bloomberg, "'Let Us Not Look Regretfully,'" __; Radke-Moss, *Women and Co-Education*, 1 (describing midwestern land grant colleges as "among the first institutions in the world to practice coeducation"), 4 (noting that the first coeducational colleges were Oberlin and "other denominational colleges in the Midwest," and then the Universities of Iowa, Wisconsin, and Michigan). In the early years of the University of Minnesota almost as many women as men were registered. Leonard, "Early College Silhouettes," 182.

140. Jill Weiss Simins, "Reluctant Renegade: Sarah Parke Morrison and Women's Equality at Indiana University," *Indiana History Blog*, October 22, 2020.

141. "Indiana State University," *Evansville Daily Journal*, December 19, 1867.

142. Simins, "Reluctant Renegade"; Gant, "'Younger and More Irreconcilable,'" 162.

143. Hevel, "Public Displays," 5–6.

144. Hevel, "Public Displays," 5–7; Radke-Moss, *Bright Epoch*, 94 (liquor); Olin, *Women of a State University*, 34 (distinguished). See also Radke-Moss, *Bright Epoch*, chapter 3.

145. Phyllis Kay Wilke, "Physical Education for Women at Nebraska University, 1879–1923," *Nebraska History* 56, no. 2 (Summer 1975), 193. In contrast to coeducational Nebraska, Oxford University did not allow women until the 1920s, as one Nebraskan highlighted. Dolores Gunnerson, "Esther Gunnison: A Nebraskan at Oxford, 1920–1921," *Nebraska History* 59, no. 1 (Spring 1978), 1–8.

146. Wilke, "Physical Education," 197, 199; Wilke, "The History of Physical Education for Women at the University of Nebraska from the Early Beginnings to 1952" (M.A. thesis, University of Nebraska, 1973), 6.

147. Nellie Snyder Yost, "Nebraska's Scholarly Athlete: Louise Pound, 1872–1958," *Nebraska History* 64, no. 4 (Winter 1983), 477–90; B. A. Botkin, "Louise Pound," *Western Folklore* 18, no. 3 (July 1959), 202 (explaining that in her scholarship Pound "remained loyal to the Middlewest"). In keeping with the civic culture of the Midwest, Pound's mother, Laura, was active as a director of the Lincoln Public Library, the City Improvement Society, the Nebraska Art Association, the Lincoln Women's Club, the Nebraska State Historical Society, and the Nebraska Daughters of the Revolution; Cochran, *Louise Pound*, 6–7, 44 (optimism). Chapter 1 of Cochran's book, telling Laura's story and drawing on a quote from her, is titled "I Have Always Been Satisfied with Nebraska." Cochran, *Louise Pound*, 12 (providing the context for Laura's comment: "I liked the altitude, the dry climate, the blue skies, the sunny days and gorgeous sunsets, the strange, new flora and the song of the prairie lark").

148. Yost, "Nebraska's Scholarly Athlete," 484.

149. Smith, "Athletics in the Wisconsin State University System," 16. On women's college sports, see also Radke-Moss, *Bright Epoch*, 190–222.

150. Bloomberg, "'Let Us Not Look Regretfully,'" __.

151. Julie Roy Jeffrey, *Frontier Women: "Civilizing" the West? 1840–1880* (New York: Hill and Wang, 1998), 6.

152. Bloomberg, "'Let Us Not Look Regretfully,'" __.

153. Griffin, "Emancipated Spirits," 34.

154. Jeffrey, *Frontier Women*, 233.

155. Griffin, "Emancipated Spirits," 33, 34 (arguing that the term "coeducation" was coined in Michigan).

156. Mabel Newcomer, *A Century of Higher Education for American Women* (New York: Harper, 1959), 19.

157. Radke-Moss, *Women and Co-Education*, 5.

158. Bloomberg, "'Let Us Not Look Regretfully,'" __.

159. Radke-Moss, *Bright Epoch*, 1, 16 (criticizing scholars for the "'fly-over approach' to women's education," for focusing on the East, and missing the history

of coeducation in the Midwest), 4 (criticizing a historiography "which has so often been focused on elite colleges in the East or on the West Coast and has ignored the state institutions of lesser renown in the Midwest and West").

160. Eleanor Flexner and Ellen Fitzpatrick, *Century of Struggle: The Woman's Rights Movement in the United States* (Cambridge, MA: Belknap Press, 1996), 116.

161. Bloomberg, "'Let Us Not Look Regretfully.'"

162. Virginia Railsback Gunn, "Industrialists Not Butterflies: Women's Higher Education at Kansas State Agricultural College, 1873–1882," *Kansas History* 18, no. 1 (Spring 1995), 6 (explaining that students' mornings focused on literary and scientific studies and the afternoons on carpentry, horticulture, farming, blacksmithing, and so on).

163. Bloomberg, "'Let Us Not Look Regretfully.'"

164. Griffin, "Emancipated Spirits," 40. In 1880, 33.4 percent of college students were women. Stevenson, *Victorian Homefront*, 112.

165. Goldin and Katz, "Putting the 'Co' in Education," 381, 379 (concluding that "coeducation varied considerably *by region*") (italics added), 378 (reminding readers that Dartmouth, Princeton, and Yale did not become coeducational until the 1970s).

166. Sylvia D. Hoffert, "Jane Grey Swisshelm and the Negotiation of Gender Roles on the Minnesota Frontier," *Frontiers: A Journal of Women Studies* 18, no. 3 (1997), 17–39, 18 (blurring), 19 (gender; also noting the factor of "expediency rather than convention" on the frontier, another way of describing midwestern pragmatism).

167. Patricia C. Gaster, "Rosa Hudspeth and the *Stuart Ledger*, 1901–1907," *Nebraska History* 79, no. 4 (Winter 1998), 171–78.

168. William D. Lock, "'As Independent as We Wished': Elizabeth Scott and Alice Fish of Blaine County, Nebraska," *Nebraska History* 82, no. 4 (Winter 2011), 138–51. For another example, see Rebecca Edwards, "Marsh Murdock and the 'Wily Women' of Wichita: Domesticity Disputed in the Gilded Age," *Kansas History* 25, no. 1 (Spring 2002), 2–13.

169. George T. Blakey, "Esther Griffin White: An Awakener of Hoosier Potential," *Indiana Magazine of History* 86, no. 3 (September 1990), 286–87.

170. Gayle Gullett, "'Our Great Opportunity': Organized Women Advance Women's Work at the World's Columbian Exposition of 1893," *Illinois Historical Journal* 87, no. 4 (Winter 1994), 274.

171. See Nancy Baker Jones, "A Forgotten Feminist: The Early Writings of Ida Husted Harper, 1878–1894," *Indiana Magazine of History* 73, no. 2 (June 1977), 79–101; Jane Stephens, "May Wright Sewall: An Indiana Reformer," *Indiana Magazine of History* 78, no. 4 (December 1982), 273–95; Ruth Van Ackeren, "Adabelle Cherry Marshall on the Ellison-White Chautauqua Circuit," *Nebraska History* 66, no. 2 (Summer 1985), 164–83.

172. Pamela Riney-Kehrberg, "Women in Wheat Country," *Kansas History* 23, nos. 1–2 (Spring/Summer 2000), 56–71; Mary Neth, *Preserving the Family Farm: Women, Community, and the Foundations of Agribusiness in the Midwest, 1900–1940* (Baltimore, MD: Johns Hopkins University Press, 1995); Katherine Jellison, *Entitled to Power: Farm Women and Technology, 1913–1963* (Chapel Hill: University of North Carolina Press, 1993).

173. Shriver, "Freedom's Proving Ground," 131.

174. Catherine B. Cleary, "Married Women's Property Rights in Wisconsin, 1846–1872," *Wisconsin Magazine of History* 78, no. 2 (Winter 1994/1995), 125, 112 (noting the surprise of European travelers at the degree of freedoms available to women); Joseph G. Gambone, "The Forgotten Feminist of Kansas," *Kansas Historical Quarterly* 39, no. 1 (Spring 1973), 12.

175. William S. Garber, "Divorce in Marion County," *Indiana Magazine of History* 6, no. 1 (March 1910), 12 (also noting the relative ease of divorces in past decades). See also Stacy Pratt McDermott, "Dissolving the Bonds of Matrimony: Women and Divorce in Sangamon County, Illinois, 1837–60," in Stowell, *In Tender Consideration*, 71–103. Women were active in the courts. Even in the antebellum era, 20 percent of the cases in Lincoln's Springfield involved women litigants. Daniel W. Stowell, "*Feme UnCovert:* Women's Encounters with the Law," in Stowell, *In Tender Consideration*, 17–45. See also Lyn Ellen Bennett, "Child Custody, Custodial Arrangements, and Financial Support in Late-Nineteenth Century Kansas," *Kansas History* 37, no. 1 (Spring 2014), 20–33.

176. In Sangamon County, Illinois, between 1837 and 1860, women filed for divorce 139 times and the court granted them a divorce 80 percent of the time. Historian Stacy Pratt McDermott has concluded that "divorce was a viable legal option for antebellum Illinois women" and that the "Illinois legislature provided liberal access to divorce, and many Illinois women chose divorce as a remedy for marital difficulties." McDermott, "Dissolving the Bonds of Matrimony," 71.

177. Davis, "'New Aspects,'" 165.

178. Robertson, *Hearts Beating for Liberty*.

179. Dykstra, "White Men, Black Laws," 436. See also Julia Wiech Lief, "A Woman of Purpose: Julia B. Nelson," *Minnesota History* 47, no. 8 (Winter 1981), 305–6.

180. Nicole Etcheson, "'Labouring for the Freedom of This Territory': Free-State Kansas Women in the 1850s," *Kansas History* 21, no. 2 (Summer 1998), 78 (tales, respect).

181. Lindsey R. Peterson, "'Iowa Excelled Them All': Iowa Local Ladies' Aid Societies on the Civil War Frontier, 1861–1865," *Middle West Review* 3, no. 1 (Fall 2016), 47–70; Ginette Aley and J. L. Anderson, eds., *Union Heartland: The Midwestern Home Front during the Civil War* (Carbondale: Southern Illinois University Press, 2013), 97–167; William E. Parrish, "The Western Sanitary Commission," *Civil War History* 36, no. 1 (March 1990), 17 (noting that the WSC "fiercely assert[ed] its independence from its better known counterpart, the United States Sanitary Commission"). See generally Judith Ann Giesberg, *Civil War Sisterhood: The U.S. Sanitary Commission and Women's Politics in Transition* (Boston: Northeastern University Press, 2000).

182. Lisa Guinn, "Annie Wittenmyer and Nineteenth-Century Women's Usefulness," *Annals of Iowa* 74, no. 4 (Fall 2015), 351–54.

183. Postel, *Equality*, 121.

184. See Bloomberg, "'How Shall We Make Beatrice Grow!,'" 170–83.

185. Buffum, "Federation Grows," 227; Mason, "Women's Clubs of Iowa," 3–4. See generally Mary Belle Sherman, *The Women's Clubs in the Middle-Western*

States (Philadelphia: American Academy of Political and Social Science, 1906), 47 (noting activities such as maintaining cemeteries, removing garbage, planting trees, cleaning streets, reducing public nuisances, and promoting hospitals).

186. Moore, "Ladies' Association for Educating Females,"166.

187. Leigh Ann Wheeler, "From Reading Shakespeare to Reforming Burlesque: The Minneapolis Woman's Club and the Women's Welfare League, 1907–1920," *Michigan Historical Review* 25, no. 1 (Spring 1999), 51 (family), 46–49, 52 (zeal, essence, yeast).

188. Maureen A. Flanagan, *Seeing with Their Hearts: Chicago Women and the Vision of the Good City, 1871–1933* (Princeton, NJ: Princeton University Press, 2002). See also Knupfer, *Toward a Tenderer Humanity*.

189. Lyon-Jones, "'They Hoed the Corn,'" 37; Brace, "Power of Porch Talks," 6.

190. Brace, "Power of Porch Talks," 5. For other relevant examples, see Ann Bowers, "White-Gloved Feminists: An Analysis of Northwest Ohio Women's Clubs," *Hayes Historical Journal* 4 (Fall 1984), 38–47; Maureen A. Flanagan, "Gender and Urban Political Reform: The City Club and the Woman's City Club of Chicago in the Progressive Era," *American Historical Review* 95, no. 4 (October 1990), 1032–50; Thomond R. O'Brien, "Alice M. O'Brien and the Women's City Club of St. Paul," *Minnesota History* 54, no. 2 (Summer 1994), 54–68; June O. Underwood, "Civilizing Kansas: Women's Organization, 1880–1920," in Nancy Cott, ed., *History of Women in the United States* 16 (New Providence: K. G. Saur, 1994), 259–82.

191. Scott, *Natural Allies*, 113.

192. Francesca Morgan, "'Regions Remote from Revolutionary Scenes': Regionalism, Nationalism, and the Iowa Daughters of the American Revolution, 1890–1930," *Annals of Iowa* 56, no. 1 (Winter 1997), 46.

193. Morgan, "'Regions Remote from Revolutionary Scenes,'" 47–48 (noting that attacks on the Iowa DAR for nativism and red-baiting during this era are incorrect). See also Eliza G. Browning, "Indiana Society Daughters of the American Revolution," *Indiana Magazine of History* 5, no. 4 (December 1909), 181–82 (noting Indiana's forty-five DAR chapters and their work to save the history of Indiana, historical records, settlers' reminiscences, and old letters). For another midwestern DAR leader, see Marjorie Kreidberg, "An Unembarrassed Patriot: Lucy Wilder Morris," *Minnesota History* 47, no. 6 (Summer 1981), 215–26.

194. Nancy G. Garner, "'A Prayerful Public Protest': The Significance of Gender in the Kansas Woman's Crusade of 1874," *Kansas History* 20, no. 4 (Winter 1997/1998), 215. See also Patrick G. O'Brien, "Prohibition and the Kansas Progressive Example," *Great Plains Quarterly* 7, no. 4 (Fall 1987), 219–31. On the state to the north, see Burton W. Folsom Jr., *No More Free Markets or Free Beer: The Progressive Era in Nebraska, 1900–1924* (Lanham, MD: Lexington Books, 1999).

195. Garner, "'Prayerful Public Protest,'" 220 (assertion), 219, n. 10 (confined, husband), 221 (low). See also John Anderson, "Lincoln, Nebraska, and Prohibition: The Election of May 4, 1909," *Nebraska History* 70, no. 2 (Summer 1989), 184–85 (describing singing temperance women descending on saloons in Lincoln, Nebraska). Some historians have argued for taking the protests of women more seriously because of the significant damage caused to family life by drunken husbands,

a matter that in previous generations was dismissed as a form of puritanism. See Lisa Ossian, "The 'I Too' Temperance Movement: A Reevaluation of Midwestern Women's Political Action at the Turn of the Last Century," in Lauck, *Making of the Midwest*, 215–29.

196. A. N. Beebe, "How a Northern Illinois Town Suddenly Became Dry," *Journal of the Illinois State Historical Society* 5, no. 2 (July 1912), 199–200.

197. Gerald Vanwoerkom, "They 'Dared to Do Right': Prohibition in Muskegon," *Michigan History* 55, no. 1 (January 1971), 48.

198. Garner, "'Prayerful Public Protest,'" 216. See also Jack Blocker, *"Give to the Winds Thy Fears": The Women's Christian Temperance Crusade, 1873–1874* (Westport, CT: Greenwood Press, 1985); Jed Dannenbaum, *Drink and Disorder: Temperance Reform in Cincinnati from the Washingtonian Revival to the WCTU* (Urbana: University of Illinois Press, 1984); Kenneth J. Peak and Jason W. Peak, "Liquor Wars and the Law: Decisions of the Kansas Supreme Court, 1861–1920," *Kansas History* 28, no. 2 (Summer 2006), 84–99; Robert E. Wenger, "The Anti-Saloon League in Nebraska Politics, 1898–1910," *Nebraska History* 52, no. 3 (Fall 1971), 267–92; Charles E. Canup, "The Temperance Movement in Indiana," *Indiana Magazine of History* 16, no. 2 (June 1920), 112–20; John Eicher, "'Our Christian Duty': Piety, Politics, and Temperance in Berne, Indiana, 1886–1907," *Indiana Magazine of History* 107, no. 1 (March 2011), 1–31.

199. Jack S. Blocker Jr., "Separate Paths: Suffragists and the Women's Temperance Crusade," *Signs* 10, no. 3 (Spring 1985), 462; Edwards, "Domesticity versus Manhood Rights," 188 (noting that "in states such as Iowa, Kansas, and Wisconsin [Republicans] led the fight for Prohibition").

200. F. M. Whitaker, "Ohio WCTU and the Prohibition Amendment Campaign of 1883," *Ohio History Journal* 83, no. 2 (Spring 1974), 84; Paul W. Glad, "When John Barleycorn Went into Hiding in Wisconsin," *Wisconsin Magazine of History* 68, no. 2 (Winter 1984/1985), 122–23; Lloyd Sponholz, "The Politics of Temperance in Ohio, 1880–1912," *Ohio History Journal* 85, no. 1 (Winter 1976), 4–5; Garner, "'Prayerful Public Protest,'" 218. Willard was president of the WCTU from 1879 to 1898. See Patricia Bizzell, "Frances Willard, Phoebe Palmer, and the Ethos of the Methodist Woman Preacher," *Rhetoric Society Quarterly* 36, no. 4 (Autumn 2006), 377–98. The WCTU started in Hillsboro, Ohio, in 1873 based on the sermons of Diocletian Lewis, and after a large-scale convention in Cleveland in 1874 it became a national organization. See Marian J. Morton, "Temperance, Benevolence, and the City: The Cleveland Non-Partisan Woman's Christian Temperance Union, 1874–1900," *Ohio History* 91 (1982 annual), 58–73. The Hillsboro founding of the WCTU was preceded by the raid by women on saloons in Greenfield, Ohio, and the resulting court trials, held in Hillsboro. Jed Dannenbaum, "The Origins of Temperance Activism and Militancy among American Women," *Journal of Social History* 15, no. 2 (Winter 1981), 245–46, 242–43 (recounting earlier assaults on saloons in Kewanee, Illinois; Winchester, Indiana; Otsego, Michigan; Farmington, Illinois; Cuyahoga Falls, Ohio; Mt. Pleasant, Ohio; Dixon, Illinois; and other places). For earlier conflict, see also Anthony Gene Carey, "The Second Party System Collapses: The 1853 Maine Law Campaign in Ohio," *Ohio History* 100 (Summer/Autumn

1991), 129–53, and Donald K. Gorell, "Presbyterians in the Ohio Temperance Movement of the 1850s," *Ohio History* 60, no. 3 (July 1951), 292–96.

201. Postel, *Equality*, 116. Willard was president of the Evanston College for Ladies, which merged into Northwestern University, where Willard became a professor and the dean of women. Postel, *Equality*, 124–25.

202. Hubbart, *Older Middle West*, 265.

203. Postel, *Equality*, 114. The petitions specifically called for the outlawing of alcohol in Washington, DC, and the territories.

204. Jeannette P. Nichols, "Contradictory Trends in Middle Western Democracy, 1865–1900," in Nichols and Randall, *Democracy in the Middle West*, 84. When Frances Willard became president of the WCTU in 1879 it had "no organization below the Mason-Dixon Line," and as a midwestern Republican she was not likely to appeal to southerners, but she tried. Postel, *Equality*, 136 (quotation), 137–38.

205. Postel, *Equality*, 123.

206. Paula Baker, "The Domestication of Politics: Women and American Political Society, 1780–1920," *American Historical Review* 89, no. 3 (June 1984), 638. The "Do Everything" policy meant that a local union could choose its direction: "It might focus its energies on educating children or prisoners about the dangers of alcohol, or on fighting tobacco or prostitution." Postel, *Equality*, 125.

207. See generally Agnes D. Hays, *A Heritage of Dedication* (Evanston, IL: Signal Press, 1974).

208. K. Austin Kerr, "Organizing for Reform: The Anti-Saloon League and Innovation in Politics," *American Quarterly* 32, no. 1 (Spring 1980), 43; Peter H. Odegard, *Pressure Politics: The Story of the Anti-Saloon League* (New York: Columbia University Press, 1928), 9–10.

209. Garner, "'Prayerful Public Protest,'" 217 (accepted, rejected, crossed), 218; Baker, "Domestication of Politics," 638.

210. Patrick G. O'Brien, Kenneth J. Peak, and Barbara K. Robins, "'It May Have Been Illegal, but It Wasn't Wrong': The Kansas 'Balkans' Bootlegging Culture, 1920–1940," *Kansas History* 11, no. 4 (Winter 1988/1989), 260; Lisa L. Ossian, "Bandits, Mad Men, and Suicides: Fear, Anger, and Death in a Troubled Landscape, 1929–1933," *Agricultural History* 80, no. 3 (Summer 2006), 302; Garner, "'Prayerful Public Protest,'" 218.

211. Martha B. Caldwell, "The Woman Suffrage Campaign of 1912," *Kansas Historical Quarterly* 12, no. 3 (August 1943), 300–326; Garner, "'Prayerful Public Protest,'" 218.

212. Postel, *Equality*, 130.

213. Elizabeth D. Katz, "'A Woman Stumps Her State': Nellie G. Robinson and Women's Rights to Hold Public Office," *Akron Law Review* 53, no. 2 (2019), 320, 322 n. 47 (other).

214. Karen Tokarz, "A Tribute to the Nation's First Women Law Students," *Washington University Law Review* 68, no. 1 (January 1990), 91–92 (generous), 101.

215. Katz, "'Woman Stumps Her State,'" 322.

216. Alice Jordan, a transfer student from the University of Michigan Law School, was allowed into Yale Law School in 1885, but soon afterward the policy was changed to make it clear that Yale law courses were "open to persons of the male

sex only." D. Kelly Weisberg, "Barred from the Bar: Women and Legal Education in the United States, 1870–1890," *Journal of Legal Education* 28 (1977), 486–87. Also, in the world of landscape architecture, "midwestern universities generally provided easier access than their East Coast counterparts, many of which were firmly closed to women applicants." Tishler, *Midwestern Landscape Architecture*, 4.

217. Katz, "'Woman Stumps Her State,'" 322, 323 (advances). When interpreting the word "persons" while determining who could become a notary public, the Nebraska Supreme Court read it widely to include women, whereas the Massachusetts Supreme Court read it narrowly to exclude women. Katz, "'Woman Stumps Her State,'" 326. See Nancy T. Gilliam, "A Professional Pioneer: Myra Bradwell's Fight to Practice Law," *Law and History Review* 5 (1987), 106 (noting that Bradwell attended school in Wisconsin and taught in Michigan).

218. Warwick v. Ohio, 25 Ohio St. 21 (Ohio 1874); Katz, "'Woman Stumps Her State,'" 329.

219. Katz, "'Woman Stumps Her State,'" 327, 334. See also Gerald R. Butters Jr., "'But I'm Only a Woman': Tiera Farrow's Defense of Clare Schweiger," *Kansas History* 25, no. 3 (Autumn 2002), 191–99 (explaining the story of Indiana-born Tiera Farrow, who rose from grain company stenographer to prominent Kansas City lawyer).

220. Caldwell, "Woman Suffrage," 300; Wilda M. Smith, "A Half Century of Struggle: Gaining Woman Suffrage in Kansas," *Kansas History* 4, no. 2 (Summer 1981), 76; Kathryn A. Nicholas, "Reexamining Women's Nineteenth-Century Political Agency: School Suffrage and Office-Holding," *Journal of Policy History* 30, no. 3 (2018), 454 (noting that "before the late 1870s, school suffrage provisions were adopted exclusively outside New England and often predated the establishment of woman suffrage organizations," and they "were included in legislation without active lobbying and without prior notice").

221. Lorraine A. Gehring, "Women Officeholders in Kansas, 1872–1912," *Kansas History* 9, no. 2 (Summer 1986), 48.

222. Hoehnle, "Iowa Clubwomen," 39. See Frederick L. Johnson, "Julia B. Nelson: 'The Rock on Which the Effort for Woman Suffrage Has Been Founded in This State,'" *Minnesota History* 67, no. 3 (Fall 2020), 104–15.

223. Kristin Mapel Bloomberg, "'A Vast Host of Consecrated Women': New Scholarship on Minnesota's Women Suffrage and Women's Rights Movement," *Minnesota History* 67, no. 3 (Fall 2020), 89.

224. Alfred Hewetson Mitchell, "America's First Woman Mayor," *Ohio History Journal* 53, no. 1 (January–March 1944), 52–54. Mitchell speculates that Salter was the first woman mayor in the world; Griffin, "Emancipated Spirits," 34.

225. Gehring, "Women Officeholders," 48–49, 57 (noting the "nearly total lack of press coverage about these women and their elections"); Griffin, "Emancipated Spirits," 34.

226. William Barlow and David O. Powell, "Homeopathy and Sexual Equality: The Controversy over Coeducation at Cincinnati's Pulte Medical College, 1873–1879," *Ohio History Journal* 90, no. 2 (Spring 1981), 101, 103. See also Barbara Sicherman, *Alice Hamilton: A Life in Letters* (Cambridge, MA: Harvard University Press, 1984) (chronicling the life of Hamilton, an 1897 graduate of University of

Michigan Medical School and professor at the Northwestern Hospital for Women and Children), and John B. Gabel, ed., "Medical Education in the 1890s: An Ohio Woman's Memories," *Ohio History Journal* 87, no. 1 (Winter 1978), 53–66.

227. Griffin, "Emancipated Spirits," 34 (sister); Lief, "Women of Purpose," 304.

228. Sara Egge, "Woman Suffrage Is a Midwestern Story: Gender, Region, and Nativism, 1880–1920," *Middle West Review* 4, no. 2 (Spring 2018), 3 (claimed), 9 (uplift), 11 (stellar). To provide broader appeal, the president of the Indiana WCTU, Zerelda Wallace, advocated "human rights" and rejected the narrow term "women's rights." Postel, *Equality*, 129.

229. Sklar, "Female Teachers," 65; Theobald, *Call School*, 65.

230. Lawrence E. Ziewacz, "Thomas W. Palmer: A Michigan Senator's 'Masterly Argument' for Women's Suffrage," *Michigan Historical Review* 26, no. 1 (Spring 2000), 31, 35 (quotation).

231. Gehring, "Women Officeholders," 49; Egge, "Woman Suffrage Is a Midwestern Story," 5; Katz, "'Woman Stumps Her State,'" 315.

232. Egge, "Woman Suffrage Is a Midwestern Story," 13–14; James E. Potter, "*Barkley v. Pool:* Woman Suffrage and the Nebraska Referendum Law," *Nebraska History* 69, no. 1 (Spring 1988), 11. See also Steven M. Buechler, *The Transformation of the Woman Suffrage Movement: The Case of Illinois, 1850–1920* (New Brunswick, NJ: Rutgers University Press, 1986); Louise R. Noun, *Strong-Minded Women: The Emergence of the Woman-Suffrage Movement in Iowa* (Ames: Iowa State University Press, 1969); Anita Morgan, *We Must Be Fearless: The Woman Suffrage Movement in Indiana* (Indianapolis: Indiana Historical Society Press, 2020); Sharon E. McHaney, "Securing the Sacred Right to Vote," *Michigan History Magazine* 75, no. 3 (March/April 1991), 38–45; Barbara Stuhler, "Organizing for the Vote: Leaders of the Minnesota Woman Suffrage Movement," *Minnesota History* 54, no. 7 (Fall 1995), 290–303; Cynthia Wilkey, "Diversity and Woman Suffrage: A Case Study of the Dayton Woman Suffrage Association in the 1912 Referendum Campaign," *Ohio History* 112 (Winter/Spring 2003), 27–37; Kristin Mapel Bloomberg, "'Striving for Equal Rights for All': Woman Suffrage in Nebraska, 1855–1882," *Nebraska History* 90, no. 2 (Summer 2009), 84–103; Kristin Mapel Bloomberg, "The Political Equality Club of Minneapolis," *Minnesota History* 60, no. 3 (Fall 2006), 113–22; Theodora W. Youmans, "How Wisconsin Women Won the Ballot," *Wisconsin Magazine of History* 5, no. 1 (September 1921), 3–32.

233. Egge, "Woman Suffrage Is a Midwestern Story," 14 (no other), 4 (civic, patriotic, pro-suffrage), 2 (rapidly).

234. McDonagh and Price, "Woman Suffrage in the Progressive Era, 416, n. 5 (calling the South "well-nigh hopeless for suffrage"), n. 3 (finding that "women in the South were slower to mobilize in support of suffrage"); Postel, *Equality*, 131 (never).

235. Cooper, "Why Wisconsin?," 15 (explaining that the "most successful and best known of [the] urban reform movements occurred" in the Midwest). On women and urban reform, see Robert Burnham, "Women and Reform in Cincinnati: Responsible Citizenship and the Politics of 'Good Government,' 1924–1955," *Ohio Valley History* 13, no. 2 (Summer 2013), 48–69. On the same city, see Zane Miller, *Boss Cox's Cincinnati: Urban Politics in the Progressive Era* (New York: Oxford

University Press, 1968); Landon Warner, "Henry T. Hunt and Civic Reform in Cincinnati, 1903–1913," *Ohio History* 62, no. 2 (April 1953), 146–61; and Robert B. Fairbanks, *Making Better Citizens: Housing Reform and the Community Development Strategy in Cincinnati, 1890–1960* (Urbana: University of Illinois Press, 1989). On Dayton, see Judith Sealander, *Grand Plans: Business Progressivism and Social Change in Ohio's Miami Valley, 1890–1929* (Lexington: University Press of Kentucky, 1988).

236. Hoyt Landon Warner, *Progressivism in Ohio, 1897–1917* (Columbus: Ohio State University Press, 1964).

237. Neil J. Lehto, *The Thirty-Year War: A History of Detroit's Streetcars, 1892–1922* (East Lansing: Michigan State University Press, 2017), 51–52; Melvin Holli, *Reform in Detroit: Hazen S. Pingree and Urban Politics* (New York: Oxford University Press, 1969).

238. Lehto, *Thirty-Year War*, 52.

239. Alexander W. Lough, "Hazen S. Pingree and the Detroit Model of Urban Reform," *American Journal of Economics and Sociology* 75, no. 1 (January 1916), 58–85; Lehto, *Thirty-Year War*, 52–56; Katzman, *Black Ghetto*, 199, 202.

240. Katzman, *Black Ghetto*, 201. See also Jack D. Elenbaas, "The Boss of the Better Class: Henry Leland and the Detroit Citizens League, 1912–1924," *Michigan History* 58, no. 2 (Summer 1974), 131–50.

241. David R. Berman, *Governors and the Progressive Movement: Publishing in Rhetoric and Composition* (Louisville: University Press of Colorado, 2019), 27 (describing the patches as "thoroughly practical").

242. Michael Megery, "Ideological Origins of a Radical Democrat: The Early Political Thought of Tom L. Johnson, 1888–1895," *Middle West Review* 6, nos. 1–2 (Fall/Spring 2019/2020), 37–61 (also noting the involvement of Frederic C. Howe and Newton D. Baker in Cleveland's reform politics); Roy Lubove, "Frederic C. Howe and the Quest for Community in America," *Historian* 39, no. 2 (February 1977), 272 (noting that Howe came to Cleveland to work in the law offices of Harry and James Garfield, the sons of the former president); Robert H. Bremner, "Tom L. Johnson," *Ohio Historical Journal* 59, no. 1 (January 1950), 1–13; Fuller, "Rural Roots of Progressive Leaders," 4–5, 9.

243. Robert Bionaz, "Streetcar Politics and Reform Government in Cleveland, 1880–1909," *Ohio History* 119 (2012), 16; Shelton Stromquist, "The Crucible of Class: Cleveland Politics and the Origins of Municipal Reform in the Progressive Era," *Journal of Urban History* 23, no. 2 (January 1997), 197.

244. Marnie Jones, *Holy Toledo: Religion and Politics in the Life of "Golden Rule" Jones* (Lexington: University Press of Kentucky, 1998). See also Arjun Sabharwal, "City, Legacy, and Reform: The Beginnings of the Toledo Humane Society," *Ohio History* 125, no. 1 (Spring 2018), 47–69.

245. Jack Tager, *The Intellectual as Urban Reformer: Brand Whitlock and the Progressive Movement* (Cleveland: Press of Case Western Reserve University, 1968); Abe C. Ravitz, "Brand Whitlock's Macochee: Puritan Theo-Politics in the Midwest," *Ohio History Journal* 68, no. 3 (July 1959), 257–75; Shirley Leckie, "Brand Whitlock and the City Beautiful Movement in Toledo, Ohio," *Ohio History Journal* 91 (1982 annual), 5–27; Neil Thorburn, "Brand Whitlock: A Public

Official as a Muckraker," *Ohio History* 78, no. 1 (Winter 1969), 5–12 (connecting Whitlock to William Dean Howells and literary realism); Robert M. Crunden, *A Hero in Spite of Himself: Brand Whitlock in Art, Politics, and War* (New York: Alfred A. Knopf, 1969). See also Neil Thorburn, "William Dean Howells as a Literary Model: The Experience of Brand Whitlock," *Northwest Ohio Quarterly* 39 (Winter 1966/1967), 22–35.

246. See Bradley Robert Rice, *Progressive Cities: The Commission Government Movement in America, 1901–1920* (Austin: University of Texas Press, 1977).

247. See chapters titled "Midwesterners Paving the Way" and "More Midwesterners" in Berman, *Governors and the Progressive Movement*, and Howard W. Allen, "Geography and Politics: Voting on Reform Issues in the United States Senate, 1911–1916," *Journal of Southern History* 27, no. 2 (May 1961), 221 (noting a sectional difference among Republican senators when voting on reform measures).

248. Charles A. Madison, "John Peter Altgeld: Pioneer Progressive," *Antioch Review* 5, no. 1 (Spring 1945), 121–22, 131; Harvey Wish, "Altgeld and the Progressive Tradition," *American Historical Review* 46, no. 4 (July 1941), 815; Berman, *Governors and the Progressive Movement*, 39; Harvey Wish, "John Peter Altgeld and the Election of 1896," *Journal of the Illinois State Historical Society* 30, no. 3 (October 1937), 354–55. See also Thomas R. Pegram, *Partisans and Progressives: Private Interest and Public Policy in Illinois, 1870–1922* (Urbana: University of Illinois Press, 1992).

249. Kathryn Kish Sklar, "Hull House in the 1890s: A Community of Women Reformers," *Signs* 10, no. 4 (Summer 1985), 658–77; Ginger, *Altgeld's America*, 11; Berman, *Governors and the Progressive Movement*, 39.

250. Fleming Fraker Jr., "The Beginnings of the Progressive Movement in Iowa," *Annals of Iowa* 35, no. 8 (Spring 1961), 582; Cooper, "Why Wisconsin?," 18; Thomas James Bray, "The Cummins Leadership," *Annals of Iowa* 32, no. 4 (April 1954), 241–96; Berman, *Governors and the Progressive Movement*, 57 (Methodist), 58.

251. Kenneth L. Smith, "Presbyterianism, Progressivism, and Cultural Influence: William M. Blackburn, Coe I. Crawford, and the Making of Civic Dakota," in Jon K. Lauck, John E. Miller, and Paula M. Nelson, eds., *The Plains Political Tradition: Essays on South Dakota Political Culture*, vol. 3 (Pierre: South Dakota Historical Society Press, 2018), 85–111; Calvin Perry Armin, "Coe I. Crawford and the Progressive Movement in South Dakota," *South Dakota Historical Collections* 32 (1964), 23–231.

252. Berman, *Governors and the Progressive Movement*, 70.

253. Robert S. Maxwell, "La Follette and the Election of 1900: A Half-Century Reappraisal," *Wisconsin Magazine of History* 35, no. 1 (Autumn 1951), 24; Kenneth Acrea, "The Wisconsin Reform Coalition, 1892–1900: La Follette's Rise to Power," *Wisconsin Magazine of History* 52, no. 2 (Winter 1968–1969), 132–57. See generally David P. Thelen, *Robert M. La Follette and the Insurgent Spirit* (Boston: Little, Brown and Company, 1976) and Thelen, *The New Citizenship: Origins of Progressivism in Wisconsin, 1885–1900* (Columbia: University of Missouri Press, 1972); Nancy C. Unger, *Fighting Bob La Follette: The Righteous Reformer* (Chapel Hill: University of North Carolina Press, 2000); John D. Buenker, "Robert M. La

Follette's Progressive Odyssey," *Wisconsin Magazine of History* 82, no. 1 (Autumn 1999), 2–31.

254. Maxwell, "La Follette and the Election of 1900," 25. The "father of Wisconsin progressivism" was Albert R. Hall, a dairy farmer from Western Wisconsin who was a farmer activist and a nephew of Oliver Kelley, founder of the Grange. David P. Thelen, "Social Tensions and the Origins of Progressivism," *Journal of American History* 56, no. 2 (September 1969), 333. President Bascom of the University of Wisconsin was also a strong supporter of coeducation. Olin, *Women of a State University*, 71–79.

255. Cooper, "Why Wisconsin?" 18–19, 22; Maxwell, "La Follette and the Election of 1900," 25; W. Elliot Brownlee Jr., "Income Taxation and the Political Economy of Wisconsin," *Wisconsin Magazine of History* 59, no. 4 (Summer 1976), 299 (noting that "Wisconsin contributed the first comprehensive, effectively administered income tax [and] served as a model for other states and for the federal government in the search for tax systems appropriate to a maturing industrial order"). On progressive politics and the rise of college football with a special focus on Wisconsin, see Brian M. Ingrassia, "Public Influence Inside the College Walls: Progressive Era Universities, Social Scientists, and Intercollegiate Football Reform," *Journal of the Gilded Age and Progressive Era* 10, no. 1 (January 2011), 59–88.

256. Burton, "Wisconsin's First Railroad Commission," 198. For a discussion of Kansas, see Robert Sherman La Forte, *Leaders of Reform: Progressive Republicans in Kansas, 1900–1916* (Lawrence: University Press of Kansas, 1974)(noting, inter alia, railroad regulations, tax reform, direct elections, prohibition, and home rule for cities).

257. Robert S. Maxwell, "La Follette and the Progressive Machine in Wisconsin," *Indiana Magazine of History* 48, no. 1 (March 1952), 58 (quotation); Tucker, "Azariah Smith Root," 283; J. David Hoeveler Jr., "The University and the Social Gospel: The Intellectual Origins of the 'Wisconsin Idea,'" *Wisconsin Magazine of History* 59, no. 4 (Summer 1976), 282–98; Benjamin G. Rader, *The Academic Mind and Reform: The Influence of Richard T. Ely in American Life* (Lexington: University of Kentucky Press, 1966); Lloyd J. Graybar, *Albert Shaw of the Review of Reviews* (Lexington: University Press of Kentucky, 1974), 35.

258. Charles Delgadillo, *Crusader for Democracy: The Political Life of William Allen White* (Lawrence: University Press of Kansas, 2018).

259. Hannah Schell and Daniel Ott, *Christian Thought in America: A Brief History* (Minneapolis: Fortress Press, 2015), 222; Paul Boyer, "An Ohio Leader of the Social Gospel Movement: Reassessing Washington Gladden," *Ohio History* 116 (2009), 88–100; Cara Lea Burnidge, *Washington Gladden's Church: The Minister Who Made Modern American Protestantism* (Lanham, MD: Rowman and Littlefield, 2019); Boyer, "Ohio Leader," 88–100.

260. Tucker, "Azariah Smith Root," 283.

261. Robert M. Crunden, "George D. Herron in the 1890s: A New Frame of Reference for the Study of the Progressive Era," *Annals of Iowa* 42, no. 2 (Fall 1973), 83–84 (highlighting the importance of "character development" to progressives and the "importance of American Protestantism in forming the world views of leading progressives"); H. R. Dieterich, "Radical on the Campus: Professor Herron

at Iowa College, 1893–1899," *Annals of Iowa* 37, no. 6 (Fall 1964), 401–15. For another example, see Thomas E. Graham, ed., "Jenkin Lloyd Jones and 'The Gospel of the Farm,'" *Wisconsin Magazine of History* 67, no. 2 (Winter 1983/1984), 121–48 (describing the Wisconsin-raised Union Army veteran who was minister of All Souls Unitarian Church in Chicago and the director of the reform organization the Abraham Lincoln Center).

262. Ross, "Religious Influences," 356. See also John Derge, "In Search of the Kingdom in Milwaukee: Judson Titsworth and the Social Gospel: 1883–1909," *Mid-America* 66, no. 3 (October 1984), 99–111; Thomas M. Jacklin, "The Civic Awakening: Social Christianity and the Usable Past," *Mid-America* 64, no. 2 (April–July 1982), 3–19.

263. Downey, "William Stead and Chicago," 156 (spiritual), 160 (devil).

264. Downey, "William Stead and Chicago," 156. Stead also wrote *If Christ Came to Chicago* (Chicago: Laird and Lee, 1894) and died on the *Titanic*. Joseph O. Baylen, "A Victorian's 'Crusade' in Chicago, 1893–1894," *Journal of American History* 51, no. 3 (December 1964), 418.

265. Morton G. White, *Social Thought in America: The Revolt against Formalism* (New York: Viking Press, 1949) (discussing midwesterners such as Charles Beard, Thorstein Veblen, and James Harvey Robinson). White also discusses John Dewey, who moved from the University of Michigan to the University of Chicago in 1894 and witnessed firsthand the social and reform movements of that time and place. Robert B. Westbrook, *Democratic Hope: Pragmatism and the Politics of Truth* (Ithaca, NY: Cornell University Press, 2005), 74. For related figures, see James L. Colwell, "The Populist Image of Vernon Louis Parrington," *Mississippi Valley Historical Review* 49, no. 1 (June 1962), 52–66, and D. G. Paz, "'For Zion's Sake, Will I Not Hold My Peace': John Williams, Radical Omaha Priest, 1877–1914," *Nebraska History* 63, no. 1 (Spring 1982), 87–107 (advocating for hospitals and churches); Andrew A. Sorensen, "Lester Frank Ward, 'The American Aristotle,'" in Illinois," *Journal of the Illinois State Historical Society* 63, no. 2 (Summer 1970), 158–66. See also Fuller, "Rural Roots of Progressive Leaders," 10. On Beard, see also David S. Brown, *Beyond the Frontier: The Midwestern Voice in American Historical Writing* (Chicago: University of Chicago Press, 2008), and Richard Hofstadter, *The Progressive Historians: Turner, Beard, Parrington* (New York: Vintage Books, 1968), 167–346.

266. See Gregory L. Crider, "William Dean Howells and the Gilded Age: Socialist in a Fur-Lined Overcoat," *Ohio History Journal* 88, no. 4 (Autumn 1979), 408–18; Fuller, "Rural Roots of Progressive Leaders," 9 (noting that the famed S. S. McClure was "a farm boy from Illinois"); Robert Stinson, "S. S. McClure's *My Autobiography:* The Progressive as Self-Made Man," *American Quarterly* 22, no. 2 (Summer 1970), 203–12 (explaining McClure's link to midwesterners such as Willa Cather and Ray Stannard Baker); J. Wayne Baker, "Populist Themes in the Fiction of Ignatius Donnelly," *American Studies* 14, no. 2 (Fall 1973), 65–83. See also Chester McArthur Destler, *Henry Demarest Lloyd and the Empire of Reform* (Philadelphia: University of Pennsylvania Press, 1963). On fantasy/utopian works, see H. Roger Grant, "Henry Olerich and the Utopian Ideal," *Nebraska History* 56, no. 2 (Summer 1975), 249; H. Roger Grant, "Henry Olerich and Utopia: The Iowa

Years, 1870–1902," *Annals of Iowa* 43, no. 5 (Summer 1976), 349–62; and Kenneth M. Roemer, *The Obsolete Necessity: America in Utopian Writing, 1888–1900* (Kent, OH: Kent State University Press, 1976).

267. Ginger, *Altgeld's America*, 11, 13. See also Guy Szuberla, "Three Chicago Settlements: Their Architectural Form and Social Meaning," *Journal of the Illinois State Historical Society* 70, no. 2 (May 1977), 114–29; John J. Grabowski, "From Progressive to Patrician: George Bellamy and Hiram House Social Settlement, 1896–1914," *Ohio History* 87, no. 1 (Winter 1978), 37–52; and Judith A. Trolander, "Twenty Years at Hiram House," *Ohio History Journal* 78, no. 1 (Winter 1969), 25–37.

268. Allen F. Davis, *Spearheads for Reform: The Social Settlements and the Progressive Movement, 1890–1914* (New York: Oxford University Press, 1967); Robert M. Crunden, *Ministers of Reform: The Progressives' Achievement in American Civilization, 1889–1920* (New York: Basic Books, 1982), 19 (arguing that the "foundations of Hull-House were laid in one woman's moral revulsion against privileged uselessness"), 17 (dating the beginning of progressivism as the founding of Hull House); Jean Bethke Elshtain, *Jane Addams and the Dream of American Democracy: A Life* (New York: Basic Books, 2002); Daphne Spain, "The Chicago of Jane Addams and Ernest Burgess," in Dennis R. Judd and Dick Simpson, eds., *The City, Revisited: Urban Theory from Chicago, Los Angeles, and New York* (Minneapolis: University of Minnesota Press, 2011), 53–55. More generally, Crunden properly emphasizes the moral zeal and Christian beliefs at the center of much progressivism. See also Lela B. Costin, *Two Sisters for Social Justice: A Biography of Grace and Edith Abbott* (Urbana: University of Illinois Press, 1983) (describing two sisters who originally worked at Hull House and then directed the Chicago Immigrants' Protective League and organized social service studies at the University of Chicago).

269. Elaine Frantz Parsons, *Manhood Lost: Fallen Drunkards and Redeeming Women in the Nineteenth-Century United States* (Baltimore, MD: Johns Hopkins University Press, 2003).

270. Postel, *Equality*, 119.

271. Leslie R. Valentine, "Evangelist Billy Sunday's Clean-up Campaign in Omaha: Local Reaction to His 50-Day Revival," *Nebraska History* 64, no. 2 (Summer 1983), 209–10.

272. S. D. Fitchie, "The Fight for Prohibition in Nebraska," *Nebraska History* 6, no. 3 (July–September 1923), 83.

273. Brace, "Power of Porch Talks," 20.

274. Kusmer, "Functions of Organized Charity," 657–62 (noting the large number of charities in Chicago and that historians tend to neglect private and volunteer relief organizations). See also Lynne Curry, *Modern Mothers in the Heartland: Gender, Health, and Progress in Illinois, 1900–1930* (Columbus: Ohio State University Press, 1999). For Ohio, see Robert M. Mennel and Steven Spackman, "Origins of Welfare in the States: Albert G. Byers and the Ohio Board of Charities," *Ohio History Journal* 92 (1983 annual), 72–95.

275. Postel, *Equality*, 134.

276. Patricia C. Gaster, "'A Fallen Victim to the Liquor Curse': The Life and Tragic Death of Samuel D. Cox," *Nebraska History* 89, no. 2 (Summer 2008), 86;

Mary E. Humphrey, "Springfield Home for the Friendless," *Journal of the Illinois State Historical Society* 20, no. 1 (April 1927), 138–54.

277. Marian J. Morton, *And Sin No More: Social Policy and Unwed Mothers in Cleveland, 1855–1990* (Columbus: Ohio State University Press, 1993).

278. Buley, *Old Northwest*, 1:73.

279. Evelyn C. Adams, "The Growing Concept of Social Responsibility Illustrated by a Study of the State's Care of the Insane in Indiana," *Indiana Magazine of History* 32, no. 1 (March 1936), 1–21; Ann Clymer Bigelow, "Cincinnati's Neglected Insane Asylum," *Ohio Valley History* 13, no. 2 (Summer 2013), 3–24; Ann Clymer Bigelow, "'The Most Appalling Forms of Degradation': Dorothea Dix Speaks Out for the Insane in Ohio Poorhouses," *Ohio Valley History* 18, no. 4 (Winter 2018), 23–41.

280. Steven R. Kinsella, "Buena Vista Sanatorium Wabasha County," *Minnesota History* 63, no. 4 (Winter 2012/2013), 131.

281. Marilyn Irvin Holt, "Children's Health and the Campaign for Better Babies," *Kansas History* 28, no. 3 (Autumn 2005), 174–87.

282. See Marilyn Irvin Holt, "'Over the Hill to the Poorhouse': Kansas Poor Relief," *Kansas History* 39, no. 1 (Spring 2016), 2–15; Thomas D. Mackie, "Over the Hill to the Poorhouse: A Glimpse at the County Farms of Southern Michigan, 1850s–1920s," *Pioneer America Society Transactions* 21 (1998), 22 (noting that by the late 1800s "nearly every Michigan county had a 'county farm' to care for the indigent of its jurisdiction"); Kayla Hassett, "The County Home in Indiana: A Forgotten Response to Poverty and Disability (M.A. thesis, Ball State University, 2013); Tom Mackie, "Stuck in the Poorhouse: The Complexity of Poverty," Indiana History Blog (July 25, 2018); Michael R. Daley and Peggy Pittman-Munke, "Over the Hill to the Poor Farm: Rural History Almost Forgotten," *Contemporary Rural Social Work Journal* 8, no. 2 (September 2016), 1–17; Bruce Smith, "Poor Relief at the St. Joseph County Poor Asylum, 1877–1891," *Indiana Magazine of History* 86, no. 2 (June 1990), 178–96; Frank Levstik, ed., "Life among the Lowly: An Early View of the Ohio Poorhouse," *Ohio History* 88, no. 1 (Winter 1979), 84–88; Elizabeth Gaspar Brown, "Poor Relief in a Wisconsin County, 1846–1866: Administration and Recipients," *American Journal of Legal History* 20, no. 2 (April 1976), 79–117; Ethel McClure, "An Unlamented Era: County Poor Farms in Minnesota," *Minnesota History* 38, no. 8 (December 1963), 365–77. See also Frederick D. Seaton, "The Long Road Toward 'The Right Thing to Do': The Troubled History of Winfield State Hospital," *Kansas History* 27 (Winter 2004/2005), 252–53 (focusing on a home for the developmentally disabled).

283. Ann Clymer Bigelow, "Dr. William M. Awl, Idealistic Founder of the Ohio Lunatic Asylum," *Ohio Valley History* 13, no. 4 (Winter 2013), 3–22; Klaus Hartman and Les Margolin, "The Nebraska Asylum for the Insane, 1870–1886," *Nebraska History* 63, no. 2 (Summer 1982), 164–82; Emil R. Pinta, "Samuel M. Smith, 'Dr. Cure-Awl's Assistant at the Ohio Lunatic Asylum: His 1841 Case-Reports on Insanity," *Ohio History* 107 (Winter/Spring 1998), 58–75. See also Robert L. Osgood, "From 'Public Liabilities' to 'Public Assets': Special Education for Children with Mental Retardation in Indiana Public Schools, 1908–1931," *Indiana Magazine of History* 98, no. 3 (September 2002), 203–20; Robert L. Osgood, "The Menace of the

Feebleminded: George Bliss, Amos Butler, and the Indiana Committee on Mental Defectives," *Indiana Magazine of History* 97, no. 4 (December 2001), 253–60.

284. "Catherine Fay Ewing, Originator of Children's Homes," *Ohio History Journal* 34, no. 2 (April 1925), 241 (noting the creation of thirty-seven children's homes for neglected or destitute children in Ohio from 1866 to 1871); Holt, "'Over the Hill to the Poorhouse,'" 9; LeRoy Ashby, *Saving the Waifs: Reformers and Dependent Children, 1890–1917* (Philadelphia: Temple University Press, 1984) (noting, inter alia, the Children's Home Society of Minnesota and the Toledo Newsboys' Association); Thomas W. Cowger, "Custodians of Social Justice: The Indianapolis Asylum for Friendless Colored Children, 1870–1922," *Indiana Magazine of History* 88, no. 2 (June 1992), 93–100; Marian J. Morton, "Homes for Poverty's Children: Cleveland's Orphanages, 1851–1933," *Ohio History* 98 (Winter/Spring 1989), 5–22; Jan Gregoire Coombs, "Indentured Children of the Wisconsin Public School," *Wisconsin Magazine of History* 100, no. 3 (Spring 2017), 40–53; Mike McTighe, "Leading Men, True Women, Protestant Churches, and the Shape of Antebellum Benevolence," in David D. Van Tassel and John J. Grabowski, eds., *Cleveland: A Tradition of Reform* (Kent, OH: Kent State University Press, 1985), 20–24. See also Megan Birk, "The Farm, Foster Care, and Dependent Children in the Midwest, 1880–1920," *Journal of the Gilded Age and Progressive Era* 12, no. 3 (July 2013), 320–42 (describing dependent children who were placed on farms).

285. LeRoy Ashby, "'Recreate This Boy': Allendale Farm, the Child, and Progressivism," *Mid-America* 58, no. 1 (January 1976), 31.

286. Holt, "'Over the Hill to the Poorhouse,'" 6, n. 7; Paul D. Nelson, "Early Days of the State Reform School," *Minnesota History* 63, no. 4 (Winter 2013/2014), 132–43; Georgina Hickey, "Rescuing the Working Girl: Agency and Conflict in the Michigan Reform School for Girls, 1879–1893," *Michigan Historical Review* 20, no. 1 (Spring 1994), 1–28; Dennis Thavenet, "The Michigan Reform School and the Civil War: Officers and Inmates Mobilized for the Union Cause," *Michigan Historical Review* 13, no. 1 (Spring 1987), 21–46; Robert M. Mennel, "'Family System of Common Farmers': The Early Years of Ohio's Reform Farm, 1840–1858," *Ohio History Journal* 89, no. 2 (Spring 1980), 279–322; Anne Meis Knupfer, "'To Become Good, Self-Supporting Women': The State Industrial School for Delinquent Girls at Geneva, Illinois, 1900–1935," *Journal of the History of Sexuality* 9, no. 4 (October 2000), 420–46. See also Ellen D. Swain, "From Benevolence to Reform: The Expanding Career of Mrs. Rhoda M. Coffin," *Indiana Magazine of History* 97, no. 3 (September 2001), 190–217.

287. Joan M. Jensen, "Sexuality on a Northern Frontier: The Gendering and Disciplining of Rural Wisconsin Women, 1850–1920," *Agricultural History* 73, no. 2 (Spring 1999), 144, 145–46 (delinquent, bad).

288. Mennel and Spackman, "Origins of Welfare in the States," 74–75.

289. Richard Schneirov, "Chicago's Great Upheaval of 1877," *Chicago History* 9, no. 1 (Spring 1980), 6 (bugs), 9, 16 (level; also describing workers invoking "terms of opprobrium" such as "aristocrats" and "monopolists" to highlight their break from egalitarian ideals). Thirty workers were killed and another two hundred injured. Most of those killed and injured were Irishmen. Schneirov, "Chicago's Great Upheaval," 15.

290. Timothy Messer-Kruse, *The Trial of the Haymarket Anarchists: Terrorism and Justice in the Gilded Age* (New York: Palgrave Macmillan, 2011); "'Eagle Forgotten': The Algeld Centenary in Illinois, 1847–1947," *Social Service Review* 22, no. 1 (March 1948), 85–86. On the role of labor groups and reform in Chicago generally, see Richard Schneirov, *Labor and Urban Politics: Class Conflict and the Origins of Modern Liberalism in Chicago, 1864–1897* (Urbana: University of Illinois Press, 1998).

291. Terry S. Reynolds, "Calm or Conflicted? Labor-Management Relations on Michigan's Iron Ranges in the Nineteenth Century," *Michigan Historical Review* 33, no. 2 (Fall 2007), 1–45; Arnold R. Alanen, "Early Labor Strife on Minnesota's Mining Frontier, 1882–1906," *Minnesota History* 52, no. 7 (Fall 1991), 246–63.

292. Richard Schneirov, "'To the Ragged Edge of Anarchy': The 1894 Pullman Boycott," *OAH Magazine of History* 13, no. 3 (Spring 1999), 27 (explaining that workers' wages were cut 33 percent though the rent of Pullman-owned housing was not reduced, pushing some workers' families into destitution and causing civic leaders to hold Pullman "responsible for that violation of the Victorian moral code").

293. Jane Eva Baxter, "The Paradox of a Capitalist Utopia: Visionary Ideals and Lived Experience in the Pullman Community, 1880–1900," *International Journal of Historical Archaeology* 16, no. 4 (December 2012), 652 (explaining that the "idyllic setting" of Pullman was designed to "elevate the moral standing and social behaviors of the factory workers"); Stanley Buder, *Pullman: An Experiment in Industrial Order and Community Planning, 1880–1930* (New York: Oxford University Press, 1967).

294. Ora Ellen Cox, "The Socialist Party in Indiana since 1896," *Indiana Magazine of History* 7, no. 2 (June 1916), 95–101. The socialist Norman Thomas grew up in Marion, Ohio, home of Warren Harding. W. A. Swanberg, *Norman Thomas: The Last Idealist* (New York: Charles Scribner's Sons, 1976).

295. Prout, *Coxey's Crusade*, 12; Carlos A. Schwantes, *Coxey's Army: An American Odyssey* (Lincoln: University of Nebraska Press, 1985); Osman C. Hooper, "The Coxey Movement in Ohio," *Ohio History Journal* 9, no. 2 (October 1900), 155–76.

296. Schneirov, "Chicago's Great Upheaval," 17; Postel, *Equality*, 120, 133 (concerned); Robert Asher, "Radicalism and Reform: State Insurance of Workmen's Compensation in Minnesota, 1910–1933," *Labor History* 14 (1973), 19–41; Richard Schneirov, "Rethinking the Relation of Labor to the Politics of Urban Social Reform in Late Nineteenth-Century America: The Case of Chicago," *International Labor and Working-Class History* 46 (Fall 1994), 93–108.

297. Roderick Nash, "Victor L. Berger: Making Marx Respectable," *Wisconsin Magazine of History* 47, no. 4 (Summer 1964), 301 (calling Milwaukee's socialist mayor the leader of the "conservative right wing of American socialism for four decades"); H. Wayne Morgan, "'Red Special': Eugene V. Debs and the Campaign of 1908," *Indiana Magazine of History* 54, no. 3 (September 1958), 212; Cooper, "Why Wisconsin?" 18.

298. David Paul Nord, "The *Appeal to Reason* and American Socialism, 1901–1920," *Kansas History* 1, no. 2 (Summer 1978), 75–89; R. Alton Lee, *Publisher for the Masses, Emmanuel Haldeman-Julius* (Lincoln: University of Nebraska Press, 2018).

299. Richard Oestreicher, "A Note on the Origins of Eugene V. Debs' 'Bending Cross' Speech," *Indiana Magazine of History* 76, no. 1 (March 1980), 56 (quotation); Hofstadter, *Age of Reform*, 240–41.

300. David A. Shannon, "The Socialist Party before the First World War: An Analysis," *Mississippi Valley Historical Review* 38, no. 2 (September 1951), 280–81 (also noting differences between eastern and midwestern socialists); John D. Buenker, "Illinois Socialists and Progressive Reform," *Journal of the Illinois State Historical Society* 63, no. 4 (Winter 1970), 368–86. See Donald T. Critchlow, ed., *Socialism in the Heartland: The Midwestern Experience, 1900–1925* (South Bend, IN: University of Notre Dame Press, 1986); Lysle E. Myer, "Radical Responses to Capitalism in Ohio before 1913," *Ohio History Journal* 79, nos. 3–4 (Summer/Autumn 1970), 193–208; William F. Zornow, "Bellamy Nationalism in Ohio, 1891 to 1896," *Ohio History Journal* 58, no. 2 (April 1949), 152–70; John Graham, ed., *"Yours for the Revolution": The Appeal to Reason, 1895–1922* (Lincoln: University of Nebraska Press, 1990).

301. Georg Leidenberger, "'The Public Is the Labor Union': Working-Class Progressivism in Turn-of-the-Century Chicago," *Labor History* 36, no. 2 (Spring 1995), 187–88 (noting that more moderate labor leaders in Chicago were later replaced by more activist unions during the early twentieth century).

302. Thelen, "Social Tensions," 335; Nye, *Midwestern Progressive Politics*, 13–14. See Paul S. Sutter, "Paved with Good Intentions: Good Roads, the Automobile, and the Rhetoric of Rural Improvement in the *Kansas Farmer*, 1890–1914," *Kansas History* 18, no. 4 (Winter 1995–96), 284–99.

303. Miles, "'Shall Woman's Voice Be Hushed?,'" 4.

304. On the trend toward a more positive understanding of the Progressive Era and its democratic nature, see Robert D. Johnston, "Re-Democratizing the Progressive Era: The Politics of Progressive Era Political Historiography," *Journal of the Gilded Age and Progressive Era* 1, no. 1 (January 2002), 78–92, and Daniel T. Rogers, "In Search of Progressivism," *Reviews in American History* 10, no. 4 (December 1982), 114. See also James T. Kloppenberg, *Uncertain Victory: Social Democracy and Progressivism in European and American Thought, 1870–1920* (New York: Oxford University Press, 1986), and Thelen, "Social Tensions," 323–41 (explaining that progressives came from all walks of life, as did stalwarts, effectively rebutting Hofstadter's claims that reformers were only those who were declining in status). See also Buenker, "Robert M. La Follette's Progressive Odyssey," 3–31 (cautioning against overhyping the moral purity of progressive leaders), and Louise E. Rickard, "The Politics of Reform in Omaha, 1918–1921," *Nebraska History* 53, no. 4 (Winter 1972), 419–45.

305. Hofstadter, *Age of Reform*, 197. Baker ghostwrote the autobiography of Robert La Follette Sr., *La Follette's Autobiography* (1913). Jorn Brondal, "The Ethnic and Racial Side of Robert M. La Follette, Sr.," *Journal of the Gilded Age and Progressive Era* 10, no. 3 (July 2011), 340.

306. Nye, *Midwestern Progressive Politics*, 4 (struggle, spirit), 14 (indigenous, moderate, practical, aimed), 32, 13.

307. John D. Hicks, "The Legacy of Populism in the Western Middle West," *Agricultural History* 23, no. 4 (October 1949), 225 (finding that "Middle Western agrarians were not socialists" but instead "small capitalists"); Nye, *Midwestern*

Progressive Politics, 13; Gene Clanton, "Populism, Progressivism, and Equality: The Kansas Paradigm," *Agricultural History* 51, no. 3 (July 1977), 565; Chester McArthur Destler, *American Radicalism, 1865–1901: Essays and Documents* (Chicago: University of Chicago Press, 1966), 222 (calling populism "at bottom a re-elaboration of the Jeffersonian tradition"); Worth Robert Miller, "*The Populist Vision:* A Roundtable Discussion," *Kansas History* 32, no. 1 (Spring 2009), 38. See also Willard Carl Klunder, *Lewis Cass and the Politics of Moderation* (Kent, OH: Kent State University Press, 1996).

308. Henry Blake Fuller, *With the Full Procession* (New York: Harper and Brothers, 1894), 245, as referenced by Hofstadter, *Age of Reform*, 166.

309. Hofstadter, *Age of Reform*, 216 (free), 5 (degenerating), 10, 137, 215 (concluding that "progressivism, at its heart, was an effort to realize familiar and traditional ideals under novel circumstances"), 217. On the transition about the time of World War I, see Henry F. May, *The End of American Innocence: A Study of the First Years of Our Own Time, 1912–1917* (New York: Alfred E. Knopf, 1959); George E. Mowry, *The Era of Theodore Roosevelt and the Birth of Modern America, 1900–1912* (New York: Harper and Brothers, 1958); Robert H. Wiebe, *The Search for Order, 1877–1920* (New York: Hill and Wang, 1967). On the cultural shifts of this era, see T. J. Jackson Lears, *No Place of Grace: Antimodernism and the Transformation of American Culture, 1880–1920* (New York: Pantheon Books, 1981), and Michael L. Berger, *The Devil Wagon in God's Country: The Automobile and Social Change in Rural America, 1893–1929* (Hamden, CT: Archon Books, 1979).

CONCLUSION

1. Robert W. Merry, *President McKinley: Architect of the American Century* (New York: Simon and Schuster, 2017), 15; Paul W. Glad, *McKinley, Bryan, and the People* (New York: J. B. Lippincott, 1964), 16 (noting that McKinley was "active in the debating societies which flourished [in Poland] as they did in even the most provincial of middle western communities").

2. H. Wayne Morgan, "William McKinley as a Political Leader," *Review of Politics* 28, no. 4 (October 1966), 417; Merry, *President McKinley*, 14 (noting that McKinley's mother Nancy Allison "personified Ohio's commitment to simple verities and the Christian values of thrift, optimism, modesty, and hard work").

3. Morgan, "William McKinley," 418.

4. Merry, *President McKinley*, 13 (320,000 Ohioans fought for the Union).

5. Glad, *McKinley, Bryan, and the People*, 18–19.

6. See William H. Armstrong, *Major McKinley: William McKinley and the Civil War* (Kent, OH: Kent State University Press, 2000).

7. H. Wayne Morgan, *William McKinley and His America* (Syracuse: Syracuse University Press, 1963), 527. On Hayes, see David P. Thelen, "Rutherford B. Hayes and the Reform Tradition in the Gilded Age," *American Quarterly* 22, no. 2 (Summer 1970), 151 (explaining Hayes's "career as a reformer" and that he "crusaded actively for public education, prison reform, Negro and Indian rights"), 152 (describing Hayes's praise of the "common virtues of order, thrift, honesty, 'the gospel of work,' the sanctity of property, 'the supremacy of law,' devotion to family,

faith in God, and a Puritanical sense of duty"), 155 (concluding that Hayes was a "good Victorian"). See also Ari Hoogenboom, *Rutherford B. Hayes: Warrior and President* (Lawrence: University Press of Kansas, 1995).

8. Mel Ayton, *Plotting to Kill the President: Assassination Attempts from Washington to Hoover* (Lincoln: University of Nebraska Press/Potomac Books, 2017), 161–68.

9. George E. Mowry, *Theodore Roosevelt and the Progressive Movement* (New York: Hill and Wang, 1946), 3 (quotation); Charles W. Calhoun, "Reimagining the 'Lost Men' of the Gilded Age: Perspectives on the Late Nineteenth Century Presidents," *Journal of the Gilded Age and Progressive Era* 1, no. 3 (July 2002), 225 (noting the stereotype of the "debility and weakness, if not utter political impotence and ineptitude, of the late nineteenth century presidents," who were commonly seen as "weak, isolated, and ineffectual"); Charles W. Calhoun, "Benjamin Harrison, Centennial President: A Review Essay," *Indiana Magazine of History* 84, no. 2 (June 1988), 136–37; Arrington, *Last Lincoln Republican*, 1–2.

10. Thomas Wolfe, *From Death to Morning* (New York: Scribner's, 1935), 121.

11. Richard Hofstadter, *The American Political Tradition and the Men Who Made It* (New York: Alfred A. Knopf, 1948), 170. On Hofstadter's cosmopolitanism and disdain for the provinces, see David S. Brown, *Richard Hofstadter: An Intellectual Biography* (Chicago: University of Chicago Press, 2006), 99–119.

12. Gilbert, *Planning Democracy*, 29.

13. Gilbert, *Planning Democracy*, 28; Jeremy Atack and Fred Bateman, *To Their Own Soil: Agriculture in the Antebellum North* (Ames: Iowa State University Press, 1987), 87. Discussing the small towns in Missouri where he grew up, George Creel said there was "no dividing line between the rich and the poor, and no class distinction to breed mean envies." George Creel, *Rebel at Large: Recollections of Fifty Crowded Years* (New York: G. P. Putnam's Sons, 1947), 24.

14. Calhoun, "Civil Religion and the Gilded Age Presidency," 656 (quotation), 654 (noting that Harrison believed that the GOP must be the "special guardian of what later generations would call the American civil religion").

15. Calhoun, "Civil Religion and the Gilded Age Presidency," 659–60.

16. For recent considerations of the Native American, African American, and women's history of the Midwest, see the three special symposia in the journal *Middle West Review* (Spring 2016, Spring 2021, and Fall 2022).

17. Marilynne Robinson, *What Are We Doing Here? Essays* (New York: Farrar, Straus and Giroux, 2018), 14.

18. Brown, "Modernization," 31.

19. Felsenstein and Connolly, *What Middletown Read*, 204. On the myth of intolerance, see Tomsich, *Genteel Endeavor*.

20. Felsenstein and Connolly, *What Middletown Read*, 205, 274–75, n. 27 (noting that censorship was weak or nonexistent in Muncie).

21. Pawley, *Reading on the Middle Border*, 79 (noting a debate over how many novels to have at the library, that these supposedly "sensational" books were readily purchased and available, and that anti-novel warnings were largely ignored), 91 (quotation) (generally finding that recommendations of the eastern cultural guardians such as the American Library Association were mostly ignored).

22. Hubbart, *Older Middle West*, 62.

23. Hubbart, *Older Middle West*, 66. See also Justin Clark, "'Invitation to the Dance': Robert Ingersoll, Dwight Moody, and the Iconoclastic Gilded Age," in Hogan et al., *Sower and the Seer*, 86.

24. Robinson, *What Are We Doing Here?* 181.

25. Van Doren, "Contemporary American Novelists X."

26. Van Doren typescript "Three Worlds," 24, 44 (happy), 35, 3, 8, 4 (easy, sober, creed, character, honest, community), Box 7, FF 6, Van Doren Papers, Princeton University.

27. Van Doren, "Three Worlds," 12, 14, 18, 45, 52 (dim), 16, 33, 47 (sly), 50, 33, 20, 66 (classless, fraternity, neighborliness, vices, normality), 80 (classic, work), 56–57 (feuds, rare, family). Of his classmates, Van Doren said, "I have never heard that any one of them all ever complained that his first school had done less for him than it should." Van Doren, "Three Worlds," 19. Even Sinclair Lewis, the supposed critic of midwestern small town life, said, "I am certain that I could have been born and reared in no place in the world where I could have had more friendliness." Lewis quoted in Barry Gross, "The Revolt That Wasn't: The Legacies of Critical Myopia," *CEA Critic* 30, no. 2 (January 1977), 7.

28. Van Doren, "Three Worlds," 63 (bored, rebellion), 72 (felt), 71 (spectator, instinct, invent), 1 (snobbishness), 83, 90, 94, 96 (Black, poet, instinct), 44 (happy, envious, abuse, unhappy), 157 (conservative, side). Van Doren "inherited many conservative reviewers" when he became literary editor at the *Nation*; he "stopped using them" and generally rejected any "dull reviewer" in favor of those more "lively." He thought the "age was irreverent, *contemptuous of the pre-war world* and rebellious toward the dead hand which still lay across the present." Van Doren, "Three Worlds," 161 (italics added). Van Doren summarized the intellectual scene: "The expatriates leaving America with large gestures to live in Paris, where they could be free. Other Americans staying home to free America." Van Doren, "Three Worlds," 163.

29. Van Doren, "Three Worlds," 164. In the original manuscript, "written out of hatred" is crossed out in favor of "early irritations."

30. Van Doren, "Three Worlds," 165. See also David Brooks, "The 'Freedom' Agenda," *New York Times*, September 20, 2010 (noting the frequent literary view that "middle-class Americans may seem happy and successful on the outside, but deep down they are leading lives of quiet desperation"), and Bailey, *Philip Roth*, 117 (noting that Maggie Martinson, Phil Roth's Michigan-born wife, was a "bohemian" who disliked the "dulness" of her hometown of South Haven).

31. Stevenson, *Victorian Homefront*, xiv.

32. Robinson, *What Are We Doing Here?* 51 (dreary), 37, 18 (explaining that "categories, woman or black or immigrant, can be encumbrances from [the writers'] point of view, obstacles to the reading of their work as something more than sociological data").

33. Tomsich, *Genteel Endeavor*, 24.

34. Wright, *Culture on the Moving Frontier*, 113.

35. Pawley, *Reading on the Middle Border*, 119.

36. Haywood, *Victorian West*, 127 (quotation), 130, 132, 133–38.

37. Judith E. Toppe, "The One-Room School and Orleans High School Valedictorians, 1926–1975," *Indiana Magazine of History* 89, no. 3 (September 1993), 246.

38. Theobald, *Call School*, 114, 132.

39. One potential large-scale research project would be to compare levels of crime and violence across regions during the nineteenth century. Such data does not now exist in a usable form, but the findings of this book suggest that the differential between regions such as the Midwest and South would be substantial, as does other research. One study found, for example, that 83 percent of lynchings occurred in the South and that the Midwest used capital punishment the least. It found 578 lynchings in Mississippi and 530 lynchings in Georgia from 1882 to 1962. During the same time period, it found eight lynchings in Michigan, six in Wisconsin, and nine in Minnesota. This same study found jail and prison incarceration rates in Mississippi and Tennessee to be roughly triple that in Wisconsin and Minnesota. Margaret Werner Cahalan and Lee Anne Parsons, *Historical Corrections Statistics in the United States, 1850–1984* (Bureau of Justice Statistics, U.S. Department of Justice, December 1986), 12, 16, 30. Another study found sixty-one lynchings in Iowa from 1840 to 1907 (including one African American and one Native American); twenty-eight lynchings in Ohio from 1856 to 1932; twenty-two lynchings in Minnesota from 1848 to 1920; seven lynchings in Michigan from 1881 to 1893; and thirty lynchings in Nebraska from 1859 to 1919.

Many of these lynching were nonracial and often related to horse stealing. See Matthew S. Luckett, *Never Caught Twice: Horse Stealing in Western Nebraska, 1850–1890* (Lincoln: University of Nebraska Press, 2020). At the same time, by way of regional comparison, Louisiana witnessed 422 lynching deaths from 1878 to 1946. The historian Michael J. Pfeifer's work has concluded that lynching in the upper Midwest was "comparatively rare." See Pfeifer, "Introduction," in Pfeifer, *Lynching beyond Dixie*, 10; Pfeifer, "Judge Lynch along the Middle Border: Lynching in the Midwest v. Other Regions," manuscript submitted to Oxford University Press for inclusion in Lauck, "The Oxford Handbook of Midwestern History" (citing lynching statistics); Lauck, *Prairie Republic*, 54, 214–15 (finding little racialized extralegal violence in Dakota Territory). See also Eric Monkkonen, "Homicide: Explaining America's Exceptionalism," *American Historical Review* 111, no. 1 (February 2006), 78 (noting "regional variations in homicide rates"). In the 1830s and 1840s, homicide rates in the rural Midwest were roughly two per hundred thousand; they were as high as twenty-eight per in the overall South, forty per in the Mexican borderlands of New Mexico and the slaveholding areas of East Texas, and one hundred per or more in California and the Hispanic areas of Texas. Randolph Roth, *American Homicide* (Cambridge: Harvard University Press, 2009), 180, 183.

Additional evidence of regional differences can be found in the apparently stronger penal and criminal justice reform efforts in the Midwest in contrast to the martial/honor culture of the South. States such as Minnesota, Michigan, and Wisconsin "were in the vanguard of national criminal justice reform." Pfeifer, "Judge Lynch along the Middle Border," __. See also David A. Gerber, "Lynching and Law and Order: Origin and Passage of the Ohio Anti-Lynching Law of 1896," *Ohio History Journal* 83, no. 1 (Winter 1974), 31–50; Albert Post, "The Anti-Gallows Movement in Ohio," *Ohio History Journal* 54, no. 2 (April–June 1945), 104–10; Paul W. Keve, "Building a Better Prison: The First Three Decades of the Detroit House of Correction," *Michigan Historical Review* 25, no. 2 (Fall 1999), 1–28; Michael J. Pfeifer, "Wisconsin's Last

Decade of Lynching, 1881–91: Law and Violence in the Postbellum Midwest," *American Nineteenth Century History* 6, no. 3 (September 2005), 229 (noting a "respect for due process of law" in Wisconsin and the existence of a "political culture rooted in the Yankee heritage of Wisconsin's most influential residents that stressed probity, regularity, and communal governance"); Michael J. Pfeifer, "Lynching in Late-Nineteenth-Century Michigan," in Pfeifer, ed., *Lynching beyond Dixie*, 211 (noting that Michigan "became the first English-speaking jurisdiction in the world to abolish the death penalty" in 1847 and highlighting the "due process" culture of Yankee-dominated Michigan and the absence of southern settlers).

40. See Tim Wu, *The Attention Merchants: The Epic Scramble to Get inside Our Heads* (New York: Knopf, 2016); Will Storr, *Selfie: How We Became Self-Obsessed and What It's Doing to Us* (New York: Overlook Press, 2018); Dhruv Khullar, "How Social Isolation Is Killing Us," *New York Times*, December 22, 2016; Benoit Denizet-Lewis, "The Kids Who Can't," *New York Times Magazine*, October 15, 2017.

41. Marty Johnson, "Protesters Tear Down Statues of Union General Ulysses S. Grant, National Anthem Lyricist France Scott Key," *The Hill*, June 20, 2020; Fran Spielman, "Statues of Four U.S. Presidents among 41 Under Microscope by Chicago Committee," *Chicago Sun-Times*, February 17, 2021; "San Francisco to remove Washington, Lincoln, and Feinstein from school names," *Associated Press*, January 27, 2021; Sidney Blumenthal and Harold Holzer, "Take Down Chicago's Lincoln Statues? It's Iconoclasm Gone Mad," *Chicago Tribune*, February 22, 2021; Lawrence Andrea, "Hans Christian Heg Was an Abolitionist Who Died Trying to End Slavery; What to Know about the Man Whose Statue Was Toppled in Madison," *Milwaukee Journal-Sentinel*, June 24, 2020.

42. Blair Whitney, "A Portrait of the Author as Midwesterner," *Great Lakes Review* 1, no. 2 (Winter 1975), 33.

43. Malcolm Cowley, "In Defense of the 1920s," *New Republic*, April 24, 1944.

44. "Remembrance: Andrew R. L. Cayton, 1954–2015," *Middle West Review* 2, no. 2 (Spring 2016), 201. See also Jon Gjerde, "Middleness and the Middle West," in Andrew R. L. Cayton and Susan E. Gray, eds., *The Identity of the American Midwest: Essays on Regional History* (Bloomington: Indiana University Press, 2001), 190 (noting that most midwesterners remembered their youth fondly). For a typical example, see Victor P. Hass, "Looking Homeward: A Memoir of a Small-Town Life in Wisconsin," *Wisconsin Magazine of History* 65, no. 3 (Spring 1982), 176–94.

45. Sandoz to Paul Hoffman, October 27, 1937, in Helen Winter Stauffer, ed., *Letters of Mari Sandoz* (Lincoln: University of Nebraska Press, 1992), 131. See also William Pratt, "Mari Sandoz: Regional Writer Never at Home," in Hogan et al., *Sower and the Seer*, 191–203.

46. Dorothy Waples, "The Middle West Finds a Voice: Mark Twain," in *Culture of the Middle West*, 40.

47. Jocelyn A. Hollander and Rachel L. Einwohner, "Conceptualizing Resistance," *Sociological Forum* 19, no. 4 (December 2004), 534.

48. Fred Hobson, "The Savage South: An Inquiry into the Origins, Endurance, and Presumed Demise of an Image," *Virginia Quarterly Review* 61, no. 3 (Summer 1985), 389–90.

49. David Bauder, "Retiring Brokaw: Journalists Should Get out of Power Centers," *Associated Press*, January 28, 2021. See also Jack Schafer and Tucker Doherty, "The Media Bubble Is Worse Than You Think," *Politico Magazine*, May/June 2017.

50. A. O. Scott, "Wallace Stegner and the Conflicted Soul of the West," *New York Times*, June 2, 2020.

51. Wallace Stegner, "Born a Square," in Stegner, *The Sound of Mountain Water: The Changing American West* (New York: Penguin Books, 1997), 170–85, 171 (unfashionable, breed). For editors and publishers, Stegner said, "Their map of the United States is shaped like a dumbbell: New York at one end, California at the other, and United Airlines in between." Stegner, "Born a Square," 177. See also Grace Olmstead, *Uprooted: Recovering the Legacy of the Places We've Left Behind* (New York: Sentinel, 2021).

52. Kasey Carlson, "Citing Discrimination, Former Associate Dean Sues MU School of Medicine," *Columbia Missourian*, December 20, 2017.

53. Tyack, "Tribe and the Common School," 4 (noting that "Most reminiscences of the rural school are highly favorable"); John E. Miller, *Small-Town Dreams: Stories of Midwestern Boys Who Shaped America* (Lawrence: University Press of Kansas, 2014); John E. Miller, "The Nostalgia Question," manuscript submitted to Oxford University Press for inclusion in Lauck, "The Oxford Handbook of Midwestern History."

54. Sohrab Ahmari, *The New Philistines* (London: Biteback, 2016), xvii (quotation); Paul Gruchow, "Discovering the Universe of Home," *Minnesota History* 56, no. 1 (Spring 1998), 36; Clay Routledge, "Remember the Good Old Days? No Need to Feel Ashamed If You Do," *Wall Street Journal*, February 26, 2021 (explaining a "growing body of research" finding that previous negative assumptions "about nostalgia are wrong").

55. Charles Lemert, *Why Niebuhr Matters* (New Haven, CT: Yale University Press, 2011), 3.

56. Lemert, *Why Niebuhr Matters*, 2; Richard Wrightman Fox, "Reinhold Niebuhr: Self-Made Intellectual," *Quarterly Journal of the Library of Congress* 40, no. 1 (Winter 1983), 50, 55 (noting Niebuhr's "formative years in the Midwest," his education in Lincoln, Illinois, and in Chicago and St. Louis seminaries, his pastorate in Michigan, and that he "never lost his midwestern accent").

57. Reinhold Niebuhr, "The Cause and Cure of the American Psychosis," *American Scholar* 25, no. 1 (Winter 1955/1956), 13.

58. Lasch, *The True and Only Heaven: Progress and Its Critics* (New York: W. W. Norton, 1991), 115; Jon K. Lauck, "Christopher Lasch and Prairie Populism," *Great Plains Quarterly* 32, no. 3 (Summer 2012), 185–205.

59. "Writer Tim O'Brien on Fatherhood and the Burden of Vietnam," Fresh Air, WHYY (Philadelphia), February 24, 2021.

60. Rita Felski, *Hooked: Art and Attachment* (Chicago: University of Chicago Press, 2020), 3 (stickiness, language, stuck, inherent), viii (sentiment, correction, value).

INDEX

Abbott, Robert, 151
abolition movement: *Dred Scott*
  decision, 97–98; evolution of,
  91–97, 128–29, 131–36; immigrant
  support of, 23, 33, 82, 90; Lincoln's
  influence, 98–99; Thirteenth
  Amendment, 102; violence against,
  129; women in, 93, 175–76, 189. *See
  also* Civil War
Adams, William Taylor, 55
Addams, Jane, 184, 185, 186, 188
Adler, Dankmar, 116
African Americans: Black press,
  151–52; community building and
  growth, 149–51; and culture of
  striving, 150–52; demographic data,
  16, 123, 124, 125, 127; women's
  groups, 167. *See also* Black civil
  rights; education, African American
agrarian culture and ideology:
  average farm size, 223n141; Black
  communities, 150; concentration of
  agribusiness, 158–59; cotton, 89–90;
  and evolution of Midwest culture,
  34–37; foods, synthetic/"counterfeit,"
  162, 307n41; Grange movement,
  36, 37, 155–56; Land-Grant College
  Act (1862), 35, 67, 101, 155, 172;
  Northern Alliance, 158, 160–61;
  north-south divide in, 12, 92, 101–2;
  reform efforts, 156–58, 160, 161–63,
  165, 190; skills, education in, 65, 67,
  68; women's involvement in, 167,
  175–76; yeoman (farmer) traditions,
  14, 35, 92, 101

alcohol/alcoholism, 186. *See also*
  temperance movement
Aldrich, Beth Streeter, 116
Alger, Horatio, 56, 57
Allen, William Francis, 81
Altgeld, John Peter, 184, 185, 188
Angell, James Burrill, 69, 70, 71, 73,
  171, 174
Antioch College, 73, 141, 170
anti-Semitism, 8, 82–83
Appalachian Mountains, 106
Appleseed, Johnny, 110
Arbor Day, 36–37
arts and culture: music, 110–11, 116;
  and regional identity, 114, 116–17;
  sculpture and murals, public, 40,
  44, 45, 46, 117, 118; theater and
  performance halls, 39–40, 47, 116;
  women's involvement in, 167
Asbury-DePauw University, 73
Ashley, James, 102
Asia, nineteenth-century profile, 9–10
Association for the Advancement of
  Women, 167
Athenaeum of Ohio (Sandusky), 108
"Athens of the Middle West," 38–39
Atwater, Caleb, 42, 110, 111

Bailey, Liberty Hyde, 36
Baker, Ray Stannard, 38, 48, 189
Barnhart, Terry, 109, 111, 112
Barnum, P. T., 59
Bascom, John, 69, 71, 73, 185
Bateman, Newton, 61–62
Bates, Edward, 98

128, 129–30, 147, 152–53; regional
variations study, 335–36n39; by
slave catchers, 120–21; and slavery,
battles over, 96; and temperance
movement, 178
voting rights: Atlantic states, 29–30;
Black suffrage, 102–3, 122–23, 129,
137, 142–46, 145–46, 146, 309–
10n63; historical global perspectives,
9–11; Native Americans, 78–79;
white male suffrage, 29, 29–30;
women's suffrage, 165–66, 180–83
Voting Rights Act, 13

Wabash College, 74, 81, 105
Wade, Benjamin, 33, 93, 95, 96, 102,
134
Waite, Morrison Remick, 157
Walker, Timothy, 22
Wallace, Lew, 60, 101
Wallace's Farmer, 35–36
War of 1812, 76
Wayne, Anthony, 44
Weaver, James Baird, 160, 164
Weber, Max, 34
Webster, Daniel, 26
Weld, Theodore, 129, 131
Western Journal, 107
Western Reserve College, 70, 71–72,
72–73, 74, 132
Western Rural, 160–61
Wheeler, Kenneth, 67
Whig Party, 90, 97
White, Esther Griffin, 175
White, Richard, 118
White, William Allen, 61, 185
white male suffrage, 29, 29–30
Whitlock, Brand, 105, 183
Whitman, Walt, 23, 46–47, 268n46
Whittier, John Greenleaf, 42

Wilde, Oscar, 195, 268n46
Willard, Francis, 179
Wilmot Proviso, 91
Wilson, James F., 102
Winks, Robin, 83
Wittenmyer, Annie, 176, 179
Wolfe, Thomas, 192
women: abolition movement, 93,
175–76, 189; in art and culture, 167,
175–76; and book culture, 167–68;
college and coeducation, 74, 169–75,
180; gender roles and Midwest
culture, 171–72, 175–76; in legal and
medical professions, 172, 175, 180,
181; societies and clubs, 39, 151,
165, 166–67; sports and recreation,
173–74; as teachers, 62, 65, 169–70;
and temperance movement, 178–80,
183, 186–87. *See also* women's civil
rights
Woman's Christian Temperance Union
(WCTU), 179, 183, 186–87
women's civil rights: activism
overview, 165–66; divorce and
property laws, 175–76; global
perspective, 9, 10; reform era
advances, 180–83, 189, 195; and
southern culture, 171–72; suffrage,
165–66, 180–83. *See also* women
Wood, Gordon S., 21
Woodward, Augustus Elias Brevoort,
127, 136–37
World War I, 18, 79, 82, 182
Wright, Frank Lloyd, 114, 116
Wyatt-Brown, Bertram, 90

yeoman (farmer) traditions, 14, 35, 92,
101
Young Men's Christian Association
(YMCA), 71

CPSIA information can be obtained
at www.ICGtesting.com
Printed in the USA
LVHW042157261122
734097LV00004B/190

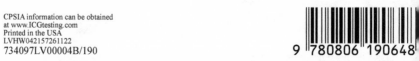
9 780806 190648